THE PRENTICE-HALL SERIES IN MARKETING
Philip Kotler, Series Editor

ABELL/HAMMOND	Strategic Market Planning
GREEN/TULL	Research for Marketing Decisions, 4th ed.
KLEPPNER/RUSSELL/VERRILL	Otto Kleppner's Advertising Procedure, 8th ed.
KOTLER	Marketing Management, 4th ed.
KOTLER	Marketing for Nonprofit Organizations, 2nd ed.
KOTLER	Principles of Marketing, 2nd ed.
MYERS/MASSY/GREYSER	Marketing Research and Knowledge Development
STERN/EL-ANSARY	Marketing Channels, 2nd ed.
URBAN/HAUSER	Design and Marketing of New Products

OTTO KLEPPNER'S

ADVER

PROCEDURE

Otto Kleppner

Thomas Russell
University of Georgia

Glenn Verrill
President, BDA/BBDO

TISING

EIGHTH EDITION

Prentice-Hall, Inc., Englewood Cliffs, NJ 07632

Kleppner, Otto, [date]
  Otto Kleppner's Advertising procedure.
  (The Prentice-Hall series in marketing)
  Bibliography: p.
  Includes index.
    1. Advertising. I. Russell, Thomas.
II. Verrill, Glenn. III. Title. IV. Title:
Advertising procedure. V. Series.
HF5823.K45 1983   659.1   82-7621
ISBN 0-13-643213-1   AACR2

OTTO KLEPPNER'S ADVERTISING PROCEDURE, 8th edition
Otto Kleppner, Thomas Russell, and Glenn Verrill
© 1983, 1979, 1973, 1966, 1950, 1941, 1933, 1925 by Prentice-Hall, Inc., Englewood Cliffs, NJ 07632

Editorial/production supervision: Susan Adkins
Interior & cover design: Maureen Olsen
Manufacturing buyer: Ed O'Dougherty
Cover photos by S. M. Wakefield

Printed in the United States of America

65th printing of the book

ISBN 0-13-643213-1

Prentice-Hall International, Inc., *London*
Prentice-Hall of Australia Pty. Limited, *Sydney*
Editora Prentice-Hall do Brazil, Ltda., *Rio de Janeiro*
Prentice-Hall Canada Inc., *Toronto*
Prentice-Hall of India Private Limited, *New Delhi*
Prentice-Hall of Japan, Inc., *Tokyo*
Prentice-Hall of Southeast Asia Pte. Ltd., *Singapore*
Whitehall Books Limited, *Wellington, New Zealand*

Otto Kleppner died just before the publication of this edition. His dedication to excellence, his pursuit of the truth, and his unflagging insistence on anticipating new directions in advertising and marketing have been a constant source of inspiration. We are deeply indebted. His influence on advertising will persist for decades to come as will his inspiration for future editions of this book.

THOMAS RUSSELL
GLENN VERRILL

CONTENTS

PART THREE
Media

PART FOUR
Creating the Advertising

PART FIVE
Managing the Advertising

PART SIX
Other Worlds of Advertising

PART SEVEN
Advertising as an Institution

About the Authors...

OTTO KLEPPNER

(1899–1982)

A graduate of New York University, Otto Kleppner started out in advertising as a copywriter. After several such jobs, he became advertising manager at Prentice-Hall, where he began to think that he, too, "could write a book." Some years later, he also thought that he could run his own advertising agency, and both ideas materialized eminently. His highly successful agency handled advertising for leading accounts (Dewar's Scotch Whisky, I. W. Harper Bourbon and other Schenley brands, Saab Cars, Doubleday Book Clubs, and others). His book became a bible for advertising students, and his writings have been published in eight languages.

Active in the American Association of Advertising Agencies, Mr. Kleppner served as a director, a member of the Control Committee, chairman of the Committee of Government, Public and Educator Relations, and a governor of the New York Council. He was awarded the Nichols Cup (now the Crain Cup) for distinguished service to the teaching of advertising.

THOMAS RUSSELL

Thomas Russell is a professor of journalism and the head of the advertising sequence at the University of Georgia. He holds a Ph.D. degree in communications from the University of Illinois. Russell is former editor of the *Journal of Advertising* and co-author of *Advertising Media: A Managerial Approach.* In addition, he has authored numerous articles and papers in a wide variety of professional and academic journals. He is an active consultant in the marketing and advertising areas and has served on the faculty of the Institute of Advanced Advertising Studies sponsored by the American Association of Advertising Agencies. He is a member of the American Academy of Advertising, the Association for Education in Journalism, and the Atlanta Advertising Club.

GLENN VERRILL

Glenn Verrill's entire career has been in advertising. He began as a copywriter and worked on the creative side of the business, rising to creative director of one of BBDO's largest agencies. He became president of BDA/BBDO in 1971, his present position, and is a member of the board of directors of BBDO International, Inc.

Mr. Verrill did his undergraduate work at Adelphi College and received his Masters degree from Harvard University. During his career he has garnered scores of creative awards, among them, Effies, Clios, and was twice cited for creating one of the ten best campaigns of the year by Advertising Age.

Mr. Verrill has been active with the American Association of Advertising Agencies. He has been a director of the Eastern region and was a national director of the 4-A's from 1973 to 1975. He was a co-founder of Atlanta's Ad Club II, a club especially formed for young people from the age of 18 to 30 interested in marketing and advertising as a career.

PREFACE

One of the legends of modern advertising, Steuart Henderson Britt, is quoted as saying, "Doing business without advertising is like winking at a girl in the dark. You know what you are doing, but nobody else does." With the growth of self-service retailing, in-home shopping, and the greater risk of doing business, advertising is more important than ever if a seller is to let customers "know what you are doing." This book is designed to introduce students to the principles and procedures of advertising that will promote a product in the most meaningful and efficient manner.

This edition has taken a perspective of advertising for the 1980s and beyond. Advertising is discussed within the new competitive environment of inflation, energy shortages, tight money, and emerging media technology. As in earlier editions, the marketing foundations of advertising are stressed. Marketing goals and objectives are viewed as a platform for discussing the procedures, planning, and execution of advertising.

This book deals with advertising on three levels. The first is the conceptual foundation which provides the necessary theoretical framework for understanding advertising. To fully comprehend advertising one must have some knowledge of a number of other fields of study. Chief among these is marketing. The overall marketing goals of a firm will largely dictate the type of advertising conducted by that company. Throughout the text we have emphasized the necessity of starting with a clear idea of marketing objectives before advertising strategy and tactics are developed. Advertising is also a people business and no one can understand advertising without also understanding human behavior. In Chapter 13, "Use of the Behavioral Sciences," we show how the disciplines of psychology, anthropology and sociology have all contributed in major ways to our knowledge of advertising.

The second level is the planning stage required for successful advertising. The single most prevalent mistake made by the advertising novice is failure to develop a strong plan as a guide to future advertising. The key to successful planning is research. This eighth edition stresses the importance of marketing and advertising research in all phases of the advertising function. The research department has become more important than ever with the current emphasis on target marketing as a primary strategy of most advertisers. With each advertiser striving to find the unfilled marketing niche, research becomes a crucial component in determining the proper marketing mix. The identification of prime prospects, the most efficient media and media schedules to reach them, and, of course, finding the best message to persuade consumers to purchase goods and services are all complex questions that require research before the advertiser can answer them.

The final level on which the text views advertising is the actual execution of advertising. We are dealing here primarily with media planning and buying and the creation of advertisements. For over fifty years this text has taken students through the several steps necessary to provide professional advertising. The current edition continues this emphasis with the intention of demonstrating to students not only the mechanics of creating advertising but how to do it in an environment which requires that advertising be both persuasive and truthful. Chapter 25 has been extensively revised to point out the growing responsibilities of the advertiser in terms of local and federal legislation and regulation, and, more importantly, in terms of the self-regulation and personal integrity of the individual advertiser on which truthful advertising ultimately depends.

We have retained the framework of earlier editions. However, virtually all examples and illustrations have been updated and some chapters have been added or reorganized to reflect current advertising practices. The intent of the final chapters is to emphasize that advertising must be studied as an institution which influences all elements of our society.

The authors feel strongly that it is the concepts of advertising that should be stressed. The planning, research, and strategy of advertising constitute the general principles that determine the ultimate success of advertising. We also realize that the specific functions and applications of these principles will vary from agency to agency and advertiser to advertiser. As we point out in Chapter 2, "Roles of Advertising," advertising is perhaps the most flexible of all business tools. The types of firms that utilize advertising, and the methods employed, cover the spectrum of the consumer, industrial, and service fields. However, a strong foundation in the basic concepts of advertising will provide students with the basic knowledge they need to adapt quickly to the various advertising problems they will encounter.

This text has been significantly updated in the media chapters (5 through 12). Obviously, most of the statistics involving the number of media vehicles and their advertising revenues have changed dramatically since the seventh edition. More importantly, the nature of media technology and the opportunities for advertisers offered by them required extensive examination of some media types. Several of these new media types were only in an experimental stage in the last edition (e.g., cable television networks). In this regard the text takes both an advertiser and media industry perspective in discussing new media technology. It is important that students understand that advertisers must choose from among the media vehicles offered by sellers of time and space. On the other hand, it is clear that many of the media innovations have been developed in reaction to demands for more efficiency on the part of advertisers. Demographic editions of magazines, specialized radio networks, and newspaper inserts are only a few of the media techniques that have been developed, at least in part, to increase advertising revenues.

This text will provide students with a pragmatic guide to advertising practice and the philosophy of advertising as a persuasive communications tool. We hope that, for some, it may also be an introduction to an exciting and fulfilling career.

ACKNOWLEDGMENTS

A book such as this could never be written without the help of numerous advertising professionals and teachers who have generously contributed their time and suggestions. While space does not permit thanking personally everyone who played a role, we would like to acknowledge those who helped in significant ways the preparation of this edition.

Alma Freedman, advertising director, Rich's, Inc., was most helpful in the preparation of the retail advertising chapter. Joseph Palastak, Transit Advertising Association, checked copy and provided the illustrations for the transit advertising discussion. Lorraine Reid, Council of Better Business Bureaus, was most cooperative in checking and updating material for that organization and the National Advertising Review Council in the legal chapter. Neil Bernstein of the Point-of-Purchase Advertising Institute obtained most of the material in that section. Fred Simon of Omaha Steaks International, Larry Frerk of A. C. Nielsen Company, and Constance Anthes of the Arbitron Company, also helped in obtaining several examples and illustrations.

John Leckenby of the University of Illinois was responsible for material concerning media planning models. Tony McGann, University of Wyoming, was particularly helpful in the areas of consumer behavior and international advertising.

We would also like to thank the many advertisers, advertising and media associations, and publications who gave their permission to reprint material throughout the book. Particular thanks are due Lou Emmanuele, Norm Campbell, Bob Johnson, and Jack Kraushaar for their help with case histories, and to Sara Glover for her invaluable help gathering material. Many advertising instructors across the country critiqued the manuscript and gave us the benefit of their expertise. Nancy Church, Plattsburgh State University; Jerry Lynn, Marquette University; Ron Taylor, Parkland College; Alan Fletcher, University of Tennessee; Richard Beltramini, Arizona State University; Arthur Winters, Fashion Institute of Technology; and Isabella Cunningham, University of Texas all made constructive suggestions which greatly strengthened the final manuscript.

Finally, we want to acknowledge the help provided by many people at Prentice-Hall, Inc., especially John Connolly, David Esner, and Susan Adkins.

THOMAS RUSSELL
GLENN VERRILL

OTTO KLEPPNER'S

ADVERTISING

PROCEDURE

The Place of Advertising

Advertising is a business of constant change: Technology, the means of communication, lifestyles, and consumer preferences have all undergone drastic alterations in the last several decades, and each of these areas (and many others) has had an effect on the advertising that we see and hear every day; society's more relaxed attitudes are evident in the products and approaches used in advertisements ("ads"). In the years between now and the twenty-first century change may be the one constant factor in our society, government, and business institutions.

Chapter 1 traces the development of advertising from its primitive beginnings on clay tablets and tavern signs to the era of satellites and cable television, superstations, and computer retrieval systems. Not only the means of advertising have changed, but also advertising has been broadened to encompass every product and service area. There is no single way to promote a product; but as Chapter 2 discusses, each product has unique requirements that must be addressed through advertising specifically designed to solve its special problems. So the many roles of advertising are covered in that chapter.

Background of Today's Advertising

What does the word *advertising* bring to mind? TV and radio commercials? Newspaper ads? Magazine ads? Outdoor signs? Supermarket displays and packages? Certainly all of these are advertising. You may, however, think of all the money spent on advertising, and you wonder how it affects the already high cost of living or whether it could better be spent on schools or in helping the poor and unemployed or for more research on disease. Or advertising may bring to mind a Hollywood picture of a Madison Avenue agency, where an advertising man or woman saves a million-dollar account by breathlessly phoning the client with a new slogan, just dreamed up. (It doesn't work that way.) You may recall advertisements that you liked or disliked. In any case one cannot help being aware of the influence of advertising in our lives.

The fact is that over $60 billion a year is spent on American advertising,* which in its various forms accosts us from early morning news programs until the late shows at night. How did advertising become so pervasive in our society? We cannot find the reasons for its importance merely by studying the ads; we must, rather, understand the economic and social forces produc-

BEGINNINGS   The urge to advertise seems to be a part of human nature, evidenced since ancient times. Of the 5,000-year recorded history of advertising right up to our present TV-satellite age, the part that is most significant begins when the United States emerged as a great manufacturing nation about 100 years ago. The early history of advertising, however, is far too fascinating to pass by without a glance at it.

It isn't surprising that the people who gave the world the Tower of Babel also left the earliest known evidence of advertising. A Babylonian clay tablet of about 3000 B.C. has been found bearing inscriptions for an ointment dealer, a scribe, and a shoemaker. Papyrus exhumed from the ruins of Thebes showed that the ancient Egyptians had a better medium on which to write their messages. (Alas, the announcements preserved in papyrus offer rewards for the return of runaway slaves.) The Greeks were among those who relied on town criers to chant the arrival of ships with cargoes of wines, spices, and metals. Often a crier was accompanied by a musician who kept him in the right key. Town criers later became the earliest medium for public announcements in many European countries, as in England, and they continued to be used for many centuries. (At this point we must digress to tell about a promotion idea used by innkeepers in France around A.D. 1100 to tout their fine wines: They would have the town crier blow a horn, gather a group—and offer samples!)

Roman merchants, too, had a sense of advertising. The ruins of Pompeii contain signs in stone or terra-cotta, advertising what the shops were selling: a row of hams for a butcher shop (Exhibit 1.1), a cow for a dairy, a boot for a shoemaker. The Pompeiians also knew the art of telling their story to the public by means of painted wall signs like this one (tourism was indeed one of advertising's earliest subjects):

Traveler
Going from here to the twelfth tower
There Sarinus keeps a tavern
This is to request you to enter
Farewell

Outdoor advertising has proved to be one of the most enduring, as well as one of the oldest, forms of advertising. It survived the decline of the Roman empire to become the decorative art of the inns in the seventeenth and eighteenth centuries. That was still an age of widespread illiteracy, and inns, particularly, vied with each other in creating attractive signs that all could recog-

---

Exhibit 1.1
One of the oldest signs known. It identified a butcher shop in Pompeii.

nize. This accounts for the charming names of old inns, especially in England—such as the Three Squirrels, the Man in the Moon, the Hole in the Wall (Exhibit 1.2). In 1614, England passed a law, probably the earliest on advertising, that prohibited signs extending more than 8 feet out from a building. (Longer signs pulled down too many house fronts.) Another law required signs to be high enough to give clearance to an armored man on horseback. In 1740, the first printed outdoor poster (referred to as a "hoarding") appeared in London.

ORIGINS OF NEWSPAPER
ADVERTISING
The next most enduring medium, the newspaper, was the offspring of Gutenberg's invention of printing from movable type (about 1438), which, of course, changed communication methods for the whole world. About 40 years after the invention, Caxton of London printed the first ad in English—a handbill of the rules for the guidance of the clergy at Easter. This was tacked up on church doors. (It became the first printed outdoor ad in English.) But the printed newspaper took a long time in coming. It really emerged from the newsletters, handwritten by professional writers, for nobles and others who wanted to be kept up to date on the news, especially of the court and other important events—very much in the spirit of the Washington newsletters of today.

The first ad in any language to be printed in a disseminated sheet appeared in a German news pamphlet about 1525. And what do you think this ad was for? A book extolling the virtues of a mysterious drug. (There was no Food and Drug Administration in those days.) But news pamphlets did not come out regularly; one published in 1591 contained news of the previous 3 years. It was from such beginnings, however, that the printed newspaper emerged. The first printed English newspaper came out in 1622, the *Weekly Newes of London.* The first ad in an English newspaper appeared in 1625.

Siquis, tack-up
advertisements
The forerunner of our present want ads bore the strange name of *siquis.* These were tack-up ads that appeared in England at the end of the fifteenth century. Of these, Frank Presbrey says:

> These hand-written announcements for public posting were done by scribes who made a business of the work. The word "advertisement" in the sense in which we now use it was then unknown. The advertising bills produced by the scribes were called "Siquis," or "If anybody," because they usually began with the words "If anybody desires" or "If anybody knows of," a phrase that had come from ancient Rome, where public notices of articles lost always began with the words "Si quis."
>
> First use of manuscript siquis was by young ecclesiastics advertising for a vicarage. . . . Soon the siquis poster was employed by those desiring servants and by

Hog in Armour

Three Squirrels

King's Porter and Dwarf

The Ape

Harrow and Doublet

Barley Mow

Hole in the Wall
"A Guide for Malt Worms"

Bull and Mouth

Man in the Moon

Goose and Gridiron

Exhibit 1.2
Signs outside seventeenth-century inns.

5

servants seeking places. Lost articles likewise were posted. Presently also to-bacco, perfume, coffee, and some other luxuries were thus advertised. The great percentage of siquis, however, continued to be of the personal, or want-ad type.*

Advertising in the English newspapers continued to feature similar personal and local announcements. The British have, in fact, shown so much interest in classified ads that the *London Times,* until a few years ago, filled its first page with classified advertising.

Advertising comes to

America
The Pilgrims arrived on American shores before the *Weekly Newes of London* was first published; so they had little chance to learn about newspapers. But later colonists acquainted them with the idea, and the first American newspaper to carry ads appeared in 1704, the *Boston Newsletter* (note the newsletter identification). It carried an ad offering a reward for the capture of a thief and the return of several sorts of men's apparel—more akin to the ad offering a reward for the return of slaves, written on Egyptian papyrus thousands of years before, than it was to the advertising printed in the United States today. By the time the United States was formed, the colonies had thirty newspapers. Their advertising, like that of the English newspapers of that time, consisted mostly of ads we describe today as classified and local.

THREE MOMENTOUS DECADES:

1870 TO 1900
Neither those ads, however, nor all the ads that appeared from ancient Egyptian days until the American industrial revolution explain the development of advertising in the United States. The history of advertising in the United States is unique because advertising took hold just as the country was entering its era of greatest growth: Population was soaring, factories were springing up, railroads were opening the West. Advertising grew with the country and helped establish its marketing system. The United States entered the nineteenth century as an agricultural country following European marketing traditions and ended the century as a great industrial nation, creating its own patterns of distribution. A new age of advertising had begun.

We pick up the story around 1870, when this era of transition was crystallizing and among the major developments transportation, population growth, invention, and manufacturing were ranking high.

Transportation
Here was a country 3,000 miles wide. It had sweeping stretches of rich farmland. It had minerals and forests. It had factories within reach of the coal mines. It had a growing population. But its long-distance transportation was chiefly by rivers and canals.

*Frank Presbrey, *History and Development of Advertising* (Garden City, N.Y.: Doubleday, 1929).

Railroads today are fighting for survival, but 100 years ago they changed a sprawling continent into a land of spectacular economic growth. In 1865 there were 35,000 miles of railroad trackage in the United States. By 1900, this trackage was 190,000 miles. Three railroad lines crossed the Mississippi and ran from the Atlantic to the Pacific. Feeder lines and networks spread across the face of the land. Where railroads went, people went, establishing farms, settlements, and cities across the continent, not limited to the waterways. The goods of the North and the East could be exchanged for the farm and extractive products of the South and the West. Never before had a country revealed such extensive and varied resources. Never since has so vast a market without a trade or language barrier been opened. This was an exciting prospect to manufacturers.

People   In 1870 the population of the United States was 38 million. By 1900 it had doubled. In no other period of American history has the population grown so fast. This growth, which included those now freed from slavery, meant an expanding labor force in the fields, factories, and mines; it meant a new consumer market. About 30 percent of the increase was from immigrants. But all the settlers before them had been immigrants or descendants of immigrants who had the courage to pull up stakes and venture to the New World, a land far away and strange to them, in search of a new and better life. The result was a society that was mobile, both in readiness to move their homes and in aspirations to move upward in their lifestyles.

Inventions and
production   The end of the nineteenth century was marked by many notable inventions and advances in the manufacture of goods. Among these were the development of the electric motor and of alternating-current power transmission, which relieved factories of the need to locate next to waterpower sources, thus opening the hinterland to development and growth. The internal-combustion engine was perfected in this period; the automobile age was soon to follow.

It was the age of fast communications; telephone (Exhibit 1.3), telegraph, typewriter, Mergenthaler linotype, and high-speed presses—all increased the ability of people to communicate with each other.

In 1860 there were 7,600 patent applications filed in Washington. By 1870 this number had more than doubled to 19,000; by 1900 it had more than doubled again, to 42,000.

Steel production has traditionally served as an index of industrial activity. Twenty *thousand* tons of steel were produced in 1867, but 10 *million* tons were produced in 1900. There is also a direct correlation between the power consumption of a country and its standard of living. By 1870 only 3 million horsepower were available; by 1900 this capacity had risen to 10 million. More current being used means more goods being manufactured; it also means that more people are using it for their own household needs—all of which is a good economic index.

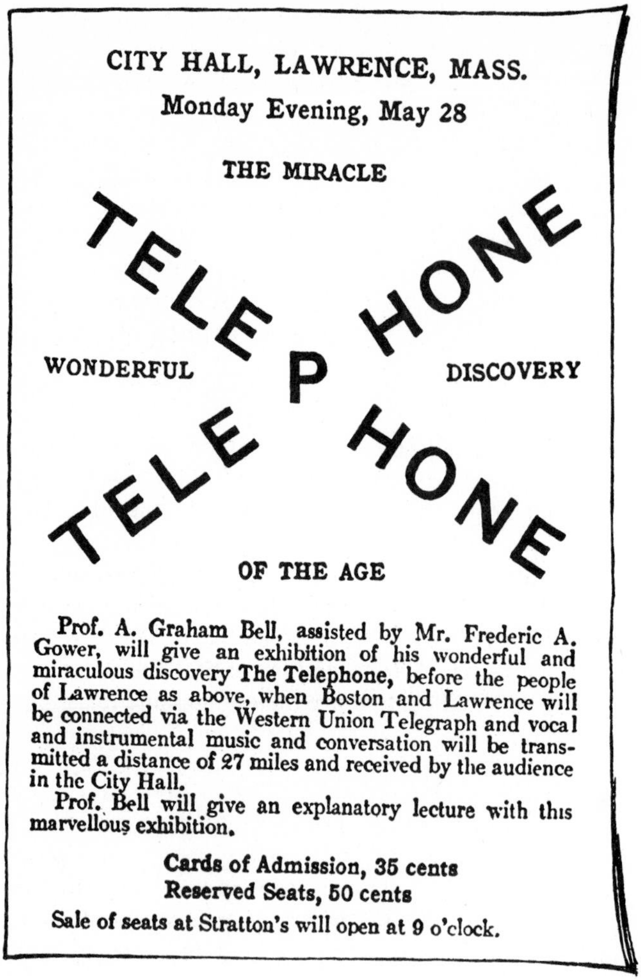

Exhibit 1.3
The first telephone ad (1877).

The phonograph and the motion-picture camera, invented at the turn of the century, added to the lifestyle of people at that time.

The Columbian exhibition in Chicago in 1893 was attended by millions of Americans, who returned home to tell their friends breathlessly about the new products they had seen.

Media   *Newspapers.* Since colonial times, newspapers had been popular in the United States. In the 1830s the penny newspaper came out. In 1846 Hoe patented the first rotary printing press, and in 1871 he invented the Hoe web press, which prints both sides of a continuous roll of paper and delivers folded sheets. By the end of the nineteenth century about 10,000 papers were being published, with an estimated combined circulation of 10 million. Ninety percent of them were weeklies (most of the rest dailies) published in the county seat with farm and local news. By 1900 twenty of the largest cities had their own papers, some with as many as sixteen pages. Newspapers were the largest class of media at this period.

To save buying paper, many editors (who were also the publishers) bought sheets already printed on one side with world news, items of general interest to farmers, and ads. They would then print the other side with local news and any ads they could obtain (forerunners of today's color insert). Or else they would insert such pages in their own four-page papers, offering an eight-page paper to their readers.

Religious publications. Religious publications today represent a very small part of the total media picture; but for a few decades after the Civil War religious publications were the most influential medium. They were the forerunners of magazines. The post-Civil War period was a time of great religious revival, marking also the beginning of the temperance movement. Church groups issued their own publications, many with circulations of no more than 1,000; the biggest ran to 400,000. But the combined circulation of the 400 religious publications was estimated at about 5 million.

Religious publications had great influence among their readers, a fact that patent-medicine advertisers recognized to such an extent that 75 percent of all the religious-publication advertising was for patent medicines. (Many of the temperance papers carried the advertising of preparations that proved to be 40 percent alcohol. Today we call that 80-proof whiskey.)

Magazines. Most of what were called magazines before the 1870s, including Ben Franklin's effort in 1741, lasted less than 6 months—and for a good reason: They consisted mostly of extracts of books and pamphlets, essays, verse, and communications of dubious value. Magazines as we know them today were really born in the last three decades of the nineteenth century, at a time when many factors were in their favor. The rate of illiteracy in the country had been cut almost in half, from 20 percent in 1870 to little over 10 percent in 1900. In 1875 railroads began carrying mail, including magazines, across the country. In 1879 Congress established the low second-class postal rate for publications, a subject of controversy to this day but a great boon to magazines even then. The Hoe high-speed rotary press began replacing the much slower flatbed press, speeding the printing of magazines. The halftone method of reproducing photographs as well as color artwork was invented in 1876, making the magazines more enticing to the public. (*Godey's Lady's Book,* a popular fashion book of the age, had previously employed 150 women to hand-tint all its illustrations.)

Intended for the upper middle classes, literary magazines now appeared—*Harper's Monthly, Atlantic Monthly, Century*—but the publishers did not view advertising kindly at first. Even when, at the turn of the century, Fletcher Harper condescended to "desecrate literature with the announcements of tradespeople," he placed all the advertising in the back of the book.

Inspired by the success of popular magazines in England, a new breed of publishers came forth in the 1890s to produce popular magazines of entertainment, fiction, and advice, forerunners of today's women's and general magazines. Magazines brought the works of Rudyard Kipling, H. G. Wells, Mark Twain, and Conan Doyle to families across the face of the land. By 1902 *Munsey's* had a circulation of 600,000; *Cosmopolitan,* 700,000; *Delineator,* 960,000. The *Ladies' Home Journal* hit the million mark—a great feat for the age. The 10-cent magazine had arrived.

The amount of advertising that magazines carried was comparable to modern magazine advertising. *Harper's* published 75 pages of advertising per issue; *Cosmopolitan,* 103 pages; *McClure's,* 120 pages. Today a typical issue of the *Ladies' Home Journal* has 100 pages of advertising; *Reader's Digest,* 75; *Better Homes & Gardens,* 125. Magazines made possible the nationwide sale of products; they brought into being nationwide advertising.

Patent-medicine
advertising
Patent-medicine advertisers had been around for a long time, and by the 1870s they were the largest category of advertisers. After the Civil War, millions of men returned to their homes, North and South, many of them weak from exposure. Many needed medical aid, and the only kind available to most of them was a bottle of patent medicine. As a result, patent-medicine advertising dominated the media toward the end of the nineteenth century, its fraudulent claims giving all advertising a bad name (Exhibit 1.4).

National advertising
emerges
Meanwhile, legitimate manufacturers saw a new world of opportunity opening before them in the growth of the country. They saw the market for consumer products spreading. Railroads could now carry their merchandise to all cities between the Atlantic and Pacific coasts. The idea of packaging their own products carrying their own trademarks was enticing, particularly to grocery manufacturers; for now they could build their business upon their reputation with the consumer and not be subject to the caprices and pressures of jobbers, who had in the past been their sole distributors. Now magazines provided the missing link in marketing—that of easily spreading word about their products all over the country, with advertising. Quaker Oats cereal was among the first to go this marketing route, followed soon by many others (Exhibit 1.5).

This was the development of national advertising, as we call it today, in its broadest sense, meaning the advertising by a producer of his trademarked product, whether or not it has attained national distribution.

Mass production
appears
The words "chauffeur," "limousine," or "sedan" remind us that some of the earliest motorcars were made and publicized in France. In the United States, as in France, they were virtually handmade at first. But in 1913, Henry Ford decided that the way to build cars at low cost was to make them of stand-

ardized parts and bring the work to the man on the assembly-line belt. He introduced to the world a mass-production technique and brought the price of a
Ford down to $265 by 1925 (when a Hudson automobile cost $1,695 and the
average weekly wage was $20). But mass production is predicated, in a free
society, upon mass selling, another name for advertising. Mass production
makes possible countless products at a cost the mass of people can pay and
about which they learn through advertising. America was quick to use both.

LEADERS IN NATIONAL ADVERTISING IN 1890's

A. P. W. Paper
Adams Tutti Frutti Gum
Æolian Company
American Express Traveler's Cheques
Armour Beef Extract
Autoharp
Baker's Cocoa
Battle Ax Plug Tobacco
Beardsley's Shredded Codfish
Beeman's Pepsin Gum
Bent's Crown Piano
Burlington Railroad
Burnett's Extracts
California Fig Syrup
Caligraph Typewriter
Castoria
A. B. Chase Piano
Chicago Great Western
Chicago, Milwaukee & St. Paul Railroad
Chicago Great Western Railway
Chocolat-Menier
Chickering Piano
Columbia Bicycles
Cleveland Baking Powder
Cottolene Shortening
Cook's Tours
Crown Pianos
Crescent Bicycles
Devoe & Raynolds Artist's Materials
Cuticura Soap
Derby Desks
De Long Hook and Eye
Diamond Dyes
Dixon's Graphite Paint
Dixon's Pencils
W. L. Douglas Shoes
Edison Mimeograph
Earl & Wilson Collars
Elgin Watches
Edison Phonograph
Everett Piano
Epps's Cocoa
Estey Organ
Fall River Line
Felt & Tarrant Comptometer
Ferry's Seeds
Fisher Piano
Fowler Bicycles
Franco American Soup
Garland Stoves
Gold Dust

Gold Dust Washing Powder
Gorham's Silver
Gramophone
Great Northern Railroad
H–O Breakfast Food
Hamburg American Line
Hammond Typewriter
Hartford Bicycle
Hartshorn's Shade Rollers
Heinz's Baked Beans
Peter Henderson & Co.
Hires' Root Beer
Hoffman House Cigars
Huyler's Chocolates
Hunyadi Janos
Ingersoll Watches
Ives & Pond Piano
Ivory Soap
Jaeger Underwear
Kirk's American Family Soap
Kodak
Liebeg's Extract of Beef
Lipton's Teas
Lowney's Chocolates
Lundborg's Perfumes
James McCutcheon Linens
Dr. Lyon's Toothpowder
Mason & Hamlin Piano
Mellin's Food
Mennen's Talcum Powder
Michigan Central Railroad
Monarch Bicycles
J. L. Mott Indoor Plumbing
Munsing Underwear
Murphy Varnish Company
New England Mincemeat
New York Central Railroad
North German Lloyd
Old Dominion Line
Oneita Knitted Goods
Packer's Tar Soap
Pearline Soap Powder
Peartltop Lamp Chimneys
Pears' Soap
Alfred Peats Wall Paper
Pettijohn's Breakfast Food
Pittsburgh Stogies
Pond's Extract
Postum Cereal
Prudential Insurance Co.
Quaker Oats

Exhibit 1.5
Leaders in national advertising in the 1890s. [Reproduced from Frank Presbrey, *History and Development of Advertising* (Garden City, N.Y.: Doubleday, 1929), p. 361.]

The advertising

agency We have been speaking of the various media and their advertising. Now a word about how the media got much of that advertising—through the advertising agency, which started out as men selling advertising space on a percentage basis, for out-of-town newspapers. Later they also planned, prepared, and placed the ads and rendered further services. The story of the advertising agency is deeply rooted in the growth of American industry and advertising. Later in the book we devote a whole chapter (Chapter 20) to the American agency from its beginnings to its latest patterns of operation. Until then we need keep in mind only that the advertising agency has always been an active force in developing the use of advertising.

AMERICA ENTERS THE TWENTIETH

CENTURY The moral atmosphere of business as it developed after the Civil War reflected laissez-faire policy at its extreme. High government officials were corrupted by the railroads, the public was swindled by flagrant stock-market manipulations, embalmed beef was shipped to soldiers in the Spanish-American War. Advertising contributed to the immorality of business, with its patent-medicine ads offering to cure all the real and imagined ailments of man. There was a "pleasing medicine to cure cancer," another to cure cholera. No promise of a quick cure was too wild, no falsehood too monstrous.

The pure food and drug

act (1906) As early as 1865, the *New York Herald-Tribune* had a touch of conscience and eliminated "certain classes" of medical advertising, those that used "repellent" words. In 1892 the *Ladies' Home Journal* was the first magazine to ban *all* medical advertising. The *Ladies' Home Journal* also came out with a blast by Mark Sullivan, revealing that codeine was being used in cold preparations and a teething syrup had morphine as its base. Public outrage reached Congress, which in 1906 passed the Pure Food and Drug Act, the first federal law to protect the health of the public and the first to control advertising.

The federal trade commission

act (1914) In addition to passing laws protecting the public from unscrupulous business, Congress passed the Federal Trade Commission Act, protecting one businessman from the unscrupulous behavior of another. The law said, in effect, "Unfair methods of doing business are hereby declared illegal." John D. Rockefeller, founder of the Standard Oil Company, got together with some other oilmen in the early days of his operation and worked out a deal with the railroads over which they shipped their oil. They arranged not only to get a secret rebate on the oil they shipped but also to get a rebate on all the oil their *competitors* shipped. Result: They were able to undersell their competition and drive them out of business. What was considered smart business in those days would be a violation of the antitrust laws today.

In time, the FTC (Federal Trade Commission) extended its province to protecting the public against misleading and deceptive advertising—a matter of which all who are responsible for advertising today are very much aware. Of this period of exposure and reform the historian James Truslow Adams said, "America for the first time was taking stock of the morality of everyday life."

Yet despite these praiseworthy efforts at self-regulation and many others in the years that followed, and general acceptance, the advertising industry was and continues to be the target of criticism for its social effects. Chapter 26 answers such criticism, and it has been placed at the end of the book so that you will have had the benefit of the advertising background that the intervening chapters provide.

ADVERTISING COMES OF AGE

Around 1905 there emerged a class of advertising men who recognized that their future lay in advertising legitimate products and in earning the confidence of the public in advertising. They gathered with like-minded men in their community to form advertising clubs.

These clubs subsequently formed the Associated Advertising Clubs of the World (now the American Advertising Federation). In 1911 they launched a campaign to promote truth in advertising. In 1916 they formed vigilance committees. These developed into today's Council of Better Business Bureaus, which continues to deal with many problems of unfair and deceptive business practices. In 1971 the bureaus became a part of the National Advertising Review Council, an all-industry effort at curbing misleading advertising. The main constituency of the American Advertising Federation continues to be that of the local advertising clubs. On its board are also officers of the other advertising associations.

In 1910 the Association of National Advertising Managers was born. It is now known as the Association of National Advertisers (ANA) and has about 500 members, including the foremost advertisers. Its purpose is to improve the effectiveness of advertising from the viewpoint of the advertiser. In 1917 the American Association of Advertising Agencies was formed to improve the effectiveness of advertising and of the advertising-agency operation. Over 75 percent of all national advertising today is placed by its members, both large and small.

In 1911 *Printers' Ink,* the leading advertising trade paper for many years, prepared a model statute for state regulation of advertising, designed to "punish untrue, deceptive or misleading advertising." The *Printers' Ink* Model Statute has been adopted in its original or modified form in forty-four states, where it is still operative.

Up to 1914 many publishers were carefree in their claims to circulation. An advertiser had no way of verifying what he got for his money. But in that year a group of advertisers, agencies, and publishers established an independent auditing organization, the Audit Bureau of Circulations, which conducts its own audits and issues its own reports of circulation. Most major publications belong to the ABC, and an ABC circulation statement is highly regarded in media circles. The ABC reports of circulation are fully accredited in most areas. (Today, similar auditing organizations are operating in twenty-five countries throughout the world.)

In June, 1916, President Woodrow Wilson addressed the Associated Advertising Clubs of the World convention in Philadelphia, the first president to give public recognition to the importance of advertising. Advertising had come of age!

Advertising in World War I

When the United States entered World War I in 1917, a number of advertising-agency and media men offered their services to the government but were turned down; for "Government officials, particularly Army chiefs, believed in orders and edicts, not persuasion."* But when these groups offered their services to the Council of National Defense, they were welcomed and became the Division of Advertising of the Committee of Public Information—the propaganda arm of the government.

Their first job, to help get all eligible men to register, resulted in getting 13 million men registered in 1 day without serious incident. The committee also succeeded in having advertisers use their own paid space to advertise Liberty Bonds and the Red Cross and to carry messages of the Fuel Administration (to use less fuel) and the Food Administration (to observe its meatless and wheatless days).

The 1920s

The 1920s began with a minidepression and ended with a crash. When the war ended, makers of army trucks were able to convert quickly to commercial trucks. Firestone spent $2 million advertising "Ship by Truck." With the industry profiting by the good roads that had been built, truck production jumped from 92,000 in 1916 to 322,000 in 1920. Trucking spurred the growth of chain stores, which led, in turn, to supermarkets and self-service because of door-to-door delivery from manufacturer to retailer.

The passenger-car business boomed, too, and new products appeared in profusion: electric refrigerators, washing machines, electric shavers, and, most incredible of all, the radio. Installment selling made hard goods available to all. And all the products needed advertising.

Radio arrives. Station KDKA of Pittsburgh was on the air broadcasting the Harding-Cox election returns in November, 1920, some months before its license to operate had cleared. Many other stations soon began broadcasting. There were experimental networks over telephone lines as early as 1922. The

---

*James Playsted Wood, *The History of Advertising* (New York: Ronald, 1958).

first presidential address to be broadcast (by six stations) was the message to Congress by President Coolidge in 1923. The National Broadcasting Company (NBC) started its network broadcasting in 1926 with six stations and had its first coast-to-coast football broadcast in 1927. That was the year, too, that the Columbia Broadcasting System (CBS) was founded and the Federal Radio Commission (now the Federal Communications Commission, FCC) was created.

Making radio sets proved to be a boon to industry (Exhibit 1.6). According to Irving Settel,

> Radio created one of the most extraordinary new product demands in the history of the United States. From all over the country, orders for radio receiving sets poured into the offices of manufacturers. Said *Radio Broadcast Magazine* in its first issue, May 1922:
>
> "The rate of increase in the number of people who spend at least a part of their evening listening in is almost incomprehensible. . . . It seems quite likely that before the market for receiving apparatus becomes approximately saturated, there will be at least five million receiving sets in this country.*

Everything boomed in the mid-1920s—business boomed, advertising boomed. The issue of *The Saturday Evening Post* of December 7, 1929, is historic. It was the last issue whose advertising had been prepared before the stock-market crash in October, 1929. The magazine was 268 pages thick. It carried 154 pages of advertising. The price: 5 cents a copy. Never again would *The Saturday Evening Post* attain that record. Never again has any magazine approached it. It was the end of an era.

The 1930s

Depression

The stock-market crash had a shattering effect on our entire economy: Millions of men were thrown out of work; business failures were widespread; banks were closing all over the country (there were no insured deposits in savings banks in those days). There was no social security, no food stamps, no unemployment insurance. Who had ever heard of pensions for blue-collar workers? There were bread lines, long ones; and well-dressed men were selling apples off the tops of boxes on street corners, for 5 cents. (Compare Exhibit 1.7). The Southwest was having its worst windstorms, carrying off the topsoil and killing livestock and crops. Farmers abandoned their farms, packed their families and furniture into old pickup trucks, and headed west. (Steinbeck wrote his *Grapes of Wrath* around this experience.) The government finally launched the Works Progress Administration (WPA) for putting men to work on public-service projects, but the bread lines continued long.

Out of that catastrophe there emerged three developments that affect advertising today:

*Irving Settel, *A Pictorial History of Radio* (New York: Citadel, 1960), p. 41.

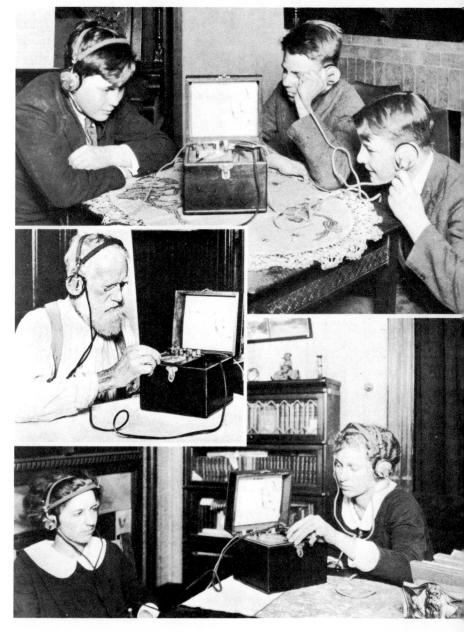

1. The emergence of radio as a major advertising medium. In March, 1933, President Franklin D. Roosevelt made the first inaugural address ever to be broadcast by radio, giving heart and hope to a frightened people. His line "We have nothing to fear except fear itself," spoken to the largest audience that had ever at one time heard the voice of one man, became historic. In one broadcast, radio showed its power of moving a nation. Radio had arrived as a major national advertising medium. It quickly became part of the life of America. The 1930s began with 612 stations and 12 million sets; they ended with 814 stations and 51 million sets.

Exhibit 1.7
Chain-store ad, 1932.

2. The passage of the Robinson-Patman Act (1936) to help protect the little merchant from the unfair competition of the big store with its huge buying power. This law is operative today.

3. The passage of the Wheeler-Lea Act (1938), giving the FTC more direct and sweeping powers over advertising, and the Federal Food, Drug and Cosmetic Act (1938), giving the administration authority over the labeling and packaging of these products. These laws, which we discuss in Chapter 25, Legal and Other Restraints on Advertising, are a pervasive consideration in advertising today and a forerunner of the government's increasing interest in advertising.

Advertising during World War II

(1941 to 1945)   With World War II industry turned to production of war goods. Since all civilian material was severely rationed, many firms curtailed their advertising. Others felt that, though they were out of merchandise, they were not out of business, and they wanted to keep the public goodwill. They applied their advertising efforts to rendering public service. The Goodyear Tire & Rubber Company's advice on how to take care of your tires in days of product shortages was akin to ads that were to appear in 1974 and 1975.

The War Advertising Council. When the government turned to the advertising industry for help in enlisting civilian aid in the war effort, the industry organized the War Advertising Council. It was composed of media, which contributed the space, agencies, which contributed the creative talent, and advertisers, who contributed management. Among the council's succession of massive public-service campaigns were those for putting workers on guard against careless talk ("The enemy is listening"), salvaging scrap metals, puchasing war bonds, writing V-mail letters, war-time recruiting (especially of women), preventing forest fires, and planting victory gardens. More than a billion dollars of space, time, and talent went into this effort. So successful was the project that it was continued after the war, to deal with public-service problems. It was renamed The Advertising Council and is very active to this day.

After World War II industry went into high gear, supplying the pent-up demand for cars, homes, appliances, and all the other postponed purchases. Many new and improved products appeared, made possible by the new materials and processes originally developed for war use, leading directly to the historic growth period of 1950 to 1975.

Advertising from 1950 to 1975: The word was

"growth"   Wrote Richard Manchester, in speaking of this period:

A surge of abundance was everywhere. Technological change had never held a greater fascination for Americans. . . . The sheer number of innovations was bewildering. . . . One by one they appeared, were assimilated into the general experience. Millions of men and women of the swing generation realized that in countless little ways life had become more tolerable, more convenient, more interesting—in a word, more livable.*

Also in discussing this era, John Crichton reported:

In 1950 many markets were either infantile or virtually nonexistent. Travel and leisure, second homes, food franchises, second, third, and fourth cars, many frozen and instant foods, many of the synthetic fabrics and combinations of them, many of the devices like color television, snowmobiles, the Sunfish and the Hobie Cat, mobile homes, and campers were all in the future. In 1950 the United States, untouched by the ravages of the Second World War, was embarked on a period of growth unparalleled in our history. It was a period of great buoyancy and confidence.†

The figures also said growth. Between 1950 and 1973‡ the population of the United States increased by 38 percent, while disposable personal income increased by 327 percent. New housing starts went up by 47 percent, energy consumption by 121 percent, college enrollment by 136 percent, automobile registrations by 151 percent, telephones in use by 221 percent, number of outboard motors sold by 242 percent, retail sales by 250 percent, families owning two or more cars by 300 percent, frozen food production by 655 percent, number of airline passengers by 963 percent, homes with dishwashers by 1,043 percent, and homes with room air conditioners by 3,662 percent.

Advertising not only contributed to the growth but was part of it, rising from an expenditure of $5,780 million in 1950 to $28,320 million in 1975—a growth of 490 percent. There were many developments in advertising during this time:

☐ In 1956 the Department of Justice ruled that advertising agencies could negotiate fees with clients rather than adhere to the then-required 15-percent commission on all media placed. This encouraged the growth of specialized companies, such as independent media-buying services, creative-only agencies, and in-house agencies owned by advertisers.

☐ The voice of the consumer became more powerful.

☐ Congress passed an act limiting outdoor advertising alongside interstate highways. Cigarette advertising was banned from television.

☐ The FTC introduced corrective advertising by those who had made false or misleading claims. Comparison advertising (mentioning competitors by name) was deemed an acceptable form of advertising.

☐ The magazine-publishing world saw the disappearance of the old dinosaurs of publishing: *The Saturday Evening Post, Colliers,* and *Woman's Home Companion.* There

---

*Richard Manchester, *The Glory and the Dream* (Boston: Little Brown, 1973), p. 946.

†John Crichton, "We're in the Last Quarter" (paper from the Western Region Convention of the American Association of Advertising Agencies, 1975), p. 3.

‡We select 1973 as the last full year before the oil embargo of 1974.

was no vacuum at the newsstands, however; that was immediately filled by the up-surge of magazines of special interests.

☐ Newspapers felt the effect of the shift of metropolitan population to the suburbs. Free-standing inserts became an important part of newspaper billings.

☐ Radio took a dive when TV came along. How it came out of that is a good example of turning disadvantages into advantages.

☐ Direct-response advertising soared from $900 million in 1950 to $8 billion in 1980, re-flecting the growth of direct marketing.

☐ The two biggest developments to emerge were TV and electronic data processing. TV has changed America's life as well as the world of advertising. Data-processing systems have brought before the eyes of management a wealth of organized information. This, together with the syndicated research services, has revolutionized the entire marketing process and the advertising-media operation.

ADVERTISING TO THE YEAR

2000   The American socioeconomic system has experienced radical changes in the last decade. All indications are that these adjustments will continue and per-haps accelerate during the latter years of the twentieth century. Advertising's role will be as vital during this period as it had been in the high-consumption economy of the post-World War II era.

Since advertising is a reflection of the economic system, changes in the way we live, work, and consume show up quickly in advertising. Three areas will be of particular importance to advertising before this century ends:

Energy

conservation   Advertising will be used to sell energy-efficient products as well as the concept of conservation. Oil companies encouraging drivers to use less gasoline, utilities stressing the proper use of insulation, and automotive com-panies selling "down-sized" cars are all indicators of a dramatic movement to responsible consumption (Exhibit 1.8). We are also likely to see more in-home shopping through catalog and direct-response advertising.

Inflation   From the 1970s Americans have had to accept inflation as a way of life. Consumers are looking to advertising for bargain air-fares, food specials, and seasonal sales on an array of consumer products. Sellers are promoting their goods to a wary, increasingly sophisticated public. Advertising is being viewed as a means of information (for both products and ideas) and product puffery, acceptable a few years ago, is being rejected by the more serious consuming public.

Changes in the social

fabric   Beyond cyclical economic adjustments advertising must relate to a society that has changed dramatically since the 1960s. The traditional modular family of working husband, housewife, and children now makes up less than 15 per-

Exhibit 1.8
Utility using advertising to advocate energy conservation. (Courtesy National Rural Electric Cooperative Association.)

cent of American households. Advertising strategy must deal with a marketplace that has more Americans over 65, fewer under 21, more educated and affluent middle-aged, and more single-person households than ever before. The ramifications of these changes will affect the purchase and promotion of everything from housing to diapers.

The future will be exciting, with many opportunities for the astute advertiser. However, in the years to come, some old marketing and advertising formulas will have difficulty working.

SUMMARY

Most of us think of advertising as having recent origins. Certainly the sophisticated marketing and advertising of the 1980s is a post-World War II phenomenon. However, the desire to persuade others through various means of communication dates back to prehistoric times. Mass advertising has its roots in the German and English handbills of the sixteenth century, which were either handed out or more frequently posted in some central locations.

The history of advertising as we know it dates from the American industrial revolution of the latter nineteenth century. During this period a growing middle class, mass production, expanded transportation, and high-speed printing presses combined to pave the way for modern marketing and advertising.

The period from 1900 to 1920 saw the introduction of a number of legal and regulatory restrictions on advertising. It was also marked by a sense of professionalism in advertising and self-regulation from within the industry as people began to understand the immense power of advertising.

The period from 1950 to 1975 was one of consolidation and growth. Advertising budgets grew at unprecedented rates and took on a new importance in the selling of virtually all products. If this period was one of growth, the present era may be known as one of change. We are starting to cope with problems of energy, inflation, and instability in all facets of society. The new communication technology, only a dream 10 years ago, is a reality. With it comes opportunities and responsibilities that advertisers of earlier periods could not have imagined.

QUESTIONS

1. When someone says, "advertising," what first comes to mind? Discuss.
2. Since advertising was used in England and Europe before it was used in the United States, what caused advertising usage to leap so far ahead in this country?

3. About when did publication advertising first appear in America? In what kind of medium?

4. Advertising was part of the great growth period of 1870 to 1900. What were the other factors that helped America's economy to grow?

5. Advertising had tremendous growth between 1950 and 1975. What were some of the causes?

6. What major changes in advertising have you observed in your lifetime?

7. Identify the FTC, War Advertising Council, the *Printers' Ink* Model Statute.

8. Identify three significant events in our nation's history in terms of their impact on advertising as we know it today. Why single out these particular events?

9. Would you regard advertising as a modern development? Why?

READINGS

CALKINS, EARNEST ELMO, and RALPH HOLDEN: *Modern Advertising* (New York: Appleton-Century, 1905).

FLEMING, THOMAS: "How It Was in Advertising: 1776–1976," *Advertising Age,* April 19, 1976, 1 *ff.* This is the feature article of a special Bicentennial section of *Advertising Age,* which has several other articles dealing with advertising history.

HOTCHKISS, GEORGE BURTON: *Milestones of Marketing.* (New York: Macmillan, 1938).

JONES, EDGAR ROBERT: *Those Were the Good Old Days: A Happy Look at American Advertising, 1880–1930* (New York: Simon & Schuster, 1959).

MORISON, SAMUEL ELIOT: *The Oxford History of the American People* (New York: Oxford University Press, 1965).

NORRIS, VINCENT P.: "Advertising History—According to the Textbooks," *Journal of Advertising,* Summer 1980, pp. 3–11.

PRESBREY, FRANK: *History and Development of Advertising* (Garden City, NY: Doubleday, 1929).

ROTZOLL, KIM B.: "Gossage Revisited: Reflections of Advertising's Legendary Iconoclast," *Journal of Advertising,* Fall 1980, pp. 6–14.

ROWELL, GEORGE P.: *Forty Years an Advertising Agent* (New York: Franklin Publishing, 1926).

SAMPSON, HENRY: *A History of Advertising from the Earliest Times* (London: Chatto & Windus, 1875).

TURNER, ERNEST SACKVILLE: *The Shocking History of Advertising* (New York: Dutton, 1953).

"Twentieth Century Advertising and the Economy of Abundance," *Advertising Age,* April 30, 1980.

2

Roles of Advertising

Advertising is a method of delivering a message from a sponsor, through an impersonal medium, to many people. (The word "advertising" comes from the Latin *ad vertere,* "to turn the mind toward.") The roles of advertising are many: Advertising is designed to dispose a person to buy a product, to support a cause, or even to encourage less consumption ("demarketing"); it may be used to elect a candidate, raise money for charity, or publicize union or management positions in a strike ("advertorials"). Most advertising, however, is for the marketing of goods and services. But regardless of its specific purpose all advertising has two common threads: a marketing foundation and persuasive communication.

Advertising functions within a marketing framework. The American Marketing Association defines marketing as " . . . the performance of business activities that direct the flow of goods and services from producer to consumer or user."* Advertising depends on a number of product, pricing, and distribution variables for its success. Yet no amount of advertising can sell an inferior product (in the long term), an overpriced product, or a product that is not available to consumers.

---

*Committee on Definitions, *Marketing Definitions: A Glossary of Marketing Terms,* (Chicago: American Marketing Association, 1960).

Advertising is *persuasive* communication. It is not neutral; it is not un-biased; it says, "I am going to try to sell you a product or an idea." In many respects it is the most honest and frank type of propaganda.

The emphasis in this chapter will be on the diversity of the advertising function and how advertising must complement other areas of marketing objectives and strategy.

CONDITIONS CONDUCIVE TO THE USE OF ADVERTISING

Advertising is not the answer to all marketing problems. It can be effective only under certain conditions. Often advertising is used to attempt to solve problems that are beyond its scope. You have only to examine the failure rate of new products (Table 2.1)—most of which were advertised—to see that advertising does not guarantee success.*

Table 2–1

SUCCESS RATES FOR MAJOR NEW PRODUCTSᵃ		
SUCCESSFUL NEW PRODUCTSᵇ, %	COMPANIES SELLING PRIMARILY TO	
	Industrial markets, %	Consumer markets, %
100	9	18
90–99	7	4
80–89	16	9
70–79	11	11
60–69	16	12
50–59	15	15
40–49	4	2
30–39	9	9
1–29	5	4
0	8	16

ᵃReprinted with permission from the February 1980 issue of *Advertising Age*. Copyright 1980 by Crain Communications, Inc.

ᵇThe success rate reported by each company represents the percentage of all major new products introduced to the market by the company during the previous 5 years that subsequently met management's expectations in all important respects.

For advertising to be effective a combination of at least some of the following conditions must be present:

The product must be good and meet a perceived need

This is of prime importance. By "good" we mean a product that consumers will want to purchase and continue to purchase in the future. If the product is a costly once-in-a-long-time purchase, like a washing machine, the buyer will

*"New Product Failures One in Three, Study Says," *Advertising Age,* February 4, 1980, p. 74.

be willing to recommend it to friends, even become a booster for it. If a product can't pass this test, then all that we say below about trying to build a business with advertising is irrelevant.

In 1979, when liquid soap was introduced, it was an immediate success. No complex explanation was necessary to tell consumers why they needed the product to prevent the mess of bar soap at the sink or in the shower. A number of liquid-soap brands have been marketed in recent years.

Benefits were not generally seen from the introduction of Nestlé's New Cookery line of low-calorie, natural-ingredient foods. Although several problems contributed to the brand's lack of success, retailers claimed that New Cookery lacked "a clear cut reason for being" in the minds of consumers. It was noted, for instance, that the New Cookery catsup was only slightly lower in calories than other brands and was priced higher.*

The potential market for the product must warrant

the cost of advertising   You could advertise toothpicks in an attractive way, but there's little hope that advertising the toothpick would ever pay for itself.

The company should have the ability and resources

to handle an increased volume of sales   There was a time when the only question asked about a proposed product was "How much can we sell?" Now a major question is "How much can we produce?"

The product should be in step with

the times   A product can be out of step with the times because of changes in style and technology, new medical discoveries, and social, economic, or government changes. About 70 years ago over 3 million men's hats were manufactured yearly; now the number is less than 20,000, chiefly because of the automobile and the move to the suburbs. No amount of advertising can restore the hat industry to its former grandeur unless there is a complete style revolution outside advertising. Until 1967 aerosol starch was one of the fastest-growing products on supermarket shelves. Along came wash-and-wear clothes and permanent-press and double-knit garments, and the aerosol-starch business grew limp. Use of aerosol spray cans for antiperspirants is out; sales of roll-on antiperspirants are up. Nonphosphate cleansers are moving up. Low-cholesterol foods are up; butter is down. Food extenders are up. For most car buyers "How many miles per gallon?" is a big question. Advertising cannot change basic trends or overcome negative consumer attitudes toward a product.

This point was confirmed by Standard Brands' attempt to introduce Smooth & Easy sauce and gravy makers. As reported in *Advertising Age,* the company fruitlessly spent some $6 million in marketing support for the brand. The company finally concluded that "consumers have ingrained a nat-

---

*"Nestle Pulls Cookery," *Advertising Age,* June 22, 1981, p. 1.

ural bias against commercial gravies which cannot efficiently be overcome by advertising."*

A producer must be interested in selling the product
under its own name
Here is a new product. Should the manufacturer put it out under its own brand name and assume the expense of marketing it, or should the company deal with just a few large outlets, such as department stores and mail-order houses, and put on their labels? In the latter case the manufacturer will have no advertising problems or expense. (There may be other problems, however.)

The product should have a unique, beneficial
differentiation for the consumer
When a new product appears on the scene, it should offer some value that existing ones do not have. If it is identical with the others already in the field, why should anyone select it? Why should dealers stock it? A sure way to lose money in advertising is to expect the difference in advertising to make up for lack of difference in value of a product.

Types of product differentiation. Product differentiation falls into four categories, each with its unique opportunities for advertising:

1. Beneficial and evident differentiation. Products with beneficial and evident contrasts from competitors are rare but are most likely to succeed. Products in this category are also relatively easy to promote since consumers must only be made aware that they exist.

2. Beneficial but obscure product differentiation. Here advertising is perhaps most crucial to a product's success. The ability to creatively promote hidden features of benefit to the consumer will usually determine the success of such a product. High-gas-mileage automobiles, low-nicotine and -tar cigarettes, and energy-efficient appliances are examples of this type of product differentiation.

3. Nonbeneficial but evident product differentiation. Perhaps the major criticism of many contemporary products is that they are changed for no reason other than to promote some insignificant feature. The adding of chrome on a car or changing labels or packaging is a common example of this category of differentiation.

4. Nonbeneficial and obscure product differentiation. When there is very little differentiation among different brands of the same product, there is very little to advertise. Sugar is a good example of a product with little differentiation among brands; result: brand advertising is minimal, especially in view of the large consumption of sugar.

The price must be
right
It must be within the range generally regarded as reasonable and competitive for that type and quality of product. If the price can be better than its immediate competition, that fact is an important differential.

---

*"Smooth & Easy Brand's Short Life Was Anything But," *Advertising Age,* September 10, 1979, p. 33.

A uniform standard of quality must be

maintainable   When people buy something sight unseen, they buy on faith. When they buy a brand of product they have bought before, they expect the same quality they had enjoyed last time. The goodwill that a trademark represents can become the company's most valuable asset. Its worth, however, can suddenly be shattered by adverse publicity following one bad production batch. The more valuable a brand becomes, the more important it is to protect its reputation by vigilance in quality control. The question to ask about a product at the outset is "Can you control its uniform quality?" Idaho potatoes are famous because the state grows uniform, large-size potatoes, which are advertisable. Otherwise, you don't see many brands of potatoes advertised (though the potato association advertises "Potatoes are good for you" to help all potato growers).

Forbes magazine once made an analysis of the American corporations whose money was best managed, based on return of stockholders' equity over a long period. It reported:

> Is there, then, any single characteristic that all of the Top Ten share? Only one, but it is highly important: Each of these companies sells clearly identifiable, branded products with high reputations in their field. . . . The products are backed in every single case by an image of quality, the kind of image that can be created only by superior advertising and promotion.

The foregoing are among the important factors to weigh before considering advertising in marketing a product. But for some products advertising—measured by the proportion of the total selling cost it represents—plays a bigger role than in other products. Why?

VARIATIONS IN THE IMPORTANCE OF

ADVERTISING   Advertising may be the most conspicuous element in the marketing mix,* but it is not necessarily equally important in all industries using advertising. In other words the ratio of advertising to sales differs among industries and among firms in the same industry. For example look at products sold through supermarkets and other self-service stores. They are all being sold:

☐ In the same trade channels
☐ In stores that are the largest distributors of nationally advertised products
☐ Where they can reach people of all economic and social levels
☐ For low purchase prices per unit

---

*A term coined in the early 1930s, by Professor Neil H. Borden of the Harvard Business School, to include in the marketing process factors such as distribution, advertising, personal selling, and pricing.

□ Where the greatest number of people daily make the greatest number of buying decisions

□ Where the interval between shopping visits in most cases is short

□ Where decisions are made quickly

But within the self-service industry there is significant variation among the percentages of sales of foods, soaps and cleansers, cosmetics, and drugs compared with expenditures for advertising. This invites further inquiry.

Influences affecting ratio of advertising to sales

Foods. Since food is a necessity, no money need be spent by advertisers to tell people that they need food. The advertising can be largely devoted to showing why the consumer should buy one product or type of product instead of another. You have never seen an ad saying why you need food, but you do see ads saying why you need a specific brand of alcoholic beverage. In particular a major portion of beer sales are created by brand switching with millions of dollars affected by small shifts in market shares among brands. This type of industry calls for more advertising than is necessary for food. Drugs are another example of products that are bought when need arises, as in the case of laxatives and cough preparations. That, too, calls for more advertising than does something bought regularly, as is food. This helps explain why it takes a greater percentage of advertising to sell drugs and alcoholic beverages than food. Among top 100 advertisers the average for food advertising as a percentage of sales is 3.1 percent, the highest being 6.4 and the lowest 1.1.

Soaps and cleansers. No one needs to be convinced of the need for food; but when it comes to soaps and cleansers, we are dealing with a cultivated lifestyle. Generations ago housewives had a choice of two cleansing agents (toilet soap and laundry soap) and two scouring powders (exemplified by Bon Ami and Old Dutch Cleanser). When Lux soap flakes first advertised "Lux your undies every night," that was an untried routine. Today we have detergents especially formulated for a wide range of specific purposes: for different types of fabrics, for flooring, windows, or woodwork, for hair, for many other purposes. To educate people in the uses of these products and to tell about improvements constantly being made in these fields takes much advertising. The average cost of advertising soap and cleanser among the 100 leading advertisers is 5.6 percent of sales. The highest is 11.7 percent; the lowest, is 2.9 percent.

Wine, beer, and liquor. Alcoholic beverages are sold on the basis of image and targeted audience appeals. Within the total alcoholic-beverage category there have been major shifts in the last decade. The beer category is increasingly concentrated among a few large brewers, such as Anheuser-Busch. However, the biggest news is the switch by young adults to wine from distilled spirits. The change in drinking habits and marketing concentrations has increased overall budgets among all three beverage categories. The industry average is 6.4 percent of sales, with the highest being 8.8 and the lowest 4.7. These figures would no doubt be higher if it was permitted to advertise liquor in the broadcast media.

Over-the-counter drugs. There is an active market for these drugs, and pharmaceutical companies are constantly trying to improve them and to develop new, more effective products. Drug companies invest a great deal of money in research and development, knowing that, if they can come out with a more effective preparation, a big market may await it. They also know that to reach such a market and thereby recoup their investment, a big advertising expenditure may be needed. Confidence in advertising is a strong inducement to take big money risks in research.

The major brands of over-the-counter drugs generally spend a higher percentage of their sales on advertising than any other product category does. Each large company already has a large following, but to hold its customers against competitive claims it needs to remind them of the benefits they derive from its products. Many products, such as those for the relief of stomach distress or headache, are used only sporadically. It is therefore important to keep the advertising of such products continually before the public to reach those people who, at any given time, may have need of them. For all these reasons advertising is a very important part of the marketing mix for drug products.

Among America's leading 100 advertisers of drugs the average percentage of advertising to sales is 5.2; the highest is 11.1, the lowest 1.6.*

Differences in advertising/sales ratios within the same industry

Among the reasons for big variations in the percentage of advertising expenditures by different companies in the same industry, these are prominent:

1. Total sales volume. Advertising/sales ratios usually decrease as sales volume increases. General Motors, with sales of over $300 billion, spends 0.5 percent on advertising, while American Motors spends 1.4 percent of its $44 billion sales on advertising.

2. Use of other elements in the marketing mix, for example, putting more money into demonstrations or sales personnel. Avon, with its door-to-door salespersons, spends much less on advertising than its competition does, such as Revlon, which depends on retail stores and self-service merchandising for its sales.

3. Management success in generating new and improved products and marketing methods. Procter & Gamble's advertising/sales ratio of approximately 6 percent is higher than would be expected, based on its sales volume of $11 billion. However, the number of new brands introduced by the company requires a higher level of advertising than its more conservative competitors feel necessary.

4. Overall management philosophy toward advertising. In a speech to stockholders W. L. Lyons Brown, Jr., President of Brown-Forman Distillers, said that Brown-Forman is

*Advertising Age, September 10, 1981, p. 8.

"a strong believer in substantial advertising support."* He went on to announce a 20-percent increase in advertising expenditures for 1982.

We now move on to the next big step, to see where and how advertising fits into the marketing process.

THE PLACE OF ADVERTISING IN THE MARKETING PROCESS

Think of a product in terms of its journey through the distributing process, from the point at which it is made to the point at which it is bought by its user. Advertising moves that product along in this journey, changing its immediate objectives along the way. This results in different forms of advertising:

Advertising to the consumer:
- ☐ National advertising
- ☐ Retail (local) advertising
- ☐ End-product advertising
- ☐ Direct-response advertising

Advertising to business and professions:
- ☐ Trade advertising
- ☐ Industrial advertising
- ☐ Professional advertising
- ☐ Corporate-management advertising

Advertising to the consumer

National advertising. The term *national advertising* has a special non-geographic meaning in advertising: It refers to the advertising by the owner of a trade-marked product or service sold through different distributors or stores, wherever they may be. It does not mean that the product is necessarily sold nationwide.

The purpose of national advertising is to make known to the consumer the name of the product or service and its uses, benefits, and advantages so that a person will be disposed to buy or order it whenever and wherever it is convenient to do so (Exhibit 2.1). It is up to the national advertiser to create the demand for the product or service. Through national advertising we have come to know products like Dial soap, Zenith TV sets, Shake 'n' Bake food mix, Avis rental cars, Suzuki motorcycles. When most people talk of advertising, they usually refer just to national advertising.

Retail (local) advertising. Retail advertising is that of a dealer who sells directly to the consumer. Chief among such advertisers are department stores, supermarkets, chain stores, discount stores, and specialty shops (Exhibits 2.2 and 2.3). No matter how big or small the store may be, its advertising will say, "This is something you should buy *here*—today."

---

*John J. O'Connor, "B-F Ready To Pour It On," *Advertising Age,* August 10, 1981, p. 4.

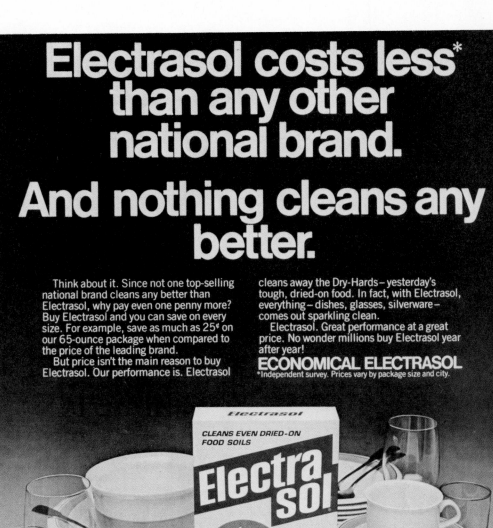

Electrasol costs less* than any other national brand.

And nothing cleans any better.

Think about it. Since not one top-selling national brand cleans any better than Electrasol, why pay even one penny more? Buy Electrasol and you can save on every size. For example, save as much as 25¢ on our 65-ounce package when compared to the price of the leading brand.

But price isn't the main reason to buy Electrasol. Our performance is. Electrasol cleans away the Dry-Hards—yesterday's tough, dried-on food. In fact, with Electrasol, everything—dishes, glasses, silverware—comes out sparkling clean.

Electrasol. Great performance at a great price. No wonder millions buy Electrasol year after year!

ECONOMICAL ELECTRASOL
*Independent survey. Prices vary by package size and city.

Exhibit 2.1
National advertising. The marketer of Electrasol tells a widespread public about the product and its chief advantages, with a view to having readers buy the product. (Courtesy Economics Laboratory.)

Exhibit 2.2
Retail advertising: supermarket. A typical supermarket ad features nationally advertised brands, private brands, and unbranded products with a common appeal—price. Purpose: to attract customers to come to the store, where they will probably buy some of the advertised items and other unadvertised ones. (Courtesy Kroger Food Stores.)

sale spring sale spring

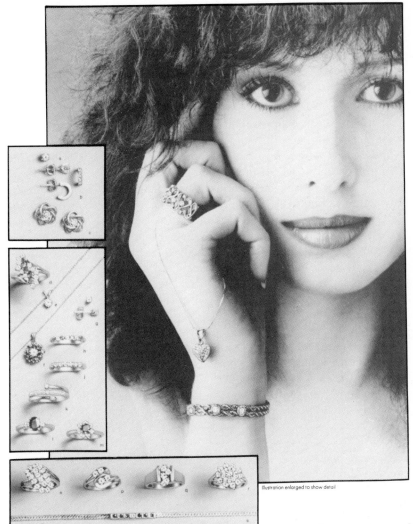

save on elegant diamond jewelry

20% off

We've slashed the price on every diamond in our Fine Jewelry department. Beautiful investments now irresistibly priced: earrings, bracelets, rings, and pendants. Some pieces feature luxurious rubies, emeralds, or sapphires, and all are set in 14K gold. All weights are total. Hurry in for best selection. Shown is only a sampling of the values. Fine Jewelry, D79, all Davison's. Sorry, no mail or phone orders.

	reg.	sale
A. Earstuds, ½ ct. of dias.	$795	$629
B. 14K gold hoops, 2/10 ct. of dias.	575	459
C. Loveknot earstuds, dias. centers	350	279
D. Emerald cluster ring, .56 ct. of dias.	1325	1059
E. 2/10 ct. dia. pendant	350	279
F. Ruby cluster pendant, .16 ct. of dias.	750	599
G. Earstuds, 1/10 ct. dias.	150	119
H. Emerald & dia. band ring	350	279
J. Band ring, .18 ct. dias.	375	299
K. Contemporary ring, .13 ct. of diamonds	450	359
L. Sapphire ring, 2 dias.	495	389
M. Ruby ring, .35 ct. dias.	625	499
N. 1 ct. dia. cluster ring	1850	1479
P. Contemporary ring, .24 ct. of dias.	575	459
Q. Contemporary ring, .42 ct. of dias.	1150	919
R. Cluster ring, 1 ct. of dias.	1775	1419
S. Bracelet, dias. & colored stones	350	279
Ring on hand: Wedding band, 2/10 ct. of dias.	875	699
Pendant on hand: ⅓ dia. heart pendant	750	599
Bracelet on hand: rope bracelet, 3/10 ct. of dias.	1150	919

Illustration enlarged to show detail

davison's

shop suburban stores sunday 12:30 to 5:30, downtown closed

Exhibit 2.3
Retail advertising: department store. A department-store ad features diamond jewelry at an attractive price. Purpose: to attract shoppers to the jewelry department, to buy earrings and perhaps other items in the store. (Courtesy Davison's, Inc.)

35

National advertising will say, "If you want good sheets, get Fruit of the Loom." A retail advertisement will say, "Now here! Latest patterns and colors in Fruit of the Loom sheets. Come early." Retail advertising also includes that of the many products not nationally advertised, especially the store's own brands. But whatever the message, the thrust of retail advertising is "Buy here, now!"

F. Mayans, vice-president of Federated Department Stores, once said:

> In my view, our kind of advertising does very little to create a demand for either goods or services that do not fulfill an already existing physical or psychic desire. . . . Retail advertising . . . should tell what options the retailer can offer—price-lines, sizes, colors, fabrics. . . .

Chapter 23 deals with retail advertising.

End-product advertising. E. I. DuPont de Nemours & Co. has sales of over $12 billion and is one of the nation's largest advertisers. The majority of DuPont's sales come from chemicals, synthetic fabrics, and plastics, which are used by other manufacturers to produce furniture (Antron nylon), lingerie (Tricot), and cooking utensils (SilverStone nonstick coating). See Exhibit 2.4.

DuPont's advertising for these products is intended to leapfrog over the manufacturer to tell DuPont's story directly to the ultimate consumer of the finished product. By building consumer demand, DuPont expects that manufacturers will be more included to use its ingredients in their products. This type of indirect advertising is referred to as *end-product advertising.*

Many makers of synthetic fabrics advertise, "Look for the name _____ whenever you buy a _____." Often such ads are cooperative ads between the fabric maker and the garment manufacturer.

Behind the scenes in any such project there is considerable sales effort to induce manufacturers to buy the advertised product for use in their own product and to get the benefit of its name on their label. End-product advertising is a variant of the usual national advertising that asks the consumer to buy a product by name.

Direct-response advertising. One of the fastest-growing sectors of our economy is direct marketing: selling a product from marketer to consumer without going through retail channels. The advertising used in direct marketing is referred to as *direct-response advertising* (Exhibit 2.5). This term is now the preferred one for what had long been known as "mail-order advertising" because an enormous amount of such advertising is now done through magazines, newspapers, television ("TV"), and radio. Direct mail continues, however, to be the most important direct-response medium—or it was before postage rates climbed steeply.

The chief characteristic of direct-response advertising is that it always bears a coupon or return card or gives a telephone number or address to which to respond to a TV or radio ad. The goal of the advertiser is to get a prompt response with the name and address of the responder. Chapter 11 is a discussion of direct-response advertising.

Exhibit 2.4
Pictured is an example of end-product advertising for SilverStone®, pointing out the availability of the nonstick surface on a wide variety of cookware types. (Courtesy E. I. du Pont de Nemours & Co., Inc.)

L.L.Bean®

Outdoor Sporting Specialties

Flannel Pajamas

Comfortably warm for cold nights. Amply cut from 100% cotton flannel. Sanforized®. Button front top with breast pocket, drawstring waist. Women's have elasticized waist. Machine wash. Colors, Red. Tan. Light Blue. Women's sizes: Sm. (30-32), Med. (34-36), Lg. (38-40). #4199W, **$16.00 ppd.** Men's sizes: A(110-135 lbs.), B(135-165), C(165-185), D(185-210). #1998W, **$16.00 ppd.** Men's Long sizes: (for 6 feet and over) B, C, and D only #1996W, **$18.00 ppd.**

Chino Pants
(For Men and Women)

You'll get more wearing pleasure from these pants than any others you own. Made of high grade combed cotton/polyester twill. Permanent crease, washable. No ironing required. Neat looking for sports or work. Color, Light Tan. Men's waist sizes: 24, 25, 26, 27, 28, 29. Inseams 30" and 32". Even waist sizes 30 to 44 plus 31 and 33. Inseams 29", 31" and 33". #1822W, **$13.00 ppd.**

Lined Chinos - Same sturdy construction but fully lined with our famous tan Chamois Cloth, a comfortably warm 100% cotton flannel. Men's even sizes 30 to 44. Inseams 29", 31" and 33". #1824W. Women's even sizes 8 to 20. #4435W. **$23.00 ppd.**

Timberline Flannel Shirt
(For Men and Women)

Rugged, warm and colorful shirts for active wear. Same sturdy construction and extra full cut as our Chamois Cloth Shirt. Long tuck-in tails (women's have squared tails), two large breast pockets with button flaps. The 8 oz. fabric of 67% cotton, 33% polyester is softly napped on both sides for extra comfort. Machine washable. Four plaids: Navy on Tan. Bright Red on Tan. Slate Blue on Tan. Forest Green on Tan. Men's whole sizes: 15, 16, 17, 18, 19. Regular Length #1626W, **$17.75 ppd.** Long Model #1627W, **$18.75 ppd.** Women's sizes: 6 to 20, #4337W, **$17.25 ppd.**

Sheeplined Slipper

Comfortably warm no-sole moccasin slipper, manufactured by us of full grain leather. Lined with soft, absorbent wool. Color, Dark Brown with Natural lining. In whole sizes only, medium width. Women's sizes: 4 to 10, #4883W, **$22.50 ppd.** Men's sizes: 6 to 13, #3631W, **$25.50 ppd.**

Ship Postpaid · ☐ **PLEASE SEND FREE CATALOG**

Item #	Qty.	Color	Size	Description	Amount
			Add 5% Sales Tax on shipments to Maine addresses	Total	

☐ Check Enclosed   ☐ Master Card   ☐ VISA   ☐ American Express

Card Number_____ Exp. Date_____

Name _____

Address _____

City_____ State_____ Zip_____

L. L. Bean, Inc., 6981 Casco St., Freeport, ME 04033

Advertising to business and
professions
There is a world of advertising that most consumers rarely see. In it one business firm tries to sell something to another; included in this category is advertising to professional people, like physicians and architects, who are in a position to specify the advertiser's product for others to buy. All this is in addition to advertising products to consumers for their personal use. Advertising to business has several different forms.

Trade advertising. All the articles in a store must be bought by someone before they are delivered to that store. The buyer may serve a whole chain of stores, or a buying committee may have to give its approval. To reach those authorities, the marketer will advertise in the trade papers of their business, giving news about the product, especially price, special deals and packaging. The advertising may describe special consumer advertising and promotions. It may tell about the success the product is having with the public and with other retailers. The theme of all the advertising is to show the profit the store can make by stocking this product now (Exhibit 2.6). Such trade advertising is an important adjunct to any national-advertising campaign.

Industrial advertising. A manufacturer is a buyer of machinery, equipment, raw materials, and components used in producing the goods he sells. Those who have machinery (Exhibit 2.7), equipment, or material to sell to other producers will address their advertising especially to them in their industry magazine. It is quite unlike consumer advertising and is referred to as *industrial advertising.*

Industrial advertising is aimed at a market that has certain characteristics: sales may run into very large sums; many people are involved in a decision to buy, each person a specialist or professional in some aspect of the total operation; decisions on a matter may take a long time. The products are not being bought for personal use.

Professional advertising. The most important person in the sale of some products is, as we've mentioned, the professional adviser to the buyer, as a physician or architect. The physician's recommendation is the best inducement to a patient to buy that product. In construction the architect's specifications are usually binding. In these areas, then, advertising is frequently directed to professionals through their professional publications (Exhibit 2.8) and by direct mail.

Corporate-management advertising. Many people within a company may join in making a decision about products the company needs. If the investment is large, the highest level of management will be involved. How to reach them? Many have found the answer by advertising the broad services of a company in the publications they read, such as *Newsweek, Time, U.S. News & World Report,* and *Fortune.* Such advertising is called *corporate-management advertising,* or *corporate institutional advertising* if it is also addressed to a wider audience (Exhibit 2.9).

Use a Bally Walk-in to build your Dairy Store sales

High's Ice Cream Company in Norfolk, Virginia, started with three stores. Now they operate forty-three throughout Tidewater Virginia and North Carolina . . . and sell one million gallons of ice cream in a year. Sales like this depend on effective merchandising . . . one of the reasons why High's selected Bally Walk-In Coolers/Freezers. Large ten-door Prefabs maintain refrigeration temperatures of −15°F., and are used for both merchandising and storage. And their large capacity enables High's to make only one delivery weekly to its stores, thus saving delivery costs.

Bally Walk-Ins can be assembled in any size from standard modular panels for storage or display. The low-cost galvanized finish can be clad with materials to match any store decor. They are easy to enlarge or relocate . . . and are subject to investment tax credit and fast depreciation. (Ask your accountant.)

BALLY   *High efficiency...low energy use*

REFRIGERATION SYSTEMS

Bally now reduces electric usage with the first systems ever designed specifically for walk-ins. Thermobalance Refrigeration Systems are made with all components ideally matched in size and balanced in capacity. The result is maximum refrigeration efficiency with lower energy consumption. Write for *free* literature, wall sample and engineering design help.

Bally Case & Cooler, Inc.
Bally, PA 19503
Phone: (215) 845-2311

©1980

Exhibit 2.6
Trade advertising. Retailers are the target here, to make them aware of the display that will help produce sales and increase profits for them. (Courtesy Bally Case and Cooler, Inc.)

Exhibit 2.7
Business advertisement of an industrial firm. The advantages of the advertiser's product are explained to other manufacturers and users of heavy machinery. (Courtesy Ammco Tools.)

41

Sea-Land is breaking up the Bill-of-Lading Bottleneck.

We're doing our best to get your bills of lading back to you in 24 hours. Or less.

At Sea-Land®, we know how waiting to get a bill of lading back from a shipping line can jam you up. So we're not about to keep you waiting.

Our systems for processing bills of lading are as streamlined as any in the industry. And our Sea-Land people are doing everything they can to push your bills of lading through fast. So fast that we can usually have them back to you in just 24 hours after your cargo is aboard our ship. Or even less.

Because we figure the better we do *our* job, the better you'll be able to do yours. Stop waiting around for bills of lading that take too long to come back. Start calling Sea-Land.

Sea Land
What we did for shipping we're doing for service.

Exhibit 2.8
Professional advertisement addressed to bank officers. Note the detailed, technical copy. (Courtesy Sea-Land Service, Inc.)

"At Gulf, we're working on a way to light lights, cook meals, and heat houses with energy stored in water."

"You probably remember from grade-school science that water is two parts hydrogen and one part oxygen," says Dr. John Norman.

"Here at General Atomic Company, a subsidiary 50% owned by Gulf Oil, a project is under way in cooperation with the Department

"There are 326 million cubic miles of water on earth, and hydrogen in every drop—a natural energy resource that won't run out."

of Energy to extract hydrogen from water for use as a fuel: for heating, cooking, or anything that now uses petroleum or natural gas.

"The extraction process is called thermochemical water-splitting. We know it works because we've done it. But it takes high temperatures — about 1600° F — so it's rather expensive.

"It may be the turn of the century before it becomes commercial. But it's an attractive idea. Hydrogen from a gallon of water has about half as much energy as there is in a gallon of gasoline.

"Hydrogen can be made into a liquid or gaseous fuel. It can be transmitted long distances more cheaply than electricity. And when hydrogen burns, it's converted back into water. Very tidy."

At Gulf, our first priority is to get all the oil and natural gas we can out of resources right here in America. But we're working on a lot of other ideas, too. Thermochemical water-splitting is one of them. We are also working on underground coal gasification, liquefied coal and other synthetic fuels, geothermal energy, and other alternative energy sources.

Basically the business we are in is energy for tomorrow.

Gulf people: energy for tomorrow.

Exhibit 2.9
Public-service (institutional) advertising, designed in this case to show how Gulf is solving the energy problem. (Courtesy of the Gulf Oil Corporation.)

Advertising of services

As examples of nationally advertised services we include airlines, rental cars, motel and hotel chains, tourist sites, tourist agencies, and fast-food chains. Banks, investment houses, and insurance companies (Exhibit 2.10) also fall into the service classification. The whole service field has been expanding greatly in recent years. The advertising of services differs from that of commodities because of the difference in the way they are marketed. The response to service advertising is meant to come directly from the prospect or at most through one intermediary, as a travel office. One interesting development in the field of service advertising has been the proliferation of franchising. Fast-food chains, for example, will grant franchises to operators who will pay a fixed sum of money to lease or own the franchise in their own communities. The company granting the franchise will usually do national advertising to spread its fame on a broad scale. The local franchise owner can then do local advertising.

SUMMARY

This chapter seeks to emphasize the diversity and unique role of each advertisement and advertising campaign. Just as no two products adhere to the same marketing and advertising strategies, no two advertisements have exactly the same purpose. Because advertising is so flexible, it is important for the advertiser to determine exactly what role advertising should play in his overall marketing program. To do this, it is important to identify those conditions conducive to successful advertising. A limited list of such conditions would include a branded product of standardized quality with beneficial differentiations from its competition and at a reasonable price.

As we examined some representative industries, it is obvious that advertising's importance varies widely from industry to industry and even among companies within the same industry. The roles of advertising also differ in where the advertising is placed. National advertising has specific roles, which differ in fundamental ways from retail advertising. For instance price is usually omitted in national promotions and emphasized in retail ads.

It is also important to note that not all advertising is intended for typical consumers. Millions of dollars are spent each year on business-to-business or professional advertisers. Advertisers must first convince retailers to stock their goods before consumers can buy them. This involves advertising to the trade. Similarly, drug companies must advertise to doctors, and makers of heavy equipment must advertise to manufacturers. By the same token not all advertising is intended to sell products. The fastest growing area of our economy is services. Obviously, advertising for airlines, banks, insurance companies, and stockbrokers is different from product advertising.

"My insurance company? New England Life, of course. Why?"

Smashing idea: we also offer mutual funds, variable annuities and investment counseling.

Exhibit 2.10
One in a long-running series of advertisements for the New England Mutual Life Insurance Company. (Reprinted by permission.)

QUESTIONS

1. How does advertising differ from other types of persuasive communication?
2. How does the marketing mix affect the level of advertising devoted to a brand?
3. Briefly discuss four factors that cause differences in advertising/sales ratios for products in the same industry.
4. Compare and contrast the role of advertising in the following: consumer-goods companies and industrial-goods companies: profit-seeking organizations and not-for-profit organizations.
5. Does advertising add value to products? If so, how? If not, why not?
6. Which is more important in achieving marketing success, the product or the advertising? Explain your answer.
7. Advertising can be effective only under certain conditions. What are conditions that are conducive to advertising? Explain why each condition is important.
8. Briefly discuss the relationship between advertising and product differentiation.
9. What is the relationship between self-service and advertising? Does advertising have a different role, depending upon whether or not the product is sold via self-service? Explain.
10. How does corporate institutional advertising differ from most branded package-goods advertising?

SUGGESTED EXERCISES

11. Choose two ads for products that demonstrate each of the four types of product differentiation discussed in the chapter.
12. Note the advertising appeals of a high-priced and a low-priced product in the same generic category. In which media were the ads placed? Is price mentioned? Are specific product features given in detail? Are competing brands mentioned by name? Other significant differences?

READINGS

AAKER, DAVID A. and JOHN G. MYERS: *Advertising Management* (Englewood Cliffs, NJ: Prentice-Hall, 1982.

"B&B Study Says Males Domestic," *Advertising Age,* October 6, 1980, pp. 53.

BARTON, ROGER, ed.: *The Handbook of Advertising Management* (New York: McGraw-Hill, 1970).

BRITT, STEUART HENDERSON, ed., *Marketing Manager's Handbook* (Chicago: The Dartwell Corporation, 1973).

DELOZIER, WAYNE M.: *The Marketing Communications Process* (New York: McGraw-Hill, 1976).

FELDMAN, SIDNEY: "Advertorials: Impact at a Premium," *Magazine Age,* May 1980, pp. 26–33.

HANES, DOUGLASS K.: "Leisure and Consumer Behavior," *Journal of the Academy of Marketing Science,* Fall 1979, pp. 391–403.

McCARTHY, E. JEROME: *Basic Marketing,* 7th ed. (Homewood, IL: Richard D. Irwin, Inc., 1981).

McCOMBS, MAXWELL E., and CHAIM H. EYAL, "Spending on the Mass Media," *Journal of Communication,* Winter 1980, pp. 153–58.

McGANN, ANTHONY F. and J. THOMAS RUSSELL: *Advertising Media / A Managerial Approach* (Homewood, IL: Richard D. Irwin, Inc., 1981), pp. 1–23.

NEAL, WILLIAM D.: "Strategic Product Positioning: A Step-by-step Guide," *Business,* May-June 1980, pp. 34–42.

POE, RANDALL: "Masters of the Advertorial," *Across the Board,* September 1980, pp. 15–28.

RUNYON, KENNETH E.: *Advertising and the Practice of Marketing* (Columbus, OH: C.E. Merrill Publishing Co., 1979).

WILSON, AUBREY, and CHRISTOPHER WEST: "The Marketing of Unmentionables," *Harvard Business Review,* January-February 1981, pp. 99–102.

Planning the Advertising

The essence of good advertising is the planning that takes place prior to execution. Although a few great advertising compaigns have resulted from an idea that "popped" into someone's head, these are rare. Effective advertising starts with an identification of the prime prospects for a product, the consumer needs that are met by such a product, and the stage of development (or as we call it, the "advertising spiral", Chapter 3) of the product and its promotion. Most products move from the introductory, or pioneering, stage to public acceptance and finally to an inevitable wear-out period. Those products which are successful over the longest period are the ones that adapt to change by constantly staying in tune with consumer needs and being positioned through product research and promotion to meet these needs. As we shall see in our discussion of target marketing (Chapter 4), the advertising process must first focus on identifying prime prospects through research. This research is then used to plan the objectives and strategy of marketing and advertising a product.

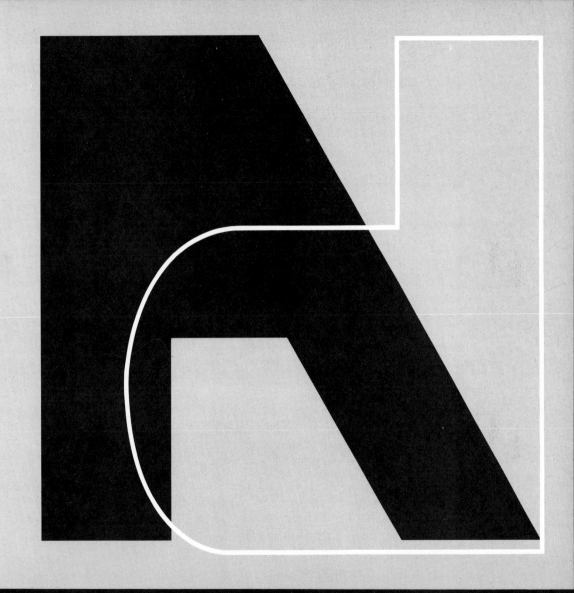

PART TWO

3

The Advertising Spiral

The following advertisement appeared in a national magazine. The name of the product is omitted. What would you guess the product to be?

> for Christmas
>
> Are you searching for a helpful, useful, practical Christmas present—for son or daughter, for brother or sister, for wife or husband, for dearest friend?
>
> Here it is! The _____ is a gift that always inspires, for it provides its owner with the modern, time saving way to _____.
>
> Remember that the _____ is the world's smallest and lightest _____, with standard keyboard weighs only 8½ pounds net and fits in a case only a few inches high. But it is complete in every feature—strong and durable—simple and easy to operate—the recognized leader—in sales and popularity.

Again, what product would you say was being advertised? A videocassette? A table-top computer? A word processor? An interactive television-computer package? None of these. It was the Remington portable typewriter, one of the earliest models marketed, advertised in a 1927 issue of *Collier's* magazine.

ADVERTISING

STAGES

There is an unmistakable similarity between the Remington portable-typewriter advertisement and those used to introduce more recent inventions because, from the time a *new type* of product first appears on the market to the time various brands of that product are household words, the product faces similar advertising stages:

- ☐ Pioneering stage
- ☐ Competitive stage
- ☐ Retentive stage

These stages depend upon the degree of acceptance accorded the product by those to whom it is being advertised. A clear understanding of these stages will be helpful in planning basic advertising strategy.

Pioneering stage

The research and development department of a large company may have been working for years on a useful new invention. When it finally succeeds and the product is ready for the market, does the public arise in elation and clamor for it? Not in most cases, because it may never have occurred to consumers to seek such a device. Until people recognize that this is something they want, a product is in the first, or *pioneering,* stage.

The advertising of products in the pioneering stage (or *pioneering advertising,* as we call it) must show that consumer needs can be satisfied in a new and more efficient way (Exhibit 3.1). Limitations tolerated as "normal" are now demonstrated to have been overcome safely. The safety razor supplanted the straight-edge razor, and the advertising said:

> If you are still depending upon the barber or an old-fashioned razor, you are in the same category as a man who climbs ten flights of stairs when there is an elevator in the building. With the Gillette Safety Razor the most inexperienced man can remove without cut or scratch in three to five minutes any beard that ever grew.

And when the electric shaver came upon the scene, its advertising proclaimed "no bother or fuss of old-fashioned soap and brush. . . . no more shaving cuts with the new electric shaver." Even color television was launched by the pioneering advertising of RCA Victor in the 1950s, which said:

> See World Series Baseball in Living Color. . . . Rarely in a lifetime can you share a thrill like this. . . . You can see baseball's greatest spectacle come alive in your own home in color. . . . You'll sense a new on-the-spot realism in every picture of the crowd, the players, the action. . . . Made by RCA—the most trusted name in electronics.

Although the early portable typewriter and color television were more than a generation apart and although the advertising techniques of their days were almost as far apart, both products attacked their common problem in much the same way: The prospective buyer was urged to add a source of utility or delight, a rare source of inspiration and thrills. These themes of new sat-

Presenting the thermostat that thinks like an accountant.

GE's new Electronic Digital Thermostat for Weathertron® Heat Pumps doesn't <u>really</u> think. But it does have a built-in microcomputer that allows it to do some rather amazing things. Not the least of which is to cut heating costs up to 15 percent*

How? For one thing, the GE Electronic Digital Thermostat allows multiple setbacks. Which means one temperature can be set for sleeping, one for waking, and yet another for periods when no one's home. So home owners won't end up paying for heating and cooling they don't need.

And while most thermostats will immediately switch to supplemental electric heat during recovery from setback times, our new thermostat is different. It monitors the house, senses if it's heating up sufficiently, and whenever possible lets the heat pump do the work. That also cuts heating bills.

And there is one other thing. When your customers buy the heat pump thermostat that thinks like an accountant, they can tell their accountant and claim the residential energy tax credit on their federal return.

Now just think how attractive all that can be to a prospective home buyer.

For further information, call your local General Electric Central Air Conditioning Zone or Independent Distributor.

*Actual savings will vary depending on consumer life-style, climate, and type of supplementary heat used for recovery.

WE BRING GOOD THINGS TO LIFE.

GENERAL 🔘 ELECTRIC

Exhibit 3.1
Computerized energy management in the pioneering stage. (Courtesy of G.E.)

isfactions in life are recurrent in pioneering advertising of new products—those which achieve a breakthrough in the principle on which the product currently operates. When the Kodak camera first came out, people had to be told, "You press the button. We do the rest." Today the Kodak Ektra camera advertises, "Big on convenience, smaller in size, just in time for Christmas." Each of such innovations adds its touch of richness to the satisfaction of life and even

Exhibit 3.2
Pioneering advertising, presenting not merely a new product but a new lifestyle. (Courtesy Casio)

The Casio Melody Calculator.
Now, anyone can carry a tune. In fact, 12 tunes. Because it's the only musical calculator that plays a different melody every day of the week, Jingle Bells on Christmas Day, Happy Birthday to remind you how young you are, the Wedding March on your Anniversary, and the Stein Song on any day you want.

Of course, this little performer is also a full-function calculator. Which means after playing a few numbers, you can then add, subtract, multiply and divide a few numbers.

And with the complete watch function, plus stopwatch and hourly time signals, you can even time your duets against your square roots and percentages.

But that's just partly why it's a true virtuoso. The real talent in a Casio ML-120 Musical Calculator is how it can be made so well, and cost so very little.

So stop in and hear one of these musical wonders for yourself. It has a repertoire that's absolutely amazing.

CASIO
WHERE MIRACLES NEVER CEASE

changes lifestyles (Exhibit 3.2). Each represents more than a minor improvement in an existing product. Each calls for a new set of tools and dies—and it calls for pioneering advertising. It is interesting to observe how often pioneering advertising uses the terms "no more this" or "no more that," referring to existing shortcomings, and "now you can do this" or "now you can do that."

Competitive stage

By the time the public accepts the idea of using the new category of product, competitors undoubtedly will have sprung up. When the public no longer wonders, "What's that product for?" but rather "Which make shall I buy?" the product enters the *competitive stage.* We speak of the advertising for a product in the competitive stage as *competitive advertising.* (This is a restrictive meaning of that term, not to be confused with the looser meaning that all ads are competitive with each other.)

Most products in everyday use are in the competitive stage: cars, detergents, toothpaste, headache remedies, razor blades, soft drinks, shampoos, TV sets, packaged foods. The purpose of advertising in the competitive stage is to show how unique features, or *differentials,* of one brand make it better than other brands (Exhibits 3.3 to 3.5). Here are some headlines:

No other video cassette recorder gives you
more than this one (RCA Selectavision 650)

All Stainless Steel Is Not Alike (Lauffer Stainless Steel)

Better Mileage Ratings Than Toyota or
Datsun Pickups. (Chevrolet Luv Pickup)

The best tonic drinks are made with Puerto
Rican white rum. Not gin or vodka. (Puerto Rican Rums)

In Germany We Sell More Rolex Watches Than
Anybody Else. Why? (Rolex Watches)

None of these ads will tell you why you should use its type of product; that is taken for granted. But each sets out to tell you why you should select that particular brand from among the others in its field.

Retentive stage

There is a third stage through which a product *might* pass, the *retentive stage.* When a brand of a product is used by a large share of the market, the goal of much of the brand's advertising may be to hold on to these customers. All over the world, for example, there are signs saying, "Drink Coca-Cola." They do not say what Coca-Cola is; they give no reason why you should drink it or why Coca-Cola is better than any other drink. The advertising is addressed to Coca-Cola drinkers to reinforce, at the least cost per message, their favorite recollection of this familiar beverage.

That best-known form of retentive advertising is often referred to as *reminder advertising,* often its chief feature. Retentive advertising, however, em-

Exhibit 3.3
Pepsi Cola features its competitive advantage over Coca-Cola. (Courtesy Pepsico, Inc.)

BIG SHAMPOO NEWS!

Try the shampoo that wins over 8 leading shampoos— New Improved Agrée Shampoo.

—the tests—

Hundreds of women across the country ages 14-45 recently tested New Improved Agree Shampoo against 8 leading shampoos. The results of these independent studies could change your mind about your current shampoo.

VS. The leading balsam & protein shampoo

Agree was preferred for lather and manageability.

VS. The leading baby shampoo

A majority of women tested preferred Agree for total performance.

VS. The leading pH shampoo

The majority of women who expressed a preference felt that their hair was cleaner with Agree.

VS. The leading herbal shampoo

The majority of women who expressed a preference felt that their hair was more manageable with Agree.

VS. The leading dandruff shampoo

The majority of women who expressed a preference felt that their hair had more body with Agree.

VS. The leading blow dryer shampoo

The majority of women who expressed a preference felt that their hair stayed clean longer with Agree.

VS. The leading economy shampoo

The majority of women who expressed a preference felt that their hair was less oily and greasy with Agree.

VS. The leading gold formula shampoo

Agree was significantly preferred for manageability.

VS. All of these shampoos

Most women said *they preferred Agree overall.*

*All comparison tests were conducted by an independent research firm using national statistical samples in 1978.

New Improved Agree shampoo helps stop the greasies.

A major problem with all hair types is that hair gets oily and greasy too soon after shampooing. We call this "the greasies."

Excess oil builds up on the scalp, spreads to the hair and attracts dirt and additional oil causing hair to lose body and become stringy and oily.

Tests prove that Agree is unsurpassed in its ability to help stop the greasies.

Unlike some shampoos, Agree shampoo contains no greasy feeling additives.

 So it cleans hair beautifully without leaving a greasy residue. That's why regular use of Agree helps stop the greasies between shampoos.

Hate the greasies?   You'll love new improved Agree.

There's a new improved Agree shampoo for your hair type.

Because everyone's hair is not alike, Agree offers you three Shampoo formulas: Regular Formula, Balsam & Protein, Oily Hair Formula.

© 1979 S.C. Johnson & Son, Inc.

New Improved Agree Shampoo helps stop the greasies.

Exhibit 3.4
Agree shampoo demonstrates its advantage over leading competitors. (Courtesy S.C. Johnson & Son, Inc.)

Exhibit 3.5
Bulova watches reacting to a price competitor. (Courtesy Bulova Watch Company, Inc.)

braces other problems of a product in the retentive stage, such as staving off imitators, an experience faced by every highly successful advertiser. Retentive advertising associates a traditional product with some consumer benefit, for example, the "smile" that comes from drinking Coke. Advertisements may also combine elements of both retentive and competitive stages (Exhibit 3.6).

Sometimes companies will use retentive advertising to maintain public awareness during product shortages. The most extended and dramatic period of this type of advertising was during World War II, when many products were either not manufactured at all or all output was diverted to the war effort. Headlines such as "It's Messerschmitts Not Mallards Today, Bill" (Winchester Repeating Arms Company, 1942) were quite common advertising themes during that war.

Exhibit 3.6
Tupperware brand products have a tremendous market so the company wants to keep its name before the eyes of the consumers. (Courtesy Tupperware Home Parties, a division of Dart Industries Inc.)

Another form of retentive advertising is used when a corporation is beset by problems that affect its existence, such as labor disputes. During the time of crisis, advertising for sales goes into limbo while the company devotes all its efforts to presenting its case to the public. This is *institutional advertising*. Here we are following the advertising stages of a product whose sales have uninterrupted, successful growth.

VARIABLES IN ADVERTISING STAGES

Shift of stage within one market

Since people may gradually change their attitudes toward a product, a product may also gradually shift from the pioneering stage to the competitive stage. Half the space of a movie-camera ad may be pioneering, telling of the joy of having moving pictures of children as they grow up; the other half may be competitive, explaining the special features of this particular camera. The

58

product could be described as half in the pioneering stage, half in the competitive stage.

Product in different stages in different

markets
In considering the advertising stages of a product, we think of it in terms of specific markets. A product may be in different stages in different markets at the same time. For example large copiers are in the competitive stage in the business-office market, but small desk copiers are in the pioneering stage for smaller offices and home usage.

Other influences on advertising stage

of product
The factor that determines the stage of a product is the attitude of the public toward it, not the recency of invention or the amount of advertising that has been done for it. Some new types of product suddenly take off like wildfire and move directly into the competitive stage—electronic calculators are an example. There had long been much publicity about the use of calculators in the scientific, technical, and business worlds. When low-priced, pocket-size calculators appeared for general consumer use, no extensive pioneering advertising was needed to teach the public about them, and they moved directly into the competitive stage. Public demand was so great that retailers immediately opened calculator departments and began extensive advertising, each ad pointing out the competitive price and other advantages of a particular model.

Products that have a special style may catch the fancy or the requirements of the public so quickly that they find themselves in a competitive price-and-style fray at an early point, without the benefit of pioneering advertising. The modern wood stove is a good example. Each marketer must make his own appraisal of the current attitude of the public toward his product or product class and must determine its advertising stage because that will determine the thrust of the advertising used.

Product in competitive stage, improvement in

pioneering stage
Not all products presented as "new" are new types of product. Many are familiar types in the competitive stage, lifted above the competition for the time being by a new, innovative feature. In that event pioneering advertising has to be done to explain the advantages of the improvement. In fact the better part of the advertisement may be devoted to that newsworthy feature (Exhibit 3.7). The product, however, is still in the competitive stage; only its differential has been changed. Competitors soon come out with their versions of that improvement plus their own new features, forcing the originator to find some other rationale for being selected.

Change is a continuum: As long as the operation of a competitive product does not change, the product continues to be in the competitive stage, despite its pioneering improvements; when, however, the principle of its operation changes, the product itself enters the pioneering stage. For example a

Exhibit 3.7
Product in the competitive stage, new feature in the pioneering stage. Sometimes a new feature of a competitive product is so radical and important that advertising attention is focused on pioneering advertising of that feature. (Courtesy Sharp Electronics.)

new feature in a pocket calculator, such as one that offers a minitypewriter, represents the pioneering stage, although the product as a whole is in the competitive stage.

DIFFERENCE IN POLICIES

The stage of a product may be determined readily enough, but two advertisers may follow different policies in interpreting the facts. One firm may recognize that there is still a large public that buys neither its article nor any like it. That firm will continue to stress pioneering appeals, winning more customers for itself and the field. The other advertiser will take advantage of the pioneering work already done in creating a market and will use only competitive advertising to get its brand selected.

Why be a
pioneer?

Since the pioneering advertiser has the expense of educating the public to the advantages of the new type of product and since others will then take advantage of that work, what benefits, if any, will compensate the pioneering advertising investor? In most instances there is little choice: One can either come into the market with pioneering efforts at the outset, or allow someone else to step in as the first in the field. In the latter case it may cost more to enter the market because it will be necessary to compete with the advertising of many others.

The only sure advantage of a pioneering advertiser is a *time* advantage, the opportunity to be a leader in the field with a head start over the followers. The leader's name is the first to come to mind for that type of product, and it establishes a following of customers before competitors get going. People know the leader's trademark better than those of the followers; they have more confidence in the product because they feel that it has the benefit of longer experience.

When Hertz rental cars first appeared on the scene, they gave the impression of being taxis in which you did the driving. But the company pioneered the idea of having Hertz cars at airports so that you could always drive a car yourself, wherever you flew in this country. And Hertz did the pioneering advertising on that idea. Then, to popularize the concept of driving your own hired car, they ran a campaign: "Let Hertz put you in the driver's seat." Car-rental companies sprang up all over the country, but Hertz was so far ahead in the public view that, when Avis set out to advertise, the best Avis could say was "We are second." Although they made the best of it by adding, "We try harder," Hertz through pioneering advertising had an invaluable, long-time benefit. They were first, in the public mind, for rental cars.

COMPARISON OF
STAGES

There is much less advertising of products in the pioneering stage than in the competitive stage because *new types,* or categories, of products—not mere minor improvements on old ones—do not appear on the scene very frequently. Most advertising is for products in the competitive stage. As we have pointed out, such advertising often introduces a new feature that is in the pioneering stage and that, for a time, gets the advertising spotlight.

The least amount of advertising is for products in the retentive stage. This stage, however, represents a critical moment in the life cycle of a product, when important management decisions must be made; hence it is important to understand the retentive stage.

After the retentive
stage?

It appears only logical that the life of a product does not end when it reaches the retentive stage; for here it is at the very height of its popularity, where, if allowed, it can coast along. But a business that coasts can coast only downward—deceptively slowly at first, then nose-diving suddenly as the impact of more aggressive competition makes itself felt.

No business can rely on old customers only. Customers die off, their patterns of living change, and they are lured away by the offerings of competitors. Just when a product is enjoying its peak years of success—when its name is the most prominent in the field—the advertising usually takes a new turn. It shows new ways of using a familiar product and reasons for using it more often. Advertising enters a new pioneering stage.

Gatorade is an example of such a product. After pioneering and dominating the health-drink market, the company sought expansion into other consumer segments. Since flu victims, especially children, often suffer from dehydration, Gatorade has been promoted to a secondary, medicinal, market. Products may also expand their markets by promoting features to different market segments as does Pillsbury in Exhibit 3.8.

The product does not actually return to the point at which it first started its career, however; instead the market stretches out to include the additional buyers now embraced (Exhibit 3.9a). After it has gone through the stages in this field, the product may repeat the movement in other fields or with new generations, with every turn enlarging the total market of buyers, the process represented by a spiral (Exhibit 3.9b). The series of ads in Exhibit 3.10 shows the Singer Company's use of this concept.

Exhibit 3.8
Pillsbury features easy lifestyle.
(Courtesy Pillsbury.)

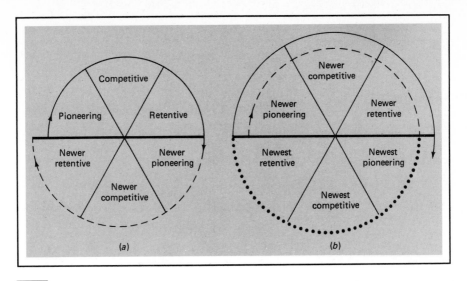

Exhibit 3.9
The advertising spiral.

Exhibit 3.10
The Singer sewing spiral. Singer introduced the electric sewing machine with this advertisement in 1927. In true pioneering fashion it explained a versatile, magic new way of sewing. (The five Singer ads on pages 63–67 are all courtesy of Singer.)

Nothing to Watch . . . .
but the Flowing Seam

SINGER, always the pioneer, has created a new sewing machine. You sit at ease before it, press a lever ever so gently with the knee, and while you merely guide your material, you watch a perfect seam flow forth, ruffles form like gathering foam or a tiny hem fall into place.

Tucking, shirring, binding, all those deft details of trimming and decoration, you do more perfectly than by hand—and in a tenth the time. Such is the versatile magic of this new Singer Electric that its very presence is a temptation to sew, and the creation of lovely things becomes a fascinating joy.

There is an easy way to prove to yourself what a modern Singer will do. The nearest Singer Shop will gladly send one to your home that you can use for thirty days, in doing your own sewing. You may have your choice of the widest variety of models—electric, treadle and hand machines. Any one of them may be yours on a convenient plan by which you will receive a generous allowance for your present machine, and your new Singer will pay for itself as you save.

The Famous Singer "S"
is one of the oldest of trade-marks. You will find it in the windows of 8,000 Singer Shops, in every city in the world. It is the identifying mark of sewing machines of enduring quality. It means, too, that every Singer Shop is ready always with instruction, repairs, supplies and courteous expert service.
When the Singer representative comes to your home let him tell you about the service Singer maintains in your neighborhood, wherever you live.

"Short Cuts to Home Sewing"—*Free*
This interesting practical book shows you how to save time in a hundred ways on your sewing machine how to do all the modish new details of trimming. It will help with your sewing no matter what make of machine you may have—or even though you have none now. The book is free. Simply phone or call at the nearest Singer Shop (see telephone directory) or send for a copy by mail, postpaid.

Singer Sewing Machine Company, Dept. 32A, Singer Bldg., N. Y.

SINGER
SEWING MACHINES
Entire contents of this advertisement copyright 1926-7 by The Singer Manufacturing Co.

Exhibit 3.10

(cont.) The Singer electric sewing machine in the competitive stage. As electric sewing machines became widely accepted, different brands entered the market, and Singer came out with improvements. The product differentials that gave it an advantage over competitors were set forth in this advertisement of the late 1960s.

Make the most of yourself—

Fit to Flatter—exclusive Speed Basting gives you stitches up to 2 inches long! Ends tedious hand-basting.

Show-Off Buttonholes are simple to make with the Built-in Buttonholer. Just set the dial—it's sew easy!

Push-Button Bobbin winds right in the machine. It's exclusive! So's the whole threading system that keeps stitching smooth, even.

Happy Ending: zig-zag your way to stronger, smoother seam finishes with The Dream Machine. Ideal for knits, synthetic fabrics.

make it with The Dream Machine.

Go ahead—cover yourself with glory! Discover how easy it is to sew up the great clothes you've dreamed of—with The Dream Machine. The newest Golden Touch & Sew® sewing machine by Singer. This fabulous zig-zag has all the special features we've shown here—and lots more! Sew on it today at the Singer Center near you.

See all 5 Touch & Sew machines. There's one priced at only $149.95. Other Singer sewing machines are priced from $69.95 at your Singer Center. And Singer has a credit plan to fit your budget.

Model 640

What's new for tomorrow is at SINGER today!*

®A Trademark of THE SINGER COMPANY

Exhibit 3.10
(*cont.*) The Singer sewing machine in a new pioneering stage—the advertising answer. Instead of basking in the retentive stage with something like "Singer for Sewing," Singer went off in two directions. From the advertising viewpoint it went into a new pioneering stage, encouraging women to sew their own clothes: "Discover how easy it is to sew up the great clothes you've dreamed of."

HOW CAN YOU BUY A SEWING MACHINE WITHOUT LOOKING AT THE SEWING MACHINES MORE PEOPLE BUY?

100 MILLION PEOPLE SEW EASIER WITH SINGER.

At Singer, we've made millions of sewing machines. Far more than anybody else in the business.

When you practice doing something that many times, you learn to do it very well.

We've learned that if the sewing machine was invented to make sewing easier, then the best sewing machine is the one that makes sewing easiest.

And that if people sew to save money, few of them will buy a sewing machine that's very expensive.

AT SINGER, OUR GOAL IS THE EASIEST POSSIBLE SEWING AT THE LOWEST POSSIBLE PRICE.

Even our least expensive machines have features for easy sewing. For example, you can buy a machine with zig-zag stitches for buttonholes and buttons, a lightweight aluminum body, push-button reverse stitching and many other features for as little as $109.99.

And our best machines have features that make sewing even easier.

Our Touch-Tronic* machines have a memory panel that remembers your stitch pattern at a touch. Instantly. No cams to change, no dials to set, no adjustments to make.

You can't buy a machine that's easier to use. Yet our Touch-Tronic machines with a memory cost no more than some less memorable ones.

Our crowning achievement. The Touch-Tronic* 2001 memory machine.

OUR TRADE-IN POLICY MEANS YOUR NEW MACHINE COSTS EVEN LESS.

If you've already got a sewing machine, bring it to Singer. We'll give you a trade-in allowance toward your new machine that'll mean the price is even lower.

It's just one more reason why today, as in every year since the sewing machine was invented, more people buy Singer* sewing machines than any other kind. Come to Singer and see why.

You'll find that once you've looked in the Singer Store, no other machines look as good.

THE SINGER STORE
WHERE SAVING IS ALWAYS IN STYLE.

*A Trademark of The Singer Company. © 1980 The Singer Company. PRICES AND TRADE-INS OPTIONAL AT PARTICIPATING DEALERS. PRICES MAY VARY IN ALASKA AND HAWAII.

Exhibit 3.10

(cont.) From the marketing viewpoint Singer's response to the problem of competition was to design a machine based upon advanced space technology and miniaturized circuitry, offering such incredible sewing performance that new pioneering advertising was called for to explain this new sewing wonder.

66

UNLIKE OUR COMPETITORS, WE THINK YOU SHOULD DECIDE HOW MUCH TO SPEND ON A SEWING MACHINE.

Model 5102 $109.99

Model 5107 $149.99

Model 833 $229.99

Model 5127 $239.99

Model 834 $269.99

Model 6105 $279.99

Model 6110 $339.99

Model 6136 $349.99

Creative Touch 1036 fashion* machine $549.99

Creative Touch 1030 fashion machine $599.99

Touch-Tronic* 2000 memory machine $949.99

Touch-Tronic 2001 memory machine $1099.99

No one else offers you the choice that Singer does. We have the largest selection of prices and features you'll find anywhere. So no matter how much you want to spend, you can afford the best. A sewing machine from Singer.

SINGER
100 MILLION PEOPLE SEW EASIER WITH SINGER

Exhibit 3.10
(*concl.*) Soon other sewing-machine manufacturers developed their own electronic features. Singer's strategy was a move toward more competitive advertising, describing how Singer machines were available in a wide range of prices.

Management decisions at the retentive

stage

As a product approaches the retentive stage, management must make some important marketing decisions:

- ☐ ***Can we make a significant improvement in a product category so that it is virtually a new type of product?*** The new feature would get the focus of attention (until it has direct competition). Many people resist wallpapering because of the mess and trouble involved; so DuPont marketed Flair Squares, preglued wallpaper in convenient 12-inch squares, to compete with traditional wallpaper strips.

- ☐ ***Should we introduce a related item, the first step in creating an expanded line?*** The makers of Aladdin oil heaters developed a complete line of designer oil-burning lamps. The Bell System started with the familiar black telephone. Today the telephone can be anything from Mickey Mouse to an executive cigar box.

- ☐ ***After gaining saturation with our primary product, can we make other things?*** That was what Golden Grain, makers of Rice-A-Roni, did. After establishing Rice-A-Roni, Golden Grain marketed a whole line of related products. Golden Grain often promotes Noodle Roni Parmesano, Stroganoff, and Romanoff, as well as Rice-A-Roni, in a single advertisement.

Thus we see that the life of a product may be affected by many conditions. If the product is to continue to be marketed, its advertising stage must be identified before its advertising goals are set.

USING THE ADVERTISING SPIRAL TO SET

ADVERTISING POLICY

The advertising spiral is a graphic representation of the advertising stages of products. It provides a point of reference for determining which stage or stages a product has reached at a given time in a given market and what the thrust of the advertising message should be. In many respects the advertising spiral parallels the life cycle of a product except that it shows what has to be done at each stage and where the product can go when it reaches a high level of success.

A product may not necessarily go through all stages. It may begin in the competitive stage and spend its life fighting for a larger share of an expanding market. But the advertising spiral forces one to answer the important questions: In which stage is the product in a given market? Do we need to do pioneering work to create a market? Must we do competitive work to get a larger share of the existing market? What proportion of the work is pioneering? What proportion competitive? As we approach the retentive stage, is it time to see whether we can expand the total market for this product or come out with a new product? These are marketing decisions as well as advertising decisions.

SUMMARY

Products are like people. They are born, mature, and die (or are significantly altered). Advertising plays a different role in each stage of product development. As we have seen in this chapter, advertising conducted in the introductory, or pioneering, stage is different in approach from that done for the established product with strong competition or the leader in the field seeking to retain its position. As a product moves from one stage to another, consumer perceptions of the product change; this must be reflected in its advertising. For instance many pioneering and competitive products use comparison advertising, although this would be an unusual approach for a product in the retentive stage.

This chapter again points out the tremendous diversity of advertising's functions. It also points out the careful evaluation of product and marketing objectives that should precede the execution of advertising strategy. As products age, so do their consumers. No product can survive without constantly attracting new customers. Long-term product success is dependent on keeping present customers while constantly creating new customers.

QUESTIONS

1. Explain the advertising-spiral concept. In what ways does it foster a better understanding of the advertising process?
2. How might product technology, modern communications techniques, and distribution methods affect a company's approach to the pioneering stage of a product?
3. What factors would make it an advantage to be the pioneering brand in a category? What factors would make it a disadvantage?
4. Discuss some factors that might require a product to skip the pioneering stage.
5. Identify two or three situations in which a product's advertising is at more than one stage at a time.
6. Cite several examples of important marketing and advertising decisions that might be considered as a product approaches the retentive stage.
7. Explain why it is important for an advertiser to determine the stage of the advertising spiral a product is in.

SUGGESTED EXERCISES

8. Make a list of two products in each of the following advertising stages: pioneering, competitive, and retentive. What was the headline in each ad?
9. Find one ad in each of the following categories: names one competitor; names two competitors; and compares a brand to unnamed competition. What is the headline of each ad? Do the ads seem to be for products in the pioneering, competitive, or retentive stage?

READINGS

DAVIDSON, J. HUGH: "Why Most New Consumer Brands Fail," *Harvard Business Review,* March-April 1976, pp. 117–22.

DeLano, LESTER A.: "Repeat Ads? Say Something New or Be Taken for Granted," *Advertising Age,* June 14, 1976, p. 48 *ff.*

FAISON, EDMUND W. J.: *Advertising: A Behavioral Approach for Managers* (New York: Wiley, 1980).

FARRIS, PAUL W.: "Advertiser's Link with Retail Price Competition," *Harvard Business Review,* January-February 1981, pp. 40–44.

FIEDLER, JOHN A.: "Choosing a Remedy for Sick Sales: Product Change or Advertising Change?" *Journal of Marketing,* April 1975, pp. 67–68.

KALWANI, MANOHAR U., and ALVIN J. SILK: "Structure of Repeat Buying for New Packaged Goods," *Journal of Marketing Research,* August 1980, pp. 316–22.

KRUGMAN, HERBERT E.: "What Makes Advertising Effective?" *Harvard Business Review,* March 1975, pp. 96–103.

LEVITT, THEODORE: "Exploit the Product Life Cycle," *Harvard Business Review,* November-December 1965, p. 81 *ff.*

URBAN, GLEN L., and JOHN R. HAUSER: *Design and Marketing of New Products* (Englewood Cliffs, NJ: Prentice-Hall, 1980).

WOLF, LAWRENCE: "How to Make Your New Product Advertising Work Harder," *Advertising Age,* October 21, 1974, pp. 57–58.

YELLE, LOUIS E.: "Industrial Life Cycles and Learning Curves: Interaction of Marketing and Production," *Industrial Marketing Management,* October 1980, pp. 311–18.

4

Target
Marketing

Target marketing is a technique designed to separate a product's prime prospects from the also-rans. The marketing executive of the 1980s must adapt to significant shifts in both demographic and product-preference patterns. The first step in this process is to identify the growth areas that will prevail to 1990 and beyond. Some examples of growth are shown in Tables 4.1 and 4.2.*

It is obvious that the consumer of 1990 will be richer and better educated, with more money for discretionary purchases, such as photographic equipment. The growth for nondurable goods will be far below the overall rate of consumption. And although growing at a slower rate, services will continue to account for almost half (47 percent) of all consumer purchases.

Target marketing is an extension of the *marketing concept,* which Philip Kotler defines as

> a management orientation that holds that the key to achieving organizational goals consists of the organization's determining the needs and wants of target markets and adapting itself to delivering the desired satisfactions more effectively and efficiently than its competitors.†

The marketing concept developed from the recognition that an emphasis solely on product production could not be continued as modern production exceeded general consumer demand.

---

*Statistics are adapted from "Target Marketing in the 1980's," *Magazine Newsletter of Research,* April, 1980, p. 3.

†Philip Kotler, *Principles of Marketing* (Englewood Cliffs, NJ: Prentice-Hall, 1980), p. 22.

Table 4-1

	1980, MILLIONS	1990, MILLIONS	CHANGE, %	INDEX
VARIOUS POPULATIONS				
U.S. population	222.2	243.5	10	100
18–44 year olds	91.5	102.8	12	120
Attended/graduated college	44.1	62.4	42	420
$25,000 or more HH income				
(1978 $)	18.3	31.8	74	740
Working women	41.8	48.7	17	170
White-collar workers	52.0	62.7	21	210
Suburban adults	64.6	76.8	19	190

Successful products would be those developed to solve a consumer problem rather than those which could be manufactured most efficiently; so companies realized that they should be creating products to solve an existing consumer need rather than forcing a product on the marketplace. Furthermore, sellers found that the best strategy was to market products that met the needs of a *specific* consumer group (or target) rather than to try to satisfy all consumers with a single product.

"The main barrier to market segmentation in recent years has been the difficulty of implementing the strategy, rather than lack of recognition of its desirability."* The research ingenuity and expense that goes into finding the unfilled marketing niche can be tremendous. Coca-Cola spent thousands of dollars determining the market feasibility of a new citrus soft drink. Only when a significant market demand was found did final product development proceed on Mello Yello, as the following article describes:

The Introduction of Mello Yello

Mello Yello, like its target audience, is growing up.

But don't think for an instant that it's adopting a mellower image, reports David C. Reddick, brand manager of the low-carbonated beverage that was introduced by the Coca-Cola Co. two years ago as "the world's fastest soft-drink." If anything, he says, that image is being toned up rather than down.

"What we have here is a brand that's irreverent when compared to others in the stable," Reddick says of Mello Yello's carefully researched and cultivated image. "And we want it to stay that way."

But the brand manager also wants to ensure that Mello Yello, which he considers "the most successful soft-drink introduction for this company and probably for the whole industry," makes an equally successful transition to its "sustaining phase." And so does McDonald & Little, the Atlanta-based agency that brought meaning to "chugalugability" when it brought out the brand's first advertising campaign.

*Ronald E. Frank, William F. Massey, and Yoram Wind, *Market Segmentation* (Englewood Cliffs, NJ: Prentice-Hall, 1972), p. 6.

Table 4–2

CONSUMER SPENDING				
	1980, BILLION $	1990, BILLION $	CHANGE, %	INDEX
Personal consumption expenditures only:	966.5	1,428.7	48	100
Durables	160.3	262.7	64	133
Nondurables	368.1	505.5	37	77
Services	438.1	660.5	51	106
Selected expenditures from all expenditures:				
Food	179.1	229.3	28	58
Clothing	75.2	110.5	47	98
Housing	159.3	237.6	49	102
Air transportation	6.7	11.4	70	146
Alcoholic beverages	11.3	15.4	36	75
Soft drinks and flavorings	6.6	9.6	45	94
Jewelry/silverware	3.0	4.9	63	131
Photographic equipment/supplies	1.7	3.0	76	158

The original campaign, which featured professional athletes in "chugging" contests, may have been aimed at teenagers in general, but it was at the younger half of the 13-to-19 age group in particular. And given the objectives, Reddick says, the campaign did everything it set out to do—and then some.

"If there was any oversight," he says, "it was possibly that we failed to think big enough." Then, speaking of all "sugar-citrus" soft drinks, he adds: "We might be on to something so big here that it could become another cola."

According to Reddick, sugar-citrus is by far the fastest-growing flavor category in the soft-drink industry. Dominated by PepsiCo Inc.'s Mountain Dew and Coca-Cola's Mello Yello, it is a category that Emanuel Goldman, beverage analyst at Sanford C. Bernstein & Co., defines as differing from conventional sugared soft drinks in that it has "a high degree of sweetness, less carbonation, and in some cases, a higher caffeine count.

"For whatever reason," he adds, "this type of drink appears to lend itself to high per capita consumption levels."

The category accounted for only about 3.4 percent of all U.S. soft-drink sales in 1980, but its compounded annual rate of growth is estimated by Reddick and others to be between 20 and 25 percent, compared with the industry's historical growth rate of between 4 and 6 percent. Further sharp gains are expected this year, reflecting in part Mello Yello's march to national distribution.

The brand was distributed in only 62 percent of the country at year-end 1980, and in only 40 percent at year-end 1979. Reddick projects 70 percent distribution should be reached in June, with more than 400 of Coke's 500 or so U.S. bottlers having added Mello Yello to their "thematic line-up" of brands Coke, Tab and Sprite.

Also expected to deliver sharp gains, however, is a new advertising campaign developed expressly to broaden the brand's core audience. "We now want to appeal to the higher end of the spectrum," Reddick says of the campaign launched locally in mid-April. "We've set as our specific target this time the 18- and 19-year-olds, and we plan to grow with them."

Supported by spending at a national rate of $20 million, the selected campaign was one of 16 tested for an ability to convey about two dozen "product attributes." Of those attributes, Reddick says, taste, low-carbonation and "chuga-lugability"—or drinkability—ranked among the top four.

But recognized as perhaps the most important attribute was "irreverent fun." "After all," Reddick explains, "it's a fun product. It's not like we're making liver pills."

Creating messages to convey irreverent fun are coveted by agencies as plum assignments, and McDonald & Little obviously regards the Mello Yello account as such. In a television spot titled "hot dog stand," for example, a beach crowd stands in awe of an attractive young woman who precedes guzzling two bottles of the soft drink with an enticing recital of the attribute-filled rhyme:

"Look out throat, watch out tongue, I've got the world's fastest soft drink and here it comes."

The statement is followed with a chorus' rendition of what Coca-Cola calls "some of the brightest music ever developed for soft drink advertising." That may be so, but it's really the commercial's sex appeal that stands out in comparison with those of the introductory campaign.

Mello Yello may still be irreverent, all right, but it's definitely grown up.*

WHAT IS A PRODUCT?

To those who are buying it a product is much more than a physical object. It represents a bundle of satisfactions. A moped may be for getting a man to work (Exhibit 4.1). It may be a way of showing how adventurous he is. Functional and psychological satisfactions combine to make the "total" product, which is what the consumer really buys. Different people have different ideas about the satisfactions that are important to them when they consider a product. Products are designed with satisfactions to match the interests of a particular group of consumers. We are judged in large measure by our physical possessions. Products we purchase say something about us and group us with people of similar taste and brand preference. Target marketing means focusing on groups of people who seek similar satisfactions from life and from a product.

Deodorants are an example of a product category that comes in a wide range of consumer preferences. Gillette advertises Soft'n Dry to women while its Right Guard brand is directed toward men. Likewise Procter & Gamble has designed its Secret brand exclusively for women. On the other hand Mennen's Speed Stick and its "Get off the can and on to the stick" theme is obviously aimed at men.

A new product faces problems breaking into the market against established competition. Since new products often lack the resources to compete against all brands in a product category, they must be selective in defining the most profitable market segments. One obvious approach—discussed later in this chapter—is to identify heavy users of the generic product.

The question confronting the new-product advertiser is how to estimate the chances of getting a heavy user of another brand to try your brand. In the package-goods field one technique is to define market segments by their brand

*Richard Morgan, "World's Fastest Soft Drink Grows Up with Market," *Atlanta Journal-Constitution,* April 26, 1981, p. 10. (Courtesy Atlanta Newspapers.)

All I need is a calculator, a credit card, and a Passport.

If you think you can't mix business with pleasure, you haven't seen Honda's C70. The Passport.

It gets up to 130 miles to the gallon.* And that could put your calculator and your credit card out of business.

It has an electric starter to get you going in a hurry. An automatic clutch to make the going nice and easy. And splash guards that help keep your suit looking good when you get there.

And talk about a good investment! At up to 130 mpg, this one's blue chip.

Last week I took my best customer to lunch on it†. She said this was the first time anyone's ever turned a tough sale into a picnic.

Get yourself a Passport. And start mixing business with pleasure.

The Honda Passport.
Get one. It'll take you almost anywhere.

*Estimated mileage calculated from results of EPA type emission tests for city riding. You may get different mileage depending on how fast you ride, weather conditions, vehicle load and trip length. †Maximum load capacity 300 pounds. ALWAYS WEAR A HELMET AND EYE PROTECTION. Specifications and availability subject to change without notice. Not available in Maryland. ©1981 American Honda Motor Co., Inc. For a free brochure, see your Honda dealer. Or write: American Honda Motor Co., Inc. Dept. 530, P.O. Box 9000, Van Nuys, California 91409.

Exhibit 4.1
This headline combines current concerns about energy conservation with a selective approach to a young audience. (Courtesy American Honda Motorcycles.)

loyalty and preference for national over private brands. Previous studies of brand loyalty have found six segments:

1. National-brand loyal. Members of this segment primarily buy a single national brand at its regular price.

2. National-brand deal. This segment is similar to the national-brand-loyal segment except that most of the purchases are made on deal (that is, the consumer is loyal only to

national brands but chooses the least expensive one). To buy the preferred national brand on deal, the consumer engages in considerable store switching.

3. Private-label loyal. Households in this segment primarily buy the private label offered by the store at which they usually shop.

4. Private-label deal. This segment shops at many stores and buys the private label of each store, usually on deal.

5. National-brand switcher. Members of this segment tend not to buy private labels. Instead they switch regularly among the various national brands on the market.

6. Private-label switcher. This segment is similar to the private-label-deal segment except that the members are not very deal prone and purchase the private labels at their regular price.*

Price, product distribution, and promotion will also affect the share of market coming from each competing brand. However, a new national brand would expect to gain most of its initial sales from segments 2 and 5, while segments 1 and 3 would normally be poor prospects to try a new brand.

Changing product styles

Few products are static in the wake of product development. For generations after the fountain pen had become a standard writing instrument, no up-and-coming young man would be without his Waterman pen. But after World War II, a new writing marvel appeared—the ballpoint pen, which was advertised as a pen that would write under water (even though no one explained why you would want to write under water). People stood in line to buy them at $5. By the 1960s prices of ballpoint pens had come way down, and they were being sold more like long-lasting pencils than as pens. Meanwhile fountain pens had entered a new life: They were offered as luxury items, often in gold and set in expensive desk stands, providing a set of consumer satisfactions different from those of the ballpoints. And while all this was happening, the fiber-tip pen came on the scene and in the 1970s had achieved a substantial share of the writing-instrument market. A pen is not just a pen; markets change with the product, and products change with the market.

WHAT IS A MARKET?

We view a market as a group of people who can be identified by some common characteristic, interest, or problem, could use our product to advantage, could afford to buy it, and can be reached through some medium. Examples of potential markets are tennis players, mothers with young children, denture wearers, coin collectors, weight watchers, newly marrieds, physicians, outdoor-sports fans, do-it-yourselfers.

The *majority fallacy* is a term applied to the assumption once frequently made that every product should be aimed at, and acceptable to, a majority of

*Robert C. Blattberg, Thomas Buesing, and Subrata K. Sen, "Segmentation Strategies for New National Brands," *Journal of Marketing*, Fall, 1980, p. 60. (Courtesy *Journal of Marketing*, a publication of the American Marketing Association.)

all consumers. Alfred Kuehn and Ralph Day have described how successive brands all aimed at a majority of a given market will tend to have rather similar characteristics and will neglect an opportunity to serve consumer minorities. They offer an illustration from the field of chocolate-cake mixes: Good-sized minorities would make a light chocolate cake or a very dark chocolate cake rather than a medium chocolate cake, which is the majority's choice. So while several initial entrants into the field would do best to market a medium chocolate mix to appeal to the broadest group of consumers, later entrants might gain a larger market share by supplying the minorities with their preferences.*

We shall pursue the question of defining a market throughout the book. At this point it is enough to say that a market is a group of potential purchasers of our product.

WHAT IS THE COMPETITION?

One of the major purposes of target marketing is to position a brand effectively within a product category or subcategory. Marketing strategy for a brand should seek to demonstrate how a product meets the needs of a particular consumer group. Your brand will gain value in a particular consumer segment by more exactly meeting its needs. Meeting the needs of a market segment will enhance the chances of success in the marketplace compared to a more generally positioned brand, which may not fully satisfy any single consumer segment. Products are normally competitive within a segment rather than across several consumer groups. In our earlier example we saw how new brands of package goods must appeal to different segments of the general market according to their product preferences and brand loyalty.

While most advertising emphasizes direct brand competition, consumers view competition in a much broader sense. We should speak of competition in the broadest sense, to include all forces that inhibit the sales of a product. The inhibiting forces may be products in the same subclass as your product or products in the same product class or another product beyond your product's class. Or the forces may not be directly related to a product.

Does the 10-speed bicycle (subclass) compete primarily with 5-, 3-, or 1-speed bicycles (product class) or with motorbikes (beyond product class)?

Does instant iced tea compete with noninstant iced tea, iced coffee, or soda pop? With hot tea or coffee? With fruit drinks or milk? With beer? With alcoholic beverages? Or with refreshment generally?

Does an electric shaver compete with other brands of electric shavers or, as a gift item, with pocket calculators?

The competitive array can widen even further as the basic price of the product increases. For example, in terms of the family budget, the real competition for a brand of life insurance may not be other brands. Rather, for

*Alfred A. Kuehn and Ralph A. Day, "Strategy of Product Quality," *Harvard Business Review,* November-December, 1962, 100*ff.*

such a purchase the competition could be general family expenses, which can't be delayed like insurance (Exhibit 4.2).

The immediate competition for a product already on the market is that of other products in its class. How does this product compare with others in differentials? In total sales? In share of the market? In the sales of this particular brand? What do consumers like and dislike about the products being offered, including the one under consideration?

PLANNING THE ADVERTISING

Market segmentation

Market segmentation means dividing a total market of consumers into groups with similar lifestyles, making them a market for products serving their special needs. The fact that a market is segmented does not preclude it from being or becoming a large market.

Speaking about market segmentation, Kotler said:

> Market segmentation . . . starts not with distinguishing product possibilities, but rather with distinguishing customer groups. Market segmentation is the subdividing of a market into distinct subsets of customers, where any subset may conceivably be selected as a market target to be reached with a distinct marketing mix. The power of this concept is that in an age of intense competition for the mass market, individual sellers may prosper through developing brands for specific market segments whose needs are imperfectly satisfied by the mass-market offerings.*

A market can also be segmented geographically, as Table 4.3 shows.

Table 4–3

PRODUCT-USAGE PROFILES (100 = NATIONAL AVERAGE)[a]		
AREA	CANDY BARS (HEAVY USERS)	PIPE TOBACCO (HEAVY USERS)
Northeast	83	102
East central	107	128
West central	106	145
South	112	74
Pacific	91	68

[a]Courtesy of Simmons Market Research Bureau, 1980.

Positioning

Positioning is another term for fitting a product into the lifestyle of the buyer. It refers to ways of segmenting a market by either or both of two ways: (1) creating a product to meet the needs of a specialized group; (2) picking the appeal of an existing product to meet the needs of a specialized group. A product can hold different positions at the same time. Arm & Hammer baking soda is featured as a refrigerator deodorizer, an antacid, and a bath skin cleaner, without losing its original market as a cooking ingredient.

Creating a product for selective markets. One of the principal ways that marketers attract a focused interest group is through variations in the conventional product. These variations are based on the idea that there exists a large

---

*Philip Kotler, *Marketing Management: Analysis, Planning, and Control,* 4th ed. (Englewood Cliffs, NJ: Prentice-Hall, 1980), p. 195.

"ANYONE WHO'S THINKING OF SPENDING $24,000 FOR A LUXURY CAR SHOULD TALK TO A PSYCHIATRIST."

—Dr. John Boston, psychiatrist
and Volvo owner, Austin, Texas

John Boston, a Texas psychiatrist, owns a '73 Volvo.

He bought that Volvo because, as he puts it: "I had admired what Volvo had done in the area of safety. The car seemed well-built. It offered solid European craftsmanship without the inflated price."

We wanted Dr. Boston's opinion of the new Volvo GLE, which has a full assortment of luxury features as standard equipment—and a price tag thousands of dollars below that of the well-known German luxury sedan.

"It's an excellent value. In my opinion, the individual buying this car would have a strong, unsuppressed need to get his or her money's worth. He or she would probably also have a strong enough self-image not to need a blatant status symbol."

When we told him that some people were actually paying five to ten thousand dollars more for a luxury car, Dr. Boston's response was characteristically succinct.

"That's not using your head."

Finally, we asked Dr. Boston if, when he was ready for a new car, he'd consider the Volvo GLE for himself.

"I'd be crazy if I didn't." **VOLVO**

A car you can believe in.

© 1980 VOLVO OF AMERICA CORPORATION.

Exhibit 4.3
A positioning headline that combines audience selectivity and a play on words. (Courtesy Volvo of America Corp.)

enough submarket with an interest in a particular product offering (as an example, see Exhibit 4.3).

To meet the needs of the small household, as well as the "single-serving" market, foods are packed in small-sized packages. Lipton's Cup-a-Soup is soup by the single serving, four individual servings in each box; similarly, Quaker oatmeal is packed in single-serving units, ten 1-ounce packets in each box. Stouffer's frozen pies are packaged for the single person.

Other products are also designed to meet the needs of particular market segments. We have Honda motorcycles, whose advertising features the road-bike as "The Honda passport." General Electric offers its Toast-R-Oven for the family that wants a second oven that "handles the small cooking jobs your big oven's too big for." Agree Creme Rinse & Conditioner emphasizes its oil-free formula, which "helps stop the greasies." Wrigley's offers Freedent chewing gum specially for denture wearers. And there is much positioning in the toothpaste product category: Crest and Colgate, for example, are formulated to prevent cavities; Ultra-Brite and Close-Up, primarily to help make teeth look brighter; Aim, to taste better to get children to brush longer and therefore acquire better brushing habits.

Positioning the product by appeal. Sometimes you can advantageously position a product or reposition it just by changing the advertising appeal, without making any physical changes in the product.

In the mid-1960s, Sterling Drug's Lehn & Fink division considered Lysol a dying brand. The disinfectant's sales were falling. Editorial, scare advertising ("Warning: Help protect babies and new mothers against dreaded staph germs") failed to stop the decline, possibly even accelerated it. So Lehn & Fink stopped advertising, and sales increased. Until that time Lysol's distribution was primarily through drugstores. Yet women were buying disinfectant cleansers in grocery stores. Research revealed that about 60 percent of homes had the product, brought into the home by new mothers and used while the children were young but collecting dust on the shelf thereafter because the mothers became less worried about germs and stopped using the product.

By repositioning Lysol as a household cleanser with germ-killing and odor-killing powers, not merely a nursery disinfectant, consumer sales response was immediate. Lysol is now a more than $20 million business, with well over 50-percent market share.

On the other hand, Clorox, long known as a liquid bleach, has been repositioned also as a disinfectant, with appeals that "you can't buy a more effective disinfectant than Clorox" and "Clorox does more than the wash." Same product, new appeals.

Johnson's Baby Oil, always known as an oil for baby's skin, is advertised also as a general cosmetic and skin-care product for women, with appeals such as "It didn't start out to be an eye make-up remover, but it sure makes a great eye make-up remover."

Salada Tea has been positioned to reach coffee drinkers, as "The Coffee-Drinker's Tea." Noxzema was repositioned from a skin medication to a beauty treatment. California raisins have been repositioned to a fruit snack that is nutritionally good for children, a substitute for candy, which is bad for their teeth (Exhibit 4.4).

Positioning to expand brand share. Positioning or, more accurately, repositioning can be an effective method of increasing brand share when a company has a very high percentage of the market for a product type. Let's as-

Sweets make her happy. But too many sweets make you unhappy. There's one to please you both. To her it's candy. To you it's fruit.

Raisins from California. Happiness by the handful.

California Raisin Advisory Board

Exhibit 4.4
Raisins now compete with candy for the children's trade.

sume our company, Acme Widgets, has 80 percent of the widget market. Shown in Tables 4.4 and 4.5 are two strategies that the company might adopt.

In Table 4.4 Acme, by engaging in direct brand competition, has increased its share very slightly. However, it is extremely doubtful that further sales can *profitably* be taken from competing brands. Future inroads into brands *A, B,* and *C* markets will probably cost proportionally more and, in fact, these costs will more than likely exceed any revenues produced by increases in advertising.

The repositioning strategy of the lower part of Table 4.5 allowed Acme to keep its overwhelming brand share in the primary market. By spending 40 percent ($4 million of its $10 million advertising allowance) of its budget to position the Acme Widget in a new market, the company gained 10 percent of this formerly untapped market segment rather than the 0.1 percent that the company would have achieved in the first strategy.

Table 4–4

STRATEGY 1: TRADITIONAL BRAND PROMOTION (NO BRAND REPOSITIONING)		
1980 BRAND SHARE, %	1981 ADVERTISING	1982 BRAND SHARE, %
A, 10 *B,* 5 *C,* 5	$10 million spent against brands *A, B,* and *C*	*A,* 9.9 *B,* 5.0 *C,* 5.0
Acme, 80		Acme, 80.1
Total 100		100.0

Johnson & Johnson Baby Shampoo is an example of a successful brand-repositioning strategy. Having dominated the baby-shampoo market, the brand was promoted to adults: first to women, "If it's gentle enough for a baby's hair . . . ," and then to men.

The common thread in the foregoing examples is that no physical changes were made in the product—only different appeals were used. This is the basis for positioning by choice of appeal.

Table 4–5

STRATEGY II: ACME WIDGET BRAND REPOSITIONING		
1980 BRAND SHARE, %	1981 ADVERTISING	1982 BRAND SHARE, %
		Primary market:
A, 10 *B,* 5 *C,* 5	$6 million spent to keep present market share	*A,* 10 *B,* 5 *C,* 5
Acme 80		Acme 80
Total 100		100
	$4 million spent to promote repositioned Acme Widget to new market	**Alternative market:** Other products and brands already in market, 85
		A, B, C, 5
		Acme 10
Total		100

THE STORY BEHIND
phillips petroleum company,
the performance company

BACKGROUND

Prior to 1973, Phillips had been a successful, growing, regional petroleum marketer. Phillips had also been a leader in developing new technology and products for petroleum-based fuels and chemicals. In fact, they were consistently a leader in new patents.

Advertising had historically been consumer product and service oriented, positioning Phillips stations as "The Performance Stop."

Just prior to the Arab oil embargo, Phillips had assigned their advertising account to Tracy-Locke. Petroleum companies faced a new, unfamiliar, and unfriendly market environment. Gasoline shortages, high prices, and long lines of irritated consumers resulted in an adversary marketplace.

Most petroleum companies either stopped advertising or launched ineffective efforts to explain and/or defend their high shortages and high profits.

STRATEGY

The advertising agency recommended that Phillips concentrate on the positive. Consumer research confirmed that the strategy could create positive consumer and public attitude toward the company.

Phillips' achievements could be demonstrated in terms of consumer benefits. The message should be what they had already done, not promises for the future.

Seven objectives were established for increasing consumer awareness and positive attitude toward Phillips in such criteria as: (a) developing new energy sources, (b) concern with the environment, (c) high-quality products, (d) good company to do business with.

With government-regulated allocations of product, Phillips could not gain market share. But, like being in an Indianapolis 500 when the yellow flag is up, they could improve their position in public awareness and attitude.

A benchmark and quarterly studies among 2000+ people would monitor progress in comparison with five other major petroleum companies in Phillips' marketing areas.

ADVERTISING

Regional network television and selected editions of national magazines afforded efficient media for Phillips. Subsequently, the agency developed and tested radio versions of the Phillips' campaign and created the first regional network radio schedules.

The format for the Phillips' campaign was the mini-drama. Commercials presented Phillips' developments such as a million-barrel storage tank for the Ekofisk oilfield under the North Sea; a pavement underliner that protected roads and bridges from deterioration; and a de-icing agent to prevent aviation fuel from freezing.

TRACY-LOCKE, INC.
Advertising & Public Relations
CLIENT: PHILLIPS PETROLEUM
PRODUCT: Performance

TITLE: Rotating Biological Discs
LENGTH: 30 Seconds
COMM'L. NO.:   POOP - 1083
FIRST AIR DATE: 7/20/81

ANNCR (VO): Clean water.

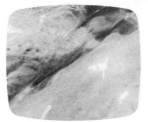

More precious to life than oil.

But it too is becoming scarce.

Because of man's pollution.

But now there's something that's helping to clean water all over the world.

A unique waste water treatment system made possible by...

this special plastic developed by Phillips Petroleum.

There are other energy sources besides oil. But there's no substitute for water.

ANNCR (VO): Caring for your car and more. That's performance. From Phillips Petroleum.

Each year more than fifty achievements are consumer concept-tested, with the highest-rated six-to-nine subjects becoming new commercials.

Capitalizing on the existing equity in Phillips' association with "performance," the advertising positioned Phillips as "The Performance Company."

After dramatizing the benefit and revealing that it was Phillips who had developed it, the early commercials had an intensifier to reinforce the unexpected fact that it was Phillips Petroleum Company. "Surprised?"

TRACY-LOCKE, INC.
Advertising & Public Relations
CLIENT: PHILLIPS PETROLEUM
PRODUCT: Performance

TITLE: Scalpel/Susan LaRue
LENGTH: 30 Seconds
COMM'L. NO.: POOP-0553
FIRST AIR DATE: 7/20/81

Susan LaRue: I recently had an operation on the nerves in my face.

If one was accidently cut, my face could have been paralyzed. In order to see better,

the surgeon used a new scalpel that reduces

bleeding by sealing off

blood vessels with heat as it cuts.

A special heat resistant plastic

developed by Phillips Petroleum insulates the blade.

And helped make all this possible. Including my smile.

ANNCR (VO): Caring for your car...and more. That's performance, from Phillips Petroleum.

RESULTS

People were surprised. And they reacted positively. Since the inception of the campaign, Phillips has moved from sixth place to first place on each criterion.

When consumers' attitudes reflected that they were no longer surprised, and in fact began to expect such achievements and performance from Phillips, the "Surprised?" was dropped.

The campaign is in its ninth year. Phillips continues to rank number one on each criterion, and the campaign shows no signs of wearing out.

The table on page 87 shows the improvement and retention of favorable attitude toward the company during the period of the campaign. The Performance Company has performance advertising.

One less complication for a surgeon can be one less complication for you.

Blood. The liquid of life. And sometimes a threat to life when excess bleeding obstructs a surgeon's field of vision. But now, a revolutionary new scalpel can seal off blood vessels using heat as it cuts. Phillips Petroleum developed the heat-resistant plastic called Ryton® that makes this possible by insulating the handle from the blade. And by holding the blade rigid for precision cutting even when it's hot.

Operations performed with this new scalpel can be virtually bloodless—one less complication for both doctor and patient to worry about. Phillips Petroleum. Good things for cars and the people who drive them. **The Performance Company** PHILLIPS 66

Courtesy Phillips Petroleum Company Advertising Agency: Tracy-Locke/BBDO

How to approach a positioning

problem   Not all products lend themselves to the type of repositioning discussed here. The advertiser must be careful not to damage the current product image by changing product appeals and expanding into new markets prematurely. Jack Trout and Al Ries say that the advertiser who is thinking about positioning should ask the following questions:

1. What position, if any, do we already own in the prospect's mind?
2. What position do we want to own?
3. What companies must be outgunned if we are to establish that position?
4. Do we have enough marketing money to occupy and hold the position?
5. Do we have the guts to stick with one consistent positioning concept?
6. Does our creative approach match our positioning strategy?*

PROFILE OF THE

MARKET   We now address ourselves to the overall market for the product. First we determine the overall usage of this type of product. Usage might be defined in terms of dollar sales, percentage of households who use such a product, or the total number of units. Has the field been growing or dwindling? What is the share of the market enjoyed by those in the business, by territories? What change has taken place in the past few years in their ranking? What is the chief product advantage featured by each brand?

The advertiser must know not only the characteristics of its market but also similar information about the advertising-media alternatives to be purchased. Most major newspapers and consumer magazines provide demographic (see next section) and product-user data for a number of advertising categories. A typical promotion from the *Richmond Times-Dispatch* is reproduced in Exhibit 4.5.

PROFILE OF THE

BUYER   The owner of a small business usually knows most of the customers personally—their age, their family status, their financial status, their life patterns. But this touch is completely lost by the time a business gets big and deals with masses of people all over the country. The best the advertiser can do is try to form a clear picture of the typical consumer of the product, to discover what kind of person must be appealed to in reaching for more business. The advertiser tries to prepare a demographic profile of such a person.

Demography is the study of vital economic and sociological statistics about people. In advertising, demographic reports refer to those facts relevant to a person's use of a product. Maybe the advertiser is interested in reaching

---

*Jack Trout and Al Ries, *The Positioning Era* (New York: Ries Cappiello Colwell, 1973). pp. 38–41.

Population and buying power

Subject	Unit	Market Served by					Market as a Percent of Virginia				
		Richmond Newspapers	Norfolk Newspapers	Roanoke Newspapers	Npt News Newspapers	Virginia Total	Rich-mond	Nor-folk	Roa-noke	Npt News	Va Total
Counties	No.	30	3	16	8	95					
Population	No.	1,007,700	875,000	592,100	418,100	5,260,900	19.2	16.6	11.3	8.0	100.0
Households	No.	349,100	274,700	211,300	138,800	1,786,100	19.6	15.4	11.8	7.8	100.0
Eff. buying income ..	($000)	6,890,676	5,432,393	3,508,243	2,572,152	36,924,599	18.7	14.7	9.5	7.0	100.0
Retail Sales	($000)	3,910,796	3,041,900	2,214,114	1,534,205	20,483,526	19.1	14.9	10.8	7.5	100.0
Food stores.......	($000)	879,666	671,568	551,034	326,115	4,604,205	19.1	14.6	12.0	7.1	100.0
Eat, drink places..	($000)	300,175	258,299	143,119	141,436	1,538,520	19.5	16.8	9.3	9.2	100.0
Gen mdse stores..	($000)	536,813	401,111	261,311	214,972	2,643,160	20.3	15.2	9.9	8.1	100.0
Apparel, acces....	($000)	166,509	150,124	83,111	76,718	895,392	18.6	16.8	9.3	8.6	100.0
Furn, appl stores .	($000)	182,094	153,418	99,702	106,164	984,812	18.5	15.6	10.1	10.8	100.0
Automotive	($000)	742,733	668,247	412,519	283,601	4,179,246	17.8	16.0	9.9	6.8	100.0
Gas stations	($000)	389,147	254,554	234,529	137,764	1,929,224	20.2	13.2	12.2	7.1	100.0
Bldg, hdw stores ..	($000)	164,998	137,069	112,396	58,147	1,066,928	15.5	12.9	10.5	5.4	100.0
Drug stores	($000)	138,162	78,594	70,467	37,639	694,579	19.9	11.3	10.2	5.4	100.0
State liquor stores ..	No.	68	36	26	21	259	26.2	13.9	10.0	8.1	100.0
Gallon sale spirits...	No.	2,313,641	1,561,768	914,474	684,935	9,325,431	24.8	16.8	9.8	7.3	100.0
New car registration.	No.	39,753	33,760	21,871	15,698	227,197	17.5	14.9	9.6	6.9	100.0

Markets based on 20 percent or more household coverage by combined dailies or Sunday as reported in Circulation '80/'81. American Newspaper Markets, Inc. Four counties in North Carolina, covered by Norfolk Newspapers, with approximately 41,000 population. 14,800 households, and $145,000,000 retail sales, are not included in Virginia totals above. New car registrations for 1979 as reported by Automotive Trade Association of Virginia. Unaudited liquor store data for fiscal year 1979-80 from Virginia ABC Board. All other data from Survey of Buying Power Data Service 1980 by Sales and Marketing Management.

Recommended Standard Breakdowns For Demographic Characteristics In Surveys of Consumer Media Audiences

I. DATA FOR HOUSEHOLDS:

	Minimum Basic Data	Additional Data Highly Desired
A. **County Size:** (see Note 1)	A County Size B County Size C County Size D County Size	

B. **Geographic Area:** (see Notes 2 & 3)	Metropolitan Area
	Non Metropolitan Area
	Farm
	Non Farm
		Urban
		  Urbanized Areas
		    Central Cities
		    Urban fringe
		  Other urban
		    Places of 10,000 or
		      more
		    Places of 2,500 to
		      10,000
		  Rural places of 1,000
		    to 2,500
		  Other rural
		
		Metropolitan Area:
		
		  1,000,000 and over
		  500,000 - 999,999
		  250,000 - 499,999
		  100,000 - 249,999
		  50,000 - 99,999

C. **Geographic Region:** (see Notes 4 & 5)	New England Metro New York Mid Atlantic East Central Metro Chicago West Central South East South West Pacific	North East North Central South West
D. **Ages of Children:**	No Child Under 18 Youngest Child 6-17 Youngest Child Under 6	Youngest Child 12-17 Youngest Child 6-11 Youngest Child 2-5 Youngest Child under 2
E. **Family Size:**	1 or 2 members 3 or 4 members 5 or more members	
F. **Family Income:**	Under $5,000. $5,000 - 7,999. $8,000 - 9,999. Over $10,000.	Under $3,000. $ 3,000 - 4,999. $10,000 - 14,999. $15,000 - 24,999. $25,000 and over

G. **Home Ownership:**	Own home
	Rent home
		Residence Five Years Prior
		to Survey Date
		  Lived in same house
		  Lived in different house
		    In same county
		    In different county

H. **Home Characteristic:**	Single family
	  dwelling unit
	Multiple family
	  dwelling unit	

I. **Race:**		White Non-White
J. **Household Possessions:**		Data on household posses- sions or purchases will pre- sumably be governed by the medium's particular selling needs.

II. DATA FOR INDIVIDUALS:

	Minimum Basic Data	Additional Data Highly Desired
A. **Age:**	Under 6 6-11 12-17 18-34 35-49 50-64 65 and over	18-24 25-34
B. **Sex:**	Male Female	

C. **Education:**	Grade school or less
	  (grades 1-8)
	Some high school
	Graduated high school
	  (grades 9-12)
	Some college
	Graduated college	

D. **Marital Status:**	Married Single Widowed Divorced	

E. **Occupation:**	Professional, Semi-
	  Professional
	Proprietor, Manager,
	  Official
	Clerical, Sales
	Craftsman, Foreman,
	  Service Worker
	Operative, Non-Farm
	  Laborer
	Farmer, Farm Laborer
	Retired
	Student
	Unemployed	

F. **Individual Possessions:**		Data on individual posses- sions or purchases will pre- sumably be governed by the medium's particular selling needs.

III. DATA FOR HOUSEHOLD HEADS:

	Minimum Basic Data	Additional Data Highly Desired
A. **Sex:**	Male Female	
B. **Age:**	34 and younger 35-49 50-64 65 and older	18-24 25-34

C. **Education:**	Grade school or less
	  (grades 1-8)
	Some high school
	Graduated high school
	  (grades 9-12)
	Some college
	Graduated college	

D. **Occupation:**	Professional, Semi-
	  Professional
	Proprietor, Manager,
	  Official
	Clerical, Sales
	Craftsman, Foreman,
	  Service Worker
	Operative, Non-Farm
	  Laborer
	Farmer, Farm Laborer
	Retired
	Student
	Unemployed	

IV. DATA FOR HOUSEWIVES:

	Minimum Basic Data	Additional Data Highly Desired
A. **Age:**	34 and younger 35-49 50-64 65 and over	18-24 25-34

B. **Education:**	Grade school or less
	  (grades 1-8)
	Some high school
	Graduated high school
	  (grades 9-12)
	Some college
	Graduated college	

C. **Employment:**	Not employed outside
	  home
	Employed outside home
	  Employed Full Time
	    (30 hours or more
	    per week)
	  Employed Part Time
	    (Less than 30 hours
	    per week)	

Exhibit 4.6
Demographic breakdowns recommended by the American Association of Advertising Agencies.

only women of a certain age, to sell them cosmetics, or young mothers who buy baby food, or mothers with big households, buyers of food products. The advertiser may want to reach men of all ages (electric shavers), or maybe the key factor is whether or not they are home owners. All advertisers will seek to prepare a profile of the kind of person they want to reach. Likewise, when a medium tries to sell space or time to an advertiser, it will supply a profile of its readers or viewers. The advertiser will then match the two profiles, to see whether that medium reaches the type of people sought. That is the basis for media selection.

To help make such matching possible, the American Association of Advertising Agencies has recommended a standardized breakdown for consumer media data so that the advertiser can prepare a list in terms of the standard classification that the media will be using. Exhibit 4.6 shows several of these categories. Advertisers make their own lists, including only facts that help identify their buyers. A simple example: *Television/Radio Age* reports that the makers of Coronet Paper Products are buying radio programs to reach women 18 to 49. Ray-O-Vac is trying to reach males 35 to 49, Rosarita Mexican Foods is interested in women 25 to 49. Each advertiser will seek the radio or TV station reaching the sex and age bracket desired. These are standard classifications. As a product gets more costly, with a more complex demographic profile (cars, for instance), you may wish to describe not only the age bracket but the income bracket and size of the family unit of the people you are trying to reach. You may even need to know the psychographic or personality characteristics of the buyer. The key point is to have clear in your mind a profile that describes potential buyers of your product.

Heavy users

For any product, a small percentage of users are responsible for a disproportionately large share of the product's sale. This principle of heavy usage is sometime referred to as the *80/20 rule.* It is not unusual for as few as 20 percent of a market to purchase 80 percent of a product.

Heavy users are identified by not only *who* they are but also *when* they buy and *where* they are located. In Table 4.6, for example, we find that the heavy users for Brand X are 55 and older women. In addition the most effective selling will be done from January through June in the East Central and Pacific regions.

Obviously, in defining your market, you must determine who the heavy users are and identify their similarities, which would define your marketing goals. Often this can be done through the nature of the appeals you use in your headline and copy. The headline for DeBeers diamond rings ("The important questions you should ask when choosing her diamond engagement ring!") immediately identifies the prospective market and eliminates non-prospects.

Table 4–6

USERS OF BRAND X			

1. TARGET AUDIENCE: CURRENT CONSUMERS

Women	Pop., %	Consumption, %	Index
18–24	17.5	5.0	29
25–34	21.9	10.0	46
35–54	30.1	24.0	80
55+	30.5	61.0	200
Total	100.0	100.0	

2. GEOGRAPHY: CURRENT SALES

Area	Pop., %	Consumption, %	Index
Northeast	24	22	92
East Central	15	18	120
West Central	17	16	94
South	27	24	89
Pacific	17	20	118
	100	100	

3. SEASONALITY

Period	Jan.–Mar.	Apr.–Jun.	Jul.–Sept.	Oct.–Nov.
Consumption, %	30	36	20	14
Index	120	144	80	56

BEYOND DEMOGRAPHICS:
PSYCHOGRAPHICS

Driving on a highway running past modest-sized back-yards of middle-class homes, one is struck first by their similarity. But a harder look is more illuminating; for behind the similarities lie differences that reflect the interests, personalities, and family situations of those who live in such homes. One backyard has been transformed into a carefully manicured garden. Another includes some shrubs and bushes, but most of the yard serves as a relaxation area, with outdoor barbecue equipment and the like. A third yard is almost entirely a playground, with swings, trapezes, and slides. A swimming pool occupies almost all the space in another yard. Still another has simply been allowed to go to seed and is overgrown and untended by its obviously indoor-oriented owners.

If you wanted to advertise to this community, you would be speaking to people with different interests, different tastes. Between two groups of buyers who have the same demographic characteristics, there may still be a big difference in the nature and extent of their purchases. This fact has led to an inquiry beyond demographics into psychographics, to try to explain the significance of such differences. According to Emanuel Demby:

—psychographics seeks to describe the human characteristics of consumers that may have a bearing on their response to products, packaging, advertising and

Exhibit 4.7
Ad based on psychographic appeal. (Courtesy Thom McAn Shoe Company.)

public relations efforts. Such variables may span a spectrum from self-concept and life-style to attitudes, interests and opinions, as well as perceptions of product attributes.*

People may have demographic similarities but yet perceive different benefits and satisfactions from the same product, whether it is clothing, magazines, vacation resorts, or carry-out fried chicken. These variations are brought to bear in the purchase decision. The advertiser tries to reach those groups whose psychographic characteristics make them likely prospects for certain products and tries to address each such group with ads appealing particularly to it. To say someone is a "single person" is talking demographics; to say a person is a "swinging single"—that's psychographics (Exhibit 4.7).

The advertisers who have long made use of psychographic thinking (without being aware of the term) are those in direct-response advertising (Chapter 11) who are always buying lists of prospects from each other. They buy book-club lists, not to sell more books but to sell some other objects or magazines for a cultured class of people. Garden-club lists are used to sell objets d'art and other fine things for the home. Psychographics, studying the life-style of a person, sharpens the search for prospects beyond the demographic data. The media are then selected, and the advertising is then directed to that special target group.

*Emanuel Demby, "Psychographics and from Whence It Came," William D. Wells, ed., *Life Style and Psychographics* (Chicago: American Marketing Association, 1974), p. 13.

THE STORY BEHIND
the lenox china campaign

Lenox Incorporated is a leading manufacturer of quality dinnerware, giftware, jewelry, and a broad line of other related products. The company's net sales volume is over $125 million per year.

In the 1880s Walter Scott Lenox created Lenox China. By 1887 it was being marketed by the Ceramic Art Company of Trenton and was the first American china to equal European porcelains. The name Lenox China was adopted as a company name in 1906. In 1917 President and Mrs. Wilson selected Lenox for the White House. Since then, two other national services were made, for Presidents Roosevelt and Truman. In 1962 the Lenox Company developed a bone china, named Oxford, for people who preferred the pure-white look over ivory. In 1965 Lenox began making and marketing Lenox Crystal. In 1973 they created an informal dinnerware and began marketing that under the name Temper-ware® by Lenox.

Lenox's traditional china business and related crystal and glassware lines account for about 40 percent of total company sales. Operating in a very competitive business, Lenox can attribute its success to its ability to define target markets and develop a media plan that effectively reaches that target audience. Lenox has done this for five of its product lines.

LENOX FINE CHINA

An ivory-colored china (as opposed to the pure white of bone china), it is selected by five out of ten brides who register for fine china at department- and jewelry-store bridal-gift registries. Of total china sales the bridal market represents approximately two-thirds, the older woman constituting the rest although in recent years the "mature" market has started to grow. Of the fifty top-selling fine-china patterns, twenty-seven are Lenox patterns. Lenox has about a 55 percent share of this market.

Advertising strategy is to present Lenox in an atmosphere of prestige in a manner reflective of the quality of the china. Three basic campaigns are used. All ads are in color and are full pages or spreads (see color plate 2).

Prebridal (early through late teens). The use of *Seventeen* magazine is to help create brand awareness among teenage girls at a time when china is a low-interest product.

Bridal (18 to 24). Two magazines, *Brides* and *Modern Bride,* claim to reach eight out of ten first-time brides. Lenox advertises in every issue of these two magazines, as well as periodically in *Glamour* and *Mademoiselle.* The objective is to give all the reasons why the bride should settle for nothing less than the finest when she registers for her china pattern. The ads are double-page spreads. Left-hand pages are full photos of things such as elegant table settings, and right-hand pages have copy on what to look for when selecting fine china and crystal patterns (product, price, where to get more information).

Mature market (women 25 to 55). Mass magazines such as *Better Homes & Gardens, McCall's, Good Housekeeping,* and *Ladies' Home Journal* and specialty publications such as *Gourmet, House & Garden,* and *The New Yorker* are used to bring the Lenox quality image to couples who are ready to replace their dinnerware, add to it, or buy fine china for the first time. The readers of these magazines are also, of course, wedding guests who buy gifts. The objective is to make Lenox synonymous with quality and prestige in the minds of homemakers.

LENOX GIFTWARE

A line of fine-china gifts, with over 100 different items ranging in price from under $10 to $100, giftware is advertised to an even broader market than dinnerware since just about anyone can afford a bud vase or candy dish. Magazines used are *Reader's Digest, Family Circle, Woman's Day,* and others. Ads are product-oriented with names and prices indicated, but presented in a prestigious way.

LENOX CRYSTAL

The major promotion of crystal is achieved by incorporating it into the Lenox China advertising. Just about every Lenox national ad, including those for giftware, carries the signature "Lenox China and Crystal." In addition, ads on crystal only—in *Vogue, The New Yorker,* and *Gourmet*—reach a fairly sophisticated audience.

OXFORD BONE CHINA

Oxford is the third best-selling fine china (Lenox is first and Royal Doulton is second). It does not carry a Lenox identification, nor does the advertising mention the fact that it is made by the same craftsmen. Retail salespeople are aware of this, however, and are urged to use this information when talking to customers. Advertising of this brand is directed exclusively to the bridal market, using *Brides, Modern Bride, Glamour,* and *Mademoiselle* magazines.

TEMPER-WARE by LENOX

Introduced in 1973, this is an informal dinnerware because of the growth of more casual entertaining. In a few years, it became the best-selling informal dinnerware (of sets costing $40 or more for service of eight). Since Temper-Ware is priced equal to, or higher than, any of the competition, this is an unusually strong success story. (A service for eight in 1982 was $450.) Magazines used include *Woman's Day, Good Housekeeping,* and *Better Homes & Gardens.*

Advertising for Lenox China prepared by Chirurg & Cairns, Inc.

SOURCES OF PRODUCT-USAGE AND DEMOGRAPHIC DATA

The syndicated research

services   Among the main sources of needed information about consumers are numerous syndicated research services, such as Simmons Market Research Bureau and Magazine Research Inc.

Different services specialize in different types of information. Each publishes reports, which it sells as a service to subscribers. The various reports involve questions of what type of product people buy, which brands, who buys them, their demographic status, and their psychographic distinctions; how people react to products and to ads; their styles of buying; what media reach them. In the TV and radio field the services report their estimates of how many TV households are listening to which programs on which stations. Among the uses of such data is helping the advertiser select the target market. In addition advertisers can order "customized" data from these services and a number of other research companies.

SUMMARY

Advertising should be like a rifle, not a shotgun. The expense of buying advertising space and time is too great to reach any but those who are current or future prospects. Modern marketing and advertising research is founded on the premise of separating prospects from nonprospects and reaching them by the most efficient means.

The marketing concept, with its emphasis on consumer satisfaction, is the key to greater efficiency in advertising. Research is also a prime component of target marketing. Market research to define prime market segments, product research to meet the needs of these segments, and advertising research to devise the most appropriate messages are mandatory for the success of a firm in a competitive environment.

We can see the importance of target marketing in current advertising. Unlike the general advertising of a generation ago, modern advertising is aimed specifically at a particular group and its needs. Working women, the young, the older retiree, and minorities are all represented in advertising in a more realistic and specific way than was the case a decade ago.

Target marketing also takes into account that market segmentation must focus not only on people but on the regions in which they live. We are starting to see a trend toward localized advertising by national advertisers. This localization takes into account the wide variance in product usage and brand preferences from market to market.

Finally, advertisers are placing more importance on lifestyle characteristics rather than just demographic factors. Advertisers recognize that purchase behavior is the result of a number of complex psychological and sociological factors that cannot be explained by a superficial list of age, sex, or occupational characteristics.

QUESTIONS

1. What is meant when a product is referred to as a "bundle of satisfactions?"
2. What are some of the advantages and limitations of psychographics compared to demographics?

3. Discuss several meanings of the term "market segment" and give examples of each.

4. Why is research a key ingredient of target marketing?

5. Products are normally competitive within a segment rather than across several consumer groups. Discuss.

6. Why do you think it is important to define the target market in planning advertising?

7. Target marketing insulates a product from competitive pressure. Explain.

8. How does the "majority fallacy" relate to target marketing?

9. What are the purposes for positioning a product? Give several examples.

10. Give examples of positioning a product by market segment, advertising appeal, and distribution.

11. What are some of the advantages and limitations of psychographics compared to demographics?

SUGGESTED EXERCISES

12. Analyze one ad that conforms to the consumer-orientation principle of the marketing concept and one that does not.

13. Find three ads in the same product category that appeal to different market segments and identify these segments.

14. Choose one ad for products in each of the six brand-loyalty segments discussed in the chapter.

READINGS

BOOTE, ALFRED S.: "Market Segmentation by Personal Values and Salient Product Attributes," *Journal of Advertising Research,* February 1981, pp. 29–36.

DHALLA, NARIMAN K.: and WINSTON H. MAHATOO: "Expanding the Scope of Segmentation Research," *Journal of Marketing,* April 1976, pp. 34–41.

MAGGARD, JOHN P.: "Positioning Revisited," *Journal of Marketing,* January 1976, pp. 63–66.

"Marketing/Advertising Research," *Advertising Age,* October 26, 1981, S–1.

McNEAL, JAMES U.: "Advertising in the 'Age of Me'," *Business Horizons,* August 1979, pp. 34–38.

MICHMAN, RONALD D.: "The Double Income Family: A New Market Target," *Business Horizons,* August 1980, pp. 31–37.

PLUMMER, JOSEPH T.: "Psychographics: What Can Go Right," *New Marketing for Social and Economic Progress and Marketing's Contributions to the Firm and to Society,* Ronald C. Curhan, ed., Combined Proceedings of the American Marketing Association, Series No. 36 (Chicago: American Marketing Association, 1974), pp. 41–44.

RAY, MICHAEL L.: *Advertising & Communication Management* (Englewood Cliffs, NJ: Prentice-Hall, 1982), pp. 225–46.

SIBLEY, DAWN, and JOEL FISHER: "The demo revolution," *Marketing & Media Decisions,* November 1981, pp. 16–26.

TOLLEY, B. STUART: *Advertising and Marketing Research: A New Methodology* (Chicago: Nelson Hall, 1977).

TROUT, JACK, and AL RIES: *The Positioning Era* (New York: Ries Cappiello Colwell, 1973). This is the reprint of a series of articles that appeared in *Advertising Age,* April 24, May 1, and May 8, 1972.

Media

This section covers the planning of media strategy and an overview of each of the major advertising media. In recent years the media segment of advertising programs has taken on much greater importance than it formerly had. Advertisers have come to realize that even the most persuasive advertising message delivered to the wrong audience will fail. In addition inflationary pressures have caused print and broadcast media to more than double their advertising rates during the last decade. The financial risks of improper media buys have led to better trained, more professional, media planners. The growing sophistication of media planning has also been a result of the explosion in communication technology. The variations and diversity of media outlets have resulted in media buying's becoming more quantitative and largely dependent on the computer to develop media plans. As we shall discuss in this section, the media planner will be faced with even more complex opportunities in efficiently utilizing the media of the future.

PART THREE

5

Basic Media Strategy

When we talk about media strategy, we mean the overall media plan for implementing a company's marketing strategy. Many media are available for delivering the message: TV, radio, newspapers, magazines, direct mail, outdoor signs, transit advertising. In each category we have hundreds, if not thousands, of individual media from which to select. This calls for a plan.

With the exception of product distribution, advertising expense is the largest variable in marketing, and media represent by far the largest part of the total advertising budget. Increases in media expenditures during the last decade have resulted in closer scrutiny of the media function than in previous years. Advertisers are demanding greater cost efficiency and less waste circulation in media buying by their agencies. Agencies, in turn, are investing more money in hiring and retaining more professional and better trained personnel in the media department. Current expenditures for the purchase of advertising media are over $60 billion. The breakdown of total United States advertising-media expenditures is approximately as shown in Table 5.1.

There can be a great difference in effectiveness per dollar spent between two media plans for the same product. The devel-

Table 5–1

ADVERTISING ALLOCATION BY MEDIA	
MEDIUM	%
Newspapers	29
Television	21
Direct mail	13
Radio	7
Magazines	6
Outdoor	1
Other	23

opment of a media plan represents a composite of many factors, including the answers to the following questions:

☐ What is the marketing goal?
☐ What is the nature of the copy?
☐ How much money is available?
☐ What are the chief characteristics of people in our target market?
☐ Where is the product distributed?
☐ Shall we stress reach, frequency, or continuity?
☐ What is the best timing for our advertising schedule?
☐ What is the competition doing?
☐ Are there any special merchandising plans in the offing?
☐ What combination of media is best?

WHAT IS THE MARKETING
GOAL?
The links between a firm's overall marketing goals and its strategy and its advertising program cannot be overemphasized. Yet advertising is only one of a number of corporate functions that must be coordinated under a marketing umbrella. So the role of advertising must be considered as a complement to the general marketing strategy.

The advertising-marketing union is a two-step process:

1. Determining what the marketer wishes to attain within a given period of time. The marketing goal can be expressed in dollar amount of sales, number of units sold, share of market, increase in distribution outlets, or share of mind (how many more people know about our product now than before we advertised?).

2. Identifying those marketing goals which can be accomplished through advertising. Advertising might have the major role in increasing the share of mind, but personal selling might be used to increase distribution outlets.

WHAT IS THE NATURE OF THE
COPY?

The type of message the advertising is to deliver may immediately suggest certain media and preclude others. If the ad is to show the beautiful design and color of drapery or floor covering, we immediately think of full-color pages in magazines or the color pages of a Sunday-newspaper magazine supplement. If it is desirable to demonstrate something, TV is usually the best medium. If there is a special coupon offer to introduce a new product, print media suggest themselves. If a supporting campaign features a slogan, trademark, or package, outdoor or bus advertising comes to mind. Not all products have such strong media predilections, but studying the copy for ideas about the best way to present the product may suggest the medium.

HOW MUCH MONEY IS
AVAILABLE?

The purchase of advertising time and space is a major decision for even the smallest advertiser. During the 1970s advertising costs increased at a rate greater than that experienced in most other sectors of the economy. Current predictions indicate that this trend will continue (see Exhibit 5.1).

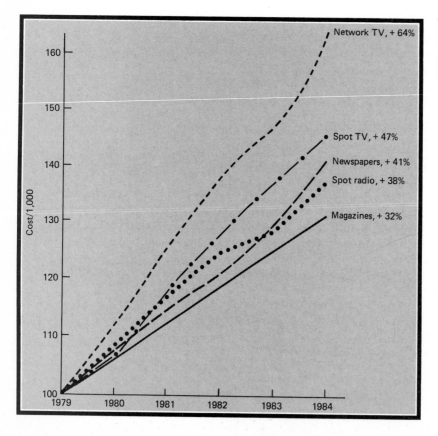

Exhibit 5.1
Media cost trends, 1979 to 1984. (From Magazine Publishers Association, Newsletter, March 1980, p. 1.)

The smaller the budget, the greater the need for resourcefulness. A small advertiser looks for media that are not commonly being used by competitive products. Another looks for special space units. Another shops intensively for TV and radio spots off prime time. Such resourcefulness is good at any level; it is particularly necessary for the small advertiser. (The term *small advertiser* means small in comparison with others in his field.) The larger the budget, the greater the risk in making decisions that entail large investments, and there is no escape from the financial day of reckoning. The first judgment to make in connection with a budget, therefore, is to see whether its size permits one to think in terms of the most costly media—TV networks and magazine color pages, for example—assuming that one would want to consider them. The advertiser must also be aware that, the smaller a medium's audience, the higher the proportionate cost. Consequently the larger, more expensive media are usually the best bargain but also may have a high level of nonprospects, or *waste circulation*. At one time many advertisers held that good intermedia planning called for concentrating on one medium of most importance to present or prospective consumers, which became the primary medium. However, the diversity of media and resulting audience segmentation make it likely that an advertiser will have to consider one or more secondary media. A goal in selecting secondary media is to create an interplay with the primary medium that will enhance the impression made by each (referred to as the *synergistic effect,* or 2 + 2 = 5).

WHAT ARE THE CHIEF CHARACTERISTICS OF PEOPLE IN OUR TARGET MARKET?

The identification of the target market is a primary function of the media planner. From the profile of people who represent the target market we want to pick out the characteristic most relevant to the use of our product. People of different ages, lifestyles, and incomes buy some products more than other people do: teenagers buy cosmetics, singles consume small servings of canned foods, young mothers buy baby food, heads of growing families purchase new cars, elderly consumers look for denture cleaners, and sports enthusiasts want tennis rackets, fishing rods, or golf clubs. What type of media would most efficiently reach such people? At a later point we can review the class of medium that reaches our prime-target audience and select the specific medium that best meets our other qualifications.

WHERE IS THE PRODUCT DISTRIBUTED?

Advertising is a part of a total marketing program that prescribes the areas in which the product is sold. We now seek to coordinate the circulation of the advertising with the geographical distribution or the special interests of the market. Four basic media plans are used: a local plan, a regional plan, a national plan, and a selective plan.

Local plan   A local plan is used when the product is on sale in only one town or community and its immediate trading zone. When a new product is being introduced, when a product is tested in different and distant markets, or when a manufacturer is building a business town by town, a local plan is appropriate. In these situations the medium must be confined to the specific geographic area in which the manufacturer has distribution. This applies no matter which media are used.

Regional plan   As the sales of a product spread to larger areas, the advertiser seeks to employ media that reach that region. He uses a regional plan, a local plan grown larger. The region may cover several adjoining markets or an entire state or several adjoining states. When the sale of a product varies with sectional differences in taste or local requirements, regional plans are used. Households buy tea more in New England than in the Middle West. More blended whisky is sold in the Middle Atlantic states than it is on the Pacific Coast. Most low-calorie soft drinks are sold in the Northeast and East Central regions. When an advertiser's product is affected by such regional preferences, he will choose media with circulations in those territories. In addition to the media used in a local plan, regional editions of national magazines and regional network TV and radio can often be used successfully.

National plan   We now jump millions of dollars ahead to the point at which the product is in widespread distribution all over the country, in every city, town, and hamlet—Coca-Cola, for example, or Crest toothpaste or Chevrolet cars. Here the task is to reach many different buyers of our product all over the country at the lowest cost per thousand prospects (CPM),* and we embark on a *national* media plan. We can now consider network TV, network radio, and full-circulation national magazines, along with the nationally syndicated Sunday supplements. Newspaper, outdoor, and transit advertising are also possibilities.

In recent years many large national advertisers have combined aspects of both local and regional plans with their overall national-advertising strategy. Marketing research has shown that even widely distributed national products and brands demonstrate significant differences in consumer acceptance from one geographical area to another. For instance, frozen-vegetable consumption is 86 percent greater in Baltimore than in Dallas, and New York is 67 percent higher in rice purchases than St. Louis is.† To account for these geographical differences advertisers often supplement national media with local advertising.

Selective plan   We now come to a fourth plan, based not on the geographical distribution of the product but on the special interest of the users of the product *wherever they may happen to be.* Boating, tennis, art, antiques, and other crafts and

---

*CPM is a means of comparing media cost among vehicles with different circulations. The formula is stated as CPM = Cost × 1,000/circulation.

†*Target Group Index,* 1977.

hobbies whose partisans may be scattered all over the country are special interests. The problem in such an instance is not the CPM of reaching people with these interests but how the greatest number of them can be reached. Most useful in reaching these people are magazines directed at specific markets *(Sports Illustrated, Photography Today, Field and Stream),* direct mail, special sections of Sunday newspapers devoted to these subjects, and selected radio and TV programs.

A selective plan is often combined with a geographical plan. If you want to reach all home owners in a certain part of the country, you may use a sectional edition of a national shelter magazine. In the South you can advertise in *Southern Living* magazine. The local, sectional, and national plans, along with the selective plan, provide a good media framework within which to work.

SHALL WE STRESS REACH, FREQUENCY, OR CONTINUITY?

Reach refers to the total number of people to whom you deliver a message; *frequency,* to the number of times it is delivered within a given period (usually figured on a weekly basis for ease in schedule planning); *continuity,* to the length of time a schedule runs. Only the biggest advertisers can emphasize all three at once, and even they seek to spread their money most efficiently.

The advantage of going for reach as the prime goal is that you get a message before the greatest number of people. A disadvantage is that you may not expose potential consumers to your message enough times to tell your full story.

In recent years most media buyers start with frequency as the first building block in a media plan. The hope is that, by estimating the number of times each prospect will be exposed to your advertising, you can evaluate the communication value of your media plan. As we shall see at the end of this chapter, computers make it economically feasible to consider several plans for both reach and frequency.

At this point we lack the scientific data to make specific generalizations in two areas crucial to the reach-frequency equation:

1. What is the optimum frequency? Most studies indicate that additional frequency will result in increases in consumer response (recall, recognition, sales, and the like) over as many as twenty exposures. However, after three to five exposures the additional increment of response tends to decrease at a rapid rate.

2. What is the reach and frequency level for a specific media plan? An estimate of optimum frequency does not necessarily allow us to determine the reach or the most efficient placement of our advertising in a media schedule. Given current research tools, we can estimate the number of different people who see consecutive issues of a particular magazine or TV show. However, our estimates are less certain in dealing with major national campaigns, which often use hundreds of insertions in several media. Even if we solve the problem of optimum frequency, we are left with the inability to determine the reach and frequency of a schedule. At this time we can only estimate the number of different people who see consecutive issues of a magazine or TV show. Just imagine the difficulty associated with a multimillion-dollar campaign with hundreds of insertions in several media.

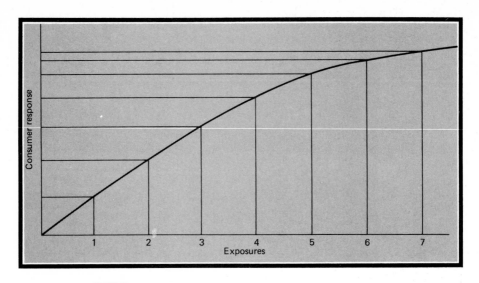

Exhibit 5.2
Consumer response to additional frequency.

The third ball in this juggling act is *continuity*. Among the clearest examples of those who make this the prime factor are the companies that engage in long-range institutional campaigns to establish favorable attitudes toward themselves.

In the absence of more scientific data many media directors apply the rule for competitive products: "Match competition and then some." If you don't have enough money to match competition on a national scale, you may be able to pick out a market or media vehicle where competition has spread itself thin and outshine it there.

There is much research being done and to be done on the criteria for evaluating reach, frequency, and continuity in a given situation. A series of recent studies reached the following conclusions:

1. One exposure of an advertisement to a target group consumer within a purchase cycle has little or no effect in all but a minority of circumstances.
2. Since one exposure is usually ineffective, the central goal of productive media planning should be to place emphasis on enhancing frequency rather than reach.
3. The weight of evidence suggests strongly that an exposure frequency of two within a purchase cycle is an effective level.
4. By and large, optimal exposure frequency appears to be at least three exposures within a purchase cycle.
5. Beyond three exposures within a brand purchase cycle, or over a period of four or even eight weeks, increasing frequency continues to build advertising effectiveness at a decreasing rate, but with no evidence of a decline.*

*"Frequency," *Marketing and Media Decisions*, April, 1980, p. 102.

WHAT IS THE BEST TIMING FOR OUR ADVERTISING
SCHEDULE?
A decision as to *when* to spend the money in advertising is one of the key elements of media strategy. A few principal timing patterns for using media are the following:

Seasonal
program
Some products' sales have seasonal fluctuations—cough drops in the winter, suntan lotion in the summer, and watches at graduation time and at Christmas. In such instances the advertising is scheduled to reflect the seasonal peaks, appearing in concentrated dosage ahead of the consumer buying season, when people might first begin thinking of such products.

Steady
program
When the sale of a product is uniform throughout the year (toothpaste, for example), the advertising could be steadily maintained. Often, however, companies choose to concentrate their advertising. Sometimes a steady schedule would have to be too thin if it were spread over 12 months, and more impressive advertising can be concentrated in shorter time periods. Sometimes money is needed to meet competitive promotional efforts or to provide for special local campaigns. During the summer, reading and watching TV decrease, and radio listening increases; so many TV-network advertisers take a hiatus or switch their advertising to radio until fall.

Pulsing
Pulsing (also called "flighting") is the technique of having comparatively short bursts of advertising in a few markets at a time rather than running a steady but weaker schedule of advertising simultaneously in many markets. Pulsing seeks to leave the consumer with the impression of a much higher level of advertising than would be possible by scheduling the same number of exposures evenly throughout some period. Pulsing also allows heavier expenditures during peak sales periods. For instance, tire companies spend at a much higher level during April and May, when consumers are preparing for vacations, and from September through November, when drivers are winterizing their cars. During other months, particularly December to March, tire advertising is cut sharply. Let's look at some specific pulsing strategies: In *radio* it is possible to purchase twice the weight (advertising exposures) in a 3-week period rather than stretch the same total weight over 6 weeks. This pattern could be followed throughout the year. In *magazines,* assuming a long enough list of publications to benefit from duplication, all insertions could be grouped within a 2-month period instead of 4. Three flights could then be scheduled at appropriate points during the year. In *outdoor* a 200 showing (daily advertising exposures equal to twice the population of the market) could be scheduled every other month for a year, rather than a 100 showing for 12 months. In *newspapers,* similarly, a series of ads can be run on consecutive days for a "burst"

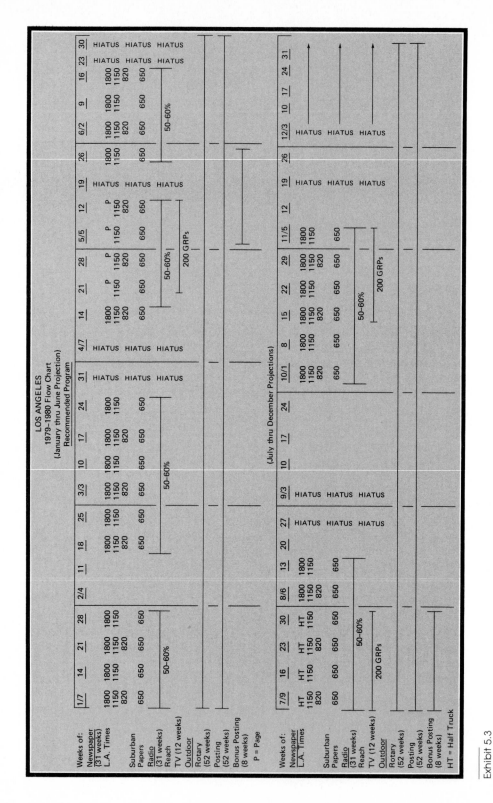

Exhibit 5.3
Delta Airlines media plan for Los Angeles, using pulsing technique. (Courtesy Delta Air Lines, Inc.)

effect, rather than spacing the ads over a month.* These strategies are illustrated in Exhibit 5.3.

WHAT IS THE COMPETITION
DOING?
In media planning we are very much interested in what our competition is doing, especially if their expenditure is bigger than ours (as it usually seems). One popular guide is not to compete with them in media that they already dominate. Instead it might be better to pick a medium in which you can dominate or hold your own against the advertising of similar products. There are numerous media in which your ad will not be overshadowed by others in your field. However, if the campaign is based on unusual copy that would be unique in any medium, go ahead and place your ad where you think it would be most effective, regardless of the competition.

There are several services available to advertisers that report competitive advertising activity. One of the leading companies in the field is Leading National Advertisers, Inc. (LNA), which provides dollar and space-time insertion figures for over 24,000 brands (Exhibit 5.4). This information can be extremely valuable in determining the relative weight of alternative media schedules compared to competitive brands.

ARE THERE ANY SPECIAL MERCHANDISING PLANS
IN THE OFFING?
By *merchandising plans* we mean special inducements offered to the buyer—cents-off coupons, premiums, prize contests, or special price reductions. These plans are usually intensive campaigns, often in special markets, designed to offset competitive pressure, to introduce new products, or to intensify demand among present customers. In such cases an entire advertising program will be built around the merchandising offer. Since merchandising plans are usually associated directly with product purchase, they are also known as "sales promotions."

WHAT COMBINATION OF MEDIA IS
BEST?
Different media can deliver the same message in different ways to different prospects. How can we combine the media available to us in the most effective way? We've seen many of the problems entering into the formulation of a media program, and we've begun to realize the complexity of media planning. Fortunately, we have tools to help us, and one of these is the computer.

Computer
thinking
By computer thinking we mean the thought of the *user* of the computer, not the supposed thinking of the computer itself. Computer thinking is thereby

---

*"Ad Men See Pulsing as a Way to Beat Soaring TV Time Costs," *Advertising Age*, July 4, 1977, p. 27. Reprinted by permission. Copyright 1977 by Crain Communications, Inc.

BRAND NAME — CLASS CODE / PARENT COMPANY (SUBSIDIARY or DIVISION)		YTD $(000)	MEDIA USED
HARTFORD NATIONAL BANK & TRUST CO	B151	$ 80.6	S
HARTFORD NATIONAL BANK & TRUST CO CONSUMER	B151	2.5	O
SERVICES			
HARTFORD NATIONAL CORP			
HARTS BREAD	F161	70.2	S
DPF INC (INTERSTATE BRANDS CORP)			
HARTS FAMILY DEPARTMENT STORES	G608	6.3	O
NATIONAL INDUSTRIES INC (BIG BEAR INC)			
HARTS SEEDS	T620	1.2	S
HART CHARLES C SEED CO			
*HARTWICK COLLEGE RESIDENTIAL	B133	1.8	M
HARTZ MOUNTAIN DOG & CAT VITAMINS	G532	877.2	S-R
HARTZ MOUNTAIN DOG CHEWS	G531	143.6	S-R
HARTZ MOUNTAIN FLEA COLLARS	G532	6,103.2	M-N-S-R
HARTZ MOUNTAIN FLEA TAGS	G932	1.8	S-R
HARTZ MOUNTAIN INDUSTRIES INC REAL ESTATE	G520	16.9	O
HARTZ MOUNTAIN INDUSTRIES INC (HARTZ MOUNTN INDUST IN)			
HARTZ MOUNTAIN PET SHAMPOO	G532	297.8	R
HARTZ MOUNTAIN WORMER	G532	639.8	S-R
HARTZ MOUNTAIN CORP			
HARVARD BED FRAMES	H120	22.8	M
RUSCO INDUSTRIES INC (HARVARD MFG CO)			
HARVARD BUSINESS SCHOOL ADVANCED MANAGEMENT	B133	21.1	M
PROGRAM			
HARVARD BUSINESS SCHOOL RESIDENTIAL	B133	6.3	M
HARVARD EXECUTIVE EDUCATION PROGRAM	B133	24.5	M
HARVARD UNIVERSITY (HARVARD BUSINESS SCHOOL)			
HARVARD JR WORLD ENCYCLOPEDIA	B410	5.0	S
EASTERN GUILD INC			
HARVARD MEDICAL SCHOOL HEALTH LETTER	B420	11.3	M-P
HARVARD UNIVERSITY PRESS	B410	4.5	M
HARVARD UNIVERSITY (HARVARD UNIVERSITY PR)			
HARVEST BLEND INSTANT HOT CEREAL	F122	36.2	M-S
RALSTON PURINA CO			
HARVEST MAID FOOD DEHYDRATOR	H220	2.6	M
ALTERNATIVE PIONEERING SYS I			
HARVEST TIME CANNING JARS & LIDS	H235	13.4	M
STONE CONTAINER CORP (NATL PKGING CONSMR GRP)			
HARVESTORE GRAIN SYSTEM	T520	3.6	S-O
SMITH A O CORP (SMITH A O HARV PRO INC)			
HARVEY PROBBER FURNITURE	H120	2.3	P
PROBBER HARVEY INC			
HARVEY RADIO	G605	4.8	M-P
HARVEY GROUP INC (HARVEY RADIO)			
HARVEYS BRISTOL CREAM SHERRY	F320	903.5	M-S
HEUBLEIN INC (HARVEY JOHN & SONS LTD)			
*HARVEYS RESORT HOTEL LAKE TAHOE NEVADA	T431	8.7	M
*HARVEYS SKINDIVING SUITS	G490	18.3	M
HARVEYS WINES	F320	23.6	S
HEUBLEIN INC (HARVEY JOHN & SONS LTD)			
HARVIE & HUDSON (APPAREL-MEN)	G607	1.8	M
HARWOOD PERFORMANCE RACING COMPONENTS	T154	6.3	M
HARWOOD PERFORM SALES INC			
HARZFELDS (JEWELRY)	G606	.9	M
HARZFELDS (APPAREL-WOMEN)	G607	22.9	M
GARFINCKEL BROOKS BRO & R I (HARZFELDS INC)			
HASBRO DOLLS & ACCESSORIES	G450	1,152.5	N-S
HASBRO TOYS	G450	1,979.1	N-S
HASBRO INDUSTRIES INC			
HASPEL SPORTSUITS MEN	A112	9.4	M
HASPEL SPORTSUITS MEN & WOMEN	A112	31.9	M-P
HASPEL SPORTSWEAR MEN & WOMEN	A115	2.1	M
HASPEL SPORTSWEAR MEN & WOMEN	A115	21.4	M-P
HASPEL SUITS MEN & WOMEN	A112	79.1	M-P
HASPEL BROTHERS INC	A112	3.9	M
HASSELBLAD CAMERA & ACCESSORIES	G230	8.1	M
GILLETTE CO (BRAUN NORTH AMERICA)			
HASSELFORS MARINE HARDWARE	G490	3.0	M
GENERAL SPORTING GOODS CORP (HASSELFORS STLES MAR D)			
HASTINGS (APPAREL-MEN)	G607	16.7	M
HASTINGS AUTOMOTIVE PRODUCTS	T154	27.0	M
HASTINGS MFG CO			
HASTINGS MUTUAL INSURANCE	B220	6.4	O
HATHAWAY SHIRTS MEN	A111	11.6	P-S
WARNACO INC (HATHAWAY C F CO)			
HATTERAS YACHTS	G430	48.2	M
AMF INC (HATTERAS YACHT CO)			
*HATTIE (APPAREL-WOMEN)	G607	12.2	M
*HAUMAN HOUSE INC (MISCELLANEOUS)	G608	66.9	M-P
HAV-A-TAMPA CIGARS	G112	15.9	M-S
ELI SECURITIES CO (HAV CORP)			
HAVAHART TRAPS	T550	4.5	M-P
ALLCOCK MFG CO			
HAVANA FLORIDA CO (MISCELLANEOUS)	G608	.9	M
HAVANA WEED OIL FRAGRANCE FOR WOMEN & MEN	D113	4.7	S
REGENCY COSMETICS INC			
*HAVERFORDS (MISCELLANEOUS)	G608	.9	M
*HAVILAND CHINA	H111	32.8	M-S
*HAWAII HOMES REAL ESTATE	G520	10.2	M
*HAWAII RESORT PROMOTION	T432	155.0	M
HAWAII STATE OF (HAWAII VISITORS BUREAU)			
HAWAIIAN CANNED & FROZEN PUNCH	F223	5.0	O
HAWAIIAN CANNED PUNCH	F223	2,243.6	P-N-S-O
REYNOLDS R J INDUSTRIES INC (RJR FOODS INC)			
*HAWAIIAN ISLANDS RESORT PROMOTION	T432	58.1	M
HAWAIIAN PUNCH POWDERED DRINK MIXES	F223	6,088.7	M-P-N-S-O
REYNOLDS R J INDUSTRIES INC (RJR FOODS INC)			
HAWAIIAN TROPIC SUN & SKI PRODUCTS	D111	18.2	M
HAWAIIAN TROPIC SUNTAN PRODUCTS	D111	19.4	S-O
TANNING RESEARCH LABS INC (RON RICE BEACH PRODS)			
*HAWK ENTERPRISES (MISCELLANEOUS)	G608	.6	M
*HAWK REAL ESTATE	G520	34.6	M-P
HAWK TUNE-UP EQUIPMENT	T154	2.3	M
PALPAC			
*HAWKER BUSINESS JETS	T300	40.5	M
HAWKER SIDDELEY GROUP LTD (HAWKER SIDDELEY AVIATI)			
*HAWORTH OFFICE FURNITURE	B411	86.3	M

BRAND NAME — CLASS CODE / PARENT COMPANY (SUBSIDIARY or DIVISION)		YTD $(000)	MEDIA USED
*HAWTHORN BOOKS	B410	$ 25.9	M
HAY-ADAMS HOTEL WASHINGTON	T431	.9	M
SHELDON MAGAZINE ENTERPRISES			
*HAYASHI GRAPHICS (MISCELLANEOUS)	G608	.9	M
HAYES-LEGER LTD (HOUSEHOLD)	G605	1.9	M
HAYES NATIONAL BANK	B151	.1	O
CHARTER NEW YORK CORP			
HAYMAKER SPORTSWEAR WOMEN	A115	15.5	M-P
GENERAL MILLS INC (HAYMAKER SPORTS INC)			
*HAYNES PUBLICATIONS	B410	10.1	M
HAYOUN SKIN CARE CLINIC	D240	7.4	M
HAYOUN CLINIC			
HAYS IGNITION SYSTEMS	T154	1.0	M
HAYS SALES			
*HAYSTACK MOUNTAIN SKI AREA	T432	.5	O
HEAD-BED BEDDING	H120	8.8	P
BOARDMAN AVERY LTD (HEAD-BED DIV)			
HEAD CAMPS RESIDENTIAL	B133	8.3	M
AMF INC (AMF HEAD DIV)			
*HEAD SHAMPOO	D142	207.2	M-S
HEAD & SHOULDERS LOTION SHAMPOO	D142	315.7	M
HEAD & SHOULDERS SHAMPOOS	D142	8,667.3	N-S
PROCTER & GAMBLE CO			
HEAD SKIS	G470	30.8	M
AMF INC (AMF HEAD DIV)			
HEAD SPORTING FOOTWEAR MEN	A132	56.5	M
HEAD SPORTSWEAR MEN & WOMEN	A115	28.2	M
AMF INC (AMF HEAD SPORTSWEAR IN)			
HEAD START KERATIN SHAMPOO	D142	9.6	M
HEAD START VITAMIN & MINERAL COMPOUND	D215	813.2	M-S
BRASWELL INC (COSVETIC LABS CO)			
HEAD STRONG 1 VITAMINS	D215	25.3	M
WEIDER COMMUNICATIONS			
HEAD TENNIS RACKETS	G490	275.1	M-S
AMF INC (AMF HEAD DIV)			
HEADHUGGER HAIR PIECES	D144	6.4	M
AMORA INDUSTRIES INC			
*HEADSTART HAIR FOR MEN HAIRPIECES	D144	9.1	M
HEALD CYCLE KITS	G440	50.9	M
HEALD LAWN & GARDEN MACHINE KITS	T610	47.5	M
HEALD INC			
HEALTH CLUB FOR WOMEN	D240	2.0	M
*HEALTH MAINTENANCE ORGANIZATION OF PENNSYLVANIA	B210	5.2	O
HEALTH-O-METER SCALES	H150	12.5	M
CONTINENTAL SCALE CORP			
HEALTH-TEX WEARING APPAREL CHILDREN	A115	752.9	M-P-S
CHESEBROUGH-PONDS INC (HEALTH-TEX INC)			
HEALTHKNIT MULTI-PRODUCT ADVERTISING MEN	A121	115.8	M
STANWOOD CORP (STANDARD KNIT MILLS IN)			
HEALTHWAYS DIVING INSTRUMENTS & ACCESSORIS	G222	6.1	M
HEALTHWAYS SCUBA EQUIPMENT	G490	2.0	M
LEISURE DYNAMICS INC (HEALTHWAYS)			
HEALTHY HAIR HAIR VITAMINS	D215	40.9	S
PALM BEACH BEAUTY PRODS CO			
*HEALY INC (JEWELRY)	G606	1.1	M
HEARST CORP NEWSPAPERS	B420	154.1	S
HEARST RADIO STATIONS	B430	357.3	S-O
HEARST TV STATIONS	B440	1.9	O
HEARST CORP			
HEART/AMERICA WOOD STAIN	H541	91.2	S
SCHERING-PLOUGH CORP			
*HEART LAND (MISCELLANEOUS)	G608	1.4	M
*HEART OF ARKANSAS RESORT PROMOTION	T432	6.1	M
HEART OF THE 60S RECORDINGS	H330	138.8	S
MISCELLANEOUS RECORD OFFERS			
HEARTLAND NATURAL CEREALS	F122	293.8	S
HEARTLAND NATURAL CEREALS SWEEPSTAKES	F122	114.8	M
HEARTLAND NATURAL SYRUP	F111	19.9	S
PET INC (PET GROCERY PROD DIV)			
*HEARTS & FLOWERS FLORIST INC WEDDING SERVICES	G602	.7	M
HEAT-CATCHER HEATING SYSTEM HOME	H522	.5	M
LASSY TOOLS INC			
*HEAT KEEPER HEATING SYSTEM HOME	H522	2.7	M
HEAT WAVE PORTABLE HEATERS	H220	16.1	S
INTERMATIC INC			
HEATH CANDY	F211	225.4	S
HEATH L S & SONS INC			
HEATH CO (MISCELLANEOUS)	G608	295.7	M-P-S-O
SCHLUMBERGER LTD (HEATH CO)			
HEATHROW HOTEL LONDON	T431	4.8	M
LEX SERVICE GROUP LTD			
HEATILATOR FIREPLACES HOME	H522	135.2	M-S
HEATILATOR FIREPLACES HOME DEALERS	H522	.3	O
VEGA INDUSTRIES INC (HEATILATOR DIV)			
HEAVEN HILL BOURBON WHISKEY	F330	50.7	O
HEAVEN HILL DISTILLERS INC			
*HEAVENLY VALLEY SKI AREA LAKE TAHOE	T431	39.2	O
HEAVY DUTY DOORS HOME	H525	.4	M
HEAVY DUTY MFG CO INC			
HEAVY METAL MAGAZINE	B420	38.3	M
TWENTY FIRST CENTURY COMM I			
*HEBREW ARTS SCHOOL RESIDENTIAL	B133	.3	M
HEBREW NATIONAL KOSHER FRANKS	F150	1,251.0	S
HEBREW NATIONAL KOSHER MEAT PRODUCTS	F150	1.7	S
COLGATE-PALMOLIVE CO (HEBREW NATL KOSHER F I)			
HECHT CO (APPAREL-WOMEN)	G607	10.4	M
HECHT CO (MISCELLANEOUS)	G608	3.5	M
HECHT CO GENERAL PROMOTION	G608	5.8	M
MAY DEPARTMENT STORES CO (HECHT CO)			
HECKERS FLOUR	F113	18.0	M
STANDARD MILLING CO			
HECKLER & KOCH GUNS	G420	1.4	M
SECURITY ARMS CO INC (HECKLER & KOCH INC)			
*HECKS (MISCELLANEOUS)	G608	73.2	S-O
*HECTORS PLANT COLLARS	T540	25.5	S
HEDDON FISHING EQUIPMENT	G410	49.8	M
KIDDE WALTER & CO INC (HEDDONS JAMES SONS)			
*HEDENKAMP CARDS AGENTS WANTED	G571	46.1	M
HEDMAN HEDDERS	T154	2.3	M
HEDMAN MFG CORP			

MEDIA USED: M - MAGAZINES,   S - SPOT TV,
P - NEWSPAPER SUPPS,   R - NETWORK RADIO,
N - NETWORK TV   O - OUTDOOR   *Company and Brand name are the same.

Exhibit 5.4

LNA ad $ summary and brand index. (Courtesy Leading National Advertisers, Inc.)

also distinguished from the incredible tasks of computer programming and operation. The greatest contribution of the computer to media planning—even to those who do not use it—is the necessity that it imposes to think in precise terms, to state problems in precise form, and to base decisions on accurately gathered information.

Use of computers. Basically, the computer speedily coordinates into a meaningful form a given set of facts from a larger set of facts. Hence the first requirement in the use of the computer for making media decisions is to define the "facts" that are fed into it; there is a familiar phrase in the computer world: "Garbage in, garbage out" (GIGO). If you speak of "users of a product," do you mean households or individuals? If individuals, do you include children? What constitutes a user? A person who has once used the product? A person who has some on hand right now?

A second characteristic of the computer is that it deals with numbers, not adjectives. All factors for a computer, therefore, must be put in numerical form, or quantified. Suppose you plan to put all the data on certain magazines into a computer—their circulation, the number of readers in different age groups, and so on. These are data already offered in numerical form. In evaluating the magazines, however, you also want to consider their editorial tone, their prestige, and the environment in which the advertisement appears. Because of this, someone must go over the different magazines and form a judgment on such qualities. That judgment must be quantified by giving each magazine a rating for "editorial tone," let us say from 1 to 5. The computer will then be able to give an end figure in which a magazine rated 4 for its editorial tone would get twice the weight of a magazine rated only 2.

There is no single computer technique for media planning. The computer does allow a number of strategies to be tested, using various statistical approaches. If ten advertising agencies developed media plans for the same client, they would probably develop ten different plans and perhaps even use ten different methods. Media planning, like most aspects of advertising, is still more art than science.

While recognizing the wide diversity of media planning most of these involve one of two general approaches:

1. Nonoptimizing approaches, such as simulation and iteration. These are forms of trial-and-error plans based to some extent on the intuition and judgment of the media planner using them;

2. the mathematical optimizing techniques, such as linear and nonlinear programming.

A nonoptimizing media problem

The nonoptimizing approaches have two primary characteristics: They are trial-and-error methods, and they provide a number of solutions but no single right answer. We'll demonstrate this with a particular problem.

Table 5–2

VEHICLE	MEDIA UNIT	COVERAGE (NO. OF WOMEN = 76,597,000)[a]	COST OF INSERTION (4-COLOR PAGE), $
1	Metropolitan Home	1,107,000	12,850
2	Better Homes & Gardens	17,517,000	49,944
3	Cosmopolitan	6,341,000	23,000
4	Family Circle	17,369,000	49,750
5	Good Housekeeping	17,239,000	39,000
6	House & Garden	8,959,000	17,500
7	Ladies' Home Journal	14,621,000	37,425
8	McCall's	17,283,000	47,500
9	MS.	1,155,000	7,925
10	National Geographic	9,487,000	74,365
11	Newsweek	6,820,000	45,665
12	House Beautiful	6,506,000	14,230
13	People	5,937,000	22,600
14	Psychology Today	2,397,000	20,990
15	Readers' Digest	23,613,000	74,550
16	Redbook	10,476,000	33,375
17	Time	7,972,000	63,895
18	TV Guide	23,177,000	61,000
19	U.S. News & World Report	2,721,000	31,250
20	Woman's Day	18,713,000	49,840
		213,910,000[b]	

[a]Reach, or unduplicated audience.
[b]Total, or duplicated, audience.

The problem is to determine what combinations of magazines will be used to reach our target audience of upscale women. The media planner has a budget of $600,000 and estimates that a frequency of four exposures will be necessary to sell the product.

The first step is to list the magazines that meet our specifications and the cost of advertising in each, as shown in Table 5.2.

Next the media planner, using the budget as a general guide, selects those magazines and the number of insertions in each that he thinks will best meet the criteria of the buy. After each selection the computer calculates (in this case using a program called "Metheringham beta binomial") the appropriate statistics. The final selection is set out in Table 5.3. And this media schedule resulted in the audience figures in Table 5.4.

Note that this is a correct solution in that it meets (within an acceptable margin) the criteria of the buy. There are, no doubt, other solutions that would also be acceptable.

Optimizing media-plan

evaluations   Unlike the trial-and-error methods, an optimizing media model has a single best solution. The problem with these models is that they offer a "best" solution based on the information, goals, and restraints imposed by the media planner. If any of these are incorrect, then naturally the solution is incorrect. It should also be obvious that, as a media plan becomes more com-

Table 5–3

MEDIA SCHEDULE AND TOTAL NUMBER OF INSERTIONS	
MEDIA UNIT	NO. OF INSERTIONS
Metropolitan Home	0
Better Homes & Gardens	2
Cosmopolitan	0
Family Circle	2
Good Housekeeping	3
House & Garden	0
Ladies' Home Journal	0
McCall's	0
MS.	0
National Geographic	0
Newsweek	0
House Beautiful	0
People	0
Psychology Today	0
Readers' Digest	4
Redbook	0
Time	0
TV Guide	0
U.S. News & World Report	0
Woman's Day	0
	11

Table 5–4

EXPOSURE DISTRIBUTIONS		
NO. OF EXPOSURES	TARGET AUDIENCE, %[a]	
0	33.2	
1	14.8	
2	10.4	
3	8.2	
4	6.8	
5	5.8	Total reach = 66.8
6	5.0	
7	4.4	
8	3.8	
9	3.2	
10 or more	4.4	

Total expenditure = $614,588
CPM (women) = $12.01
Frequency = 4.2

[a]33.2 percent of the audience was not exposed, 14.8 percent was exposed once, 10.4 percent twice, and so on.

Source: Tables 5–2, 5–3 and 5–4 are courtesy Dr. John D. Leckenby, Dept. of Advertising, University of Illinois.

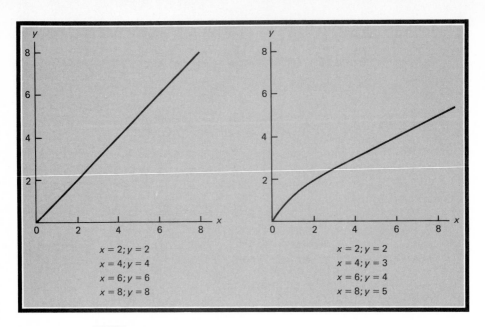

Exhibit 5.5
Examples of linear and nonlinear models.

plex, the practical application of a trial-and-error solution decreases. Let's look at how an optimizing model might work.

Optimizing media models can find a maximum solution (for example the greatest number of TV households reached for a given budget) or a minimum solution (for example the lowest cost per household for a given set of media alternatives). One major advantage of optimizing models is that they force a precise statement of the problem. For instance assume that a media planner wishes to maximize the number of households reached in a TV advertising campaign.

He or she would have to provide (at a minimum) the following information:

1. Budget
2. Media alternatives
   a. TV stations in the market
   b. Day parts available to the advertiser (prime time, daytime)
3. Cost of commercials in these day parts for each station
4. Some other constraints
   a. Client will not advertise on certain shows with excessive sex and violence
   b. All stations in the market must be used a minimum number of times
   c. At least 20 percent of the budget must be allocated to daytime commercials

After the data and constraints have been given to the computer (stated in mathematical language), the computer offers the single best solution. That is the combination of stations and buys that will deliver the greatest number of households.

The simplest types of optimizing models are called "linear." Linear models, as their name implies, assume a constant proportion between variables. Nonlinear models assume varying relationships between variables (Exhibit 5.5).

It should be pointed out that linear models, for all their simplicity, have many problems in media planning. They assume that all commercials exposures have equal value, they do not take into account media discounts, they cannot calculate audience duplication among media, and, finally, they do not indicate when the commercials should be placed.

A MEDIA DIRECTOR LOOKS AT MEDIA

When faced with a media-planning problem for a new product, a media director has various fields from which to draw:

☐ For a local campaign, as a test to be run in different markets:

Local newspapers

Local TV

Local radio

Local cable TV

☐ For a regional campaign:

Local newspapers

Newspaper magazine supplements, bought sectionally

Regional magazines

Regional editions of national magazines

Parts of regional radio networks

Outdoor advertising

Transit advertising

☐ For a national campaign:

TV network

Cut-ins, or for testing purposes substituting local commercials for network commercials

Cable-distributed "superstations"

Radio network

TV and radio commercials, alone or to fill gaps

National magazines

Series of selected magazines

Newspapers

Newspaper magazine supplements

Outdoor advertising

Transit advertising

☐ Selective campaign to reach only people with special interests (such as handicrafts, tennis, photography, or antiques):

Magazines devoted to that specialty

Newspapers with sections devoted to that interest
(possibly on Sunday only)

TV and radio programs attracting devotees of that subject

Direct-response advertising

This is summarized in the three parts of the work plan of Exhibit 5.6.

MEDIA WORK PLAN

SECTION I -- MEDIA OBJECTIVES

*Section I must include the Creative Work Plan and a marketing background statement.

1. **ADVERTISING PERIOD:**
January-December 1977

2. **MEDIA BUDGET:**
$5,000,000

3. **KEY MARKETING OBJECTIVE:** (As it relates to Media Planning)
Increase volume and share by using a product quality improvement to attract current non-users.

4. **KEY COMPETITIVE MEDIA CONSIDERATION:**
$37 million spent in this category, with 5 major brands. Tv is primary medium, with % tv ranging from 60% to 90%. (Exhibit attached for detailed competitive summary.)

5. **PROSPECT DEFINITION:** (If more than one category assign % effort for each)

A. Demographic	% U.S. Base	% Effort
women 18-24	8.6%	30%
women 25-34	10%	70%

B. **Psychographic:**
Women who are more venturesome in trying new products and concerned about approval received from family for meals and food.

6. **KEY MEDIA OBJECTIVES & RATIONALE:**
Provide continuous pressure on a predominantly national basis to maintain an awareness level as prospects come and go out of marketplace. New product will be distributed nationally and continuous pressure is needed to convince prospects that improvement is really significant.

Food product "X"	January 1, 1977	*Peter Planner*
PRODUCT	DATE	PLANNING SUPERVISOR

Exhibit 5.6
On this and the next two pages, a work plan from Young & Rubicam. (From *Media Decisions*, December 1976, pp. 110, 112, 114. Courtesy of Media Publications, Inc.)

MEDIA WORK PLAN

SECTION II -- STRATEGY

1. GEOGRAPHIC: (Identify emphasis as to National, Regional, Local)

Emphasis predominantly national (89% of budget). Local spending will be placed in markets with brand development at least 20% better than national average (11% of budget is local).

2. SEASONALITY: (Identify seasonal concentration, if any)

No seasonality for brand, but we will invest 40% of funds during first quarter to build faster awareness of improved product.

3. REACH & FREQUENCY GOALS:

Effective reach 5+ messages during average 4-week period in introductory phase; 3+ thereafter (Exhibit for frequency goal rationale attached). Anticipated reach of prime prospects 70-80% in introductory period; 50-60% thereafter.

4. OTHER STRATEGIC CONSIDERATIONS: (Include creative units if they are a strategic consideration)

(A) Environment--food prep editorial and high visibility positions.

(B) Commercial length--100% 60-second commercials in first 8 weeks; 50% 60-second/50% 30-second on next 6 weeks; all 30's thereafter.

5. BASIC STRATEGIC DIRECTION: (Check Media classes being considered)

CLASS

DAY NETWORK TV	X	NETWORK RADIO	
PRIME NETWORK TV	X	MAGAZINES	X
LATE NIGHT NETWORK TV		SUPPLEMENTS	
NETWORK SPECIALS	X	NEWSPAPERS	
NETWORK SPORTS		OUTDOOR	
SPOT TV (Identify Daypart)		OTHER (Identify)	

6. MEDIA RATIONALE: (Rationale for Media classes being considered)

Prime network to optimize reach, etc. Day network to provide efficiency against target. Specials to supply high impact at outset of campaign. Magazines to provide new package registration and strong food environment. Etc., etc.

Food product "x"	January 1, 1977	*Peter Planner*
PRODUCT	DATE	PLANNING SUPERVISOR

Exhibit 5.6 (cont.)

117

MEDIA WORK PLAN

SECTION III -- EXECUTION

*Section III must include the Media Plan Budget detail
and Flow Chart. Detail should include % Spending by
media and by quarter.

1. MEDIA MANDATORIES & LIMITATIONS:

Avoid tv violence. Maintain competitive separation.

2. KEY EXECUTIONAL FACTORS AND THEIR EFFECTS: (Scheduling)

Concentrate on daytime serials. Schedule primetime and daytime
activity to coincide. Heavier prime network at start of campaign,
with daytime level consistent throughout.

3. MEDIA PURCHASE GUIDELINES: (Include techniques)

Schedule net activity on at least 2 networks to maximize reach.
Execute road-blocks wherever possible. Negotiate print positions
adjacent to high-readership, pertinent editorial. (Detailed spot
specifications in separate exhibit attached.)

4. PERFORMANCE DATA: (How the MP accomplished strategies,
                        such as R&F, and seasonality. Identify
                        R&F period (4 wks. or quarterly) and
                        indicate national, regional if pertinent)

(Estimated performance delivery shown in exhibit attached)

5. MEDIA TESTING ACTIVITY:

Plan for all-magazine test in two key markets as a media mix
alternative to recommended plan.

Peter Planner
PLANNING SUPERVISOR

Exhibit 5.6 (concl.)

SUMMARY

As we shall stress throughout this book, the essence of successful advertising is planning. Planning is certainly crucial to the media-buying process. The media options (number of vehicles, space and time availabilities, discounts, and the rest) are so numerous that a trial-and-error approach to media strategy will not work. The media planner must move systematically from the overall marketing goals to advertising objectives, including budgets, creative considerations, and target markets, to the actual media plan.

Media plans operate on a number of levels, sometimes simultaneously. National media plans are different in many ways from regional or local plans. Media availability, costs, and tactics will change as we go from the broad national approach to the more individualized regional or local plans.

Regardless of the type of media plan, certain basic principles remain constant. The media planner must consider reach, frequency, continuity, and time of the media schedule. Most of the mechanics of the media-buying process are being done by computers. However, it is important to realize that computers are only as good as the information they are given. Using computers incorrectly will give you faster wrong answers.

QUESTIONS

1. The strategy of creating a media plan for a product is based upon a variety of factors. Identify these factors; what is the importance of each in the overall media plan?
2. How does advertising relate to corporate marketing goals?
3. Discuss media segmentation and waste circulation in media planning.
4. What is the relationship of creative elements to media selection?
5. Discuss the difference between a primary medium and a secondary medium. How does the synergistic effect come into play in selecting primary and secondary media?
6. How are media costs affected by the decision to use a local, regional, national, or selective plan?
7. Define and analyze the significance of reach, frequency, and continuity in planning media schedules.
8. Do some general principles of advertising frequency exist? Discuss.
9. What is the typical consumer response rate after three to five advertising exposures?
10. What future trends are likely to occur in advertising space and time costs?
11. To what extent should a media plan be flexible? How does an advertiser build flexibility into the media plan?
12. What is the major limitation of a nonoptimizing media-planning approach?

SUGGESTED EXERCISES

13. Analyze a brand's advertising in at least three media. Specifically, look for similarities or differences in headlines and copy, product visualization, and target market(s) appealed to.

14. Find at least two examples of sales promotion (such as point-of-purchase displays) that mention that a brand has been advertised elsewhere.

READINGS

AAKER, DAVID A.: "ADMOD: An Advertising Decision Model," *Journal of Marketing Research,* February 1975, pp. 37–45.

BARBAN, ARNOLD M.: *Essentials of Media Planning: A Marketing Viewpoint* (Chicago: Crain Books, 1975).

CANNON, HUGH M., and C. RUSSELL MERZ: "A New Role for Psychographics in Media Selection," *Journal of Advertising,* Spring 1980, pp. 33–36.

JUGENHEIMER, DONALD W., and PETER B. TURK: *Advertising Media* (Columbus, OH: Grid Publishing, 1980).

LIEBMAN, L., and E. LEE: "Reach and Frequency Estimating Services," *Journal of Advertising Research,* August 1974, pp. 23–25.

MANELOVEG, HERBERT D.: "Media Research's Future: Is There Any?" *Advertising Age,* July 15, 1974, p. 23 *ff.*

"Media Outlook," *Advertising Age,* November 9, 1981, S-1.

RAY, MICHAEL L. and PETER H. WEBB: *Advertising Effectiveness in a Crowded Television Environment* (Cambridge, MA: Marketing Science Institute, 1978).

SURMANEK, JIM: *Media Planning* (Chicago: Crain Books, 1980).

6

Using
Television

From 1950, when 70 percent of TV households tuned in Mr. Television, Milton Berle, every Tuesday night, to a nation asking the question "Who shot J. R.?" in 1980, TV has been the prime entertainment medium for millions of Americans; and for all its potential as a medium of education, culture, and information, it continues to be primarily a source of mass entertainment.

Consequently, TV is sold on the basis of audience size. Up to this time no other medium has been consistently able to deliver such a large and diversified audience. Each night almost 60 million households engage in some TV viewing. The success of the medium can be gauged by the fact that a network prime-time program that is seen by *only* 15 million households is usually considered a failure and removed from the schedule.

TV has never been more popular. Part of this popularity is caused by the medium itself, but social forces such as inflation and a home-oriented entertainment style have contributed to its popularity. While TV statistics tell only a part of the story of this social force, they are impressive.* Table 6.1, which is a comparison of a few statistics from 1970 and 1980, will put TV's growth into perspective.

---

*These and subsequent statistics in this chapter, unless otherwise credited, were obtained through the courtesy of the Television Bureau of Advertising (TvB).

Table 6–1

TV STATISTICS		
	1970	1980
TV households, %	95.3	98.2
Multiset households, %	32.2	51.2
Color-set households, %	35.7	85.2
Average daily household viewing, hours:minutes	5:56	6:36
TV advertising expenditures, billion $	3.6	11.3
Commercial TV stations	677	734
Cable households, %	7.6	22.6

We could cite many other figures pointing to TV's growth and popularity. However, they would only reinforce the point made here that TV continues to take a larger share of our time and advertisers' money.

THE MANY FACES OF TELEVISION

Buying a TV set as a self-contained entertainment and information appliance will soon become a thing of the past. Even today some customers buy a set as only one of a number of components in a complete home-entertainment center. In the near future a color set receiving local over-the-air signals will constitute the "stripped-down" model. From this basic unit the household may add a videocassette recorder, a videodisc player, a home computer with two-way communication capability, a TV camera, hi-fi systems, satellite antenna, and of course basic cable service.

Since we can't tell the players without a scorecard, a brief description of the new technology and new services offered by television may prove helpful.

Cable TV

The oldest of the "new" technology, cable began shortly after World War II as a means of improving TV reception to isolated communities. Currently almost 30 percent of homes are wired for cable, and this figure is increasing about 10 percent a year. Cable has been largely deregulated in recent years, and this deregulation opens up major markets to cable and allows more diversified programming. As an advertising medium, cable is still very small, with only $50 million spent in 1981 according to the Cabletelevision Advertising Bureau. However, cable's ability to reach special-interest markets and target individual households may make it a major advertising force in the future.

Pay Cable. In addition to basic cable service most cable systems offer noncommercial auxiliary services for a supplemental fee. Movies are the staple of the services, with "Home Box Office" and "Showtime" the two largest. In the future pay cable will include home security services (already available in a few markets) and a number of information services. Pay-cable services worry advertisers since they provide a noncommercial alternative for an upscale viewing audience, the very people advertising is trying to reach through traditional TV outlets.

Subscription television

A potential competitor to pay cable is subscription television (STV). A decoding device takes jumbled broadcast signals and lets the subscriber see first-run movies and other material similar to that offered by pay cable. The advantage of STV is that it doesn't require the capital investments of cable since the signal is broadcast and no wiring is needed. On the other hand the subscriber gets only a single channel rather than the large number delivered by cable.

Cable networks

A hybrid cable service, included as part of a cable system's basic service but available only through cable, is the cable networks. These networks are delivered by satellite to the cable operator and then sent to cable subscribers in that community. Among the better known cable networks are the Cable News Network (CNN) and Entertainment and Sports Programming Network (ESPN; Exhibit 6.1), both 24-hour services. Cable networks are a major growth area. The three major TV networks all have plans to expand into this area, in effect competing with themselves. Large multiple-cable-system operators (MSO) also plan to produce programs for their cable systems, thus adding advertising revenue to their subscription fees.

Superstations. Closely related to the cable networks are the so-called superstations. These are independent UHF stations whose programs are carried by satellite to cable operators, giving these stations not only coverage within their own markets but also national coverage. The first of the superstations was WTCG-TV in Atlanta, Exhibit 6.2, whose owner, Ted Turner, is generally credited with making the concept a success. Other well-known superstations are WGN-TV, Chicago, and WOR-TV, New York.

Information services

Many people think TV information services are the growth industry of the future. If your TV set is a part of an interactive system tied into a central computer, it can provide a theoretically unlimited amount of information. These systems, called "videotext," provide words rather than pictures. Soon we'll be reading our TV as well as watching it. Not only could a person obtain stock reports, TV schedules, and home-study courses but, by using the same system, could order merchandise, reserve airline tickets, and make bank transactions.

Since this information is going to a self-selected audience, advertising can play a major role in the system, with virtually no waste circulation. For instance, when a person asks to see movie schedules, ads for movies could be shown with their schedules, much like a Yellow Pages listing except with updated information.

Why is Datsun driven to ESPN?

Because SportsCenter gives them a franchise on TV's most complete sports newscast.

That's why Datsun's Vice President of Marketing Services, Robert Kent, bought SportsCenter on ESPN, the 24-hour cable sports network. And there are other reasons:

Five SportsCenters daily bring viewers 30 or 60 minutes of the most comprehensive sports news coverage on television. With updates throughout the day, SportsCenter provides an entirely new dimension to the traditional sports or sports news media buy. Datsun also receives billboard identification.

SportsCenter affordably reaches a national upscale audience of over 11 million homes, almost 15% of all TV households.

In short, ESPN gets Datsun in on the ground floor of the cable boom. SportsCenter advertisers already include Anheuser-Busch, Firestone, Gillette, and Xerox, to name a few.

To see how ESPN and SportsCenter can drive up your sales, call Mike Presbrey today at (212) 245-6650.

The 24-hour total sports network (ESPN)

©1981 ESPN

Exhibit 6.1
Promotion for ESPN. (Courtesy Entertainment and Sports Programming Network.)

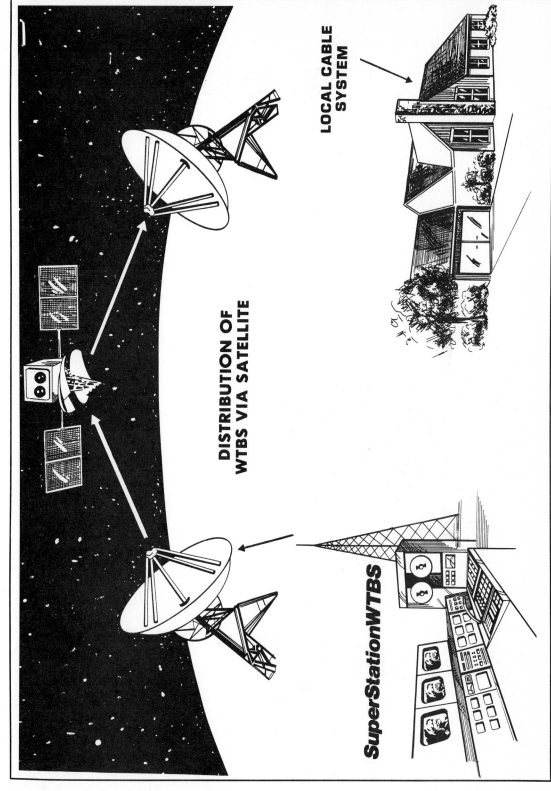

DISTRIBUTION OF WTBS VIA SATELLITE

LOCAL CABLE SYSTEM

SuperStationWTBS

Exhibit 6.2
Distribution of WTBS via satellite. (Courtesy Turner Broadcasting Company.)

THE FRAGMENTED TELEVISION
AUDIENCE
It is difficult to guess what TV will be like in 1990 even though it is less than a decade away. What specific technologies, some probably not yet invented, will ultimately determine the service, quality, and availability of programming and information we shall receive is still unclear. The implications for advertising are many and involve the efficient allocation of billions of dollars.

The one thing advertisers can be certain of is that the audience for any single program will be smaller and much more costly to reach on a CPM basis. Offsetting this higher cost will be greater selectivity of market segments, less waste circulation, and perhaps a lower cost per *prospect* figure. Advertisers will also be able to coordinate commercials with specific types of programming. Advertisers will then be able to coordinate their advertising with editorial content in much the same way they use specialized magazines today. This matching of commercial with program will make the creative message more appropriate to the audience but also will result in higher commercial production costs. Advertisers and their research departments will have to decide whether better communication and sales will justify these higher costs.

Coca-Cola has been among the leaders in producing commercials to fit specific programs. The famous Mean Joe Greene Coke commercial was originally made for the 1980 Super Bowl. Other Coke commercials have had Olympic themes for the 1980 Olympics and rock singers for various musical shows and radio spots.*

TELEVISION AS AN ADVERTISING MEDIUM

Features and
advantages
The major advantage of TV is that it is an indispensable social institution for millions of American families; almost everyone, regardless of socioeconomic status, watches some TV regularly.

TV presents the advertiser's message in the most spectacular way possible, combining sight, sound, motion, and color. A product story can be presented most dramatically on TV. With the aid of live performers and appropriate settings, it provides an unmatched opportunity to demonstrate the merits of a product in the intimacy of the home. It is a fast-acting medium, especially for a new product or an important new feature of an already well-known one. Being on a popular network program is a respected argument in getting dealer support for the product.

Advertising Age, March 10, 1980, p. 6

Limitations and
challenges   With all its effectiveness TV advertising has its problems.

Costs. Despite the efficiency of TV in reaching mass audiences, it is not an inexpensive medium. Network commercials often run as high as $200,000 to produce, and 30-second commercials on top-rated prime-time shows may sell for almost $200,000. The 1982 Super Bowl was the first time a network (CBS) charged over $300,000 for a 30-second commercial.

Clutter. Nonentertainment use of the screen for announcements of forthcoming programs ("promos"), long lists of credits, and a variety of other nonentertainment presentations dilute viewers' attention and therefore hurt advertising.

Increasing profusion of commercials. In the 10-year period from 1970 to 1980 the average weekly number of network commercials rose from 2,633 to 4,088, largely as a result of substituting 30-second for 60-second commercials. Another 25,000 commercials are run on local stations each week. The more commercials that are jammed on top of each other in limited broadcast time, the less attention each of them receives. The kaleidoscope of clutter and commercials produces confusion among viewers and a high rate of misidentification of brands.

Forms of television
usage   An advertiser can buy TV time through a network *(network TV)* or from individual stations *(spot TV)*. If a national advertiser buys spots, they are, strictly speaking, national spot TV; but they are generally referred to as spot TV.* When a local advertiser uses spot TV, it is, strictly speaking, local spot TV, but it is referred to as local TV. This is the standard classification established by the FCC and followed by the industry. In 1980, 45 percent of all TV expenditures was for network, 28.8 percent for spot, and 26.2 for local. In this discussion we deal chiefly with network and spot, saving our discussion of local TV for Chapter 23, Retail Advertising.

Network television. A *TV network* is defined as two or more stations simultaneously broadcasting a program originating from a single source. As a practical matter, 98 percent of all network programming comes from one of the three major networks: ABC, CBS, and NBC, each with approximately 200 affiliates. In addition to these national networks there are also regional and state networks. Often these networks exist only for special events such as bas-

---

*The word "spot" is another of those terms in advertising that are used in two senses: (1) time-buying use, a way of buying time on a nonnetwork show, and (2) creative use, "We need some 30-second spots."

ketball games. The Hughes Sports Network is an example of such a special-event network. Hughes signs up a number of stations for a sports event. The stations may be independent or an affiliate of one of the major networks, but during the event they are the Hughes Sports Network. (Unless otherwise noted, our discussion of networks will be confined to the three national networks.)

The national networks arrange for their affiliates to carry their programming. This is called *clearance* since the local station clears its schedule for network programming. The local affiliate is paid approximately 30 percent of its *program-time* charges.* If a station sells an hour of programming time for $1,000, the network would pay the station $300. In addition the station is allowed to sell some time during network programs and, of course, between programs. Stations do not have to take any particular network show. They can fail to clear the program and broadcast a locally produced show or movie and keep all the advertising revenue. An affiliate that continually failed to clear its network's programming would probably lose its affiliation and substantially reduce its viewing audience.

Network advertising is concentrated among a relatively few advertisers. In 1980 only 558 companies bought network commercials for 2,522 brands. This concentration is partly due to cost, with regular prime-time 30-second commercials ranging from $50,000 to $150,000, depending on ratings. Another important factor in this concentration is the relatively few advertisers who can make use of the large and diverse audience reached by network TV. To use network advertising efficiently, products must have extensive distribution and appeal to a major segment of the buying public.

Network time is bought on a supply-and-demand basis, with prices usually negotiated between the networks and a few large advertising agencies. The agency negotiator must be able to hold out for the lowest price without losing a time slot to a competitor. A major-agency network negotiator can make as much as $100,000.

The networks announce their fall schedules in late spring, and the largest network advertisers make a number of buys at that time to get the best programs. These early purchases are called *up-front buys.* As the fall season approaches, prices are more negotiable, but the premium spots have been bought. You don't buy "60 Minutes" or "The Dukes of Hazzard" in August.

Prime-time network advertising is bought in packages of commercials spread across a number of shows called *scatter plans* (the exceptions would be specials such as those solely sponsored by Hallmark Greeting Cards). Daytime network dramas (soaps) are often sponsored by a single advertiser, who may produce and own the rights to the show.

A final characteristic of network-TV advertising is its inflexibility of scheduling. Advertisers must generally commit large sums of money months in

---

*As contrasted with commercial time. Program-time fees are the rates a political candidate or religious group would be charged for airing an hour or half-hour program.

advance. This long-term planning negates last-minute adjustments to changing market conditions.

Spot television. Spot-TV advertising is time bought by national advertisers from individual stations. Spot advertising is a flexible medium. With it an advertiser can choose particular cities at particular times. Often an advertiser uses TV spot schedules along with a network schedule in markets where the local affiliate of the network may not be the strongest station. Spot schedules are also useful in markets where an advertiser wants to put on a full-scale drive for a limited period of time.

The disadvantage of spot advertising has been chiefly in the problem of handling it. To place a schedule, the advertiser has had to deal with many markets. In each market one must select a station. Then for each station it is necessary to: (1) determine whether the desired time is available, (2) negotiate for price, (3) place an order, (4) make sure the commercial was played as scheduled or, if preemptible, learn when it was played, (5) follow up on a make-good if it appeared at a wrong time, and (6) check the bills. In fact paperwork has been the bane of spot TV. Advertisers simplify the spot-buying process by working through sales representatives who have up-to-date computerized information on each of their client stations. Some large advertising agencies have installed direct hookups with major sales representatives. Spot-TV advertising is much more expensive than network on a CPM basis. A national spot buy will cost as much as 60 percent more than the same stations bought on a network basis.

Of all TV spots 85 percent run for 30 seconds and 4 percent for 60 seconds, with the remainder running varying lengths from 10 to 120 seconds. The 10-second spot, just long enough for a short message identifying the product, was born of the FCC requirement that every station identify itself every hour. It is usually referred to as an ID (short for "identification"), or station-break, announcement. The visual part of the commercial may last 10 seconds; the audio, 8 seconds. When an advertiser sponsors a special 2-hour performance, six 2-minute announcements are sometimes made.

Since spot-TV advertising is often used as a supplement to network advertising, spot advertising investment closely follow network, as shown in Table 6.2. Table 6.3 summarizes and predicts TV costs for the 1980s.

Table 6–2

TOP FIVE SPOT AND NETWORK TELEVISION ADVERTISERS		
RANK	SPOT ADVERTISERS	NETWORK ADVERTISERS
1	Food and food products	Food and food products
2	Automotive	Toiletries and toilet goods
3	Toiletries and toilet goods	Automotive
4	Confectionery and soft drinks	Proprietary medicines
5	Beer and wine	Confectionery and soft drinks

Table 6-3

| | TELEVISION-ADVERTISING REVENUE IN THE 1980s | | | | | | | | | | | |
| | TV AD VOLUME | | NETWORK | | | SPOT | | | LOCAL | | |
Year	$, millions	Chge., %	$, millions	Chge., %	TV, %	$, millions	Chge., %	TV, %	$, millions	Chge., %	TV, %
1981	12,630	11.5	5,720	12.0	45.3	3,620	11.0	28.7	3,290	11.0	26.0
1982	14,400	14.0ᵃ	6,520	14.0ᵃ	45.3	4,100	13.0ᵃ	28.5	3,780	15.0ᵃ	26.2
1983	16,410	14.0	7,430	14.0	45.3	4,630	13.0	28.2	4,350	15.0	26.5
1984	18,710	14.0	8,470	14.0	45.3	5,240	13.0	28.0	5,000	15.0	26.7
1985	21,330	14.0	9,660	14.0	45.3	5,920	13.0	27.7	5,750	15.0	27.0
1986	24,320	14.0	11,010	14.0	45.3	6,700	13.0	27.5	6,610	15.0	27.2
1987	27,720	14.0	12,550	14.0	45.3	7,570	13.0	27.3	7,600	15.0	27.4
1988	31,600	14.0	14,310	14.0	45.3	8,550	13.0	27.0	8,740	15.0	27.7
1989	36,020	14.0	16,310	14.0	45.3	9,660	13.0	26.8	10,050	15.0	27.9
1990	41,070	14.0	18,600	14.0	45.3	10,910	13.0	26.6	11,560	15.0	28.1

ᵃEstimated average annual growth rate through 1990; does not represent expected growth for any given year.

Television syndication

Among the most popular local advertising outlets are syndicated programs. Syndicated shows can be either network reruns or new shows. Some shows, such as "Lawrence Welk" (now all in reruns), are sold to almost 200 stations, while others, such as "Wonder Woman," may be sold to fewer than 20. These shows are sold on a station-by-station basis, and the stations in turn sell time on these programs to local and national spot advertisers. In some cases syndicated shows are given free to stations with some commercials included. This is called *barter syndication*. Among the most popular syndicated shows are "M*A*S*H," "Family Feud PM," the "Muppet Show," and the long-running "Hee Haw."

UHF stations

A glance at the sketch, Exhibit 6.3, of the wavelengths over which all electronic communication by air takes place will show you that TV and radio are only two of the many claimants for frequency allocations. They have competition from other users. When TV came along, the FCC, which is the responsible government authority, assigned to it what were then the best available channels, now known as channels 2 through 13. These twelve channels are in the very-high-frequency band of the spectrum and are referred to as VHF stations. Today they are the TV stations most people get on their sets.

But the demand for more TV frequencies grew faster than had been anticipated. The FCC did not want to repeat its mistake of not allowing room for expansion. They leapfrogged into the ultrahigh-frequency band, where they made room for 70 channels: channels 14 to 83, referred to as UHF. It takes a different type of receiving set to tune in on these channels; so since 1965, by law, all new TV sets have had to be capable of receiving UHF as well as VHF.

UHF stations are normally found in smaller markets or operate as independents (not affiliated with a major network) in the largest markets. Of the 757 commercial TV stations 238 (31.4 percent) are UHF.

Exhibit 6.3
Frequencies in this range of wavelengths are allocated for different purposes by the FCC. Note that the scale increases by factors of 10 (a linear scale would consume too much space). To get an idea of how much of the spectrum is assigned to AM and FM radio and to VHF and UHF TV, compare the frequency bands beside each heading.

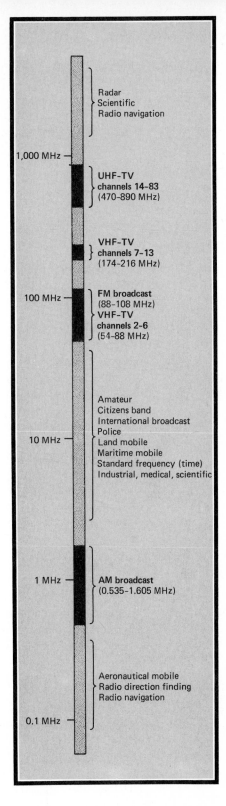

Radar
Scientific
Radio navigation

1,000 MHz

UHF-TV
channels 14–83
(470–890 MHz)

VHF-TV
channels 7–13
(174–216 MHz)

100 MHz

FM broadcast
(88–108 MHz)
VHF-TV
channels 2–6
(54–88 MHz)

Amateur
Citizens band
International broadcast
Police
Land mobile
Maritime mobile
Standard frequency (time)
Industrial, medical, scientific

10 MHz

AM broadcast
(0.535–1.605 MHz)

1 MHz

Aeronautical mobile
Radio direction finding
Radio navigation

0.1 MHz

ELEMENTS OF TELEVISION

PLANNING

Since TV schedules can run into a lot of money and since there are many alternative choices available for use in TV, it is important to start with a plan, embracing considerations such as those in the following sections:

Define the target

audience

All media planning should start with an identification of the target market.

Establish the

budget

The budget tells us whether we can think in terms of network, spot, or a combination of the two.

Set a goal: reach or

frequency

The TV advertising plan is a projection of the marketing plan. What is the goal of that plan? To introduce a new product? To get a greater share of the present market? To keep our product before the many who know it (retentive advertising)? Is there anything newsworthy about the product? Is there a special promotion program being planned to run at the same time? The answers to these questions are translated into terms of reach and frequency. (As we discussed in Chapter 5, reach refers to getting a message before as many people as possible and frequency refers to getting a message before people as often as possible.) Most TV schedules set optimum frequency levels and then determine reach. In a widely quoted study by Herbert Krugman of General Electric he suggested that three exposures were optimum. Each exposure over three reinforced the message but at a diminishing rate.*

Determine duration of

flights

The duration of a TV advertising effort is referred to as a *flight*. Most TV advertising is done in a series of flights of different durations during the year. As we mentioned in Chapter 5 in discussing pulsing, flights are designed to give maximum awareness and yet be less expensive than a continuous advertising schedule. (See Exhibit 6.4.)

Define the television

territory

Before the advent of TV a company traditionally established sales and advertising territories by state boundaries and arbitrary geographical areas within them. But a TV transmission wave goes in many directions for varying

---

*Herbert E. Krugman, "Why Three Exposures May Be Enough," *Journal of Advertising Research,* December, 1972, pp. 11–14.

Business Briefly

Elanco □ Treflan (agricultural product). Begins Jan. 4 for 19 weeks in 43 markets. Day, news, prime and sports times. Agency: Creswell, Munsell, Fultz & Zirbel, Cedar Rapids, Iowa. Target: men, 35 and over.

Underwood □ Accent (flavor enhancer). Begins Jan. 4 for first quarter in 47 markets. Day, fringe and weekends. Agency: Kenyon & Eckhardt Advertising, Boston. Target: women, 18-49.

White Lily □ Flour. Begins Jan. 11 for first quarter in 17 markets. Day, early fringe, news and prime access times. Agency: Tucker Wayne & Co., Atlanta. Target: women, 18-49.

Kal Kan □ Crave cat food. Begins Jan. 4 for 10 weeks in about 14 markets. All dayparts. Agency: D'Arcy-MacManus & Masius, St. Louis. Target: women, 25-54.

Amtrak □ Travel. Begins Jan. 11 for eight weeks in 26 markets. Fringe, prime, sports and specials. Agency: Needham, Harper & Steers, New York. Target: men, 18-49.

Delta Airlines □ Begins in January for approximately eight weeks in six markets. All dayparts. Agency: Burke Dowling Adams/BBDO, Atlanta. Target: adult, 35 and over.

Blessing Corp. □ Diaper service. Begins Jan. 11 for six weeks in 15 markets. Day, early fringe, late fringe and prime times. Agency: Howard Marks Advertising New York. Target: women, 18-34, women, 18-49.

Poulan Chain Saws □ Begins Dec. 28 for five weeks in four Southern markets. News, prime access and sports times. Agency: Smith & Associates, Charlotte, N.C. Target: men, 25-54.

Bank of America □ IRA savings accounts. Begins Dec. 28 for four weeks in all California markets. Agency: Grey Advertising, San Francisco. Target: women, 25-54.

Holland International Foods □ Savory sticks. Begins Jan. 18 for four weeks in five markets. All dayparts. Agency: Burton-Campbell, Atlanta. Target: adults, 25-49.

Robinson-Humphrey □ Brokerage firm. Begins Jan. 4 for three weeks in 17 markets. All dayparts. Agency: Bowes/Hanlon Advertising, Atlanta. Target: adults, 25-49.

Murphey's Oil Soap □ Begins Jan. 11 for two weeks in under 10 markets. Day and early fringe times. Agency: Media Buying Services, New York. Target: women, 18-49.

Glidden □ Paints. Begins Feb. 22 for one week in 88 markets. All dayparts. Agency: Meldrum & Fewsmith, Cleveland. Target: men, 25-54; women, 25-54.

Dillard Department Stores □ After-Christmas promotion. Begins Dec. 25 for one week in about 22 markets. Day, fringe and news times. Agency: Faulkner & Associates, Little Rock, Ark. Target: adults, 25-54.

Eckerd Drug Stores □ English Leather/Houbigant fragrances. Begins this week for one week in 41 markets. Day, news and prime access times. Agency: William B. Doner and Co., Southfield, Mich. Target: women, 25-54.

Ralston-Purina □ Various children's cereals. Begins Jan. 4 for various flights in about 140 markets. Children's programing. Agency: CPM Inc., Chicago. Target: children, 6-11.

TG&Y stores. □ Begins Jan. 4 for varying flights in 52 markets. Day, early fringe and late fringe times. Agency: Saffer, Cravit & Freedman Advertising,

Exhibit 6.4
Reports of spot schedules. Note differences in length of flights, selection of markets, audiences, and times. (Reprinted with permission from the December 21, 1981 issue of *Broadcasting.*)

distances; it is no respecter of man-made maps. How to coordinate sales territories with TV planning for advertising was the problem on which two major research firms worked.

The A.C. Nielsen Company developed a marketing map based upon important (designated) marketing areas. It selected stations that reached those areas best and referred to these selections as designated marketing areas, or DMA.

The Arbitron Company based its solution on its concept of areas of dominant influence (ADI). The ADI, as the company defines it, "is a geographic market design which defines each market, exclusive of another, based on Measurable Viewing Patterns. The ADI is an area that consists of all counties in which the home market stations receive a preponderance of viewing. Each county in the U.S. (excluding Alaska) is allocated exclusively to only one ADI. There is no overlap." (The ADI system has also been adopted by newspapers and other media to describe which part of the TV ADI their circulation covers; see Exhibit 6.5.) It is used also for radio, outdoor, and magazine scheduling. The ADI rankings underwent substantial change in the spring of 1981 based on 1980 census data.

Exhibit 6.5
Use of ADI. (Courtesy Chicago *Sun-Times.*)

Determine the profile of our audience

Having determined which geographical area we want to work in, we take the next step by making a broad determination of what sex or age group we wish to reach. As you can see from Table 6.4, audience profiles do not remain constant and must be constantly updated.

Table 6–4

PROFILE OF TELEVISION AUDIENCE (ALL ADULTS = 100)				
	REACHED DAILY			
	1975		1980	
	%	Index	%	Index
All adults	85	100	87	100
Age:				
18–34	83	97	85	98
35–49	85	100	84	97
50+	86	101	90	103
18–49	84	99	85	98
25–49	84	99	84	97
25–54	—	—	85	98
Household income:				
Under $10,000	85	100	90	103
$10,000–14,999	85	100	89	102
$15,000+	83	97	84	97
$15,000–24,999	85	100	86	99
$25,000+	77	91	82	94
$30,000+	—	—	81	93
Education:				
Grade school	85	100	90	103
High school	86	101	89	102
Any college	82	96	83	95
College graduate	81	95	82	94
Occupation:				
Working adults	81	95	84	97
Prof./teacher	82	96	81	93
Mgr./offcl./prop.	79	93	86	99
Clerical/sales	84	99	82	94
Nonwhite collar	81	95	85	98
Housewife	85	100	91	105

THE RATING-POINT

SYSTEM

TV time is bought on the basis of gross rating points (GRP). A *rating point* is 1 percent of the total number of households in a specified area (either nationally or in a selected ADI) that have TV sets. A rating of 12 for a program means that 12 percent of all TV households in a particular area have their sets tuned to that station. Prime-time network programs generally achieve a rating of between 14 and 30, with the average around 20.

As discussed earlier, TV advertising is rarely bought on a program-by-program basis. TV advertisers buy a number of commercials and measure the weight of their schedules in terms of the total ratings for all the commercial spots bought (the GRP's). Let's look at Table 6.5 (next page) for a weekly buy for an advertiser in a single market.

Advertisers also use GRP's as the basis for examining the relationship between reach and frequency. These relationships can be expressed mathematically:

Table 6–5

NO. OF SPOTS/ONE PER SHOW	HOUSEHOLD RATING/SPOT
1 ("Today Show")	10
2 ("News at Noon")	14
3 ("Evening News")	11
4 ("Merv Griffin")	12
5 ("Gilligan's Island")	13
6 (prime-time variety show)	20
GRP's	80

$$R \times F = \text{GRP}$$

$$\frac{\text{GRP}}{R} = F \quad \text{and} \quad \frac{\text{GRP}}{F} = R$$

where R = reach and F = frequency.

To use these relationships, you must know (or be able to estimate) the unduplicated audience. That is, out of the 80 GRP's how many of these households are different? If we assume that 40 of the 80 GRP's were unduplicated, then the frequency would be 2.0:

$$F = \frac{80}{40} = 2.0$$

Now we know that of the six possible exposures each household in the audience was exposed an average of two times.

One of the principal merits of the GRP system is that it provides a common base that proportionately accommodates markets of all sizes. One GRP in New York has exactly the same relative weight as one GRP in Salt Lake City. GRP's can't be compared from one market to another unless markets are of identical size. However, the cost of TV commercial time varies by city size. Exhibit 6.6 gives an idea of the range of costs per TV rating points in major markets.

The advertiser has to decide how much weight (how many GRP's) he or she wishes to place in his or her markets and for how long a period. This is a matter of experience and of watching what the competition is doing. Say he or she selects 100 to 150 per week as the GRP figure (considered a good working base). Within this figure the advertiser has great discretion in each market. How to allocate the time: Put it all on one station? Divide it among all the stations? With what yardstick? The answers depend on whether the goal is reach or frequency. (In the next chapter we shall see how the computer is used to present the various alternatives possible with a given number of GRP's.)

Nielsen market rank		Prime time '80 vs. '79
1.	New York	$316 (+ 7.8%)
2.	Los Angeles	241 (+ 7.6%)
3.	Chicago	172 (+ 11.0%)
4.	Philadelphia	141 (+ 7.6%)
5.	San Francisco	152 (+ 9.4%)
6.	Boston	145 (+ 5.4%)
7.	Detroit	105 (+ 8.2%)
8.	Cleveland	66 (+ 6.5%)
9.	Washington	90 (+ 5.9%)
10.	Dallas	97 (+ 5.4%)
11.	Pittsburgh	72 (+ 7.5%)
12.	Houston	96 (+ 9.1%)
13.	Minneapolis	96 (+ 35.2%)
14.	St. Louis	63 (+ 10.5%)
15.	Miami	89 (+ 6%)
16.	Atlanta	92 (+ 19.5%)
17.	Seattle	73 (+ 10.6%)
18.	Tampa	70 (+ 7.7%)
19.	Baltimore	70 (+ 7.7%)
20.	Indianapolis	53 (+ 12.8%)

Market combinations
at a glance

Ranked by market size	Prime time cpp	cpm
1–10	$1,525	$6.10
11–20	774	8.12
21–30	471	6.96
31–40	295	5.47
41–50	242	5.28

Source: Spot Quotations & Data. 950 Third Ave., New York 10022. Average cpps for a 30-second spot were determined from ad agency conventional buys on affiliates as of Aug. 29. Excluded are spots bought on a 52-week basis or calling for 150-plus gross rating points weekly. These averages are a yardstick and not a listing of the market's lowest price. Ratings used are an Arbitron/Nielsen average. Those guides can be applied to 60s—200%—and 10s—50%. Percentage gains over September, 1979, are shown in parentheses.

Important though the GRP is, however, it has its limitations. Consideration must be given to the number of prospects for the product that are being reached by a program, regardless of rating. But the GRP concept provides a unified dimension for making scheduling judgments.

Additionally, GRP's alone cannot tell how effectively a broadcast schedule is performing. If an advertiser's target audience is women aged 18 to 49, for example, it is often the case that 5 GRP's will deliver more women 18 to 49 for the advertiser than will 10 GRP's. This, as you would suspect, is a function of where the GRP's are scheduled. Five GRP's scheduled during a Sunday-night movie will almost always deliver many times more women 18 to 49 than 10 GRP's scheduled on a Saturday morning will.

One method that appears well received among advertisers whose products have wide appeal (such as packaged goods) is arbitrarily to determine the number of GRP's required to make an impact on a market. If the budget cannot accommodate the cost of providing this number of GRP's, the schedule may be reduced to the desirable level of frequency. Or the budget may be reexamined to determine additional dollars needed to increase frequency to desired level.

SHARE OF
AUDIENCE

While the rating is the basic audience-measurement statistic for TV, another measure, the *share of audience* (or simply *share*), is often used to determine the success of a show. The share is used by advertisers to determine how a show is doing against its direct competition. The share is defined as the percentage of households using TV that are watching a particular show.

Let's assume that the "Today Show" has 5,000 households watching it in a market with 50,000 households. In this case we know that the rating for the "Today Show" would be 10:

$$\text{Rating} = \frac{\text{``Today'' viewers}}{\text{total TV households}} \times 100 = \frac{5,000}{50,000} \times 100 = 10$$

The share calculates the percentage of *households using TV* (HUT) who are tuned to the program. Let's assume that of the 50,000 TV households 25,000 are watching TV. In this case the share for the "Today Show" would be 20:

$$\text{Share} = \frac{\text{``Today'' viewers}}{\text{HUT}} \times 100 = \frac{5,000}{25,000} \times 100 = 20$$

It is understood that both the ratings and share of audience are expressed as percentages (hence the factor of 100 in the equations). Therefore, we do not use decimal points or refer to either as, say, "10 percent." Instead we say, as in this example, that the rating is 10 and the share is 20.

THE SYNDICATED RESEARCH
SERVICES

In the big business of TV ratings two companies dominate: A.C. Nielsen Company and The Arbitron Company issue a number of reports dealing with local and network ratings. The most well known of these services is the Nielsen Television Index (NTI), Exhibit 6.7, which provides continuing estimates of TV viewing and national sponsored network-program audiences, including national ratings 52 weeks per year.

Local market ratings are primarily available through the Nielsen Station Index (NSI) and Arbitron Television (Exhibit 6.8) reports. These services pro-

Nielsen NATIONAL TV AUDIENCE ESTIMATES EVE.THU. OCT.29, 1981

TIME	7:00	7:15	7:30	7:45	8:00	8:15	8:30	8:45	9:00	9:15	9:30	9:45	10:00	10:15	10:30	10:45

WEEK 1

ABC TV

TOTAL AUDIENCE (Households (000) & %)

	8:00	8:30	9:00	9:30	10:00
Households (000)	18,420	15,890	13,770	15,240	14,750
%	22.6	19.5	16.9	18.7	18.1
Program	MORK & MINDY	BEST OF THE WEST	BARNEY MILLER	TAXI (OP)	20/20

AVERAGE AUDIENCE

	8:00	8:15	8:30	8:45	9:00	9:15	9:30	9:45	10:00	10:15	10:30	10:45
Households (000) & %	15,650 / 19.2		13,940 / 17.1		12,310 / 15.1		13,120 / 16.1		10,350 / 12.7	13.2*		12.2*
SHARE OF AUDIENCE %	31		28		24		26		23	23*		23*
AVG. AUD. BY ¼ HR %	18.0	20.5	17.5	16.8	15.1	15.1	16.0	16.2	13.4	13.0	12.0	12.3

CBS TV

TOTAL AUDIENCE (Households (000) & %)

	8:00	9:00	10:00
Households (000)	20,950	27,220	
%	25.7	33.4	
Program	── MAGNUM, P.I. (OP) ──		BLAZING SADDLES

AVERAGE AUDIENCE

	8:00	8:15	8:30	8:45	9:00	9:15	9:30	9:45	10:00	10:15	10:30	10:45
Households (000) & %	16,460 / 20.2	18.7*		21.8*	17,360 / 21.3	23.1*		21.7*		20.5*		19.9*
SHARE OF AUDIENCE %	33	30*		35*	36	37*		35*		35*		37*
AVG. AUD. BY ¼ HR %	18.5	18.9	21.7	21.9	23.2	23.0	22.2	21.3	20.5	20.6	20.4	19.3

NBC TV

TOTAL AUDIENCE (Households (000) & %)

	8:00	8:30	9:00	9:30	10:00
Households (000)	12,550	12,800	13,940	13,690	19,320
%	15.4	15.7	17.1	16.8	23.7
Program	HARPER VALLEY	LEWIS AND CLARK (OP)	DIFF'RENT STROKES	GIMME A BREAK (SUS-OP)	── HILL STREET BLUES ──

AVERAGE AUDIENCE

	8:00	8:15	8:30	8:45	9:00	9:15	9:30	9:45	10:00	10:15	10:30	10:45
Households (000) & %	11,250 / 13.8		11,080 / 13.6		12,710 / 15.6		11,980 / 14.7		14,910 / 18.3	18.7*		18.0*
SHARE OF AUDIENCE %	22		22		25		24		33	32*		34*
AVG. AUD. BY ¼ HR %	14.0	13.6	14.0	13.3	15.1	16.2	14.2	15.1	18.4	19.0	18.6	17.3

WEEK 2

ABC TV

TOTAL AUDIENCE (Households (000) & %)

	8:00	8:30	9:00	9:30	10:00
Households (000)	18,170	16,870	16,220	15,970	18,990
%	22.3	20.7	19.9	19.6	23.3
Program	MORK & MINDY	BEST OF THE WEST	BARNEY MILLER	TAXI (OP)	20/20

AVERAGE AUDIENCE

	8:00	8:15	8:30	8:45	9:00	9:15	9:30	9:45	10:00	10:15	10:30	10:45
Households (000) & %	15,810 / 19.4		14,830 / 18.2		14,340 / 17.6		14,750 / 18.1		13,280 / 16.3	18.0*		14.7*
SHARE OF AUDIENCE %	31		29		27		28		29	31*		27*
AVG. AUD. BY ¼ HR %	18.9	19.8	17.8	18.5	17.3	17.9	17.4	18.8	19.2	16.7	14.9	14.5

CBS TV

TOTAL AUDIENCE (Households (000) & %)

	8:00	10:00
Households (000)	25,840	14,510
%	31.7	17.8
Program	── MAGNUM, P.I. (OP) ──	── JESSICA NOVAK ──

AVERAGE AUDIENCE

	8:00	8:15	8:30	8:45	9:00	9:15	9:30	9:45	10:00	10:15	10:30	10:45
Households (000) & %	18,010 / 22.1	19.9*		22.4*		23.1*		23.0*	10,920 / 13.4	13.7*		13.2*
SHARE OF AUDIENCE %	34	32*		35*		35*		35*	24	23*		25*
AVG. AUD. BY ¼ HR %	19.7	20.0	21.9	22.8	23.1	23.1	23.5	22.4	14.0	13.4	13.5	12.8

NBC TV

TOTAL AUDIENCE (Households (000) & %)

	8:00	8:30	9:00	9:30	10:00
Households (000)	11,080	9,780	13,450	12,550	19,150
%	13.6	12.0	16.5	15.4	23.5
Program	HARPER VALLEY	LEWIS AND CLARK (OP)	DIFF'RENT STROKES	GIMME A BREAK (SUS-OP)	── HILL STREET BLUES ──

AVERAGE AUDIENCE

	8:00	8:15	8:30	8:45	9:00	9:15	9:30	9:45	10:00	10:15	10:30	10:45
Households (000) & %	10,190 / 12.5		8,560 / 10.5		11,900 / 14.6		11,330 / 13.9		14,910 / 18.3	18.2*		18.4*
SHARE OF AUDIENCE %	20		17		22		21		33	31*		34*
AVG. AUD. BY ¼ HR %	12.4	12.5	10.6	10.3	13.8	15.3	13.6	14.1	17.6	18.9	18.7	18.0

TV HOUSEHOLDS USING TV (See Def. 1)

	7:00	7:15	7:30	7:45	8:00	8:15	8:30	8:45	9:00	9:15	9:30	9:45	10:00	10:15	10:30	10:45
WK. 1	58.4	59.7	59.3	59.8	61.1	62.6	62.4	61.6	61.8	62.5	61.5	61.3	59.1	57.1	55.0	52.2
WK. 2	58.9	61.1	60.9	61.7	62.1	62.7	62.9	64.3	65.4	66.6	65.8	64.7	59.7	57.9	55.1	52.3

U.S. TV Households: 81,500,000

For explanation of symbols, See page A.

EVE.THU. NOV.5, 1981

Exhibit 6.7
National Nielsen Television Index Example. (Courtesy A. C. Nielsen Company.)

vide audience estimates in over 200 TV markets and are the basis of spot and local advertising-buying decisions. With the exception of the very largest markets local ratings are conducted three times a year in 4-week periods known as *sweeps*. The sweep periods are November, February, and May.

Weekly Program Estimates   Time Period Average Estimates

PORTLAND, OR — FEBRUARY 1981 TIME PERIOD AVERAGES — TPA-39 — SAT/SUN

DAY AND TIME / STATION / PROGRAM	WK1 2/4	WK2 2/11	WK3 2/18	WK4 2/25	ADI RTG	ADI SHR	NOV '80	JUL '80	MAY '80	FEB '80	METRO RTG	METRO SHR	TV HH	P 18+	P 12-24	P 12-34	W TOT 18+	W 18-49	W 12-24	W 18-34	W 25-49	W 25-54	WKG WMN 18+	M TOT 18+	M 18-49	M 18-34	M 25-49	M 25-54
RELATIVE STD-ERR THRESHOLDS (1σ) 25%	8	8	8	8	2						3		14	22	29	25	17	17	28	20	14	14	17	16	17	21	14	15
▲ 50%	2	2	2	2							1		3	5	7	6	4	4	7	5	3	3	4	4	4	5	3	5
SATURDAY																												
11:45P-MDNGHT (CNTD)																												
KPTV WRESTLING	7	6	10	4	7	32	**	**	**	**	8	31	57	75	18	29	29	10	3	5	9	11	7	47	26	15	18	19
HUT/TOTAL	20	23	24	19	22		**	**	**	**	25		167	208	61	116	86	45	18	27	41	49	27	123	81	59	57	65
MDNGHT-12:15A																												
KATU MLN $ MV FEA	4	3	5	5	4	22	**	**	**	**	5	25	30	35	9	17	17	7	3	5	6	8	4	19	12	9	8	10
KOIN TV6 LT MV SA	2	4	3	2	3	14	**	**	**	**	3	12	21	23	5	10	12	8	4	3	8	10	6	11	5	3	4	5
KGW SAT NGT LIVE	5	8	4	6	6	31	**	**	**	**	7	35	40	51	27	47	18	13	7	9	9	12	9	33	30	27	17	19
KPTV WRESTLING	7	6	10	3	6	35	**	**	**	**	7	33	54	70	15	26	26	9	3	4	7	9	6	45	25	15	19	19
HUT/TOTAL	19	19	20	16	18		**	**	**	**	21		145	179	56	100	73	37	17	21	30	39	25	108	72	54	48	53
12:15A-12:30A																												
KATU MLN $ MV FEA	4	4	5	5	4	23	**	**	**	**	5	25	30	37	8	17	18	8	2	4	7	10	5	19	11	8	8	11
KOIN TV6 LT MV SA	2	3	3	3	3	14	**	**	**	**	3	13	21	24	7	12	14	10	6	5	8	10	7	11	5	3	4	5
KGW SAT NGT LIVE	5	8	4	4	5	29	**	**	**	**	7	34	37	46	25	40	16	11	7	9	8	10	9	30	27	23	13	16
KPTV WRESTLING	7	6	10	3	6	36	**	**	**	**	7	33	53	69	15	24	26	9	3	4	7	9	7	43	24	14	17	18
HUT/TOTAL	19	19	20	14	18		**	**	**	**	21		141	176	55	93	74	38	18	22	30	39	28	103	67	48	42	50
12:30A-12:45A																												
KATU MLN $ MV FEA	3	5	5	5	5	33	**	**	**	**	6	37	33	40	6	15	18	6	2	3	6	10	4	22	12	8	9	13
KOIN TV6 LT MV SA	3	3	3	3	3	22	**	**	**	**	3	18	24	29	9	14	15	9	6	5	8	9	7	14	6	4	4	5
KGW SAT NGT LIVE	4	5	3	4	4	27	**	**	**	**	5	32	27	36	19	30	12	9	3	7	8	8	6	24	21	17	8	11
KPTV SOLID GOLD R	4	1	3	2	2	18	**	**	**	**	3	16	18	24	10	13	10	8	3	4	5	5	5	14	12	6	9	9
HUT/TOTAL	15	14	14	13	14		**	**	**	**	17		102	129	44	72	55	32	14	19	27	32	22	74	51	35	30	38
12:45A-1:00A																												
KATU MLN $ MV FEA	3	5	5	5	5	38	**	**	**	**	6	41	33	38	6	14	17	5	2	2	5	9	4	21	11	8	8	12
KOIN TV6 LT MV SA	3	3	3	2	3	22	**	**	**	**	3	17	21	25	6	12	13	8	4	3	8	9	6	12	5	3	4	5
KGW SAT NGT LIVE	4	5	3	4	4	30	**	**	**	**	5	35	26	34	19	29	11	9	3	7	8	8	6	23	20	17	8	10
KPTV SOLID GOLD R	3	1	1	1	1	12	**	**	**	**	1	10	11	13	8	12	4	3	2	2	2	3	3	9	9	6	6	6
HUT/TOTAL	13	13	12	11	12		**	**	**	**	15		91	110	39	67	45	25	11	14	23	28	19	65	45	34	26	33
1:00A-1:15A																												
KATU MLN $ MV FEA	3	5	5	5	5	46	**	**	**	**	5	50	33	35	5	13	18	9	2	3	9	12	8	16	8	5	6	10
KOIN AMER TOP 10	2	3	3	1	2	25	**	**	**	**	2	21	19	21	5	11	10	5	2	2	5	6	3	11	6	3	6	5
KGW SECOND CITY	2	1	2	2	2	18	**	**	**	**	3	25	12	15	9	11	2	2		2	2	2	1	13	12	10	3	3
KPTV SOLID GOLD R	3	-	1	1	1	13	**	**	**	**	1	10	9	10	6	9	2	1		1	1	1	1	8	8	5	5	5
HUT/TOTAL	11	10	9	8	9		**	**	**	**	11		70	81	25	45	32	17	4	8	17	21	14	48	34	23	20	25
1:15A-1:30A																												
KATU MLN $ MV FEA	3	6	5	5	4	48	**	**	**	**	5	52	30	35	5	13	17	8	2	3	8	11	7	17	9	5	7	11
KOIN AMER TOP 10	2	3	3	1	2	25	**	**	**	**	2	22	19	20	5	10	10	5	2	2	5	6	3	11	6	3	6	7
KGW SECOND CITY	1	1	2	1	1	15	**	**	**	**	2	21	10	13	8	10	1	1		1	1	1	1	12	11	9	3	3
KPTV SOLID GOLD R	2	-	1	1	1	10	**	**	**	**	1	7	7	7	3	5	1			1				5	5	3	3	3
HUT/TOTAL	9	10	9	8	9		**	**	**	**	10		66	75	21	38	29	14	4	6	14	18	11	45	31	20	19	24
1:30A-1:45A																												
KATU MLN $ MV FEA	3	4	3		4	46					5	48	25	32	1	11	16	9		4	9	11	8	16	10	7	8	11
M $ MV FEA 2				3	3	48					5	64	22	19		1	12	1				4		6				9
--4 WK AVG--					3	48	**	**	**	**	5	51	24	29	1	8	15	7		3	7	9	7	14	7	5	6	9
KOIN AMER TOP 10	1				1	12					1	10	10	10	1	7	2	2				2		8	8	8	8	8
NIGHTWTCH TH		4	2	1	2	33					3	33	19	20	2	8	8	5	1	1	5		4	11	8	4	8	8
--4 WK AVG--					2	27	**	**	**	**	2	28	16	17	2	8	7	4	1	1	4		3	10	8	4	8	8
KGW CH8 PRESENTS	3	-	1	1	1	18					2	18	9	13	5	6	3	2	2	2				9	6	4	2	3
HUT/TOTAL	8	9	7	5	7		**	**	**	**	9		49	59	8	22	25	13	3	6	11	13	10	33	21	13	16	20
1:45A-2:00A																												
KATU M $ MV FEA 2	3	4	2	3	3	51					4	57	20	21	1	6	11	5		2	5	8		16	6	4		6
MLN $ MV FEA		4			4	56					6	64	21	36		8	12	8				8		25	13			21
--4 WK AVG--					3	52	**	**	**	**	4	56	23	25	1	6	11	6		2	6	8	6	13	8	4	7	9
KOIN NIGHTWTCH TH		4	2	1	2	25	**	**	**	**	2	26	13	14	2	5	5	3			3	3	3	8	6	3	6	6
KGW CH8 PRESENTS	2	-	1	1	1	15	**	**	**	**	1	15	7	9	3	4	2			2				7	3	3	1	2
HUT/TOTAL	6	8	5	5	6		**	**	**	**	8		43	48	6	15	18	9		2	9	11	8	28	17	10	14	17
SUNDAY																												
6:00A-6:30A																												
KATU CHRISTOPHERS	-		-	1									1	1		1								1	1	1	1	1
KOIN UNTAMED WRLD	-		-	1									1	2			1	1			1	1		1			1	
SUN MORNING																												
--4 WK AVG--							**	**	**				1	1		1	1	1			1	1		1	1	1	1	1
HUT/TOTAL	-		-	1							1		2	2		1	1	1			1	1		1	1	1	1	1
6:30A-7:00A																												
KATU HLLELUJH SUN	1		-	-									1	1			1							1				
KOIN INTNL ZONE	-		-	1									2	1			1	1			1	1		1			1	
SUN MORNING																												
--4 WK AVG--								**					1	1			1	1			1	1		1			1	
KGW DOXOLOGY	-		-	-									1	1														
SOUND TRUMPT																												
--4 WK AVG--	-		-	-									1	1														
KPTV N.O.A.	-		-	-									1															
NEWS HILITES													1															
--4 WK AVG--	-		-	-									1															
HUT/TOTAL	1		-	1	1		1		1		1		3	2			1	1			1	1		1	1	1	1	1
7:00A-7:30A																												
KATU DIRECTIONS	-		1	1			20	32	51	48			3	2			1											
KOIN HR OF POWER	2		-	1	1	35					1	41	7	7			4							2	1		1	1
SUN MORNING		1			1	68					2	71	12	19			11	5				5		8				3
--4 WK AVG--					1	43	29	38	28		1	52	8	10			6	1		1	1	1		4				1
KGW SIGN OF LIFE	-		-	1									2	2	1	1	2	2	1	1	2	2						
DAVY-GOLIATH													3	2	3	4	2	2	2	1	1	2						
--4 WK AVG--													3	2	2	3	2	2	1	1	2	2						
KPTV GOSPEL HOUR	1	1	1	-			34		15	36	2		4	4			3							1				
HUT/TOTAL	3	2	2	2	2		3	4	5	5	2		18	18	2	3	12	3	1	1	3	3		5				1
7:30A-8:00A																												
KATU KIDS ARE PEO	3	2	1	3	3	58	52	44	66	55	3	59	25	10	14	9	6	1	3	5	3		2	16	12	10	5	5
KOIN HR OF POWER	2	2		1	1	24	19	28	20		1	26	11	13			6	3		2	3	3			5	2	1	2	3

Exhibit 6.8

* SAMPLE BELOW MINIMUM FOR WEEKLY REPORTING
** SHARE/HUT TRENDS NOT AVAILABLE
- DID NOT ACHIEVE A REPORTABLE WEEKLY RATING
‡ TECHNICAL DIFFICULTY
+ COMBINED PARENT/SATELLITE
▲ SEE TABLE ON PAGE iv

TV program audience estimates for San Antonio. (Courtesy The Arbitron Company.)

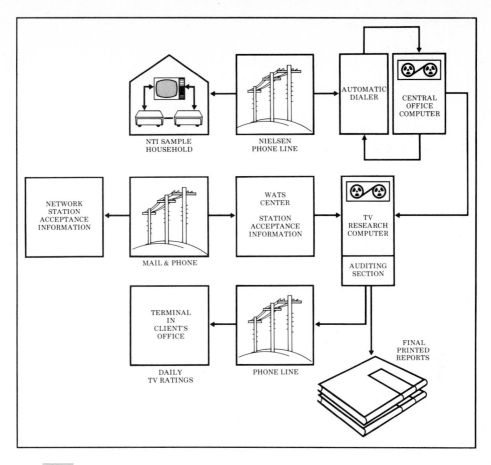

Exhibit 6.9
The Nielsen measurement system. (Courtesy A. C. Nielsen Company.)

Research techniques

Metered audience measurements. Since 1950, when Nielsen introduced the Nielsen Storage Instantaneous Audimeter (referred to as either SIA or simply Audimeter), metered audience measurement has been the principal method of obtaining national ratings. The meters provide a direct tie-in, through telephone lines, between each TV set in a household and a central computer (Exhibit 6.9). In the case of Nielsen these meters give minute-by-minute information concerning set usage. Information is provided to clients through printed reports or, for an extra charge, by computer terminal. A major drawback to meters is that they cannot tell who, if anyone, is actually watching the TV set. In 1959 Nielsen began local metered service in the New York market. By 1978 both Nielsen and Arbitron (through its Arbitron Television Meter) were using meters in New York, Los Angeles, and Chicago.

During the last several years San Francisco, Philadelphia, and Detroit have been added to the list of metered markets, with as many as ten other markets scheduled for metered ratings by 1985. Some TV experts expect the meter to replace the diary (see below) as the major source of local TV ratings by the early 1990s.

The major detriment to further expansion of meters is cost. It is estimated that metered ratings will run four to five times more than similar ratings obtained by diaries. In a large market a station may pay $300,000 or more for metered ratings from either Nielsen or Arbitron. To justify these added costs, several major advantages are cited for meters over diaries as a ratings-measurement technique:

1. Meters are generally regarded as more accurate.
2. Meters overcome the problem of illiteracy and can monitor viewing habits of small children.
3. Meters are more practical for monitoring cable markets with thirty to fifty channels.
4. Meters are faster, allowing for daily feedback regarding advertising and programming decisions.

Telephone coincidental method. The telephone coincidental method uses calls made during a particular program or daypart. The coincidental method is often used when an advertiser needs information quickly or wants additional information concerning specific market or demographic data.

Diary method. Having been selected according to a carefully planned sampling pattern, families agree for a fee to keep a notebook (Exhibit 6.10) next to their TV sets. Members of the family record the stations and programs they watch and answer questions about themselves as current purchasers. The diaries are returned regularly to the research firm, and results are tabulated and reported to subscribers. The advantage is its low cost and ability to provide personal (rather than household) information.

SPECIFICS OF BUYING TELEVISION TIME

The television day

TV has many audiences, differing in character and size according to the time of day. The cost for that time will vary with the size of the audience. The first question to ask is what time of day you can reach the people in whom you are most interested.

Preemption rate

A considerable proportion of spot-TV advertising time is sold on a preemptible (lower-rate) basis, whereby the advertiser gives the station the right to sell his time slot to another advertiser who may pay a better rate for it or who has a package deal for which that particular spot is needed. Although some stations offer only two choices, nonpreemptible and preemptible, others allow advertisers to choose between two kinds of preemptible rate. If the station has the right to sell your spot to another advertiser any time up until the time of the telecast, your rate is called the immediately preemptible (IP) rate (the low-

HERE'S HOW TO BEGIN YOUR ARBITRON DIARY . . .

- Fill in the first name of the Male Head of Household and Female Head of Household in the appropriate boxes at the top of the fold-out portion of the Wednesday page. (If there is no Male or Female Head of Household, write NONE and do not enter any viewing in this column.)

- Then fill in the first name of each person living in your household who is 24 months of age or older . . . whether or not they plan to watch television during the survey week. If you have more than one set, you probably received an Arbitron diary for each set. Please fill in the names in the same order for each diary.

- Now, fill in the age and sex of each person listed.
  [EXAMPLE]

MALE HEAD OF HOUSE — FIRST NAME ONLY: *Tom*
FEMALE HEAD OF HOUSE — FIRST NAME ONLY: *Jane*

OTHER FAMILY MEMBERS

TIME	TV SET		STATION TUNED IN		NAME OF PROGRAM	AGE →	35	31	6	8					VISITORS	VISITORS
QUARTER HOURS	OFF	ON	CALL LETTERS	CHAN. NO.		SEX →	M	F	F	M						

6:00 A.M. | 6:00- 6:14

HERE'S HOW TO MAKE VIEWING ENTRIES . . .

The example in the lower part of this page shows you how to make the entries.

When the set is OFF . . .
❶ Draw a line in the "Set Off" column for ALL quarter-hours the set is OFF.

When the set is ON . . .
❷ Draw a line in the "Set On" column and ask yourself these questions:

What Station?
❸ Opposite the correct time period, write in the station call letters, channel number and the name of the program, whenever this set is on for 5 minutes or more in a quarter-hour.

Who is watching?
❹ **Household Members**
Put an X in the proper columns to indicate the persons who are watching or listening to this set for 5 minutes or more in a quarter-hour.
❺ **Visitors**
If a visitor watches or listens to this set, fill in the visitor's age and sex in a VISITORS column (see example).
❻ **No one watching or listening but the set is on.**
If the set is on but no one is watching or listening, opposite the correct time period, write in the station call letters, channel number and "0" under all family member columns (see example).

How long?
❼ When the information from one quarter-hour to another remains the same, draw lines or use ditto marks (") . . . as shown in the example.

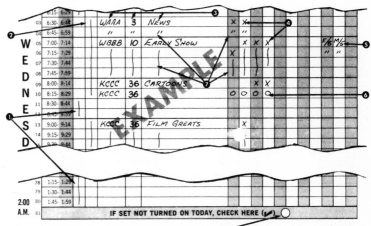

If your set was not turned on during an entire day, check the circle at the bottom of the evening page.

YOUR ARBITRON DIARY STARTS ON THE NEXT PAGE . . .

est rate). If the station can preempt only if it gives the original advertiser 2 weeks' notice, the rate is designated "preemptible with 2 weeks' notice" and is sold at a higher rate. The highest rate is charged for a nonpreemptible time slot; the two weeks' preemptible rate is the next highest; and the immediately preemptible rate is the lowest. Preemption rates are listed on the rate card (see summary in Exhibit 6.11), along with the basic rate for 30 seconds. Table 6.6 is a quotation from a rate card. The three columns show the preemption rates, column I listing the nonpreemptible rate, column II the rate for preemption on

---

NEW YORK

New York (N. Y.)-Northeastern New Jersey—W N J U-TV—Continued

Cancellation: 70j, 71, 72, 73b.
Prod. Services: 80, 83, 84, 86.
(*) 5 months for continuous advertisers.
Product Protection: 10 minutes.

6. TIME RATES
No. 22 Eff 6/1/81—Rec'd 6/22/81.

8. PARTICIPATING ANNOUNCEMENT PROGRAMS
Rec'd 6/22/81.
30 SECONDS

MON THRU FRI:	F	P
Daytime Programming—11 am-3 pm	125	100
PM:		
Variety/Comedy—3-5	175	150
Novela—5-6	225	200
Novela—6-7	400	375
Novela—7-8	550	500
Luis Vigoreaux Presenta—8-9 Mon.	450	400
Show de Nydia Caro—8-9 Tues.	450	400
Show de Chucho Avellanet—8-9 Wed.	450	400
Noche de Gala—8-9 Thurs.	450	400
En Casa de Wiwi—8-8:30 Fri.	450	400
El Show de Rosita Peru—8:30-9 Fri.	450	400
Novela—9-10	550	500
Novela—10-10:30	400	350
El Informador (News)—10:30-11	350	300
Sports/Comedy/Musical Variety—11-midnight	200	175
Sports—2-4:30 pm Sat	325	300
El Show de Menudo—4:30-5 pm Sat.	275	250
Sonido de Miami—6-6:30 pm Sat.	275	250
Sabado Salsa—6:30-7 pm Sat.	275	250
Santo Domingo Invita—7-8 pm Sat.	275	250
Los Garcia—6-7 pm Sun.	325	300
Su Show Favorito—7-8 pm Sun.	325	300
KaKu Komicos—8-9 pm Sun.	325	300

9. PACKAGE ANNOUNCEMENT RATES
EARLY-LATE FRINGE COMBO: Mon thru Fri, 11 am-6 pm, 8 per wk; 11 pm-midnight, 2 per wk; 6-11 pm, 5 per wk 2200
NOVELA PACKAGE: Mon thru Fri, 6-7 pm, 1 per wk; 7-8 pm, 2 per wk; 9-10 pm, 1 per wk; 10-10:30 pm, 2 per wk.
6 spots per wk 1850
MEN'S PACKAGE: 10:30-11 pm Mon thru Fri, El Informador (News), 5 per wk; 11-midnight Mon thru Fri, Wrestling, 2 per wk; 2-4:30 pm Sat, Sports, 3 per wk 1500
Advertisers purchasing preemptible rate may be preempted by fixed rates after 2 weeks notice.
60 sec: double the 30 sec.
10 sec: 1/2 30 sec.

10. PROGRAM RATES

	1 hr	1/2 hr	1/4 hr	10 min	5 min
6-11 pm Mon thru Sun	2500	1600	980	720	600
4-6 pm & 11 pm-sign-off Mon thru Sun	1700	1100	700	575	490

11. SPECIAL FEATURES
COLOR
Schedules network color, film, slides, tape and live.
Equipped with high band VTR.

WPIX

NEW YORK CITY, N. Y.
(Airdate June 15, 1948)

TvB

Subscriber to the NAB Television Code
Media Code 6 233 0800 4.00
WPIX, Inc., 11 WPIX Plaza, New York, N. Y. 10017. Phone 212-949-1100. TWX 710-581-2768.

1. PERSONNEL
President—Leavitt J. Pope, 212-949-2300.
Senior Vice-President of Sales—Gerard Mulderrig.
212-949-2340.
Vice President, Sales—Larry Linehan, 212-949-2350.
Vice-President, Sales—Gerard Puccio, 212-949-2360.

2. REPRESENTATIVES
TeleRep.

3. FACILITIES
Video 100,000 w., audio 20,000 w.; ch 11.
Antenna ht.: 1,410 ft. above average terrain.
Operating schedule: 6:30-1:30 am daily. EST.

4. AGENCY COMMISSION
15% to recognized agencies; no cash discount.

5. GENERAL ADVERTISING See coded regulations
General: 1a, 2a, 3a, 4a, 5, 6a, 7b, 8.
Rate Protection: 10k, 11k, 12k, 13k, 14k.
Contracts: 20b, 21, 27c, 29, 31b, 31c.
Basic Rates: 40a, 41b, 41c, 42, 43b, 45a, 52.
Cancellations: 70a, 70g, 73a.
Prod. Services: 80, 82, 83, 84, 85, 86, 87a, 87b, 87c.
Announcements and station breaks may be rescheduled if product conflicts arise as the result of time segments, otherwise they may be cancelled upon notice to the agency or advertiser.
Station's prior approval is required if a multi-product advertiser wishes to substitute another of its products after the commitment for a specific product is made.
Although station will make every effort to give reasonable separation to products that might be considered competitive, we cannot guarantee to do so, nor will we offer credit or make-goods on that basis.
All rates quoted herein apply only to products of a single advertiser.
The station in all cases reserves the right to determine the rotation of all spots.
The spot rotations include exposure in adjacent breaks.

6. TIME RATES
Rates have been temporarily withdrawn by station.

11. SPECIAL FEATURES
COLOR
Schedules, film, slides, tape and live.
Equipped with high and low band VTR.

12. SERVICE FACILITIES
Address all commercial films or other commercial material to:
WPIX Operations,
220 E. 42nd St.,
New York, N. Y. 10017.
Address all program films, program material and tape to:
WPIX Film Department,
220 E. 42nd St.,
New York, N. Y. 10017.

13. CLOSING TIME
72 hours prior copy, scripts, film, recordings, slides, material and music, artwork 5 days, program scripts 1 week.

Exhibit 6.11

Partial page of TV rates from Standard Rate & Data Service. Here all rate cards are published in full, giving information in standardized numerical sequence for each medium. (Courtesy of SRDS.)

Table 6–6

RATE-CARD EXCERPT			
	I	II	III
Tues., 8–9 A.M.	$135	$125	$115

2 weeks' notice, and column III the rate for preemption without notice. Observe how the rate goes down.

When a spot is preempted, an advertiser must be given a spot of equivalent value, known as a *make-good*.

Special features

News telecasts, weather reports, sports news and commentary, stock-market reports, and similar programming are called *special features*. Time in connection with special features is sold at a premium price.

Run of schedule (ROS)

An advertiser can earn a lower rate by permitting a station to run his commercials at its convenience whenever time is available rather than in a specified position (comparable to ROP in printed advertising; see Chapter 8).

Package rates

Every station sets up its own assortment of time slots at different periods of the day, which it sells as a package. The station creates its own name for such packages and charges less for them than for the same spots sold individually. The package rate is one of the elements in negotiation for time.

Rate negotiation

At this point it is opportune to bring up the recognized trade practice of negotiation between buyers of TV or radio spots and the broadcasting stations for better rates than those published on the rate cards. This practice is nurtured by the fact that the only asset a broadcaster has for sale is time—a most ephemeral asset indeed. Every second during the broadcasting day or night for which there is no commercial buyer means a dollar loss to the station. The station must broadcast continually during its allotted broadcast time to keep its license. The stations know this; the time buyers with big schedules know this as they bargain for a deal better than that on the rate card. It may be for a lower rate, beginning with the package deals that stations always offer, or for better time slots for a given rate, or for more spots for the same money. Much depends on how much open time the station has, as well as on the expertise of the buyer. But there is never any harm in asking, "What's the best package you can work out for x dollars?" or "I may be interested in buying x rating points in your market. What's your best proposal?"

Rotation: horizontal and vertical. Rotation of a schedule refers to the place-ment of commercials within a schedule to get the greatest possible showing (see Exhibit 6.12). If you bought two spots a week for 4 weeks on a Monday-to-Friday basis, but all the spots were aired only on Monday and Tuesday, your rotation would be poor. You would miss all the people who turn to the station only on Wednesday, Thursday, or Friday. Your horizontal rotation should be increased.

Vertical rotation assures differences in time at which a commercial is shown within the time bracket purchased. If we bought three spots on the "Tonight Show," which runs from 11:30 P.M. to 1:00 A.M., but all our spots were at 12:45 A.M., we'd be missing all the people who go to sleep earlier than

Exhibit 6.12
Availability chart. (Courtesy of Petry Television, Inc., and Vitt Media International, Inc.)

PETRY TELEVISION INC.

FOR AGENCY USE

AGENCY	BUYER	ADVERTISER	PRODUCT	SCHEDULE DATES	MARKET BUDGET
Vitt Media	Alice Benson	ITT Cont Bkg	Various	Cal Yr 1977	

STATION/MARKET	CHANNEL/NETWORK	RATING SERVICE	SALESMAN	TEL. NO.	DATE
KSAT/San Antonio	CH 12/ ABC	NSI, Nov'75,F/M'76,May'76	Gene McHugh	688-0200	10/8/76

AG'Y USE	DAY	TIME FROM	TO	TYPE	PARTICIPATION OR ADJACENCY	CODE	DMA RATING	W18-49 HOMES 25-	W	W35+	W50+	K6-11	COST INFORMATION FIXED	PREEMPTIBLE	IDENT.	AG'Y USE
	M-F	7	9A	30	Good Morning America	N	3	6	7	10	6			$30		
						F/M	4	8	9	8	5					
						M	5	8	12	14	9					
	M-F	9	1030A	30	Mike Douglas	N	8	22	21	18	8			$50		
						F/M	7	17	16	16	9					
						M	7	14	15	15	10					
	M-F	1030	330P	30	ABC Rotation	N	7	22	16	13	8			$65		
						F/M	8	23	19	16	10					
						M	8	22	19	13	8					
	M-F	330	4P	30	Mickey Mouse	N	7					24		$95(TP=Merv)		
						F/M/tp6						3				
						M/tp	7					1				
	M-F	4	5P	30	Emergency	N/tp 6		13	9			9		$135(TP=Adam 12/FBI)		
						F/M/tp6		11	13			3		(TP=Merv)		
						M/tp	7	12	16			2				
						E	9	22	21			24				

The popular Emergency comes to daytime this fall. With the additional kids programming, there will be an increased number of available kids, and Emergency will pick them up and maintain the kids from Mouse. May'76 prime shrx Nov'75 HUT=9 rtg/32 shr. Demos to Emergency May'76.

AG'Y USE	DAY	TIME FROM	TO	TYPE	PARTICIPATION OR ADJACENCY	CODE	DMA RATING	W18-49 HOMES 25-	W	W35+	W50+	K6-11	COST INFORMATION FIXED	PREEMPTIBLE	IDENT.	AG'Y USE
	M-F	5	530P	30	Partridge Family	N/tp 4		12	8	7	4	6		$125(TP=FBI)		
						F/M/tp6		14	12	10	16	3		(TP=Adam 12)		
						M/tp	7	17	14	10	6	8				
						E	13	21	17	19	12	24				

(R) = ROTATION   * = NO PIGGY BACK

TP = TIME PERIOD   PT = PARTIAL TIME PERIOD
ES = ESTIMATED   PR = PROGRAM
ALL HOMES AND DEMOS IN THOUSANDS

AAAA-SRA RECOMMENDED FORM

AGENCY COPY

ALL AUDIENCE MEASUREMENT DATA ARE ESTIMATES ONLY–SUBJECT TO DEFECTS AND LIMITATIONS OF SOURCE MATERIAL AND METHODS, HENCE MAY NOT BE ACCURATE MEASURES OF THE TRUE AUDIENCE

that. To avoid this situation, we schedule one spot in each half hour of the program, vertically rotating our commercial to reach the largest possible audience.

Other trade practices

Closing time. Tapes and films that are to be part of a commercial must be in the station's hands 72 hours in advance although stations are usually capable of accommodating a request for a shorter closing time in special instances. To be sure that the right commercial goes on in the right sequence, agencies' traffic departments issue standard coded instructions on the sequence in which films are to be run.

Certificate of performance. Station invoices for spot-TV time include a certificate of performance (station affidavit) attesting that the commercials were run on the days and time enumerated. (A similar statement appears on network bills, too.) A system for electronically coding TV commercials has been developed that, with the help of computer tape, provides an exact record.

Product protection. Every advertiser would like to keep the advertising of competitive products as far away as possible. That brings up the question of what "protection" (against competition) an ad will get. Although some stations say that they will try to keep competing commercials 5 to 10 minutes apart, most say that, while they will do everything possible to separate competing ads, they guarantee only that they will not run them back to back.

Station-representative system. Persons with offices in the main advertising centers act as sales and service agents for stations around the country. These station representatives provide the time buyer with data about the market, the station's programming, and the audience of the station. They find out for the time buyer (often by computerized hookup, otherwise by telephone or teletype) what spots are available, and they help set a firm schedule. A number of representatives, each handling many stations, have lined up their stations into transcription networks to handle spot sales. From their list an advertiser can select the stations of his or her choice. The advertiser supplies one transcription of the commercial, and the representative makes duplicates as needed, sending them to all the scheduled stations. The advertiser places only one order and receives only one bill—an expedient way of handling a big spot list.

Barter. Besides purchasing TV time directly from the station, many advertisers make a practice of purchasing it through barter houses. We discuss this practice in Chapter 20, "The Advertising Agency: Media Services and Other Services."

All the preceding material on purchasing TV time can be summarized in the following TV-planning checklist and in Exhibit 6.13:

VITT MEDIA INTERNATIONAL, INC.

PART I - BUYING AUTHORIZATION FORM

BUYING SPECIFICATIONS

DATE: _____

AUTH.#:_____

Parent Company: _____ Agency: _____ Product: _____

Dates: Start: _____ End: _____ No. of Wks: _____ No. of Markets _____ (Attach Part III)

_____ _____ _____ _____ _____

_____ _____ _____ _____ _____

Target Audience: Primary _____ Secondary _____

Weekly GRP's _____ Total GRP's _____ ☐ ARB ☐ NSI _____ Month(s)

Weekly Gross Budget _____ Total Gross Budget _____

APPROXIMATE % OF GRP'S BY DAY PARTS AND COMMERCIAL LENGTHS

DAYPARTS	EASTERN AND PACIFIC TIME ZONES*		60's	30's	10's	OTHER
Daytime:	Sign on to 4:30P	Mon. - Fri-				
Early Fringe:	4:30 to 7:29P	Mon. - Fri.				
	12N to 7:29P	Sat. - Sun.				
Prime:	7:30 to 11:00P	Mon. - Sun.				
Late Fringe:	11:01 to Sign Off	Mon. - Sun				
	TOTALS					

*Adjusted for Central and Mountain Time Zones

INCLUDE ONLY THOSE SPECIFICS THAT ARE REQUIRED FOR THIS BUY

Days of the Week Preferred_____ Maximum No. of Spots in one Program per week _____

Adjacency Exceptions _____ Station Exceptions _____

Desired No. of Stations per Mkt. _____ Min. Rating/Spot _____ Min. No. Spots/Wk._____

Tags Required? ☐ YES ☐ NO Bill Tags to: _____ Salesman's Sheets ☐ YES ☐ No (Attach format)

Makegood Policy : _____

_____

Rotation Policy : _____

_____

Cancellation Policy: _____

_____

Traffic Instructions: _____

_____

Schedules ☐ FORMS SUPPLIED ☐ VMI FORMS (Sample Attached)

Other Requirements: _____

_____

APPROVED VMI	DATE	APPROVED CLIENT	DATE

Exhibit 6.13
Notice how this chart asks key questions for planning and purchasing time. (Courtesy of Vitt Media International, Inc.)

☐ The basic plan:

What is the budget?

What is the relative importance of reach and frequency?

What geographic area (ADI or DMA) do we want to cover? Over what period of time?

What audience do we want to reach? Sex? Age?

What is the weight in GRP's we want for a market?

Shall we use network and/or spot? What proportion of each?

☐ The network buying plan:

What are the availabilities of each network for the time we want? What programs?

What are the ratings of available programs? Cost per point per program?

What is the share of market of individual stations in their respective markets?

What is the reputation of the network for product protection? For other helpful services?

Network programs must be planned well in advance—often a year ahead.

☐ The spot buying plan:

How do stations compare in share of audience?

What are station ratings by quarter-hour periods?

Which single program best reaches the audience we are seeking?

What are all the programs that best reach the audience we are seeking?

What is the station's history of reliability for handling spots, product protection, make-goods?

What is the best deal we can work out to get the spots we want at the least cost?

These are among the considerations in making a TV spot schedule.

TRENDS IN TELEVISION
ADVERTISING

TV in the next decade will be more expensive to advertisers, more diverse in its programming, and unpredictable in its capacity for technological innovation. We shall see a greater per-household investment in TV as part of a complete home entertainment-information center. A TV set will be only the primary ingredient in a complex two-way communication system.

TELEVISION AND
SOCIETY

We can't leave the subject of TV without noting its controversial aspects. Hardly a month goes by that some group doesn't issue a "rating" of TV's treatment of some subject. Groups as diverse as the PTA, gay-rights organizations, and the Moral Majority have all found TV falling short of their expectations. Most groups critical of TV have concentrated their efforts in the areas of sex and/or violence. Over the last decade most of these groups have protested to the networks their concerns over TV's portrayal of moral issues. Indeed, in the spring of 1981 Rev. Donald Wildmon's Coalition for Better Television threatened a boycott of companies that advertised on programs the Coalition termed "offensive"; and shortly thereafter several major corporations, led by Procter & Gamble, either met with Wildmon or announced a review of their advertising practices. Wildmon then announced that the threat of a boycott was at least temporarily suspended.

The Coalition episode is important in that it raises several fundamental questions: Does such a boycott impinge on the free-speech guarantees of the Constitution? Does Wildmon or any other group represent a consensus of viewer opinion, or is he or it simply a well-organized vocal minority? Should advertisers be censors or neutral participants in network programming? If sexually oriented shows are obviously offensive, why do "offenders," such as "Dallas," consistently top the ratings?

There are no definitive answers to these questions. The controversy over TV programming and advertising is an indication of their importance and pervasiveness in our lives. The very elements that make TV controversial also contribute to its importance as an advertising medium.

SUMMARY

TV is a medium in flux. From the family-oriented, small-screen, black-and-white set of the 1950s we have entered an era of cable TV with more than 50 channels, computer linkages, specialized programming, and a set for every member of the household. This new technology's implications for advertising are many, with both risks and opportunities.

While no one can predict TV's future with absolute certainty, there are several areas where we can safely make some assumptions for the future:

1. Cable will continue to grow, with household-penetration levels of 60 to 70 percent likely by 1990.
2. We shall have more choices of programming, with a smaller audience for each channel.
3. Network dominance of TV programming will lessen.
4. Advertisers will pay more to reach this fragmented audience, but these higher costs will be partly offset by more efficiency in reaching prospects through programming and advertising designed for them.
5. TV will become a medium of information as well as entertainment, with the lines between the two blurring.
6. TV ratings will give more emphasis to individual viewership rather than household data.

QUESTIONS

1. What is network TV? Spot TV? Local TV? What are the advantages and limitations of each?
2. It has been suggested that the decade of the 1980s will be the era of cable. Discuss.

3. How does subscription TV differ from cable? What are its major advantages and disadvantages compared with cable?

4. What is the potential of cable TV for direct-response advertising?

5. Define DMA and ADI. How do they apply to TV advertising? How do other media use the ADI concept?

6. Describe the telephone coincidental, diary, and mechanical-recorder methods of TV audience research. What are the advantages and limitations of each?

7. What is the difference between a rating of 20 and a share of audience of 20?

8. What is the difference between spot TV and a TV spot?

9. Give a brief definition, explanation or description of the following:

a. Superstation	l. Package rate
b. Clutter	m. Rate negotiation
c. Clearance	n. Rotation: horizontal, vertical
d. Reach	o. Closing time
e. Frequency	p. Certificate of performance
f. Flight	q. Product protection
g. Rating point	r. Station representative
h. Gross rating point (GRP)	s. Barter syndication
i. Preemption rate	t. Scatter plan
j. Run of schedule (ROS)	u. Up-front buy
k. Frequency discount	

SUGGESTED EXERCISES

10. If your library keeps back issues of the Spot Television Standard Rate and Data Service find a current issue and one from 10 years earlier. From each volume list the independent (nonnetwork-affiliated) TV stations in the top ten markets. Also compare the cost of a prime-time 30-second commercial on the network affiliates in these same markets from each year.

11. Using the current Spot Television SRDS figure, calculate the number of households that would be bought with 60 GRP's in the following cities: New York, Atlanta, Orlando, and Jackson (Mississippi).

READINGS

BELCH, GEORGE E.: "An Examination of Comparative and Noncomparative Television Commercials: The Effects of Claim Variation and Repetition on Cognitive Response and Message Acceptance," *Journal of Marketing Research,* August 1981, pp. 333–49.

"Consumer VCR Business Booming Despite Court Order, but Video Disc Sales Progress Is Slow," *Television/Radio Age,* November 16, 1981, pp. 44–46.

COSNER, DWIGHT M.: "Coping with the Complexity of New Video Technologies," *Admap,* May 1980, pp. 237–39.

EDWARDS, MORRIS: "Videotext/Teletext Services Seek Haven in USA Homes," *Communications News,* August 1980, pp. 38–42.

GENSCH, DENNIS and **PAUL SHAMAN:** "Models of Competitive Television Ratings," *Journal of Marketing Research,* August 1980, pp. 307–15.

"Good News, Bad News in DBS Spacerush," *Broadcasting,* July 20, 1981, pp. 23–27.

"NATPE cable contingent hints at new program trends," *Television/Radio Age,* March 9, 1981, p. 150.

REISS, CRAIG: "Syndicator Split over Barter's Im-pact on Programming," *Marketing & Media Decisions,* June 1981, pp. 76–78.

"There's a Satellite in your Future," *Marketing & Media Decisions,* November 1981, pp. 880–89.

"TVB Keeps Focus Downward—On the Bottom Line," *Broadcasting,* November 16, 1981, pp. 28–29.

"Videotech," *Advertising Age,* November 16, 1981, S-1-24.

7

Using Radio

Table 7

Radio was the bright star of the media world from the early 1920s to the early 1950s. It had created network shows, soap operas, and nighttime shows, which became part of the American scene. Sunday-night shows, particularly, provided the country with conversation pieces for the week. Radio also became the favorite source of news, particularly during World War II, when many people kept the radio on all day to catch the latest war news. Then in the early 1950s TV came upon the scene and took away big parts of the radio audience—and the advertisers. Radio was hurt. But soon, working on the old principle "Sell what you've got," the industry realized that it could successfully adapt to a changing marketplace. Rather than competing with nighttime TV, radio has become a local daytime medium directed toward individual listening with numerous selective formats. Table 7.1 shows what has happened since radio shifted to a primarily local medium.*

Set-ownership and audience-listenership statistics for radio are impressive. Almost 500 million radios are in circulation, with another 40 million purchased each year. Approximately one-third of these radios are out-of-home receivers, making it the

*All data in this chapter, unless otherwise credited, are used through the courtesy of the Radio Advertising Bureau.

		RADIO ADVERTISING EXPENDITURES (in thousands)[a]					
YEAR	NETWORK, $	% OF TOTAL	NATIONAL NONNETWORK, $	% OF TOTAL	LOCAL, $	% OF TOTAL	TOTAL
1981[b]	205,000	5.1	915,000	22.7	2,900,000	72.1	4,020,000
1978	126,400	4.3	592,100	20.2	2,208,400	75.5	2,926,900
1975	72,500	3.8	416,300	22.0	1,403,300	74.2	1,892,100
1970	48,800	3.9	355,300	28.3	852,700	67.8	1,256,800
1960	35,000	5.6	202,100	32.5	385,300	62.0	622,400
1950	131,200	28.9	119,100	26.3	203,200	44.8	453,500

[a]From *Broadcasting Yearbook*, 1981.
[b]From *Broadcasting*, August 17, 1981, p. 50. Note the big drop in network revenues and share after 1950 and the slight resurgence predicted for the 1980s. (Reprinted permission of *Broadcasting*.)

only medium that goes with the audience. Over 90 percent of automobiles are radio equipped, drive time (morning and evening) being the peak audience period for most radio stations. On a weekly basis radio reaches 95 percent of all persons 12 or more years old.

FEATURES AND ADVANTAGES

Radio is a personal medium

When you listen to a voice on the radio, you are hearing it on a one-to-one basis. Usually you are alone with it. Someone is speaking directly to you. Many people have a close rapport with a radio personality to whom they listen faithfully. Radio also brings a wide range of sound effects to involve the listener's imagination in the script. You can hear a plane leave the airfield as vividly as if you saw it off. A majority of Americans—men, women, and teenagers—have transistor sets for personal use, which goes way up in the summertime, when people are outdoors.

Radio is broadly selective

There are more than ten times as many radio stations as TV stations (7,937 commercial radio stations to 763 commercial TV stations).* That means a greater choice of stations from which to select. Even in small towns there are more radio than TV broadcasts available. Each station will seek to acquire a loyal following by virtue of its programming, its announcer, its talk shows, or other program qualities. Because different programming attracts different types of audiences, the advertiser can pick the stations that attract the kind of audience desired, such as housewives, men or women of different age groups, teenagers, farmers, or ethnic groups (Exhibit 7.1). Radio is a friendly, warm way of delivering a message at a low CPM.

Broadcasting, August 3, 1981, p. 83.

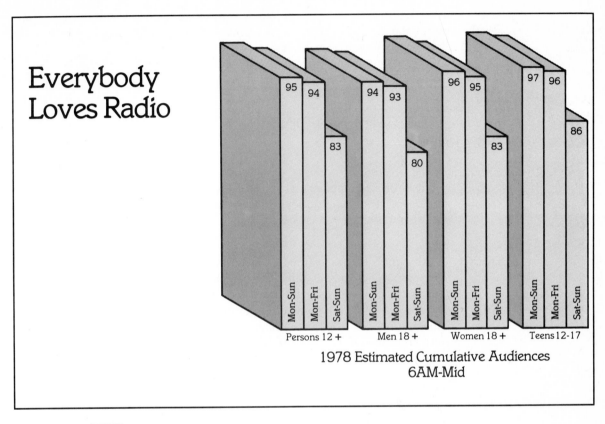

Everybody
Loves Radio

1978 Estimated Cumulative Audiences
6AM-Mid

	Persons 12 +			Men 18 +			Women 18 +			Teens 12-17		
	Mon-Sun	Mon-Fri	Sat-Sun	Mon-Sun	Mon-Fri	Sat-Sun	Mon-Sun	Mon-Fri	Sat-Sun	Mon-Sun	Mon-Fri	Sat-Sun
	95	94	83	94	93	80	96	95	83	97	96	86

Exhibit 7.1
Everybody loves radio: Each week, radio reaches 95 percent of all people age 12 and over. (The Arbitron Company, *Today's Radio Audience*, 1979, p. 7.)

LIMITATIONS AND CHALLENGES

Because there are so many radio stations (many cities of under 300,000 population have eight radio stations each), the audience is highly fragmented. It may take a number of stations to cover a market.

Since radio is an aural medium, you cannot use it for couponing, showing styles, or picturing new models. You cannot show a package or trademark to a shopper so that he or she can quickly identify your product on the shelf.

The chief complaint about radio is that it has too many commercials per hour. This frequency lessens the impact of all commercials and makes it much more difficult to position a commercial away from that of a competing product, even though stations try to separate them. The need for getting immediate attention in commercials, however, has inspired some of the most imaginative writing in the field of mass communication.

The paperwork in putting through a schedule of national radio spots, as in TV, can be quite overwhelming, involving checking and gathering availabilities, confirming clearances, ordering, checking appearances and make-goods, approving bills for payment, and billing to clients with proper credits, as in the case of TV spots. But great advances have been made in computerizing the entire operation.

Yet with all its limitations radio ad expenditures more than doubled between 1970 and 1980.

A FEW USEFUL TECHNICAL POINTS
ON RADIO

The signal   The electrical impulses that are broadcast, whether by radio or TV, are called the *signal*. If a certain station has a good signal in a given territory, that means its programs and commercials come over clearly in that area.

Frequency   All signals are transmitted by electromagnetic waves, sometimes called *radio waves*. These waves differ from each other in *frequency* (the number of waves that pass a given point in a given period of time). Frequencies are measured in terms of thousands of cycles per second (*kilohertz,* or *kHz,* formerly called *kilocycles,* or *kc*) or millions of cycles per second (*megahertz,* or *MHz,* formerly called *megacycles,* or *Mc*). Every station broadcasts on the frequency assigned to it by the FCC so that it does not interfere with other stations. The FCC, in fact, acts as the traffic director of the air, assigning frequencies to all users of broadcasting, including TV, police radio, citizens' band, navigational aids, and international radio. Exhibit 6.3 shows present usage. A radio station assigned a frequency of 850,000 cycles per second, or 850 kHz, is identifed by 85 on the radio dial (the final zero is dropped for convenience).

Differences between AM and FM radio. All electromagnetic waves have height, spoken of as *amplitude,* like the difference between an ocean wave and a ripple in a pond; and they have speed, measured by the *frequency* with which a succession of waves passes a given point per minute or per second. If a radio station operates on a frequency of 1,580 kilohertz, for example, it means that 1,580,000 of its waves pass a given point per second.

Based upon these two dimensions—amplitude and frequency—two separate systems have been developed for carrying the sound waves: The first system carries the variations in a sound wave by corresponding variations in its amplitude; the frequency remains constant; this is the principle of *amplitude modulation* (AM), Exhibit 7.2a. The second system carries the variation in a sound wave by corresponding variations in its frequency; the amplitude remains constant; this is the principle of *frequency modulation* (FM), Exhibit 7.2b.

There are approximately 4,800 AM and 4,000 FM stations (including 1,100 noncommercial stations). Establishment of new AM stations has stabilized at 1 percent annual growth, while FM stations are increasing at a yearly rate of almost 8 percent. Each system offers different values to the listener and

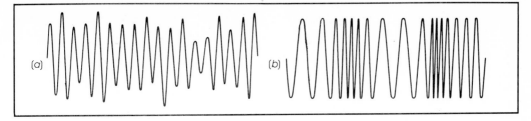

Exhibit 7.2

In amplitude modulation (a) waves vary in height (amplitude); frequency is constant. Frequency modulation (b) varies the frequency but keeps the height constant. These drawings, however, are not made to scale, which would reveal that width is the significant difference between AM and FM. The FM wave is twenty times wider than the AM wave. That fact helps to explain how FM captures its fine tones.

to the advertiser. So the technical structure of AM and FM radio has created what is in effect two distinct media. AM signals carry farther but are susceptible to interference. FM has a fine tonal reception, but signal distances are limited. Reception of a particular station is determined by atmospheric conditions and station power (broadcast frequency). Station rate cards give hours of operation, frequency, and signal-coverage areas.

SELLING RADIO COMMERCIAL TIME

Like TV time, radio advertising is divided into three categories—*network, spot,* and *local* (Exhibit 7.3). However, the radio networks are a minor source of advertising revenues, with local advertisers dominating the medium, as indicated in Table 7.2.

Table 7–2

NETWORK	AFFILIATES
American Broadcasting Company (ABC)*	
Contemporary	407
Entertainment	505
FM	203
Information	611
Columbia Broadcasting System (CBS)	340
Mutual Broadcasting System (MBS)	900
National Black Network	90
National Broadcasting Company (NBC)	
Basic network	355
The Source (for stations programming to 18–24 year olds)	176
RKO Radio Network	86
RKO Radio Network 2	[Began operation in fall, 1981]
Sheridan	103
Associated Press Radio	720
United Press International Audio Network	1,000

*Courtesy of Broadcasting, August 17, 1981, p. 48.

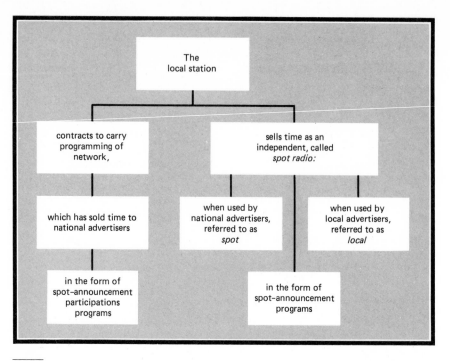

Exhibit 7.3
The radio structure.

Network radio has recently experienced tremendous growth in both number of affiliates and advertising revenues. Although network advertising accounts for only 5 percent of total radio revenues, it grew almost 30 percent from 1980 to 1981. Several factors have combined to create this healthy situation for radio networks: Satellite technology has made multiprogram distribution feasible; advertisers are drawn to radio's opportunities for audience segmentation and specialized formats; furthermore, daytime TV viewership has been static for the last few years, causing advertisers to examine other media alternatives.

Radio networks operate much differently than TV networks do. Most importantly, networks provide only a small amount of programming for local stations. They do, however, provide national news, specials, live remotes, and other features that a single station could not afford to produce. Since most network programming is short, stations may belong to more than one network, each providing specialized programming to fill out a station's schedule.

In the future we shall probably see a higher percentage of network programming particularly in small and medium markets. In some cases we may see networks providing most of the programming for some stations. If this occurs, then the network-affiliate relationship might take on many of the features we now find in TV.

Quality, not quantity, is the measure of the value of a radio network's affiliates. In the future we'll see networks placing greater emphasis on commonality of audience demographics among their affiliates rather than acquiring the largest number of affiliates. All the major networks offer a long list of stations with which they are, or can be, interconnected, in combinations designed to reach all parts of the country and flexible enough to meet the advertiser's needs. As in TV, there are state and regional networks, interconnected but not part of a national network.

We also have *nonwired networks,* formed by leading stations' representatives, who line up a large number of stations from which the advertiser can pick those most appropriate to his needs. The advertiser supplies one transcription and a schedule to the network, which handles all details of ordering the time, delivering the commercial, and handling the billing.

These networks are not interconnected and an advertiser cannot simultaneously have his message broadcast over a number of stations, as in regular network broadcasting. The term network is used in this context to emphasize the fact that an advertiser can buy many stations with one insertion order (to the representative) and pay a single bill.

Spot radio   When an advertiser buys time on an individual station, the usage is called *spot radio.* The program originates at the station from which it is broadcast; it is not relayed from a network broadcast. As in TV, when a national advertiser uses spot radio, it is, strictly speaking *national spot radio;* however, by FCC usage and trade custom it is called simply *spot radio.* Similarly, when a local advertiser uses spot radio, it is, strictly speaking, *local spot radio;* but it is referred to as *local radio.* (We discuss local radio in Chapter 23, Retail Advertising.)

Spot radio represents the height of radio flexibility. An advertiser has 8,000 stations from which to tailor a choice to fit the market, for as long or short a flight as desired. The schedule can be pinpointed to the weather (for suntan lotion) or to house paint or to holiday seasons(for gift suggestions). Spot radio is often used to build the frequency of a campaign running locally in other media or to reach specific demographic segments. An advertiser can move fast with spot radio. Although some stations ask for 2 weeks' closing, most specify 72 hours' closing for broadcast materials. When asked his closing time, one candid station manager replied, "Thirty minutes before broadcast!"

FM as an advertising
medium   The story of radio in the 1970s is one of the emergence of FM as a viable commercial medium. Since 1978 over half of the leading metro radio stations in audience ratings have been FM outlets.* From 1970 to 1980 FM revenues grew more than 600 percent from $85 million to over $500 million. It is expected that FM will continue to gain in audience popularity and advertising revenues throughout the coming decade.

Television/Radio Age, March 24, 1980, p. A–3. Leading stations are defined as the top ten stations in the top ten markets and the top five in the remaining eighty markets—for a total of 500 leading stations. Among these 500 stations FM outlets account for 278.

In many respects AM has become the medium on the defensive in competing with FM for the radio advertising dollar. Innovations such as AM stereo broadcasting are seen as giving AM the potential for competition (or at least parity) with FM. However, few observers think AM stations can erode the audience gains made by FM stations during the 1970s.

Time classifications—

dayparts

The broadcast day is divided into time periods called *dayparts,* as set out in Table 7.3.

Weekends are regarded as a separate time classification. Most radio spot time is sold in 60-second units. The cost varies with the daypart.

Table 7–3

DAYPART	CHARACTERISTICS
6 A.M.–10 A.M.	Drive time, breakfast audience, interested chiefly in news
10 A.M.– 3 P.M.	Daytime, programs characteristic of station, talk, music or all-news
3 P.M. – 7 P.M.	Afternoon, drive time; radio prime time and same as morning drive time
7 P.M.–12 M	News, music, talk shows
12 M – 6 A.M.	Music, talk shows

Types of

programming

Because there is great competition among the radio stations in a town, each station, by means of its programming, tries to reach a certain type of audience. Programs are addressed to men or to women of different age groups and to teenagers. The magnet for drawing the desired audiences is chiefly music, but it is also the personality of a particular announcer who becomes popular with an audience. Talk shows and local sports events are other program features through which various stations seek to be identified. Table 7.4 shows the wide range of radio formats and the popularity of each.

RADIO RATING SERVICES

Arbitron

The Arbitron Company totally dominates the local-radio-ratings business. Arbitron Radio ratings are determined by use of a 7-day self-administered diary (Exhibit 7.4) with a local market sample of individuals 12 years or older. In markets with significant black or Hispanic populations telephone surveys supplement diary placements.

Arbitron conducts surveys from one to four times a year depending on market size. Arbitron Radio measures the metropolitan survey area (MSA), the total survey area (TSA), and in larger markets the area of dominant influence (ADI). See, for example, Exhibit 7.5.

Media

statistics
Media Statistics, Inc., publishes several Mediastat reports on radio-audience listening habits. The major report is the Mediatrend report based on same-day telephone interviews. These reports are used to show preferred program formats among various demographic segments. Traditionally the reports have been used primarily by station programmers. However, advertisers have become interested in the service to predict future audience trends.

Regional Acceptance Monitor (RAM)

research
RAM, like Mediastat, has generally been regarded as a programming service to stations. RAM uses a daily-diary technique administered to each household member 12 years or older. The monthly RAM report provides average and cumulative audience data by dayparts. The RAM Qualitative/Usage Estimates Report is published annually and combines audience measurements and product consumption data for each radio station in the survey.

Network radio

ratings
Radio All-dimension Audience Research (Radar). Radar measures radio-network audiences by means of the telephone-coincidental technique. The Ra-

Table 7–4

FORMAT SHARES OF RADIO STATIONS, ALL MEASURED MARKETS[a]						
	STATIONS, %[b]			LISTENING, %[b]		
Format	AM	FM	AM + FM	AM	FM	AM + FM
Easy listening	2.6	10.4	6.5	3.1	19.4	12.0
Adult contemporary	9.2	4.9	7.0	11.0	8.1	9.4
Classical	0.5	2.0	1.3	0.1	2.3	1.3
Country and western	3.9	1.8	2.8	2.1	1.2	1.6
Black	5.3	2.2	3.7	5.7	3.4	4.4
Disco	1.7	3.3	2.5	1.1	9.2	5.5
Middle of the road	7.3	3.4	5.4	10.7	3.5	6.8
Modern country	7.8	4.1	5.9	8.4	3.7	5.8
News	2.7	0.0	1.4	10.3	0.0	4.7
Contemporary	6.4	9.4	7.9	8.9	12.2	10.7
Spanish	2.3	0.8	1.5	3.7	0.6	2.0
Talk	3.9	0.2	2.0	10.0	0.3	4.7
Various	1.7	0.2	0.9	5.6	0.0	2.6
Standard	2.6	2.6	2.6	4.6	4.0	4.2
Religious	5.4	2.5	4.0	1.4	0.5	0.9
Golden oldies	1.3	1.1	1.2	1.2	2.1	1.7
Progressive	0.1	1.1	0.6	0.0	1.9	1.1
Soft contemporary	0.4	2.0	1.2	0.1	3.1	1.7
Album-oriented rock	1.2	7.3	4.2	0.5	10.0	5.7

[a]From *Television/Radio Age*, March 24, 1980, p. A–4.
[b]By total persons age 12 and over, Monday to Sunday from 6 A.M. to midnight.

Exhibit 7.4
A pocket-size Arbitron Radio diary for recording time spent in listening. It is to be carried around all day and returned at the end of a week, when it will be replaced by a new diary. (Courtesy of The Arbitron Company.)

dar report views the entire country as a single population with no market-by-market data available.

Arbitron. Arbitron reports for network radio audiences are provided by summing individual market data. Consequently Arbitron network radio reports can provide advertisers with individual market breakouts for network-rating measurements.

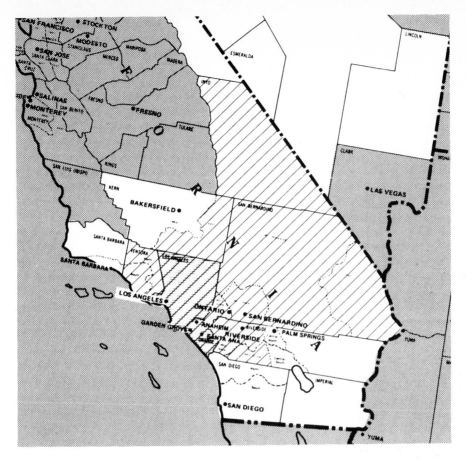

Exhibit 7.5
Coverage areas for the Los Angeles Arbitron Radio report. The area in which listing data were gathered for this survey in this radio market is shown on the map. The TSA of this market is shown in white. The MSA is shown by horizontal hatching. The ADI is shown by diagonal hatching (Copyright American Map Corporation, NY, reprinted with permission. Further reproduction is prohibited.)

RATE
CLASSIFICATIONS
Every station establishes its own classifications and publishes them on its rate card (Exhibit 7.6). The negotiated cost of time depends on those classifications, which are typically:

- ☐ *Drive time.* The most desired and costly time on radio, it varies by the community and usually has the highest ratings.
- ☐ *Run-of-station (ROS).* The station has a choice of moving the commercial at will, wherever it is most convenient. Preemptible ROS is the lowest on the rate card.
- ☐ *Special features.* Time adjacent to weather signals, news reports, time signals, or traffic or stock-market reports usually carries a premium charge.

Package plans
Most spot time is sold in terms of weekly package plans, usually called *total audience plans,* or TAP. A station offers a special flat rate for a number of time slots divided in different proportions over the broadcast day. A typical TAP plan distributes time equally through the broadcast day:

163

☐ 25%, 6 A.M.–10 A.M. (morning drive time)

☐ 25%, 10 A.M.–3 P.M. (housewife time)

☐ 25%, 3 P.M.–7 P.M. (afternoon drive time)

☐ 25%, 7 P.M.–12 M. (nighttime)

Exhibit 7.6
Spot-radio rates and data. (Courtesy Standard Rates and Data Service, Inc.)

GEORGIA

Albany—W G P C—Continued

6. SPOT ANNOUNCEMENTS

	1 min.			30 sec		
PER WK:	1-6	10 ti	20 ti	30 ti	1-6	10 ti 20 ti 30 ti
DT	11.00	10.00	9.00	8.00	8.00	7.00 6.00 5.00
*OT	9.00	8.00	7.00	6.00	7.00	6.00 5.00 4.00

	1 min			30 sec		
PER YR:	156x	260x	312x	156x	260x	312x
DT	4.50	4.00	3.30	3.60	3.20	2.20
*OT	4.00	3.50	2.75	3.20	2.80	2.20

(*) All other times.

W G P C–FM
1963
NAB

Subscriber to the NAB Radio Code

Media Code 4 211 8441 5.00
Albany Broadcasting Co., 2011 Gillionville Rd., Albany, Ga. 31707. Phone 912-888-6500.
See affiliated AM station for additional information.

W J A D (FM)
BAINBRIDGE

City of license, Bainbridge, Ga.
See listing under Bainbridge, Ga.

W J A Z
1952

Modern Country

RAB

Media Code 4 211 0495 1.00
Dr. Charles Finney, dba WJAZ Radio, Box 505, 2700 N. Slappey Blvd., Albany, Ga. 31702. Phone 912-432-9181.
1. PERSONNEL
General Manager—William L. Pope.
Program Director—John Hart.
2. REPRESENTATIVES
Jack Bolton Associates.
3. FACILITIES
5,000 w. days 960 kc. Directional.
Operating schedule: 6 am-local sunset. EST.
4. AGENCY COMMISSION
None; all rates net to station.
5. GENERAL ADVERTISING See coded regulations
Member: The Tobacco Radio Network.
TIME RATES
AAA—6-9 am, 3:30-7 pm/any special time placement.
AA—Throughout Broadcast day.
6. SPOT ANNOUNCEMENTS

	AAA		AA	
	1 min	30 sec	1 min	30 sec
6 ti	10.95	6.90	8.00	5.60
12 ti	9.90	6.25	7.60	5.00
18 ti	9.45	5.80	7.00	4.70
24 ti	8.90	5.30	6.60	4.30
30+	8.00	4.85	6.25	3.75

W J I Z (FM)
1986
Media Code 4 211 0550 3.00
James R. Rivers, Inc., Box 545, Slappey Dr., Albany, Ga. 31702. Phone 912-432-7447.
1 min rate 1x: 16.00.

W M G R
BAINBRIDGE
City of license, Bainbridge, Ga.
See listing under Bainbridge, Ga.

W Q D E
1962

NAB   RAB

Media Code 4 211 0605 5.00
Dave Mack Broadcasting Co., Inc., Box 1634, 2804 N. Jefferson, Albany, Ga. 31702. Phone 912-436-0544.
STATION'S PROGRAMMING DESCRIPTION
WQDE: MUSIC: pop/adult. Personalities. NEWS: business reports & commentator, network news. Contact Representative for further details. Rec'd 8/3/81.
1. PERSONNEL
Pres. & Gen'l Mgr.—Dave (Mack) McGriff.
Sales Manager—Gary Monroe.
2. REPRESENTATIVES
Savalli & Schutz, Inc.
3. FACILITIES
1,000 w. days; 1250 kc. Non-directional.
Operating schedule: 6 am-local sunset. EST.
4. AGENCY COMMISSION
15%.
5. GENERAL ADVERTISING See coded regulations
General: 3a, 4a, 5, 8a.
Rate Protection: 10b, 11c, 12c, 13c, 14c.
Basic Rates: 21b, 21c, 22a, 23a, 25c, 29a.
Contracts: 42a, 45, 46.
Comb.; Cont. Discounts: 60b, 60k.
Cancellation: 70c, 71a, 73a.
Affiliated with MBS.

222

TIME RATES
NATIONAL AND LOCAL RATES SAME
No. 4 Eff 9/1/81—Rec'd 8/3/81.
AAA—Mon thru Sun 6-10 am, 11 am-1 pm & 3-7 pm.
AA—BTA.

6. SPOT ANNOUNCEMENTS

	AAA			AA	
PER WK:	10 ti	20 ti	30 ti	10 ti	20 ti 30 ti
1 min	11.77	10.59	10.00	10.00	8.82 7.65
30 sec	8.24	7.06	6.47	7.06	5.88 5.29

WWCW (FM)
STEREO COUNTRY 101
#1 COUNTRY STATION
IN 13 COUNTY TSA
Mar. 19/June 10, 1981 ARB

W W C W (FM)
1972

Modern Country

NRBA

Media Code 4 211 0632 9.00
Albany Radio, Inc., Box W. Albany, Ga. 31702. Phone 912-435-9929.
STATION'S PROGRAMMING DESCRIPTION
WWCW (FM): Programmed for adults 18-64 with emphasis on 25-55.
MUSIC: modern country with concerts. NEWS: local at 7:30 am, 12:30 & 5:30 pm; network at :60; state at 6:30, 9:30, 10:30, 11:30 am, 1:30, 2:30, 3:30, 4:30, 6:30 pm; network personalities; commentator at 8:20 am, 12:35 & 5:40 pm. SPORTS: commentator at 7:35 am & 5:35 pm, NASCAR races Sun; high school, college & pro football & bowl games. Contact Representative for further details. Rec'd 2/9/81.
1. PERSONNEL
General Manager—Mark Shor.
Traffic Coordinator—Melissa Shor.
Program Director—Don Michaels.
2. REPRESENTATIVES
Jack Masla & Co., Inc.
Busby, Finch, Lathom & Widman.
3. FACILITIES
ERP 3,000 w. (horiz.), 3,000 w. (vert.); 101.7 mc. Stereo.
Operating schedule: 24 hours daily. EST.
Antenna ht.: 300 ft. above average terrain.
4. AGENCY COMMISSION
15%.
5. GENERAL ADVERTISING See coded regulations
General: 1a, 2b, 3a, 4a, 4d, 5, 8.
Rate Protection: 15b.
Basic Rates: 20b, 22a, 24b, 25a, 28c.
Contracts: 40a, 45, 51a.
Comb.; Cont. Discounts: 60l, 62d.
Cancellation: 71a.
See affiliated AM station for additional information.
AM facilities: WALG.
Affiliated with American Information Network.
Member: Georgia Network, Inc.
TIME RATES
Rates have been temporarily withdrawn by station.

ALMA
Bacon County—Map Location E-9
See SRDS consumer market map and data at beginning of the State.

W U L F
1957
See SRDS Spot Radio Small Markets Edition.

AMERICUS (2 AM; 2 FM)
Sumter County—Map Location C-8
See SRDS consumer market map and data at beginning of the State.

W A D Z (FM)
1964

Z 94

Media Code 4 211 0687 3.00
Americus Broadcasting Co., Box 1307, 605 McGarrah St., Americus, Ga. 31709. Phone 912-924-1290.
STATION'S PROGRAMMING DESCRIPTION
WADZ (FM): Programmed adult contemporary, 18-49.
MUSIC: adult contemporary, best 40 singles of wk. heavy promotion & personality announcers. Wkly countdowns, album group features & specials. NEWS: local at :20 & :50 through both drives. SPORTS: at :40 through both drives; college play-by-play basketball; high school play-by-play football. Contact Representative for further details. Rec'd 1/5/81.
1. PERSONNEL
Gen'l & Sales Mgr.—Joseph Langworthy.
Program Director—J. Arthur.
2. REPRESENTATIVES
South—Dora-Clayton Agency, Inc.
Southwest—C. K. Beaver & Associates, Inc.
3. FACILITIES
ERP 3,000 w. (horiz.), 3,000 w. (vert.); 94.3 mc.
Operating schedule: 24 hours daily. EST.
Antenna ht.: 300 ft. above average terrain.
4. AGENCY COMMISSION
None; all rates net to station.

An advertiser can buy the total plan or parts of it. In all instances there is a quantity- or dollar-discount plan, depending upon the total number of spots run during a given period of time (Table 7.5).

Table 7–5

TOTAL AUDIENCE PLAN[a]					
Number of times	8	12	20	32	40
1 minute, $	110	100	92	86	79
30 seconds, $	88	80	74	69	63

[a]Per week (¼ A.M., ¼ P.M., ¼ housewife, ¼ night).

Negotiation

In buying spot-radio time, as in buying spot-TV time, negotiation is the rule rather than the exception.

Gross rating points (GRP) in radio

One rating point represents 1 percent of the total potential audience within a specified area, as defined by the rating service used. A GRP is the rating a program gets (reach) multiplied by the number of times the program is played (frequency).

If in a community of 10,000 people research indicates that 160 are listening to one particular program on a certain station, that station is given a rating of 1.6 for that time period. If you were to run a commercial five times per week in that same daypart, the GRP would be represented by the following formula:

$$1.6 \text{ (rating)} \times 5 \text{ (frequency)} = \text{(GRP)}$$

National advertisers planning to enter markets across the country can determine how many GRP's they plan to buy in each market and use that as a yardstick in actually scheduling stations and programs in a city.

Cumes

A *cume* represents the accumulated number of different people who have been exposed to a commercial that ran more than once. Say a commercial runs on a station three times a week for a 4-week period and reaches 10,000 listeners each time it appears. That does not mean that it has reached 120,000 people; for every time it appeared, some of the previous audience were listening, and some new listeners joined the audience. The audience cume is the unduplicated audience *accumulated* over some period of time. In Exhibit 7.7 we see the average number of people listening to the stations and the number of different people (the cume) listening during the time period covered.

Average Quarter-Hour and Cume Listening Estimates

||| Adults |||

This table reports Average Quarter-Hour and Cume listening estimates by demographic group (ADULTS 18+, ADULTS 18-34, ADULTS 18-49, ADULTS 25-49, ADULTS 25-54, ADULTS 35-64). For each group, figures are shown for TOTAL AREA (AVG PERS (00), CUME PERS (00)) and METRO SURVEY AREA (AVG PERS (00), CUME PERS (00), AVG RTG, AVG SHR).

ADULTS 18+

STATION CALL LETTERS	TOTAL AREA AVG PERS (00)	TOTAL AREA CUME PERS (00)	METRO AVG PERS (00)	METRO CUME PERS (00)	METRO AVG RTG	METRO AVG SHR
*WASC	22	64	22	64	5	2.2
WCKI	7	43	7	43	.2	.7
WEAB	6	47	6	47	.1	.6
WELP	9	48	9	48	.2	.8
WESC FM	53	461	39	277	3.6	9.9
WESC FM	317	1394	153	693	15.1	15.1
TOTAL	370	1720	192	871	19.0	24.4
WFBC	73	450	52	328	5.1	2.5
WFBC FM	327	1464	148	723	14.6	14.6
TOTAL	400	1761	200	948	19.7	19.7
WFIS	10	40	10	40	1	1.0
WHYZ	80	396	43	221	4.3	4.3
WKDY	14	85	14	85	1.4	1.4
WMRB	25	103	25	103	2.5	2.5
WMUU	13	60	13	60	1.3	1.3
WMUU FM	23	153	13	94	1.3	1.3
WORD	51	355	32	291	3.6	3.6
WQOK	36	211	36	211	3.6	3.6
WSPA	109	509	102	450	10.1	10.1
WSPA FM	168	886	97	507	9.6	9.6
WAIM FM	76	474	24	239	2.4	2.4
WANS FM	68	565	40	300	4.0	4.0
WAGI	16	122	6	55	1	1
WMIT	18	112	5	31	1	.5
WKIT	27	235	7	45	2	2
WLOS	52	328	10	76	1.0	1.0
WSSL	113	581	39	241	3.9	3.9
WBCY	39	347	5	35	1	.5
METRO TOTALS	1011	3524	1011	3524		23.5

Metro Totals by demographic

Demographic	AVG PERS (00)	CUME PERS (00)	AVG SHR
ADULTS 18+	1011	3524	23.5
ADULTS 18-34	390	1530	21.0
ADULTS 18-49	689	2443	23.8
ADULTS 25-49	527	1767	25.2
ADULTS 25-54	599	2014	25.3
ADULTS 35-64	505	1592	26.9

Footnote Symbols: (*) means audience estimates adjusted for actual broadcast schedule
ARBITRON

Exhibit 7.7
Average quarter-hour and cume listening estimates. (Courtesy The Arbitron Company.)

PLANNING REACH AND FREQUENCY SCHEDULES
IN A MARKET

At this point we again take a good look at the copy to be broadcast. Will the product be familiar to most people? Are you chiefly interested in telling one sharp story, as in a slogan, to as many customers as possible? Then you will be interested in *reach*. If you have a product or a feature of a product to be carefully explained, *frequency* may be preferable. In either case the problem of how much time and frequency is required to establish a message in a person's mind determines the proportion of reach and frequency that is best for you.

Numath 80
programming*

There are several sources of radio audience information. One of the best known and most sophisticated is Radio Advertising Representatives' (RAR) NUMATH 80. NUMATH 80 is a comprehensive group of reports that provides the user with easy to use, reliable information.

One of the NUMATH 80 reports is the Comparative Demo Profile Report (Table 7.6, on page 168). This report presents the penetration of any user specified age demo within the Arbitron framework, separately for male, female and total listeners, as well as male/female distribution. The penetration base may be 12 + or 18 +, at the user's option.

The report may be requested for the top 5, 10, 15 or 20 stations in respect to the user specified age demo. Alternately, the user may select specific stations, irrespective of rank.

Both quarter-hour and cume data are included. MSA, ADI and TSA areas are available. The report may be based on individual surveys or averages of two to four surveys.

Reports are available for the four "standard" dayparts for Monday-Friday, Saturday and Sunday as well as for Monday-Friday AM Drive + PM Drive, Monday-Friday 6AM-7PM, Monday-Friday 6AM-Midnite, Monday-Friday 6AM-3PM, Monday-Friday Combined Drive + Weekend, Monday-Friday 3PM-Midnite Weekend-Only and Total Week (Monday-Sunday 6AM-Midnite).

INTERMEDIA SCHEDULING IN A
MARKET

One important question in scheduling a campaign in a market is whether the advertising can get better results by using a combination of media rather than just one. If a combination is used, what media and what proportion will give the best results per dollar? In response to this question the Radio Advertising Bureau has done considerable research on the use of radio network and radio spots in conjunction with TV network and TV spots and/or newspapers,

*Courtesy Radio Advertising Representatives, Inc.

Table 7–6

NUMATH 80 COMPARATIVE DEMO PROFILE REPORT
A SERVICE OF RADIO ADVERTISING REPRESENTATIVES

MARKET: SAN FRANCISCO RATING SERVICE: ARBITRON 1525–02–001
DEMO: 25–54 STATIONS: TOP 10 11/23/81
REPORT DATES: SPRING 81, WINTER 81, AVERAGE
AREA: MSA DAYPART: M-F AM DRIVE + PM DRIVE

| | —Penetration: Base = 12 +— | | | —26–54 Distribution— | | |
	Male %	Female %	Total %	Male %	Female %	Total %
Quarter Hour Report						
KAPL-F	*	52.1	50.4	*	60.3	100.0
KPLX	61.3	*	59.2	54.4	*	100.0
KCBS-A	53.1	44.3	48.9	58.8	41.2	100.0
KFRC	42.6	37.8	39.7	43.3	56.7	100.0
K60	49.9	40.8	44.9	49.4	50.6	100.0
KIOI	68.6	63.9	66.7	49.4	50.6	100.0
KLOK	*	68.7	*	*	69.3	*
KMEL	36.2	*	*	65.8	*	*
KNBR	76.1	67.0	72.0	55.6	44.4	100.0
KNEW	69.1	54.7	62.5	58.5	41.5	100.0
KSFO	61.3	64.1	62.8	47.6	52.4	100.0
KYUU	73.3	57.8	64.9	49.0	51.0	100.0
PUR	54.1	49.7	51.8	50.2	49.8	100.0
Cume Report						
KABL-A	*	45.3	*	*	63.3	*
KABL-F	*	52.3	54.5	*	57.0	100.0
KCBS-A	56.3	48.6	52.9	59.1	40.9	100.0
KFRC	43.1	41.0	41.8	42.4	57.6	100.0
KGO	53.9	44.3	48.8	52.0	48.0	100.0
KIDI	62.2	57.6	59.7	45.7	54.3	100.0
KMEL	37.1	*	*	66.4	*	*
KNBR	66.5	60.6	63.8	55.4	44.6	100.0
KNEW	68.5	57.1	62.7	53.2	46.8	100.0
KSAN	61.9	*	61.7	58.8	*	100.0
KSFD	56.3	57.6	56.9	53.2	46.8	100.0
KYUU	65.0	55.9	59.7	46.0	54.0	100.0
PUR	51.4	48.9	50.1	49.5	50.5	100.0

(*Does not meet RAMP criterion)

in different combinations. More than that, it studied different classifications of buyers because the formula that worked for one group would not necessarily work for other groups. This is the Arms II study, Arms being an acronym for All-Radio Marketing Study. The research was conducted equally in New York and Los Angeles, with a total of 10,000 respondents.

The scope and complexity of this thoroughly computerized study are considerable. The project has generated 145 million bits of information that have been stored on fifty-six reels of computer tape prepared from over 570,000 IBM punch cards. It now can make available over 4,000 tables of information to supply advertisers with information they need to pick the best

HOW 3 MEDIA STRATEGIES COMPARE IN TOTAL IMPRESSIONS DELIVERED AS WELL AS REACH AND FREQUENCY

STRATEGY 1	STRATEGY 2	STRATEGY 3
ALL TV BUY COMBINING NETWORK AND SPOT TV	NET TV REMAINS SAME: 50% OF SPOT BUDGET IN TV, 50% RADIO	NET TV REMAINS SAME: 100% OF SPOT BUDGET TO RADIO

Target audience measured: Men who purchased new car in past 4 model years
Equal weekly budget for all strategies

3,304,000 impressions

Reach **72.8%** Frequency **2.5**

5,324,000 impressions

Reach **84.2%** Frequency **3.5**

6,221,000 impressions

Reach **85.4%** Frequency **4.0**

HOW 3 MEDIA STRATEGIES COMPARE IN DELIVERING NEW CAR BUYERS WHO ARE LIGHT, MEDIUM AND HEAVY TELEVISION VIEWERS

NEW CAR BUYERS REACHED WHO ARE:	REACH	FREQUENCY	IMPRESSIONS	% IMPRESSIONS GAINED WITH RADIO
● **LIGHT**-VIEWERS OF TELEVISION				
Strategy 1—Network Tv & Spot Tv	51.9%	1.5 times	476,000	**+221%**
Strategy 3—Network Tv & Spot Radio	77.9	3.3 times	1,526,000	
● **MEDIUM**-VIEWERS OF TELEVISION				
Strategy 1—Network Tv & Spot Tv	76.9%	2.3 times	1,110,000	**+101%**
Strategy 3—Network Tv & Spot Radio	86.9	4.1 times	2,228,000	
● **HEAVY**-VIEWERS OF TELEVISION				
Strategy 1—Network Tv & Spot Tv	89.2%	3.2 times	1,718,000	**+ 44%**
Strategy 3—Network Tv & Spot Radio	91.4	4.5 times	2,467,000	

DETAILS OF 3 MEDIA STRATEGIES AND CUSTOM TAB COSTS

In each strategy the network Tv schedule was 9 participations in prime and late night. A $22,600 weekly spot budget was used in the New York ADI. Strategy 1 is spot Tv in early and late fringe and was an actual buy by an automotive advertiser. In Strategy 2, $11,300 of original spot budget remains in Tv, $11,300 goes into morning and afternoon drive Radio. In Strategy 3, Radio gets total $22,600 spot budget. In Tv 30's are used, in Radio 60's. Further details available from Radio Advertising Bureau Research Department. Cost of reach/frequency analysis only (top half of page): $35. Cost of full analysis including light, medium and heavy viewers breakdown (entire page): $100.

Exhibit 7.8
Comparison of intermedia strategies (cont. p. 170). (Courtesy of Radio Advertising Bureau.)

combination of media for their purposes. They do not have to work on hunches or precedent. The pages reproduced here (Exhibit 7.8) are samples of the type of information gathered.

HOW 4 MEDIA STRATEGIES COMPARE IN TARGETING WOMEN 25-49

The analysis below is from ARMS II for the Los Angeles ADI. The first table shows varying combinations of Reach and Frequency achievable on a $13,300 weekly budget. The second shows how frequency distributes and how ability to achieve more frequent repetition of the advertiser's message improves with changes in media strategy.

Strategy	Net Reach	Average Frequency	Total Impressions
All TV	45.9%	2.1 Times	1,531,000
2/3 TV, 1/3 Radio	62.1%	2.5 Times	2,412,000
1/3 TV, 2/3 Radio	60.0%	3.1 Times	2,925,000
All Radio	48.3%	4.4 Times	3,336,000

HOW REACH DISTRIBUTES AMONG WOMEN 25-49 BY FREQUENCY

Strategy	1 or More Times	2 or More Times	3 or More Times	4 or More Times	5 or More Times
All TV	45.9%	24.4%	14.9%	7.0%	3.8%
2/3 TV, 1/3 Radio	62.1%	38.4%	24.2%	14.7%	3.5%
1/3 TV, 2/3 Radio	60.0%	40.1%	27.0%	17.6%	12.8%
All Radio	48.3%	35.8%	27.1%	20.9%	16.6%

HOW 3 MEDIA STRATEGIES COMPARE IN TARGETING MEN 18+

The analysis below is based on a computer run of ARMS II data for the New York ADI. A weekly budget of $10,000 was available to reach the target audience.

Strategy	Net Reach	Average Frequency	Total Impressions
All TV	26.7%	1.2	1,689,000
Half Radio, Half TV	41.0%	2.0	4,478,000
All Radio	49.2%	2.4	6,464,000

Note: Frequency distributions are also available for all above cross-tabs where only Reach and Frequency are shown.

ALTERNATIVE WAYS TO REACH PRESTIGE STORE SHOPPERS

What happens if a newspaper advertiser puts half his weekly budget into Radio? Tabulation of New York ADI ARMS II data, given a weekly budget of $7,500 and a target audience of prestige department store shoppers, shows Reach, Frequency and total impressions.

REACH/FREQUENCY/TOTAL IMPRESSIONS (PRESTIGE STORE SHOPPERS)

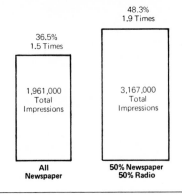

36.5%
1.5 Times

1,961,000
Total
Impressions

All Newspaper

48.3%
1.9 Times

3,167,000
Total
Impressions

50% Newspaper 50% Radio

HOW 4 MEDIA STRATEGIES COMPARE IN TARGETING TEENAGE GIRLS

Here is an analysis of ARMS II data for the Los Angeles ADI. A weekly budget of $6,600 was available to reach girls 12-17.

Strategy	Net Reach	Average Frequency	Total Impressions
All TV	27.7%	1.3	193,000
2/3 TV, 1/3 Radio	46.8%	1.8	464,000
1/3 TV, 2/3 Radio	50.3%	2.6	715,000
All Radio	50.6%	3.6	986,000

For information on other available customer and demographic audience cross-tabulations, contact RAB Research Department or ARMS II subscribing radio stations.

Exhibit 7.8
(cont.)

TRENDS IN RADIO ADVERTISING

Radio will continue to emphasize audience selectivity. Formats will demonstrate added diversity at the local level. We will also see more network-distributed and syndicated programming to supplement the all-music format of most stations. Along with more format options will come greater research sophistication to identify these audience segments and their preferred stations. Greater competition for the radio advertising will lead to a larger investment in audience measurement, particularly out-of-home ratings.

On the technical side AM is working hard on a new technical system, to overcome the FM stereophonic superiority. FM is developing a quadraphonic system to strengthen its claim to the finest tone on the air. A second generation brought up on FM tone will soon be coming along, strengthening the position of FM in the future.

SUMMARY

Radio is in some ways what TV is becoming. That is, it is a medium designed for the individual with a number of formats and many stations to choose from, particularly in larger markets. Through satellite transmission we are starting to see the resurgence of radio networks linking stations with a wide diversity of programming and permitting small market stations to have very sophisticated programming.

Perhaps the most impressive thing about radio is its penetration. There are almost six radios per household, with a third of these out of home. The mobility of the medium gives it a great advantage in reaching a mobile audience while they are in the marketplace.

For the foreseeable future FM radio will continue to grow at a phenomenal rate. The audience for FM will probably pass that of AM by 1985. Advertisers will find even more sophisticated means of identifying and reaching the diverse audience of radio. In many respects radio is the prototype medium of the segmented society of the 1980s.

QUESTIONS

1. What are the major advantages of radio for the national advertiser? Its limitations?
2. Discuss the broad appeal and penetration of radio.
3. What is FM's future as an advertising medium?
4. How have radio networks changed over the last 5 years?
5. Name and briefly describe the major radio rating services.
6. Discuss the major considerations involved in buying radio network time and radio spot time.
7. What types of products and services does radio best serve as an advertising medium?
8. Compare and contrast radio with TV in terms of potential effectiveness for an advertiser.
9. How important is radio's basic inability to create visual impact in advertising messages?
10. What do you see as the future of radio, both as an entertainment and as an advertising medium?

11. One important question in scheduling a campaign in a market is whether the advertising can get better results by using a combination of media rather than by using just one. Explain fully.

12. Describe the following:
    a. spot advertising
    b. TSA
    c. AM, FM
    d. nonwired networks
    e. dayparts
    f. preemptible versus nonpreemptible time
    g. ROS
    h. drive time
    i. cume
    j. reach

SUGGESTED EXERCISES

13. List the stations you can receive in your market. How many are local? How many from further than 25 miles? How many distinct formats can you identify?

14. Using Exhibit 7.7, find the top station in terms of average rating for adults 18 to 34, 25 to 54, and 35-64.

15. Using Figure 7.4, keep a rating diary for 2 days.

READINGS

"ARMS II: Will It Lift Radio in the Media Mix?" *Media Decisions,* June 1976, p. 60 *ff.*

"Black Radio Market Study," *Television/Radio Age,* February 23, 1981, A-1.

GARDNER, FRED: "The Revival of Network Radio," *Marketing & Media Decisions,* November 1981, pp. 191–206.

Radio Corporation of America, *The First 25 Years of RCA.* (New York: Radio Corporation of America, 1944).

"Radio: State of the Art 1981," *Broadcasting,* August 17, 1981, pp. 39–87.

8

Using
Newspapers

Think of the United States not as one big market but as 1,600 individual markets. The focal point of each market is a city or town where one or more newspapers are published. At the editorial desk of each paper sits someone who has lived in that community for many years, someone who was probably born in that region and who knows the people, their ethnic background, where they live, how they live, how they make a living, and what kind of news interests them most. No wonder 70 percent of the population over the age of 18 reads a newspaper daily. The average newspaper is read by slightly under two people.* More advertising money is spent in newspapers than in any other medium.

Newspaper readership goes up with educational level and income. Among individuals with incomes of over $25,000, 84 percent read a newspaper daily while 79 percent of college graduates report daily newspaper readership.†

People go through a newspaper in a news-seeking frame of mind—a good environment for any advertisement.

In the United States there are over 1,760 daily newspapers, of which about 1,400 are evening papers, 350 morning papers, and 20 all-day, or continuous-edition, papers. There are also

---

*Unless otherwise stated, the source of statistical data in this chapter is the Newspaper Advertising Bureau.

†Simmons Market Research Bureau, *1979 Study of Media & Markets.*

slightly more than 700 Sunday newspapers. These are in addition to weekly papers, which we consider separately.

THE CHANGING
NEWSPAPER

The newspaper of the 1980s is a different medium from that of its predecessors of the last 250 years. The newspaper of today must adapt to two major types of pressure: changes in society and changes in the competitive situation with other media.

Changes in
society

Americans of the 1980s are better educated, more affluent, and older than any past generations were. They marry later, are more likely to be childless, and are less tied to either the geography or mores of their parents. Over half of all women work, and the occupational alternatives for women and minorities have never been greater.

These changes have created a population more concerned about *self* and less about the society as a whole. Newspapers are adapting to these new readers with innovative content, "self-help" features, and an approach to the news that is more relevant to the individual. Newspapers are also improving their graphics and engaging in sophisticated readership surveys to find out what the public wants.

Changes in the competitive
situation

Daily newspapers face more competition for readers and advertisers than ever before. The growing suburban press, regional magazine editions, additional radio stations, and cable TV are all competing for the reader's or listener's time and the advertiser's money.

Successful newspaper publishers have met these challenges with a basic marketing strategy. They have identified their audiences' needs and gone about the task of providing a product to meet these needs. The Saturday newspaper has become a feature and entertainment vehicle; publishers have expanded marketing and informational services to advertisers; and many newspapers have been redesigned and more tightly edited to reflect shorter newspaper reading time.

A major innovation in the last decade or so is the mininewspaper. These newspapers, also called *zoned editions,* are delivered to different sections of a metropolitan market as part of the "mother" paper (Exhibit 8.1). They are usually published weekly, but in a few major markets twice-weekly editions are used. These mininewspapers provide several advantages to the metropolitan daily:

1. Readers want more local news of their neighborhood and suburb, and this is a way to do it without cluttering up the big paper.

Exhibit 8.1
Ad for a zoned edition, showing how metropolitan newspapers reach into the suburbs.

2. As advertising gets more expensive in the downtown paper, minipapers are a way to serve smaller advertisers and increase revenue.

3. Minipapers can be a circulation tool to increase penetration—or at least maintain current levels.

4. They can provide effective competition against weeklies and shoppers.*

---

*The Changing Newspaper, Report of the Changing Newspaper Committee New York: Associated Press Managing Editors Association, 1980, p. 17.

Despite the challenges faced by newspapers, the overall industry is extremely healthy. Newspaper advertising revenues are over $15 billion and make up almost 30 percent of all advertising sold. By combining traditional strengths with new marketing techniques and technology the future of the newspaper looks bright indeed.

CATEGORIES OF NEWSPAPER ADVERTISING

The two major categories of newspaper advertising are classified advertising and display advertising. We'll discuss them in turn.

Classified advertising

Classified advertising constitutes a major part of a newspaper publisher's income. Classified advertising accounts for approximately 30 percent ($5 billion) of all newspaper revenue. The three major categories of classified are employment, real estate, and automotive. Altogether these three categories account for 75 percent of all classified advertising. In addition there are classified advertisements for lost and found, legal notices, pets, and a number of other categories. Each category has a column heading describing its special offering; all are set in uniform type without illustrations. These are the classic examples of classified advertising.

Newspapers also carry advertisements in the classified section with illustrations. These are known as classified display and are normally run in the automotive and real-estate sections. All come under the heading of classified advertising, which has its own rate card and is usually a department in itself.

Display advertising

All newspaper advertising except classified falls into two classes: *local,* or *retail,* and *national,* or *general.*

Local (retail) advertising. This refers to all the advertising placed by local businesses, organizations, or persons. Chief among them are the department stores and supermarkets; but the local category includes other local stores and service operations—banks, beauty shops, travel agencies, morticians. Strictly speaking, retail advertising is only one form of local advertising, but the terms are frequently interchanged. Local is more inclusive.

It is the local-advertising offerings, prices, and coupons that shoppers scan before going to the supermarket or the department store; and the nearer their decision to buy, the more carefully they search the local ads.

Local advertising represents 85 percent of all newspaper advertising. Classified advertising is usually included as part of the local-advertising figure when media comparisons are made.

National (general) advertising. National newspaper advertising refers to the advertising done by any marketer who seeks to send readers to ask for a branded product or identified service at any store, showroom, or agency office dealing in such products or services.

National newspaper advertising serves three primary purposes:

1. It builds and maintains a demand for branded goods and services that can be obtained from outlets throughout the country.
2. It demonstrates that national advertisers are complementing local retailers' promotional efforts and thus can help increase distribution and local retailer support.
3. National newspaper advertising supplements other national media by pinpointing advertising in high potential markets.

Regardless of the purpose, the spirit of all newspaper ads, local or national, is news. The ad may combine these announcements with cents-off coupon promotions, usually for a short time, to get quick action in a market. Often coupons are offered in response to a competitor's sales drive. Such promotional drives are often inherent parts of a widespread marketing plan.

Occasionally the term "general" (instead of "national") is used on some newspaper rate cards. National newspaper advertising represents 15 percent of all newspaper advertising.

Local rates versus national rates. A different set of rates prevails for local advertising and for national advertising; each has its own rate card. (Only a handful of newspapers do not follow this practice.) Since retail advertisers have traditionally been the steadiest and largest newspaper advertisers and since their advertising is placed directly, without agency commission or the need for special representatives in the major advertising centers, they are charged less than national advertisers. In fact, in the largest cities, national rates are as much as 60 percent higher than local ones. (This difference has nurtured cooperative advertising, which we discuss in Chapter 12.)

In 1979 the Newspaper Advertising Bureau (NAB) initiated Newsplan. The program was designed to increase national newspaper advertising by encouraging individual newspapers to offer discounts to national advertisers. While Newsplan does not solve the problem of the local-national rate differentiation, it lessens the gap among heavy national advertisers and their local counterparts.

FEATURES AND ADVANTAGES

Newspapers are a basic local medium, with all the advantages of local media for the national advertiser: freedom to advertise to a widespread audience when and where desired and the ability to conduct a national campaign, adapting the headline to each city market or running test ads in a number of markets. Reading newspapers is a daily ritual in most homes and on commuter trains. Family shoppers carefully read supermarket ads for prices, cents-off coupons, and offerings. They study department-store ads not only for planned purchases but to keep abreast of fashion and lifestyle trends. While reading world and local news, financial pages, and sports and entertainment sections, newspaper readers may stay to look at ads for cars, household and sports equipment, family purchases, and clothing. That all these can be illustrated and described in detail is one of the great advantages of newspapers. Even full-page, beautiful color reproductions can be carried.

A national advertiser can get his ad in a newspaper quickly—overnight if necessary—an advantage much prized by advertisers who sometimes have to act very fast to get a special announcement in the paper.

Free-standing (loose) inserts, which we discuss later, have become increasingly important to local advertisers, national advertisers announcing news and promotions, and direct-response advertisers.

LIMITATIONS AND CHALLENGES

Although much of the population reads a daily newspaper, the average time so spent is fairly small—an important deficiency of the medium as an advertising vehicle. A late-1970s study indicated that average readership time is declining among all age groups, with young adults spending the least time with their newspaper (Table 8.1).

With an average reading time of 15 minutes, creating an ad that can compete for attention with news headlines and other ads can be a challenge!

Buying newspaper space can be very difficult for national advertisers. The different page formats, rates, and discounts make buying newspaper advertising on a national basis a cumbersome task. Newspapers, national advertisers, and advertising agencies envision a single order for all newspapers in the near future. Under such a plan the advertiser or agency would submit an insertion order to a national clearinghouse, pay one bill, and be able to buy space in a number of newspapers simultaneously.

Table 8–1

AVERAGE 1965–1975 DIFFERENCES IN PRIMARY-ACTIVITY TIME SPENT READING PAPERS (URBAN-EMPLOYED SAMPLES)[a]			
	1965–1966 (SAMPLE = 1,244),	1975–1976 (SAMPLE = 786),	
Age Group	Minutes	Minutes	Decline in Time, %
18–24	9	6	33.3
25–34	17	10	41.2
35–44	22	16	27.3
45–54	28	16	42.9
55–65	34	22	35.3
Average total	22	15	31.8

[a]John P. Robinson, "Daily News Habits of the American Public," *ANPA News Research Report, 15,* September 22, 1978, p. 6. Courtesy American Newspaper Publishers Association.

HOW NEWSPAPER SPACE IS BOUGHT

Measuring

space

The width of newspaper space is measured in terms of *columns.* The depth from top to bottom is measured in agate lines per column, referred to just as *lines,* of which there are fourteen to the inch. Newspapers come in a variety of sizes and formats. However, the full-size newspaper is approximately 21½ inches long and 13½ inches wide and is divided into eight columns. A full page would be about 2,400 lines in the typical newspaper. In recent years many newspapers have changed from the standard eight-column page width to either a nine- or six-column page (Exhibit 8.2).

The size of an ad is specified in terms of lines time columns. An ad 5 inches deep by two columns wide is written "70 × 2" and is a 140-line ad. The width of the column varies from paper to paper but has no bearing on the line rate of display advertising. (Want ads, however, are sold per line or per word of copy.) Nor does the number of lines of type in a display ad have anything to do with the measurement of space in terms of lines. Rates are usually quoted by the line. (In small-town papers of low circulation, space may be sold by the column inch.) Just remember: fourteen lines to the column inch.

Exhibit 8.2
Basic newspaper formats.

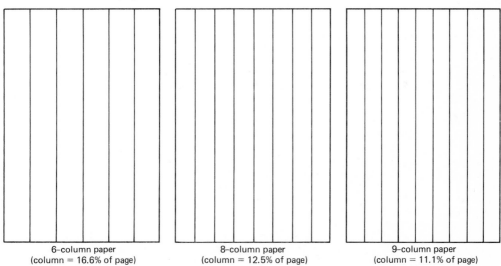

6–column paper	8–column paper	9–column paper
(column = 16.6% of page)	(column = 12.5% of page)	(column = 11.1% of page)

Newspaper space

restrictions

Most newspapers require an ad to be at least fourteen lines deep for every column width. They set a break point in column depth, beyond which the advertiser must pay for the full column depth even though the ad may not use all of it. Each paper sets its own break point, usually about 270 lines on a

300-line page. If you run 280 lines, you are charged for a full column (300 lines). On a 200-line tabloid page you are charged the amount of a full column for any ad over 175 lines. Newspapers insist on this provision because they would have a hard job selling a small fringe of unused space.

Between 1973 and 1975 the whole newspaper world was shaken by a 50-percent increase in paper costs—and they have continued going up. Among the steps many papers have taken to meet costs is the change in width of their columns, for instance, putting nine advertising columns on a page that formerly had eight columns. The smaller columns cost as much as the larger ones did. Although column width has never been standard, recent reductions have resulted in so much disparity that the American Newspaper Publishers Association has proposed a Standard Advertising Unit (SAU) System. The system makes it possible for individual national advertisers to use any of twenty-four advertising sizes that can be accepted by any full-size newspaper regardless of its format. Within these standard units sixteen can also be used by tabloid newspapers. See Exhibit 8.3.

To have an ad dominate a page without having to pay for a full-page ad, advertisers will often run an ad to its break point. Instead of taking all nine columns on a page, they will take only eight columns on a nine-column page, saving the cost of the space they haven't bought but nevertheless dominating the page. For example:

$$300 \text{ lines} \times 9 \text{ columns} = 2,700 \text{ lines}$$
$$270 \text{ lines} \times 8 \text{ columns} = 2,360 \text{ lines}$$
$$\text{Saving} = 340 \text{ lines}$$

On a large schedule, in large markets, that may mean a lot of money.

The rate structure

Publishers set their own rates. Many papers offer a uniform *flat rate* to all national advertisers. However, as mentioned earlier, Newsplan has encouraged approximately half of American newspapers to offer a *quantity* discount or an alternative *time* or *frequency* discount. The advertiser elects whichever discount structure is best for him.

The highest rate, against which all discounts are figured, is called the *open* rate, or *basic* rate, or *one-time* rate, as shown in the examples in Table 8.2 on page 182.

ROP and preferred-position rates. The basic rates quoted by a newspaper entitle the ad to a *run-of-paper* (abbreviated ROP) *position* anywhere in the paper that the publisher places it although the paper will be mindful of the advertiser's request and interest in getting a good position. An advertiser may buy a choice position by paying a higher, *preferred-position rate*—similar to paying for a box seat in the stadium instead of general admission. A cigar advertiser, for example, may elect to pay a preferred-position rate to be sure of getting on the sports page. A cosmetic advertiser may buy preferred position on the women's page. There are also preferred positions on the page itself. An

NEWSPAPER STANDARD AD UNITS

| No. 15 | No. 11 | No. 9 | No. 4 | No. 1 |

← 13" →

| | | | No. 5 | No. 2 |

| | | | No. 6 | |

| No. 16 | No. 12 | | No. 7 | |

| No. 17 | No. 13 | No. 10 | | No. 3 |

| No. 21 | 21A | No. 18 | | No. 8 |

| No. 22 | 22A | No. 19 | No. 14 | |

| No. 23 | 23A | No. 20 | | |

| No. 24 | 24A | | | |

| No. 25 | 25A | | | |

21"

NOTE:
Unit No. 7 is a tabloid full page.
Units marked (∗) fit tabloid formats,
as well as broadsheets.
Units marked (•) are 1-column ads in
6-column broadsheet formats.

Each number describes a standard ad unit, covering the
area below and to the left of the number. Refer to the
table on the adjoining page.

ANPA RESEARCH INSTITUTE

Exhibit 8.3
Newspaper SAU. (Courtesy of the American Newspaper Publishers Association.)

Table 8–2

DISCOUNTS	
QUANTITY, $	TIME, $
Open rate 0.78	Open rate 0.78
2,500 lines within 1 year 0.74	13 times within 1 year 0.74
5,000 lines within 1 year 0.68	26 times within 1 year 0.68
10,000 lines within 1 year 0.62	52 times within 1 year 0.58
20,000 lines within 1 year 0.56	156 times within 1 year 0.56

advertiser may pay for the top of a column or the top of a column next to news reading matter (called *full position*). Each paper specifies its preferred-position rates; there is no consistency in this practice. (A familiar position specification for which you do not have to pay extra is "Above fold urgently requested.")

Combination rates. In a number of cities the same publisher issues a morning paper and a separate evening paper, in which you can buy space individually or at a better combination price for both. The same space and copy must be used in both papers. In some instances, however, the papers are sold on a *forced combination basis.* Such publishers usually require the ads to be run the same day, but you may be able to get them to run the ads a few days apart to get the advantage of a wider time spread.

The rate card

A publisher's rate card contains more than rates; on it is all the information that an advertiser needs to place an order (including copy requirements and mechanical requirements), set in a standardized, numbered sequence (Exhibit 8.4). Most advertising offices subscribe to the Standard Rate & Data Service, which publishes in full all the rate-card information in monthly volumes, kept up to date by monthly supplements (Exhibit 8.5).

The changing milline rate

For over a half century the standard means of comparing the cost of newspaper space has been a measure called the *milline* rate. The milline rate is a hypothetical figure that measures what it would cost per line to reach a million circulation of a paper, based on its actual line rate and circulation. The formula is

$$\text{Milline} = \frac{1,000,000 \times \text{rate per line}}{\text{circulation}}$$

In recent years the milline rate is being replaced by the CPM calculation as a means of comparing newspaper rates. The change has been brought about primarily because of the introduction of six- and nine-column newspapers.

Exhibit 8.4
Anatomy of a rate card. This is a model rate card, widely used by newspapers and based on the recommendation of the American Association of Advertising Agencies. The chief feature of the card is that all information is given in standardized numbers and is listed in standardized sequence. All newspapers follow the same numbering system and sequence of information. If they have no information under some classification, they skip the number but do not change the numbering of the rest of the card. (Card continues on next page.)

Published Morning, Evening, Sunday
Publication Address
Telephone Number

NAME OF NEWSPAPER

Rate Card Number
Issue Date
Effective Date

1—PERSONNEL

a. Name of publisher.
b. Names of advertising executives.
c. Name of production supervisor.

2—REPRESENTATIVES

a. Names, addresses, and telephone numbers of advertising representatives.

3—COMMISSION AND CASH DISCOUNT

a. Agency commission.
b. Cash discount.
c. Discount date.

4—GENERAL

a. Policy on rate protection and rate revision notice.
b. Regulations covering acceptance of advertising.
c. Policy regarding advertising which simulates editorial content.

5—GENERAL ADVERTISING RATES

a. Black and white rates for standard space units. Bulk and/or frequency discounts.
b. Starting date if sold in combination.

6—COLOR — ROP

a. Color availability — days of week and number of colors available.
b. Minimum size for ROP Color advertisements.
c. Rates for standard units — 1 page, 1500 lines, 1000 lines — with black and white costs as base for comparison.
d. Rates for non-standard units—black and white line rate plus applicable flat or % premium.
e. Closing dates for reservations and printing material.
f. Cancellation dates.
g. Leeway on insertion dates, if required.

h. Number of progressive proofs required.
i. Registration marks on plates and mats.
j. Full page size for direct casting, in inches.
k. Number of mats required for direct casting.
l. Running head and date line for direct casting, if required.
m. Bulk or frequency discounts on color.

7—MAGAZINE SECTIONS
(Name of Section and when issued)

a. Rates for letterpress — black and white, color.
b. Rates for rotogravure — monotone, color.
c. Minimum depth and mechanical requirements.
d. Closing and cancellation dates.

8—COMIC SECTIONS (When issued)
a. Rates for color units.
b. Minimum depth and mechanical requirements.
c. Closing and cancellation dates.

9—CLASSIFICATIONS
a. Rates for special classifications
 (amusements, financial, political, etc.,
 and special pages.)

10—SPLIT RUN
a. Availabilities and rates.

11—POSITION CHARGES
a. Availabilities and rates.

12—DAILY COMIC PAGES
a. Rates.
b. Minimum requirements.
c. Regulations covering acceptance of
 advertising.
d. Closing and cancellation dates.

13—CLASSIFIED
a. Rate per word, line or inch; number of words
 per line.
b. Minimum requirements.

14—READING NOTICES
a. Available pages.
b. Rates and requirements.

15—CONTRACT AND COPY REGULATIONS
a. Regulations not stated elsewhere in **rate card.**

16—CLOSING AND CANCELLATION DATES
(Black and White)

17—MINIMUM DEPTH ROP

18—MECHANICAL MEASUREMENTS
a. Type page size before processing —
 inches wide by inches deep.
b. Depth of column in lines.
c. Number of columns to page.
d. Number of lines charged to column and to page.
e. Number of lines charged to double-truck and
 size in inches.
f. Requirements as to mats, originals and
 electros.

g. Screen required.
h. Address for printing material.
i. Other mechanical information.

19—CIRCULATION INFORMATION
a. Circulation verification (details in Publisher's
 Statement and Audit Report).
b. If unaudited, basis for circulation claim.
c. Milline rates, if desired. Daily .... ,
 Sunday ....

20—MISCELLANEOUS
a. Year established.
b. Subscription price; single copy price.
c. News services, e.g. AP, UP.
d. Other information not listed elsewhere.

(Standard Form Rate Card recommended by the American Association of Advertising Agencies, Inc.).

Exhibit 8.4 (*cont.*)

For example, let's assume that we wish to compare three newspapers with six, eight, and nine columns each with a line rate of $2.00 and a circulation of 2 million. By the standard milline rate it would appear that the advertiser will get equal value per dollar in each paper (that is, milline = $1.00).

Since this calculation is obviously incorrect, we must adjust for the different formats. The simplest adjustment is to use the full-page cost instead of the rate per line in computing the milline rate.

We could then compute the comparative figures for the three formats as shown in Table 8.3, assuming each paper is 21 inches in depth.

The milline rate does not allow direct comparison with other media that use the CPM comparison. Because of this disadvantage and the multiformat

Exhibit 8.5
Part of a page of newspaper rates. (Courtesy of Standard Rate & Data Service, Inc.)

NASHUA

Hillsborough County—Map Location F-8
See SRDS consumer market map and data at beginning of the State.

TELEGRAPH

60 Main St., Nashua, N. H. 03060.
Phone 603-882-2741.

band BOSTON AREA NEWSPAPER DAILIES

Media Code 1 130 8910 6.00

EVENING (except Sunday).
(Not published Jan. 1, Washington's Birthday, 4th Monday in April, Memorial Day, July 4, Labor Day, Thanksgiving or Christmas.)
Member: Newspaper Advertising Bureau, Inc.

1. PERSONNEL Publisher—J. Herman Pouliot.
Assistant Gen. Mgr.—William Bean.
Advertising Mgr.—Walter D. McLaughlin.

2. REPRESENTATIVES and/or BRANCH OFFICES
Landon Associates, Inc.

3. COMMISSION AND CASH DISCOUNT
15% to agencies; no cash discount.

4. POLICY—ALL CLASSIFICATIONS
30-day notice given of any rate revision.
Alcoholic beverage advertising accepted.

ADVERTISING RATES
Effective January 1, 1980.
Received November 1, 1979.

5. BLACK/WHITE RATES

	Open per line	1 page	1,500 lines	1,000 lines
	.33	893.97	495.00	330.00

NEWSPLAN—Linage Equivalent.

	6 pgs.	13 pgs.	26 pgs.	52 pgs.
Eve.	.3135	.297	.2805	.264
Lines	16,254	35,217	70,434	140,868

6. GROUP COMBINATION RATES—B/W & Color
Boston Area Newspaper Dailies—see listing at beginning of the State of Massachusetts.

7. COLOR RATES AND DATA
Minimum size 1,000 lines. Non-commissionable.
Use b/w line rate plus the following applicable costs:

	b/w 1 c	b/w 2 c	b/w 3 c
Extra	180.00	265.00	325.00

Closing dates: Reservations 1 week in advance; printing material and cancellation date—3 days in advance.

11. SPECIAL DAYS/PAGES/FEATURES
Best Food Day: Wednesday.

12. ROP DEPTH REQUIREMENTS
As many inches deep as columns wide. Copy exceeding 281 lines deep charged full column.

13. CONTRACT AND COPY REGULATIONS
See Contents page for location of regulations—items 1, 2, 5, 7, 9, 10, 12, 13, 16, 18, 19, 20, 22, 24, 25, 28, 30, 31, 32, 34, 35.

15. MECHANICAL MEASUREMENTS
PRINTING PROCESS: Photo Composition Stereotype Letterpress.
For complete, detailed production information, see SRDS Print Media Production Data.
9/9/6—9 cols/ea 9 picas/6 pts betw col.
Lines to: col. 301; page 2709; dbl. truck 5117.

16. SPECIAL CLASSIFICATION/RATES
Amusements, Radio, TV, Sports: per line, flat .34.
POSITION CHARGES
Full position, extra 25%; first page, flat, per line 1.90 last page per line, flat .74.

17. CLASSIFIED RATES
For complete data refer to classified rate section.

20. CIRCULATION
Established 1832, per copy .15.
Net Paid—A.B.C. 9-30-79 (Newspaper Form)

	Total	CZ	TrZ	Other
Eve	26,888	21,711	4,464	713

Max-Min rate: Eve 12.27.
For county-by-county and/or metropolitan area breakdowns, see SRDS Newspaper Circulation Analysis.

NEW HAMPSHIRE

PORTSMOUTH

Rockingham County—Map Location G-7
See SRDS consumer market map and data at beginning of the State.

HERALD

band BOSTON AREA NEWSPAPER DAILIES
A Thomson Newspaper
111 Maplewood Ave., Portsmouth, N. H. 03801.
Phone 603-436-1800.

Media Code 1 130 9900 6.00

EVENING (except Sunday) & SATURDAY MORN.
(Not published Jan. 1, Washington's Birthday, Memorial Day, Independence Day, Labor Day, Veteran's Day, Thanksgiving or Christmas.)
Member: INAE; Newspaper Advertising Bureau, Inc.

1. PERSONNEL
General Manager—Azio J. Ferrini.
Advertising Manager—H. L. Clark.

2. REPRESENTATIVES and/or BRANCH OFFICES
Thomson Newspapers, Inc.

3. COMMISSION AND CASH DISCOUNT
15% to agencies 15th following month. No cash discount.

4. POLICY—ALL CLASSIFICATIONS
60-day notice given of any rate revision.
Alcoholic beverage advertising accepted.

ADVERTISING RATES
Effective January 1, 1980.
Received November 5, 1979.

5. BLACK/WHITE RATES
Flat, per line 27

6. GROUP COMBINATION RATES—B/W & Color
Also sold in combination with the Seacoast Pilot (Wed.) per line .07.
Circulation—Sworn 3-31-80: Total Non-Paid 12,100.
Boston Area Newspaper Dailies—see listing at beginning of the State of Massachusetts.

7. COLOR RATES AND DATA
Available b/w 1 or 2 c daily (except Sunday).
No minimum or leeway required.
Use b/w rate plus the following applicable cost:

	b/w 1 c	b/w 2 c
Extra	50%	100%

Closing dates: Reservations 4 days in advance, printing material—4 days in advance. Cancellation date 2 days in advance.

11. SPECIAL DAYS/PAGES/FEATURES
Best Food Day: Wednesday.
Society, Church Notices, Saturday.

12. ROP DEPTH REQUIREMENTS
As many inches deep as columns wide.

13. CONTRACT AND COPY REGULATIONS
See Contents page for location of regulations—items 1, 2, 3, 10, 11, 12, 13, 15, 19, 24, 28, 30, 31, 32, 34, 35, 39, 41, 42, 44, 45, 46.

14. CLOSING TIME
Noon, 2 days before publication for all copy regardless of size

15. MECHANICAL MEASUREMENTS
PRINTING PROCESS: Photo Composition Direct Letterpress (Merigraph).
For complete, detailed production information, see SRDS Print Media Production Data.
9/9/8—9 cols/ea 9 picas/6 pts betw col.
Lines to: col. 297; page 2673; dbl. truck 5643.

16. SPECIAL CLASSIFICATION/RATES
Political —general rate applies. Cash in advance.
POSITION CHARGES
Next to reading, extra 10%: full position or top of column, extra 15%: any specific page or top of column next to reading, extra 25%: last page, extra 50%: broken column layouts, extra 75%.

17. CLASSIFIED RATES
For complete data refer to classified rate section.

20. CIRCULATION
Established 1880. Per copy .20.
Net Paid—A.B.C. 3-31-80 (Newspaper Form)

	Total	CZ	TrZ	Other
Eve	18,311	9,559	8,385	367

Max-Min rate: Eve 14.75.
For county-by-county and/or metropolitan area breakdowns, see SRDS Newspaper Circulation Analysis.

Table 8–3

NEWSPAPER FORMAT, COLUMNS	COST/LINE, $	LINES/PAGE[a]	PAGE COST, $	MILLINE RATE/PAGE, $	CPM/PAGE, $[b]
9	2	2,646	5,294	2,647	2.65
8	2	2,352	4,704	2,352	2.35
6	2	1,764	3,528	1,764	1.76

[a]Lines per page = columns × lines per column (in this example lines per column = 21 inches × 14 lines per inch, or 294)
[b]When advertisers use the full-page cost, they usually compute the CPM rather than the milline rate.

problem, the milline rate is used less frequently than previously. In the near future the milline rate will probably be replaced by the CPM as a means of comparing newspaper costs.

The space contract; the short rate

If a paper has a flat rate, all you need do is send in an insertion order, specifying the space, date, and rate. But if the paper gives a scale of discounts depending on the amount of linage run during the next 12 months, you must first enter upon a *space contract*. Such a space contract is not a guarantee for the amount of space you will run but an agreement of the rate you will finally pay for any space that has been run during the year in question. It involves two steps: First, you estimate the amount of space you think you will run and agree to any rate adjustments needed at the end of the year, and you are then billed during the year at the selected rate; second, at the end of the year the total linage is added, and if you ran the amount of space you had estimated, no adjustment is necessary, but if you failed to run enough space to earn that rate, you have to pay at the higher rate charged for the number of lines you actually ran. That amount is called the *short* rate.

For example, a national advertiser plans to run advertising in a paper whose rates are as follows:

- ☐ Open rate, $1.45 a line
- ☐ 1,000 lines, $1.42 a line
- ☐ 5,000 lines, $1.39 a line
- ☐ 10,000 lines, $1.36 a line

The advertiser expects to run at least 5,000 lines and signs the contract at the $1.39 (5,000-line) rate (subject to end-of-year adjustment). At the end of 12 months, however, only 4,100 lines have been run; therefore the bill at the end of the contract year is as follows:

Earned rate: 4,100 lines @ $1.42 per line = $5,822
Paid rate: 4,100 lines @ $1.39 per line = 5,699

Short rate due $123

or

Lines run × difference in earned and billed rates = 4,100 lines × $1.03 = $123

If the space had reached the 10,000-line rate ($1.36), the advertiser would have received a rebate of $300. Some papers charge the full rate and allow credit for a better rate when earned.

THE AUDIT BUREAU OF CIRCULATION

(ABC)

Publishers list their rates on a standardized rate card, which includes a statement of circulation. Since advertising rates are based on circulation (see, for example, Exhibit 8.6), verification of circulation statements is at the heart of the publisher-advertiser relationship. As long ago as 1914, the industry recognized the problem by forming an independent auditing group representing and supported by the advertiser, the agency, and the publisher. The Audit Bureau of Circulation (ABC), whose members include only paid-circulation newspapers and magazines, audits the complete circulation methods and figures of each publication member. Rate cards marked "ABC" are accorded top confidence by the industry.

Over 95 percent of the daily papers and most of the significant magazines belong to the ABC. Available to all advertisers, the ABC circulation statement of a newspaper contains much other useful information, including:

☐ Net paid circulation
☐ Amount of circulation in city zone, trading zone, other
☐ Number of subscribers obtained through cut prices, contests, premiums
☐ Number of papers sold at the newsstands, sent by mail, home delivered. (Home or mail distribution is considered advantageous to advertisers because it promises leisurely reading by several members of the family.)

The ABC reports have nothing to do with the rates a paper charges. They deal with circulation statistics only. Publishers will be glad to supply demographic data of their users. The ABC, however, now has a separate division giving demographic data for many of the markets in the United States. All data are computerized and quickly available as their accompanying ad reports. The ABC also audits paid-subscription magazines, a service we'll discuss in Chapter 9.

TEAR SHEETS AND CHECKING

COPIES

When a national ad has been run in a newspaper or magazine, the publisher forwards to the agency a copy of the page bearing the ad. Torn out of the newspaper, this page is called a *tear sheet;* the magazine page is called a *checking copy.* To *check* a tear sheet is to examine the page and record on a form (Exhibit 8.7) whether the ad ran according to the instructions and standards of the agency, particularly in respect to position in paper, position on page, and reproduction quality. If the ad is satisfactory, payment is approved. If not, the advertiser may be entitled to an adjustment. Should there be a serious error, the publisher may agree to a corrected rerun of the ad, called a *make-good,* without additional cost.

Most newspapers forward their sheets through a private central office, the Advertising Checking Bureau.

TELEVISION VIEWING AREA (ADI) PRINT ANALYSIS

	Total Daily within ADI	Penetration	Morning or All Day within ADI	Penetration	Evening within ADI	Penetration	20% MAC DAILY Counties within ADI with at least 20% coverage Circulation	Penetration	Hslds (000)	Sunday within ADI	Penetration	20% MAC SUNDAY Counties within ADI with at least 20% coverage Circulation	Penetration	Hslds (000)

ABILENE-SWEETWATER ADI
POPULATION 304,000 HOUSEHOLDS 111,700 RETAIL SALES $ 1,424,000,000 AVG HSLD INC $18,787 20 COUNTIES

TEX BROWN 11.3%,CALLAHAN 3.8%,COKE 1.2%,COLEMAN 3.8%,CONCHO 1.0%,EASTLAND 7.0%,FISHER 2.0%,HASKELL 2.7%,JONES 5.7% KING 0.2%,MC CULLOCH 3.0%,MENARD 0.8%,MITCHELL 3.0%,NOLAN 4.0%,RUNNELS 4.0%,SCURRY 5.8%,SHACKELFORD 1.3%,STONEWALL 0.9% SUTTON 1.5%,TAYLOR 35.2%

Newspaper	within ADI	Pen	Morn within ADI	Pen	Even within ADI	Pen	Circ	Pen	Hslds	Sunday within ADI	Pen	Circ	Pen	Hslds
★ ABILENE REPORTER-NEWS	49,840	45%	33,909	30%	15,931	14%	47,775	57%	84	51,682	46%	49,573	59%	84
★ BROWNWOOD BULLETIN	8,497	8%			8,497	8%	7,995	63%	13	9,571	9%	8,904	71%	13
DALLAS MORNING NEWS	1,734	2%	1,734	2%						2,621	2%			
FT WORTH STAR-TELEGRAM	1,243	1%	1,227	1%	16	%				2,149	2%			
SAN ANGELO STANDARD,TIMES	6,011	5%	5,849	5%	162	%	5,272	47%	13	6,445	6%	5,768	45%	13
★□ SNYDER NEWS	N.A.													
★□ SWEETWATER REPORTER	N.A.													
TOTAL NEWSPAPERS	68,307	61%					53,677	58%	92	73,829	66%			
HH HARTE-HANKS TEXAS GROUP	56,025	50%					58,365	52%	92	55,957	61%	92	

FM WKLY	7,147	6.4%	ANR WN	59,788	53.5%	FORTN	373	3%	NEWSWK	2,443	2.2%	R DGST	31,952	28.6%	TV GUI	12,480	11.2%
PARADE	2,209	2.0%	BET HO	11,319	10.1%	GDHSK	6,748	6.0%	NWYRKR	90	1%	RED BK	7,513	6.7%	USNEWS	2,848	2.5%
SUNDAY	3,003	2.7%	COSMO	2,154	1.9%	LHJ	8,573	7.7%	PENTHS	3,396	3.0%	17	2,033	1.8%	VOGUE	765	7%
METRO C	2,729	2.4%	F CIRC	8,955	8.0%	MCCL	11,832	10.6%	PEOPLE	1,751	1.6%	SPRTIL	2,005	1.8%	WO DAY	8,629	7.7%
PUCK CW	61,583	55.1%	FARM J	3,394	3.0%	N GEO	9,493	8.5%	PLAY B	3,761	3.4%	TIME	2,005	1.8%			

ALBANY, GA. ADI
POPULATION 328,000 HOUSEHOLDS 109,100 RETAIL SALES $ 1,093,000,000 AVG HSLD INC $16,719 15 COUNTIES

GA ATKINSON 1.8%,BAKER 1.1%,BEN HILL 5.3%,BERRIEN 4.3%,COFFEE 8.3%,COLQUITT 11.4%,COOK 4.2%,DOUGHERTY 31.1%,IRWIN 2.8% LANIER 1.7%,LEE 3.5%,MITCHELL 6.0%,TIFT 10.1%,TURNER 2.8%,WORTH 5.4%

★ ALBANY HERALD	28,095	26%			28,095	26%	25,699	55%	46	30,454	28%	27,295	59%	46
ATLANTA JOURNAL,CONSTITUTION	4,282	4%	4,003	4%	279	%				7,680	7%			
JACKSONVILLE FLA TIMES-UN,JRNL	813	1%	813	1%						1,241	1%			
★ MOULTRIE OBSERVER	7,425	7%			7,425	7%	7,425	60%	12					
★□ TIFTON GAZETTE	N.A.									1,241	1%			
VALDOSTA DAILY TIMES	3,055	3%			3,055	3%	2,989	27%	11	2,970	3%	2,894	26%	11
TOTAL NEWSPAPERS	44,471	41%					25,815	56%	46	43,136	40%			
GG GEORGIA GROUP	28,659	26%								31,222	29%	27,401	59%	46
JS JACKSONVILLE/ST. AUGUSTINE GR	813	1%								1,241	1%			

FM WKLY	33,507	30.7%	ANR WN	45,493	41.7%	FORTN	298	3%	NEWSWK	1,674	1.5%	R DGST	18,651	17.1%	TV GUI	18,402	16.9%
PARADE	1,926	1.8%	BET HO	6,967	6.4%	GDHSK	4,559	4.2%	NWYRKR	83	1%	RED BK	5,561	5.1%	USNEWS	2,220	2.0%
SUNDAY	7,680	7.0%	COSMO	2,250	2.1%	LHJ	6,204	5.7%	PENTHS	2,752	2.5%	17	1,279	1.2%	VOGUE	492	5%
METRO C	8,921	8.2%	F CIRC	6,667	6.1%	MCCL	8,801	8.1%	PEOPLE	1,700	1.6%	SPRTIL	1,439	1.3%	WO DAY	7,043	6.5%
PUCK CW	768	7%	FARM J	3,738	3.4%	N GEO	5,728	5.3%	PLAY B	10,325	9.5%	TIME	1,989	1.8%			

ALBANY-SCHENECTADY-TROY ADI
POPULATION 1,276,000 HOUSEHOLDS 462,600 RETAIL SALES $ 5,494,000,000 AVG HSLD INC $21,391 14 COUNTIES

MASS BERKSHIRE 11.4%
N Y ALBANY 23.3%,COLUMBIA 4.7%,FULTON 4.4%,GREENE 3.3%,HAMILTON 0.4%,MONTGOMERY 4.3%,RENSSELAER 11.5%,SARATOGA 11.5% SCHENECTADY 12.2%,SCHOHARIE 2.1%,WARREN 4.3%,WASHINGTON 3.9%
VT BENNINGTON 2.6%

★ ALBANY TIMES-UNION,KNICK NS-US	130,172	28%	79,838	17%	50,334	11%	108,699	55%	198	142,141	31%	137,184	38%	365
★ AMSTERDAM RECORDER	14,143	3%			14,143	3%	12,565	63%	20					
★□ BENNINGTON BANNER	7,278	2%			7,278	2%	6,678	55%	12					
BOSTON GLOBE @	1,204	%	1,204	%						3,512	1%			
BOSTON HERALD AMERICAN	1,345	%	1,345	%						3,646	1%			
★ GLENS FALLS POST-STAR	30,389	7%	30,389	7%			24,958	66%	38					
★ GLOVERSVILLE LEADER-HERALD	13,443	3%			13,443	3%	12,295	60%	21					
★ HUDSON REGISTER-STAR	12,077	3%			12,077	3%	12,077	56%	22					
□ LITTLE FALLS TIMES	1,298	%			1,298	%								
NEW YORK NEWS	28,067	6%	28,067	6%						55,370	12%	7,211	21%	35
NEW YORK POST @	1,644	%			1,644	%				20,187	4%			
★ NORTH ADAMS TRANSCRIPT	11,639	3%			11,639	3%								
□ PITTSFIELD BERKSHIRE EAGLE	29,848	6%	29,848	6%			12,106	23%	53					
RUTLAND HERALD	1,164	%			1,164	%	29,387	56%	53	998	%			
★ SARATOGA SPRINGS SARATOGIAN	11,850	3%			11,850	3%	11,409	21%	53	18,260	4%	14,443	27%	53
★ SCHENECTADY GAZETTE	69,556	15%	69,556	15%			61,936	44%	139					
SPRINGFIELD UNION, NEWS	3,991	1%	3,965	1%	26	%				8,168	2%			
★ SYRACUSE HERLD-JRNL,POST-STDRD	5	%	4	%	1	%				1,057	%			
★ TROY TIMES RECORD	46,060	10%			46,060	10%	27,107	51%	53	44,893	10%	26,020	49%	53
TOTAL NEWSPAPERS	428,835	93%								299,883	65%			
AD ALBANY A.D.I. NEWSPAPER NETWO	81,902	18%					81,585	53%	153	18,260	4%	14,443	27%	53
HD HUDSON VALLEY NEWSPAPER NETWO	12,077	3%					12,077	56%	22					
RB RUTLAND,BARRE,MONTPELIER GROU	1,164	%								998	%			
SY SYRACUSE AREA NEWSPAPER NETWO	1,298	%												
WM WESTERN MASSACHUSETTS NEWSPAP	42,857	9%					41,493	79%	53					
WS WESTERN N E NEWSPAPER NETWORK	50,877	11%					49,586	76%	53					

FM WKLY	114,775	24.8%	ANR WN	78,867	17.0%	FORTN	2,649	6%	NEWSWK	19,075	4.1%	R DGST	114,982	24.9%	TV GUI	72,647	15.7%
PARADE	155,211	33.6%	BET HO	48,262	10.4%	GDHSK	37,680	8.1%	NWYRKR	3,992	9%	RED BK	25,928	5.6%	USNEWS	10,472	2.3%
SUNDAY	63,890	13.8%	COSMO	16,950	3.7%	LHJ	31,243	6.8%	PENTHS	18,836	4.1%	17	18,732	3.0%	VOGUE	4,388	9%
METRO C	112,110	24.2%	F CIRC	65,225	14.1%	MCCL	32,636	7.1%	PEOPLE	14,118	3.1%	SPRTIL	13,732	3.0%	WO DAY	70,396	15.2%
PUCK CW	147,149	31.8%	FARM J	4,306	.9%	N GEO	51,633	11.2%	PLAY B	22,819	4.9%	TIME	30,006	6.5%			

ALBUQUERQUE ADI
POPULATION 1,018,000 HOUSEHOLDS 345,900 RETAIL SALES $ 4,142,000,000 AVG HSLD INC $19,449 28 COUNTIES

ARIZ APACHE 3.8%
COLO ARCHULETA 0.4%,CONEJOS 0.7%,COSTILLA 0.3%,DOLORES 0.2%,LA PLATA 2.9%,MONTEZUMA 1.7%,RIO GRANDE 1.0%,SAGUACHE 0.4%
N M BERNALILLO 45.2%,COLFAX 1.4%,GRANT 2.5%,GUADALUPE 0.4%,HARDING 0.1%,LINCOLN 1.2%,LOS ALAMOS 1.9%,MC KINLEY 4.4% MORA 0.4%,OTERO 4.3%,RIO ARRIBA 2.7%,SANDOVAL 3.2%,SAN MIGUEL 2.2%,SANTA FE 7.9%,SIERRA 1.1%,SOCORRO 1.2%,TAOS 1.9% TORRANCE 0.8%,VALENCIA 5.8%

★□ ALAMOGORDO NEWS	N.A.													
★ ALBUQUERQUE JOURNAL,TRIBUNE	115,937	34%	75,297	22%	40,640	12%	104,319	55%	189	116,200	34%	104,719	54%	195
DENVER POST	4,692	1%			4,692	1%	4,692	50%	9	6,338	2%	267	21%	1
DENVER ROCKY MOUNTAIN NEWS	3,315	1%			3,315	1%				1,662	%			
★ DURANGO HERALD,CORTEZ HERALDLD	5,744	2%			5,744	2%	5,054	50%	10	6,994	2%	6,106	60%	10
EL PASO HERALD-POST,TIMES	3,907	1%	3,596	1%	311	%				5,137	1%			
★ GALLUP INDEPENDENT	10,500	3%			10,500	3%	8,054	53%	15					
★□ GRANTS BEACON	N.A.													
★□ LAS VEGAS OPTIC	N.A.													
★□ LOS ALAMOS MONITOR	4,174	1%			4,174	1%	4,174	64%	7					
PHOENIX REPUBLIC,GAZETTE	623	%	621	%	2	%				1,080	%			
PUEBLO CHIEFTAIN,STAR-JOURNAL	1,875	1%	1,875	1%			1,598	27%	6	1,823	1%	1,474	25%	6
★□ RATON RANGE	N.A.													
ROSWELL RECORD	763	%			763	%				1,038	%	1,038	24%	4
★ SANTA FE NEW MEXICAN	17,481	5%			17,481	5%	15,029	44%	34	20,924	6%	19,805	46%	43
★□ SILVER CITY PRESS&INDEPENDN-N	N.A.													
TOTAL NEWSPAPERS	170,995	49%								162,421	47%			

FM WKLY	34,968	10.1%	ANR WN	84,219	24.3%	FORTN	1,638	5%	NEWSWK	14,536	4.2%	R DGST	80,428	23.3%	TV GUI	76,580	22.1%
PARADE	122,999	35.6%	BET HO	26,656	7.7%	GDHSK	16,268	4.7%	NWYRKR	2,306	.7%	RED BK	18,462	5.3%	USNEWS	10,362	3.0%
SUNDAY	7,418	2.1%	COSMO	13,876	4.0%	LHJ	21,954	6.3%	PENTHS	15,579	4.5%	17	6,404	1.9%	VOGUE	3,204	9%
METRO C	7,418	2.1%	F CIRC	28,798	8.3%	MCCL	25,186	7.3%	PEOPLE	9,536	2.8%	SPRTIL	8,707	2.5%	WO DAY	30,846	8.9%
PUCK CW	123,137	35.6%	FARM J			N GEO	24,762	12.9%	PLAY B	17,046	4.9%	TIME	20,358	5.9%			

NOTE: ARBITRON credits 79.6% of Apache County to the Albuquerque ADI, and 20.4% to the Tucson ADI. CIRCULATION '81/'82 assigns 100% of Apache County to the Albuquerque ADI.

ALEXANDRIA, LA. ADI
POPULATION 251,000 HOUSEHOLDS 81,500 RETAIL SALES $ 737,000,000 AVG HSLD INC $18,433 4 COUNTIES

LA AVOYELLES 16.9%,GRANT 7.2%,RAPIDES 56.1%,VERNON 19.8%

★ ALEXANDRIA TOWN TALK	33,255	41%			33,255	41%	31,840	49%	65	33,692	41%	32,258	49%	65
SHREVEPORT JOURNAL,TIMES	2,783	3%	2,581	3%	202	%				2,692	3%			
TOTAL NEWSPAPERS	37,947	47%								38,474	47%			
SH SHREVEPORT MONROE NEWSPAPER M	2,783	3%								2,692	3%			

FM WKLY	34,209	42.0%	ANR WN	16,840	20.7%	FORTN	186	2%	NEWSWK	1,344	1.6%	R DGST	14,703	18.0%	TV GUI	12,531	15.4%
PARADE	3,893	4.8%	BET HO	4,761	5.8%	GDHSK	3,018	3.7%	NWYRKR	77	.1%	RED BK	3,790	4.7%	USNEWS	1,495	1.8%
SUNDAY	107	.1%	COSMO	1,405	1.7%	LHJ	4,213	5.2%	PENTHS	2,870	3.5%	17	827	1.0%	VOGUE	533	.7%
METRO C		%	F CIRC	4,663	5.7%	MCCL	5,011	6.1%	PEOPLE	1,176	1.4%	SPRTIL	1,005	1.2%	WO DAY	4,806	5.9%
PUCK CW	3,246	4.0%	FARM J	1,220	1.5%	N GEO	4,989	6.1%	PLAY B	2,606	3.2%	TIME	1,834	2.3%			

★ Published within ADI   **CIRCULATION '81/'82**   □ Non-ABC newspaper

---

Exhibit 8.6
To simplify multimedia scheduling, newspaper circulation in geographical markets is converted into ADI territories and used in schedules requiring both TV and newspapers. (Courtesy of Standard Rate & Data Service, Inc.)

Copyright 1920 American Association of Advertising Agencies   (Blank No. 4)

CHECKING RECORD

MONTH	1	2	3	4	5	6	7	8	9	10	11	12	13	14	15	16	17	18	19	20	21	22	23	24	25	26	27	28	29	30	31	TOTAL	

TO PUBLISHER OF   ORDER NO.

CITY AND STATE   DATE

PLEASE PUBLISH ADVERTISING OF (advertiser)
FOR (product)

┌──── SPACE ────┐   ┌── TIMES ──┐   ┌────── DATES OF INSERTION ──────┐

POSITION

COPY   KEY   CUTS

ADDITIONAL INSTRUCTIONS

RATE

LESS AGENCY COMMISSION   PER CENT ON GROSS   LESS CASH DISCOUNT   PER CENT ON NET

PER ------------------------------

MONTH	1	2	3	4	5	6	7	8	9	10	11	12	13	14	15	16	17	18	19	20	21	22	23	24	25	26	27	28	29	30	31	TOTAL	

NEWSPAPER MARKETING AND MERCHANDISING
SERVICES
To show what an attractive market their paper offers the national advertiser, most newspapers, especially in the larger cities, can usually provide helpful marketing and demographic data about their city and its people. Lured by the prospect of a large schedule, newspapers may also be helpful in preparing material to send out in advance to the trade. This material tells about the forthcoming schedule and can help "merchandise the advertising." (Put "merchandising" down among the numerous words that have many meanings.) The *Milwaukee Journal,* for example, has for years published an annual household inventory of consumer product usage. In addition to showing the total usage of each type of product studied, it shows the rank of different brands in each category (see Exhibit 8.8).

Frozen Potatoes

Buying within 30 Days

Percent and Number of Buyers

Year	Percent	Number
1981	40.7%	200,800
1980	40.3	197,200

Household Use of Leading Brands in Metro Milwaukee

	Percent			Number
Brand Last Purchased	1981	1980		1981
All Brands	100%	100%	....	200,800
Ore-Ida	72	75	....	144,600
Heinz	8	9	....	16,100
Carnation	5	....	....	10,000
Farmer's Choice	2	....	....	4,000
Okray's	2	5	....	4,000
Roundy's	2	....	....	4,000
Don't Know	3	2	....	6,000
Miscellaneous*	6	10	....	12,000
Total Sample	1,527	1,547	......	
Sample Base	621	624	......	

*Used by less than 2%

Snack Crackers

Buying within 30 Days

Percent and Number of Buyers

Year	Percent	Number
1981	59.9%	295,500
1980	65.4	320,000
1979	62.0	299,400

Household Use of Leading Brands in Metro Milwaukee

	Percent			Number
Brand Last Purchased	1981	1980	1979	1981
All Brands	100%	100%	100%	295,500
Nabisco Miscellaneous*	29	30	28	85,700
Nabisco Ritz	25	29	29	73,900
Keebler Miscellaneous*	10	9	12	29,600
Nabisco Triscuit	7	6	6	20,700
Keebler Town House	6	8	10	17,700
Nabisco Wheatsworth	5	4	....	14,800
Nabisco Wheat Thins	4	4	3	11,800
Sunshine Biscuit	3	....	....	8,900
Keebler Tucs	2	2	....	5,900
Ralston Rye Crisp	2	....	....	5,900
Don't Know	4	5	5	11,800
Miscellaneous*	8	9	13	23,600
Total Sample	1,527	1,547	1,529	
Sample Base	914	1,011	948	

*Used by less than 2%

Canned Shoestring Potatoes

Buying within 30 Days

Percent and Number of Buyers

Year	Percent	Number
1981	7.1%	35,000
1980	6.5	31,800

Household Use of Leading Brands in Metro Milwaukee

	Percent			Number
Brand Last Purchased	1981	1980		1981
All Brands	100%	100%	....	35,000
Pik-nik	35	41	....	12,300
Durkee/O&C	15	14	....	5,300
Roundy's	12	13	....	4,200
Kohl's	3	7	....	1,100
Butterfield	2	....	....	700
Food Club	2	3	....	700
Don't Know	27	19	....	9,500
Miscellaneous*	5	3	....	1,800
Total Sample	1,527	1,547	......	
Sample Base	108	100	......	

*Used by less than 2%

Exhibit 8.8
Milwaukee Journal consumer analysis. (Courtesy Milwaukee Journal.)

NEWSPAPER-DISTRIBUTED MAGAZINE

SUPPLEMENTS

How could we be sure it was a week end if we didn't have newspaper supplements? When we open our Sunday papers, many of us find two kinds of supplements: *syndicated* and *local*.

Syndicated supplements are published by an independent publisher and distributed to papers throughout the country with the publisher's and local paper's logotypes printed on the masthead. Best known are *Family Weekly*, with a national circulation of about 12 million sold through 350 newspapers, *Parade*, with a national circulation of about 21 million, distributed through about 130 newspapers, and *Sunday Metropolitan's Sunday Newspaper Group*, with about 22 million circulation. The various supplements differ in respect to the proportion of big cities and smaller cities in which they are distributed. The advertiser can select the combination that best fits his marketing plan.

Magazine supplements in newspapers reach a large audience that many magazines do not reach. They offer beautiful color reproductions comparable to those of magazines, and they provide a medium for distributing cents-off coupons. Another great advantage to the advertiser of a campaign in a syndicated magazine supplement is that the campaign involves only one order and the handling of only one bill for all the markets in which the ad appears.

There are also local magazine supplements printed by a newspaper or group of papers in the same locality. These supplements concentrate on the advertising of department stores and other local advertisers. Many newspapers have both a syndicated and a local magazine supplement. Of the Sunday magazine supplements published 29 million copies are syndicated, and 26.6 million are locally published.

In recent years newspapers have provided specialized supplements on days other than Sunday. For instance, *Food* and *Taste* are weekly food supplements in the *Boston Globe* and *Minneapolis Star*, while *Sportsweek* and *Action* are weekly sports "magazines" in the *Chicago Tribune* and *Louisville Times*. Advertisers find these excellent outlets to reach specific target markets within a newspaper's total readership.

NEWSPAPER COLOR

ADVERTISING

Advertisers buy color advertising in newspapers either on an ROP basis or through free-standing inserts. At one time national advertisers used preprinted color pages. The ad was printed on one side of a roll of newsprint. The roll was then shipped to the newspaper, which printed the obverse with regular editorial and advertising material. The increase in costs of this process and the popularity of free-standing inserts have largely rendered obsolete this type of color advertising.

ROP

color

In ROP the color is printed by the newspaper on its own presses as a part of the regular press run. This is referred to as *ROP color*, meaning that it is printed on the same presses that print the rest of the paper. An ad printed in black ink is referred to as a black-and-white ad. If one color is added, it is a two-color ad (black is counted as one of the colors); if a second color is added, it is a three-color ad; and so forth. In ROP color the color is used mostly for attracting attention by a mass effect, as a background, border, or a strong design or headline, rather than for a picture of the product, unless it is in a flat-colored package. (In *flat color* red is red, blue is blue, and yellow is yellow; the three are not mixed to give effects of orange, purple, and so on. The opposite of flat color is *process color,* which is demonstrated in color insert Chapter 17; also see Print Production.)

FREE-STANDING (PREPRINTED OR LOOSE) INSERTS

Since the early 1970s, the free-standing, preprinted insert (also known as a "loose insert") has zoomed in importance as a medium for advertisers and a source of income for newspapers. Ranging from a single card to a tabloid-size enclosure running to thirty-two pages or even more, it is prepared by an outside printer and delivered to the newspaper before the newspaper itself is printed. Then it is loosely inserted into the regular edition of the paper. In recent years the NAB's insert division has permitted advertisers to buy a number of newspapers simultaneously with a single insertion and purchase order (Exhibit 8.9).

Because of postal regulations, the words "Supplement to (logotype)" must appear on the masthead. It is the advertiser's responsibility to supply these printed inserts to the newspaper. In some cities an advertiser can buy circulation in specific sections of the city at a fixed CPM.

The loose insert is designed for quick response. It is being used widely by retail stores, by national advertisers in promotions with coupon-redemption offers, and by direct-response advertisers as a reaction to increasing postal rates for direct mail. Some now have a reply card tip-in, which is mechanically affixed to the advertising page. Loose inserts must be planned and scheduled well in advance.

BLACK AND ETHNIC NEWSPAPERS

Black newspapers primarily reach the black, urban population. The black press is diversified in terms of content and audience appeal. The great majority of these papers are weeklies although a few, such as the *Atlanta Daily World* and the *New York Daily Challenge,* are published more frequently. Black newspapers achieve high readership and offer advertisers an alternative communication channel to the black community.

Ethnic newspapers are published in over thirty languages in the United States. In addition some ethnic newspapers are printed in English but appeal to a specific ethnic segment. Like black newspapers, they are concentrated in urban centers with large ethnic populations. Most of these newspapers are published weekly and have circulations of 5,000 or less. However, a few, such as New York's *China Post,* are dailies with over 20,000 circulation.

Exhibit 8.9
Newspaper insertion and purchase order. (Courtesy Newspaper Advertising Bureau, Inc.)

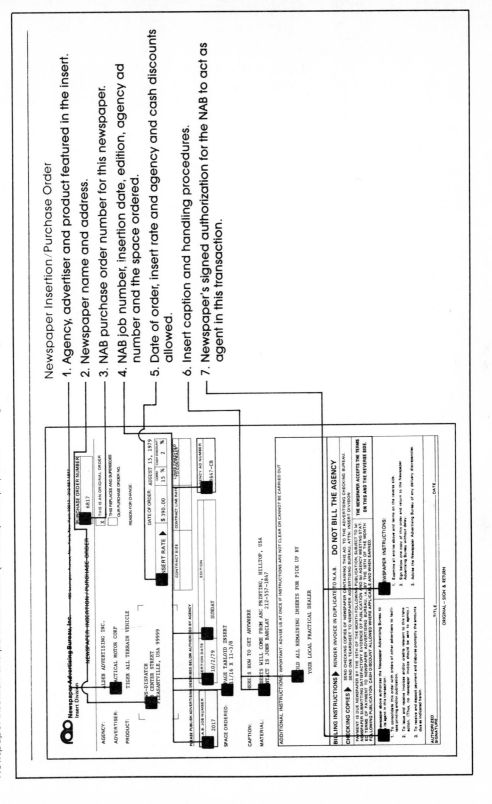

Newspaper Insertion/Purchase Order

1. Agency, advertiser and product featured in the insert.

2. Newspaper name and address.

3. NAB purchase order number for this newspaper.

4. NAB job number, insertion date, edition, agency ad number and the space ordered.

5. Date of order, insert rate and agency and cash discounts allowed.

6. Insert caption and handling procedures.

7. Newspaper's signed authorization for the NAB to act as agent in this transaction.

WEEKLY NEWSPAPERS

America was a country of weekly newspapers before it became a daily-newspaper land, and to this day there are about 9,000 weekly newspapers published, five times the number of dailies. (A weekly paper is sometimes published twice a week.) About two-thirds of the papers are urban oriented, published in communities in the metropolitan areas or in the suburbs and in the satellites of the suburbs; one-third are published in farm communities. Ranging from paid subscriptions to partially paid or even free circulation, weeklies have high readership because they offer so much local news. They also have local shopping information; in fact many are known as "shopping newspapers" because they contain less than 25 percent news.

National advertisers often use suburban papers to round out a promotion they are running in the dailies of the nearby cities. Weeklies are often offered as part of a group of papers within the same geographical market. The Pioneer Press of Chicago, for example, offers a flat rate of $3.89 for a group of 17 separate suburban papers with a combined circulation of more than 98,000.

COMICS

The Sunday comic supplement that comes with most week-end newspapers is a family institution. Well over 100 million people read the comics, a figure that may surprise you until you discover that 59.3 percent of them are adults 18 years or older. Children 2 to 12 make up 22.2 percent, and teenagers 18.5 percent of the audience.

Comics are syndicated, and space in the comic supplement is sold by national or sectional groups of papers although space is also sold by individual papers. The chief national comics are *Puck,* in 160 papers with a national circulation of 18 million, and *Metro,* in 68 papers with 23 million circulation. The advantage of the group purchase is that the advertiser places only one order and receives one bill. Space in the comic publications is usually sold in terms of a page or fraction of a page.

SUMMARY

Newspapers will continue their marketing emphasis and expansion of services to compete for the increasingly competitive advertising dollar. Newspapers will continue to standardize ad sizes, discounts, and billing systems to increase national advertising linage. We will also see more newspapers going to **total market coverage**. Total market coverage means that all households in a market will be reached with the entire newspaper, an advertising supplement, or even direct mail to nonsubscribers.

Someday we shall tune in our newspaper either on specially equipped TV sets or on home computers. Instead of having a package of information delivered to our driveways, we shall choose ads and information from an index and read it off a screen. With an accompanying printer we shall be able to have "hard copy" or recipes, stock-market reports, and even advertising coupons.

The newspaper of the future will eliminate the high costs of physical distribution and greatly reduce costs of paper and ink. From an advertising standpoint the electronic newspaper will mean that we shall be able to target our prospects with more precision. However, it will also give control of the communicative process to the audience. This two-way—instead of one-way—mass communication may make the introduction of new brands more difficult as people ask only for information with which they are familiar.

QUESTIONS

1. How have changes in society affected the content of the daily newspaper in recent years?
2. What are the differences between the two major categories of newspaper advertising: classified and display?
3. Describe the advantages of the mininewspaper to the newspaper advertiser.
4. Discuss some reasons for the CPM comparison's replacing the milline rate in newspapers.
5. What is meant by an ABC newspaper report? What is special about it? What is the importance of the ABC report for an advertiser? How does he use it? How does it differ from a Standard Rate & Data Service report?
6. How has the competitive situation changed for newspapers in the last several years?
7. Discuss some reasons for newspapers' increasing the merchandising of their advertising in recent years.
8. What are the two types of newspaper magazine supplement? What is their chief difference as far as the advertiser is concerned?
9. What steps are being taken by newspapers to encourage more national advertising?
10. How has the character of the weekly newspaper changed in the last 20 years?
11. Give a definition, explanation, or description of the following:

    a. open rate
    b. flat rate
    c. ROP
    d. SAU System
    e. space contract
    f. tear sheet
    g. combination rates
    h. Newsplan
    i. split run
    j. electronic newspaper

SUGGESTED EXERCISES

12. Collect the free-standing inserts in your newspaper for a week. How many coupons did they contain? How many were for national franchise operations? For department or specialty store? How many were in color?
13. Take a daily newspaper and measure the column inches devoted to: local display advertising (including local operations of national chains), national advertising, classified advertising.
14. Using the same newspaper and a current Daily Newspaper SRDS, estimate the cost of four national ads of different sizes. Assume the advertiser has paid the full national rate with no discounts.

READINGS

BURROUGHS, ELISE: "Modern Marketing Makes its Mark," *Presstime,* December 1981, pp. 4–9.

"Food Shoppers Shop Newspaper Ads: FTC," *Advertising Age,* September 15, 1980, p. 4.

"Get Ready for the Video Publishing Explosion," *Marketing & Media Decisions,* April 1981, pp. 59–63.

"How 12 Agencies View Newspapers," *Media Decisions,* September 1976, pp. 124–40.

JAIN, CHAMAN L.: "Newspaper Advertising: Preprint vs. R.O.P.," *Journal of Advertising Research,* August 1973, pp. 30–32.

"Neuharth Tackles Turner on Future of Newspapers," *Broadcasting,* May 25, 1981, p. 65.

WHITE, KENNETH R., CHRIS T. ANZALONE, and DAVID BARBOUR: "The Effectiveness of Shopper Guides," *Journal of Advertising Research,* April 1980, pp. 17–24.

Using
Magazines

National advertising first became possible in the 1870s, when railroads opened the West. Trains carried magazines to people all across the country, telling them of the new products made in the East. In the 100 years since then, magazines have continued to be a major advertising medium. But when TV came along, in the 1950s, people's reading habits became viewing habits, and national magazines had to change to survive.

National advertising in the days before TV meant advertising in *Life, Look,* or the old *Saturday Evening Post,* the traditional, big-page general magazines designed to appeal to everyone. But people began turning to TV by the millions, and advertisers followed the crowd. After spending years and fortunes to hold their audiences and advertisers, the big giants of the general-magazine world folded, one by one, victims of TV and rising paper and postage costs, which particularly hurt the large-size, enormous-circulation magazines. By coincidence the demise of *Life* magazine,* the last of the old giants, occurred at the end of 1972, just when the sixth edition of this book went to press. No single event could have more clearly marked the turn-

---

*Time, Inc., currently publishes a monthly version of *Life,* with a circulation of 1.3 million readers.

ing point in the revolution that had been taking place in the magazine world since the advent of TV.

Many people hold the mistaken idea that the demise of these magazines was caused primarily by a loss of readership. In fact the large-circulation publications—even at the end—had respectable circulations; rather, a loss of advertising revenue was the major culprit in their deaths. For advertisers who wanted a mass audience TV was the obvious answer. To reach a specialized audience, advertisers looked to an alternative to the mass magazine. Consequently the mass-circulation magazines were caught in an advertising and financial no-man's land.

Meanwhile, a new generation of now-successful magazines had appeared on the scene: *Playboy, Psychology Today, Money, Rolling Stone, Ms., Smithsonian, Sports Illustrated,* and others. They all have one thing in common: Each appeals to a specific group of people who share the same interest, taste, hobby, or special point of view. The older magazines that survive appeal also to people who share a common interest. *Good Housekeeping, Vogue, Seventeen, House Beautiful,* and *Cosmopolitan* all go to women, but each stresses different aspects of women's lives. Also among today's older successful magazines are *Time, Fortune, Popular Mechanics, Field and Stream, Ebony,* and *National Geographic,* each appealing to a specific economic, social, or cultural level or special interest.

Today there are only two magazines with circulations above 10 million. Ironically, the largest, *TV Guide,* with almost 20 million circulation, is a magazine about TV. The other circulation giant is, of course, *Reader's Digest.* In the last several years the only successful new general-editorial publications have been the "personality" publications, such as *People,* and the tabloids, such as the *National Enquirer.* These publications appeal to female audiences (with *People* more oriented to an upscale audience) and are not comparable to the general-interest magazines of the pre-TV era.

Magazines reflect changes in lifestyles. Greater sexual freedom, greater interest and participation in sports, more women in the work force, more and easier travel—all find expression in today's magazines. On the desk of every magazine editor are manuscripts to be read with one question in mind: "Is this for my readers?"

AUDIENCE QUALITY

In the last several years magazines have emphasized the quality rather than quantity of their circulation. The Magazine Publishers Association (MPA) has taken a leadership role in promoting magazines to national advertisers. Most of the MPA-sponsored research is designed to show how buying additional magazine space increases the efficiency of a predominantly TV media schedule.

Media imperatives

Since 1975 a major selling tool of magazines has been the *Media Imperatives,* based on research by Simmons Media Studies. The system is in-

Table 9-1

| | | GRP/$1 MILLION | |
IMPERATIVE SEGMENT	SHARE OF TARGET MARKET, %	ALL TV	⅔ TV, ⅓ MAGS.
	THE MEDIA IMPERATIVES YOUNG UPSCALE MARKET ADULTS 18 TO 49 WITH $15,000 + HOUSEHOLD INCOME[a]		
Magazine	44	119	264
TV	25	246	246
Dual[b]	18	290	395
Non (light/light)[c]	13	76	105

[a]W. R. Simmons, MPA, *Magazine Newsletter of Research*, January, 1979. Courtesy Magazine Publishers Association.
[b]Heavy users of both TV and magazines.
[c]Light users of both TV and magazines.

tended to show that, by using TV exclusively, advertisers will miss a sizable group of heavy-magazine–light-TV users. As the target market becomes more educated and affluent, the more imperative the use of magazines. A typical example, Table 9.1, shows how the Imperatives are used as a sales tool to a specific market.

Media

involvement   In addition to the MPA's selling the quality of magazine circulation, it also sells the quality of exposure or attention to the medium. In a MPA-sponsored study the Opinion Research Corporation found that attentiveness to magazine advertising rose as the socioeconomic status of the reader increased (Table 9.2).

LEISURELY

READING   When you get a magazine, you look forward to reading it at leisure. You have plenty of opportunity to select ads of interest and to read all their details, no matter how much copy is involved. You have a chance to study a picture along with the copy and become familiar with the appearance of the product or the package. Time for leisurely reading is particularly important for new, pioneering products, for products with new features, and for other products about which the advertiser has an important story to tell. Your leisurely reading time is also valuable to the advertiser offering suggestions for wider uses of the product. The more you read about a product in an ad, the better the chance is that you will remember the brand name. All this adds up to the cumulative value of magazine advertising.

Some years ago General Foods ran a massive series of tests of five products in six cities and compared the effects of magazine advertising with those of TV advertising. One outstanding finding was the high memorability of brand names among magazine readers as opposed to the high misidentifica-

Table 9–2

DISPOSITION TO SEEK OUT THE ADVERTISING (ATTENTIVENESS TO ADVERTISING IN MAGAZINES AND TV)[a]				
	MEN		WOMEN	
	MAGAZINES	TV	MAGAZINES	TV
Total U.S.	45	45	53	43
By education:				
Did not graduate high school	37	43	48	47
Graduated high school	48	49	54	40
Attended/graduated college	51	42	54	40
By household income, $:				
Under 5,000	34	47	44	51
5,000– 7,999	36	43	50	48
8,000– 9,999	46	43	47	47
10,000–14,999	52	46	51	39
15,000–24,999	46	46	57	38
25,000–34,999	50	46	57	34
35,000 and over	53	36	57	42
By age:				
18–24	49	50	56	42
25–34	53	48	57	42
35–44	51	46	53	36
45–54	43	43	51	45
55–64	40	40	52	38
65 and older	29	37	44	46
By occupation:				
Exec/Prof/Mgr	48	43	52	38
White Collar	55	46	55	36
Skilled	52	49	52	41
Unskilled	38	47	53	46
Retired	33	37	51	47
Prime Prospects[b]	52	43	54	38

[a]A Study of Media Involvement (conducted by Opinion Research Corporation for MPA), p. 29. Courtesy Magazine Publishers Association.
[b]Adults 18 to 49 years of age, have attended or graduated from college, and have household income of $15,000 or more.

tion among TV viewers. Result: a major shift to magazine advertising, doubling General Foods' magazine investment from $6 million to $12 million.

Quality of controlled color
reproduction   Some of the most outstanding contemporary color work appears in magazines. When color is important in depicting or enhancing a product (carpets, draperies, printed sheets, lipsticks, and nail polish, for example), exquisite color work is significant. Color work is so common these days that not using color may put a product at a disadvantage with competitive products that do use color advertising.

Coupon and direct-response

advertising   Magazines are an excellent medium for ads calling for a coupon or card response with coupon. Since a magazine will probably be around the house for days, weeks, or even months, it is a good place to put a color photograph of a product, with ample space for copy. The reader will have time to read the ad and cut out a coupon. For these reasons magazines are a favorite medium for direct-response advertisers.

LIMITATIONS AND

CHALLENGES   It is a costly process to provide a selected audience, as magazines do. The value of this service is lost if all you want to do is get a short message about a familiar product before the widest possible audience. Magazines are most economical in sending a message about a specialized product to a specialized audience. They are usually least economical in delivering to the general public just the name and a short message about a widely distributed type of product.

Most magazines have closing dates long before publication; so they may not be the best medium for making news announcements, such as a change in an airline schedule. Many magazines close 5 to 7 weeks before publication for black-and-white ads, 8 weeks for color ads. The closing date is even further ahead for special editions.

However, in recent years several major magazines have introduced "late-close" or short-notice ad closings. These permit advertisers to take advantage of timely events that tie in with their products or changes in marketing or competitive strategy. When Chrysler Corporation gained approval for its government loan-guarantee program, it placed eight-page ads in five weekly magazines that ran within a week of the announcement.

In most cases there is no extra charge for this service. Advertisers are not guaranteed a position nor even that the ad will run. To assure space, some advertisers will submit an insertion order but not send the actual ad until the last minute. For instance, a tire company may order space the week after the Indianapolis 500. If a car using its tires wins the race, then an ad announcing this will run; if not, another standard ad will be used. Among the magazines providing some type of late close are *Time, U.S. News & World Report, Sports Illustrated,* and *Newsweek* (see Exhibit 9.1).

Geographic and demographic

editions   One of the great recent developments in magazines has been the ability, by the use of a computer, to split the nationwide circulation of a magazine into geographic and demographic classifications.

Geographic Editions. In more than 100 of the largest-circulation national magazines you do not have to buy the entire national circulation to run an ad. In their *sectional,* or *regional,* editions you may buy circulation in whatever

Exhibit 9.1

An ad for a late-close service. (Used by permission of *Newsweek*. Copyright *Newsweek*, 1980.)

markets you wish to select. The tremendous advantage is that you do not have to pay for running the ad in markets that are of no interest to you. *Time,* for example, has divided its circulation into 127 separate markets, from which the advertiser can make up his own list. The special edition usually consists of a special section inserted as a part of the magazine. Schedule for a minimum number of markets is required.

Among its many other advantages the geographical edition

☐ Permits a marketer to relate advertising to territories in which the product is sold

☐ Supports promotions being run in different parts of the country

☐ Tests a campaign in various markets before embarking on a national campaign

☐ Reaches a scattered set of markets with one order

☐ Encourages local retail support since retailers' names are listed as distributors in their home markets

☐ Is ideal for local and sectional advertisers

There are some disadvantages to contend with in the geographical edition, however:

☐ CPM is higher than in a national edition.

☐ Forms close much sooner.

☐ Ads for a given market may not run in every issue.

☐ Orders must be placed well in advance.

☐ All local ads may be run back to back in an insert—a situation not conducive to high readership. (It is better to place an ad in one of the regional editions with a special localized editorial section for each major split.)

Demographic Editions. There is another type of split, the *demographic* edition, for subscribers who have similar lifestyles and can be identified from a subscription list as belonging to a particular group (Exhibit 9.2). *Time* is an outstanding example. It has over 200 special geographic and demographic editions. Included in this number are editions to all fifty states, major markets, high-income zip codes, as well as student-educator, top-management, and professional editions. Most consumer magazines confine their special editions to advertising. However, in the future we should see some magazines offering editorial material as well as advertising on an edition-by-edition basis.

The proportion of geographic and demographic editions in relation to the total circulation has been around 20 percent for a number of years. These editions are now referred to as *less than full run.*

MAGAZINE ELEMENTS

Sizes   The *page size* of a magazine is the type area, not the size of the actual page. For convenience the size of most magazines is characterized as *standard size* (about 8 by 10 inches, like *Time*) or *small size* (about 4⅜ by 6½ inches, like *Reader's Digest*). When you are ready to order plates, you must get the exact sizes from the publisher's latest rate card, as sizes keep changing.

Space-buying designations. The front cover of a magazine is called the *first cover page.* This is seldom if ever sold in American consumer magazines (though it is sold in business magazines). The inside of the front cover is called

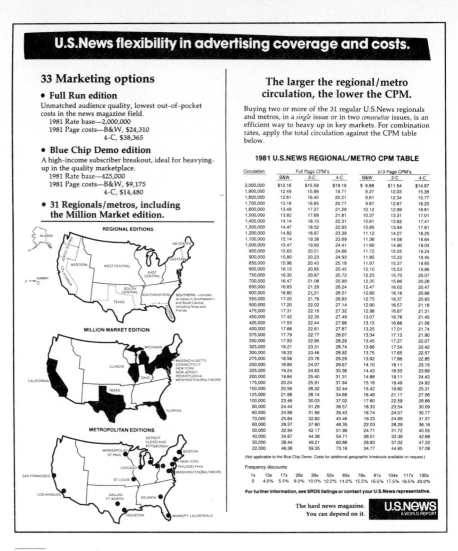

Exhibit 9.2
How you may buy demographic editions. (Courtesy *U.S. News and World Report*.)

the *second cover page,* the inside of the back cover the *third cover page,* and the back cover the *fourth cover page.* For the second, third, and fourth cover positions, you must pay a premium price and may have to get your ad on a waiting list.

Space in magazines is generally sold in terms of full pages and fractions thereof (half pages, quarter pages, three columns, two columns, or one column; see Exhibit 9.3). Small ads in the shopping pages in the back of many magazines are generally sold by the line. Most magazines are flexible in allowing one-page or double-page ads to be broken up into separate units.

Gatefolds. Sometimes, when you open a magazine, you find that the cover or an inside page opens to reveal an extra page that folds out and gives the ad a big spread. Advertisers use these *gatefolds* (Exhibit 9.3) on special oc-

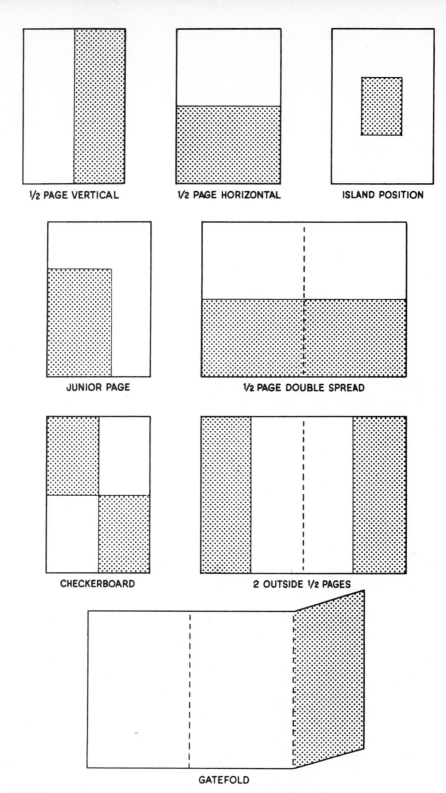

½ PAGE VERTICAL   ½ PAGE HORIZONTAL   ISLAND POSITION

JUNIOR PAGE   ½ PAGE DOUBLE SPREAD

CHECKERBOARD   2 OUTSIDE ½ PAGES

GATEFOLD

Exhibit 9.3
Various ways of using magazine space.

casions to make the most spectacular presentation in the magazine, usually to introduce a colorful product like a new model car. Not all magazines offer gatefolds because plans for them must be made well in advance, and they are expensive.

Bleed Ads. When an ad runs all the way to the edge of the page, leaving no margin, it is called a *bleed ad* (Exhibit 9.4). Designed to get extra attention, the ad may bleed on only three sides, or it may bleed on two sides, leaving the white space on the other two sides open for copy if desired. Although some publications, especially new ones, do not charge for bleeds, usually you must pay an extra 15 to 20 percent whether the ad bleeds on one, two, three, or four sides.

Inserts. These are the return cards, coupons, recipe booklets, and other kinds of outside material bound into magazines in connection with an adjoining ad. They are never sold separately. Return cards, effective in getting prompt response from an advertisement, are widely used in direct-response advertising; they are also an effective way of distributing coupon offers. As we shall see in Chapter 11, when we discuss magazine inserts, they can be an effective part of a sales-promotion campaign. We mention magazine inserts here to recognize that they are an important feature of magazine advertising.

Position an important consideration

On the question of position in magazines, no one has more accurate information than the direct-response advertisers. They know exactly what response they get from each advertisement. Bob Stone, an authority in that field, reports:

> Decades of measured direct response advertising tell the same story over and over again. A position in the first seven pages of the magazine produces a dramatically better response (all other factors being the same) than if the same insertion appeared farther back in the same issue. . . .
>
> Here is about what you may expect the relative response to be from various page positions as measured against the first right-hand page arbitrarily rated at a pull of 100:

POSITION	RANKING
First right-hand page	100
Second right-hand page	95
Third right-hand page	90
Fourth right-hand page	85
Back of book (following main body of editorial matter)	50
Back cover	100
Inside third cover (inside of back cover)	90
Page facing inside third cover	85

A panty is only a panty.

Till you discover the soft, silky luxury of Lycra.®

You'll love the difference Lycra® spandex makes in a panty—the silky, sensuous feeling—the freedom to bend and stretch without panties binding or creeping up. Available in brief, hipster and bikini styles, cotton and nylon blends. Ask for panties with "Lycra" at fine stores everywhere.

Panties with LYCRA®
DU PONT SPANDEX

DU PONT

Exhibit 9.4
An ad which bleeds on two sides. (Courtesy E. I. du Pont de Nemours & Co., Inc.)

207

Right-hand pages are more visible than left-hand pages; right-hand pages pull better than left-hand pages—by as much as 15 percent. Insert cards open the magazine to the advertiser's message, and thereby create their own "cover" position.*

Exceptions: A position in front of any article relevant to your product is good. A page facing reading matter is better than an ad facing an ad. In many magazines only the cover positions and possibly the pages facing them are preferred positions that can be reserved at a premium. This need not prevent you, as an advertiser, from letting your view on positioning up front be known to the publisher.

HOW SPACE IS SOLD

Magazine rate

structure   Publishers issue rate cards quoting the costs of advertising space in their magazines. The rate card of one weekly reads like this (also see Exhibit 9.5):

Black/White	1 time
1 page	$31,710
2 columns	24,100
½ page (horizontal)	19,025
1 column	12,365
½ column (vertical)	6,340
Agate line	92.10

The listing above is the one-time rate. The card continues, to give the rates for 13, 26, 39, and 52 insertions and the corresponding rates for color. (Weeklies' rates are quoted in units of 13.)

Whereas newspaper rates are compared by millines, magazine rates are compared by *cost per page per thousand circulation* (CPM). As mentioned earlier, the formula is

$$CPM = \frac{cost/page}{circulation\ (thousands)}$$

Discounts   The one-time, full-page rate of a publication is referred to as its *basic,* or *open,* rate. All discounts are computed from that. There are two familiar types of discount:

---

*Bob Stone, *Successful Direct Marketing Methods* (Chicago: Crain Books, 1975), p. 78.

36A News - Weeklies

Newsweek

A Newsweek, Inc., Publication

Media Code 8 572 0500 9.00 **Mid 000906-000**
Published weekly by Newsweek, Inc., 444 Madison Ave., New York, NY 10022. Phone 212-350-2000
For shipping info., see Print Media Production Data.

PUBLISHER'S EDITORIAL PROFILE

NEWSWEEK is a magazine of news and commentary. News is categorized into National Affairs, International, science, Sports, Business, Medicine, Religion, Entertainment, the Graphic and Performing Arts, and encompasses the week's developments on the newsfronts of the world and of the nation. Articles are usually illustrated with relevant charts, maps, cartoons and photographs. The reader's views are amplified by a number of columns of opinion on national and international trends in politics, the economy, personal business, the Washington scene, current affairs, life styles. Rec'd 8/24/78.

1. PERSONNEL

Vice President/Adv. Dir.—James W. Allbaugh.
Vice President/Advertising Services—Art Karlan.
Assoc. Adv. Dir.—John G. Alexander.
Assoc. Adv. Dir.—Eric Bruhn.
Director, Advertising Services—Richard F. Bausch.

2. REPRESENTATIVES and/or BRANCH OFFICES

New York 10022—John F. King, Executive Sales Mgr., James D. McVey, Mgr., Virginia Mueller, Newsweek Woman Sales Mgr., 444 Madison Ave. Phone 212-350-2000.
Boston 02110—J. Devereux de Gozzaldi, Bay 121 Lewis Wharf. Phone 617-523-8181.
Chicago 60601—Newton J. Friese, Mgr., Jerome J. Maroney, Associate Mgr., 200 E. Randolph Dr., Suite 7948. Phone 312-861-1180.
Cleveland 44113—William E. Nieman, 1 Public Square. Phone 216-696-3565.
Southfield (Detroit), Mich. 48075—William E. Ross, Mgr., 3000 Town Center, Suite 1940. Phone 313-355-3333.
Atlanta 30326—James Baillie, Tower Place, Suite 2990, 3340 Peachtree Rd., N.E. Phone 404-237-6943.
Washington, D. C. 20006—Douglas P. Jeppe, Suite 1220, 1750 Penneylvania Ave. Phone 202-393-3200.
Dallas 75240—George W. Lodge, Mgr., 810 Carillon Tower West, 13601 Preston Rd. Phone 214-980-1821.
San Francisco 94111—Huntley Bennett, Suite 1501, 505 Sansome St., Phone 415-788-4321.
Los Angeles 90067—Lemuel C. Hall, Suite 380, 10100 Santa Monica Blvd. Phone 213-553-0910.
London—Michael Warburton, 25 Upper Brook St.
Paris—Max G. Bouchard, 162 Faubourg St., Honore.
Tokyo—Keiichi Kato, 1, 6-4, 1-chome Marunouchi, Chiyoda-ku.
Sydney—Michael Groves, 55 Elizabeth St.
Manila—Frank Ramos, 1350 Roxas Boulevard, Ermita.
Amsterdam—Lars-Erik Malmgvist, 687 Prinsengracht.
Frankfort—Heribert Striewe, Gerard Bouteiller, Friedrichstrasse 10-12, D-6000.
Geneva—Hans Fluijt, 6 Place des Eaux-Vives.
Hong Kong—Ian Leonard, 71 Des Voeux Road Central.
Chicago—Edwin W. J. Keil, 200 E. Randolph Dr.

3. COMMISSION AND CASH DISCOUNT

15% of gross to recognized agencies. Cash discount 2% of net allowed for payment 10 days or less from invoice date. Net 30 days. Bills rendered on or before issue date and due within 10 days from date of invoice.

ADVERTISING RATES

Rates effective January 4, 1982.
Rates received November 30, 1981.

5. BLACK/WHITE RATES

	1 ti	13 ti	17 ti	26 ti	39 ti
1 page	40,930.	39,295.	38,680.	37,655.	36,835.
2 cols.	31,105.	29,860.	29,395.	28,615.	27,995.
* 1/2 page	24,965.	23,965.	23,590.	22,970.	22,470.
1 col.	15,965.	15,325.	15,085.	14,690.	14,370.
1/2 col.	8,185.	7,860.	7,735.	7,530.	7,365.
Line rate	121.65	116.80	114.95	111.90	109.50

	52 ti
1 page	36,180.
2 cols.	27,495.
* 1/2 page	22,070.
1 col.	14,115.
1/2 col.	7,235.
Line rate	107.55

(*) Limited availability.

DISCOUNTS
FREQUENCY DISCOUNTS

Rates determined by number of insertions contracted for and used during a 12 month period. Schedules composed of mixed space units of 1/2 column or larger entitled to standard frequency discounts except when use of smaller units lowers cost of campaign below amount which larger units would reach at their earned rate. Schedules composed of National and Regional and/or Executive Newsweek insertions may be combined to earn frequency discounts except when use of Regional and/or Executive Newsweek space lowers cost of campaign below amount which National insertions cost at their earned rates.
Schedules composed entirely of Regional advertising may combine various regions to earn frequency discounts except when use of smaller region lowers total cost of campaign below amount which larger regions would cost at their earned rates.
Regional combinations count as only 1 insertion if combination discount is used.

HIGH VOLUME SPACE CREDIT PLAN

Advertisers purchasing 78 or more national equivalent pages during a contract year at the 52-time rate are eligible for the following additional space credits:

National equivalent pages:	Space Credit
78	4%
104	8%

As an alternative to the space credit, advertisers who purchase 65 or more National equivalent pages will qualify for the following additional cash discounts off the 52-time rate:

National Equivalent Pages:	(*)
65	1%
78	2%

continued

36A News - Weeklies

Newsweek—cont

National Equivalent Pages:	(*)
91	3%
104	4%
117	5%

(*) Cash discount off 52-time rate.

MULTIPLE PAGES

Multiple Page Discounts: Advertisers purchasing four or more pages in a single issue and in a single printed form or on consecutive pages will be granted a special multiple page discount. Pages must run as part of the same printed form, or as consecutive pages, or as supporting space for a less-than-page-size insert, and may be any combination of black & white, black and one-color or four-color. Advertisers running either two or more eight page consecutive units or three or more six page consecutive units within a contract year will be granted a maximum multiple page discount of 25%. Regular frequency discounts apply in addition to the special multiple page discount with each page counting as one insertion. Units of eight or more pages will be limited to one per issue. Discount will not apply to special units or four-page units in Regional and/or Top Ten, College Student, Newsweek Woman, Half Newsweek, Hometown and Metro editions.

Pages	Discount	Pages	Discount
4 pages	10%	32 pages	30%
8 pages	15%	48 pages	33%
12 pages	20%	64 pages	36%
16 pages	25%		

TIE-IN DISCOUNT

Insertions in Newsweek by dealers, franchise operators or members of Associations may adopt, as a base, the earned frequency discount of the Company or Association with which they are affiliated provided:
A. The company or association runs a minimum of 13 pages.
B. The affiliated advertiser's copy runs within the same contract year and geographic areas as the company or association.
C. The dealer or franchise operator features, exclusively, the product or service of the company advertising in Newsweek.
Qualifying advertisers, affiliated with multiple associations or companies, may tie-in with only one for discount purposes. Granting of the Affiliation Discount will be further governed by Newsweek's basic discount policies as set forth in the preceding paragraphs. Special discounts to philanthropic, public interest, advertising agencies and other qualifying organizations are available.

6. COLOR RATES

Black and 1 color:

	1 ti	13 ti	17 ti	26 ti	39 ti
1 page	51,735.	49,665.	48,890.	47,595.	46,560.
2 cols.	39,320.	37,745.	37,155.	36,175.	35,390.
*1/2 page	31,555.	30,295.	29,820.	29,030.	28,400.
1 col.	20,630.	19,805.	19,495.	18,980.	18,565.
1/2 col.	10,805.	10,375.	10,210.	9,940.	9,725.

	52 ti
1 page	45,735.
2 cols.	34,760.
*1/2 page	27,895.
1 col.	18,235.
1/2 col.	9,550.

4 color:

1 page	63,850.	61,295.	60,340.	58,740.	57,465.
* 2 cols.	50,345.	48,330.	47,575.	46,315.	45,310.
*1/2 page	39,905.	38,310.	37,710.	36,715.	35,915.
* 1 col.	25,950.	24,910.	24,525.	23,875.	23,355.

1 page	56,445.
* 2 cols.	44,505.
*1/2 page	35,275.
* 1 col.	22,940.

(*) Limited availability.

7. COVERS

4 color process:

	1 ti	13 ti	17 ti	26 ti	39 ti
2nd & 3rd cover	63,850.	61,295.	60,340.	58,740.	57,465.
4th cover	81,860.	78,585.	77,360.	75,310.	73,675.

	52 ti
2nd & 3rd cover	56,445.
4th cover	72,365.

8. INSERTS

Insert Cards: Units consisting of a minimum of a page and a 2 color insert card are available, on a limited basis, in National, Regional and Metro Group I Editions. Minimum size: 6" x 4-1/4".
Rates for National card, 51,730.00 plus applicable supporting space rate. Rates for other than minimum size, Regional Editions and other situations are available. Note: a 5% margin must be allowed in the distribution of insert cards. Closing: 10 weeks. Insert Stock: Black and white, black and 1 process color, 2 process colors, 3 process colors, and 5 process colors (4 process) ads are available on 4-color insert stock for special purposes. Prices are available and are subject to frequency discounts. Contract must be received 9 weeks prior to issue date. Closing date for plates is the same as standard 4-color units. Gatefolds: 1/2 page and full page gatefolds are available, as well as other special ads. Mechanical details and dimensions should be confirmed with Newsweek prior to preparation of original art for engraving. Premium charges for these units are available. All premiums are non-commissionable.
Closing 9 weeks prior to issue date.

9. BLEED

Bleed pages, 2 Columns, 1 column and 1/2 page horizontal accepted at earned rates plus 10%. No charge for bleed across gutter in 4 column and larger ads.

12. SPLIT-RUN

On a limited basis, advertisers, purchasing national or regional circulation may tailor copy to different geographical areas. Split runs should follow state lines, except when influenced by regional edition distribution patterns. States are to be contiguous. Premiums vary according to number of geographical splits, coloration and regional unit boundaries that are followed. On cycle of College Student Editions, a limited number of advertisers may purchase the non-student portion of the National Edition at a special rate. 5% margin for distribution error required on all split-run contracts. Send for premium charges and issue availabilities. Closing: Regional close required on regional and national split runs. All premiums on split-runs are non-commissionable.

13a. GEOGRAPHIC and/or DEMOGRAPHIC EDITIONS

DEMOGRAPHIC EDITIONS
COLLEGE STUDENT EDITION

BLACK AND WHITE RATES:

	1 ti	13 ti	17 ti	26 ti	39 ti	52 ti
1 page	8,510.	8,170.	8,040.	7,830.	7,660.	7,525.
2 cols.	6,470.	6,210.	6,115.	5,950.	5,825.	5,720.
1 col.	3,405.	3,270.	3,220.	3,135.	3,065.	3,010.

COLOR RATES:
Black and 1 color:

	1 ti	13 ti	17 ti	26 ti	39 ti
1 page	10,755.	10,325.	10,165.	9,895.	9,680.
2 cols.	8,175.	7,850.	7,725.	7,520.	7,360.
1 col.	4,305.	4,135.	4,070.	3,960.	3,875.

	52 ti
1 page	9,505.
2 cols.	7,225
1 col.	3,805.

4 color:

1 page	13,275.	12,745.	12,545.	12,215.	11,950.
2 cols.	10,465.	10,045.	9,890.	9,630.	9,420.

1 page	11,735.
2 cols.	9,250.

ISSUE AND CLOSING DATES:
Available in 2nd cycle: Jan. 11, Feb. 8, Mar. 8, Apr. 5, May 3, May 31, June 28, July 26, Aug. 23, Sept. 20, Oct. 18, Nov. 15, Dec. 6.
Closing—black and white and 2 color, 5 weeks; 4 color, 7 weeks preceding date of publication. No cancellations accepted after contract closing dates.
CIRCULATION:
A.B.C. 6-30-81—384,557.
Publisher states: "Effective January 5, 1981 issue, circulation rate base 400,000."

EXECUTIVE NEWSWEEK

BLACK AND WHITE RATES:

	1 ti	13 ti	17 ti	26 ti	39 ti
1 page	15,050.	14,450.	14,220.	13,845.	13,545.
* 2 cols.	11,440.	10,980.	10,810.	10,525.	10,295.
*1 col.	6,020.	5,780.	5,690.	5,540.	5,420.
*1/2 page	9,180.	8,815.	8,675.	8,445.	8,260.

	52 ti
1 page	13,305.
* 2 cols.	10,115.
*1 col.	5,320.
*1/2 page	8,115.

(*) Limited availability.

COLOR RATES:
Black and 1 color:

	1 ti	13 ti	17 ti	26 ti	39 ti
1 page	19,025.	18,265.	17,980.	17,505.	17,125.
*2 cols.	14,460.	13,880.	13,665.	13,305.	13,015.
*1 col.	7,610.	7,305.	7,190.	7,000.	6,850.
*1/2 page	11,605.	11,140.	10,965.	10,675.	10,445.

	52 ti
1 page	16,820.
*2 cols.	12,785.
*1 col.	6,725.
*1/2 page	10,260.

Exhibit 9.5
A magazine rate card. (Courtesy Standard Rates and Data Service, Inc.)

Table 9–3

PAGES	DISCOUNT, %
13 or more	7
26 or more	12
39 or more	16
52 or more	20

Table 9–4

VOLUME, $	DISCOUNT, %
83,000 or more	8
125,000 or more	11
180,000 or more	17
260,000 or more	20

The frequency discount. Not to be confused with "frequency" in scheduling an ad, a frequency discount results in a lower cost per unit the more often the advertiser runs ads within the contract year (Table 9.3).

Volume (dollar) discount. The more total space an advertiser uses within a contract year, measured in dollars, the lower the rate. The figures in Table 9.4 will serve to demonstrate this. Sometimes frequency and volume discounts are combined to give the advertiser the best possible rate, but this must be planned and contracted for in advance.

Other discounts. Publishers are always alert to give special rates to large advertisers and to other advertisers they are anxious to attract. Among different magazines we find various special discounts: *mail-order* discount, *travel* discount, *trade-book* discount, *multiple-page* discount, *seasonal-adjustment* discount, and *consecutive-page* discount. Blanketing all these is a *corporate,* or *total-dollar,* discount. This overall discount, above all the others earned, is based on the total dollars spent by all of a corporation's divisions in a year. There is obviously no such thing as a standard trade discount or standard use of terms. It pays to ask a lot of questions when buying space.

Remnant space. A number of publishers, especially those with geographic or demographic editions, find themselves with extra space in some editions when they are ready to go to press. Rather than run an empty space, the publisher often offers this *remnant space* at a big discount. For direct-response advertisers, whose ads are not part of a continuing campaign but stand on their own, remnant space is an especially good buy. Of course, material for the ad must be ready for instant insertion.

Table 9–5

NO. TIMES	COST/INSERTION %
1	2,000
3	1,975
6	1,950
9	1,925
12	1,900

The magazine short

rate   When an advertiser and a publisher sign a noncancellable, nonretroactive space contract at the beginning of the year, they agree to make adjustments at the end of the year if the advertiser's estimates are off. If the advertiser uses less space than estimated, the publisher charges more. If more space is used, the publisher gives a rebate.

Take a magazine with the page rates shown in Table 9.5. The advertiser believes ads will be run twelve times during the year, qualifying for the $1,900 rate, and the contract is entered tentatively at that figure. If ads are run twelve times, all is well; there is no problem. But if the ads run only ten times, the advertiser would get a bill like this:

Ran 10 times. Paid the 12-time rate of $1,900 per page	$19,000
Earned only the 9-time rate (there is no 10-time rate) of $1,925 per page,	19,250
Short rate due 10 insertions × $250 =	$ 2,500

If the advertiser had earned more than the rate contracted for, the publisher would give a rebate.

Some publishers charge the top (basic) rate throughout the year but state in the contract, "Rate credit when earned." If the advertiser earns a better rate, the publisher gives a refund. If the publisher sees that an advertiser is not running sufficient pages during the year to earn the low rate on which the contract was based, the publisher sends a bill at the short rate for space already used. Further ads are billed at the higher rate earned. Failure to keep short rates in mind when you reduce your original schedule can lead to unwelcome surprises.

PLACING THE

ORDER   Placing advertising in a magazine on a 12-month schedule may entail two steps: the *space contract* and the *insertion order*. An advertiser who plans to advertise in a particular magazine during the coming 12 months will sign a space contract in order to get the best rate. This is not an order for a specific amount of space but merely an agreement to pay at the current rate schedule for whatever space is used. The advertiser estimates how much space might be run during the year and is billed for the discount rate charged for that amount of space. The contract usually allows the publisher to raise the rates during the contract year with, however, a 2- or 3-month notice. The advantage to the advertiser is that during those months no increase in rates is permitted. When the advertiser is ready to run an ad, he or she sends an insertion order to the publisher, specifying date of issue, size of ad, and contract rate.

MAGAZINE DATES

There are three sets of dates to be aware of in planning and buying magazine space:

1. *Cover date,* the date appearing on the cover
2. *On-sale date,* the date on which the magazine is issued (the January issue of a magazine may come out on December 5, which is important to know if you are planning a Christmas ad)
3. *Closing date,* the date when the print or plates needed to print the ad must be in the publisher's hands in order to make a particular issue.

Dates are figured from the cover date and are expressed in terms of "days or weeks preceding," as in the following example:

New Yorker
Published weekly, dated Monday
Issued Wednesday preceding
Closes 25th of 3rd month preceding

MAGAZINE NETWORKS

A publisher may gather into one selling group a number of publications, his own and those of other publishers reaching readers with similar general interests and lifestyles. Space in groups of these publications (usually three or more) is then sold at lower rates per publication than for any single member of the network. Ziff-Davis, for example, offers an advertiser a choice among seven magazines: *Flying, Car and Driver, Boating, Popular Mechanics, Stereo Review, Skiing,* and *Cycle.* Publishers who offer their magazines through a network are still free to pursue any other circulation and advertising sales effort they wish to make. Magazine networks offer publishers an efficient way to build circulation and sell advertising space, and they offer advertisers an economical way to buy space (Exhibit 9.6). Because of these advantages, the use of magazine networks has been spreading.

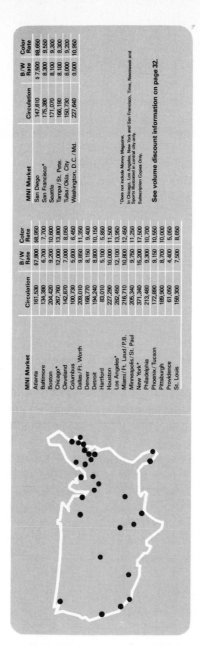

MNI Market	Circulation	B/W Rate	Color Rate
Atlanta	161,530	$7,000	$8,950
Baltimore	134,380	6,700	7,700
Boston	204,420	9,200	10,600
Chicago*	267,760	12,000	13,900
Cleveland	142,870	7,000	8,050
Columbus	100,730	5,600	6,450
Dallas/Ft. Worth	209,010	9,850	11,350
Denver	168,770	8,150	9,400
Detroit	194,240	8,800	10,150
Hartford	83,010	5,100	5,850
Houston	227,290	10,000	11,500
Los Angeles*	282,450	12,100	13,950
Miami/Ft. Laud./P.B.	216,710	10,800	12,450
Minneapolis/St. Paul	205,340	9,750	11,250
New York*	371,340	15,200	17,500
Philadelphia	213,460	9,900	10,700
Phoenix/Tucson	172,690	9,150	10,550
Pittsburgh	189,900	8,700	10,000
Providence	61,050	4,400	5,050
St. Louis	159,300	7,500	8,650

MNI Market	Circulation	B/W Rate	Color Rate
San Diego	147,610	$7,500	$8,660
San Francisco*	175,390	8,300	9,550
Seattle	171,070	8,100	9,300
Tampa/St. Pete.	166,190	8,100	9,300
Tulsa/Okla. City	150,730	8,000	9,200
Washington, D.C./Md.	227,640	9,500	10,950

*Does not include Money Magazine.
In Chicago, Los Angeles, New York and San Francisco, Time, Newsweek and Sports Illustrated in central city only.
Subscription Copies Only.

See volume discount information on page 32.

Business Network
BusinessWeek
Dun's **BUSINESS MONTH**
Money
Nation's Business
Newsweek
Sports Illustrated
TIME
U.S.News &WORLD REPORT

Exhibit 9.6
Magazine rates from MNI rate and data service. (Courtesy Media Networks, Inc.)

SPLIT-RUN
ADVERTISING

Just as Sunday-newspaper magazine sections offer split-run advertising, so do many magazines and for the same purpose: to test different ads against each other. Many magazines also have *split-run editions,* or more specifically they divide a geographic edition for testing purposes. In the simplest of such tests the advertiser supplies two different ads of the same size and shape, each running in the same position in half an edition and each calling for a coupon response. The publisher arranges to distribute both sections equally in the same territory or in two adjacent territories with the same demographics. The advertiser can then readily compare results. The basic principle is that there is to be no difference whatever between places where the ad is run; the only difference is in the two ads. In our discussion of split-run tests in Chapter 11, we shall see how this principle can be applied to test four ads at one time.

MAGAZINE CIRCULATION; THE AUDIT BUREAU OF
CIRCULATION

When advertisers buy space in magazines, they are really buying the delivery of their ad to as many people as possible, expressed in terms of circulation. All rates are based on the circulation that a publisher promises to provide, referred to as *guaranteed circulation.* How many copies of the magazine were really distributed, and how was that circulation obtained? These are key questions every space buyer asks. To help answer these questions, the Audit Bureau of Circulation (ABC) collects and evaluates data about magazines just as it does about newspapers. Briefly, the bureau audits the magazine's books and checks how many copies were printed, sold at newsstands, and returned, how many were sold by subscription, and how the subscriptions were obtained, measured in terms of cut-rate sales and delinquent subscribers. It also determines the rate of renewal. These vital facts all help evaluate the worth of the magazine as a medium.

Primary circulation versus pass-along
circulation

Advertisers are also interested in how many copies of the magazine are read by *primary* (original) buyers and how many copies are passed along from one friend to another or read in beauty parlors or doctors' waiting rooms. At least one study indicated that in consumer magazines primary readers had double the advertising response of pass-along readers, and this response increased to four times greater in business and news magazines.* But sometimes pass-along circulation is especially valuable. Circulation to beauty parlors is just what advertisers want if they are selling hair and beauty preparations. The woman who gets *Good Housekeeping* from a friend may be watching her budget more closely than her friend does, but she may be all the more avid a

---

Fortune Magazine, *The 80–20 Rule in Advertising Response* (a report), pp. 6–7.

reader for money-saving suggestions. Total readership (paid plus pass-along readers) is available from most of the major syndicated magazine-audience services.

MAGAZINE MERCHANDISING
SERVICES

Magazines offer a variety of services to help advertisers *merchandise** their advertising. They may prepare mailings and counter display cards for advertisers to send to dealers. With this service, advertisers profit because dealers are notified of forthcoming advertising, and magazines profit because display cards often include lines like "as advertised in _____ Magazine." The service may extend to store promotions. In its "Fashion Locator," *Esquire* lists department stores carrying fashions featured in the current issue. The August issue of *Mademoiselle* is famous for its back-to-school fashion predictions, and the magazine holds a fashion show in New York in June, attended by stores' buyers and coordinators. *Reader's Digest* has a computerized marketing service that helps readers find local outlets via a single nationwide phone number. Many a magazine campaign has been successful because the manufacturer's salespeople could present the advertising to buyers and show them the advantage of building their merchandising efforts around it.

Merchandising services vary from magazine to magazine; their scope depends upon the size of the advertiser's schedule. Because of ever-rising costs, however, magazines have greatly reduced their expenditures for merchandising aids.

CRITERIA FOR SELECTING
MAGAZINES

Choosing the best magazine(s) for a specific advertiser is a complex task. The number of publications and incompatible data make direct comparisons of magazines difficult. In March, 1980, the American Association of Advertising Agencies published a *Checklist for Evaluating Consumer Magazines* (Exhibit 9.7). The questionnaire was to be sent by advertising agencies to consumer magazines. The agency is then able ". . . to synthesize and collate in an orderly and uniform manner the significant data needed to evaluate consumer magazines."† The checklist asks for eight types of information:

1. Background (general editorial focus)
2. Research and information services
3. Editorial and makeup
4. Cost-rate structure

---

*This is one of the many uses of the term. In this context it means the action and materials supplied by the publisher to help the dealer get direct benefit from magazine advertising.

†*Checklist for Evaluating Consumer Magazines* (New York: American Association of Advertising Agencies, March, 1980), cover letter.

5. Circulation
6. Advertising
7. Flexibility (for example, availability of regional editions)
8. Merchandising services

Exhibit 9.7
Sample page from *Checklist for Evaluating Consumer Magazines.* (Courtesy American Association of Advertising Agencies.)

CIRCULATION

1. a) Current Rate Base: _____

   b) Effective Date: _____

2. Current Actual Total Circulation: _____

3. Circulation Trend Data: *(Most recent three years)*

Year Ending	19__ No.	%	19__ No.	%	19__ No.	%
Total Paid USA						
Subscriptions						
Single Copy						
All Other Paid Circ.						
Grand Total Circ.						
Rate Base Circ.						

   Source: _____

4. ABC Statement

   Are you ABC audited? _____ If not, have you applied? _____ When? _____

   Date of last ABC audit *(white sheet)* _____

5. If not ABC, please provide other verification/substantiation regarding your circulation claims. Please include latest copy of audit.

   Certified Audit Circulation _____

   Verified Audit Circulation _____

   Publisher's Sworn Statement _____

   Any Other? _____

6. If you have demographic editions, are they audited? Please list all demographic editions below.

Demographic Editions	Circulation	Last Audit
_____	_____	_____
_____	_____	_____
_____	_____	_____

With standardized information the advertiser is better able to answer the following questions:

☐ Does the magazine reach the type of reader to whom we are trying to sell our product?
☐ How does distribution of the circulation compare with our product's distribution?
☐ What is the cost of reaching a thousand prospects (not merely the cost per thousand readers)?
☐ How do readers regard the magazine?
☐ Will the advertisement be in acceptable company?
☐ How cooperative is the publisher in giving good position?
☐ How important are merchandising aids, and what aids are available?
☐ How do other magazines compare with this one with respect to the above points?

Despite their problems, the future for magazines is bright. The Magazine Publishers Association has addressed both the short- and long-term prospects for the industry. Magazines will be successful in the near future because:

1. The printed word is a more efficient way to communicate information. It communicates more quickly and in greater depth, and it is retained longer (Exhibit 9.8).
2. For the public at large, magazines and TV serve quite different needs: Magazines are information machines; TV is our entertainment machine.

Finally, magazines will be successful in the long term by adapting to their electronic environment. For instance, see Exhibit 9.9.

BUSINESS AND PROFESSIONAL
JOURNALS

Most of the remainder of this chapter will concentrate on publications devoted to interests other than those of the individual consumer. While consumer magazines occupy a place of prestige among the media, business publications are the less familiar workhorses of the magazine industry. There are three times as many business publications as consumer magazines (2,700 versus 900). However, business publications have much lower circulations and advertising rates but higher CPM's. They are also much more specialized in terms of editorial content and readership.

Under "business advertising," the Standard Rate and Data Service includes advertising to the following:

☐ Distributive trades (*trade*)
☐ Manufacturers and builders (*industrial*)
☐ Top officers of other corporations (*management*)
☐ Physicians, dentists, architects, and other professional people (*professional*)

GM Goes Exclusively with Magazines For New Image-Building Campaign

There are factors in the market gains of imported cars that go beyond list prices and gas mileage estimates. One element that relates to those practical concerns, but is more subtle and philosophical in impact, is the average American's attitude not toward a General Motors car but rather the *idea* of a General Motors or *any* giant profit-making institution. And it's probably impossible to say to what extent, if any, the increased buying of foreign cars by Americans has been the cause or the effect of changing public attitudes toward United States automakers and their products.

Still, General Motors is concerned not about which came first, but with the situation itself. American automakers undoubtedly need an image boost. And GM, notwithstanding the fact it has held its domestic market share over the past 10 years, understands that its success could become reason enough for some public displeasure. These considerations triggered the increase in magazine spending for corporate promotional advertising that accompanied GM's X-car introductions.

In 1977 GM spent $4.4 million in corporate automotive general promotion, only $103,000 of it in magazines and nearly $3 million in network tv, according to PIB/LNA Service. The following year its overall corporate expenditure was $4.9 million, with $1.8 million in magazines and $2.7 million in television. For just the first nine months of 1979, this same corporate program was up to $4.5 million, with $4.3 million of it in magazines, and GM had added a special image building campaign that cost an additional $1 million, exclusively in magazines. Television was omitted from this corporate program during the January-September period in 1979, and Sunday magazines accounted for $1.5 million of the overall magazine expenditure.

The unique element in the 1979 program was General Motors' Customer Information campaign, designed to improve the GM public image with both timely and far-

HOW TO SAVE YOUR LIFE AND THE ONE NEXT TO YOU

No illustrations, no photos, no color. Just basic information designed to help consumers and convey the fact that GM cares about people. Agency was N W Ayer ABH International, New York.

sighted discussion of automotive trends, improvements, suggestions for safety, and so forth. The whole effort conveys the message that General Motors is not some cold mechanism gone wild, but rather a group of people concerned with people.

Last October, General Motors executive vice president Roger B. Smith gave a speech in which he stressed the need for using advertising to rebuild corporate images, and to convey corporate competence, consumer information, and, above all, *humanity.*

"Credibility and acceptance are as fleeting as a one-point lead in the National Football League," he said. "When special interest groups are bombarding the public with violent campaigns. When the surveys we were taking revealed that business ranked somewhere between politicians and carnival barkers in terms of credibility, a lot of us got religion. . . . What it boils down to is this: Over and above the selling of our products, in this day and age we have to sell ourselves, too. And that is the thrust of the public affairs advertising program we have designed—to sell the *human* attributes of General Motors."

In an effort to convey this theme of humanity and public concern, Mr. Smith stated, the ads should truly inform the reader while suggesting that "the customer's best friend when it comes to information about our company is not the government or the consumerists or the environmentalists—it's General Motors."

But television alone could not carry this message, he said. "Some of the information we wanted to get across is fairly complicated, too much for a television spot. Therefore, we designed what we call a consumer advertising campaign as a counterpoint to our tv campaign. There are no pretty girls, no shiny cars, no pictures of any kind. They discuss problems. They answer questions. They inform."

As Smith also stated, the GM Customer Information campaign in magazines risked being visually uninviting in order to deliver solid information. There's no white space, and there *are* large blocks of print. According to GM, the ads regularly achieve over 30 percent in readership scores. More importantly, 91 percent of the readers think the ads are a good idea, and 89 percent say the information is useful to them.

"We conclude that people will read honest, helpful, informative advertising," said Mr. Smith. "I think our customer information campaign has done a lot to dampen some of the hostility and criticism of a company as large and as much in the limelight as ours. To be sure, the campaign is not over. I guess it can never be over."

Ironically, though, amid all this work to convince the American consumer that a corporation like GM can be of service and sell a car that's just as good as—or better than—an import, it was reported in February that customer complaints about engine stallouts in the X-cars while traveling at low speeds or idling could lead to the recall of 250,000 of the year-old vehicles. Perhaps it's only a minor adjustment, perhaps not. Either way, it isn't good news for an image-conscious company trying to sell dependability. —R.C.

Exhibit 9.8
Magazine advertising: a case study. (Courtesy *Magazine Age,* April 1980. Copyright 1980 by Magazine Age Publishing Co.)

Trade papers Because most nationally advertised products depend upon dealers for their sales, we give trade-paper advertising our first attention. Usually this advertising is prepared by the agency that handles the consumer advertising, and in any new campaign both are prepared at the time time. The term *trade papers* is applied particularly to business publications for those who buy products for resale, such as wholesalers, jobbers, and retailers. Typical trade papers are *American Druggist, Supermarket News, Chain Store Age, Hardware Retailer, Modern Tire Dealer, Women's Wear Daily,* and *Home Furnishings,* their points of view revealed in their titles.

Magazines of the Future

It is the year 2020 and your grandson's wife or co-habitant has just entered her home information/entertainment room. She slips gracefully into her home information/entertainment chair. She presses the proper three buttons on the arm of the chair. This brings her favorite magazine into focus on her home information/entertainment wall. She examines the cover, presses the change-page-button and peruses the first advertising spread. It's a delicious array of wonderful desserts. She presses her print-out-food-button and a recipe goes directly into her food file, recipe scanner where it is read by her computerized-ingredient mixer. Ingredients slide down to the oven and activate the bake button. Your grandson is lucky to have a wife who cooks so well. She punches her turn-page button and continues her magazine reading experience, much as she did in 1980.

We think ours is a happier, more logical scenario: Paper companies will be happy because they will be supplying print-out-paper to every household. The cable and satellite companies will be happy because they will have found a way to make a profit from print. Editors will be happy because they will be supplying the software for the electronic marvels. *Readers will be happy because by reading, they will still be able to acquire 3½ times as much information twice as fast and remember it longer.* Only the Post Office remains unhappy.

Exhibit 9.9
The prospect for magazines. [Courtesy of *Magazine Newsletter of Advertising* (New York: MPA, June 1980), pp. 3–4.]

Hardly a business engaged in distributing goods does not have a trade paper to discuss its problems. Trade papers are the great medium for reporting the merchandising news about products and packaging, prices, deals, and promotions of the manufacturers who cater to their particular industries. The chain-store field alone has more than twenty such publications. Druggists have a choice of over thirty and more than sixty different publications are issued for grocers. There are many localized journals, such as *Texas Food Merchant, Michigan Beverage News, Southern Hardware, California Apparel News,* and *Illinois Building News.*

Trade-paper copy. No matter what the field, all trade papers have a common editorial objective: to tell the dealer how to make more money. Whether the magazine is for sporting-goods, hardware, grocery, or service-station dealers, articles deal with how to increase stock turnover, how to get the most out of window displays, finding, training, and motivating salespeople, the use of contests to attract new business, how to buy merchandise that will sell, how to get the most out of available selling space, and a host of merchandising ideas designed to increase store profits.

The advertising discusses not how good a product is—that is taken for granted—but how it will help the profit picture of a store. Among the subjects promoted are new aspects of the product, such as a new:

- ☐ feature of the product
- ☐ style of packaging
- ☐ display idea
- ☐ consumer deal
- ☐ store deal
- ☐ plan for a new advertising campaign involving the retailer (couponing)
- ☐ promotional idea
- ☐ in-store suggestion for improving sales of the advertised and related products
- ☐ idea that will help sales and reduce expense

Industrial

advertising

As we move into the world of a member of one industry selling its materials, machinery, tools parts, and equipment to another company for use in making a product or conducting operations, we are in an altogether different ball game—the *industrial-marketing* arena.

There are fewer customers than in the consumer market, and they can be more easily identified. The amount of money in making a sale may be large, hundreds of thousands of dollars, maybe even millions. Nothing is bought on impulse. Many knowledgable executives with technical skills often share in the buying decision. The sales representative has to have a high degree of professional competence in dealing with the industrial market, in which personal selling is the biggest factor in making a sale. Advertising is a collateral help in paving the way for or supporting the salesperson; hence it receives a smaller share of the marketing budget.

Advertising addressed to people responsible for buying goods needed to make products is called *industrial advertising*. It is designed to reach purchasing agents, plant managers, engineers, comptrollers, and others who have a voice in spending the firm's money.

Uniqueness of industrial advertising. Industrial advertising speaks to people who have their own approach to making business decisions. For example:

☐ Buying is done with a sense of professional responsibility that asks, "Will this prove to be the best choice?" A poor decision will be around to haunt all who shared in it.

☐ Buyers purchase to meet predetermined specifications, not on impulse.

☐ Many people may be involved in a decision—a scientist, a designer, an engineer, a production manager, a purchasing agent, a comptroller—each approaching the problem from a special viewpoint.

☐ Decisions are made after many demonstrations, much inquiry, and many meetings.

☐ With so many individuals involved, so many actions to be taken, so much money at stake, there is often a big time lag between the moment it was decided to consider a purchase and the final decision.

A report issued by Time, Inc., reveals some of the complexity in an industrial buying decision:

An air-conditioning exhaust system—the kind found in office buildings and factories, as opposed to a room air-conditioner for home use. The process of purchasing an air-conditioning exhaust system can be very complicated. Some 16 actions were taken by six individuals within the company.

A case loader—a packaging machine used for loading small, package bottles into corrugated containers. Some 13 actions were taken by 9 individuals or groups of individuals in middle management, top management, and purchasing.

An encoder drum—part of an electrical system needed in a Department of Defense project. Some 12 actions were taken by 3 individuals within the company.

In addition, 4 suppliers were involved, as well as the U.S. government offices concerned with this project.

A desk calculator—the kind normally found in offices throughout the United States. It is a lightweight, semiportable, and highly versatile machine small enough to be placed on a desk, as opposed to a special "table" by the desk. Some 8 actions were taken by 4 individuals or groups of individuals within the company.

Carpeting—the kind of floor covering normally found in offices and reception rooms. Some 10 actions were taken by 11 individuals within the company.*

From three to eleven people had a say in those final buying decisions. Advertising's problem is to reach all who may be involved.

Effectiveness of industrial advertising. Studies have been done to measure the impact of industrial advertising. Typical study results are reported by the Arthur B. Little Company from its survey of 1,100 studies:

- ☐ Companies that maintain their advertising in recession years have better sales and profits in those and in later years.
- ☐ Industrial advertising reaches purchasing influences not normally reached by salesmen.
- ☐ It reduces the cost per sales dollar by supplementing the salesman's efforts.
- ☐ Industrial product advertising increases the share of potential buyers who consider the brand.
- ☐ Industrial advertising reaches prospective purchasers the salesman can't find or does not have adequate time to cover.

Industrial-advertising copy. Industrial advertising speaks to engineers and to other people who are technically trained. They read their trade or professional journals because of a constant challenge to keep informed of the latest developments affecting their field; they have to fight professional obsolescence. They read advertisements with the same critical curiosity with which they read the editorial matter. They are looking for news of products and experiences relevant to their problems, expressed in specific, factual form. They are interested in problems and their solution; they are most interested in case reports showing how some problem was successfully met. They seek confirmation or other proof of all claims made. They will read long copy and welcome any charts or photographs that help explain matters.

Most advertisements make a strong bid to the reader to write for further information. Industrial advertising adheres closely to the copy structure discussed earlier—promise of benefit, amplification, proof, action.

The case history is widely used in industrial advertising as a publicity release, as a fact sheet for salespeople, as direct mail, and as an ad.

---

*Based on a study conducted by Dr. Emanual Demby, Fairleigh Dickinson University and reprinted through the courtesy of Time, Inc.

BPA Buyer's Guide No. 000

This Publication Is Reporting On A Comparable Basis

PUBLISHER'S STATEMENT
For 6 Month Period Ending
JUNE 19 —

▽BPA

BUSINESS PUBLICATIONS AUDIT OF CIRCULATION, INC.
360 Park Avenue South, New York, N.Y. 10010

No attempt has been made to rank the information contained in this report in order of importance, since BPA believes this is a judgment which must be made by the user of the report.

THE CRITERION

Criterion Publishing Company
360 Park Avenue South, New York, N.Y. 10010
(212) 487-5200

OFFICIAL PUBLICATION OF	None
ESTABLISHED 1931	ISSUES PER YEAR 12

FIELD SERVED

THE CRITERION serves the field of data processing systems and procedures in manufacturing industries, service organizations, finance, insurance companies, government, utilities, retail and wholesale trade and transportation, communication, printing and publishing firms.

DEFINITION OF RECIPIENT QUALIFICATION

Qualified recipients are corporate officials, controllers, data processing and accounting personnel, purchasing and other management personnel in the above field.

Also qualified are a limited number of library addressed copies.

AVERAGE NON-QUALIFIED DISTRIBUTION

	Copies
Advertiser and Agency	443
Non-Qualified Paid	28
Rotated or Occasional	26
Samples	122
All Other	242
TOTAL	**861**

U.S. POSTAL MAILING CLASSIFICATION ...... SECOND CLASS

1. AVERAGE QUALIFIED CIRCULATION BREAKDOWN FOR PERIOD

	Qualified Non-Paid		Qualified Paid		Total Qualified	
	Copies	Percent	Copies	Percent	Copies	Percent
Single	7,007	34.1%	12,917	62.9%	19,924	97.0%
* Group	–	–	523	2.5	523	2.5
Association	–	–	–	–	–	–
Gift	–	–	–	–	–	–
* Bulk	–	–	100	0.5	100	0.5
*See Para. 11 **TOTALS**	7,007	34.1%	13,540	65.9%	20,547	100.0%

2. QUALIFIED CIRCULATION BY ISSUES WITH REMOVALS AND ADDITIONS FOR PERIOD

19— Issue	Qualified Non-Paid	Qualified Paid	Total Qualified	Number Removed	Number Added	19— Issue	Qualified Non-Paid	Qualified Paid	Total Qualified	Number Removed	Number Added
January	6,936	13,546	20,482	778	533	April	7,049	13,485	20,534	651	684
February	6,696	13,899	20,595	351	464	May	7,286	13,278	20,564	528	558
March	6,857	13,644	20,501	523	429	June	7,215	13,388	20,603	345	384
						TOTALS				3,176	3,052

Exhibit 9.10
Publisher's statement, showing paid and nonpaid circulation. Turnover is indicated by numbers removed and numbers added, keeping the list fresh. (Courtesy Business Publications Audit of Circulation, Inc.)

Business publications—general

practices

The following practices relate to trade papers as well as to industrial publications (which have their own special problems to be discussed after this general discussion).

Controlled circulation. Business publications include *paid circulation* and *controlled circulation.* Controlled circulation is free circulation to a carefully selected list of those who are in a position to influence sales; furthermore, they must annually express in writing a desire to receive, or continue to receive, the publication in order to qualify for the list. They must also give their titles and functions. Most business papers are sent out in controlled circulation, but some are paid for. Paid circulations are usually smaller than controlled circulations, but their publishers hold that the paying audience is more select.

Circulation audits. The leading trade and industrial publications belong to the Business Publications Audit of Circulation, Inc. (BPA), which audits approximately 700 business publications (Exhibit 9.10). In their audit of circulation, BPA pays particular attention to the qualifications of all those on the controlled list and when they last indicated that they wanted the publication.

In addition to BPA, the Audit Bureau of Circulation (ABC) performs essentially the same function (for over 200 paid-circulation publications), although its main effort is in the consumer field. Some publications have both ABC and BPA audits. (Many business publications, especially the smaller ones, do not offer any circulation-audit report).

A third auditing group is the Verified Audit Circulation Company (VAC). Its standards are less strict than those of BPA.

Circulation-audit reports provide the business advertiser with information and statistics to use in selecting the best publications for carrying a product's advertising.

Industrial publications—special

practices

Vertical or horizontal publications. Industrial publications designed to reach people who make purchasing decisions for industry may be classified as *vertical* and *horizontal.*

Vertical industrial publications discuss problems of a single industry. *Manufacturing Confectioner,* for example,

is intended for management and departmental executives of firms manufacturing confectionery, chocolate, cough drops, nut products, marshmallows, chewing gum, etc. Editorial content covers production, formulation, quality control, materials handling, storage, packaging, shipping, marketing, merchandising, new ingredients, supplies, equipment, business management and others, including association news.

The Glass Industry

is edited for those who engage in the manufacture of glass from raw materials and those who fabricate finished glass products from purchased glass. It answers technical and manufacturing questions and indicates the trends that the industry is following.

Each industry will have several publications devoted to its problems. In the engineering-construction classification in the Standard Rate and Data Service over eighty publications are listed; the automotive and brewing categories each list more than sixty; there are over fifty publications listed for the grocery classification.

Horizontal publications are edited for people who have similar functions in their enterprises, regardless of industry. Consider *Grounds Maintenance,*

edited for landscape architects and for landscape contractors and grounds superintendents, serving industrial plants, parks, colleges and schools, golf courses, cemeteries, shopping plazas, highways, institutions, public works, and recreational areas. It provides technical and management information about landscape beautification, care of turf, trees, and ornamentals. Articles cover such subjects as plant selection, seeding, planting, transplanting, fertilizing, irrigating, pruning, controlling weeds and pests, selection and service of equipment.

Consulting Engineer

edited for engineers in private practice in mechanical, electrical, structural, civil, sanitary, and allied engineering disciplines who have authority over the specifications of products and systems for their firms, projects.

Purchasing "provides news and ideas for today's purchasing professional."

There are also a large number of state industrial publications. Many of the larger publications have geographic and demographic editions, and some have international editions.

Standard Industrial Classification System. One thing that greatly facilitates the industrial marketing process is the Standard Industrial Classification System (SIC), a numbering system established by the United States government. SIC classifies more than 4 million manufacturing firms into ten major categories, further subdivided into more specific groups. The code numbering system operates as follows: All major business activities (agriculture, forestry, and fisheries; mining; construction; manufacturing; transportation, communication, and public utilities; wholesale; retail; finance, insurance, and real estate; services; government) are given a two-digit code number. A third and a fourth digit are assigned to identify more specific activities within each major business category, in much the same way that the Dewey Decimal System works.* For example:

---

*The *Standard Industrial Classification Manual* is available from the Superintendent of Documents, United States Government Printing Office, Washington, D.C.

☐ 25   Manufacturers of furniture and fixtures
☐ 252   Manufacturers of office furniture
☐ 2521   Manufacturers of wood office furniture
☐ 2522   Manufacturers of metal office furniture

The great value of the SIC system is that it enables the advertiser to identify and locate specific target markets. Industrial publications usually provide an analysis of circulation by SIC classifications. The advertiser can then pick the publication reaching the greatest number of the appropriate classification, or the information can be used in buying lists for direct mailings.

Professional publications

The Standard Rate and Data Service, in its special business-publications edition, includes journals addressed to physicians, surgeons, dentists, architects, and other professionals who depend upon these journals to keep abreast of their professions. Their editorial content ranges from reporting new technical developments to discussing how to meet client or patient problems better and how to conduct their offices more efficiently and more profitably. Those professional people are great influences in recommending or specifying the products their patients or clients should order. Much advertising of high technical caliber, therefore, is addressed to them.

Farm magazines

We have a big farm population, and it has its own, special magazines. These may be classified as *general farm magazines, regional farm magazines,* and *vocational farm magazines.* These classifications overlap, however, because a number of the larger magazines have geographical and demographic splits.

General farm magazines. The largest of these is *Farm Journal,* with a circulation of about 3 million. Two-thirds of its editorial content is devoted to farm production, management, and news; one-third, to the needs of women and families. It is published in a series of regional editions.

Regional farm magazines. These publications specifically aim at farmers in different regions of the country. They discuss problems relating to farmers' chief crops, their general welfare, and governmental activity affecting them. Publications such as *Ohio Farmer, California Farmer,* and *Dakota Farmer* are obviously regional.

Vocational farm magazines. Many farm publications are devoted to certain crops or types of farming. They are really vocational papers and include such publications as *The Dairyman, American Fruit Grower, Poultry Press,* and *Better Beef Business.* Classifications overlap in magazines like the

New England Dairyman, Washington Cattleman, and *Gulf Coast Cattleman.* Whatever the farmer's interest may be, there are a number of publications edited for him. Many farm homes get several publications.

SUMMARY

We can expect a continuing flow of new magazines, each devoted to a specialized interest that its publishers think has not been reached effectively.

The major problems facing all magazines are the rising costs of paper, printing, and postage. To offset high paper costs, magazines that have not already done so will trim their size—but this is a limited solution. To meet rising printing costs, magazines will continue to raise per-copy prices and will use newer, less expensive composition and printing methods. Magazines face continuing postage increases, which may affect circulation methods, advertising costs, and the very character of magazines. So publishers are finding ways of reaching consumers without having to pay high postal costs: Some deliver their magazines in bulk to distributors, who put the magazines in plastic bags and hang them on subscribers' doorknobs (they are prohibited by law from using mailboxes); others have discovered the importance of supermarket distribution; electronic delivery is a possibility for the future, particularly for business publications. And magazines have a continuing competitive problem of establishing their importance on every media schedule.

In the next several years business publishers will see themselves more as sources of information than publishers of ink-on-paper magazines. This is not to suggest that the traditional magazine format will fall by the wayside. Instead, magazine publishers will diversify and supplement their magazines with a number of other information-delivery systems. These may include things as simple as newsletters or as innovative as computer-retrieval data bases and same-day trade-show newspapers.

Already major publishers, such as Dow Jones, provide their publications via computers along with other financial and business information. Earlier in this chapter and in our discussion of TV (see Chapter 6) we mentioned some future applications of in-home electronic communication now largely in the experimental stage. Business publishers predict that general electronic communication will be a reality in a much shorter time frame. This will be primarily based on the fact that business can afford to spend a great deal more on computer hardware and financial services than the average household can. The ability to retrieve baseball scores electronically from a home computer is a luxury few households can afford. However, for a business the competitive advantage gained from immediate access to marketing information will make the same investment a minimal business expense.

Cable TV is a potential threat; for, like magazines, it can reach selected audiences. Only 30 percent of TV households have cable TV now, however, and there will probably always be a great many advertisers and consumers who do not use cablecasting.

QUESTIONS

1. What are the major advantages and limitations of magazines for the national advertiser?
2. Discuss the Media Imperatives as they relate to audience selectivity.
3. How did TV contribute to the demise of several leading general-circulation magazines?
4. There are three sets of magazines dates one must be aware of in planning and buying space. What are they?
5. What steps have magazines taken for their advertisers to be more timely?
6. How do demographic and geographic editions differ?
7. What is a magazine network?
8. What is the major problem with combining primary and pass-along circulation in the evaluation of magazines?
9. What is the difference between a frequency discount and a volume discount in buying magazine space?
10. What is the major advantage of the American Association of Advertising Agencies *Checklist for Evaluating Consumer Magazines*?
11. Discuss the relationship between the guaranteed circulation and the magazine rebate.
12. Distinguish among trade advertising, industrial advertising, and professional advertising.
13. How are business publishers following the lead of major newspapers in adapting to new electronic technology?
14. What is the difference between vertical and horizonal industrial publications?
15. Distinguish among general, regional, and vocational farm publications.
16. Consumer magazines view TV as their major competitor for advertising dollars while business publications see direct mail in this role. Discuss.
17. Define the following:

   a. split run
   b. controlled circulation
   c. fourth cover page
   d. gatefolds
   e. bleed ads
   f. SIC

   g. CPM
   h. space contract
   i. magazine network
   j. late close
   k. remnant space
   l. basic rate (open rate)

SUGGESTED EXERCISES

18. Take a general consumer magazine directed toward women and one toward men. Categorize the full-page ads in each according to product class (automobile, cigarettes, cosmetics, and so on). How many ads are in each category?
19. Take a copy of *Progressive Farmer* and *Southern Living*. Compare and contrast the advertising for plants, fertilizer, and the like in the two publications.

READINGS

"ABP hails U.S. freeze," *Advertising Age,* April 27, 1981, p. 2.

BRIN, GERI: "How Special Interest Publications Capture Specialized Audiences," *Magazine Age,* September 1980, pp. 64–69.

"Magazines," *Advertising Age,* October 19, 1981, S-1.

MOTT, FRANK LUTHER: *A History of American Magazines,* 3 vols. (Cambridge, MA: Harvard University Press, 1930–1938).

STERN, BRUCE L., DEAN M. KRUGMAN, and ALAN RESNIK: "Magazine Advertising: An Analysis of its Information Content," *Journal of Advertising Research,* April 1981, pp. 39–46.

REVETT, JOHN: "Magazines Seen Next Censor Target," *Advertising Age,* October 26, 1981, p. 3.

URBAN, CHRISTINE D.: "Correlates of Magazine Readership," *Journal of Advertising Research,* August 1980, pp. 73–84.

WHITE, GORDON: *John Caples: ADMAN* (Chicago: Crain Books, 1977), pp. 71–88.

WOOD, WALLY: "Old MacDonald Has an Agribusiness," *Magazine Age,* September 1981, pp. 44–49.

10

Outdoor Advertising; Transit Advertising

Despite high gasoline prices and recent conservation efforts, America is still a country on wheels. As people go to and from work, shopping, visiting, and touring, they are greeted on different parts of their trip by out-of-home advertising, one of today's major advertising media. Outdoor advertising is often defined as *any* ad or identification sign located in a public place, such as signs of varying sizes, shapes, and colors that mark eating places, bowling alleys, motels, movies, and the like. In fact outdoor advertising is a medium made up of some 270,000 standardized posters and painted signs. Laid flat,, these standardized posters would not cover the pavement at Chicago's O'Hare Airport. There are actually fewer outdoor posters today than there were a decade ago, with most of these in areas zoned for business or industry.

OUTDOOR ADVERTISING

The outdoor-advertising industry is self-regulated by its trade association, the Outdoor Advertising Association of America (OAAA).* Over 80 percent of all outdoor posters adhere to the OAAA's Code of Practices, which states:

---

*Unless otherwise identified, information in this chapter is from the Outdoor Advertising Association of America, Inc.

As owners and operators of standardized outdoor advertising displays, we the members of Outdoor Advertising Association of America, Inc., have voluntarily pledged strict adherence to a rigid code of practices, and endorse adoption of these principles by state or local governments, as follows:

We share the public interest in natural scenic beauty, parks, and historical monuments. We do not erect our advertising displays in such areas.

We believe in and support zoning based on sound community planning.

We locate our structures in urban areas only where business exists or is permitted under zoning.

We build displays in rural areas along highways only where other business exists or is permitted by state or local regulation.

We place outdoor advertising displays only upon property we own or lease for that purpose.

We observe rigid standards of design, construction, and maintenance so that our displays will be attractive.

We only display outdoor advertising which is truthful in every respect and in accordance with high moral standards.

We actively and continuously support worthy public causes through our contribution of outdoor advertising displays.

We locate our structures with discretion and good taste with respect to frequency and concentration.

Features and advantages

Outdoor advertising provides the largest and most colorful display for an advertiser's trademark, product, and slogan. It offers the most spectacular use of lights to attract attention and has shown special effectiveness in getting a name known.

It is geographically flexible; and for its more than 9,000 markets computerized market data are available. An advertiser can reach his market nationally, regionally, and locally. In many cities advertisers can reach special ethnic neighborhoods. Outdoor advertising offers both frequency and reach at low cost.

Used with other media, outdoor advertising can round out a campaign by providing extra frequency or reach. Local advertisers, especially those handling institutional or service accounts, blanket their markets with outdoor ads.

Limitations and challenges

Creative considerations. Since cars pass outdoor signs quickly, copy is limited to a message that can be told in a few words. Creating a design that can tell its story in pictures is the greatest challenge for outdoor advertisers. Not all messages are suited to such compression. Although outdoor advertising reaches a wide audience, an advantage for a product in widespread sale, its use is quite limited for advertisers trying to reach a segmented market (such as women age 25 to 49).

Legal considerations. The Federal Highway Beautification Act of 1968, banning outdoor signs within 660 feet of a federally financed highway, permits signs within that area if it is locally zoned for business and industrial use. The act was revised in 1976 to permit identification, directional, and distance signs for services. In addition, most states and municipalities also have laws restricting outdoor advertising to business and industrial areas, a policy the OAAA has long supported.

The Beautification Act never accomplished the full intent of the environmental groups that originally supported it: Congress has been unwilling to provide the funds needed for compensating billboard owners for the removal of their signs. With the removal of some nonconforming signs, however, the remaining locations have often gained in value. In some markets outdoor is more profitable now than it was before passage of the act.

Energy considerations. Recent gasoline shortages and price increases have been accompanied by decreased automobile usage. Any diminution in driving is a potential threat to the outdoor-advertising industry although current decreases in automobile mileage affect highway driving more than they do city transportation, where most outdoor signs are located. If gasoline shortages continue to occur, they would severely damage outdoor revenues, perhaps in favor of mass-transit and station-poster advertising.

Outdoor plant

The basic business unit of the outdoor industry is the local outdoor company, the *outdoor plant*. Its stock in trade is the location it has leased or bought under local zoning regulations permitting the erection of signs. Having acquired a location, the plant operator builds a structure at his own expense, sells the advertising space on it (technically, leases the space), posts or paints the advertiser's message, and is responsible for maintaining the board and the ad in good condition during the life of the advertiser's contract.

The two forms of standardized outdoor advertising handled by outdoor plants are the poster panel and the painted bulletin.

Poster panels

Frequently called "posters," these outside structures have blank panels on which preprinted advertisements can be gummed (Exhibit 10.1). Posters can be illuminated (for the more important locations) or unilluminated (for the less costly ones). A standard-size poster panel is 12 by 25 feet. (In outdoor advertising the height is given first, then the width.) It has a standard construction and frame. A distinguishing feature of poster panels is the ease and simplicity of replacing the message. They are the lowest-cost method of buying outdoor advertising and are the most widely used form.

Poster sizes. Poster sizes are measured in terms of *sheets.* The term originated in the days when it took twenty-four of the largest sheets the presses

Exhibit 10.1
Four designs from a most provocative series in which a "bite" was removed from the original poster each week for 13 consecutive weeks. (All outdoor examples in this chapter are courtesy of the Institute of Outdoor Advertising.)

could hold to cover a sign 12 by 25 feet. The presses have become much larger, but the designation has stuck. Today all poster ads are still mounted on standard boards, 12 by 25 feet. The most popular size is the *thirty-sheet poster,* which consists of a metal frame around the outside, a margin of blank paper acting as a mat, or border, and the message mounted on a standard-size panel in the center. If the artwork extends all the way to the metal frame, without a margin, it is called a *bleed poster.* Since it costs the least, a *twenty-four-sheet poster* is generally used for noncommercial purposes. See Exhibit 10.2.

In addition to the standard posters we have been discussing, there is another sector of the industry, which deals in eight-sheet posters, 6 feet high and 12 feet wide. (Often called "junior posters," the eight-sheet designation is preferred to indicate their proportion to the more popular thirty-sheet posters.) In the past they were used to reach specific groups in neighborhoods where pedestrians would see them on walls adjacent to stores. However, in recent years the eight-sheet poster has grown in popularity since advertisers can buy locations at a tremendous savings in both space and production costs. In addition, the eight-sheet is more likely to meet local outdoor-advertising regulations than standard-size posters are.

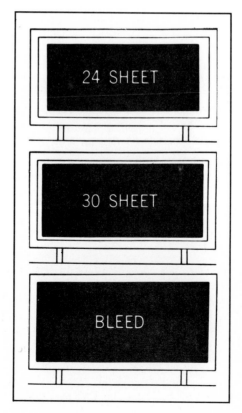

Exhibit 10.2
The standard-size structure, 12 feet high by 25 feet long, is the most popular size. Within this framework are ads in three sizes, depending upon how much white space is left between the ad and the frame. There is no difference in cost among any of these sizes. The most popular is the 30-sheet; the bleed is second.

Eight-sheet posters are handled by special poster plants and frequently appear concurrently with thirty-sheet showings in a market. The Eight-Sheet Outdoor Advertising Association (ESOAA) was recently founded to promote the interests of the eight-sheet poster medium.

Buying poster advertising;

GRP units

Until 1973 the traditional way of selling outdoor posters of uniform size was in a *showing*, a package or assortment of different poster locations. The price of a showing depended on the number of posters and the quality of the locations. There was a 100 showing; there was a 50 showing and a 25 showing. Obviously, the 25 showing was half the 50 showing, and the 50 showing was half the 100 showing. What then, you might ask, was a 100 showing? A 100 showing was each plant owner's private opinion of what would make an excellent impression on that particular market. This system clearly caused problems for advertisers: How could they compare the values of showings in different markets when different plant owners did the rating?

Because of these problems, in 1973 the industry moved to the practice of selling posters in *GRP (gross-rating-point) units,* preselected by the plant owner; the showing is priced according to its *GRPs.* (Posters are rarely sold individually.)

A rating point is equivalent to the exposure of an ad to 1 percent of the population of a market per day. A 100-GRP package consists of the number of poster panels required to deliver exposure opportunities to 100 percent of the population of the market in 1 day; a 50-GRP buy offers exposure opportunities to 50 percent of the population of a market. A 100-GRP showing in one city may include fewer posters than in another larger city, but it will provide the same intensity of market coverage. A study of the accompanying page (Exhibit 10.3) of the *Buyer's Guide to Outdoor Advertising* will show you the difference in the number of posters in a 100 showing in different cities.

When the actual time comes to purchase posters, the outdoor-space buyer rides through the area with a plant operator or his representative, who has a map spotting the prepared sites included in a package. Posters are sold on a monthly basis, and copy can be changed monthly.

Audience measurement

services

Traffic Audit Bureau. The sale of space in the outdoor-advertising industry is based on a count of automobile traffic passing a sign every day. The traffic count ignores duplication (people who pass a sign twice a day), but it does provide a yardstick for comparing values of different locations. The central source of all such information is the Traffic Audit Bureau (TAB), a tripartite organization formed years ago by the advertisers, agencies, and plant owners who constitute its membership. Its field employees are continually gathering the latest traffic data from local, state, and federal authorities, and they make their own checks as well. (The TAB audits some 100,000 panels per

PLANT NO	MARKET NO.	MARKET NAME	COUNTY NAME	POP.	EFF. DATE	GRP SHOW	POSTERS NON ILL	POSTERS ILL	COST PER MONTH	DIS.
		RIVERSIDE, PA SHICKSHINNY, PA WASHINGTONVILLE, PA								
1784.0	03900	BETHEL PHL SEE MARKET NO. 37-48050**	BERKS	.6	09/01/9	*100	1		151.00	67
1784.0	04100	BIRDSBORO-BAUMSTOWN MKT PHL SEE MARKET NO. 37-48050**	BERKS	3.5	09/01/9	*100 * 50	2 1		297.00 151.00	67 67
9211.0	04150	BLAIN HAR SEE MARKET NO. 37-45170**	PERRY	.3	09/01/0	*100	1		72.00	
6175.0	04250	BLAIRSVILLE PIT	INDIANA	4.4	01/01/1	100	1		170.00	50
1784.0	04400	BLANDON PHL SEE MARKET NO. 37-46980** SEE MARKET NO. 37-48053**	BERKS	1.1	09/01/9	*100	1		151.00	67
6072.0	04700	BOALSBURG JOH SEE MARKET NO. 37-56870**	CENTRE	.8	09/01/0	*100	1		174.00	16
1784.0	05000	BOYERTOWN PHL SEE MARKET NO. 37-41800**	BERKS	4.4	09/01/9	*100 * 50	2 1		297.00 151.00	67 67
5925.0	05200	BRADFORD COUNTY MKT. BIN	BRADFORD, PA.- TIOGA, N. Y.	65.9	01/01/1	100 50	10 5		1203.00 600.00	30 30
5945.0	05250	BRADFORD MKT BUF	MCKEAN, PA.- CATTARAUGUS, N. Y.	27.7	01/01/1	100 50	6 3	2 1	1000.00 500.00	30 30
6072.0	05550	BRIAR CREEK WIL SEE MARKET NO. 37-03750**	COLUMBIA	.5	09/01/0	*100	1		168.00	16
9211.0	05800	BROAD TOP CITY JOH SEE MARKET NO. 37-27470**	HUNTINGDON	.3	09/01/0	*100	1		72.00	
5360.0	05900	BROOKVILLE PIT	JEFFERSON	4.3	01/01/1	*100 * 75 * 50 * 25	4 3 2 1		600.00 450.00 300.00 150.00	
5095.0	06420	BUCKS COUNTY MKT PHL	BUCKS	474.0	01/01/1	100 75 50 25	4 3 2 1	32 24 16 8	8868.00 6651.00 4434.00 2217.00	14 14 14 14
6072.0	06550	BURNHAM HAR SEE MARKET NO. 37-32520**	MIFFLIN	2.6	09/01/0	*100	1		168.00	16
6170.0	06800	BUTLER METRO MKT PIT	BUTLER	75.3	01/01/1	100 75 50 25	6 4 3 1	6 5 3 2	1930.00 1470.00 965.00 505.00	50 50 50 50
6080.0	07150	CAMBRIDGE SPRINGS ERI SEE MARKET NO. 37-36250**	CRAWFORD	2.0	09/01/0	100	1	1	420.00	16
6090.0	07450	CARLISLE-GETTYSBURG MARKET HAR SEE MARKET NO. 37-66450**	ADAMS-CUMBERLAND	89.0	09/01/0	100 75 50 25	5 5 3 3	9 6 4 2	2822.00 2230.00 1537.00 1126.00	16 16 16 16
9211.0	07800	CASSVILLE JOH SEE MARKET NO. 37-27470**	HUNTINGDON	.2	09/01/0	*100	1		72.00	
6072.0	08000	CATAWISSA WIL SEE MARKET NO. 37-03750**	COLUMBIA	1.7	09/01/0	*100	1		168.00	16
6072.0	08350	CENTRE HALL JOH SEE MARKET NO. 37-56870**	CENTRE	1.3	09/01/0	*100	1		174.00	16
9064.0	08450	CHAMBERSBURG-WAYNESBORO-FRANKLIN WAS	FRANKLIN	105.6	01/01/1	100 75 50 25	24 18 12 6		2448.00 1836.00 1296.00 684.00	55 55 55 55
		--SUB MKTS. (ALSO SOLD SEPARATELY) GREENCASTLE MKT, PA MERCERSBURG MKT, PA WAYNESBURG MKT, PA								
5945.0	09570	CLARION MKT PIT	CLARION-VENANGO	7.6	01/01/1	100 50 25	8 4 2		920.00 460.00 230.00	30 30 30
5360.0	09650	CLEARFIELD-PHILIPSBURG JOH	CLEARFIELD	58.1	01/01/1	100 75 50 25	12 9 6 3		1800.00 1350.00 900.00 450.00	
6087.0	09700	CLEARFIELD-PHILLIPSBURG MKT. JOH SEE MARKET NO. 37-01060**	CENTRE-CLEARFIELD	58.1	09/01/0	100 75 50 25	12 9 6 3		2088.00 1562.00 1042.00 521.00	16 16 16 16
6080.0	11200	CONNEAUT LAKE ERI SEE MARKET NO. 37-36250**	CRAWFORD	.7	09/01/0	100	1	1	420.00	16
6080.0	11250	CONNEAUTVILLE ERI SEE MARKET NO. 37-36250**	CRAWFORD	1.0	09/01/0	100	1	1	420.00	16
6175.0	11300	CONNELLSVILLE MKT PIT	FAYETTE	11.5	01/01/1	*100 * 50	2 1		340.00 170.00	50 50
5945.0	11950	COUDERSPORT MKT BUF	POTTER-TIOGA	8.0	01/01/1	100 50	2 1		250.00 125.00	30 30
6080.0	12550	CROSSINGVILLE ERI SEE MARKET NO. 37-36250**	CRAWFORD	.2	09/01/0	100	1	1	420.00	16
6072.0	13150	DALMATIA WIL SEE MARKET NO. 37-58220**	NORTHUMBERLAND	.5	09/01/0	*100	1		174.00	16

ADI CODE SEE NOTE TO BUYER
**FIRST 2 DIGITS INDICATE STATE
9000.0+ OAAA NON-MEMBER

GRP GROSS RATING POINTS, EXCEPT **SHOWING

JANUARY 1981

Exhibit 10.3

Page from outdoor-advertising rate book. All markets offer 100 GRPs and smaller units, but the number of posters in a 100 GRP and the price vary by community. The number of GRPs per dollar is easily calculated. (Courtesy FC & A, Inc., publishers of the *Buyers Guide to Outdoor Advertising*.)

year.) TAB reports are a key part of all outdoor buying because they accumulate and update market information as well as mass traffic statistics in all markets where outdoor advertising is being used.

SMRB/TGI. In 1978 Target Group Index (TGI) measured and syndicated outdoor audience information for the first time. When TGI merged with the Simmons Market Research Bureau (SMRB), the TGI information was presented in the SMRB report. The report includes audience reach and frequency (Exhibit 10.4) as well as demographic and product cross tabulations.

Telecom. Telecom Research simulates an actual driving situation. The respondent sees a moving scene while eye movements are measured by an eye-movement recorder. The system measures impact, viewer involvement, and brand-name awareness.

OHMS   Out-of-Home Media Services (OHMS) provides a national outdoor buying service for both outdoor and transit advertising. OHMS can buy on a market-by-market basis, with the advertiser paying a single bill and being guaranteed proper installation and maintenance of the posters.

Criteria for selecting outdoor

locations   Among yardsticks besides circulation to take into consideration in picking a location are:

Exhibit 10.4
Measuring (a) outdoor reach (percentage of total adults reached in 30 days by 100 showing in average market) and (b) outdoor frequency (number of times each adult is reached in 30 days by 100 showing in average market). (Courtesy Outdoor Advertising Association of America, Inc.)

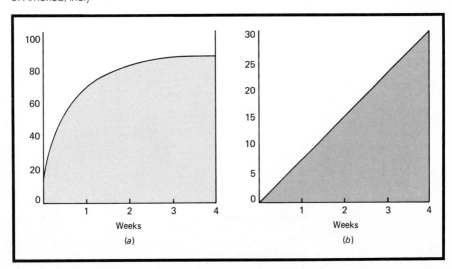

☐ *Length of unobstructed approach:* the distance from which the location first becomes fully visible to people driving.

☐ *Type of traffic:* the slower the better. Is it all auto, or is it also pedestrian, bus, or a combination of these? Is the traffic toward the location or away from it, as happens on a one-way street?

☐ *Characteristics of placement:* angled, parallel to line of traffic, or head-on. *Angled* is easily seen as cars approach in one direction; *parallel* can be viewed by traffic traveling in both directions but better by people sitting in the car at the near side; *head-on* is viewed by traffic approaching a location on the outside of a curve or where traffic makes a sharp turn.

☐ *Immediate surroundings:* Is it close to a shopping center? Is there competition from surrounding signs? Is the sign by a traffic light? Red lights give people more time to read the sign.

☐ *Size and physical attractiveness of the outdoor sign.*

☐ *Price:* an area of comparative values and negotiation.

Painted bulletins

Painted bulletins are permanent structures, larger (usually 14 by 48 feet) and costlier than posters. Erected at choice locations, these structures are made of prefabricated steel with a standardized or specially constructed border trim (Exhibit 10.6*a*). The advertisements are either hand-painted or mounted on separate panels in the shop and then assembled at the bulletin site.

Painted bulletins can be illuminated for night traffic. Often extending from them are clocks, thermometers, or electric time and temperature units known as *jump clocks.* Some signs have revolving units or rotating panels to attract attention. Others display three-dimensional styrofoam structures or enlarged, extending cutouts of packages or trademarks displayed in lights (Exhibits 10.5 and 10.6). Local ordinances limit the size of extensions allowed.

Exhibit 10.5
A powerful product identification ensures important recognition at the point of sale.

Exhibit 10.6
An eye-stopping example of a painted bulletin with extensions. Extensions to the basic painted bulletin are limited to 5 feet 6 inches at the top and 2 feet at the sides and bottom with a 200-square-foot combined maximum.

Buying painted bulletins. Painted bulletins are bought individually, unlike posters, which are bought by GRP units. Contracts run for a year or more, especially if the bulletins require extra construction. The advertiser or a representative visits a territory to inspect each location offered by the local plant operator, who supplies a traffic-flow map of the locations. The advertiser judges the ad's circulation, the distance from which it is visible, the amount of traffic, competing signs and distractions, and any special features affecting its visibility. If shortcomings are found, the price quoted for the individual painted bulletin may be subject to negotiation. About three times a year, the advertiser can change the copy and supply the design and artwork to the plant operator, who is responsible for reproducing it and maintaining the sign in good condition.

Rotary plans. With a *rotary plan,* an advertiser may buy painted bulletins in three different favorable locations. The faces of the boards are removable, and the copy is different on each one. Every 30, 60, or 90 days the bases of the boards are rotated in sequence so that each board gets a different audience each time and each audience gets a different message. The panels may even be moved to different markets (Exhibit 10.7).

Inspecting the outdoor signs

After the outdoor signs are up, the advertising agency is notified. A representative of the agency drives around to inspect the signs (called *riding a showing*) to make sure that all boards are in proper working order. The boards are inspected regularly to verify that the traffic flow has not changed, that no obstruction (such as foliage or new construction) impedes the view of the sign, and—if posters are used—that the posters are not peeling and all flashing and

239

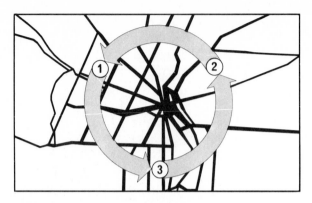

Exhibit 10.7
Rotary-plan map. Every 30 or 60 or 90 days painted bulletin 1 is moved to site 2, bulletin 2 is moved to site 3, and
bulletin 3 is moved to site 1. Later the process is repeated,
but bulletin 1 is moved to site 3.

lighting arrangements are working properly. In national buys purchased
through OHMS, verification is performed by a Field Inspection Service employee of that organization.

Advertising and creating copy for outdoor
advertising

The outdoor advertising of a national advertiser is usually part of a
campaign appearing also in other media. The problem is to create an effective
tie-in with the total campaign theme. Whether you are adapting copy to tie in
with other advertising or creating copy to stand on its own, it is well to remember that outdoor advertising should contain no more than three elements:

☐ *Clear product identification:* The trademark may appear alone or on a package. Can it
be immediately recognized? How clear is it at a distance?

☐ *Large illustration size:* Size gets attention. The picture should tell the story. Colors
should be bold and bright, not pastel. Figures should be distinct and silhouetted (backgrounds usually interfere with illustrations).

☐ *Short copy:* The copy, if any, should be concise, the words short, the message unam-
biguous. Read the copy out loud. If it takes more than 8 seconds, it's too long. The
typography should be large, preferably heavy sans serif, liberally spaced. The best
color combination for legibility is black on yellow.

The secret of outdoor-advertising design is simplification.

In an industry with its own special jargon, it is refreshing to come upon a
word that literally means what it says—the outdoor *spectacular* sign (Exhibit
10.8). This is not a standardized sign; it is made by specialists in steel
construction. Spectaculars are the most conspicuous and the costliest in terms
of cash outlay (but low cost per person reached) of all outdoor advertisements.

Exhibit 10.8
A spectacular, built to order.

Placed in prime day-and-night locations and designed to attract the greatest number of passers-by, they are built of steel beams, sheet metal, and plastics. They utilize bright flashing lights and technically ingenious designs. (Everything is subject to local zoning laws and limitations on energy use, of course). Spectaculars are individually designed; the cost of space and construction is individually negotiated. Changes are costly because they may entail reconstruction of steelwork and neon lighting; so new advertisers often use the construction of existing spectaculars to erect their own designs. Because of the high cost of construction, spectaculars are usually bought on a 3- to 5-year basis. It takes an experienced and skilled buyer to handle negotiations involving engineering and legal problems as well as the usual advertising considerations. Large outdoor advertisers often use poster displays, painted bulletins, and spectaculars in large cities.

Agency commission and
fees   The advertising agency commission in outdoor is 16.67 percent rather than the traditional 15 percent. If the agency goes through OHMS to buy outdoor, a fee of 3.5 percent is charged, which is deducted from this commission. An agency using the services of OHMS nets 13.17 percent (16.67 percent less 3.5 percent OHMS fee). However, the savings in agency staffing and overhead would provide a savings to the agency.

Trends   Since outdoor joined other media in adopting the GRP system, advertisers have a better base for intermedia cost comparison. The industry's huge investment in outdoor research and computerization, along with the adoption of the GRP system, will greatly expand the stature and use of outdoor advertising planning (Table 10.1).

This new stature will also be reflected in continued growth in outdoor advertising. Outdoor accounts for just over 1 percent of total United States advertising, or approximately $600 million. Outdoor should continue to grow at a rate of 10 percent a year during the 1980s. With the fragmentation of the TV audience we can expect to see mass advertisers, including major package goods, increase their outdoor-advertising investment. The major categories of outdoor advertising will continue to be cigarettes and liquor, which often use outdoor by default because of TV's exclusion of these products.

The future will see greater diversity of outdoor advertising. Already the term "outdoor," referring to posters, is being replaced by *out-of-home,* which covers new formats in transit advertising as well as the traditional forms of outdoor advertising shown in Exhibit 10.9.

Exhibit 10.9
When space is scarce, a one-pole bulletin like this special construction can be erected at a good traffic point. (Courtesy of E. T. Legg & Co.)

Table 10–1

COMPARISON OF OUTDOOR ADVERTISING

| | STANDARDIZED | | NONSTANDARDIZED |
	POSTER PANELS	PAINTED BULLETINS	SPECTACULARS
Description	Permanent structure, 12 by 25 feet, on which reprinted ads are mounted. Most frequent size of poster panel is 30-sheet, with small white margin, or bleed, with no margin. 8-sheet poster gaining in popularity in urban areas.	Permanent structure, usually 14 by 48 feet, on which the message is painted or mounted.	Special steel construction, built or altered to order.
Chief characteristics	Least costly per unit of standardized outdoor advertising. Standard size, nationwide. Most popular form of standardized outdoor advertising.	Placed in higher traffic locations. No uniform size, but proportion always 1:3½.	Placed only in busiest locations. Each one is specially fabricated. The costliest and most conspicuous form of outdoor advertising.
How bought	By ready-made assortments, according to the size of GRP units, as 100 GRP units, 50 GRP units, 25 GRP units. Bought by the month.	Individually. Price individually negotiated. Bought on 1- to 3-year basis.	Individually. Price of construction, rental, and maintenance individually negotiated. Usually bought on 3- to 5-year basis.
Special features	Illuminated or unilluminated boards. Illuminated ones in best locations.	Illuminated. Jump clock, oversize bottle, scenes that rotate, neon-lit trademarks, and many other extra construction features possible.	Everything is constructed to order.
Comments	Formerly sold as arbitrary showings. Practice changed since 1973. Copy changeable monthly.	Placed in more important locations. Costlier per unit than posters. Copy usually repainted every 4 to 6 months.	Change of copy difficult and costly.

Exhibit 10.10
Interior bus cards. Car cards offer advertisers excellent exposure to an out-of-home audience. (Courtesy of Transit Advertising Association.)

TRANSIT ADVERTISING

As we travel in buses, commuter trains, or subways, we find ourselves reading and rereading the overhead advertising cards facing us. As we wait for a train at the station or walk to a plane through the airport, we glance at the posters and displays. All of these are *transit advertising*, as are posters on the sides, rears, and fronts of buses and other transit vehicles.

Importance

Forty million individual people, including many who have their own cars, now travel in buses. The biggest gains have been in cities of over 500,000 with bus lines reaching ever outward. The average ride is 22 minutes; the average rider takes twenty-four rides a month. There are 8 billion rides a year on transit vehicles.

In the New York City subways, 5.3 million different adults are exposed to subway ads more than 160 million times a month, and now the passengers of the Washington subway and the BART subway in San Francisco must be added to the roster of those exposed to transit advertising.

When we include suburbanite commuters and airline passengers, we have listed the markets that advertisers are investing about $100 million per year to reach. Of that huge sum 30 percent is invested in local advertising and 70 percent in national.

Bus advertising, the most widely used form of transit advertising,

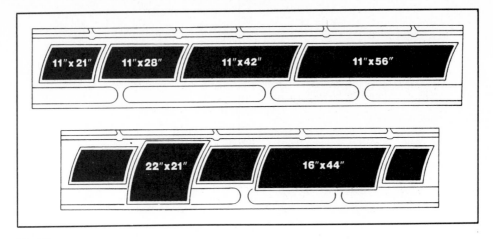

Exhibit 10.11
Standardized sizes of interior bus cards. (Courtesy of Transit Advertising Association.)

actually includes two separate transit media; *interior* transit advertising (28 percent of ad expenditures; Exhibit 10.10) and *exterior* transit advertising (72 percent).*

Interior transit advertising

Card sizes. We speak of interior bus advertising in terms of the cards on which the ads are printed. Some of the standard sizes are the following (also see Exhibit 10.11):

☐ Overhead rack card, 11 inches high by 28 inches wide†
☐ Overhead rack card, 11 by 42 inches
☐ Overhead rack card, 11 by 56 inches
☐ A large unit near the door, 22 by 21 inches

Service values. We now meet a new term in the space-buying world. *Service values* are units for buying interior transit space. Each plant owner decides how many cards will give an advertiser excellent coverage in a market. That number of cards is "full service" and has a certain price. "Half service" and "quarter service" may command correspondingly lower prices. All this is published on the rate card (Exhibit 10.12). Prices are quoted on a 1-month-per-card basis with discounts for longer contracts. Because each plant owner sets the terms, there is no such thing as a standard service value in transit advertising. Plant owners give individual rates for their cards on their own rate cards. An advertiser buying card space in interior transit advertising specifies the card size, the service unit, the length of time the ad will run, and the price.

Figuring circulation. The key question in buying any medium is "How many people will this message reach, and am I getting the circulation I'm pay-

---

*This and the following data in this section, unless otherwise credited, are from the Transit Advertising Association.

†In transit advertising, as in outdoor advertising, the height is given first, then the width.

MINNESOTA
MINNEAPOLIS/ST. PAUL

OPERATOR: TDI/WINSTON NETWORK
NATIONAL SALES MANAGER: DONALD E. DWYER
NATIONAL OFFICE: 275 MADISON AVE., NEW YORK, N.Y. 10016
                 (212) 599-1100
LOCAL MANAGER: BEN J. WALTERS
LOCAL OFFICE: 6950 FRANCE AVE. S., SUITE 218, MINNEAPOLIS, MN. 55435 (612) 920-1657
SHIPPING ADDRESS: TDI/WINSTON NETWORK, C/O MTC/TRANSIT OPERATING DIV.,
                  32ND ST. & NICOLLET, LOADING DOCK, MINNEAPOLIS, MN. 55408

EXTERIOR RATES

Size	Showing/# Units		1 Mo.	3 Mos.	6 Mos.	12 Mos.
30 x 144	#100	200	14,600	13,800	13,000	11,600
	# 50	100	7,300	6,900	6,500	5,800
	# 25	50	3,650	3,450	3,250	2,900
	Unit	1	73.00	69.00	65.00	58.00
21 x 72	#100	200	10,600	10,000	9,600	8,400
	# 50	100	5,300	5,000	4,800	4,200
	# 25	50	2,650	2,500	2,400	2,100
	Unit	1	53.00	50.00	48.00	42.00
21 x 44	#100	200	6,600	6,212	6,000	5,200
	# 50	100	3,300	3,106	3,000	2,600
	# 25	50	1,650	1,553	1,500	1,300
	Unit	1	33.00	31.00	30.00	26.00

INTERIOR RATES

Size	Showing/# Units		1 Mo.	3 Mos.	6 Mos.	12 Mos.
11 x 28	Full	900	4,500	4,275	4,050	3,600
	Half	450	2,250	2,138	2,025	1,800
	Unit	1	5.00	4.75	4.50	4.00
11 x 42	Full	900	6,300	5,985	5,670	5,040
	Half	450	3,150	2,993	2,835	2,520
	Unit	1	7.00	6.65	6.30	5.60
11 x 56	Full	900	7,200	6,840	6,480	5,760
	Half	450	3,600	3,420	3,240	2,880
	Unit	1	8.00	7.60	7.20	6.40
22 x 21	Full	900	7,470	7,110	6,750	5,940
	Half	450	3,735	3,555	3,375	2,970
	Unit	1	8.30	7.90	7.50	6.60

No. Vehicles Operating: 900
Transit System: Metropolitan Transit Commission/Twin City & Suburban Lines
Area Served: Minneapolis, St. Paul
Avg. Monthly Rides: 7,105,068 (Source: Transit System)
SMSA Population: 2,030,800

Exhibit 10.12
Transit rates from TAA Rate Directory. (Courtesy of Transit Advertising Association, October 1981.)

ing for?" To answer the question, the industry has established a system of measuring inside audience by a fare-box count defined as "one person riding a display-carrying vehicle for one trip." All references to circulation are in terms of estimated monthly rides. This does *not* mean that all riders see every card or that riders are different people each trip. Special research services are available in some markets to judge how many riders see and remember specific ads.

Take one. A special card called a *take one* has a pad of direct-response return cards attached. The rider is invited to take one and mail it in for further information or for an application blank to join something. This is an effective way for direct-response advertising to reach many prospects.

Features and advantages.

- ☐ Because of the length of the ride, a rider gets a chance to read the copy in the ad. The cards permit more copy than exterior cards or outdoor signs do.
- ☐ A rider can usually see and read three adjacent ads. During rush hour attention may well be fixed on one ad.
- ☐ Because the rider goes back and forth on the same route, an ad may make two impressions a day, expanding the frequency of the ad in another medium.
- ☐ In large cities advertisers may be able to choose buses that pass supermarkets or travel through neighborhoods with the ethnic audience they particularly want to reach.

Limitations and challenges.

- ☐ Bus riders present a wide audience, but it is nonselective. Ads for everyday products suited to middle-class lifestyles can reach a fine concentration of consumers. It is possible, however, to buy ad campaigns in sectors of a market because buses operate from specified garages in specified areas. Also, on subway and railroad platforms you can buy posters in a given locale or area.
- ☐ It takes time to produce the cards needed in transit advertising. Furthermore, there must be plenty of time to put the cards where they belong. Plans for this type of advertising must be made well ahead.
- ☐ Costs must be compared with other local media.

Exterior transit advertising

Ads carried on the outside of buses are the most conspicuous form of transit advertising and the largest part of bus advertising.

Forms of exterior transit advertising. Exterior space comes in various sizes, some of which are shown in Exhibit 10.13:

- ☐ King size (side of bus), 30 inches high by 144 inches wide
- ☐ Busorama (side of bus), 22 by 144 inches
- ☐ Queen size (side of bus), 30 by 88 inches
- ☐ Traveling display (side of bus), 21 by 44 inches

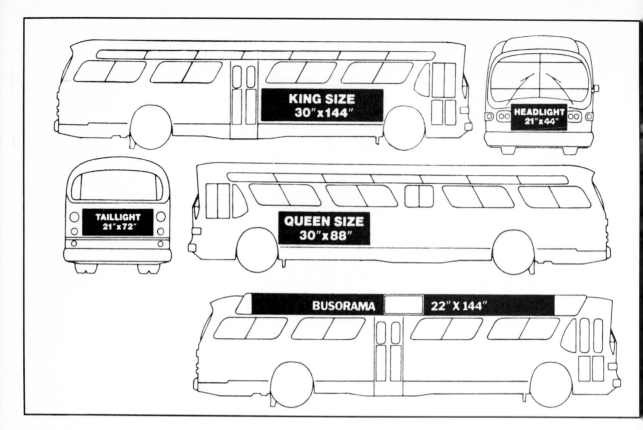

Exhibit 10.13
Some examples of standardized sizes for exterior bus signs. (Courtesy of Transit Advertising Association.)

☐ Taillight spectacular (rear of bus), 21 by 72 inches
☐ Headlight (in front), 21 by 44 inches

    King size, traveling display, headlight, and taillight spectacular are more widely used than queen size. Next time a bus passes by, see how many of these different forms you can recognize.

    The important thing to carry away from this discussion of sizes is the resourcefulness of the transit-advertising operators in creating standard sizes to fit the different available areas of a bus. Among the options offered the advertiser may chose those which best fit the message to the budget.

Features and advantages.

☐ Buses pass through the neighborhoods where people live, shop, and work (Exhibit 10.14).
☐ They provide great reach for any message.
☐ Ads are seen by passersby on the street and by riders in passing cars and buses.

☐ In larger cities the advertiser can select routes that best reach particular demographic groups.

☐ The ads are virtual traveling outdoor signs, reaching many who never travel inside buses. They represent media values different from those of interior advertising.

Limitations and challenges.

☐ Exterior ads must be limited in copy, usually to brand names, package, and slogan.

☐ They reach a wide, unclassified audience; consequently they are not suitable for a segmented market unless bought on a sector-plan basis.

☐ Time is needed to prepare and schedule them; so they are not appropriate for news flashes. Good location on buses must be scheduled well in advance.

☐ Circulation is estimated.

☐ Cost (including production) must be compared with other available local media.

How exterior space is sold. Exterior space is sold on a basis completely different from that of interior transit space. Exterior space is sold by the number of displays, or "units." Each plant owner determines how many displays would make a strong impression on a market (a 100 showing) and sets a price. Then half showings are offered for sale and in large cities even quarter showings, as outdoor advertising formerly offered. Space is sold in terms of such packages. The rate card tells how many units go into a showing. Since some advertisers may want two displays on opposite sides of one bus, space is not sold in terms of number of buses. In smaller markets the price is also quoted in terms of a number of units.

The chief information sought in exterior-transit-advertising rate cards is the following:

Exhibit 10.14
Sign carries the advertiser's message throughout a metropolitan area. (Courtesy of Transit Advertising Association.)

☐ Number of displays
☐ Availability of one or two side panels
☐ Quantity of units per 100 showing
☐ Basis for charging (showings or number of units)
☐ Cost

The basic bus; the total bus; the total

total bus

Instead of selling their advertising space to different advertisers, transit-advertising companies have developed the idea of selling advertising space in one bus to one advertiser at a time. Advertisers may use the space to sell different products made by one company, or they may concentrate all the ads on one product. No rider leaving the bus, no matter how long or short the ride, will be unmindful of the advertiser's product or products.

The use of an entire bus *interior* by one advertiser is referred to as a *basic bus.* Basic buses are not available everywhere, but more and more cities are selling the arrangement.

An advertiser may also buy all the advertising space on the *exterior* of a bus—front, back, sides, and top. This is called a *total bus* and is also sold on an exclusive basis to one firm in an industry at a time.

If you combine a basic-bus buy with a total-bus buy, you are said to have bought a *total total bus.* You can't buy more advertising on a bus than that.

Commuter trains and stations; air

terminals

One sector of the transit-advertising industry specializes in commuter trains and terminals. There are such train stations in about 50 cities, serving over 400 communities.

In New York, Philadelphia, and Chicago two out of three executives commute from home to office by train. The level of affluence of commuters is higher than that of riders in subways and buses, and the average length of rides is 44 minutes. Usually commuters have seats and plenty of opportunity to see the signs in the trains or stations. Since most commuters ride 5 days a week, there is also the advantage of frequency of exposure to the signs. In the sale of station and platform advertising the number of posters is identified in terms of showings, but here they are called *intensive* showings, *representative* showings, and *minimum* showings. In each instance the plant operator announces how many posters are involved in each bracket.

Airline terminals provide another opportunity for reaching a large, upper-income audience. Of all airline passengers 86 percent are executives, businesspeople, or professionals on business trips. And to the airports come not only passengers but people seeing them off or awaiting their arrival. Advertising space and display-unit space (Exhibit 10.15) in terminals are sold on a per-unit basis.

Exhibit 10.15
It must have been 3:00 Sunday morning when this round island display at an air terminal was photographed. That is about the only time a terminal is not busy. (Courtesy of Transit Advertising Association.)

A characteristic of major train and airline terminals is the variety of
advertising forms: floor exhibits, two-sheet posters, dioramas (three-
dimensional scenes), island showcases, illuminated signs, and clocks. If ever
you find yourself in an air terminal with time on your hands (that does happen), you can make good use of it by seeing how many different forms of
advertising you can spot.

Station and platform posters. Poster space is available on the walls of
many bus, train, and subway stations (Exhibit 10.16), where passengers have
time to read while waiting for transportation. They can read all the copy on

Exhibit 10.16
A subway-station transit poster. (Courtesy of Transit Advertising Association.)

these posters; and since people pass through these stations regularly, advertisers can build the frequency of their ads.

The New York subway system, the largest user of station posters, has reduced the number of one-sheet posters. Now advertisers can use a smaller number of two-sheet posters and get better exposure with improved overall appearance.

Copy for transit
advertising
Because passengers have time to read signs in a bus, copy for interior bus signs can be fuller, more like magazine copy than outdoor copy. It is a good idea, though, to place the name of the product on the lower part of the card, close to the rider.

Copy for exterior bus advertising is similar to outdoor advertising, except that the shape is different and units are more compressed (since they are read at closer range).

TRENDS IN TRANSIT
ADVERTISING
The major force that promises to increase the importance of transit advertising is the pressure for more public transportation, particularly around large cities. Increasing gasoline prices have popularized riding the bus. Within the industry the trends will be to create more attractive cards and to encourage the use of more scientific data for making buying decisions. By 1990 transit advertising (excluding production) will probably exceed $175 million.

Pressure-sensitive vinyl displays are on the increase. These can be directly applied to the outer surfaces of transit vehicles (for example, bus, articulated bus, or trolley bus). No frame is needed. The vinyl display can also be applied to hardboard, which is inserted into frames attached to the bus.

Under the sponsorship of the TAA, transit research is also increasing. Not only are gross exposure figures available to advertisers, but reach and frequency estimates have been calculated (see Exhibit 10.17).

Exhibit 10.17
Team II Transit Estimated Audience Measure, prepared for the TAA by Marketmath, Inc., 1981.

MARKETMATH, INC.   SUMMARY TABLE   TEAM II -- 1981

MARKET	POPULATION 18+ (000)	#100 SHOWING - ONE MONTH				#50 SHOWING - ONE MONTH			
		REACH (%)	AVERAGE FREQUENCY	GRP	GROSS EXPOSURES (000)	REACH (%)	AVERAGE FREQUENCY	GRP	GROSS EXPOSURES (000)
1. AKRON, OHIO	380	79.8	9.6	762	2896	70.6	5.6	396	1506
2. ALBANY/SCHENECTADY/TROY, NEW YORK	438	86.9	24.2	2101	9197	80.9	13.0	1050	4598
3. ALLENTOWN/BETHLEHEM/EASTON, PENNSYLVANIA	379	77.0	7.9	608	2303	66.2	4.6	304	1152
4. ASHEVILLE, NORTH CAROLINA	123	83.0	13.6	1132	1390	74.8	7.6	566	695
5. ATLANTA, GEORGIA	782	86.5	30.5	2633	20598	80.9	16.3	1317	10299
6. ATLANTIC CITY, NEW JERSEY	144	91.5	44.0	4023	5799	87.3	23.0	2011	2899
7. BALTIMORE, MARYLAND	1338	85.1	20.5	1744	23336	78.5	11.1	872	11668
8. BATTLE CREEK, MICHIGAN	102	87.1	18.1	1579	1606	NOT AVAILABLE			
9. BAY CITY, MICHIGAN	84	88.8	23.1	2054	1721	83.6	13.1	1095	918
10. BERGEN COUNTY, NEW JERSEY	640	85.7	14.9	1274	8161	78.2	8.2	637	4081
11. BERGEN COUNTY, NEW JERSEY	640	91.2	32.9	3003	19237	86.6	17.4	1511	9677
12. BINGHAMTON, NEW YORK	156	86.1	17.3	1487	2316	79.1	9.4	743	1158
13. BIRMINGHAM, ALABAMA	485	81.2	11.7	951	4612	72.4	6.6	476	2306
14. BOISE, IDAHO	124	79.4	9.4	744	921	69.5	5.4	372	461
15. BOSTON, MASSACHUSETTS	2435	86.9	21.9	1903	46343	80.7	11.8	951	23172
16. BUFFALO, NEW YORK	891	84.7	18.4	1558	13881	77.7	10.0	779	6940
17. CAMDEN, NEW JERSEY	1020	82.6	13.6	1123	11453	74.4	7.5	561	5727
18. CANTON, OHIO	274	82.8	12.7	1049	2878	74.9	7.3	546	1496
19. CHARLOTTE, NORTH CAROLINA	294	85.1	16.4	1398	4104	77.7	9.0	699	2052
20. CHATTANOOGA, TENNESSEE	209	84.4	15.7	1329	2781	76.9	8.6	664	1390
21. CHICAGO, ILLINOIS	3800	88.2	17.9	1576	59887	81.6	9.7	788	29943
22. CINCINNATI, OHIO	631	86.5	21.4	1848	11657	80.1	11.5	924	5829
23. CLEVELAND, OHIO	1099	89.3	26.4	2360	25931	83.9	14.1	1180	12966
24. COLUMBUS, OHIO	628	85.1	16.2	1381	8669	77.9	9.0	700	4392
25. DALLAS, TEXAS	1123	83.3	13.5	1123	12605	76.4	8.0	612	6876
26. DES MOINES, IOWA	219	87.9	23.7	2082	4566	82.0	12.7	1041	2283
27. DETROIT CITY, MICHIGAN	1657	85.3	15.0	1282	21251	77.8	8.2	641	10626
28. DETROIT/SUBURBS, MICHIGAN	1205	81.9	11.5	939	11322	73.0	6.4	470	5661
29. DURHAM, NORTH CAROLINA	116	84.9	16.4	1396	1613	77.6	9.0	698	807
30. ESSEX/MORRIS COUNTIES, NEW JERSEY	921	90.0	41.8	3764	34670	85.5	22.0	1882	17335
31. FLINT, MICHIGAN	309	86.7	16.9	1467	4540	79.6	9.2	734	2270
32. FORT WAYNE, INDIANA	205	87.8	25.4	2226	4570	82.0	13.6	1113	2285
33. FRESNO, CALIFORNIA	368	84.4	14.9	1253	4606	76.7	8.2	627	2303
34. FT. LAUDERDALE, FLORIDA	818	64.7	4.4	286	2342	51.1	2.8	143	1171
35. FT. WORTH, TEXAS	629	79.6	9.1	728	4582	73.2	6.2	455	2864
36. GRAND RAPIDS, MICHIGAN	315	85.9	17.0	1460	4602	78.8	9.3	730	2301
37. GREENSBORO/WINSTON-SALEM, NORTH CAROLINA	416	84.4	14.4	1213	5045	67.3	4.9	331	1376
38. HAGERSTOWN, MARYLAND	85	80.3	10.1	815	697	70.8	5.8	408	348
39. HARRISBURG, PENNSYLVANIA	305	79.1	9.4	747	2282	69.2	5.4	374	1141
40. HOUSTON, TEXAS	1704	80.8	9.9	803	13680	73.6	6.4	468	7980

SUMMARY

The 1980s will be a time of consolidation and growing prestige for out-of-home media. New developments in the use of light-intensity materials will heighten the visual appeal of both outdoor and transit posters and will lower energy costs. Energy-conservation concerns will also bring a greater use of mass transit, which will increase the use of out-of-home advertising by major national companies. We shall also see more diversity in the medium. Bus shelters, trash containers, taxi signs, and pedestrian benches are just a few of the commercial opportunities for out-of-home advertising. Finally, a greater investment in sophisticated research techniques will continue to increase the credibility of out-of-home audience data.

QUESTIONS

1. Outdoor advertising includes any advertising or identification signs located in a public place. Do you agree? Discuss.
2. Briefly discuss the primary advantages and disadvantages of outdoor advertising.
3. Discuss the three major categories of outdoor advertising and when each would most likely be used by an advertiser.
4. Discuss the current status of the Highway Beautification Act.
5. What is a Gross Rating Point Buy in buying outdoor advertising? What are its advantages over the previous way of buying poster advertising?
6. What is the role of the Out-of-Home Media Services in buying outdoor advertising?
7. What is the standard agency commission in outdoor advertising?
8. What are the three main copy considerations recommended for designing outdoor advertising?
9. What are the two major forms of transit advertising?
10. Discuss the advantages and limitations of transit advertising, for both interior and exterior advertising.
11. How is interior transit advertising circulation computed? Exterior transit advertising?
12. What are the forms of exterior transit advertising? Which are most widely used?

SUGGESTED EXERCISES

13. Make a list of the outdoor signs on a major street of your town. How many of these are standardized outdoor signs?
14. Using the same list of outdoor signs, categorize them by generic product class.
15. Other than outdoor posters, how many other forms of out-of-home advertising can you identify in your neighborhood? What does each advertise?

READINGS

The Big Outdoor (New York: Institute of Outdoor Advertising, 1981).

JOHNSON, J. DOUGLAS: *Advertising Today* (Palo Alto: Science Research Associates), pp. 231–45.

"Out-of-Home Explosion!" *Media Decisions,* July 1977, pp. 70–71.

"Outdoor's AMMO," *Media Decisions,* August 1976, pp. 72–74.

Direct-Response Advertising; Direct-Mail Advertising

Who, at one time or another, has not sent in a coupon from an ad for a book or record album or a bird feeder or some other item of interest? The firm that ran the ad was engaged in the business of selling by *direct marketing.* Direct marketing is often regarded as a minor field by consumers who only glance at the many small ads selling different types of merchandise. However, as we will see, direct marketing is a multi-billion dollar industry. The advertising used in direct marketing is called *direct-response advertising,* a field consisting of a number of distributive methods, media, trade practices, and tradition. Hence we begin with some definitions.

DEFINITIONS

Direct marketing   Direct marketing is the selling of goods directly to consumers without using a retailer or trade channel. It is one of the fastest growing and profitable types of marketing activity. It is estimated that direct marketers average profits three times higher than most retail outlets. Direct marketing is a huge business, with sales in excess of $100 billion, led by J. C. Penney, with direct-marketing sales approaching $1 billion.

The term direct marketing is supplanting the term "mail-order business" because today so much of the business is initiated or shipped by means other than mail.

Direct-response
advertising

Any advertising form used in selling goods directly to consumers can be called direct-response advertising. The message doesn't have to come through the mails (though it often does); it can be an ad with a coupon in a newspaper or magazine or even a telephoned solicitation. That is why the well-known description *mail-order advertising* is now less frequently heard than direct-response advertising when this general advertising mode is intended.

When we wish to specify the one of several direct-response advertising techniques that involves mailing, we speak of *direct-mail advertising.* Currently direct mail accounts for $9 billion in advertising expenditures, ranking third behind newspaper and TV advertising. However, more dollars are spent in direct-mail advertising than in radio, magazines, and outdoor *combined.*

Difference between direct mail and sales promotion. If a recipe booklet is sent through the mails, it is direct-mail advertising. If, however, the same booklet is sent to dealers to put on their counters for their customers to pick up, it is regarded as *sales promotion* (discussed in Chapter 12, Sales Promotion). In this chapter we deal with direct mail as a direct-response medium.

GROWTH OF DIRECT-RESPONSE
ADVERTISING

Direct marketing, with its direct-response advertising, has been a major growth area in marketing since 1970. Many factors have contributed to this growth, but we will discuss the ones that have had the biggest effects.

Societal
factors

The working woman, with disposable income and little time for shopping, is one of the obvious societal changes contributing to the growth of direct marketing. In addition, cost of transportation and desire for convenience have added to the popularity of direct marketing. As direct marketing grows and major corporations enter the field, customers have more confidence in direct purchasing, which in turn will bring even greater growth.

Credit
cards

The widespread use of credit cards has simplified payment and encouraged purchases of expensive items. Recent consumer legislation regarding credit-card purchases also give customers more protection in receiving refunds if merchandise is unsatisfactory.

How many pieces of mail will you send to Mr. Liles today?

Ten may be nine too many!

```
02
01                              Mr. C. E. Liles
        Mr. Charles E. Liles    823 Grndvw. Dr.
        823 Grandview Drive     Anderson, Indiana 46017
        Anderson, Indiana 46017
                                04
03
        Mr. Charles E. Liles            Mrs. Katie Liles
        283 Grandview Dr.              823 Grandview Dr.
        Anderson, Indiana 46017        Anderson, Indiana 46017

05                                06
        Mr. Chas. Liles                Mr. & Mrs. Chas. E. Liler
        823 Grandvew D.               823 Grandview Drive
        Anderson, Indiana 46011        Anderson, Indiana 46017

07                                08
        Mr. Charles E. Liles           Mr. Chas. E. Liles
        Kingston Apts. 312            P. O. Box 1011
        2505 E. 10th St.             Anderson, Indiana 46015
        Anderson, Indiana 46012

                                  10
09                                Mr. C. E. Liles
        Mr. Charles E. Liles          Universal Products
        Universal Products Corp.      P. O. Box 1788
        100 West 11th                Anderson, Indiana 46014
        Anderson, Indiana 46016
```

Perhaps you already know which variations in Mr. Liles' labels you want eliminated from your mailings. But let's take a minute to look at some of the reasons variations like these crop up in the first place.

#01 Mr. Liles with his name spelled out and his address listed correctly.

#02 The name and street are abbreviated.

#03 The correct street number is transposed.

#04 Mr. Liles' wife.

#05 This time the street address is right but someone recorded the zip code incorrectly.

#06 Mr. & Mrs. Liles with their last name misspelled.

#07 Their old apartment, the one they had before buying their house.

#08 Mr. Liles' personal post office box.

#09 His business address.

#10 The company post office box.

Now Mr. Liles may be receiving mail at more addresses than the average person. But when you see **MATCHMASTER** go to work, you realize that many, many people use more than one address. And when you throw in both valid and erroneous variations in the same address, you begin to appreciate how **MATCHMASTER** lets you get a grip on things.

MATCHMASTER is better than any other Merge/Purge System on the market for two simple reasons.

1. It has the capability to find these different types of duplicates.

2. Once they are identified, **you** decide which types to eliminate.

To schedule your job, or for more information on how we can help you, call collect right now.

Wiland & Associates Inc.

1101 International Parkway, P.O. Box 5445, Fredericksburg, VA 22401   (703) 752-2541
1263 Lincoln Building, Sixty E. 42nd St., New York, NY 10165 (212) 986-8798
One Skyline Place, 5205 Leesburg Pike, Suite 509, Falls Church, VA 22041 (703) 931-1026
1688 Conestoga St., Boulder, CO 80301 (303) 447-1870

Exhibit 11.1
Computer technology can quickly purge a list of unwanted duplication. (Courtesy Wiland and Associates, Inc.)

Computers   Perhaps the most important single advance in direct response is the adaptation of computer technology. Computers allow audience segmentation to a degree that would have been impossible only a few years ago. By identifying prime prospects, the computer justifies the higher cost of direct response by eliminating the waste circulation that occurs in much mass advertising. Computers also quickly determine duplication among several lists (Exhibit 11.1). Finally, the computer-generated letter has added to the personalization of direct-response messages.

Exhibit 11.2
Credit-card capabilities and toll-free numbers enhance direct marketing. (Courtesy Riehl Time Corp.)

Telephone   In recent years the telephone has become an important tool in direct marketing. The "800" toll-free number is a convenient supplement to mail-order selling (Exhibit 11.2). Many ads offer a customer the choice of mailing in a coupon or buying by phone.

Another, somewhat controversial, use of the telephone is for direct-sales solicitation. No accurate figures exist for how many sales calls are made, but estimates run as high as 7 million daily. With the use of random-dialing machines and tape-recorded messages some think this technique is an invasion of

Exhibit 11.3
Catalog buying is popular in many fields. Firms specialize in becoming the center for certain types of merchandise presented in their catalogs, which become steady salespeople for them. (Courtesy The Edmund Scientific Catalog.)

privacy in a way direct mail is not. Congress and the Federal Trade Commission have studied the feasibility of restricting telephone sales calls. However, barring legislation against them, we shall see more telephone selling in the future.

WHAT MAKES A "GOOD" DIRECT-RESPONSE

PRODUCT? Not every product is suitable for direct-response advertising. Broadly speaking, it should not be the usual product available at a neighborhood store, unless it is offered at a very special price. It should have some distinguishing quality or render a useful service not generally convenient to buy. It should be small, for mailing, unless it is a costly purchase. It should open the door to repeat business. If it comes with a well-known name back of it, so much the better. Above all, it should be a good value. The advertiser must be geared to handle repeat business; for it is on repeat business that the total-marketing business rests (Exhibit 11.3).

TYPES OF DIRECT-RESPONSE OFFERS

One-step purchase of specific

product   The simplest examples of this type of direct-response advertising are the small ads one sees in the back of the shopping section of many magazines or in the Sunday-newspaper shopping-section supplement.

Whoever responds to a mail-order ad will probably receive the product with one or more circulars in the package, offering other merchandise of related interest. *Bounce-back* circulars, as these are called, often produce as much as 20 to 40 percent additional sales from the same customers and often launch the buyer on the path to becoming a steady customer.

The two-step sales

operation   For more expensive items direct-response advertising often uses a two-step sales presentation (Exhibit 11.4). The first step in such a campaign is to determine potential consumers. Then a follow-up, second step, is used to close the sale. This second step often consists of a personal or telephone sales call. However, companies may also send more detailed literature or even a product sample in this second step. The problem is to generate leads from your most profitable customers. Many companies screen their audiences by charging a fee for a catalog or brochure instead of offering it for free. Other companies request that inquiries be made on letterhead stationery with the person's title. Large mail-order houses often send their catalog for a $2 charge but include a $2 credit certificate toward the first purchase.

Negative

options   Another direct-response technique used by record and book clubs is the negative option. Book-of-the-Month Club is credited with inventing this method of "one-package-a-month" selling. The advantage to the seller is that, once the customer joins the plan, the merchandise is sent automatically unless the customer notifies the company that he does not wish to receive it.

Life of Georgia's Flexible Annuity.
So you can be ready for the 21st century.

The year 2001 is only twenty years away. Now is the time to start planning for your financial security.

Life of Georgia's Flexible Annuity offers you a practical way to begin. It features a choice of premium payments, maturity dates and monthly incomes. And it provides all the advantages of a conventional annuity such as tax deferred accumulations, guaranteed interest rate, guaranteed accumulating cash values and guaranteed monthly income.

Our Flexible Annuity can be tailored to meet your needs today, while providing the flexibility to allow for change tomorrow.

To help you plan for the 21st century, contact your nearest Life of Georgia office or send us the coupon.

 **Life of Georgia**®
Working hard to insure your future.

Yes, I want to be ready for the 21st century. Please send me information about Life of Georgia's Flexible Annuity.

Name_____

Address_____

City_____

State_____Zip_____

Home phone_____

Business phone_____

Mail to: Hugh Rickenbaker, Executive Offices, Life Insurance Company of Georgia, Life of Georgia Tower Atlanta, GA 30365

A GeorgiaUS Company

Exhibit 11.4
A two-step offer to buy an annuity program. The first step is to generate inquiries. The second step is to follow up with mailings designed to complete the selling process. (Courtesy Life of Georgia.)

TELEVISION
ADVERTISING

LIBERTY MUTUAL

"SWING EASY"

For every golfer

who ever had a drive take a bad turn. . .

or an iron game that was a bit rusty. . .

or who just couldn't shake that trapped feeling. . .

Liberty Mutual Insurance Company has some very good news.

As sponsor of this spring's Liberty Mutual Legends of Golf Tournament, we'll send you the secret to developing a smoother swing. . .

the techniques that made this man, Julius Boros, one of golf's living legends.

How to develop a smoother swing.

It's all here, in Swing Easy, Hit Hard by Julius Boros.

To get this $2.95 value, mail your name and address plus one dollar for postage and handling to:

Julius Boros, c/o Liberty Mutual, Box 777, Boston, Mass. 02116.

At Liberty, we put a lot of effort

into insuring your car, your home, your business and your life.

CADDIE: Down the middle!
GOLFER: Of course.

Now we're putting some effort into insuring you a better game of golf.

XLMA9056
Quinn & Johnson/LM 98-11

Exhibit 11.5
Direct-response offers can be made in broadcast as well as print media. (Courtesy Liberty Mutual Insurance Company.)

Business-to-business direct

marketing Direct-response advertising is not confined to the consumer market-place. In recent years direct marketing has been used more and more in business-to-business selling. Most business direct marketing is intended to introduce a company, product, or salesperson rather than to complete a sale. Personal selling to business may cost as much as $150 per contact. Businesses must introduce themselves to the market before calling on customers. Direct marketing offers an excellent way to "prepare the way" for a company's sales force.

TIMING OF DIRECT-RESPONSE

ADVERTISING Direct-response advertising has its good months and poor months for getting responses. For most (not all) offerings the best months are January and February. Other good months are August, September, October, November, and December. The low months for most products are June, March, April, May, and July. Direct-response advertisers always plan their tests well in advance to be able to come out strong with their best mailings and ads in the best months of their sales calendars.

USING DIRECT

MAIL The biggest medium used in direct-response advertising is direct mail, an institution built on a structure of mailing lists, which the advertiser has to gather. This is the only medium for which the advertiser must provide the circulation. There are two types of list: *compiled* and *mail-derived.*

Exhibit 11.6
Time schedule for a typical promotion mailing. [Bob Stone, *Successful Direct Marketing Methods* (Chicago: Crain Books, 1975).]

PROJECT: ABC MAILING — REVERSE TIME SCHEDULE — PROJECTED DROP DATE: **January 15th**

ELEMENT	LAYOUT DUE	COPY DUE	TYPE DUE	FINAL ART DUE	SEPARATIONS DUE	PRINTING DUE	DELIVERY TO MAILING SERVICE	LABELS TO BE AFFIXED BY MAIL SERV.	AFFIXING TIME	PRE-ADDRESSED MATERIAL	DROP DATE
	Creative			Production				Mailing			
CIRCULAR 17 x 11—4/c-2/s Fold to 8½ x 5½	11/20	11/25	11/29	12/5	12/19	1/4	1/5				J A
BONUS SHEET 8½ x 5½—2/c-1/s	12/1	12/7	12/10	12/8	12/26	1/4	1/5				N
LETTER 17 x 11—2/c-2/s Fold to 8½ x 5½	12/1	12/7	12/10	12/18		1/4	1/5				U A
ORDER CARD 11½ x 5½—2/c-2/s Die-cut fold to 8½ x 5½	12/1	12/5	12/8	12/14		1/4	1/5				R Y
OUTER ENVELOPE 9 x 6—2/c-1/s Open side die-cut perforated cellophane window	11/20	11/25	12/2	12/4		1/3	1/4				15
REPLY ENVELOPE 6¾ x ?—1/c-1/s	11/20	11/25	12/2	12/4		1/3	1/5				
ADDRESSING MATERIALS								12/30	1/5-1/7	1/5-1/7	

Compiled lists Lists of names gathered from published sources, such as lists of car owners, people recently married, new-home buyers, boat owners, or people by trade or profession. The Standard Rate and Data Service reports over 27,000 compiled lists for sale by *mailing-list houses* all over the country, who specialize in assembling them from many sources and who sell them at so much per thousand (Exhibit 11.7).

There are changes taking place in every list all the time. One of the first questions to ask about any list is "How old is it?" or, more specifically, "When was the last time it was used?" because presumably it would have been corrected at that time for all returned mail.

Mail-derived lists Many mailing-list houses sell lists of names of people who have ordered something by mail or have responded to an ad for further information. People on mail-derived lists are those who are prone to order by mail; therefore these lists are more productive than compiled lists. A mail-derived list can be your own house list or a response list that you rent from some other advertiser.

House lists. The finest asset that any direct-marketing firm can have is its own list of customers. These customers have shown that they buy by mail, have had dealings with the house, and have confidence in its integrity and wares. By the nature of the purchase they have made they reveal what type of product might hold further interest. Besides, there is no extra cost for the use of their names.

Renting lists from other advertisers. A major profit center for many firms is the renting of lists of their customers to other companies. Most record and book clubs, magazines, and major direct-response firms have formed subsidiaries to sell or rent their lists. (See Exhibit 11.8.)

Many firms sell a number of lists or parts of lists. Playboy offers lists of *Playboy* and *Oui* subscribers, Playboy Book Club members, and Playboy Club keyholders. Columbia House (a division of CBS) has twenty lists available from among its direct-response customers. Even professional associations like the American Bar Association provide lists of members by region, birthdate, admission to the bar, and areas of specialization. These lists often identify not only prospects for your product but also those consumers who may have responded to direct-response advertising in the past. For instance a record-club member might be an excellent prospect for a book-club or magazine offer.

List brokers Another important industry within an industry is that of the *list broker,* who acts as a clearing house of lists and as a consultant. Rose Harper, president of the Kleid Company, one of the leading brokers in the field, describes the list broker's work in this way:

EXECUTIVES & BUSINESSMEN
STATE Quantities

Big Business Executives	Presidents Big Business	Presidents Mfg. Cos.	Metalworking Executives	Businessmen Self-Employed	States	Financial Executives	Personnel Executives	Purchasing Executives	Sales Executives	Women Executives
6,150	1,200	500	1,463	10,000	ALABAMA	1,090	483	500	392	1,751
650	150	1,000		8,500	ALASKA	147	91	209	27	284
3,060	590	1,449	643	7,400	ARIZONA	758	558	280	227	1,235
4,040	900	1,224	860	6,300	ARKANSAS	740	283	361	269	1,707
37,490	2,990	14,046	12,564	77,500	CALIFORNIA	8,863	3,397	6,551	4,354	13,237
6,820	1,340	2,634	1,037	9,700	COLORADO	1,719	535	700	483	1,687
10,570	1,640	3,525	3,429	11,900	CONNECTICUT	2,978	737	1,390	1,143	1,736
1,200	350	0	34	4,200	DELAWARE	830	616	42	172	1,044
2,570	200	120	188	2,400	D.C.	336	97	98	0	291
14,370	2,840	4,410	2,529	33,500	FLORIDA	3,411	1,444	1,110	945	5,820
9,230	1,830	3,304	1,471	16,500	GEORGIA	1,995	885	690	934	2,444
1,820	80	626	65	2,700	HAWAII	558	165	65	98	473
1,680	410	161	161	3,200	IDAHO	314	209	76	94	457
38,040	6,700	16,592	9,126	42,900	ILLINOIS	10,124	2,383	3,545	3,950	7,830
13,310	2,520	7,794	3,348	19,900	INDIANA	2,592	659	1,106	1,050	2,719
8,100	1,670	2,314	1,439	12,400	IOWA	1,626	376	580	574	1,500
7,060	1,480	0	1,234	9,200	KANSAS	1,315	357	763	402	2,255
6,540	1,330	1,787	1,291	10,100	KENTUCKY	1,302	294	549	439	1,961
6,750	1,370	899	857	10,700	LOUISIANA	1,439	345	1,231	324	2,155
2,090	400	740	287	3,500	MAINE	483	108	141	109	520
7,140	1,240	2,225	1,161	14,600	MARYLAND	1,730	925	634	583	2,060
18,850	2,980	4,780	4,740	20,300	MASSACHUSETTS	4,931	861	1,919	1,658	2,724
19,350	3,540	6,864	7,188	33,500	MICHIGAN	4,173	1,166	2,736	1,756	3,658
11,670	2,120	3,582	2,016	13,800	MINNESOTA	2,565	906	1,020	1,079	2,256
3,450	780	1,773		6,200	MISSISSIPPI	593	175	335	0	1,480
12,950	2,360	4,322	1,867	18,100	MISSOURI	2,645	1,122	958	1,251	3,806
1,590	400	532	90	2,600	MONTANA	278	54	90	41	536
5,000	970	1,120	526	5,600	NEBRASKA	916	246	280	302	1,246
840	190	0	97	2,500	NEVADA	216	115	45	53	267
2,420	430	758	469	2,700	NEW HAMPSHIRE	569	111	252	170	487
17,560	3,070	7,362	5,287	26,800	NEW JERSEY	4,540	1,416	2,430	2,285	3,730
1,790	390	713	190	3,800	NEW MEXICO	316	161	230	68	732
50,410	7,110	13,977	8,148	60,900	NEW YORK	12,982	2,789	4,570	5,337	10,412
11,390	2,190	3,120	1,764	16,800	NORTH CAROLINA	2,346	805	941	824	2,366
2,010	470	532	116	2,300	NORTH DAKOTA	352	67	70	62	514
26,290	4,730	14,576	8,801	38,600	OHIO	6,288	2,143	3,799	2,853	4,854
7,330	1,520	2,829	1,094	8,700	OKLAHOMA	1,551	275	1,272	321	2,444
4,350	900	3,011	826	1,300	OREGON	980	627	1,465	377	1,207
27,740	4,850	10,962	6,480	39,000	PENNSYLVANIA	6,190	1,819	3,109	2,641	5,013
4,470	490	1,897	818	3,500	RHODE ISLAND	663	115	402	234	525
4,470	1,000	550	729	8,000	SOUTH CAROLINA	851	436	390	311	986
1,710	1,420	0	128	2,300	SOUTH DAKOTA	272	57	70	58	506
9,210	1,680	4,050	1,501	14,300	TENNESSEE	1,833	579	737	733	2,567
32,270	6,000	8,895	4,437	43,000	TEXAS	7,583	1,631	4,750	1,822	8,269
2,910	650	300	337	3,800	UTAH	587	209	187	122	541
1,070	190	582	161	1,700	VERMONT	213	44	95	76	294
8,890	1,680	1,280	917	16,400	VIRGINIA	1,928	1,172	600	625	2,380
6,230	1,200	3,979	1,041	13,200	WASHINGTON	1,439	1,053	646	435	1,364
3,360	770	864	331	5,300	WEST VIRGINIA	583	132	180	143	1,113
14,180	2,540	3,086	2,941	16,100	WISCONSIN	2,803	982	1,309	1,334	2,439
860	220	707	48	1,100	WYOMING	152	47	205	33	246
501,210	91,490	172,870	112,630	750,000	Totals	115,720	36,360	54,870	43,750	122,136

13

Exhibit 11.7
Part of a compiled list in a catalog that lists thousands of classifications. (Courtesy of Zeller & Letica, Inc.)

Exhibit 11.8
Selling and renting lists has become big business. (Courtesy MRS Associates, Inc.)

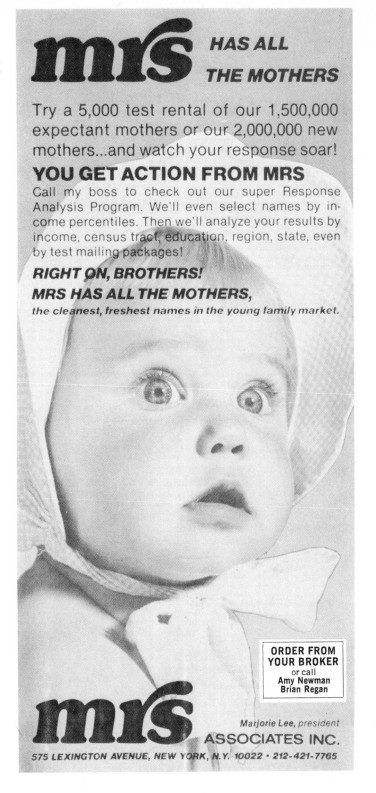

267

The list broker functions as an intermediary between list owners and prospective renters of these lists. The typical list broker handles from 3000 to 10,000 lists or list segments. The average cost of a list is $30 per 1000 names, but more specialized lists can cost three or four times that amount.

When a list is selected the owner of the list pays the broker a commission (usually 20 percent). The broker normally guarantees the accuracy of the list and an undeliverable rate of over 7–10 percent will qualify the user of the list to a rebate.

Usually these rented lists do not actually come into the advertiser's possession. A third party, such as a *letter shop,* which we shall discuss later, undertakes to address company *A*'s mailing pieces with the names on company *B*'s list. Company *A,* therefore, never actually sees the mailing list it uses. Only those names that respond ever become known to the mailer.

Almost 95 percent of the available lists are now being reproduced on labels and magnetic tape. The magnetic tape is also used for computer letter writing and for eliminating duplication among the lists being mailed.

List brokers can supply their own collections of choice lists; or they may serve as consultants to list buyers, participate in the planning, prevent the use of lists that do not appear appropriate, and bring to bear the latest experiences in the field.

Merge/purge

One of the big problems involved in using a number of lists is that the same name may be on several of them. One person may receive two, three, or even four copies of the same mailing, an annoyance to the recipient, an extra cost to the advertiser, and perhaps the loss of a prospective customer. To advertisers who send out millions of pieces a year this loss and expense is considerable.

To offset duplication, computerized systems have been developed whereby all lists for a mailing are sent directly to a central service equipped to handle what is known as a *merge/purge* operation. This results in having all duplicates removed from the list so that the recipient gets only one mailing. Numerous firms are equipped to handle a merge/purge operation, but it can be used only on response-derived lists with names on magnetic tape.

Other direct-mail techniques

The constant increase in postal cost has inspired different ways of getting a message to a list of prospects. Among them are the following:

Package inserts. It has long been the custom to enclose a bounce-back circular when an order is filled. The circular advertises another of the firm's products that might interest the purchaser. But in recent times it has become possible to contract for package inserts in the shipments of other companies, much as one would buy space in a magazine. These inserts are called *ridealongs* and can be sent at a fraction of the cost of an independent mailing. They are also another approach to the high cost of list rental.

Cooperative (joint) mail advertising. There are firms who specialize in sending out mailings to selected lists, each mailing carrying the offer and return-order form of a group of direct marketers who want to reach the described audience. The joint mailing may be made in an envelope, or it may be a full-page ad in a magazine, the page consisting entirely of couponlike ads of different firms. The arrangement divides postage and mail-handling costs.

Syndicate mailings. Here a marketer prepares a direct-mailing piece offering a product or service; but instead of mailing it, he or she makes financial arrangements with other mail-order companies to mail the offer under their letterhead. The marketer supplies material that the mail-order people can use to sell the product under the name of the mail-order house. Thus Meredith Publishing Company, which publishes the *Better Homes & Garden Family Medical Guide,* might syndicate it to Doubleday Book Clubs, Encyclopaedia Britannica, and others that may be able to sell it to their lists of prospective customers. Each of these direct-marketing companies might adapt the syndicator's letter copy to some extent. Most of them will use that circular without change. An important factor in such arrangements is to keep down the weight of the mailing piece.

What makes a good name

Some people are more responsive to mailings than others are. Among the more responsive are

Customers who have recently ordered or who order frequently

Buyers of similar products

Volume buyers

People who have shown interest in a related product, for example, book-club members or record and tape buyers

People who have a demographic interest in a product, for example, parents, who buy encyclopedias, young marrieds, who buy insurance

Those who are known to reply to direct mail (in contrast to those whose response is unknown)

DIRECT-RESPONSE COPY

The difference between direct-response copy written for direct mail and copy for publication advertising is chiefly in format, not in substance. Because we have already become familiar with preparing print publication copy, we shall discuss the subject in that framework. Then we shall discuss the special needs of the direct-mail format and how to adapt copy for it.

Direct-response publication copy invariably has a strong promise-of-benefit headline to attract immediate attention. It is usually news of a special value to attract a certain type of audience. This is not the place for subtlety nor for a play on words—seldom for humor. Subheads appear frequently, describing the offer in a different way. This is immediately followed by an abundance of clear copy, spelling out details of the offer. This is the place for all forms of evidence available to give assurance to the reader, specify money-back guarantees, and close with a special bonus for promptness in replying. All this will be recognized as following the PAPA formula: promise, amplification, proof, action.

The order form should be big enough for the reader to fill out easily. Terms should be clearly presented, including handling and shipping charges, approval offers or money-back guarantees, and use of credit cards.

The formula is applied in a different way to direct-mail pieces, especially if they are not single cards but part of a package of different pieces sent in the same envelope.

THE DIRECT-MAIL PACKAGE

All the different pieces that go out in one mailing are referred to as its "package." When you get a direct-mail envelope, you may think someone had an envelope addressed, then stuffed a lot of various advertising into it. But the chances are that it was all one unit of carefully selected pieces, each with its purpose. It may include the following elements:

Envelope

The selling effort begins on the outside of the envelope. Everything depends upon rousing interest and curiosity so that the recipient will open it. In fact 15 percent of the people who receive unsolicited mail coming in an envelope throw it away because they think they already know what is inside and they are not interested. The message should not make any false pretense; otherwise the reader will feel tricked and toss the whole mailing away. The envelope must break through that barrier by what it says.

Letter

The addressee's name may be computerized on it, but it is usually a personal letter, establishing contact directly with the reader. It explains the importance of getting the full details given on the handsome brochure enclosed. The job of the letter is to interest the reader in such an enclosure. In recent years the computer has allowed direct mail letters to be truly personalized by including the name of the recipient in the salutation and even in the body of the letter. This technique heightens interest in the message and increases readership.

Brochure

This is the big selling part of the mailing—a booklet, folder brochure, or broadside, perhaps with color pictures and charts to illustrate everything discussed. This is the workhorse of the team.

Order form Requirements for this form are the same as those for the publication advertisement. The order form may, however, be considerably larger and may have the addressee's name computerized on it, needing only a signature.

Act now The act-now enclosure may be a different-colored slip, offering a special bonus for a prompt reply.

Reply

envelope A very important standard practice, based on experience, is to enclose a return envelope when an order is requested. Convenience encourages the reader to reply.

COPY TESTING

Direct-mail

tests One of the great advantages of direct-response advertising is that you can test everything on a small but meaningful scale before proceeding on a very large scale. Testing is especially simple in direct mail. You may want to test which of two propositions or two appeals or two different formats is better. You prepare the materials to be tested the way they are to go out. Every other name on a list is sent mailing *A*; the other half is sent mailing *B*. All order cards have a code or key number by which replies are identified and tabulated. But to get statistically meaningful differences, you must use a big enough sample of a mailing list. You must receive enough responses to show clearly which is the better ad. If mailing piece *A* produces fourteen orders while mailing piece *B* produces eleven, the result of the test is meaningless. And in order to make our test beds, or mailing, large enough, we have to have some idea of the percentage of response to expect. This will vary enormously by medium and by proposition. You must make sure that the names chosen for a direct-mail test are a fair sample of the rest of the list.

Split-run

tests For magazine ads split-run tests are used. We met them briefly in Chapter 9, Using Magazines. By this method the advertiser runs two different ads in the same position, on the same date, in alternate copies of the same publication. Ads in newspapers are placed in papers distributed equally in the same area. Magazine ads may appear in geographic editions split for testing or in mailings to different but equivalent areas. Each ad carries a coupon with its own key number. The advertiser can then tell whether ad *A* or ad *B* brings in more responses.

As a practical matter, advertisers will usually test a number of ads at one time, in the hope of finding at least one real jewel among them. The one-at-a-time system is a very slow one. Therefore, in conducting such tests, advertisers will pick out one of the successful ads they already have and regard that as a *control* against which all their other ads are separately tested. You can thus plan a series of tests such as these: ad *A* versus control ad; ad *B* versus control ad; ad *C* versus control ad; ad *D* versus control ad. You will then run the series in one of the magazines with geographic editions that accept split-run advertising, running different sets of ads (new versus control) in various editions at the same time (Exhibit 11.9). Thus you can test four, six, or any number of ads at one time, a great saving in the total time taken for testing.

Exhibit 11.9

This is a control ad used successfully by Omaha Steaks International for its direct-response business. The following four ads were tested against this control. Rank the four ads in the order you think they were best in producing sales. What actually happened is noted at the end of the summary of this chapter. (All five ads courtesy of Omaha Steaks International.)

**Phone order
Toll FREE—
(800) 228-9055**

charge to major
credit card

(In Nebr. call
collect 402-
391-3660)

Try a little tenderness

There are so many special occasions. One of the best is shared by just the two of you. Candlelight, wine and magnificent aged Omaha Steaks. Luscious corn-fed beef with an inimitable flavor. Perfect.

Experts select and prepare each filet from the choicest tenderloins. Their artistry in cutting and aging is your assurance of the utmost in enjoyment. Try a little tenderness soon. Phone or mail your order. Shipped frozen in a reusable styrofoam box. Arrival in perfect condition guaranteed.

Save! Six 6-oz. Filet Mignons, 1-1/4" thick (reg. $39.95)...$29.95
(plus $2 shipping/handling)

Save $10.00. Limit 2 per customer. Valid only in 48 connected States. Offer expires Dec. 2, 1979.

James A. Beard, noted food authority, says: "Omaha Steaks are everything I expect a good steak to be."
Recipe booklet including James Beard favorites and 24-page catalog of our complete line free with order. For catalog only send $1

Omaha Steaks International
CALL TOLL FREE (800) 228-9055
Dept. 1340. 4400 So. 96th St., Omaha, NE 68127

Exhibit 11.9
(*cont.*) Ad 2.

Exhibit 11.9
(*cont.*) Ad 3.

IT'S LOVE AT FIRST BITE!

And no wonder. It's a choice, succulent and oh-so-delicious Filet Mignon from Omaha Steaks. It's naturally-aged, corn-fed Midwestern beef at its finest. Fact is, nowhere else (except in some of America's finest restaurants) will you sink your teeth into anything quite as good. But see and taste the difference for yourself...

SAVE $10 on introductory offer. Get six 6-oz. Filet Mignons 1¼" thick (reg. $39.95) for only $29.95 (plus $2 shipping and handling.)

Call 800-228-9055 toll-free day or night (Nebraska residents call 402-391-3660 collect) and charge your order to any major credit card. Or write and send your check or money order to the address below. Your steaks will be shipped frozen in a reusable styrofoam box. We guarantee arrival in perfect condition.

We'll also include *James Beard's Favorites* recipe book, and our 32-page full-color catalog. Limit 2 orders per customer and you must order before December 7, 1979.

Omaha Steaks International ™

Dept. 1370, 4400 S. 96th St. • Omaha Nebraska 68127

Exhibit 11.9 (*cont.*) Ad 4.

Attention: Steak Lovers

This special offer saves you $10 on the finest steak you can buy.

Ever wonder where the Filet Mignons served in the fine restaurants came from? Quite possibly from us. But we also reserve some Filet Mignons for private sale to discriminating gourmets. And that's why we're inviting you to discover the unforgettable taste of these superb Filet Mignons...*and save $10 in the bargain.*

SAVE $10 on introductory offer. Get six 6-oz. Filet Mignons 1¼" thick (reg. $39.95) for only $29.95 (plus $2 shipping and handling.)

Call 800-228-9055 toll-free day or night (Nebraska residents call 402-391-3660 collect) and charge your order to any major credit card. Or send your check or money order to the address below. Your steaks will be shipped frozen in a reusable styrofoam box. We guarantee arrival in perfect condition.

We'll also include *James Beard's Favorites* recipe book, and our 32-page full-color catalog. Limit 2 orders per customer and you must order before November 30, 1979.

Omaha Steaks International ®

Call Toll Free (800) 228-9055
Dept. 1365, 4400 S. 96th St. • Omaha, Nebraska 68127

Exhibit 11.9 (*concl.*) Ad 5.

Guidelines for copy
testing
Here are a few guidelines for copy testing, whether for publication ads or for direct-mail use:

- ☐ Test most important differences first, such as offers, prices, formats, and appeals. Then, if you have time, patience, and money, test small refinements.
- ☐ There should be a conspicuous difference between new ads or elements being tested against each other.
- ☐ Set a quota of replies per dollar before you start.
- ☐ Keep careful records of replies.
- ☐ Test only one variable at a time. Make sure that ads or mailings are identical in every respect except the one being tested. Don't try to test several variables at one time to save time or money. Neither is saved.
- ☐ Make no final judgments based on small percentage differences. They may represent simply a normal statistical variation.
- ☐ Do not change or attempt to improve the mailing or condition of the ad or mailing once a test has proved satisfactory. If any improvement suggests itself, test it out before using it further. The test may show that it is no improvement at all.

PLANNING THE DIRECT-MAIL
PIECES
The creator of direct mail has a wide latitude in format: It may be a single card encompassing a coupon; it may be a letter with a return card, a small folder, a brochure, or a folded broadside with an order form and return envelope. Each has a different function and use depending on the cost of the product being sold, the importance of pictures, and the nature and length of the copy. As a rule, a warm letter, even if not personalized, should accompany any request for the order, stressing the benefits, describing the key features and importance, and asking for the order. No matter what material is to be sent, there is always the possibility of presenting it in a more interesting form, within postal limitations.

PRODUCING DIRECT
MAIL
What a different world direct-mail production is, compared to that of magazine ad production! In production for magazine ads the publisher is responsible for the total printing and delivery of the publication. In direct mail, however, the advertiser has the complete burden of having all the material printed, which involves selecting the paper and the type, establishing prices, and selecting the printer. It involves also selecting a letter shop, whose functions we discuss below. All this is the burden of direct-mail production.

A mail-production
program
Perhaps the clearest way to see what is involved is to work through a schedule and touch upon some of the key points:

Checking weight and size with post office. Everything begins upon receipt of a complete dummy of the mailing unit, including copy and artwork from the creative department, along with quantities and mailing dates. First—and most important to do—is to check with the post office on weight and size.

Selecting the printing process. In Chapter 16, Print Production, we discuss the three major types of printing: letterpress, offset, and gravure. For the time being, we can say that most direct-mail advertising is printed by the offset method, except very big runs, which may use rotogravure.

Selecting the paper. Here we have to pause to become familiar with some important things about the choice of paper, as this is not covered elsewhere in the book. The three chief categories of paper ("stocks") used in advertising are writing stocks, book stocks, and cover stocks.

WRITING STOCKS. These cover the whole range of paper meant to write or type on. Quality varies from ledger stock, used to keep records, to bond stock for top-level office stationery to utility office paper to memorandum paper. If you wanted to include a letter in a mailing, you would find a paper stock in this class.

BOOK STOCKS. With many variations, book stocks are the widest classification of papers used in advertising. Chief among them are:

- ☐ *News stock:* the least costly book paper, built for a short life and porous so that it can dry quickly. Takes line plates well. Used for free-standing inserts in magazines. Not very good for offset.
- ☐ *Antique finish:* a paper with a mildly rough finish. It is a soft paper, widely used for offset. Among the antique classifications are *eggshell antique,* a very serviceable offset paper, and *text,* a high-grade antique used for quality offset books, booklets, and brochures (it is often water-marked and *deckle-edged*).
- ☐ *Machine finish:* most books and publications are printed on machine-finish paper. It is the workhorse of the paper family.
- ☐ *English finish:* has a roughened nonglare surface. Widely accepted for direct-mail and sales-promotion printing. Especially good for offset lithography and gravure.
- ☐ *Coated:* this is a paper that is given a special coat of clay and then ironed. The result is a heavier, smoother paper. Not usually used for offset. It can take 150-screen halftones very well for letterpress printing and is therefore frequently used in industrial catalogs, where fine, sharp reproduction is important and where there will be continuous usage over a period of time.

COVER STOCKS. Here is a strong paper, highly resistant to rough handling and used not only for the cover of booklets but sometimes by itself in direct-mail work. Although it has many finishes and textures, it is not adaptable for halftone printing by letterpress but reproduces tones very well in offset.

There are many other types of paper used for many purposes, but writing, book, and cover are the chief ones in advertising. The printer will submit samples of paper suitable for a given job.

Basic weights and sizes. Paper comes off the machine in large rolls. It is then cut into large sheets in a number of different sizes. In that way many pages can be printed at one time. Paper is sold by the ream of 500 sheets, and its grade is determined by weight. To meet the problem of trying to compare the weight of paper cut to different sizes, certain sizes have been established for each class as the basic ones for weighing purposes. These are:

- [ ] For writing paper, 17 by 22 inches
- [ ] For book paper, 25 by 38 inches
- [ ] For cover stock, 20 by 26 inches

Hence, no matter how large the sheet may be into which the paper has been cut, its weight is always given in terms of the weight of that paper when cut to its basic size. Thus one hears a writing paper referred to as a "20-pound writing paper," a book paper referred to as a "70-pound paper," or a cover stock identified as a "100-pound cover."

Paper has to be selected in relation to the printing process to be used and the plates to be used.

Paper is usually procured by the printer, after a specific choice has been made. In large cities it may also be bought directly from paper jobbers. Each will be glad to submit samples. Before paper is finally ordered, check once more with the post office for weight, shape, and size of envelope. Check the total package.

In planning direct mail, you must know basic paper sizes and plan all pieces so that they may be cut from a standard sheet size without waste. Before ordering envelopes, be sure to check with the post office to learn of their latest size restrictions. These are subject to change.

Selecting the printer. The big problem in selecting a printer is, first of all, to consider only those printers who have the type of presses and the capacity to handle the operation that you have in mind. They may not be located near you. In any case experience has shown that it's always best to get three estimates. Of course, in the selection of a printer, the reputation of the firm for prompt delivery is important.

Have finished mechanicals with type and illustrations or else photographic negatives ready to turn over to the printer. Proofs should be carefully checked and returned promptly to the printer.

Selecting the letter shop (mailing house). Once all the material has been printed—including the envelope, which has to be addressed, a letter possibly calling for a name fill-in, a folder that has to be folded, and a return card, also perhaps with the name imprinted—it goes to a mailing house (called in many quarters a "letter shop"). Many letter shops are mammoth plants where everything is done by computer. Their computerized letters not only mention the addressee's name but include a personal reference. The name is also printed

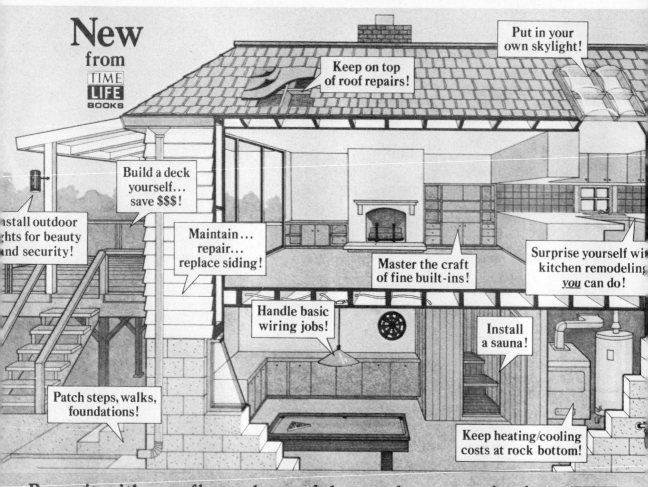

Exhibit 11.10
This illustration, in color, was on the back of a mailing envelope that contained the enclosure pictured on the facing page. The run has exceeded 10 million mailings. (Courtesy of Time/Life Books.)

on the return order form. Machines automatically address various units, fold all pieces that need to be folded, collate all material, and insert it in the envelope, which is sealed, arranged geographically for postal requirements, and delivered to the post office (for example, Exhibit 11.10). (There is always a question of which is more wonderful: the machines with their swinging arms that do all these things or the production director, who has all the material ready in one place, on time.)

Since the letter shop and the printer must work closely together, it is desirable to have them near each other.

Exhibit 11.10
(*concl.*)

Production schedule for direct

mail   The planning and execution of a direct-mail campaign is not an overnight operation. The advertiser must work backward from the date he wishes the customer to receive the mailing piece to determine the necessary lead time. A reverse production timetable can be helpful in planning each step of a project (see Exhibit 11.11).

USING MAGAZINES FOR DIRECT-RESPONSE

ADVERTISING   Magazines are the second largest medium used by direct-response advertisers, but the direct-response advertisers' approach to buying space in them is different from that of national advertisers. Many magazines have mail-order sections in the back of the book; and judging by advertisers' continued use of them, we can assume that results on the whole are good. Many a small business has grown to be a big one through these ads. In direct-response advertising the question is not what is the CPM of the magazine but what will be the cost per order or inquiry. You work both for good position and for good prices.

This means at the outset a very close matching of the media to the type of person you want to reach. *House and Garden* is a good magazine for seeds and plants; *Popular Mechanics,* for a new wrench set. Any promising magazine is worth testing if the space cost is low enough.

In direct-response magazine advertising, small ads have paid because it does not take too many orders to show a profit. Big ads have paid because of the attention they get and—very important—because of the position they get. But medium-size ads can be expensive. You lose priority in negotiations when you reduce from full-page to smaller than full-page ads. You no longer can bargain for position in the book, and you cannot bargain for position on the page. You not only pay a higher premium for the smaller space but lose any bargaining power you might have.

Some publications will accept a *per inquiry* (PI) space ad, to run at no initial cost. The publisher charges for the ad at so much per response received, whether the respondents buy or just make an inquiry.

Most direct-response advertisers expect a full-page magazine ad to pull from 0.05 percent to 0.20 percent of circulation, in other words, from one-half of a response per thousand to two responses per thousand. This is a typical range of figures, but results vary enormously. According to Frank Vos, an authority on the subject, direct-mail results will usually range between 0.7 percent and 5.0 percent of names mailed, in other words, from seven orders per thousand to fifty orders per thousand. You will notice that the ratio of response per thousand between direct-mail and magazine space is roughly on the order of 10 or 20:1. However, the same ratio applies to the CPM of the two kinds of media. Therefore many advertisers find that their *cost per order* for both space and direct mail is about the same.

280

DESCRIPTION OF ITEM OR PROJECT: _____

<u>REVERSE TIME TABLE</u>

(The purpose of which is to work backwards to make
sure enough time is allowed for proper completion.)

FINAL DATE **DUE IN HANDS** **OF RECIPIENTS** _____	This is when you expect the mailing to reach the people who are going to read it and act upon it.
MAILING **DATE** _____	When you must release it to get it there on time. Avoid disappointment by allowing enough time for the P. O.
ASSEMBLY **DATE** _____	All material must be in on this date to allow sufficient time for the mailing operations.
PRINTING **COMPLETION** **DATE** _____	This could be same as ASSEMBLY DATE except where time is required for shipment to out–of–town point.
FINAL ARTWORK **APPROVAL** **DATE** _____	This is the date the artwork must be ready to turn over to the printer.
ARTWORK **COMPLETION** **DATE** _____	Although most details should have been okayed before work actually began, quite often several people must approve the finished artwork. Allow enough time for this approval.
FINISHED **ARTWORK** **ASSIGNMENT** **DATE** _____	This is the day the artist or art department gets the job. Allow at least a week. If no type has to be set, the interval can be cut short.
CONSIDERATION **AND APPROVAL** **DATE** _____	Allow four or five days for staff members, including legal department if necessary, to see finished copy and layout.
COPY AND **LAYOUT** **ASSIGNMENT** **DATE** _____	Allow a week or more to give the copy and layout people time to do their jobs. Give more time when you can; they will more readily come through for you when a rush job is really critical.
STARTING **DATE** _____	You need some time to think about the job and draw up a set of instructions.

Exhibit 11.11
(From *The Direct Mail Marketing Manual,* Release 4005, July 1976. Courtesy Direct Mail/
Marketing Association, Inc., New York, N.Y.)

Importance of position in

magazines   Direct-response advertisers are particularly fussy about position in the regular part of the magazine, for one good reason: They are the only advertisers who can figure exactly what the differences are in various positions (see Stone's precise figures in the section on magazine elements in Chapter 9).

Inserts   One of the important features of magazines is the fact that an advertiser can have a special insert bound into the magazine opposite his page, greatly increasing the response from an ad. The trend to physical flexibility is pronounced. There are bound-in response cards, full-page inserts, and multipage inserts of various kinds provided by the advertiser, who pays an extra space charge and possibly a charge for binding. The insert might also be a recipe booklet or a miniature catalog. Position in the magazine, again, is of great importance. Table 11.1 is Stone's ranking of effectiveness of position order on the pull of inserts. From that we see that the second insert card in a magazine is 95 percent as effective as the first, the third 85 percent as the first, and so forth.

Table 11–1

INSERT-CARD EFFECTIVENESS[a]	
INSERT-CARD POSITION	RANK
First	100
Second	95
Third	85
Fourth	75 (if after main editorial)
Fifth	70 (if after main editorial)

[a]Bob Stone, *Successful Direct Marketing Methods* (Chicago: Crain Books, 1979), p. 122.

It is important to make sure that your coupon ad is not backed up by another. Publishers usually watch out for this.

Discounts   Before placing an ad, ask whether there is a special mail-order rate or a special mail-order section. Rates can be substantially lower than for other classes of advertising. Also ask if they have remnant space, which we discussed in Chapter 9. Check all other discounts offered. If your advertising is for a company that is an affiliate of a large advertiser see whether you can get in under "corporate discounts." Also look into the question of barter space, which we discuss in Chapter 20.

USING OTHER MEDIA FOR
DIRECT-RESPONSE ADVERTISING

Newspapers   Newspapers are the third largest medium in the use of direct-response advertising. The Sunday-magazine supplements have long been a favorite medium for direct marketers. They are also ideal for split-run testing, with the supplements distributed in cities all over the country. The use of free-standing inserts is an important medium for direct-response advertising, devices being borrowed from direct mail: business-reply envelopes, die cuts, and punch-out tokens.

Radio   Like TV, radio for direct-response advertising is bought by cost per order, not by ratings, as national advertisers buy it. Hence there is always a search for a good time buy. Direct-response advertisers can be more venturesome in radio than can national advertisers. They can test their commercials at low cost. And at those low nighttime rates you can afford to take 60-second spots to deliver your story.

One of the greatest contributions that radio makes to direct-response advertising lies in connection with a massive mailing that a firm is going to make in the area reached by the radio station. *Reader's Digest,* for example, has an elaborate sweepstakes package with a computerized letter, computerized check, and mailing form. Just prior to the mailing, a heavy radio schedule is launched, telling people to be sure to watch for this mailing. The technique, though costly on the face of it, has been so effective that this plan has been repeated in *Reader's Digest's* drives for subscribers. Radio has proved to be of great value as a back-up for direct-mail campaigns, as well as directly in getting orders by mail and by toll-free telephone.

Direct response and
television   TV direct-response advertising is much different from traditional TV advertising. Direct-response advertisers are more likely to buy spots at off hours when they can negotiate for low rates. By buying spots at these low prices, they increase the return per dollar.

Other methods of placing direct-response advertising are PI and *bonus-to-payout.* As in magazines, PI means that the station runs the ad as often as it wishes and receives a percentage of the money received or so much for each inquiry. In bonus-to-payout a fixed schedule of spots is bought with the station and advertiser agreeing on a certain return. If the advertising fails to generate this level, the station is obligated to run additional spots or provide a rebate to the advertiser. Both PI and bonus-to-payout advertising are usually placed on independent stations or during late fringe time.

Two-way television and direct

response   Many direct-response practitioners see two-way TV (or home computer terminals) as offering a bright future to the industry. The convenience of viewing merchandise on your home TV and then pushing a button to order it while simultaneously having your bank account debited for the purchase price would seem to be the shopping pattern of the future. Already consumers can see the Sears Roebuck catalog on videodiscs complete with product demonstrations.

However, a major study conducted by Benton & Bowles, a leading advertising agency, indicated substantial resistance to shopping at home by TV. Among the reasons given were liking to go out to shop, cost of in-home technology for shopping, and fear of invasion of privacy, especially with in-home banking services.*

SUMMARY

In the 1980s direct-response advertising will begin to fulfill its potential and become an integral part of the marketing process. Transportation expense, increase in working women, new direct-response techniques, and a desire for added shopping convenience will combine to increase direct marketing.

The direct-marketing industry will continue to make a concentrated effort to upgrade its image and combat any unethical practices. The Direct Mail Marketing Association (DMMA) has for several years reviewed complaints about direct marketers through its Committee on Ethical Business Practice. When outright fraud exists, legal avenues are open through the postal service and state attorney generals' offices. However, the key to ethical practice is through self-regulation of direct marketers and the media that accept their advertising.

Ingenuity and new technology will continue to make direct marketing profitable to an expanding market. Despite some apprehension, electronic in-home shopping will become more widespread in the next decade. Computers will allow advertisers to identify a market more precisely and profitably reach it with a made-to-order offer.

ORDER OF SPLIT-RUN ADS

☐ Control cost of ad to sales produced = 100%†
☐ Ad 2   28
☐ Ad 3   29
☐ Ad 4   74
☐ Ad 5   76

---

*"Only 10% of Consumers Interested in Shopping at Home Via 2-way TV," *Marketing News,* May 29, 1981, p. 1.

†Courtesy of Omaha Steaks International.

The control ad performed better than any of the new ads did. Ad 5 produced 76 percent of the sales-to-cost ratio of the control ad and was the best of the four ads tested.

QUESTIONS

1. Discuss the major changes in society that will contribute to the growth of direct marketing.
2. What is the difference between one-step and two-step direct-response offers?
3. What is a bounce-back circular? A ride-along?
4. Distinguish between compiled lists and mail-derived lists; between house lists and outside lists.
5. Discuss the use of the computer in direct-response advertising.
6. What is a negative-option direct-response technique?
7. Discuss the importance of a merge/purge operation.
8. Why is direct-response advertising usually more wordy than other advertising?

SUGGESTED EXERCISES

9. Get three direct-response magazine ads. Compare the headline and copy approach with three non direct-response ads in the same magazine.
10. Find two examples of direct-mail advertising pieces that follow the PAPA formula and two that do not.

READINGS

CAPON, NOEL and JOHN U. FARLEY: "The Impact of Message on Direct Mail Response," *Journal of Advertising Research,* October 1976, pp. 69–75.

COHEN, WILLIAM: *Mail Order Marketing* (New York: John Wiley & Sons, 1982).

PIRONTI, A. R., MORTON M. VITRIOL, and ANDREW THURM: "Consumer Interest in Mail-Order Purchasing," *Journal of Advertising Research,* June 1981, pp. 35–40.

POPE, JEFFREY: "Ringing Up Industrial Sales by Phone," *Sales & Marketing Management,* October 12, 1981, pp. 50–51.

STONE, BOB: *Successful Direct Marketing Methods* (Chicago: Crain Books, 1979).

SWINYARD, WILLIAM R., and MICHAEL L. RAY: "Effects of Praise and Small Requests on Receptivity to Direct-Mail Appeals," *Journal of Social Psychology,* August 1979, pp. 177–84.

"Targeting In on America's Prime Consumers," *ZIP,* March 1981, pp. 28–30.

WEINTZ, WALTER: "Ideas in Copy and Creativity Change Only With Environment," *Direct Marketing,* January 1976, pp. 31–32.

"When's the Best Time to Mail?" *ZIP,* September 1981, p. 33.

WOODSIDE, ARCH G., and WILLIAM H. MOTES: "Image Versus Direct Response Advertising," *Journal of Advertising Research,* August 1980, pp. 31–37.

12

Sales
Promotion

Sales promotion is a supplement to advertising, other promotional efforts, and personal selling. Sales promotion is included here because of its close relationship to advertising. Effective sales promotion must be planned simultaneously with the advertising campaign so that each complements the other. It is the most diverse type of promotion, with a limitless number of plans used at all levels of the trade channel. Annual expenditures for all sales-promotion activities is more than $40 billion.

Sales promotion is generally divided into two types: plans directed to ultimate consumers, called *promotions*, or sales-promotion plans, and those directed to wholesalers or retailers, usually referred to as *dealer programs*, or *merchandising plans*.

No matter which category your sales promotion falls into it must be coordinated with the overall marketing goals and advertising program of the firm if it is to be successful. It is tempting to use "cute" ideas in sales promotion, but unless they have an obvious relevance to the product and its prime prospects, the effort (and considerable expense) will be wasted. Successful sales promotion demands the same degree of planning and expertise as the advertising and promotional techniques discussed earlier.

FORMS OF SALES
PROMOTION

The most frequently used forms of sales promotion (sometimes used in combination) are:

- ☐ Points-of-purchase advertising
- ☐ Premiums
- ☐ Coupons
- ☐ Sampling
- ☐ Deals
- ☐ Contests and sweepstakes
- ☐ Advertising specialties
- ☐ Cooperative advertising
- ☐ Booklets, brochures, mailing pieces

Regardless of the type of promotion used, the purpose is the same. Sales promotion is designed to promote product sales by providing additional incentives in the form of money (cents-off coupons) or merchandise (towels packed in detergent). Sales promotions are also used as substitutes for engaging in price competition.

Point-of-purchase advertising

P. Jan Anstatt, Chairman of the Board of the Point-of-Purchase Advertising Institute, describes the value of point-of-purchase advertising by pointing out that

> companies have recognized that the real worth of p-o-p advertising lies in its natural partnership with the big media dollar. Often, in fact, an effective point-of-purchase campaign is developed as a logical extension of the pre-sell approach and can dislodge the message being carried around in the back of the shopper's mind. Of course, signs and displays are often the only means of advertising a product or service and perform their job without any outside marketing support.*

Point-of-purchase advertising displays are placed in retail stores to identify, advertise, or merchandise a product. The effective use of point-of-purchase advertising is based on an understanding of shopping habits of the consumer, needs of the retailer, forms of displays, the display idea, and ways to use the display.

Shopping habits of the consumer. Dependence on retail self-service and the tendency of shoppers to make unplanned purchases have given point of purchase added importance in sellers' marketing and advertising strategies. A

287

*P. Jan Anstatt, "Chairman's Message," *POPAI Marketplace*, 1981, p. 5.

major study of supermarket shoppers found that 64.8 percent of all purchase decisions were made in the store.*

The study indicated that product-buying decisions fall into the following categories:

Specifically planned	Generally planned		Substitute		Unplanned		Store decisions
35.2%	14.8	+	3.0	+	47	=	64.8%

It was also noted that the percentage of specifically planned purchases increased 13 percent over a 12-year period. This increase may indicate that the effects of inflation are being seen in more careful shopping behavior. There was a wide variance in the type of product whose purchase was specifically planned. Of the supermarket items studied, laundry detergents and soaps had the highest rate of planned purchases (56.2 percent) while candy and gum had the lowest (15.2 percent).

Which items should be promoted with point-of-purchase advertising? The retailer uses the following criteria:

☐ Sale of product accounts for a good dollar volume.
☐ Theme of the display is exciting (often it is one used in mass media).
☐ Appropriate display is well-adapted to the character and size of the store.
☐ Related items may be sold by the promotion.
☐ Promoted merchandise has a good markup.
☐ The promotion fits in with the retailer's own schedule of promotions.†

Needs of the retailer. The manufacturer and retailer can make the most of point-of-purchase materials when they realize that advertising at the point of sale is part of the total advertising program. A study made for Campbell Soup Company indicated that, by tying in point-of-purchase advertising to related TV advertising, display productivity (in terms of sales) could be increased significantly. Point-of-purchase displays that were tied in with TV advertising sold 15.5 percent more soup than did similar displays without the TV tie-in.

Forms of displays. If someone has not thought of a display for every dimension and area, someone will. Maybe you will. There are point-of-purchase signs for outdoors, indoors, windows, and overhead. These displays come in every imaginable format. Some are intended for short duration, as in promoting a special sale, while others may be used for years, such as clocks (Exhibit 12.1).

---

*Point-of-Purchase Institute/DuPont Consumer Buying Habits Study.
†"The Value of In-Store Support," The Point of Purchase Advertising Institute, Inc., 1971.

PERMANENT SIGNS. A sign in front of a gas station, one surrounding a clock in a restaurant, and a glass sign that frames an expensive watch are familiar examples of permanent displays. If they are illuminated, they attract more attention and are reserved for good spots since they are usually designed to be effective even when they are not lighted.

MOTION DISPLAYS. In a succession of tests, displays with motion were favored by 70 percent of the dealers, were given 88 percent of the prime in-store locations (compared with 47 percent for nonmotion displays), and produced an 83-percent average gain above normal shelf sales. Motion displays are especially effective in attracting the consumer's attention.

PERMANENT MERCHANDISE TRAYS, RACKS, AND CASES. Many dealers welcome displays that will occupy little space on a counter or floor (Exhibit 12.2), will serve as a showcase for merchandise, and provide a self-service feature (Exhibit 12.3). The display may be an open-face stand from which merchandise such as paint brushes can be picked out. Small, costly items such as watchbands or lipsticks may be displayed to the customer but made accessible only from the dealer's side of the counter in a pilferproof arrangement. In recent years there has been a trend toward display of hard goods, such as electric irons and washing machines (Exhibit 12.4).

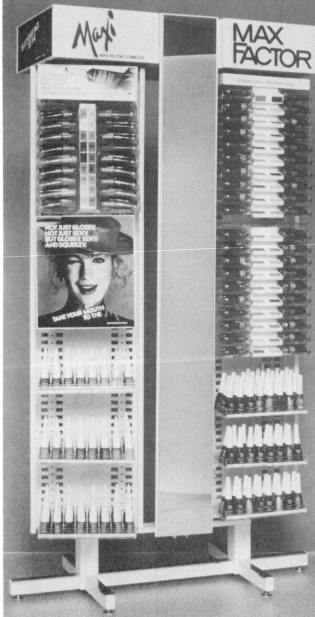

Exhibit 12.2
Trico windshield wipers are featured in wall-mounted displays that hold uneven-sized blades.

Exhibit 12.3
A self-service display. Max Factor used a floor merchandiser to market the complete Max Factor and Maxi lip and nail lines. The company wanted all products to be self-service in an environment that segregates each product line and uses minimum floor space.

Exhibit 12.4
The Sears Lady Kenmore Washer/Dryer display demonstrates that point-of-purchase is not confined to small package-goods items.

The display idea. The heart of the display is the campaign selling idea, designed to generate purchases. Here we can think in terms of three dimensions, and—subject only to size limitations and need for construction simplicity and cost—the creative person has the world of shapes and materials with which to work. Among the directions we can go are these:

PRODUCT ITSELF. The most important display piece in a store is the product itself, and any idea that focuses attention on it is helpful. The solution

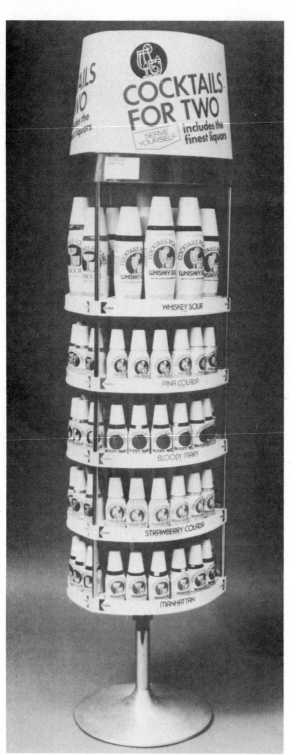

Exhibit 12.5
The Cocktails For Two rotating floor stand allows customers to see the entire line of flavors and sizes and uses minimal floor and shelf space.

may be a large stack of the packaged product on the floor, with a sign stating an advantage and the price (Exhibit 12.5). Or the merchandise can be tumbled in a large box from which the shopper is invited to pick one (a relic of our childhood grab-bag days, no doubt); it also will have a sign stating an advantage.

CURRENT ADVERTISING THEME. Point-of-purchase advertising is a projection of the current advertising theme, whatever it may be. The challenge is to reduce it to its simplest elements and then to dramatize it in three dimensions.

TIE-IN WITH OTHER PRODUCTS. This idea promotes other products, related to the one advertised, that the store also sells. A display of beer suggests pretzels and potato chips. Cold-cereal displays feature appetizing dishes of cereal with berries and other fruit on sale in the store.

STOREWIDE PROMOTION. Some displays are based on a storewide promotion, as back to school, cook-out, spring cleaning, fall festival, and vacation needs. Here the manufacturer provides thematic point-of-purchase material that can apply to all departments in the store, with special emphasis, of course, on his own products.

TIE-IN WITH NATIONAL ADVERTISING. For the smaller independent stores, window displays based on the national-advertising theme may be particularly helpful in reminding the passerby that here is the place to get the product she or he saw advertised.

DEMONSTRATING THE PRODUCT. Often the display can invite the shopper to try out features of the product by pressing a button, looking through an opening, or turning a knob (Exhibit 12.6). This is especially good for new types of products.

In summary: point-of-purchase advertising displays can help create an atmosphere conducive to buying, and they can reinforce an advertising campaign at the retail level (see Table 12.1).

Table 12–1

PRODUCTS DISPLAYED BY MAJOR USERS OF POINT-OF-PURCHASE MATERIALS[a]		
Apparel	Drugs	Recreational
Automobiles	Food	products
Automotive parts and	Hardware and paints	Services
accessories	Home furnishings	Soaps and
Beer	Household appliances	detergents
Confectionary products	Notions and sundries	Soft drinks
Cosmetics and toiletries	Office supplies and stationery	Tobacco

[a]From *POPAI News*, Point-of-Purchase Advertising Institute, Inc., June 29, 1976, and September 24, 1976.

Exhibit 12.6
The Texas Instruments display not only gains eye-catching counter space for these new models but involves the customers in the use of the product by providing sample problems.

Getting displays used. One of the main problems with displays is getting them used. There should be a plan, and the retailer should know about it in advance. In the majority of cases, whether in independent or chain stores, the store manager authorizes the use of point-of-purchase display materials, and the manager's cooperation must be enlisted by the manufacturer's salesperson. Usually display materials come with the order, and store personnel set them up. But many displays are not used because they are not in accordance with the promotion or merchandising policy of the store. Sometimes tailor-made displays are needed to fit the store's requirements.

Having displays made. Firms that create and manufacture displays sometimes specialize according to the materials used for those displays: cardboard, metal, wood, plastic, or glass. Some companies combine these materials or subcontract parts of the work. A display company will usually submit a sketch that portrays an idea. Then a handmade model, or dummy, follows with an estimate of complete costs of production.

Many firms serve as consultants and brokers in the sale of displays. They supply the idea; and if they get the order, they will have the display produced through a manufacturer.

Before you deal with either-type firm, you must have a clear understanding about the conditions under which you are doing business. You may, for example, be presented with an idea that you like but find too expensive. Perhaps the creating firm will agree to manufacture the first run at their price but allow you to get competing bids for reruns. Whatever the deal, it must be made before any work is done.

Most large firms that continually require displays create ideas for them in their own display departments. Manufacturing, however, is done elsewhere, and the costs are handled through the advertiser's purchasing department.

Premiums

A *premium,* as the term is used in advertising, is an item offered in exchange for some consumer action. Normally the consumer must purchase a product to qualify for a premium, but other premiums are given for visiting a retailer, real-estate development, or automobile dealer. These are known as *traffic-building premiums.* Among the most popular of the various types of premium plans are *self-liquidators, direct premiums, free mail-ins, continuity coupon premiums,* and *free giveaways.*

Self-liquidating premiums. A *self-liquidating premium* is one offered upon proof of purchase and payment of a charge (usually handled by mail). The charge covers the cost of the premium, handling, and mailing. Self-liquidators are best used when the advertiser wants to give some new excitement to a mature brand and when the objective is to pick up new or occasional users of his product or to reward loyal users. Examples of self-liquidating premiums:

☐ Golden Graham cereal offers a kite for $1.75 and proof-of-purchase label.
☐ Litter Green cat litter offers a litter tray and litter lifter for $5.75 and proof of purchase.
☐ Customers can purchase a Sun Maid cookbook with raisin recipes for $2.

Sometimes premiums are offered on a cooperative basis by two companies or by two brands of the same firm. This approach is particularly effective when there is a logical tie-in between two products. For example,

☐ Chef Boy-Ar-Dee allows consumers to buy either a *Better Homes & Gardens* cookbook or Corning Ware products for a fee and proof of purchase of specific Chef Boy-Ar-Dee products.
☐ Kellogg 40% Bran Flakes offers Vaughn seed packets for $2 and proof of purchase.
☐ Minute Rice offers 15-cent coupon for Kraft Cheese to promote rice and cheese recipes.

Direct premiums. *Direct premiums* are usually free, given to the consumer at the time of purchase. There are several types of direct premiums, including *on-pack, in-pack, near-pack,* and *container* premiums.

ON-PACK PREMIUMS. On-pack premiums are affixed to the outside of the package or may be part of a double package to hold both the advertised product and the premium. The double package also overcomes security problems with on-packs that are not securely fastened to the package. Denture-Creme doubled-packed its toothbrush premium to prevent this problem.

Another potential problem with some on-pack premiums is that they don't fit easily on retailer shelves or take up additional shelf space. In either case a weak brand runs the risk of having retailers buy another brand that will be more profitable or easier to stock.

IN-PACK PREMIUMS. The oldest and most familiar direct premiums are the in-pack premiums. These premiums give the consumer immediate satisfaction and are easier to deal with than the on-pack premium. The enclosure can be either the premium itself or a coupon that can be redeemed. Some successful in-packs include:

☐ Cocoa Pebbles cereal includes a superhero poster.
☐ Wheaties cereal offers puzzle pieces for sports-spectacular sweepstakes.

NEAR-PACK PREMIUMS. Near-pack premiums are items offered by the advertiser, but they are located in a separate display, usually adjacent to the product. Such inducements have good display potential; and since they are usually distributed by the retailer, they help to increase the store's business.

CONTAINER PREMIUMS. Container premiums, the final form of direct premiums, are reusable containers that serve as the package for the product. It is a good way for the advertiser to increase consumer trials of his product, and the containers act as a constant reminder of the brand. For example:

☐ Shedd's Whipped Margarine comes in a plastic drinking glass.
☐ From time to time most of the fast-food chains offer drinking-glass promotions, such as McDonald's Ronald McDonald glasses.
☐ Sanka coffee is packed in a decorative cameo tin for cookies, flour, and so on.

Free mail-ins. Free mail-ins are premiums that the consumer gets by mailing in to the advertiser a request for the premium and some proof of purchase. Since most free mail-ins require several proofs of purchase, the advertiser uses such premiums to stimulate product (or product-line) sales. And the consumer benefits since there is no payment involved. Hamburger Helper gives a hamburger cookbook with proof of purchase. In some cases a manufacturer will give a premium without even requiring a purchase. Kraft Barbecue Sauce and Two Fingers Tequila both send appropriate recipe books without requiring purchase of the products.

Continuity coupon premiums. Continuity coupon premiums are those that the consumer gets by saving coupons or special labels that come with the product. It is an on-going program, and the premiums normally are selected from a catalog. Premiums vary according to the number of coupons redeemed. Continuity premiums are used to promote a product. Raleigh cigarettes is an example of this approach to building continuing consumer loyalty. Retailers, especially grocery stores, use premiums such as S & H Green Stamps to promote their stores.

Free giveaways. Sometimes the premium is given to the consumer directly by the dealer at the time of purchase. This is known as a *free giveaway,* and it is used to build store traffic. A sporting-goods store might give a baseball bat to those who buy a set value of other sporting goods, or a fast-food outlet might hand out glasses to people who buy a certain item or amount of food. *Farmer's Almanac* has long been a favorite giveaway for drug stores.

Use of premiums

Premiums are among the most used and flexible of all promotional techniques. Premiums can be as simple and inexpensive as a child's toy in a cereal box or as elaborate and expensive as the copperware set offered as a self-liquidating premium by Taster's Choice. In any case the purpose of a premium is to create immediate sales. It may help to introduce new products. It may be used nationally or in a local territory where strong competitive pressure has developed. It may be an effort to increase the unit of sales or to get traffic into the store. It may be used to offset seasonal slumps and to attract repeat purchasers. It can get people to try a product or to use it more often.

Regardless of its use, the premium selected should be appropriate to the job it is intended to accomplish. Unsuccessful premium promotions can most often be traced to one of the following causes:

☐ Inappropriate premium selection. Choosing a premium without regard for a logical tie-in with the product it is promoting will usually lead to unsatisfactory results.

☐ Using premiums in an inappropriate way. Premiums are not normally appropriate for products that are bought only occasionally, as people buy tires, nor for products like cough preparations, bought only when a special need arises.

☐ Ignoring marketing conditions in using premiums. Premiums are not helpful when a product's sales have been steadily declining because the cause for such a downtrend is usually far too critical to be offset by premiums.

What makes a good premium? To judge the value of a premium the advertiser should ask the question "Would this item appeal to my target audience?" Is the premium

☐ useful to my customers?
☐ unique from other competitive promotions?
☐ related to my product?
☐ easily promoted with the product?
☐ of a quality expected by consumers at a price I can afford?

If the answer to any of these questions is no, then the premium may be inappropriate for your purpose. The exception is that sometimes you will be forced into a follow-the-leader promotion (for example, when many of the major airlines gave reduced-fare coupons to meet competitive pressure).

Different premium offers will frequently be tested in various markets to determine which holds the most promise.

But premiums have their problems too. An in-pack premium in a package of food must meet the requirements of the Food and Drug Administration, to make sure it does not impair the foodstuff. In-pack coupons must meet the regulations of the Federal Trade Commission. On-pack premiums are not favored by the trade on account of pilferage.

There is one guide that should be followed in advertising premiums: *The advertising must so clearly and correctly describe and picture the premiums and must state the terms so clearly that the person receiving it will not be disappointed.* This also applies to prompt delivery. If a child, especially, has been disappointed, the whole family feels his sadness.

Fulfillment firms   The physical work of handling premiums, including opening the mail, verifying payment, packaging, addressing, and mailing, is often handled on a fee basis by firms who specialize in "premium fulfillment." They also handle contest responses and prizes.

Premiums as trade

incentives   The desire of consumers to win prizes or receive cash in exchange for purchasing a product is no less appealing to members of the trade channel, that is, wholesalers, retailers, brand managers, and others. Premiums offered to the trade are known as *incentives* and are used to encourage sales through the marketing channel.

The most common incentive to wholesalers or retailers is price reductions in the form of promotional allowances. In effect this is comparable to the cents-off promotion at the consumer level. In addition sweepstakes, contests, and continuity promotions (some with prize catalogs) based on sales volume are all used at the trade level.

Cents-off

coupons   The most used promotional techniques is the cents-off coupon. More than 100 *billion* coupons are distributed each year. Most coupons range from 10 to 30 cents, with a few offering a dollar or more toward the purchase of a product. The manufacturer reimburses the retailer (from 5 to 7 cents per coupon) as a handling fee above normal profit.

Couponing is done for a variety of reasons. It attracts new users and brings back previous users who have switched brands. The desirability of the product is reinforced for present users while competition is reduced. Coupons complement the regular advertising done by the manufacturer. Coupons also let the manufacturer meet price competition without adjusting the actual product price.

Approximately 80 percent of households report redeeming one or more coupons during the last year. Consumer income or education seem to make little difference in the use of coupons although middle- and high-income families have slightly higher usage.

Coupons are distributed in a number of ways. They appear in the daily newspaper (lowest average redemption rate of all media carrying coupons). They appear in the Sunday supplements, the syndicated or independent magazine sections included with the newspaper. Many advertisers distribute their coupons through free-standing inserts that contain several different coupons on the sheet, which is inserted in the Sunday newspaper. Often coupons are issued through magazines, as a magazine on-page (a coupon printed as part of the ad) or a magazine pop-up (a coupon bound into the magazine separately, on heavier stock, and usually facing an advertisement). Many coupons are of the in-pack or on-pack variety. Here the coupons are either in the product package or imprinted on it and redeemable on a later purchase of the same product or a different product (a cross coupon). Package coupons have the highest redemption rate, 17 percent. Finally, coupons may be sent by direct mail. Because of the high postage costs, those advertisers using direct mail often share in a joint mailing with coupons for noncompetitive products.

Table 12.2 compares the various couponing media according to distribution and redemption.

Table 12–2

	COMPARISON OF COUPONING MEDIA[a]		
MEDIUM	TOTAL COUPON DISTRIBUTION, %	TOTAL COUPON REDEMPTIONS, %	AVERAGE REDEMPTION RATE, %
Newspapers	56.3	32.6	2.9
Magazines	11.8	17.3	7.3
Sunday supplements	8.6	3.6	2.1
Package	8.4	28.2	17.0
Free-standing inserts	11.8	11.9	5.0
Direct mail	3.1	6.4	10.5

[a]Adapted from *The Nielsen Researcher 4*, 1979, p. 11.

Despite recent increases in the use of coupons, manufacturers are concerned about misredeemed coupons. An unscrupulous retailer can make a great deal of money by clipping hundreds of coupons and sending them in for the handling charge. It is estimated that approximately 20 percent of all money spent on coupon promotions goes toward misredemptions.[*]

In 1980 the Audit Bureau of Circulation established the Coupon Distribution Verification Service to monitor and report on newspapers' practices in couponing. Participating newspapers will submit a statement outlining the handling, storage, and disposition of free-standing inserts, advertising supplements, and newspaper copies containing ROP coupons.[†] Unless the misredemption problem can be solved, some manufacturers see the use of couponing sharply curtailed in the future.

Sampling Back in the first chapter of this book there is a report of the way the French innkeepers around A.D. 1100 attracted trade to their taverns. They had the town crier go out, blow his horn, attract a crowd, and give samples of the wine of the inn. That is the first recorded use of *sampling*. Giving the consumer a free trial of a product, or sampling, has today become an established technique of promoting sales, along with the use of advertising. The sample is often a smaller version of the product—say, a 4-ounce bottle of dishwashing liquid or a 3-ounce tube of toothpaste.

While sampling can be very effective, it is an expensive form of sales promotion (national sampling campaigns can run up to $5 million for a single product). New formula Crest toothpaste used extensive sampling as part of a $45 million introductory campaign.[‡] Sampling was used since the product met the following conditions:

---

[*]*Advertising Age*, December 15, 1980, p. 44.

[†]*Advertising Age*, May 26, 1980, p. 1.

[‡]*Advertising Age*, March 16, 1981, p. 1.

☐ The product appealed to a broad segment of the population.
☐ The product was backed by a large budget.
☐ The product had a benefit that was not obvious through advertising.

Sampling is usually done by door-to-door delivery through distributing firms geared to handle assignments. Or samples may be mailed (the expensive way, especially in light of escalating postal rates). Sometimes the sample is provided in a magazine, or a coupon is to be sent in for a free sample. A sample might be attached to another package. In any case one of the problems of sampling is the inclusion of nonprospects.

Lipton tea offered free-in-the-mail samples of five new flavored teas to consumers requesting them. By sending the tea only on request, Lipton was able to focus on serious prospects and eliminate the expense of a door-to-door canvas.*

A trade practice has developed whereby an advertiser's product is sold in sample-size minipackages through retail stores. To the consumer it is a good value and minimizes the risk of purchasing a heretofore unknown or untried product. To the store it is a high-margin profit. To the advertiser it is an economical way of distributing the sample. But the value of the sample-package contents lies in the reputation the product has built through customer usage and advertising. (Regardless of how the sample is distributed, it is common for sample packages to be miniatures of regular product packages, thereby allowing greater package recognition.)†

Retailer support, in the form of adequate inventory and special displays, can go a long way in determining the success of an advertiser's sampling campaign.

The basic philosophy underlying sampling of a repeat product is rather simple: The best ad for a product is the product itself.

Deals   There are two types of deal: consumer deals and trade deals.

Consumer deals. A *consumer deal* is a plan whereby the consumer can save money in the purchase of a product. It may be a direct price reduction, of which the cents-off deal is the most familiar form. Or it may be a merchandising deal, in which three bars of soap are wrapped together and sold at a reduced price. Or a package of a new member of the product family is attached to a package of the older product at little or no extra cost—an effective way of introducing a new product.

Sometimes the advertiser uses a deal to spread out the buying season for certain products, such as Carrier's offering a color-TV set for $119 with the purchase of a central air conditioner as part of an "Early Buyer Bonus" sale. Another type of deal is illustrated by this headline: "Buy two, get three! A real

---

*Advertising Age, April 7, 1981, p. 54.
†Richard E. Stanley, *Promotion* (Englewood Cliffs, N.J.: Prentice-Hall, 1977), p. 328.

deal from Playtex on selected styles." Or the deal might be a straight "20 percent off" on General Electric washers or dryers.

In a study of price deals, Charles Hinkle has reported:

- ☐ The closer deals are to each other, the less effective they are. Brands that deal frequently encourage even regular customers to stock up and wait for the next deal.
- ☐ The majority of annual price reductions occur in high-volume periods, but off-season deals are more effective.
- ☐ Dealing is effective more for newer brands than for old.
- ☐ Deals are as much as two to three times more effective when a brand's advertising share level is maintained.
- ☐ Deals are fruitless for products whose sales have been going off steadily.

An assessment should be made of the more basic corrective measures.*

Deals may provide the theme for a strong local advertising campaign. Cents-off deals must meet Federal Trade Commission requirements.

Trade deals. A *trade deal* is a special discount to the retailer for a limited period of time. It may involve free goods or a minimum purchase. It may be a sliding scale of discounts, depending on the size of the purchase. It may be in connection with a consumer merchandising deal, offering a discount on the purchase of a given number of consumer deals and size assortments. Counter displays may be included to help sell the product to the consumer. (All trade deals are subject to the Robinson-Patman Act, which we discuss in Chapter 25.)

Trade deals, which are extensively advertised in the trade papers, are used to achieve or expand distribution of the advertiser's product. And because the retailer stands to gain from trade deals, they are usually effective (although rather expensive) in enlisting merchandising support of retailers.

Contests and sweepstakes

Each year more than $100 million is awarded to consumers in promotional sweepstakes. Contests (those promotions which require some skill) and sweepstakes (promotions based on luck) are used by hundreds of companies annually. Prizes range from Super Bowl vacations by *Sports Illustrated* to a free month of air travel by American Airlines.

Contests are also used as trade incentives to supplement normal sales commissions. Scott Paper Company uses trips and a continuity-type promotion as incentives to salespeople. Multiline companies often use incentives to focus on a single segment or brand within the product line.

---

*Charles L. Hinkle, "The Strategy of Price Deals," *Harvard Business Review,* July-August, 1965, pp. 75–84.

THE STORY BEHIND
the kellogg instant-win premium ball-game

Background   The Kellogg Cereal Company required a notable promotion for its presweetened line of cereals during the first half of 1981. An instant-winner game was a consideration, especially since Kellogg's agency, Don Jagoda Associates, had extensive successful experience with that type of sweepstakes drive. There was an expressed desire by the client to maximize consumer involvement in the game and to ensure that all consumers had an opportunity to obtain a prize or award.

Program Objectives

☐ Effect cross-brand trial.

☐ Stimulate multiple cross-brand purchasing for an extended time period.

☐ Foster Kellogg-only households.

☐ Create maximum awareness for the promoting of Kellogg brands, leading to increased purchasing.

☐ Maximize trade sell-in and display support.

Strategy   The strategy adopted was to implement an instant-winner game utilizing a unique, reusable pressure-sensitive game card that would have some intrinsic value. The game would also need to contain a collection device to enable all noninstant-winning participants to save for a special bonus prize. The instant-winner game was selected for its ability to achieve the promotion objectives at a highly cost-efficient level, preempting major competition with a state-of-the-art sales-promotion device.

Promotional implementation   Kellogg's presweetened line of cereals contained a pressure-sensitive peel-back instant-win ball-game card in each of 63 million packages (Exhibit 12.7); they were put on grocery shelves beginning January 1, 1981. Each game card had a reusable Kellogg's Kid character on the face, with complete rules on the reverse. Consumers were instructed to peel back the front illustration to reveal whether or not a prize was instantly won. Prize information was printed on the backing to the pressure-sensitive reusable sticker.

Noninstant-winning game cards stated that the participant could obtain a special bonus prize by collecting and submitting five nonwinning cards. A second-chance sweepstakes to award all unclaimed instant-winner prizes was the third executional element, providing the consumer with another prize-winning chance.

The instant-win ball game offered an extremely simple and easily communicated prize structure—100,000 Wilson balls—including:

☐ 25,000 baseballs

☐ 25,000 playground balls

FORTIFIED WITH 10 ESSENTIAL VITAMINS AND MINERALS

Kellogg's
FROSTED MINI-WHEATS

BROWN SUGAR CINNAMON
Whole Wheat biscuits

NET WT. 16 OZ. (1 LB.)
(454 GRAMS)

Game card inside!
100,000 WINNERS in
INSTANT WIN BALL GAME
(See back panel)
(No purchase necessary)

Wilson

OFFICIAL RULES
No purchase necessary

1. One game card will be packed in each specially marked package of Kellogg's cereals. No purchase necessary. You may also obtain a game card by writing to: Instant Win Ball Game, P.O. Box 2888, Westbury, New York 11591. Game card requests must be received by July 15, 1981.

2. If the message under the peel-off portion of the game card indicates you are a winner, you may claim your prize by signing your name in the space provided and sending your game card along with your complete address for verification to: Kellogg's Winners, c/o NATIONAL JUDGING INSTITUTE, INC., 800 Shames Drive, Westbury, New York 11590. Sweepstakes ends and prize claims must be received by July 31, 1981. Please allow eight weeks for delivery of prize. Any game card that is altered, defaced, mutilated or tampered with in any way, or contains printing or other errors, is automatically void. Decision of the judges is final on all matters relating to this sweepstakes. No responsibility is assumed for lost, misdirected or late mail.

3. Odds of winning one of 100,000 balls are: One in 600. Number of prizes and odds of winning by ball type are: Baseballs (25,000), one in 2,400 odds; Playground Balls (25,000), one in 2,400 odds; Softballs (20,000), one in 3,000 odds; Basketballs (15,000), one in 4,000 odds; Footballs (5,000), one in 12,000 odds; Soccerballs (5,000), one in 12,000 odds; Volleyballs (5,000), one in 12,000 odds. No substitution of prizes permitted. Retail value of prizes is estimated at $700,000.

4. All prizes not claimed will be awarded in a Second Chance random drawing under the supervision of NATIONAL JUDGING INSTITUTE, INC., an independent judging organization. To participate, hand-print your name, address and zip code on a plain, 3" x 5" piece of paper, and mail it along with an Instant Win game card, or with a plain 3" x 5" piece of paper on which you have hand-printed the words Kellogg's Instant Win Ball Game, to: Kellogg's Second Chance Sweepstakes, P.O. Box 2800, Westbury, New York 11591. Enter as often as you wish, but each entry must be mailed separately and received by July 31, 1981.

5. BONUS: Collect five non-winning game cards and receive a free plastic Wiffle ball and automatically be entered in the Second Chance Sweepstakes. To claim the bonus, mail your five game cards to: Kellogg's Bonus, P.O. Box 3000, Westbury, New York 11591. Bonus offer ends July 31, 1981.

6. Offer open to all residents of the U.S. except employees of Kellogg Company, its affiliates, subsidiaries, advertising agencies, printers and Don Jagoda Associates, Inc. Void wherever prohibited by law. All federal, state, and local regulations apply. Prizes are not transferable and may not be exchanged or substituted. Taxes, if any, are the responsibility of the winners.

Exhibit 12.7
Rules and premiums for the Kellogg promotional game. (Courtesy of The Kellogg Company and Don Jagoda Associates.)

- ☐ 20,000 softballs
- ☐ 15,000 basketballs
- ☐ 5,000 footballs
- ☐ 5,000 soccerballs
- ☐ 5,000 volleyballs

Advertising Support   Advertising support included 30-second TV commercials reaching 95 percent of the audience 2 to 17 years of age and 60 percent of the 18 to 49 year olds. A total of 60 GRP's was carried on network prime-time TV to the 18 to 49 age group, and 360 GRP's on children's week-end network TV. All commercials scored well in day-after recall testing. In addition Kellogg provided 5,000 retail displays and two teaser mailings to the trade.

Results   The total sales volume for the participating cereals significantly exceeded the volume for January and February, 1980. In-store display activity was at an all-time high. Requests for Wiffle Ball (the collection prize requiring five losing game cards) exceeded projections, indicating a high level of multiple and continuity purchase.*

*Courtesy of The Kellogg Company and Don Jagoda Associates.

A typical promotion prize structure (normally a "pyramid" structure) might be a grand prize of $10,000 plus a new automobile, two first prizes (new cars), twenty second prizes (2-week, all-expenses-paid vacations), fifty third prizes (color-TV sets), eighty fourth prizes (digital watches), one hundred fifth prizes (AM-FM radios), two hundred sixth prizes (electric toasters), and three hundred seventh prizes (1-year subscriptions to a magazine).

In a highly competitive, highly advertised field, prize promotions may be a welcome change of pace from head-on competitive claims. They bring fresh interest in the product to its present customers. They reach out for new customers. Promotions may be run locally to meet competition or to serve as a test before expanding the program regionally or nationally. They may generate new interest among dealers by bringing traffic into their stores. As in the case of other inducements, contests and sweepstakes are not the solution to a company's steadily declining sales picture; something more basic then requires correction.

A continuing problem of sweepstakes is the professional entrant. (An advertiser may urge entrants to buy the product to get a proof of purchase but cannot make this a requirement for participation in the sweepstakes.) It is estimated that in some promotions 80 percent of entries are facsimiles rather than proof of purchase. Some companies have sought to overcome this problem by requiring greater participant involvement. Gillette's World Series sweepstake uses a playing device delivered in a magazine, but it must be taken to a retail display to determine whether it is a winner.*

Historical trends in prize promotions.   There are vogues in forms of promotions that award prizes. In 1950 most contests were for trademarks and slogans. In 1966 sweepstakes were 65 percent of all contests; 23 percent required

*_Advertising Age_, January 7, 1980, p. 66.

Win your dog's weight in gold up to $100,000 from Chuck Wagon.®

*Price of gold subject to fluctuation.

You could win your dog's weight in pure gold in Chuck Wagon dog food's Win Your Dog's Weight In Gold contest. With gold selling for about $2,000* a pound, even a five-pound Chihuahua could win you $10,000! (Maximum prize: $100,000.)

How do you get a chance to win all this gold? Just carefully read the rules on the adjoining page or on specially marked packages of Puppy Chuck Wagon® or Chuck Wagon at your grocer. Enter today. It's your golden opportunity.

For your pet's health . . .
See your veterinarian regularly.

306

Exhibit 12.8
Even dogs get into contests.

explanations such as "Why I like. . . ." In 1971 *Incentive Marketing* magazine reported that 84 percent of all contests were sweepstakes. Completing statements were not even mentioned. By 1975 the preference for sweepstakes over contests had increased still further to the point where, according to Thomas J. Conlon, president of D. L. Blair Corporation, the world's largest sales-promotion agency, sweepstakes represented 89 percent of all prize offers (Exhibit 12.8), with skill contests accounting for only 11 percent. By 1980 serious concerns were expressed by advertisers about the proliferation of contests and sweepstakes. The "clutter" problem brought on by overuse raised questions about the impact and competitive advantage of such promotions.

A contest or a sweepstakes may provide a theme for the whole advertising and sales-promotion program. Each must be planned well in advance. All contests and sweepstakes are subject to federal and state laws (discussed in Chapter 25).

Handling contests and sweepstakes replies. As we have mentioned, firms that specialize in the design and execution of contests and sweepstakes *(fulfillment firms)* are equipped to handle every detail of the promotion, including receiving entries and selecting and notifying winners. But the success of the contest or sweepstakes greatly depends on advertising support.

Advertising specialties

An *advertising specialty* is a useful object bearing the advertiser's name or message. It is given to carefully defined recipients as goodwill offerings, without any cost or obligation to them. The category includes calendars, pens, matchbooks, and thousands of other things. The industry claims that there are more than 10,000 advertising specialties. Current advertising investments in specialty items is over $2.5 billion.

An advertising specialty differs from a premium in that a premium requires a proof of purchase, often accompanied by a charge. The advertiser's name, as a rule, does not appear on the premium. An advertising specialty is an advertising medium carrying a name and a message. It is given free and is usually quite inexpensive. It is a useful, goodwill gift that keeps the advertiser's name before selected recipients for a long time. Calendars are the ideal specialty items since they act as effective promotional reminders throughout the year.

Limitations of the advertising specialty are the shortness of the message it can deliver, the problem of getting it into the right hands, and checking of the results. Because of the expense of specialty promotions, it is important to avoid waste circulation by choosing items and methods of distribution appropriate to your prospects. For instance, a company whose products were sold by jobbers who also handled competing products sent them an expense-keeping notebook with the name of the firm.

Planning the use of specialties. Specialties may well be considered when there is a specific, limited group of people whose goodwill you wish to develop.

The group may be prospective customers, present customers, or those in a position to influence important sales—like architects, physicians, and certain corporate officials. The use of the specialty should be part of an organized plan for reaching these defined audiences.

The Specialty Advertising Association International has suggested the following list of marketing opportunities that can be enhanced by using specialty-advertising items:

☐ Promoting branch openings
☐ Introducing new products
☐ Motivating salespeople and sales-department employees
☐ Opening new accounts
☐ Stimulating sales meetings
☐ Developing trade-show traffic
☐ Balancing improper product mix
☐ Activating inactive accounts
☐ Changing names of products
☐ Using sales aids for door openers
☐ Motivating consumers through premiums
☐ Moving products at dealer level
☐ Improving client or customer relations
☐ Building an image
☐ Motivating employees
☐ Promoting new facilities
☐ Introducing new salespeople*

Cooperative advertising

In cooperative advertising a national advertiser reimburses a retailer or local distributor for an ad placed in local media. Based on the volume of business, the repayment may be 100 percent, 50 percent, or whatever terms are agreed upon. But whatever the terms are, they must be available to all other distributors in the market on the same proportionate basis. That is the crux of the federal Robinson-Patman Act governing cooperative advertising and enforced by the Federal Trade Commission. (We discuss this at greater length in Chapter 25.)

The major media used in cooperative advertising are newspapers (about 75 percent of cooperative advertising), radio, and TV. Usually the national advertiser will provide reproduction proofs for newspaper advertising (Exhibit 12.9), videotape for TV, scripts and recordings for radio, and printed matter for any direct mail, in each instance allowing room for the dealer's name.

---

*Dan S. Bagley, *Specialty Advertising: A New Look* (Irving, TX: Specialty Advertising Association International, 1979), p. 6.

Exhibit 12.9
Dealer cooperative advertising. Mats or prints like these for use in newspapers are supplied to dealers, who may insert their own names.

More than 50 percent of all department-store newspaper advertising is cooperative, but the store may not use advertisers' reproduction proofs. Instead, it uses its own logo and receives a cooperative allowance. In an *omnibus* ad, a store uses reproduction proofs from different manufacturers and creates a full-page ad over its own name. Each manufacturer then pays a pro-rata share of the total cost.

The idea for cooperative newspaper advertising was originally spawned by the fact that in many papers the local rate was much lower than the national rate so that, even if the national advertiser reimbursed the retailer 100 percent, money might still be saved.

The retailer might also be disposed to provide room for store displays for the product if it is advertised over his name and to make sure the item is in stock if a special cooperative ad on it is run.

Retailers are paid for advertising when they submit documentation or proof of performance. For newspaper advertisements, they show tear sheets giving the name of the newspaper, the date the ad ran, and the exact ad copy as it ran. This can be matched with the newspaper invoice stating its cost. For radio and TV cooperative ads, proof of performance used to be a perennial problem until the Association of National Advertisers and the Radio and TV Advertising Bureau developed affidavits of performance (Exhibit 12.10) that document in detail the content, cost, and timing of commercials, as discussed in Chapter 23, Retail Advertising.

Among the advantages of cooperative advertising are that it helps defray selling costs and creates local prestige by additional advertising. Furthermore, space used by a manufacturer's cooperative advertising may help to earn a better rate for all of that firm's advertising. The disadvantage is that, even if a store has to pay only 50 percent of the cost, that sum may not be justified by the profits on the sale of that product or the manufacturer's ads may not meet the special style of the store.

What's the catch to all this? There are a number. There are often difficulties and disparities for the advertiser in the store's billing procedure. A serious problem in cooperative advertising is *double billing*. Double billing can take many forms, but basically it involves the retailer's paying one fee to the medium for advertising space and charging the manufacturer with a different, higher reimbursement. Often the medium will bill the retailer at the lower charge and provide a higher bill for the retailer to send to the manufacturer. This higher bill is supposed to be a copy of the original bill to the retailer, but in fact it is a different, double bill. It should be noted that double billing is regarded as an unethical practice; only a small minority of retailers and media are involved.

In addition, stores may not use the manufacturer's ad; rather, they may prepare an ad in the store style, charging the manufacturer the production cost (called a vendor fee) and changing the image of his advertising. An ad may be placed in the weaker paper in town to help the store earn a quantity discount there. As a result, the manufacturer may lose strict control over the format of the advertising as well as over the choice of media.

Use This ANA/RAB "Tear-Sheet To get retailers paid faster

ANA/RAB FORM FOR SCRIPT (IF TAPE IS USED, PREPARE SCRIPT FROM TAPE)

W___

ANA/RAB RADIO "TEAR-SHEET"
FORM AT BOTTOM OF SCRIPT PERMITS KNOWING HOW MANY TIMES THIS SCRIPT RAN, AT WHAT COST.

Client: _____   For: _____

Begin: _____   End: _____   Date: _____

HERE'S NEWS FOR YOU HANDY HOMEOWNERS. IF YOU'D LIKE TO LEARN HOW TO PUT UP A BEAUTIFUL NEW ARMSTRONG CEILING IN YOUR HOME, COME TO ACE LUMBER THIS SATURDAY AT 10 A.M. ACE LUMBER IS HOLDING A HOME IMPROVE-MENT CLINIC. IT WILL TEACH YOU EVERYTHING YOU NEED TO KNOW. YOU'LL LEARN HOW EASY IT IS TO INSTALL ARMSTRONG CEILING TILE IN BASEMENTS, ATTICS, OR ANY ROOM IN YOUR HOME. YOU'LL SEE HOW TO CUT AND FIT BORDER TILES AND HOW TO DO A NEAT JOB AROUND LIGHTING FIXTURES. YOU'LL ACTUALLY INSTALL PRACTICE CEILING TILES YOURSELF. ACE LUMBER IS HEADQUARTERS FOR ALL THE NEW AND EXCLUSIVE ARMSTRONG CEILING DESIGNS, SO IF YOU'RE PLANNING TO REMODEL OR REDECORATE YOUR HOME, IT WILL PAY YOU TO ATTEND THIS CEILING CLINIC. AND THERE'S NO OBLIGA-TION TO BUY A SINGLE THING. WRITE IT DOWN. THE PLACE IS ACE LUMBER. THE TIME IS THIS SATURDAY AT 10 A.M.

▼ (STAMP OR PRINT THIS FORM ON THE BOTTOM OF YOUR SCRIPT PAPER)

Hand Billing Form

STATION DOCUMENTATION STATEMENT APPROVED BY THE CO-OPERATIVE ADVERTISING COMMITTEE OF THE ASSOCIATION OF NATIONAL ADVERTISERS

This announcement was broadcast _____ times, as entered in the station's program log. The times this announcement was broadcast were billed to this station's client on our invoice(s) number/dated _____ at his earned rate of:

$_____ each for _____ announcements, for a total of $_____
$_____ each for _____ announcements, for a total of $_____
$_____ each for _____ announcements, for a total of $_____

Signature of station official

(Notarize above) _____   Typed name and title _____   Station _____

▼ (STAMP OR PRINT THIS FORM ON THE BOTTOM OF YOUR SCRIPT PAPER)

Computer Billing Form

This announcement was broadcast a total of _____ times at the dates and times coded _____ on our at-tached invoice(s) numbered/dated _____ as entered in the station's program log. This announce-ment was billed to this station's client at a total cost of $_____

Sworn to and subscribed before me and in my presence on this _____ day of _____ . 19 _____ .

Signature of station official

(Notarized above) _____   Typed name and title _____   Station call letters _____

For details on using this verification document—preferred by hundreds of manufac-turers—ask RAB's Co-op Department.

When a manufacturer plans a budget for advertising, cooperative adver-tising is also budgeted. Most of it is expected to appear as part of a store's ef-fort to build the consumer's image of the brand. Each store, however, decides for itself whether or not it will run the ad and how much of that cooperative advertising it will use. Therefore the manufacturer never has complete control over how much of his name advertising will be seen by consumers.

Booklets, brochures, mailing

pieces   In the sale of household appliances, cars, motorcycles, and other costly items that give the customer a choice of models or styles, the manufacturer will usually supply colorful booklets or other descriptive pieces printed for distribution by the dealer. Such material, with clear technical information, is especially helpful to distributors who have a high turnover in personnel and a consequent lack of experienced help. Some sales-promotional material will also be offered in connection with do-it-yourself equipment sold in hardware stores, where there may be special racks to hold it. In some specialized fields producers may offer booklets: recipe booklets, for example, to liquor stores or booklets on planting or lawn care where seed and garden equipment is sold. Often such booklets have space for the dealer's imprint, becoming a part of the cooperative-advertising plan. Counter space for booklets is a problem for stores that are offered such material, and waste is a problem for the producer who offers the material without charge. The quantities supplied must be distributed and used as planned.

TRADE SHOWS AND

EXHIBITS   Trade shows and exhibits, effective complements to a regular advertising program, are particularly important in industrial fields, but they are also staged by manufacturers of consumer products. A trade show is a particularly good forum in which to demonstrate new products and to interest prospective buyers. At a boat show, for example, consumers and dealers both see the latest innovations in marine craft and equipment; advertisers develop sales leads (see Chapter 24).

CASH

REFUNDS   Money refunds primarily encourage people to try a particular product. The refunds are sent by mail to consumers from whom the advertiser has received (by mail) proof of purchase. Although most refunds for package-goods items are $1 or less, it is not uncommon to find some for $2 or $3. Rebates of larger sums are given for appliances; and for automobiles, $200 to $500 have been paid back to buyers. It is a way of cutting price without affecting the dealer's discount structure.

CONCLUDING THOUGHTS

It is important to recognize what promotion can and cannot do. It cannot overcome either too little or poor advertising. It is best used as an adjunct to brand-sell advertising, not as a replacement.*

Successful sales promotion, like successful advertising, depends on a clear statement of objectives, careful planning, and above all coordination with the other aspects of the advertising and marketing program.

*Eugene Mahany, "Package Goods Clients Agree: Promotion Importance Will Grow," *Advertising Age*, April 14, 1975, p. 48.

SUMMARY

As we have seen, sales promotion takes many forms: Premiums, specialities, directory advertising, coupons, and trade shows are just a few of the many types of sales promotions offered to both consumers and dealers. The major ingredient that separates sales promotion from other forms of advertising and promotion is that it is a direct, usually short-term, device to encourage sales. It is not carried through another communication medium but is normally directly associated with the sale of the product. Point of purchase is the most obvious type of sales promotion with this particular feature.

Sales promotion is a multibillion-dollar business, with more money spent in it than in TV, newspapers, and magazines combined. Sales promotion is an area where uniqueness and creativity play a major role. The opportunities for sales promotion are limited only by the creativity of the advertiser.

QUESTIONS

1. What is the relationship between advertising and sales promotion?
2. Why is point of purchase so important in modern retailing?
3. Briefly discuss the difference between premium and specialty promotion.
4. Give an example of a marketing strategy that might use each of the following types of premiums: self-liquidators, direct premiums, free mail-ins, continuity coupons, and free giveaways.
5. What are the similarities and differences between contests and sweepstakes?
6. Why does the coupon redemption rate vary so widely among newspapers, magazines, direct mail, and in-pack distribution? How do the media affect the target market reached?
7. Briefly discuss the problems of coupon misredemption.
8. What are some of the major causes for premium promotions failing?
9. Discuss the concept of cooperative advertising, and explain the advantages and limitations of cooperative advertising for the advertiser and for the retailer.
10. What are the major advantages and limitations of product sampling?
11. What are the factors that determine how much money an advertiser should allocate to sales-promotion activities?

SUGGESTED EXERCISES

12. Next time you are in a grocery store note the number of premium offers available. Name two in-pack, free mail-ins, self-liquidators, and coupon promotions.
13. For the next week count the number of coupons in your daily newspaper. How many were on free-standing inserts? How many were ROP coupons?
14. Of two specialty items directed to college students give examples you have seen or been given this year.

READINGS

"A New Look at Coupons," *The Nielsen Researcher* (Chicago: A.C. Nielsen Company (No. 1), 1976).

ALTER, STEWART: "Coupons, Premiums, and Recipes: Why They're Still Potent Lures." *Magazine Age,* November 1981, pp. 22–34.

BROWN, R. G.: "Sales Response to Promotions and Advertising," *Journal of Advertising Research,* August 1974, pp. 33–38.

CALLO, JOSEPH F.: "Send Me," *Magazine Age,* January 1981, pp. 14–18.

CROOKE, ROBERT: "The Serious Game of Sports Promotion: How Advertisers Reach Consumers," *Magazine Age,* August 1980, pp. 56–62.

DEMPSEY, WILLIAM, F. ANTHONY BUSHMAN, and RICHARD E. PLANK: "Personal Inducement of Industrial Buyers," *Industrial Management,* October 1980, pp. 281–89.

DENNERLEIN, JOHN M.: "Trade Promos New Two-Way Benefits," *Advertising Age,* May 5, 1980, S-2.

HOPPER, L. C.: "How Advertising and S.P. Can Make or Break Your New Product," *Industrial Marketing,* September 1976, pp. 132–35.

RAUCH, ROBERT D.: "The Supplier Perspective: Manufacturers Seek Tighter Coupon Controls as Yearly Cost of Misredemption Tops $175m," *Supermarket Business,* July 1980, p. 48.

ROBINSON, WILLIAM A.: "12 Basic Promotion Techniques: Their Advantages—and Pitfalls," *Advertising Age,* January 10, 1977, pp. 50–51.

TEEL, JESSE E., ROBERT H. WILLIAMS, and WILLIAM O. BEARDEN: "Correlates of Consumer Susceptibility to Coupons in New Grocery Product Introductions," *Journal of Advertising,* Summer 1980, pp. 31–35.

13

Use of the Behavioral Sciences

Have you ever thought in detail about what happens when you pick, say, a can of soup off the supermarket shelf—how it happens that you've chosen Campbell's instead of Lipton's, why you chose beef noodle instead of beef barley? Your decision to buy a product or service can be influenced in many ways, and the behavioral sciences—anthropology, sociology, and psychology—attempt to determine what these influences are and how they work. Although the behavioral sciences are not concerned solely with consumer behavior, they can help us understand why people buy what they do. Anthropology studies the way people are influenced by their cultural heritage, as they might be when they prefer one kind of food to another. Sociology examines the structure and function of organized behavioral systems, which include our economic system. Psychology determines how people's needs and drives influence their buying habits. Although these behavioral sciences often overlap, they are all of interest to the advertiser. The field of consumer behavior brings together all the behavioral sciences in the study of how and why we make buying decisions. Understanding consumer behavior is the key to learning what makes advertising work.

ANTHROPOLOGY AND ADVERTISING

The word "anthropology" usually brings to mind the study of primitive societies. But anthropologists study the cultures of all societies, and from their work they have found that certain needs and activities are common to people wherever they are: Bodily adornment, cooking, courtship, food taboos, gift giving, language, marriage, status, sex, and superstition are present in all societies although each society attaches its own values and traditions to them.

The anthropologist sees the United States as a pluralistic society made up of an array of subcultures. In each subculture lives a different group of people, who share its values, customs, and traditions. In our culture thirty-nine radio stations currently broadcast entirely in a foreign language, and more than fifty languages are broadcast at least 1 hour a week; 500 radio stations carry black-oriented programs. These figures bear witness to the strength of cultural identification in the United States. Even if we move into another culture later, the one we were brought up in permanently influences our tastes and behavior. Studies of media-usage patterns show major differences among groups. Blacks and Hispanics tend to be heavier listeners to radio than the general population is. Working women demonstrate distinct differences in magazine readership from their nonworking counterparts.

Anthropologists make major contributions to advertising through their study of the distinctive living patterns of cultural groups and subgroups. Ethnic, religious, and racial subgroups all have identities that can affect food preferences, language, customs, styles of dress, and roles of men and women. All these preferences may in turn affect the advertising addressed to members of the subgroup.

Some ethnic groups prefer highly spiced foods (Polish or Italian sausage) or distinctively flavored foods (Louisiana chicory-flavored coffee). Indeed, many dishes favored in certain parts of the country identify people in that area with their cultural past: Pennsylvania Dutch cookery, with its fastnachts and shoofly pie, has roots mainly in the valley of the Rhine; in North Carolina the serving of lovefeasts (sugar cake, Christmas cookies, and large white mugs of coffee) reflects people's Czechoslovakian heritage; in Rhode Island tourtière (meat pie) reflects the French-Canadian influence; Mexico's influence is revealed in the taco and other Mexican-style foods served in southern California and the Southwest.

There are regional variations in the American language, too. A sandwich made of several ingredients in a small loaf of bread is a "poor boy" in New Orleans, a "submarine" in Boston, a "hoagy" in Philadelphia, a "hero" in New York City, and a "grinder" in upstate New York. A soft drink in Boston is a "tonic," while in Syracuse it is a "soda," and in Phoenix a "pop." Creamed cottage cheese is known as "schmierkase" around Cincinnati, while what is cottage cheese to most Americans is "cream cheese" in New Orleans. "Salad" in Virginia means kale and spinach. In Key West evaporated milk is referred to as "cream," and sweetened condensed milk is called "milk." In Minnesota a "rubber band" is a "rubber binder." Advertisers make use of their knowledge of cultural differences in food preferences, terminology, and subgroup identities when they advertise their products (Exhibit 13.1).

Rites of
passage
Every society celebrates certain milestones of life. In ours we mark births, birthdays, confirmations, bar mitzvahs, graduations, weddings, and anniversaries, usually celebrating them with appropriate gifts. Marketers often relate their advertising to these milestones (Exhibit 13.2).

Exhibit 13.1
Ad relating product to the he-man image. (Courtesy Pepsi-Co, Inc.)

Dad,
  You often told me I should
seek my goals with passion; but
enjoy the rewards in moderation.
  It's that kind of thinking that
makes Father's Day as special
to me as _you_ are.
              Happy Father's Day!
                    Love
                    Jerry

June 7

Crown Royal

We tip our hat
to all the fathers
of the world
who've taught their
children the values
of drinking only
in moderation.

Exhibit 13.2
Ad for product purchase based on a specific celebration. (Courtesy of Crown Royal.)

Changing role of
women
In the past few years there has been an astounding change in the way women perceive their role in life:

> The most important social development in our nation, with tremendous impact on our businesses, will be the continuing rise to positions of power and influence of women. What we used to call women's lib, but what we now refer to more accurately as the feminist movement or the women's movement, has spread dramatically. It started in a few cities on both coasts and in a handful of campus communities, but it has moved from the big cities to the small towns, from the coast inland, from the North to the South, so that there is no woman in this country, whatever her position on the cutting issues, who remains unaffected.*

Because women have access to higher-level jobs and a greater variety of jobs, they have more discretionary income than ever before. Fundamental changes in the marketplace will result from these changes in women's status. A study conducted by Batten, Barton, Durstine & Osborn, Inc., predicted that by 1990 female lifestyle changes will influence many basic consumption patterns.

Research among working women indicates that by far the greatest problem they face is a lack of time. With time at a premium, it's more than likely that demand will grow substantially for convenience and time-saving products and services. These include microwave ovens, toaster ovens, crock pots, fast-cook foods, cleaning and maintenance services, door-to-door delivery, and any time-saving innovations research can develop.

Indicators also show working women buy substantially more leisure products than nonworking women do. And they travel more, eat out more, go to the theater and movies more, drink more, buy more cosmetics and clothes, and also buy many more automotive products. Nearly 50 million women will be working by 1990.

The changing role of women in the work force has important implications for advertisers and the means they use to reach these women. Table 13.1 shows the differences among working and nonworking women in terms of both media usage and opinions toward advertising.

With more options than ever before, the contemporary woman continues to search for a better quality of life, one that allows her to be an individual in her own right. Women's new attitudes and roles represent a basic cultural change in our society, and advertising reflects that change (Exhibit 13.3). For consumers of both sexes there is growing evidence that advertising that appears to exploit women (via sexually explicit illustration) is counter-productive.†

Anthropology helps sharpen our understanding of, and insights into, differences in cultural heritage, regional variations, rites of passage, and chang-

---

*Marshall Loeb, "America in the 1980s: Ten Major Changes," *Journal of Advertising Research*, February 1980, p. 8.

†Robert A. Peterson and Roger A. Klein, "The Female Role in Advertisements," *Journal of Marketing*, October, 1977, pp. 59–63.

Table 13–1

	WORK STATUS FOR ALL RESPONDENTS			MARRIED RESPONDENTS	
MEDIA CHARACTERISTICS	NOT WORKING, %	WORKING PART TIME, %	WORKING FULL TIME, %	"WORKWIFE," %	NOT WORKING, %
Watch TV:					
Rarely	5	7	13	12	5
Less than 3 hours a day	47	64	61	59	49
More than 3 hours a day	48	29	26	29	46
Read newspaper:					
Rarely	1	2	4	4	1
Once a day	86	87	76	80	85
During the week	12	9	19	17	13
Only when I am looking for something	1	2	1	2	1
Opinion of advertising:					
Useful, informative	36	26	27	23	36
Fair	44	48	39	43	46
Useless	17	22	26	27	16
No opinion	3	4	8	7	2

USE OF MEDIA AND OPINION OF ADVERTISING BY WORK STATUS[a]

[a]Suzanne H. McCall, "Meet the 'Workwife.' " Courtesy *Journal of Marketing*, a publication of the American Marketing Association. July, 1977, p. 61.

ing cultural roles. Because it does, anthropology has great relevance for marketing and advertising.

SOCIOLOGY AND ADVERTISING

Sociology is the scientific study of human relationships. The sociologist examines groups and their influence and interaction with the individual. Research dating back to the 1930s has recognized that group influences play major roles in the use of media, adoption of new ideas, and consumer-product behavior. In recent years advertising has borrowed from sociology to predict the probability of product purchase by various consumer groups.

Social class and stratification

Just about any society is clustered into classes, which are determined by such criteria as wealth, income, occupation, education, achievement, or seniority. We sense where we fit into this pattern; we identify with others in our class ("these are my kind of people"); and we generally conform to its standards. People's aspirations often take on the flavor of the social class immediately above their own; experienced advertisers do not go above that.

An understanding of social-class structure helps explain why data on income, occupation, education, and other demographic categories sometimes fail to provide meaningful insights into consumer characteristics. Numerous studies indicate that income and social class must be considered together in deter-

320

There are people more famous we insure.
But none more important.

In this country, there are 8.5 million women who are sole heads of household. Their need for life insurance has always been obvious.

Of course, there are also millions of married working women who are joint heads of household. It's only been in recent years that the economic value of the housewife or the working mother has even been talked about.

The Travelers and its independent agents, though, have not been Jane-come-latelies in life insurance for women. As evidenced by the fact we were one of the first major companies to offer lower life insurance rates for women.

To get in touch with an independent Travelers agent, check your local Yellow Pages. They are there to help you; whether or not you even need insurance.

Women don't need any more help from insurance companies than men. Just the same help.

THE TRAVELERS

We offer life, health, auto, and homeowners insurance, and mutual funds and variable annuities for individuals, and virtually all forms of insurance for businesses. The Travelers Insurance Company, The Travelers Indemnity Company, Travelers Equities Sales Inc., and other Affiliated Companies of The Travelers Corporation, Hartford, Connecticut 06115.

Exhibit 13.3
Ad aimed at the "new" woman. (Courtesy The Travelers Insurance Companies.)

mining lifestyle and consumption. To consider only income assumes that how we think and behave is solely a function of money. The no-longer wealthy aristocrat may demonstrate more sophisticated tastes than a sports figure with ten times more income. A rich person is not simply a poor person with money. The reference group a person identifies with is at least as important as money in determining behavior.

How different people view new products

Extensive research has been done on the ways people learn about and accept new products. Generally, consumers can be divided into five groups:

1. *Innovators:* highly venturesome, cosmopolitan people who are eager to try new ideas and willing to accept the risk of an occasional bad experience with a new product.
2. *Early adopters:* people in the community with whom the average man or woman checks out an innovation; a successful and *careful* innovator, the early adopter is influential with those who follow.
3. *Early majority:* a group that tends to deliberate before adopting a product; its members are seldom leaders, but they are important in legitimizing and innovating.
4. *Late majority:* a cautious group that adopts ideas after the bulk of public opinion is already in favor of an innovation.
5. *Laggards:* past-oriented people who are suspicious of change and of those who bring it; by the time they adopt a product, it may already have been replaced by yet another.*

It is crucial that advertisers identify and reach innovators to introduce products and maintain sales. The media recognize the importance of promoting themselves as sources of information for innovators. In recent years we have seen a number of media promoting the innovative nature of their audiences as well as the demographic segments they deliver (Exhibit 13.4).

Opinion leaders. Although not every early buyer of a new product is considered a reliable source of new-product ideas, those people whose ideas and behavior serve as models to others are of special interest to advertisers. These *opinion leaders* can speed the acceptance of new products by their own purchases. Of course, opinion leaders in one field are not always influential in others. The friend whose opinion you value when buying new clothes may not be much help when you're shopping for an air conditioner.

When General Motors introduced the energy-efficient X cars, they used magazines to reach opinion leaders. Ted Miller, advertising manager of the Pontiac Division of General Motors, explaining the advertising plan for the Pontiac Phoenix said, "We saw the magazine advertising as directed to opinion leaders. A lot of our spending went into the buff books, *Road & Track* and *Motor Trend.* We wanted to present this car to people who really know about cars."†

---

*Everett Rogers, *Diffusion of Innovations* (New York: Free Press, 1962), pp. 168–171.

†"How GM Alone Holds the Fort against the Imports," *Magazine Age,* April, 1980, p. 32.

Klaus Lucka

THE NEW ACHIEVER
A Tough Man To Ignore

Communications Satellite Engineer.
Annual Income: $32,000.

He's the New Achiever. The hero of the '80s.
A man who's in control of his environment. On the
job. At home. And in the community.

He's a man that knows how to get things done.
Like having his own personal computer. And
because he knows how things work, he seeks the
best. And finds it in Popular Mechanics, the
magazine for the New Achievers.

Popular Mechanics is in the forefront, informing,
guiding and motivating him. Take home computers.
He's been reading about them in Popular Mechanics
since 1976.

And there's more. The New Achiever owns
weekend and vacation homes, buys 35mm cameras
and rides in private planes to a greater extent
than the readers of Playboy, Newsweek and
Sports Illustrated.

Popular Mechanics
reaches over 5,100,000*
New Achievers. Men who
spend big. Depend on
themselves and Popular
Mechanics.

Popular Mechanics
THE MAGAZINE FOR
THE NEW ACHIEVERS.

*Simmons 1981

Exhibit 13.4
Ad showing a medium's audience as progressive and innovative. (Reprinted by permission
of *Popular Mechanics Magazine* 1981 by The Hearst Corporation. All rights reserved. *Popular Mechanics* is a publication of Hearst Magazines, a division of The Hearst Corporation.)

Traditionally, advertisers have used opinion leaders to give testimonials: Movie stars endorse cosmetics and perfume; TV personalities promote soft drinks and cars; politicians, socialites, and business people ask you to donate to charitable causes. There are, however, Federal Trade Commission restrictions on the use of testimonials. For instance, if a person gives an expert endorsement of a product, that person must have the qualifications implied in the commercial. You can't use a model dressed as a doctor to endorse a product unless you specifically note that the ad is a dramatization.

A common advertising technique is to seek status for a product or service through association with the institutions that use it. American Express advertising aligns itself with major airlines and hotel chains. Dun & Bradstreet ads point out that Rockwell International Corporation uses their computer information services to keep top management up to date.

The advantages of understanding and using opinion leadership are easily understood. However, equally important are the concepts of "followership" and "information seeking." That is, among what market segments do opinion leaders exercise their influence and what type of information would be most accepted by opinion leaders? Research indicates that opinion leaders tend to exercise their leadership in one or very few areas: The person whose judgment we trust about movies is not the same person we turn to for fashion or financial advice. Likewise, leaders and followers change roles, depending on the topic. Identifying the opinion leader on one subject will not help the advertiser to identify opinion leaders for other product categories.

Family life cycle and buying

behavior   The basic unit of buying behavior is the family. As Table 13.2 shows, most households pass through an orderly progression of stages, and each stage has special significance for buying behavior. Knowledge about the family life cycle permits you to segment the market and the advertising appeal according to specific consumption patterns and groups. Also it must be recognized that nontraditional living arrangements are becoming more numerous. In the 1980 census the most rapidly increasing household type was the single-adult household.

PSYCHOLOGY AND

ADVERTISING   Psychology is the study of human behavior and its causes. Three psychological concepts of importance to consumer behavior are motivation, cognition, and learning. Motivation refers to the drives, urges, wishes, or desires that initiate the sequence of events known as "behavior." Cognition is the area in which all the mental phenomena (perception, memory, judging, thinking, and the rest) are grouped. Learning refers to those changes in behavior that occur through time relative to external stimulus conditions.* These three

*James A. Bayton, "Motivation, Cognition, Learning—Basic Factors in Consumer Behavior," *Journal of Marketing*, January, 1958, p. 282.

Table 13–2

AN OVERVIEW OF THE LIFE CYCLE AND BUYING BEHAVIOR[a]	
STAGE IN LIFE CYCLE	BUYING BEHAVIORAL PATTERN
Bachelor stage: young, single people not living at home	Few financial burdens. Fashion opinion leaders. Recreation-oriented. Buy basic kitchen equipment, basic furniture, cars, vacations.
Newly married couples: young, no children	Better off financially than they will be in near future. Highest purchase rate and highest average purchase of durables. Buy cars, refrigerators, stoves, sensible and durable furniture, vacations.
Full nest I: youngest under 6	Home purchasing at peak. Liquid assets low. Dissatisfied with financial position and amount of money saved. Interested in new products. Buy washers, dryers, TV, baby food, chest rubs and cough medicines, vitamins, dolls, wagons, sleds, skates.
Full nest II: youngest child 6 or over	Financial position better. Some wives work. Less influenced by advertising. Buy larger-sized packages, multiple-unit deals. Buy many foods, cleaning materials, bicycles, music lessons, pianos.
Full nest III: older couples with dependent children	Financial position still better. More wives work. Some children get jobs. Hard to influence with advertising. High average purchase of durables. Buy new, more tasteful furniture, auto travel, nonnecessary appliances, boats, dental services, magazines.
Empty nest I: Older couples, no children living with them, head in labor force	Home ownership at peak. Most satisfied with financial position and money saved. Interested in travel, recreation, self-education. Make gifts and contributions. Not interested in new products. Buy vacations, luxuries, home improvements.
Empty nest II: Older married couples, no children living at home, head retired	Drastic cut in income. Keep home. Buy medical appliances, medical-care products that aid health, sleep, and digestion.
Solitary survivor, in labor force	Income still good, but likely to sell home.
Solitary survivor, retired	Same medical and product needs as other retired group. Drastic cut in income.

[a]Source: William D. Wells and George Gubar, "Life Cycle Concept in Marketing Research," *Journal of Marketing Research,* November, 1966, pp. 355–63. Reprinted with permission.

factors working within the framework of the societal environment create the psychological basis for consumer behavior. Advertising research is interested in cognitive elements to learn how consumers react to different stimuli, and research finds learning especially important in determining factors such as advertising frequency (see Chapter 5). However, in recent years the major application of psychology to advertising has been the attempt to understand the underlying *motives* that initiate consumer behavior.

Nature of motivation

Understanding the reasons for consumer behavior will allow marketers to develop products and advertising appeals to satisfy consumer demands. What are these motives? One classification divides them into *physiological* motives (those, like hunger, thirst, and mating, whose satisfaction is essential to survival) and *secondary* or *social* motives (those whose satisfaction is unrelated to survival: the desire to be socially accepted, to win a tournament, to get a promotion).

Another classification describes motives in terms of people's needs:

- [ ] *Affectional:* the need to form satisfying relations with others
- [ ] *Ego bolstering:* the need to enhance one's personality
- [ ] *Ego defensive:* the need to protect one's personality

Ads are full of examples of fulfilling basic consumer motives, including:

- [ ] *Security:* personal safety (Genie ads for its automatic garage-door opener say, "Genie Puts an Extra Touch of Safety in the Palm of Your Hand")
- [ ] *Conserving:* to save energy and money ("Common sense says the Magic Chef gas range that saves energy saves money")
- [ ] *Ego enhancement:* gaining status (Seagram's V.O. ads say, "Some People Set Their Sights Higher Than Others")
- [ ] *Health:* importance of weight control (Bumble Bee tuna ads say, "Packed with water. Not calories")

Other lists contain as many as sixty separate motives. Although no single set of classifications has been recognized as a standard in the field, the point is clear. At all times people are crying (even though the world does not often hear them), "Please understand me!" The advertiser has to *understand the buyers,* not merely the product. To be successful, advertising must empathize with the goals, needs, wants, desires, drives, and problems of the people it's addressing. American Airlines tells customers it understands their needs: "We don't fly airplanes, we fly people." Holiday Inn does the same when it advertises, "Number 1 in People Pleasin'."

Differences in motivation. Predicting behavior from psychological motives is an extremely difficult task. There are three reasons why knowing the motives of an individual will not necessarily allow an advertiser to predict consumer behavior:

1. The reason a person *says* he buys a certain product may have nothing to do with his *real* reason for buying it. A man may say he bought a car because he likes its looks; the real reason may be that he likes the youthful way it makes *him* look. A woman may say she took up tennis for its health benefits; perhaps she really took up the game because it provided her entry into the "in" crowd of her neighborhood.

2. Two persons exposed to the same motivational stimulus may behave in markedly different ways. An ad for a diamond engagement ring will evoke different reactions from a recent divorcee, a person contemplating marriage, and a person living at the poverty level.

3. People don't fully understand their motivations and behavior. Why did you buy the shoes you are wearing or eat at a certain restaurant last night? There are probably a number of motives for any particular behavior we exhibit. Since we cannot analyze our behavior, it should not be surprising that researchers have difficulty in linking motives and behavior.

Self-images and roles

Our motivations are closely related to the way we see ourselves—our self-images and the different roles we play. Through the products we buy we tell the world how we'd like to have it think of us. In this way products serve as symbols of who and what we think we are. Virginia Slims cigarette ads emphasize their symbolic positioning for the modern woman: "You've come a long way, baby."

All of us have a number of roles, many of which we play at the same time. The same 35-year-old man may be a husband, a father, an employee, and a youth baseball-team manager. Advertising addresses each of these roles when it urges gifts for his wife, toys for his children, furniture for his office, equipment for his team. Just as we buy products that serve our self-image, our buying behavior tends to be consistent with our roles.

CONSUMER LIFESTYLES

Each of the behavioral sciences we have touched upon offers its own contributions. They can also work in combination, as is the case in the study of consumer lifestyles. Advertisers are interested in lifestyles as they reflect the way individuals see themselves and their living patterns. Lifestyle research is linked to social trends and how people fit themselves into them. Since the future of virtually any consumer product is affected by one or more of these trends, they can also affect the direction and tone of advertising.

Daniel Yankelovich, who has extensively studied American lifestyles, has identified thirty-one social trends that he believes can change the overall patterns of American life and of buying behavior.* These trends do *not* push in a single direction, and they do *not* affect all people. They have been categorized into five major groupings:

1. Trends that are effects of the psychology of affluence, particularly felt among consumers who seek fulfillment beyond economic security. Included are trends toward personalization (expression of one's individuality through products), new forms of materialism (deemphasis on money and possessions), and more meaningful work (work satisfactions aside from money).

---

*"What New Life Styles Mean to Market Planners," *Marketing/Communications,* June, 1971, pp. 38 *ff.*

2. Trends that reflect a quest for excitement and meaning beyond the routines of daily life. Included are trends to novelty (constant search for change), to sensuousness (emphasis on touching and feeling), and to mysticism (new spiritual experience).

3. Trends that are reactions against the complexities of modern life. Included are trends toward life simplification, toward return to nature (rejection of the artificial and chemical in dress and foods), toward stronger ethnic identification (new identification in one's background), and away from bigness.

4. Trends that reflect new values pushing out traditional ones. Included are trends toward pleasure for its own sake and living for today, toward blurring of the sexes (and their roles), and toward more liberal sexual attitudes.

5. Trends reflecting the personal orientations of those now in their teens and twenties. Included are trends toward tolerance of disorder (such as against fixed plans and schedules, affecting shopping and eating habits), toward rejection of hypocrisy (affecting attitudes toward exaggeration in communication), and toward female careers (away from traditional home-and-marriage roles as sufficient for women).

Effects of lifestyle

trends   To reflect these changing trends and values *and* their effect on marketing and advertising, Yankelovich offers two vignettes:

> An older married couple whose children are grown move from their big home to a smaller, brand-new apartment. With fewer home repairs, with more labor-saving appliances, they have more time and money for leisure pursuits. Their efforts at "life simplification" are relevant to marketers of such products as home appliances, prepared and frozen foods, and travel.
>
> A young professional, about 30, married, with two children, wonders how meaningful his job really is, how important the traditional home-family-job "rat race" is. He buys new stereo equipment, trades in his American sedan for a foreign car, and is an avid reader of publications about how people are changing their lives.

Dramatically different lifestyles and attitudes are reflected in the ad shown in Exhibit 13.5. Only a few years ago the motorcycle had the connotation of antisocial tough guys—hardly the image most advertisers would want to associate with their products. Today, however, motorcycles project an image of youthful adventure and products associated with them one of currency.

In their responses to a survey company presidents showed how important they consider lifestyle research. Asked the specific purpose of their companies' formal or informal "early-warning system" of monitoring changes in social attitudes and opinions, 73.1 percent answered, "to evaluate changes in consumer attitudes and life-styles."*

MULTIPLE

DIRECTIONS   Although new social values and lifestyle trends can change the overall patterns of American life and buying behavior, they do not affect everyone equally. Indeed, many Americans are not caught up in patterns of

---

The Gallagher Report, supplement to June 2, 1975, issue.

The jeans that hang in there.
Longer.

THEY'RE TOUGHER! Jeans beefed up with
Dacron® polyester outwear ordinary jeans. By far!
THEY'RE NEATER! Jeans with "Dacron" don't
wrinkle or pucker like ordinary jeans.
Yet they fade and soften the way you like.
THEY'RE COMFORTABLE! Jeans with "Dacron"
fit to size; don't shrink up or sag out.
GET INTO JEANS WITH DACRON®
the jeans that hang in there, Longer!
Jeans shown: 65% cotton, 35% Dacron® polyester.
Du Pont registered trademark.
Du Pont makes fibers, not fabrics or jeans.

denim
DACRON®

DUPONT

Exhibit 13.5
Ad relating product to new, adventuresome lifestyle. (Courtesy DuPont.)

change at all. Some people cling to the old value system. One study of a broad sample of married middle-class Americans shows that this "large segment of U.S. society portrays itself as happy, home-loving, clean and square. . . . For most Americans it is indeed a Wyeth, not a Warhol world."*

UNDERSTANDING PEOPLE—A CONTINUING STUDY FOR ADVERTISING

All advertising seeks to influence people's behavior. Sometimes its goal is simply to reinforce a consumer's existing pattern, to encourage the repurchase of a frequently bought brand. Sometimes the goal is to modify a consumer's behavior, to bring about a switch in brands or to replace an older model of a product with a newer one. Sometimes, especially in the case of truly new products, it can be to change a behavior pattern, to get someone to substitute a new way of doing something for an old one. All this points up the most important element of effective advertising—understanding people.

SUMMARY

Advertising is a people business. Successful advertisers know who their prospects are and, to whatever extent is practical, their needs and motives, which result in the purchase of one product and the rejection of another. Consumer behavior is the result of a complex network of influences based on the psychological, sociological, and anthropological makeup of the individual.

Advertising rarely, if ever, changes these influences but rather channels the needs and wants of consumers toward specific products and brands. Advertising is a mirror of society. The advertiser influences people by offering solutions to their needs and problems, not by creating these needs. The role of the advertiser is to act as a monitor of the changing face of society.

QUESTIONS

1. Why must advertisers have a broad knowledge of the social sciences?
2. We often hear the statement "The world is getting smaller." Does this mean advertising will be more standardized in the future?
3. Discuss the fundamental differences between a sociological approach and an anthropological approach to the marketing of goods and services.
4. Discuss the role of opinion leaders in product introduction.

---

*William D. Wells, "It's a Wyeth, Not a Warhol World," *Harvard Business Review*, January-February, 1970, p. 26.

5. How is an understanding of consumer motivation related to the marketing concept discussed earlier?

6. "A product may mean different things to different people." Comment.

7. "The goal of marketing and advertising is to provide consumer satisfaction." Discuss this statement.

8. What are some of the factors that prevent motives from being used as accurate predictors of consumer behavior?

SUGGESTED EXERCISES

9. Find and discuss an example of current advertising illustrating two of the following: reference group, social class, innovators, opinion leaders.

10. What was the last item you purchased costing over $25? Analyze the reasons for making the purchase. What role, if any, did advertising, salespersons, or acquaintances play in the decision?

11. Find an example of an ad primarily directed to five of the nine states in the life cycle.

READINGS

AAKER, DAVID A., and GEORGE S. DAY: "Dynamic Model of Relationship Among Advertising, Consumer Awareness, Attitudes and Behavior," *Journal of Applied Psychology*, June 1974, pp. 281–86.

ARMSTRONG, GARY M., and LAURENCE P. FELDMAN: "Exposure and Sources of Opinion Leaders," *Journal of Advertising Research*, August 1976, pp. 21–27.

BEARDEN, WILLIAM O., and JESSE E. TEEL: "An Investigation of Personal Influences on Consumer Complaining," *Journal of Retailing*, Fall 1980, pp. 3–20.

CLAXTON, JOHN D., J. R. BRENT RICHIE, and JUDY ZAICHKOWSKY: "The Nominal Group Technique: Its Potential for Consumer Research," *Journal of Consumer Research*, December 1980, pp. 308–13.

DAVIS, HARRY L.: "Decision Making Within the Household," *Journal of Consumer Research*, March 1976, pp. 241–60.

ENGLE, JAMES F., ROGER D. BLACKWELL, and DAVID T. KOLLAT: *Consumer Behavior* (3rd ed.) (Hinesdale, IL: The Dryden Press, 1978).

GREEN, ROBERT T., and ISABELLA C. M. CUNNINGHAM: "Feminine Role Perception and Family Purchasing Decisions," *Journal of Marketing Research*, August 1975, pp. 325–32.

HIRSCHMAN, ELIZABETH C.: "Innovativeness, Novelty Seeking and Consumer Creativity," *Journal of Consumer Research*, December 1980, pp. 283–95.

LAMBERT, ZARREL V.: "Consumer Alienation, General Dissatisfaction, and Consumerism Issues: Conceptual and Managerial Perspectives," *Journal of Retailing*, Summer 1980, pp. 3–24.

LEVY, SIDNEY J.: "Interpreting Consumer Mythology: A Structural Approach to Consumer Behavior," *Journal of Marketing*, Summer 1981, pp. 49–61.

RAJU, P.S.: "Optimum Stimulation Level: Its Relationship to Personality, Demographics, and Exploratory Behavior," *Journal of Consumer Research*, December 1980, pp. 272–82.

ROBIN, DONALD P., and LOUIS M. CAPELLA: "Attitudes of Advertising Executives Toward the Consumer Behavior Course," *Journal of the Academy of Marketing Science*, Fall 1979, pp. 404–13.

Creating the Advertising

The most dynamic and exciting manifestation of advertising for most of us is the ads and commercials. TV, radio, magazines, and newspapers are filled with all types of advertising messages that influence us to buy things and try to change our attitudes about issues, a subject taken up in our discussion of behavioral science in Chapter 13.

This part also deals with the making of ads: writing copy (Chapter 14), visualizing the layout (Chapter 15), and creating TV and radio messages (Chapters 17 and 18). It covers all aspects, from putting words on paper to producing the ads (Chapter 16) and filming or taping the commercials; for nothing in advertising receives as much attention and criticism as the ads themselves. There are many and varied techniques to use in creating ad messages. All are discussed in this part.

Finally, Chapter 19 deals with a very important aspect of the advertising process: trademarks and packaging, things vital to every successful product but usually taken for granted by most consumers.

PART FOUR

14

Creating the Copy

The remarkable thing about advertising is that it can prompt people to buy a specific product voluntarily. Advertising has no authority to compel a person to buy anything; it exercises no mystical power. To the most vigorous exhortation of an advertiser the meekest of us can yawn and say, "No, thank you!" Nevertheless, people buy specific goods and services because of advertising. Since it has neither the power nor the authority to compel a person to do anything, just how does advertising work?

In discussing advertising, we deal with big numbers: billions of dollars, millions of TV sets, thousands of radio stations. But whether it's directed toward a reader, a viewer, or a listener, an ad deals with only one person at a time. If a person feels an ad is speaking directly to him or her, that person pays attention, otherwise not. In either case he or she is indifferent to the fact that the ad is addressing millions of others at the same time. The person's interest depends upon the degree to which the ad speaks about his or her interests, wants, goals, problems.

NATURE AND USE OF APPEALS

An appeal is any statement designed to motivate a person to action. To motivate anyone to action, the statement must relate to that person's interests, wants, goals, or problems; for the reason

334

anyone buys anything is for the benefit he or she expects to derive from it. Perhaps a homemaker wants the satisfaction of providing a nutritious meal for the family on a limited budget. Both men and women may buy clothes and jewelry to make them look their best. One consumer responds to the joy of being able to take the whole family off on a trip in a trailer; another is attracted by the freedom of riding a motorcycle. Regardless of the product, it is the benefit the buyer will receive that prompts him or her to buy it. The life-giving spark of an ad is its promise of the special significant benefit the product will provide—a promise the product must be able to fulfill. That special significant benefit becomes the *appeal* of an ad. For example:

Kodak Service—good training, good tools, good people.

Selecting the appeal

Many appealing things can be said about any product, but we want to put our effort behind the appeal that has the most significance. Since selecting the appeal is a key decision in any campaign, many research techniques have been developed to find out which appeal to use. These techniques usually fall into two categories: structured research and unstructured research.

Structured research. In structured research the inquirer prepares a list of questions and choices and asks the respondent to select the choice that appeals most to him or her. The consensus of findings serves as a basis for deciding which appeal to use.

A company planning a promotional campaign for a new house-plant food listed seven appeals that might influence growers of house plants to try the product:

1. A complete feeding program for your plants
2. A uniform timed-release application that keeps feeding your plant for 3 months
3. Just the right amount of nitrogen, phosphorus, and potassium
4. No danger of burning or overfeeding
5. No mess, no waste
6. No mixing or measuring
7. Quick-starting nitrogen for immediate benefit

The question was which advantage meant the most to house-plant owners. Research revealed that two benefits stood out: no danger of burning or overfeeding and no mixing or measuring.

The advantages of structured research are that it is clear, simple, and easy to administer and that it can be mathematically computed. The disadvantages are that the research is limited to predetermined questions and does not elicit spontaneous reactions to the product category from the respondent. Often the spontaneous reactions of consumers can suggest a problem with the product, which in turn suggests a new product entirely. One method to elicit reactions on a spontaneous basis is *focus-group interviewing.* This method uses a trained leader with a group of ten or twelve consumers, usually prime-prospect consumers, those who consume a relatively large amount of the product being researched. In the food category, for example, it would be the 27 percent of the women who buy 79 percent of the prepared cake mixes or the 20 percent of the men who buy 70 percent of the airline tickets.

The leader of the group directs the conversation among the prime prospects to determine what problems, what "hang-ups," might be associated with the product. In this manner the answers are not predetermined by the advertiser or the researcher into neatly categorized niches. Rather, they are direct responses to the product and the benefits and problems these prime-prospect consumers see in the product. Further, because the research is done in a group, there is less inhibition by each member of the group. The result is usually a good evaluation of what the problems, attributes, and particular strengths and weaknesses of the product are from the consumer's point of view.

The Gillette Company used this method in conjunction with their advertising agency to evaluate a new women's deodorant they were thinking of marketing. Results of the interviews with women showed that a particular problem no manufacturer had addressed was very important to prime prospects: irritation of the underarm by a deodorant, especially just after shaving the underarm. Based on this discovery in the focus-group interviews, Gillette developed a roll-on deodorant that would not sting or irritate, gentle enough to apply right after shaving underarms. The agency named it Soft 'n Dry. It became one of the leading women's deodorants almost overnight and remains so today.

Another example of the value of this type of research is Delta Air Lines. Their agency, BBDO, interviewed prime-prospect men to determine what was most important when they planned and took a trip by air. The interviews elicited hundreds of responses. But one important factor stood out: Prime prospects were most concerned about schedule convenience—what time does the plane leave and what time does it arrive? That was more important than anything else. Delta had a ready answer for that problem because in most cities they serve they have more frequent flights at more convenient times than the competition does. The product, in effect, solves the prime-prospect problem. BBDO came up with the phrase "Delta is ready when you are." The campaign has been running for several years.

Unstructured research. Unstructured research, also known as *motivational research* or *depth-interview research,* is undertaken in a relaxed interview in the respondent's home. Not confining themselves to yes or no answers, the interviewer and the respondent discuss attitudes about the use of the product. From such conversations a true picture of the respondent's feelings about the product may emerge. The interviewer often discovers the best appeal and may even elicit suggestions for a product change. Because it is very costly to conduct such research on a one-to-one basis, researchers more often use focus groups.

Sometimes a project starts off as structured research but evolves into unstructured research—with interesting results. In one such project, the Cy Chaikin Research Group was given a proposal for structured research:

> The product class was a liquid dishwashing detergent. The objective of the research was to ascertain which of three proposed copy themes would be the most effective in developing interest and action on the product. Each theme began and ended with:

> This Amazing Dishwashing Discovery
> [new line to come here]
> and is extra kind to hands.

> The three themes being considered were:

> *Gets you away from the sink faster.*
> *Keeps your hands out of greasy dishwater.*
> *Powerful, effective, gets it all out.*

> We raised the question of where would we be if all we learned was that none of these themes appealed to the consumers. We recommended that we approach the problem, instead, via depth interviews; the proposal was accepted.

> We undertook a series of depth interviews and focus group discussions and learned there was confusion and some misunderstanding in the consumers' minds on each of the three proposed themes. Some said, "How can you get away from the sink faster if the dishes are stacked a mile high?" Others wondered how they could possibly keep their hands out of greasy dishwater. With respect to the third theme, homemakers wondered how a powerful product could be "extra kind to hands." The conclusion of this research was that none of these three themes was effective.

> At this point intuition suggested a different approach. In the course of the study many questions were discussed. One of them was, "What do you find easiest to do?" Consumers generally replied, "The dishes and the glasses." That led to another question: "And what do you find most difficult to do?" The response was, "The greasy pots and pans."

> These answers led to the creative leap that resulted in a new appeal:

> This Amazing Dishwashing Discovery
> Does Pots and Pans as Easy as Glasses
> —and is extra kind to hands.

> The theme was further tested against those used by leading competitors. It was also tested for believability with respect to all themes under consideration. The findings showed that the "Pots and Pans as Easy as Glasses" approach in the slogan scored best with housewives and had a high credibility quotient.

> This copy strategy was adopted in all media, particularly TV and radio. The theme appeared on the facing of the package, and the share-of-market increased from 3 percent to nearly 9 percent.*

---

*Direct Communication with Cy Chaikin, Cy Chaikin Research Group, New York.

The most important part of any research, structured or unstructured, is interpreting the findings. In making interpretations, we find that intuition and creative imagination often play vital parts. Support for the role of intuition in this scientific age comes from Lord Brain, late president of the British Association for the Advancement of Science, who said:

> The contributions which science can make to the interpretation of something as complex as human nature are at present limited, and in unscientific theories, as in art, there may be insights, intuition, and illuminations, which are of value for practice as well as for theory.*

It is good that we begin our creative work with the "insights, intuition, and illuminations" of which we are possessed and which are of practical value.

It was an intuitive idea—not the result of research—that prompted the Doyle Dane Bernbach Agency to use Volkswagen's small size as the appeal for an advertising campaign to launch the car nationwide. While all the other cars were outdoing each other in size, this agency made a creative leap to the headline "Think small," and a new car with a new size was launched across America.

Whether created by research or in other ways, the appeal provides the basis of the advertising structure. That appeal can be expressed in words, a picture, or both. In this chapter we discuss how to make use of words, called *copy*, in presenting the appeal.†

STRUCTURE OF AN ADVERTISEMENT

In some instances the promise is the whole advertisement.

Freedent gum won't stick to most dentures.

Usually, however, a fuller exposition is required, in which case the promise can act as the headline—the first step in the structure of the advertisement. Most ads are presented in this order:

- ☐ **Promise** of benefit (the headline)
- ☐ **Amplification** of story (as needed)
- ☐ **Proof** of claim (as needed)
- ☐ **Action** to take (if not obvious)

---

*Lord Brain, "Science and Behavior," *The Listener*, August 27, 1964, p. 294.

†The term "copy" is a carryover from the days in printing when a compositor, given a manuscript to set in type, was told to copy it. Before long the manuscript itself became known as copy. In the creation of a printed ad, copy refers to all the reading matter in the ad. However, in the production of printed ads, copy also refers to the entire subject being reproduced—words and pictures alike. This is one of the instances in advertising when the same word is used in different senses, a practice that all professions and crafts seem to enjoy using as a way of bewildering the uninitiated.

The headline The headline is the most important thing in an ad. It is the first thing you read, and it should arouse the interest of the consumer so that the person wants to keep on reading and get to know more about the product you are selling. The headline has to arouse the interest of that particular group of prime prospects you want to reach. If it doesn't, the rest of the ad probably will not be read.

The major kinds of headlines fall into the following classifications:

☐ Headlines that present a new benefit
☐ Headlines that directly promise an existing benefit
☐ Curiosity-invoking and provocative headlines
☐ Selective headlines (often combined with one of the others)

Headlines that present a new benefit. The moment of peak interest in a product is when it first offers a new benefit. That is why, in our innovative society, you often see headlines such as these:

Introducing the clean air machine. Fresh from Norelco	(Norelco)
New! The Incredible talking clock!	(Sharp)
Sony Introduces a Cassette Deck for people who would only consider reel to reel	(Sony)

Headlines that directly promise an existing benefit. Products can't be offering new benefits all the time, of course, so headlines often remind consumers of existing features about their products.

Washes while you sleep	(Whirlpool)
Every day aboard a Princess is like no other day in your life	(Princess Cruises)
The best course after the last course	(Crest Tooth Paste)
PPG reflective glass holds down the cost of keeping cool	(PPG Industries)

Curiosity-invoking and provocative headlines. As a change of pace from the direct-promise headlines, an advertiser may challenge the curiosity of the reader, prompt him or her to read further, and lead to the key message. Tacitly the message promises helpful information for the reader.

How to build a city that runs on sun and wind instead of oil and gas	(Matsushita Electric)
How to cut travel costs without cutting travel	(Beechcraft)
Now we give men another reason to stay fit: lower insurance costs	(New York Life)

Remember, however, that readers should not feel tricked into reading something that fails to answer the questions or relate the challenge to their self-interest.

Selective Headlines. Readers looking through a magazine or newspaper are more likely to read an ad that concerns them personally, rather than one that talks to a broad audience. The selective headline aimed at a particular prime prospect that would be most interested in the product is often used.

Here are four headlines:

To All Men and Women

To All Young Men and Women

To All College Men and Women

To All College Seniors

The first headline is addressed to the greatest number of readers, but it would be of least interest to any one of them. As each succeeding headline reduces the size of the audience it addresses, it improves the chances of attracting that particular group.

Besides addressing them directly, headlines can appeal to a particular group by mentioning a problem they have in common:

Get fiber into more foods your family will like   (Kellogg's)

You can't bake chicken in a toaster, but you can
in a GE Toast-R-Oven   (General Electric)

Another vital quality in headlines is that they be specific. "A sewing machine that's convertible" is better than "A sewing machine with an unusual feature." In fact, being specific is vital not only in headlines but in the rest of the copy as well.

Subheadline

A headline must say something important to the reader. The actual number of words is not important; long headlines have been known to work as well as short ones. If the message is long, it can be conveyed with a main headline and a *subheadline*. The subheadline can spell out the promise presented in the headline. It can be longer than the headline. It can invite further reading, and it serves as a transition to the opening paragraph of the copy. As examples:

Headline:
Packed with water. Not Calories

Subheadline:
Bumble Bee Tuna packed in water has 50%
less calories than tuna packed in oil   (Bumble Bee Tuna)

Headline:
A spoon that tells the temperature

Subheadline:
Perfect for candy, icing, sauces, jams,
custards—deep-fat frying, too!
Accurate readings from 80°F to 450°F.   (McCall's thermometer spoon;
Exhibit 14.1)

Headline:
For the best pops . . . moms, brothers, nieces, friends

Exhibit 14.1
A promise-of-performance headline that is clear, direct, and enthusiastic. (Courtesy of McCall's.)

Subheadline:

**Presto Pop Corn new continuous hot air corn popper . . .
the gift people want the minute they see it** (Presto Industries)

Amplification

After the headline comes the body copy of the ad. Here we present our case for the product and explain how the promise in the headline will be fulfilled. What we say, how deep we go, depends on the amount of information our prime prospect needs at this point in the buying process. A high-cost product, such as a refrigerator or electric range, probably calls for more explanation than a low-cost product, such as a soup with a new flavor. If a product has many technical advances, such as a new home computer, there probably will not be room enough to give a detailed explanation of all the features. In this case explain just enough so that your prime prospect will want to go to a dealer to see a demonstration and be sold in the store.

Technical features of a product should be presented in terms of what they will do for the user. A Litton microwave oven ad described its features in this manner:

Microwave speed.
Cook a complete meal or a quick snack in the eye-level microwave oven. Or rely on automatic defrost to thaw frozen foods fast. Either way, you save time and energy with microwave speed.

Self-cleaning ease.
Save clean-up time, too. Litton Micromatics have a self-cleaning oven system that removes even the toughest baked-on stains. And a one-piece smoothtop that keeps spills from dripping away.

Cooks four ways.
So now there's always time for complete meals. Cook with microwave speed in the eye-level oven. Bake or broil in the conventional oven. Stir up something saucy on the smoothtop. Or prepare one dish or a complete meal using both ovens for a combination of conventional browning and microwave speed.

Before we conclude this section of the ad, it is wise to offset any potential objections that might inhibit a prospect from buying the product. Hair-preparation ads say, "Leaves the hair soft, not sticky." Janitor-in-a-Drum cleanser advertised "Contains no concentrated phosphates, and is biodegradable so that it will not pollute water."

Before coloring the hair became stylish, many women hesitated for fear their friends would know they were dying their hair. Clairol shampoo built a multimillion-dollar business with the slogan

**Does she or doesn't she?
Only her hairdresser can tell for sure.**

Proof

There comes a point in the consideration of a new product or costly purchase where the prospective buyer wonders, "But how much can I count on all these claims?" Proof supporting the promises made is especially important for high-priced products, health products, and new products offering a special feature.

The reputation of the maker is very important. Other evidence, however, is often necessary too.

Warranties. Eveready dramatizes its new flashlights with a dramatic 10-year warranty:

"Eveready" introduces flashlights for the 80s
with a warranty for the 90s

Car and tire companies continually seek to outdo each other with their warranties. We discuss the legal aspects of warranties in advertising in Chapter 25.

TRIAL OFFERS. Widely used for such low-cost, nonconsumable products as books and small tools, trial offers show consumers that the company is confident about its product.

MONEY-BACK GUARANTEES. These are the basic assurance for low-priced products.

SEALS OF APPROVAL. From accredited sources, such as *Good Housekeeping, Parents' Magazine,* the American Medical Association, and Underwriters Laboratories, seals of approval allay consumers' fears about product quality.

Demonstrations. Simple demonstrations, like those for paper towels, can be performed live on TV. When demonstrations are performed outside the field, under impartially controlled conditions (tests of car brakes, for example), they can be shown on TV and in print ads. It is important to show convincingly that such tests were fairly conducted. Of course, if the product was used in a public competition, as is the case when tires are used in the Indianapolis 500, excellent evidence is automatically available.

Testimonials. Testimonials should come from persons competent to pass judgment on the subject or whose judgment, for other reasons, is respected. A golf champion's opinion of a golf ball is meaningful; but on the finetuning of a TV set his or her opinion may be worth no more than that of an ordinary person. Health testimonials are unacceptable to the government.

The entire ad as dramatic proof. Although we have listed proof as fourth in the hierarchy of elements of a comprehensive ad, often whole campaigns are devoted to establishing the validity of one important claim. We have discussed this strategy in Chapter 3.

Action   Before you begin to write an ad, ask yourself exactly what you want the readers to do. Whatever you may want them to do must be consistent with their normal procedures in buying a product like the one you are advertising. Sometimes you simply want to dispose consumers favorably toward the product so that, when they are next in the market, they will turn to your brand.

For most low-priced products widely sold in supermarkets, you want consumers to buy them next time they go shopping. Lest they forget the name, an urge line may be added: "Enjoy _____ for dinner tonight." Many advertisers include a cents-off coupon as an incentive to buy the product on the next shopping expedition.

For more costly products, such as household appliances, there is more deliberating, more shopping. The ad aims to get the reader to visit a dealer. "See your dealer" or "Visit your dealer for demonstration or trial run" are familiar closing lines. The ad may also invite the reader to send for a booklet giving more information; that inquiry can then be passed on to the local dealer for follow-up by a sales representative.

COPY STYLE

Like people, ads have personalities all their own. Some say what they have to say in a fresh way. They make an impact. Others, although they try to say the same thing, are boring. Unfortunately, while many of us may be polite to a dull person, no one is polite to a dull ad. We simply pass it by.

Up to now we have been discussing how the building blocks of copy are put together. We now discuss how the way we say what we have to say can lift it out of the humdrum. That's style. The creative essence in writing copy is to see a product in a fresh way, to explore its possible effects upon the reader, to explain the product's advantages in a way that causes the reader to view the product with new understanding and appreciation.

Most ads end in the same way, by asking or suggesting that the reader buy the product. The difference between a lively ad and a dull one lies in the *approach* to the message at the outset.

The lens through which a writer sees a product may be the magnifying glass of the technician, who sees every nut and bolt and can explain why each is important. It may be the rose-colored glasses of the romanticist, who sees how a person's life may be affected by the product. Therefore we speak of *approaches* of ads, rather than types of ads. The chief approaches in describing an article may be characterized as the factual approach and the emotional approach.

Factual approach

In the factual approach we deal with reality, that which actually exists. We talk about the product—what it is, how it's made, what it does. Focusing on the facts about the product that are of most importance to the reader, we explain the product's advantages. An interesting thing about a fact, however, is that it can be interpreted in different ways, each accurate but each launching different lines of thinking. The most familiar example is that of the 8-ounce glass holding 4 ounces of water, of which it could be said, "This glass is half full" or "This glass is half empty."

Both statements are factually correct. The difference is in the interpretation of the reality and in the viewpoint projected, as the Chivas Regal ad in Exhibit 14.2 so aptly illustrates. The skill in presenting a fact is to interpret it in the way that means most to the reader.

A job is what you do with your days.
A career is what you do with your life.

You won't find jobs at General Electric, but you will find many different careers.

One of the most important ingredients in the growth of your career is the growth of the company you go to work for.

Today, one of the biggest areas of growth in engineering is microelectronics. It's an area that GE is totally committed to across the board in all our businesses.

We've backed up this commitment with an investment of more than 500 million dollars. We're building a fifty-million-dollar microelectronics research and manufacturing center.

We've also recently acquired Intersil and Calma, two of the leaders in microelectronics and CAD/CAM technology.

Microelectronics and computer applications are two areas of growth at General Electric.

Our decentralized structure and diverse businesses give us a depth in management and a wide range of career opportunities. From jet engines to the Computerized Tomographic Scanner, from energy-conserving technologies to spaceflight systems.

You'll also be able to help your career grow by continuing your education. We offer both internal courses and a college-tuition refund program.

If you would like to learn more about microelectronics, computer applications and other career opportunities at GE, we'd like to talk to you. We'll be on your campus on Sept. 30 and Oct. 1, 1981.

If we can't get together at your school, please write to us. We'd be happy to send you a pamphlet on career opportunities. Write General Electric, Educational Communications, Fairfield, CT 06431.

GENERAL ⓖⓔ ELECTRIC

An Equal Opportunity Employer

University of Illinois

Exhibit 14.3
Recruiting ad with a dramatic, thought-provoking headline. (Courtesy of G.E.)

A BMW ad could have said, "Driving a BMW is an exhilarating experience." But how much more interesting and provocative a statement is "Driving a luxury car doesn't have to be a boring experience"!

General Electric could have said, "Finding a job is the most important decision you'll ever make." Instead they said, "A job is what you do with your days. A career is what you do with your life." (Exhibit 14.3)

Imaginative copy can be used to sell more than products. Facts about services, ideas, places—anything an ad can be written for—can be presented with a fresh point of view. The Economic Development Department of Memphis, Tennessee, ran an ad to encourage industries to move there. The writer could have said, "Memphis—a city of 650,000," but instead interpreted the city's size this way:

Memphis—a city of manageable size

Imaginative approach

A fact is no less a fact if it is presented with imagination. The art of creating copy lies in saying a familiar thing in an unexpected way.

A workshop bench could be advertised on its practical value. How much more imaginative to picture a window in the vise and say, "It even does windows." (Exhibit 14.4)

Campbell's soups could have said, "When you have guests, serve Campbell's Soup." Instead, they said:

Give Me the Campbell Life
It's an Informal Party
Where Guests
Help Themselves to a Good Time

Both these ads appeal less to our reason than to our emotions. Like ads taking a factual approach, they tacitly make a promise, but the promise is emotional satisfaction.

Emotional approach backed by factual copy

Although people may become interested in an ad because of the emotional approach of its headline, they may also want to know some specific facts about a product before deciding to buy it. Often the copy approach begins with an emotional presentation and ends with a factual one. Some of the most effective ads combine an emotional headline and picture with factual copy. A factual statement interpreted imaginatively, backed up by factual copy, can also be persuasive. We avoid speaking of factual ads or emotional ads; we say ads are using a factual or emotional *approach*.

Copy for special-interest groups

Much advertising is devoted to people who have specialized interests: tennis, cars, gardening, hunting, sailing, or photography. In ads for special-interest groups the copy promises to solve specific problems common to members of the group.

Exhibit 14.4

A good example of the imaginative approach. (Courtesy Black and Decker.)

SAVE A TOMATO'S LIFE.

THESE TOMATOES STAYED FRESH FOR 15 DAYS IN THE GE FOOD SAVER. It's easy to keep tomatoes this fresh and firm for that long in a General Electric Food Saver refrigerator. Because its Moist 'n Fresh drawer lets you keep foods at the right temperature <u>and</u> humidity. So vegetables and your other moisture-loving foods thrive in it.

Fruits keep fresh for 15 days, too. Grapes, strawberries, oranges, all keep better in the lower humidity of our Cool 'n Fresh drawer.

Even meat and cheese can stay fresh. Because the sealed, high-humidity Snack Pack adds extra life to your unwrapped cold cuts and other uncovered snacks.

We can't think of a better feature than keeping your food fresh so long. (After all, that's what you buy a refrigerator for!) But, there's even more! This Food Saver has adjustable glass shelves, an energy-saver switch and gives you crushed ice, ice cubes and chilled water through the door. And there are other Food Savers in a selection of sizes and styles too, all equipped for an automatic icemaker. So don't be a food waster. Get a GE Food Saver.

Model TFF24R

Unretouched photos were taken of tomatoes and other food stored in Food Saver drawers after 15-day test.

WE BRING GOOD THINGS TO LIFE.

GENERAL ⓖⓔ ELECTRIC

Exhibit 14.5
Unusual headline for a household appliance. (Courtesy of G.E.)

COMPARATIVE ADVERTISING

The term *comparative advertising* means advertising in which the advertiser's named product is directly compared with one or more competitive named or readily identified products. It was long held by most advertisers that naming competitive products was just giving free advertising to the competitor. Moreover, the networks banned its use until in 1973 the Federal Trade Commission held that naming competitors' brands was not unfair competition, provided the statements made were all supportable. Since that time comparative advertising has become a familiar technique. There are legal problems in comparative advertising, however, as we shall see in Chapter 25.

"How good is comparative advertising, anyway?" The question will be answered only with time and experience. As of now, we have learned these things:

- [ ] The leader in a field has never embarked on such campaigns.
- [ ] The most successful comparison ads are those comparing the advertised product with products identical in every respect except for the specific differential featured in the ad. The stronger the proof that products are otherwise identical, the better.
- [ ] The different features should be of importance to the consumer.

One unexpected advantage that comparative advertising has brought to consumers is this: When product *A* comes out with an advantage over product *B*, the makers of product *B* often set out to improve their product so that it may be even better than product *A*. That is the creative competitive impact of the free-enterprise system at work.

SLOGANS

Originally from the Gaelic *sluagh-ghairm*, "battle cry," the word *slogan* has an appropriate background. Slogans sum up the theme of a company's advertising to deliver an easily remembered message in a few words.

Used even more often on TV and radio than in print, slogans may be combined with a catchy tune to make a *jingle*. They are broadly classified as either *institutional* or *hard-sell*.

Institutional

Institutional slogans are created to establish a prestigious image for a company. Relying on this image to enhance products and services, many firms insist that such slogans appear in all their advertising and on their letterheads. An entire ad may feature the slogan. Some institutional slogans are familiar:

You're in good hands with Allstate	(Allstate Insurance Company)
The quality goes in before the name goes on	(Zenith television)
Where science gets down to business	(Rockwell Industries)

Such policy slogans are changed infrequently, if at all. Stating the platform or virtues of the candidate in a few words, slogans used in political campaigns likewise fall into the institutional-slogan classification. Such campaigns expire on election day, as, regrettably, do many of the promises.

Hard-sell

These capsules of advertising change with campaigns. They epitomize the special, significant features of the product or service being advertised, and their claims are strongly competitive:

Let your fingers do the walking	(Bell System Yellow Pages)
The best of France to all the world	(Air France)
We try harder	(Avis Rent-a-Car)
Wait'll you get your hands on my ribs	(Beefsteak Charlie's)

Slogans are widely used to advertise groceries, drugs, beauty aids, and liquor. These are products that are bought repeatedly at a comparatively low price. They are sold in direct competition to consumers on the shelves of supermarkets, drugstores, and department stores. If a slogan can remind a shopper in one of those stores of a special feature of the product, it certainly has served its purpose. Slogans can also remind shoppers of the name of a product from a company that they respect. Not all advertising needs slogans. One-shot announcements, sale ads for which price is the overriding consideration, usually don't use slogans. Creating a slogan is one of the fine arts of copywriting.

Elements of a good slogan

A slogan differs from most other forms of writing because it is designed to be remembered and repeated word for word, to impress a brand and its message on the consumer. Ideally, the slogan should be short, clear, and easy to remember.

Rhyming helps:

A title on the door rates a Bigelow on the floor	(Bigelow Carpets)

Parallelism helps:

New York Life For all your life	(New York Life)

Aptness helps:

The canned dog food without the can	(Gainesburger Dog Food)

Alliteration helps:

Progress for People	(General Electric Company)

The name of the product in a slogan is a great advantage:

Delta is ready when you are	(Delta Air Lines)

Slogans are not easy to create. Sometimes they "pop out" of a piece of copy or a TV commercial. Most often, they are the result of hard work and days and months of thinking and discussions by not only creative but marketing people.

REVIEWING THE COPY

After the copy has been written, review it with these questions in mind:

- ☐ Is it arresting?
- ☐ Does it clearly state a promise to solve a problem or a significant benefit?
- ☐ Is the ad clear?
- ☐ Does it give the information that the prospective buyer would seek at that point in the buying process?
- ☐ Are all factual claims supportable?
- ☐ Is it believable?

SUMMARY

Good copywriting begins with an understanding of what will motivate a person to action. We discover prime prospects' problems and what motivates them by doing research. Structured research uses a preselected set of choices; unstructured research uses in-depth interviews to determine what problems prime prospects are most likely to respond to. Write something that strikes at a problem your prime prospect has and you will capture interest. Headlines should get attention, subheadlines support the headline statement, and body copy explain and amplify the headline and subhead. You may cite proof of a product's effectiveness, use a manufacturer's warranty to guarantee performance, use testimonials by reputable and/or famous consumers. In some campaigns, comparative advertising is employed—making direct comparisons among different brands in the same category. Slogans are easily remembered messages about a company or product. Good slogans are short, clear statements that can be repeated word for word by consumers.

QUESTIONS

1. What is an advertising appeal? On what is it based? What is the appeal supposed to do?

2. Select a product category in which there are several competing brands. From current advertising see how many different specific appeals are used by the various brands. In each case what is the advertiser trying to accomplish?

3. What do you see as the qualities of an effective advertising appeal?

4. The most important part of any research is the way the findings are interpreted, often a blend of facts, intuition, and creative imagination. Discuss how these were used in the examples cited in this chapter.

5. Advertising copy generally has a basic structure. What are the elements of that structure?

6. Describe the purpose of a focus-group interview.

7. Why is the headline the most important statement in an ad? What are the major forms of headlines? Find two examples illustrating each type.

8. What is the function of the subheadline?

9. What does amplification specifically seek to accomplish? What determines the extent of amplification?

10. When is proof important in an ad? Describe the various ways to substantiate claims. How much proof is required in an ad? Can you suggest some guidelines for deciding how much proof to include?

11. Distinguish between the factual and emotional copy approaches. Find three examples of each.

12. Under what circumstances is comparative advertising beneficial? Find an example of effective and ineffective comparative ads.

13. What is the emotional approach backed by factual copy? Illustrate with two examples.

14. Describe situations in which slogans are particularly useful.

15. Identify and discuss (including an example of each) the major types of slogans.

16. What are the elements of a good slogan?

17. What are the questions you should keep in mind when reviewing the copy?

18. From current advertising, find and analyze the copy approaches used by two different brands of the same product.

19. Identify what you think are the most desirable qualities of good copy. Select an ad that illustrates some of these qualities and explain why.

20. What kind of background and training do you think a copywriter should have?

SUGGESTED EXERCISES

21. Pretend you are the copywriter at an agency serving the Universal Electric Corporation; Universal Electric has assigned the agency the task of coming up with a new slogan. Universal Electric has several divisions: They manufacture small appliances (hair dryers, toasters, and microwave ovens), large appliances (refrigerators, dishwashers, freezers, electric stoves, central-heating systems, and air conditioners), plus special products for use by NASA and the military, aircraft components, electrical systems for cars, nuclear power plants, and hydroelectric systems. Thus they serve the public directly with goods for use in the home and indirectly by producing systems that ultimately benefit individual persons.

Universal Electric needs a slogan that tells the public two basic things: how large and diversified Universal Electric is and how much they help the individual in his day-to-day living. Remember that a good slogan is no more than eight words, usually fewer.

READINGS

BAKER, STEPHEN: *Systematic Approach to Advertising Creativity* (New York: McGraw-Hill, 1979).

BOGART, LEO: "Mass Advertising: The Message, Not the Measure," *Harvard Business Review,* September-October, 1976, pp. 107–116.

BURTON, PHILIP WARD: *Advertising Copywriting* (Columbus, Ohio: Grid Publishing, 1978), pp. 51–62.

HOLBROOK, MORRIS B., and DONALD R. LEHMANN: "Form Versus Content in Predicting STARCH Scores," *Journal of Advertising Research,* August, 1980, pp. 53–62.

HOPKINS, CLAUDE: *Scientific Advertising* (New York: Crown, 1966).

KEISER, STEPHEN K.: "Awareness of Brands and Slogans," *Journal of Advertising Research,* August, 1975, pp. 37–43.

McMAHAN, HARRY WAYNE: "Alltime Ad Triumphs Reveal Key Success Factors Behind Choice of '100 Best,'" *Advertising Age,* April 12, 1976, pp. 74–78.

SCHWAB, VICTOR O.: *How to Write a Good Advertisement* (New York: Harper, 1962).

VAUGHN, RICHARD: "The Consumer Mind: How to Tailor Ad Strategies," *Advertising Age,* June 9, 1980, pp. 45–46.

"Wirthlin: Steel companies like Presidents," *Advertising Age,* September 28, 1981, p. 74.

15

Layouts: the Headline-Visualization Match

So far we've been discussing ideas in terms of copy. Now we want to think of copy and art—or visualization—at the same time, as a *total concept*. "Concept" is defined as "an idea of something, mentally combining all its elements." In the creation of an ad the chief elements are headlines and visual. Sometimes the headline and visual need each other to make sense; or the visual gives a realistic picture of what the headline says. They reinforce one another. Or the picture interprets what the copy says. The result is a total concept.

The importance of thinking of ideas in terms of a total concept was emphasized by an advertising agency seeking two art directors. The ad in *Advertising Age* read:

> We want total concept people who believe they can write as good a headline as some of our writers (because our writers, more often than not, have great visual ideas).

Usually an agency art director is teamed with a copywriter to develop a concept for a new campaign. Sometimes the art director suggests a headline, and the copywriter suggests a visualization. In any case, when you ask creative people how they

Exhibit 15.1
An interesting headline—visualization match. (Courtesy of Pepsico, Inc.)

create their ideas, they answer, "We go off in all directions, and—flash!—there it is!" That flash usually doesn't come easily or quickly but is the result of dozens of starts, changes of thought, irrelevant ideas, and dull perceptions. But once the idea hits, you know you've come up with a good one, the "creative leap," as some call it. Behind that creative leap is a well-thought-out strategy and disciplined thinking.

WHAT IS VISUALIZING AN IDEA?

To visualize an idea, you form a mental picture of it. Suppose you were asked to suggest a visualization of golfing. You might think of a player blasting out of a sand trap or completing a beautiful swing. You might show a locker-room scene. The scope of visualizing is boundless (just for fun, how would you visualize success?). In creating an ad, you can describe your visualizing idea in words or in the crudest sketch for an artist to carry out—unless you are the artist creating the ad. The important thing in visualizing is to imagine the kind of picture you think would express your idea.

Now you don't.

One-Calorie
Diet Pepsi

MARKETING APPROACH TO
VISUALIZING
Before you embark on any creative project, spend time with the marketing department and get agreement on

- ☐ the special, significant benefit the product offers
- ☐ the marketing problem to be overcome with the competition and in getting acceptance of the public.

When you have this information, write a statement of the one thing you would say about the product if that were all you could say. This is your basic statement, or theme.

THE CREATIVE
LEAP
Try making different types of headline out of that statement, in as many ways as you can. Suggest any visual ideas you may want to go with the headlines, or try a reverse deal: Think of a picture in which the product would fit, and try

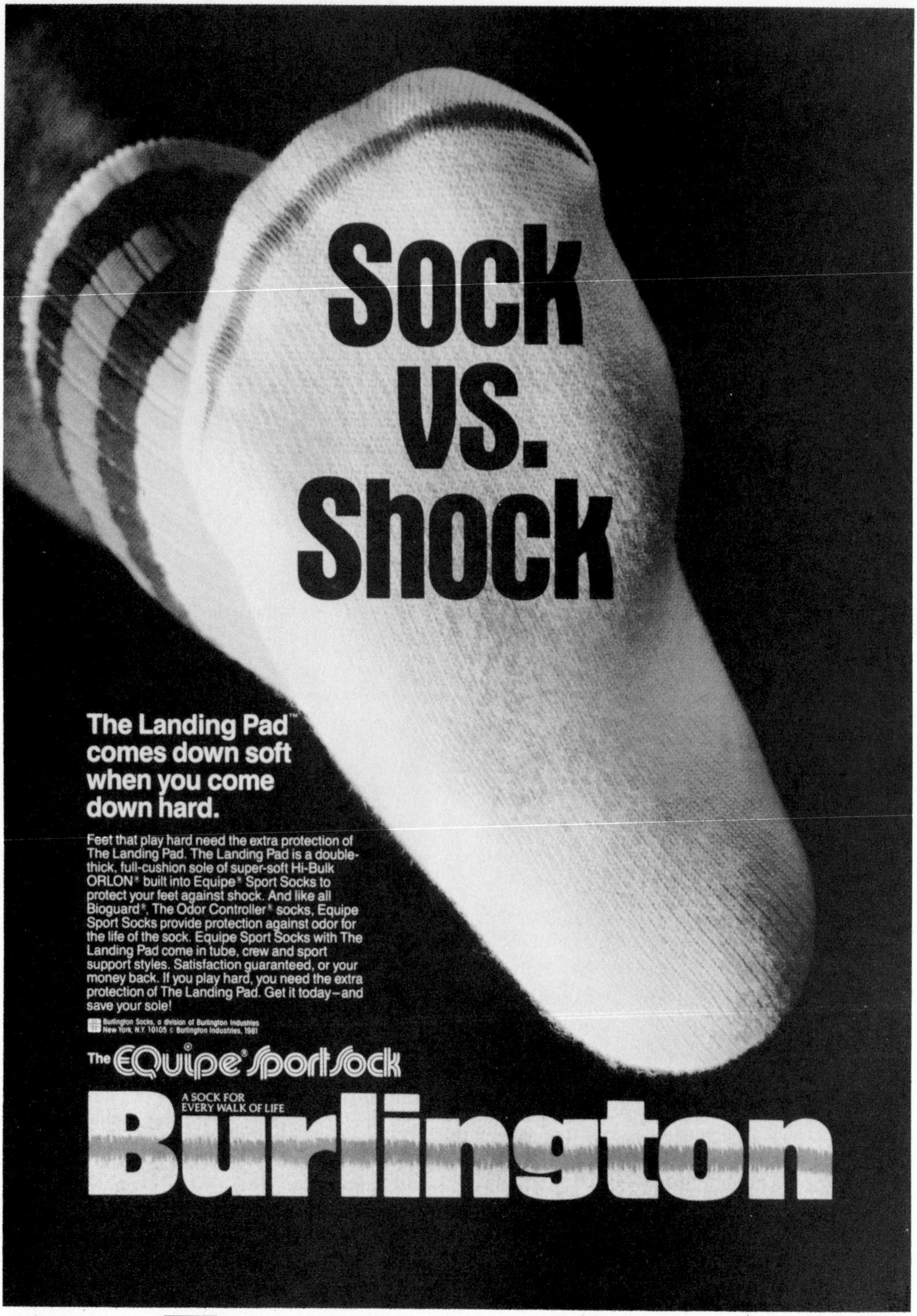

Exhibit 15.2
A dramatic use of picture and headline that shocks the reader into attention. (Courtesy of DuPont.)

writing a headline to go with it. You will find that ideas beget ideas. Make as many versions of the basic idea as you can. Be as imaginative as you want to be, provided the end result delivers the basic message (Exhibit 15.2). Take from this collection the concept that delivers the message best. That is the concept for the ad.

You might say that's a lot of work. You have now learned the first lesson in creating for a good ad a total concept on which the copy can be written and an illustration prepared. You have made the creative leap.

The purpose of this approach is to guide your thinking so that whatever creative ideas you offer will help to solve the marketing problem. They will make good "selling" ads. Some examples are shown in Exhibits 15.3 to 15.7 and the full color plates following page 366.

LAYOUTS

An ad is made up of parts: headline, illustration, copy, and logotype; there may also be a subheadline, several different illustrations of varying importance, long or short copy, a coupon—an infinite variety. Putting these together in an orderly form is called the *layout* of the ad. The term "layout" is one of the many used in advertising in two senses: It means the total appearance of the ad, its design, the composition of elements; it also means the physical rendering of the design of the ad, a blueprint for production purposes. You will hear someone say, "Here's the copy and the layout," as he or she hands another person a typed page and a drawing. Right now we are talking about the layout as the overall design of an ad.

Layout person as editor

Although the person who created the visual idea may be the same as the one who makes the layout, the two functions are different. The visualizer translates an idea into visual form; a layout person takes that illustration and all the other elements that are to go into the ad and makes an orderly, attractive arrangement.

Before putting pencil to paper, however, the layout person—usually an art director—and the writer review all the elements. The first task is to decide what is most important. Is it the headline? The picture? The copy? How important is the package? Should the product itself be shown, and, if so, should it be shown in some special environment or in use? Is this ad to tell a fast story with a picture and headline, or is it a long-copy ad with illustration only an incidental feature? The importance of the element determines its size and placement within the ad.

Getting meaningful attention

Every ad in a publication directly competes for attention with every other ad and the editorial matter. It is axiomatic in advertising that a person must first pay attention to your ad if it is to be read. Many sins have been committed in the name of this oversimplified directive because you can use an odd

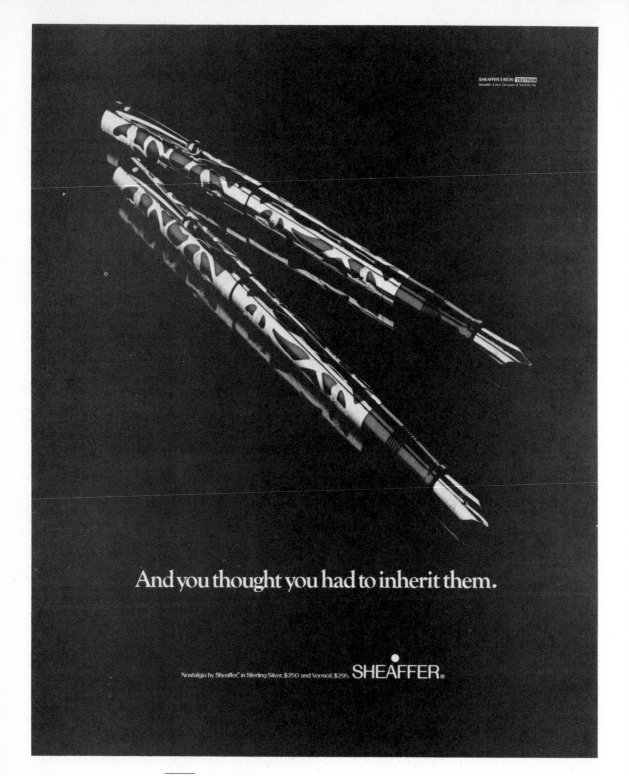

And you thought you had to inherit them.

Nostalgia by Sheaffer, in Sterling Silver, $250 and Vermeil, $295.

SHEAFFER.

Exhibit 15.3
How to say something is elegant without saying it in so many words. (Courtesy Sheaffer pen.)

12 YEAR OLD BLENDED SCOTCH WHISKY, 86.8 PROOF. BOTTLED IN SCOTLAND. IMPORTED BY SOMERSET IMPORTERS, LTD. N.Y. © 1981   DIAMONDS BY HARRY WINSTON, INC.

Give her something expensive with rocks.
If you're lucky, she'll do the same for you.

Johnnie Walker®
Black Label Scotch
YEARS 12 OLD

Exhibit 15.4
A feeling of affluence for a premium-priced Scotch whiskey. (Ad created by Smith/Green-
land, Inc. for Somerset Importers, Ltd., importers of Johnnie Walker Black Label Scotch.)

ONCE THE EQUIPMENT GETS INTO YOUR NEW PLANT, YOU'LL NEED WORKERS WITH A HEAD FOR THE BUSINESS.

You need employees with the know-how to do your work—the way you want it done. But if those workers aren't ready when you are, the lost production time will cost you money.

In Alabama, there's a state-financed Industrial Development Training Program that can help you get the qualified workers you need. When you need them. And there's no cost to you for the tailor-made planning, recruiting, screening, and training. You can also get labor and training data as well as help with management orientation. Alabama is ready to meet all your industrial needs. And we can put you in touch with all the right people. Write G.T. Nelson, Vice President, Industrial Development, Alabama Power Company, Box 2641, Birmingham, Alabama 35291.

Then when your plant is ready to open, you'll have all the resources you need to get it off to a profitable start.

Alabama Power

ALABAMA'S OPEN FOR BUSINESS.

Exhibit 15.5
Provocative headline-visualization match. (Courtesy Alabama Power Co.)

Japan, now only $3.75

It's the new low price. $3.75 for a 3-minute call to Japan when you dial the call yourself any time on Sunday.

If you don't have International Dialing in your area, you still get the same low rate as long as it's a simple Station phone call. (Person-to-person, credit card and collect calls, for example, cost more because they require special operator assistance.) Just tell the local Operator the country, city, and telephone number you want.

Here's how to dial Tokyo:

011 + 81 + 3 + LOCAL NUMBER

(If you are calling from a Touch-Tone*telephone, press the "#" button after dialing the entire number. This will speed your call along.)

$3.75! What a nice surprise! Or, as they say in Japan, "Wow-ie, How Wonderful!" *Trademark of AT&T Co.

Want to know more? Then call our International Information Service, toll free:

1-800-874-4000

In Florida, call 1-800-342-0400

◉ **Bell System**

INITIAL 3-MINUTE DIAL RATES			
FROM THE U.S. MAINLAND TO:	DAY RATE	LOWER RATE	
American Samoa	$4.05	$3.15	A
Australia	4.95	3.75	A
Fiji	4.50	—	C
Guam	4.50	3.60	B
Hong Kong	4.50	—	C
Indonesia	4.95	—	C
Japan	4.95	3.75	A
Korea, Rep. of	4.95	—	C
Malaysia	4.95	—	C
New Caledonia	4.95	—	C
New Zealand	4.50	—	C
Philippines	4.95	3.75	A
Singapore	4.95	—	C
Tahiti	4.95	—	C
Taiwan	4.95	3.75	A

A) Sunday only (all day)
B) Saturday and Sunday only
C) No lower rate period

The charge for each additional minute is 1/3 the initial 3-min. dial rate. Federal excise tax of 2% is added on all calls billed in the United States.

Exhibit 15.6

Special benefit: New low rates to foreign countries. *Marketing problem:* To increase awareness of low telephone rates overseas. *Basic statement:* New rates to foreign countries are lower than ever. *The creative leap:* An ad that imitates travel advertising by featuring destination and price commands attention because the price is so incredible. (Courtesy Bell System.)

363

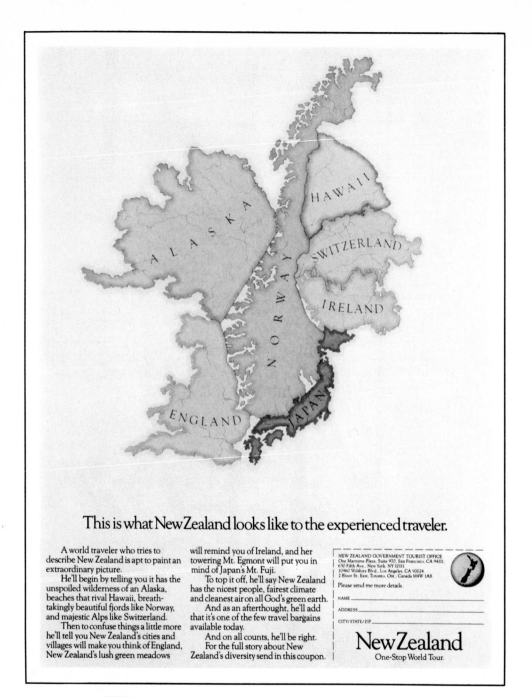

This is what New Zealand looks like to the experienced traveler.

A world traveler who tries to describe New Zealand is apt to paint an extraordinary picture.

He'll begin by telling you it has the unspoiled wilderness of an Alaska, beaches that rival Hawaii, breathtakingly beautiful fjords like Norway, and majestic Alps like Switzerland.

Then to confuse things a little more he'll tell you New Zealand's cities and villages will make you think of England, New Zealand's lush green meadows will remind you of Ireland, and her towering Mt. Egmont will put you in mind of Japan's Mt. Fuji.

To top it off, he'll say New Zealand has the nicest people, fairest climate and cleanest air on all God's green earth.

And as an afterthought, he'll add that it's one of the few travel bargains available today.

And on all counts, he'll be right.

For the full story about New Zealand's diversity send in this coupon.

NEW ZEALAND GOVERNMENT TOURIST OFFICE
One Maritime Plaza, Suite 970, San Francisco, CA 94111.
630 Fifth Ave., New York, NY 10111.
10960 Wilshire Blvd., Los Angeles, CA 90024.
2 Bloor St. East, Toronto, Ont., Canada M4W 1A8.

Please send me more details.

NAME

ADDRESS

CITY/STATE/ZIP

New Zealand
One-Stop World Tour.

Exhibit 15.7
Special benefit: The one country that has so many natural attractions within its borders. *Marketing problem:* To make prospects aware of the diverse attractions available in New Zealand. *Basic statement:* If you want to go to one country that has all the attractions of seven different areas, come to New Zealand. *The creative leap:* An unusual map joining seven lands and a headline that says this is what New Zealand seems like once you've been there. (Courtesy New Zealand Tourist Office.)

device or a freak drawing that will catch a person's eye only long enough for him or her to discover that it was merely a misleading lure. The result is mistrust of the ad and the product. The real art in advertising lies in getting meaningful attention to an idea that relates the product to the reader's life.

Composing the elements

The skill in making a layout is to assemble all the elements of the ad into one pleasing arrangement. Here are some guides that may be helpful:

Unity. All creative work begins by seeing a subject as a whole unit. A face is more than eyes and nose and mouth; it is a complete expression of personality. People smile not only with their mouths but with their eyes. A layout must also be conceived in its entirety, with all its parts related to each other, to give one overall, unified effect.

Balance. By balance we usually mean the relationship between the right-hand side and the left-hand side of the ad.

When objects at the right and left sides of the page match each other in size, shape, and intensity of color and are placed opposite each other, the balance is called *formal* balance. This kind of balance is the easiest to achieve. It makes the easiest reading, but it tends to be static.

Informal balance. The optical center of a page, measured from top to bottom, is five-eighths of the way up the page; thus it differs from the mathematical center. (To test this, take a blank piece of paper, close your eyes, then open them, and quickly place a dot at what you think is the center of the page. The chances are that it will be above the mathematical center.) Imagine that on the optical center a seesaw is balanced. We know that a lighter weight on the seesaw can easily balance a heavier one by being farther away from the fulcrum. (The "weight" of an element in an ad may be gauged by its size, its degree of blackness, its color, or its shape.) Objects are placed seemingly at random on the page but in such relation to each other that the page as a whole feels in balance. This type of arrangement requires more thought than the simple bisymmetric formal balance, but the effects can be imaginative and distinctive, as illustrated by Exhibit 15.8.

Color in advertising

Color is a great tool in print advertising. It brings brightness and attractiveness to any ad, and it is particularly important for ads of products that are sold because of color: cosmetics, drapery, jewelry, fashion, carpeting, appetizing foods. With most full-page and half-page ads in magazines in color, there is pressure on the competition—and from the advertiser's own trade—to use color for ads that can be enhanced by it. Color talks its own psychological language. To make a drink look cool, there will be plenty of blue in the background; to make a room look warm (for heating), there will be plenty of red in the background. Springtime suggests light colors; autumn, dark tones. A clue

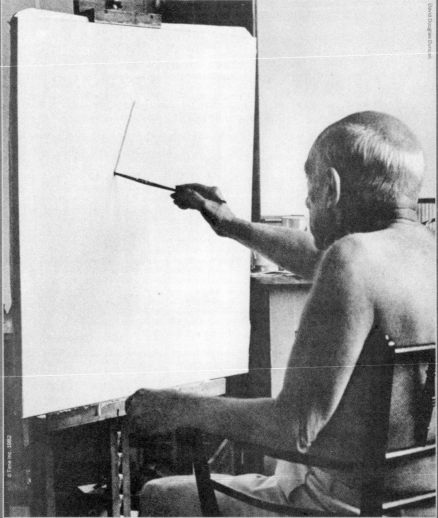

VISION

© Time Inc. 1982

He had the eyes of a child.
Even at 90, he saw the world as fresh, miraculous...new.
And what he saw and created in his long life forever
changed the way we see. A TIME cover story provided
an illuminating perspective on the most important artist
of the 20th century. Week after week, TIME gives you
more than news and information. It brings insight and
understanding to subjects that matter to you.

Read TIME and understand.

TIME

Exhibit 15.8
A dramatic use of informal balance. (Courtesy *Time* Magazine.)

Bacardi rum mixes with everything.

Except driving.

Plate 1 The Creative Leap: A striking arrangement of bottle caps shows the variety of mixers with which the product may be used, . . . and avoided. (Courtesy Bacardi Imports, Inc.)

At home at the most beautiful dinners in America.

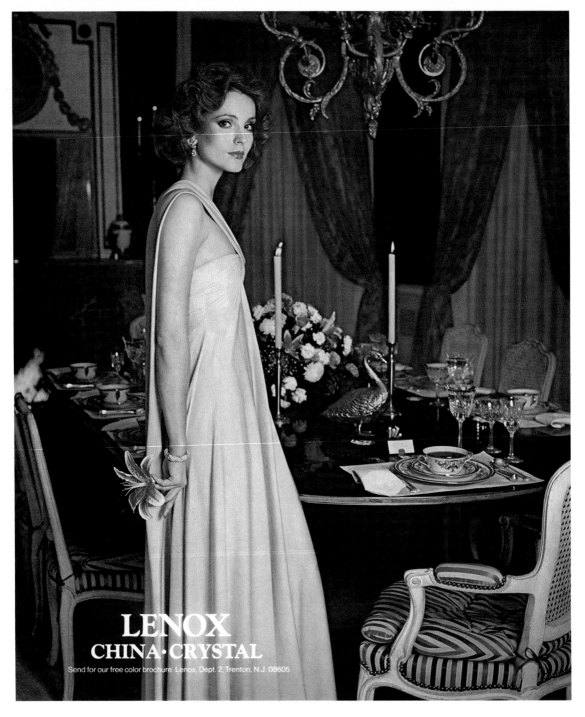

LENOX
CHINA·CRYSTAL

Send for our free color brochure. Lenox, Dept. 2, Trenton, N.J. 08605.

Plate 2 The Creative Leap: Positioned to attract brides, this ad uses an elegant setting to establish the quality of the product. (Courtesy Lenox China)

DELTA'S HAUTE CUISINE AT 30,000 FEET
served on our daily Atlanta-London nonstops

Typical First Class menu, Delta
Medallion Service. (Fine dining
in Economy Class, too.)

Cocktails Wines Liqueurs

Hors D'Oeuvres
Smoked Salmon Pheasant Galantine
Sweetbread of Veal Swedish Meatballs
Stuffed Mushrooms

Soups
Vichysoisse Beef Barley
Puffed Cheese Sticks

Salad
Caesar Salad
Assorted Breads and Sweet Butter

Entrées
Beef Wellington
Lobster Americaine
Cornish Hen Veronique

Vegetables
Fresh Carrots Fresh Zucchini
Parisienne Potatoes Wild Rice

Desserts
Bombe Napolitaine French Pastries

Assorted Cheeses Fruits in Season

Your jet:
the Delta Wide-Ride™
L-1011 TriStar

DELTA IS READY WHEN YOU ARE®

Plate 3 The Creative Leap: Beautiful 4-color pictures of gourmet food served in flight serves to win the prime prospect trans-Atlantic traveler. A much more compelling sales tool than the usual in-flight pictures. (Courtesy Delta Air Lines)

IN YOUR SEARCH FOR A LONGER LASTING CAR, REMEMBER LONGEVITY IS HEREDITARY.

As car prices have spiralled, so have people's expectations of what they should get for their money.

A recent study by the Roper organization, for instance, has shown that Americans plan to keep their cars longer.

Which could explain why more and more people are buying Volvos.

For 55 years, Volvo's philosophy has been to produce durable, well-built automobiles. Nowhere is that philosophy better embodied than in the Volvos of today.

Recent findings show that Volvo's life expectancy is 1/3 longer than the average life expectancy of all other cars on the road.*

So if you expect your next new car to last a long time, make sure you marry into the right family. **VOLVO** A car you can believe in.

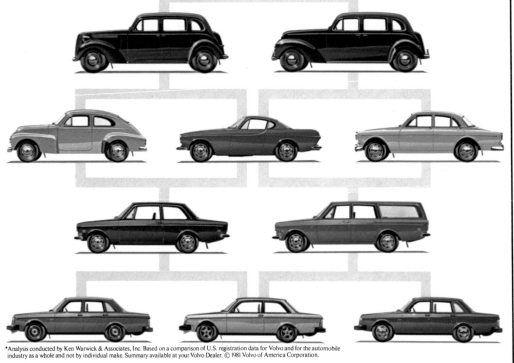

*Analysis conducted by Ken Warwick & Associates, Inc. Based on a comparison of U.S. registration data for Volvo and for the automobile industry as a whole and not by individual make. Summary available at your Volvo Dealer. © 1981 Volvo of America Corporation.

Plate 4 Volvo cars last longer. In these times of rapidly rising car prices, a long-lasting car has special significance. The Creative Leap: The picture along with the headline shows how Volvo has a reputation for longevity. (Courtesy Volvo)

Plate 5 The Creative Leap: The headline offers a benefit and a challenge. Sandwiches are stacked to attract attention and tell the whole story quickly, without confusion. Numbered and identified below the picture, the sandwiches tempt the reader to try them soon. (Courtesy Hormel)

Plate 6 The finished product of the thumbnail and layout on pages 372 and 373. (Courtesy DuPont)

AMERICA'S BEST KNOWN BEER DRINKERS TALK ABOUT **Lite** BEER...

COMM'L NO.: MOTK 0930   TITLE: "ALUMNI BOWLING"

JONES: Deacon's my name, and bowling's my game.

MADDEN: Gutter Ball! Gutter Ball!

BUTKUS: (VO) How you going to score that?
MARTIN: Come on, three strikes and you're out.

HEINSOHN: We just won another round of Lite Beer from Miller.

RED AUERBACH: Well, Lite sure tastes great!

CROWD: LESS FILLING!!! TASTES GREAT!!!

POWELL: Hold it! Hold, it, Jim.

You're going the wrong way. There it is down there.

MIZERAK: Eight ball in the pocket.

BUTKUS: Hey Bubba, this ball doesn't have any holes in it.

SMITH: Now it does.

MEREDITH: The score is all even.
NITSCHKE: Last frame. Who's up?

CARTER: Rodney...

CROWD: RODNEY???
BUTKUS: Got to be a mistake.

DANGERFIELD: Hey you kidding. It's a piece of cake.

DAVIDSON: All we need is one pin Rodney.

ANNCR: (VO) Lite Beer from Miller. Everything you always wanted in a beer. And less.

MADDEN: I didn't get my turn yet. I'm gonna break this tie.

Plate 7 Most light beers stress quality and flavor. The Creative Leap: Lite beer uses famous personalities to make their product distinctive and memorable. (Courtesy Miller Brewing Company)

Plate 8 The Creative Leap: The product benefit for Diet Pepsi is perfectly expressed in illustration and headline. No more need be said. (Courtesy Pepsi-Co, Inc.)

to the choice of the dominating color may often be found in the mood in which the product is being shown.

Search for
distinction
One goal in creating a layout is to have the ad stand out among all the ads in a medium, particularly all ads for similar products. The first step in creating national advertising (there are different rules of the game for other forms of advertising) is to break away from the layout trend among others in the same field. There are styles in layouts, and great waves of following the leader sweep over advertisers, with the result that all ads in the field are in the same mold. Pretend you are the first person in your field to advertise. Create a layout to fit the mood and nature of your message.

Among the techniques for creating distinction is size. You get more attention if you take a full-page rather than a half-page ad in a newspaper. A double-page spread in a magazine is obviously more attractive than a single page. The great problem is cost. Twice as much space does not give you twice as much attention, and it soon chews up the budget. The only time that use of space may be worth the cost is those exceptional times when you have a special announcement to make.

Other techniques may use an extralarge headline (Exhibit 15.9) or the reverse; and when everyone is using large-size type, set the headline smaller with lots of white space around it. You can establish a different style of artwork or establish a distinctive art subject (Exhibit 15.10). Marlboros were once known as a lady's cigarette: They came in white boxes with delicate lettering. The positioning was changed to a man's cigarette; and the company reached out for the most masculine type of man, the cowboy who rides around in what is now Marlboro Country—a valuable visual property, setting Marlboros apart from other cigarette advertising. Another example of breaking away from tradition is found in the liquor field, for which four-color pages are the standard magazine formula. Yet Jack Daniels broke away from the tradition by running all its ads in black and white (Exhibit 15.11). Those ads not only stand out among all the four-color liquor ads but represent a tremendous savings in costs. Sometimes a product will become known for always having a fresh-looking ad, each clearly delivering the same story in a different way. But at least the reader will not confuse the brand with others in the field.

This is not meant to be a catalog of techniques for achieving distinction (compare Exhibit 15.12). It merely lists a few of the myriad devices for making layouts distinctive.

PREPARING THE
LAYOUTS
Now we refer to layouts as the actual drawings used in planning the final design of the ad. Different types of layout represent different stages in the development of the ad. For the first ad of an important new campaign of color magazine ads, an elaborate step-by-step series of layouts may be prepared:

NOW, AS ALWAYS,

Delta is flying to every city we serve. And most of our flights are running as scheduled. There are few, if any, delays. If you have reservations on Delta there's no need to call. Just come to the airport as you usually would, and be prepared to enjoy a carefree trip. If you don't have reservations check your Travel Agent or call Delta now. There are plenty of seats available on most of our flights. In fact, if you have tickets on another airline we'll accept them. Now, more than ever, Delta is ready when you are. **▲DELTA**
The airline run by professionals.

DELTA IS READY WHEN YOU ARE.

Exhibit 15.9
Big type becomes the message and illustration. (Courtesy Delta Air Lines, Inc.)

The Great Indoors.

With an average yearly income of $42,000, Smithsonian's 1,800,000 subscribers buy the finest in home furnishings.

Smithsonian

Exhibit 15.10
An unusual illustration to make readers take notice and read the short copy. (Courtesy Smithsonian Magazine.)

If you enjoy our whiskey, drop us a line. We'd like to hear from you.

SOME OF AMERICA'S happiest cows live just down the road from Jack Daniel's Distillery.

We distill our whiskey from a mash of America's choicest grain. Then, after distilling, we sell what's left over to neighboring farmers. And they use it in liquid form to fatten up their cows. Thanks to our choice grain, we've got some highly contented cattle here in Moore County. And, we believe, some highly contented customers most everyplace else.

CHARCOAL
MELLOWED

DROP

BY DROP

Tennessee Whiskey • 90 Proof • Distilled and Bottled by Jack Daniel Distillery
Lem Motlow, Prop., Inc., Route 1, Lynchburg (Pop. 361), Tennessee 37352
Placed in the National Register of Historic Places by the United States Government.

Exhibit 15.11
(Courtesy Jack Daniel Distillery.)

The New Tax-Deferred Individual Retirement Accounts—IRAs.

You'll be putting in years of hard work between now and retirement.

And when you finally retire, you shouldn't have to struggle just to make ends meet.

Social Security can help. So can a company pension.

But an insured Individual Retirement Account—or IRA—managed by the professionals at A FULL SERVICE BANK® could help provide the financial security that can make you truly independent.

For the first time, new government regulations allow FULL SERVICE BANKS to offer IRAs to almost everyone. Including individuals already covered by a company pension or profit-sharing plan.

With the new IRAs, you're able to invest any amount up to $2,000 a year towards a high-yield retirement account.

Making deposits by the week, by the month, or whatever plan suits you best.

And because A FULL SERVICE BANK'S IRAs are tax-deferred, you deduct your IRA investment from your taxable income every year. So you'll pay no federal taxes on your IRA until you start withdrawing funds (minimum age: 59½).

Then, when you do retire, you'll probably be in a lower tax bracket. Paying lower taxes.

But more importantly, your total deposits at A FULL SERVICE BANK are insured by the FDIC up to $100,000. While many other places promoting

IRAs can't offer you this kind of insurance.

So, with an insured IRA at A FULL SERVICE BANK, you'll have fewer taxes to pay today. And less to worry about tomorrow. Plus, you'll be able to keep that gold watch.

For professional guidance with your financial future, talk to the professionals at A FULL SERVICE BANK.

They'll help make your golden years just that.

Golden.

WE'VE GOT THE ANSWERS.

Exhibit 15.12
Some ads have a provocative headline and long copy. (Courtesy American Bankers Association.)

Exhibit 15.13

Thumbnail sketches: miniature drawings, trying out different arrangements of the layout elements (Exhibit 15.13). The best of these will be selected for the next step.

Rough layouts: drawings, the actual size of the ad. All elements are presented more clearly, to simulate the way the ad is to look (Exhibit 15.14). The best of these will be chosen for the next step.

The comprehensive, or mechanical, layout (often just called the comp, or the mechanical): all the type set and pasted in place exactly as it is to appear in the printed ad. Because artwork is drawn one and a half times the actual size it will be in the ad (to be reduced by one-third for sharper reproduction) and is prepared separately, it is precisely indicated on the comprehensive by blank boxes of the exact final size. This layout will be used not only for client approval but also for making the final print or plate (Plate 6).

Once a basic ad for a campaign has been approved, layouts for subsequent ads usually consist of just a rough layout and a finished layout.

Layouts for small
advertisements

Small ads are usually one-column ads up to 4 inches deep. They appear in many magazines, and numerous businesses have been built by them. Successful small ads usually have a strong promise in a selective headline with a functional picture. The eye takes in all of a small ad at one time so that a liberal part of the space is used merely to be noticed. A small ad is not a big ad reduced; it is created by abstracting the one or two most essential elements of a big ad (if one has already been created) and emphasizing one of them.

The artist's
medium

The tool or material used to render an illustration is the artist's *medium,* the term being used in a different sense than it is in "advertising medium" (as TV or magazines). The most popular medium in advertising is photography. Other popular ones are pen and ink, pencil, crayon, and wash. Perhaps a photograph may be used as the main illustration for an ad, but for the smaller, secondary illustration pen and ink will be used. The choice of the artist's me-

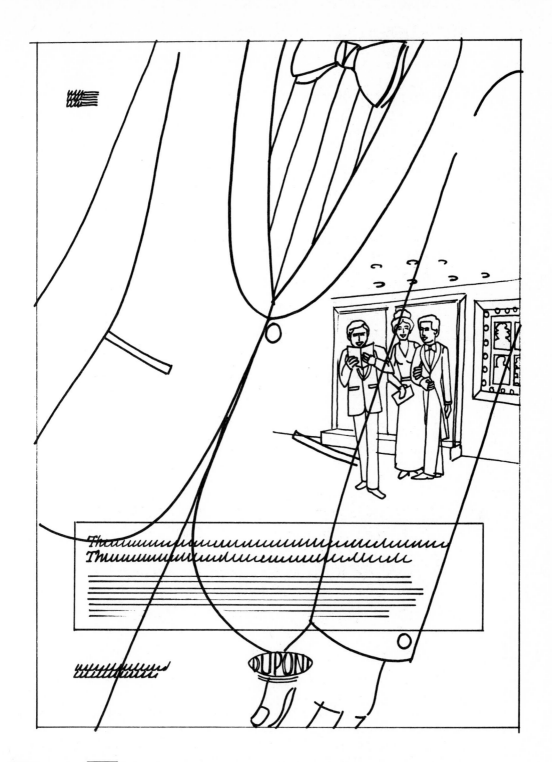

Exhibit 15.14

READERSHIP REPORT

83 ADS 1/2 PAGE AND OVER
READER'S DIGEST   NOVEMBER 1976   MEN READERS

PAGE	SIZE & COLOR	ADVERTISER / PRODUCT CATEGORIES	COST PENNIES PER READER	RANK IN ISSUE BY NUMBER OF READERS	RANK IN ISSUE BY COST PER READER	PERCENTAGES NOTED	PERCENTAGES ASSOCIATED	PERCENTAGES READ MOST	READERS PER DOLLAR NOTED	READERS PER DOLLAR ASSOCIATED	READERS PER DOLLAR READ MOST	COST RATIOS NOTED	COST RATIOS ASSOCIATED	COST RATIOS READ MOST
		(CONT.) CAMERAS/PHOTOGRAPHIC SUPPLIES												
100	1P4B	KODAK EK4 INSTANT CAMERA	1.0	12	6	56	50	20	112	100	40	187	200	400
213	V1/2P4	EASTMAN KODAK COMPANY G P	.9	33	3	36	31	13	131	112	47	218	224	470
		LUGGAGE/LEATHER GOODS												
238	1P4B	AMERICAN TOURISTER LUGGAGE	1.4	28	22	38	35	12	76	70	24	127	140	240
		PETS/PET FOODS/PET SUPPLIES												
77	1P4B	TABBY CANNED CAT FOOD OFFER	2.6	49	58	30	19	2	60	38	4	100	76	40
		BUSINESS PROPOSALS/RECRUITING												
282	V1/2P	QSP INC BUSINESS PROPOSITION	1.8	64	34	17	13	5	74	57	22	123	114	220
		FLOOR COVERING												
267	1P4B	CONGOLEUM SHINYL VINYL FLOOR	2.0	40	41	34	25	9	68	50	18	113	100	180
		MAJOR APPLIANCES												
8	1P4	SEARS KENMORE COMPACTORS	2.2	45	50	27	23	5	54	46	10	90	92	100
40 X	1S4B	WHITE-WESTINGHOUSE RANGE	4.0	48	71	31	21	4	36	25	5	60	50	50
55	1P4B	K-MART/WHIRLPOOL WASHER & DRYER	1.6	32	27	41	32	1	82	64	2	137	128	20
206	1P	WHIRLPOOL CORPORATION G P	2.4	58	55	19	17	*	46	41	*	77	82	*
248	1P4	KITCHENAID DISHWASHER	3.1	60	65	20	16	2	40	32	4	67	64	40
		SMALL HHLD. APPLIANCES/EQUIP.												
7	1P4	WESTCLOX CLOCKS	1.5	30	25	39	33	2	78	66	4	130	132	40
48	1S4B	K-MART/SMALL APPLIANCES	2.0	17	45	52	46	6	56	49	6	93	98	60
287	1P4B	MR. COFFEE BREWER/FILTERS	1.4	27	20	39	36	9	78	72	16	130	144	160
		RADIOS/TV SETS/PHONOGRAPHS												
20	1P4B	MAGNAVOX TOUCH-TUNE COLOR TV	1.4	28	22	38	35	10	76	70	20	127	140	200
51	1P4B	K-MART/CAPEHART STEREO SYS	1.1	17	10	52	46	11	104	92	22	173	184	220
53	1P4B	K-MART/CAPEHART 1000 STEREO ENSEMBLE	1.0	14	8	54	49	18	108	98	36	180	196	360
57	1P4B	K-MART/PORTABLE RADIO & CASSETTE RECORDER	1.1	19	11	48	45	13	96	90	26	160	180	260
89	1P4B	ZENITH CHROMACOLOR II TV	.9	6	2	60	58	15	120	116	30	200	232	300
229	1P4B	ZENITH ALLEGRO CONSOLE	1.2	22	13	46	43	16	92	86	32	153	172	320
		BUILDING MATERIALS												
17		OWENS-CORNING FIBERGLAS INSULATION/AMERICAN GAS ASSOCIATION SEE COMMUN/PUBLIC UTILITY												
		BLDG. EQUIP./FIXTURES/SYSTEMS												
90	1P4	GE HOME SENTRY SMOKE ALARM	1.0	14	8	51	49	27	102	98	54	170	196	540
		* LESS THAN 1/2 OF ONE PERCENT.												
		MEDIAN READERS/DOLLAR							60	50	10			

READERS PER DOLLAR ARE BASED ON 12,965,000 MEN READERS AND PUBLISHED ONE-TIME SPACE RATES. READER FIGURES ARE OBTAINED FROM 18,006,799 U.S. A.B.C. CIRC. TIMES MEN PRIMARY READERS PER COPY FROM STARCH ESTIMATES.

Exhibit 15.15
A Starch Report, showing how well ads get attention and readership.

dium depends upon the effect desired, the paper on which it is to be printed, the printing process to be used, and, most important, the availability of an artist who is effective in the desired medium.

Trade practice in buying
commercial art
Creating an ad usually requires two types of artistic talent: the imaginative person who helps create the visual idea, with a copywriter or alone, and who makes the master layout; and an artist who does the finished art of the illustrations. In larger agencies staff art directors and layout people visualize and create original layouts and also have studios and artists to handle routine work.

In the largest advertising centers—New York, Chicago, Los Angeles, Dallas, San Francisco, and Atlanta—a host of free-lance artists and photographers specialize in certain fields for preparing the final art of such subjects. In fact, agencies in other cities go to one of the major art centers to buy their graphic artwork for special assignments.

There are two important points to observe in buying artwork, especially photographs: First is the *legal release.* You must have written permission from anyone whose picture you will use, whether you took the picture or got it from a publication or an art file. (In the case of a child's picture you must have a release from the parent or guardian.) The second point is to *arrange all terms in advance.* A photographer may take a number of pictures, from which you will select one. What will be the price if you wish to use more than one shot?

"HOW ARE WE DOING?"—STARCH
REPORTS
In Chapter 16 we shall get back to ads, but now we are going to leapfrog into the future. The new ad on which we have been working is appearing in a magazine, and everyone connected with the ad—management as well as the creative team—asks, "How are we doing?" especially against competition. One method of obtaining answers to that question is through the Starch Reports.

Starch is the pioneer service for appraising magazine ads at the primary level of effectiveness, to see how many people noted the ad, associated it with who was doing the advertising, and read most of it. Starch publishes these results for all ads in the magazine issue being researched so that advertisers can make comparisons (especially with the competition). Starch gets its information through personal interviews. A large staff of women calls upon householders, by appointment, and goes through copies of the magazines with them, page by page. This method of research is *aided recall.* The information compiled is published in reports, such as the one in Exhibit 15.15, which are issued to subscribers.

The Starch Reports are limited to just one aspect of advertising effectiveness: how well the ad gets attention and gets the reader into the ad. The total effectiveness of the ad depends at the outset on its performing well on this level. Studies like those reported on Exhibit 15.15 are made separately for each issue of each magazine on the list to be studied. Drawing conclusions about the effectiveness of a campaign in getting attention and readership takes a number of successive reports.

SUMMARY

The total concept of an idea is the complete ad—headline and visualization. To visualize an idea, you form a mental picture of it. To capture the essence of what you wish to say, you find the single most important thing you can say. Then you write that statement as many different ways as you can. Try visualizing the ideas as well in many different ways. The result of your efforts will be a good idea, or the creative leap.

The art director and copywriter must take the idea and make it an attention-getting ad. Elements must be composed so that they are pleasing, yet unusual enough to stand out among other ads. Balance, unity, informal balance, and color are some of the techniques used; size is another way of giving distinction.

Ads are usually begun as thumbnail sketches, and subsequent steps are rough layouts, finished layouts, and comps. Layouts for small ads are essentially a strong promise headline with a functional illustration. In most ads "art" is usually photography, bought from specialized photographers on a free-lance basis.

To find out how effective an ad is, we use Starch Reports. Starch does personal interviews of readers and, by projecting results, determines how many people who read the publication noted your ad, associated it with the product, and read most of it.

QUESTIONS

1. Distinguish between visualization and layout.
2. What is meant by a "total concept"? Why is it important to think in terms of a total concept?
3. Explain what is meant by "visualizing an idea."
4. What is the creative leap?
5. Name several ways in which the visualization of an idea and the headline need each other. Illustrate with examples from recent advertising.
6. Find several examples from current advertising that you think have excellent visualization. Explain why you think so.
7. What are some of the major guides to developing an effective layout?

8. From contemporary advertising find three examples reflecting what you consider to be excellent layouts. Explain why you selected the ones you did.

9. Discuss the particular layout problems of small ads. From present-day advertising can you find three excellent examples of small ads (not over 4 inches)?

10. Describe some of the techniques for creating distinction in ads. Pick out three ads with distinctive layouts. What makes them distinctive?

11. Distinguish among the following types of layout: thumbnail, rough, and comprehensive (or mechanical). Must every ad have all these forms? Explain.

12. In your newspapers and magazines find three different art media used by artists in ads.

13. Does Starch advertising measurement of an ad indicate the quality of the idea?

SUGGESTED EXERCISES

You and your creative partner have just been asked to come up with a campaign for a new nutritious soft drink named TODAY. One twelve ounce serving gives you all the essential vitamins recommended daily by the Food and Drug Administration, yet it is as sweet and refreshing as the usual soft drink. How would you visualize the new product? Who will you picture in the illustration? What is the headline? The subhead? What are the dominant elements in the ad—words or pictures? Is the slogan an important part of the ad? Do a rough layout of the ad and write the headline, subhead, and slogan.

READINGS

Art Directors of New York, *Annual of Advertising Art* (New York: 1982).

BURTON, PHILIP WARD: *Which Ad Pulled Best?* 4th ed. (Chicago: Crain Communications, 1981).

CAPLES, JOHN: *Tested Advertising Methods,* 4th ed. (Englewood Cliffs, N.J.: Prentice-Hall, Inc., 1974).

ERNST, SANDRA: *The Creative Package* (Columbus, Ohio: Grid, Inc., 1979).

Graphics Annual 80/81 (Washington, D.C.: Print, 1981).

"1981 Art Award," *Communicative Arts,* July/August, 1981.

"Printers and Designers: Adversaries or Partners?" *Communicative Arts,* March/April, 1981, pp. 84–96.

ROSSITER, JOHN R., and LARRY PERCY: "Attitude Change Through Visual Imagery in Advertising," *Journal of Advertising,* Spring 1980, pp. 10–16.

TAYLOR, ROBERT C., and R. D. PETERSON: "A Textbook Model of Ad Creation," *Journal of Advertising Research,* February, 1972, pp. 35–41.

"Trends: Winter Whites," *Art Direction,* January 1980, pp. 55–56.

TURNBULL, ARTHUR T., and RUSSEL N. BAIRD: *The Graphics of Communication* (New York: Holt, Rinehart and Winston, 1980).

"The Visual Messengers," *Advertising Age,* September 7, 1981, pp. 40–44.

16

Print Production

When the copy for an ad has been written, the layout has been made, and the illustrations have been prepared, the material must be assembled into a form that the printer can use for his presses. This conversion process, which is the responsibility of the advertiser or agency, is called *print production.*

The planning of print production is a management function involving much money and many people: the production department, the copy and art departments, the media department, the account executive, and finally the management executive who will be called upon to approve all expenditures. Anyone entering the marketing and advertising world would do well to understand certain basics of print production, and this is a good time to learn.

You will find that the careful planning of print production can result in both cost savings and also the best possible finished ad. In most cases the media, rather than the advertiser, will determine the printing process to be used. However, in many areas such as sales promotion, direct mail, and print inserts the advertiser must make the final decision regarding print production. In order to deal effectively with printers the advertiser must have some knowledge of the basic printing techniques and when each is most appropriate.

378

SELECTING THE PRINTING
PROCESS
The first step in print production is to select one of the three major processes by which advertising is printed:

- ☐ Letterpress printing (from a raised surface)
- ☐ Offset lithography (from a flat surface)
- ☐ Rotogravure (from an etched surface)

All the work of print production depends upon the process used. In publication advertising each publisher has already decided on the printing process, and the advertiser must plan his work accordingly.

Letterpress printing
Whoever has used a rubber stamp has applied the principle of *letterpress printing*—printing from a raised surface. The surface to be printed stands out in relief from the rest of the stamp and gets the ink when pressed against the ink pad. Then, when the stamp is pressed against paper, the message is reproduced. The same principle applies to anything printed by letterpress, whether a rubber-stamped mailing piece or a book of many pages. In letterpress printing the advertiser or agency must supply photoengravings for all artwork or duplicates of such plates.

For generations all presses did their printing from raised type and from relief plates; some still do (Exhibit 16.1) But in advertising and in general publication printing, letterpress has given way to offset and rotogravure.

Offset lithography
Offset is the most popular printing process in the United States. It can print illustrations on rougher paper than letterpress can, and its plates cost less than those of the other major processes. It makes the best use of the photo-

Exhibit 16.1
Letterpress.

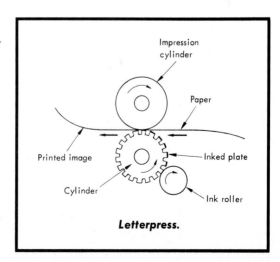

Impression cylinder

Paper

Printed image

Inked plate

Cylinder

Ink roller

Letterpress.

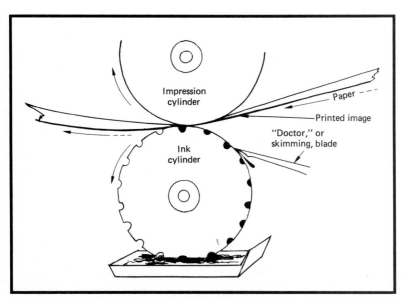

Exhibit 16.2
Offset lithography.

Dampening
(water rollers)

Ink rollers

Plate wrapped
around cylinder

Blanket cylinder

Paper

Printed
image

composition process. Most periodicals, books, and large runs of direct mail are now printed in offset. This book was printed by offset; earlier editions were printed by letterpress.

Offset printing is done on a rotary press with a thin sheet of aluminum or zinc wrapped around the cylinder. By a photomechanical process an image is transferred to this plate. The principle of lithography is that oil and water do not mix: The plate is chemically treated so that the nonprinting areas accept water while the greasy printing ink adheres only to the portions to be printed. In *straight lithography* the printing is done directly from the plate (originally, from the stone) onto the paper. In *offset lithography* we go a step further: Instead of the design's being printed directly onto a sheet or roll of paper, an intermediate cylinder is introduced, covered with a rubber "blanket," which, in turn, *offsets* it onto the paper (Exhibit 16.2).

The advertiser or the agency must supply the artwork and mechanicals or films from which offset plates can be made.

Exhibit 16.3
Rotogravure.

Impression
cylinder

Paper

Printed image

"Doctor," or
skimming, blade

Ink
cylinder

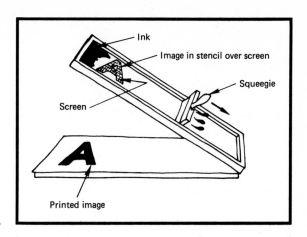

Exhibit 16.4
Screen printing.

Rotogravure Rotogravure printing utilizes the photographic method of transferring the printing image to a large copper cylinder used on a rotary printing press (Exhibit 16.3). In this process the etching of the cells, or wells (tiny depressed printing areas created by means of a screen), is only 0.001 to 0.002 inch deep; nevertheless, it is an etching. Rotogravure is the printing method for long-run printing, as mail-order catalogs, Sunday-newspaper supplements, a growing number of consumer magazines, packaging, and other material with an abundance of photographic copy. It is characterized by relatively high preparatory costs. Yet it is economical for long runs since it provides excellent color quality, with inexpensive inks, on paper stocks usually less costly than those used for letterpress or offset. Major corrections on press, however, are expensive. Rotogravure cylinders are made by the printer, usually from films or art and copy supplied by the advertiser.

Screen printing

There is also one minor, economical process worth knowing about, especially when you work only in broad, flat colors, as for car cards, posters, and point-of-purchase displays. This is *screen printing*, also known as *silk-screen printing* (Exhibit 16.4). It is a stencil process, especially good for short runs. The stencil of a design can be manually or photographically produced and then placed over a textile or metallic-mesh screen. Ink or paint is spread over the stencil and, by means of a squeegee, is pushed through stencil and screen onto the paper. This can be done by hand, for short runs, or by machine.

PLANNING THE TYPOGRAPHY

Typography is the art of using type effectively. It entails selecting the style (typeface) of type to use, deciding upon the sizes in which different elements of the copy are to be set, and preparing the specifications for the typesetter.

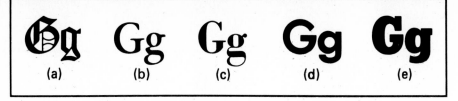

Exhibit 16.5
Styles of typefaces: (a) black letter, (b) oldstyle, (c) modern roman, (d) sans serif, (e) square serif. Courtesy Typographic Communications, Inc., who set this and the other type specimens in this chapter.

Typefaces   Type does not merely convey the words of a message; it can enhance and complement pictures and words. If you were advertising jewelry, you might use a light, decorative typeface, reflecting the beauty of the jewelry. If you were advertising chain saws, you might use a heavier, straighter face. For products and services that do not have such sharp typographic personalities, you would probably seek a face compatible with the creative tone of the ad.

The earliest letter, now known as "black letter," or "text," and four other styles of type—oldstyle roman, modern roman, sans serif, and square serif—have had a lasting influence on the types of today.

Text, or black letter. Johannes Gutenberg, in the fifteenth century, invented printing from movable type. He fashioned the letters after the hand-lettering style of the scribes in German monasteries, who used wide-pointed reed pens. These types, called *text,* or *black letter* (Exhibit 16.5a), are seldom seen today in English-speaking countries except in diplomas or ceremonial announcements or for captions.

Oldstyle Roman. During the Renaissance, type designers seeking to get away from black letter found inspiration in letter forms chiseled on old Roman stone monuments. The stone cutters had marked the top and bottom of their letters with a little bar called a *serif. Oldstyle Roman,* often called *oldstyle,* is characterized by graceful serifs and by relatively little contrast between thick and thin strokes (Exhibit 16.5b).

Modern Roman. Late in the eighteenth century there appeared another version of a Roman letter, called *modern Roman,* or just *modern.* It differs from oldstyle in that there is a decided contrast between the thicks and thins, and the horizontal serifs are cut sharply, as if by a pointed tool, rather than drawn gracefully by a pen (Exhibit 16.5c).

Sans serif. This group is characterized by the absence of serifs and by relatively even weighting of the entire letter (Exhibit 16.5d). Some common examples in this group have become associated with functional, contemporary design. The marginal heads in this book are set in a sans-serif type.

Square serif. This is a group of typefaces with strongly pronounced square serifs and evenly weighted strokes (Exhibit 16.5e).

ABCDEFGHIJKLMNOPQRSTUVWXYZ
abcdefghijklmnopqrstuvwxyz
1234567890 &?/!$("'"-:;—.,)

THIS LINE IS SET IN ROMAN CAPS.
This line is set in roman, initial cap and lowercase.
THIS LINE IS SET IN ITALIC CAPS.
This line is set in italic, initial cap and lowercase.
THIS LINE IS SET IN CAPS AND SMALL CAPS.

Type fonts and families

Type font. An individual letter, numeral, or punctuation mark is called a *character*. (In copy casting, which means counting the number of characters, space between words is usually also counted as a character.) For any face and size of type a *font* consists of all the lower-case and capital characters, as well as numerals and the usual punctuation marks (Exhibits 16.6 and 16.7). Some fonts also include small capitals, which are capitals in lower-case height. THIS SENTENCE IS SET IN SMALL CAPITALS.

A font may be roman or italic. A *roman* (with a lower-case ar) type refers to the upright letter form, distinguished from *italic,* which is oblique. Roman (capital ar) denotes a group of serifed typeface styles, as explained earlier.

Type family. From a single roman typeface design a number of variations are possible by altering letter slant, weight (stroke thickness), and proportion. Each one, however, retains essential characteristics of the basic letter form. There may be italic, semibold, bold, bold condensed, expanded, and so forth. These variations are called a *type family.* A family of type may provide a harmonious variety of typefaces for use within an ad (Exhibit 16.8).

TYPE MEASUREMENT

Type sizes are measured in *points,* about 72 to the inch. They are determined by the depth of the metal body on which the type character was traditionally cast, including the metal shoulder at top and bottom (Exhibit 16.9). Thus the printed letter, measured from the top of an ascender to the bottom of a descender, is slightly smaller than its point size (Exhibit 16.10).

Helvetica Thin
Helvetica Light
Helvetica Light Italic
Helvetica
Helvetica Italic
Helvetica Italic Outline
Helvetica Regular Condensed
Helvetica Regular Extended
Helvetica Medium
Helvetica Medium Italic
Helvetica Medium Outline
Helvetica Bold
Helvetica Bold Compact Italic
Helvetica Bold Outline
Helvetica Bold Condensed
Helvetica Bold Condensed Outline
Helvetica Bold Extended
Helvetica Extrabold Condensed
Helvetica Extrabold Condensed Outline
Helvetica Extrabold Ext.
Helvetica Compressed
Helvetica Extra Compressed
Helvetica Ultra Compressed

Exhibit 16.8
A family of type retains its basic letter-form and style characteristics through all its variations. Some type families consist of only roman, italic, and bold versions. Others, like the popular Helvetica family, have many variations and different stroke thicknesses.

Exhibit 16.9
Foundry type used in hand setting. Note shoulders on type. Point sizes measures the whole block, which explains why a printed letter is slightly less than point size.

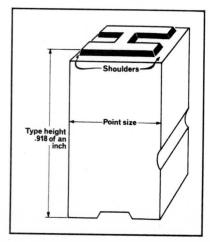

Exhibit 16.10
The size of type is determined by the height of the face (not the height of its letter *x* alone) and includes ascenders, descenders, and shoulders. A point measures almost exactly 1/72 inch. This word is photoset in 72-point Times Roman.

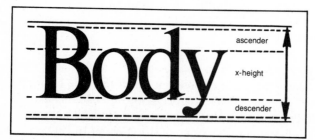

You may have two lines of letters of the same point size, and yet one appears larger because it has a larger lower-case or *x* height (the size of the letter *x*) and short ascenders and descenders. It looks bigger than one with a small *x* height and longer ascenders and descenders. Moral: Before you specify size of type, check a type specimen sheet to see the face in the size you require (Exhibits 16.11, 16.12, and 16.13).

Type sizes below 18 points are normally referred to as *text types,* while sizes from 18 points up are called *display types.* In phototypesetting the type is photographed, and its size can easily be changed; yet the traditional system of denoting type sizes has largely been retained.

Pica (pica em). The width of the line in which type is to be set is stated in *picas.* There are 12 points to the pica and approximately 6 picas to the inch. Areas of composition are usually given in picas (width first, then depth). Pica was the name originally given to 12-point type when all type sizes had names rather than numbers. An *em* is the square of any point size, usually formed by

Exhibit 16.11
Point sizes.

SIZE of type	6-point
SIZE of type	8-point
SIZE of type	10-point
SIZE of type	12-point
SIZE of type	14-point
SIZE of type	18-point
SIZE of type	24-point
SIZE of type	30-point
SIZE of type	36-point
SIZE of type	48-point

Relative size
Relative size
Relative size

Exhibit 16.12
These words are set in the 24-point size of three different typefaces: Bodoni, Century Schoolbook, and Avant Garde medium. Although the point size is identical, the relative size of these three typefaces varies substantially, owing to differences in the *x* height. Relative size of a typeface influences its readability.

This line is spaced with en spaces.

This line is spaced with 4-to-the-em spaces.

This line is spaced with 5-to-the-em spaces.

Exhibit 16.13
Readability of type is also affected by word spacing. If words are spaced too widely, the line lacks coherence; but conversely they should not "hang at each other's tails." The space between sentences should be the same as the word space within that line.

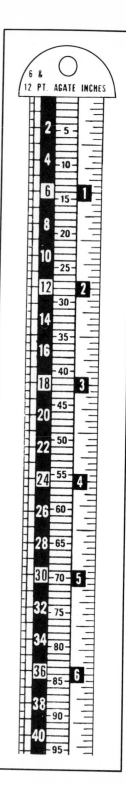

Exhibit 16.14
A pica ruler.

the capital letter M. The 12-point em (which is 12 points wide and 12 points deep) is also known as the *pica em.* An *en* is half of an em. You measure these items with the ruler shown in Exhibit 16.14.

When lines are all set to the same width, as they are on this page, they are said to be *justified.* When the lines are set to irregular, free-form widths (usually at the right) they are said to be *unjustified,* or *ragged*—a style often seen in print ads. The part opening pages of this book show type set ragged left and right. It is necessary to specify the width only once for all type in one block of copy to be set. This paragraph, for example, is set 28 picas wide.

Agate line. In newspaper advertising and in small-space magazine advertising the *depth of space* (height of the ad) is measured in terms of *agate lines,* of which there are 14 to a column inch, regardless of how wide a column is. Newspaper space is referred to as depth (agate lines) and width (number of columns): For "100 × 2" read "one hundred lines deep by two columns wide."

Line spacing. To increase the normal space between lines of metal type, a thin strip of lead, measured in points, was inserted between the lines, giving rise to the term *leading* for increasing line space in type. The term has spread to phototypesetting although measurements are also made from the base of one letter to the base of the letter below. Lines are leaded, as a rule, to make the type more readable. The extra space is usually specified as "10 pt. with 2-pt. leading" or "10 on 12," denoting 10-point type with 2-point leading. To summarize the foregoing material:

- ☐ *Height (size) of type* is expressed in *points,* 72 to the inch.
- ☐ *Width of a line of type* is measured in *picas,* 6 to the inch.
- ☐ *Depth of newspaper space* is measured in *agate lines* per column, 14 to the inch.

TYPE SPECIFICATIONS AND COPY
CASTING

The type of most national advertising is set by *advertising typographers,* firms that specialize in photo- or metal composition, but generally they do not print. Recently, some advertisers and advertising agencies have installed their own photographic display- or text-typesetting equipment.

Copy sent to a typographer or publication carries the type specifications marked on the typescript (Exhibit 16.15) and is usually accompanied by a rough or comprehensive layout.

Before the size of type can be chosen, the number of characters in the copy typescript must be determined (*cast off*). Published tables show how many characters of various typefaces and point sizes fit into different line widths. In advertising agencies type specifications and casting off might be handled by art directors, print-production personnel, or specialized *type directors.*

CLIENT   __METROPOLITAN LIFE__

PRODUCT   __PB-40889A__

MEDIA   __NATIONAL GEOGRAPHIC 9/7__

SIZE/
COLOR   __Page B/W non-bleed__

DATE   __6/18/7__   WRITER _____

YOUNG & RUBICAM INTERNATIONAL INC.

285 MADISON AVENUE • NEW YORK, NEW YORK 10017

*Headliners Neo Tribune Medium NM162N
3 lines flush left, 3 1/16" on wide line
set tight with line spacing as close as
ascenders and descenders permit.*

3/8" indent

Before they can even tell time,
they're always reminding you how
quickly it passes.

1 pica indents

If you're like most parents, you measure time
in outgrown sneakers and jackets.
    Children are a constant reminder of the
obvious: that time waits for no man, or woman, or wardrobe. And while you and your
family are racing toward the future, it helps
to take a moment to consider what it might be
like once you arrive. That's where Metropolitan Life can help.
    We think insurance should be more than
just security for your family. While one
third of all the money Metropolitan pays out
goes to beneficiaries, the other two thirds
goes to living policyholders. And that's
money you can use to help pay for your future.
    Take the time to listen when a Metropoli-
tan representative calls. We can help design
not just an insurance program for you, but a
secure future. And it's never too soon to begin.
    Because your Size-2 will soon be Size-4.
    Then a Size-6. Then a Size-8. Then...

*10/10 Plantin
VIP set on track 1
flush left
rag right
X 10 picas max
2 columns align
with logo and
headline, see
layout. 12 point
gutter.*

*METROPOLITAN
Where the future is now

*Pick up logo
shoot to 10 picas wide
align at base of right col.
See layout.*

122274/16ams

SELECTING THE TYPESETTING

PROCESS   There are three methods of setting type: by hand, which has mostly passed into history; by purely mechanical means, which are passing into history; and by photographic methods, which is now making history.

The hand-setting

method   Exhibit 16.16 is almost a collector's item, showing the hand-setting method used before machine typesetting was invented. The type was set by hand, letter by letter out of a "job case" (Exhibit 16.16*a*), assembled in a composing stick (Exhibit 16.16*b*), and then placed in a long tray or *galley* until the entire passage had been set. Then it was assembled into columns and pages. After the job was done, each letter had to be returned by hand to its cubicle. It is not hard to perceive the laboriousness of this operation. And this was the only way in which type was set from Gutenberg's day until mechanical typesetting came along in the nineteenth century.

Exhibit 16.16
(*a*) California job case; (*b*) composing stick. [From David Hymes, *Production in Advertising and Graphic Arts* (New York: Holt, 1966).]

Mechanical typesetting: the
Linotype

In 1886 Ottmar Mergenthaler invented a machine that not only set type but molded a whole line at one time. The *Linotype* made possible the mass production of books, newspapers, and magazines all over the world. A Linotype is operated by one person sitting at the keyboard of a machine. From a pot of molten metal attached to the machine the type is cast (Exhibit 16.17). Because Linotype is being displaced by phototypesetting—in fact, its manufacture has been discontinued in the United States—there is little point in describing the ingenious mechanism. But we must recognize the tremendous leap forward it gave to typesetting, helping the literacy of the world, the wealth of its publications, and the growth of advertising.

Phototypesetting

The development of equipment to set type photographically, having accelerated since the end of World War II, has made phototypesetting dominant in advertising. It is being further advanced by electronics and computer technology, a complex field; but those who are just beginning the study of print production enjoy the advantage of not being burdened and confused by all the limitations and problems of metal typesetting.

Phototypesetting has numerous advantages. Phototypesetting equipment, especially when computerized, works considerably faster than does metal typesetting machinery. It fits right in with all photoplatemaking processes. The image quality is excellent, and there is utmost flexibility in spacing and shaping (Exhibit 16.18) of letters and words. Display type (18 points and up) that requires fine optical spacing is usually set on *photodisplay* equipment. Text type (below 18 points) is usually set on *phototext* equipment. However, there are exceptions: Some of the phototypesetting machines normally used for phototext can set type as large as 72 points.

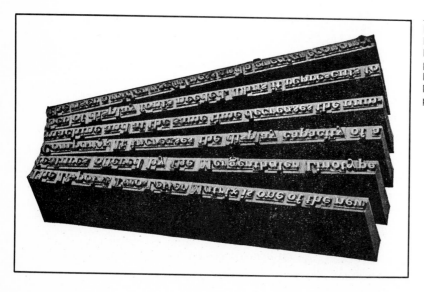

Exhibit 16.17
Linotype slugs. Easy to handle, but to correct one letter or punctuation mark, the whole line must be recast. (Courtesy of Mergenthaler Linotype Company.)

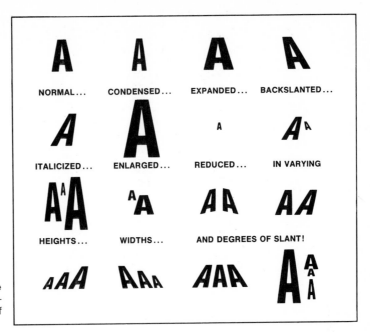

NORMAL... CONDENSED... EXPANDED... BACKSLANTED...

ITALICIZED... ENLARGED... REDUCED... IN VARYING

HEIGHTS... WIDTHS... AND DEGREES OF SLANT!

Exhibit 16.18
All of these were from the same letter *A,* but with different positioning of the lens. (Courtesy of Visual Graphics Corp.)

Principle of phototypesetting. Phototypesetting-machine systems consist of two units: a *keyboard* for input of the copy to be set into type, and a *photounit* for output of the copy so set. On a typewriterlike keyboard the operator produces a perforated paper tape (Exhibit 16.19*a*) or magnetic tape that contains the text and all typographic instruction codes. These tapes are loaded into a separate machine, the photounit. Exhibit 16.19*b* may help explain how everything works synchronously within the photounit.

Phototypesetting is a continually developing process. Advances such as the following are constantly being made. These are cited in an effort not to explain how they operate but to show the endless possibilities now unfolding.

Computerized composition. Some of the phototypesetting systems work with *counting keyboards.* Here the operator justifies the lines and tells the machine where to break lines and whether or not to hyphenate the last word.

Other systems operate from *noncounting keyboards,* which do not justify the lines. The text is keyboarded in continuous sequence. The resulting tape is subsequently run into a computer that can be either separate (*stand-alone*) or built into the photounit.

This computer, on the basis of rather complex *software* (that is, a program, as opposed to the machine itself, which is termed *hardware*), makes all line-end decisions and implements many other typographical instructions. Hyphenation programs can be based on logic (rules of grammar) or on dictionaries stored in the computer.

Exhibit 16.19

(*a*) Typical photocomposition perforated tape. It transmits copy and type instructions to photounit. (*b*) Operation of the photounit: 1 A high-intensity flash lamp that can be turned on instantly by signal from computer tape. 2 A spinning disk, with photographic negatives of an entire type font (or several fonts) around its rim [see (*c*)]. Any letter or other character on the disk can instantly be moved into the line of light from the lamp by instruction from the perforated tape. Some machines use negative font grids or film strips instead of disks, but the principle is the same. 3 A lens turret with different lenses or a single zoom lens that can be moved to set that font of type in different point sizes. No need to have a different font image master for each size. 4 On the far left, a prism moves along synchronously with the flash of light and casts the image onto film so that the letters are placed in position to form lines and blocks of type. The film stays still, but the letters move. 5 This is the film (or photosensitive paper) onto which the copy is exposed. The film is developed in a separate processor and can be used in making photoplates and photoprints for all major printing processes. (C. P. Palmer. Courtesy of E. I. duPont de Nemours & Company.) (*c*) A Fototronic spinning-type disk that contains two fonts of type, 120 characters each, 240 characters per disk. The characters can be exposed in any size from 5 points to 72 points. A punched paper tape signals the disk to spin to the required character, which is instantly photographed as positive on film or paper. The size is also determined by a punched-tape signal that selects the size of lens. The Fototronic photographic units each accommodate 5 disks and have output speeds of up to 150 newspaper equivalent lines per minute. The square holes on the disk are part of the computer code-signaling system. No light goes through them. The spinning-type disk is one kind of font image master used in phototypesetting machines. Others are rectangular grids or film strips. (Courtesy Tri-Arts Press, Inc.)

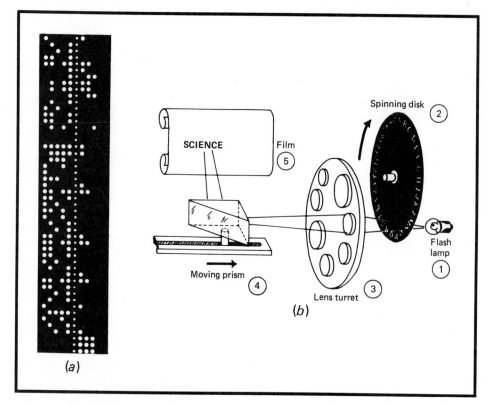

(*a*)

SCIENCE Film 5 Spinning disk 2 Flash lamp 1

Moving prism 4 Lens turret 3

(*b*)

(c)

Exhibit 16.19
(continued)

Computerized composition is particularly useful where identical (or nearly identical) text is utilized, especially for newspaper ads of different sizes. The computer can tell the photounit how to set in different point sizes and measures from a single unjustified tape. Airlines that advertise retail copy in newspapers often use the same basic ad in many cities, but change the text to reflect different schedules, fares, and reservation numbers. Their ad agencies use computerized composition to incorporate changes without respecifying the entire copy for each ad.

Optical character recognition (OCR). Electronic devices have been created to "read" typewritten copy. The typewriter faces used are stylized to facilitate their recognizability by the machine. These "reading machines" produce perforated paper tape of the text, which, via computer, can be used directly for phototypesetting, thus avoiding double keyboarding.

Cathode-ray-tube composition (CRT). The most advanced development in phototypesetting at this time is cathode-ray-tube composition, or laser technology. CRT machines can generate type characters at speeds of thousands or characters per second. Such composition is increasingly used for books and other publications and is also used in the advertising field.

CRT composition also permits the operator to "customize" the type spacing as the ad designer specifies. Many typefaces have visual peculiarities that make the absolutely even spacing of each letter undesirable. By *kerning* (overlapping) letters or customizing the space between them, an operator makes the type fit better than if it were left to the computer alone.

Video display terminals (VDT). When the copy has been set, it is presented in film form or photopaper setting. If corrections have to be pasted (stripped) into the original film or paper setting, they can be slow and costly; but VDT provides a quick method for making corrections in type set on film. It accepts previously keyboarded tapes and displays sizable blocks of text on a TV-like screen. The operator can insert corrections by tapping an attached keyboard. The terminal thereupon produces a new, clean, corrected tape. This tape is used for a quick resetting of the text.

This is not the time or place to elaborate on these technical developments. It is enough to know that such resources are available, along with others still on the drawing board.

Photoproofs. Most advertising phototypesetting is done on film rather than on photopaper, especially when multiple proofs are required. For proofreading, photoproofs—also called *submission,* or *reading proofs*—are usually made on sensitized paper, which is chemically developed.

MECHANICALS AND ARTWORK

After the copy fit has been checked and all corrections have been made, the type shop can make reproduction-quality photoproofs (*photorepros*). They can be used in making camera-ready, pasted up mechanicals, with copy all pasted in place.

Before an ad can be turned over to a photoplatemaker, the advertiser has to review the mechanical and artwork. The mechanical is the master from which the photoplatemaker works.

If a *photomechanical* (film makeup) has been made of photographically set type, illustrations may be positioned on a final photoproof of that mechanical. On a camera-ready mechanical there are several ways of showing the platemaker where the illustrations must be placed. Although artwork is usually prepared larger than printing size, a photoprint or photostat of the illustration, reduced to the proper size, can be pasted on the mechanical; or the illustration can merely be indicated by lines. Scaling (size indication) and cropping (shape indication) instructions can be given separately.

Exhibit 16.20
Line plate made from illustration with solid lines.

Besides the mechanical with all the type stripped or pasted in place, the photoplatemaker needs the actual artwork, unless a prescreened photoprint has been used in the mechanical. The artwork is usually prepared larger than printing size so that photographic reduction may help remove imperfections.

PHOTOPLATEMAKING

Typesetting is normally the first step in the production of an ad. The second step deals with the preparation of the artwork for the printing process. This is *photoplatemaking,* that is, producing a printing plate or other image carrier for publication printing. In offset and gravure films are normally sent to the publication printers, from which they will produce their own plates or cylinders. For letterpress printing, the advertiser will order *photoengravings* (combining photography and chemical engraving).

The two major forms of photoengraving are *line plates* and *halftone plates.* In offset and gravure photoplatemaking the basic principles are very similar.

Line plates (or line cuts)

The least costly form of photoengraving, these can be printed even on rough paper. How a message on a flat piece of paper can be converted into a printing block with the message standing out clearly for printing, like the letters on a rubber stamp, is indeed interesting. Typical results can be seen in Exhibit 16.20.

Line-tint plates. To give a line subject some variation in shades between different areas, the photoplatemaker can break up solid areas with screen (see the section on halftone plates, below) tints, for instance, 20 percent of black or 70 percent of black, providing variations in shading. The platemaker can also take a clearly defined blank area on the artwork and, in the film-stripping stage, lay over it a pattern of geometric or irregular lines and dots—often used in making subdivisions of a chart. Such plates are referred to as *line-tint plates* (see Exhibit 16.21).

Line color plates. To produce line plates in two, three, or more flat colors, the artwork itself need not be colored. Each extra color is marked on a separate tissue or acetate overlay on the base art. The platemaker then makes a separate plate for each color. Line color plates provide a comparatively inexpensive method of printing in color with effective results.

Exhibit 16.21
(*a*) Line drawing, (*b*) a selection of tint patterns, (*c*) line drawing with tint laid in.

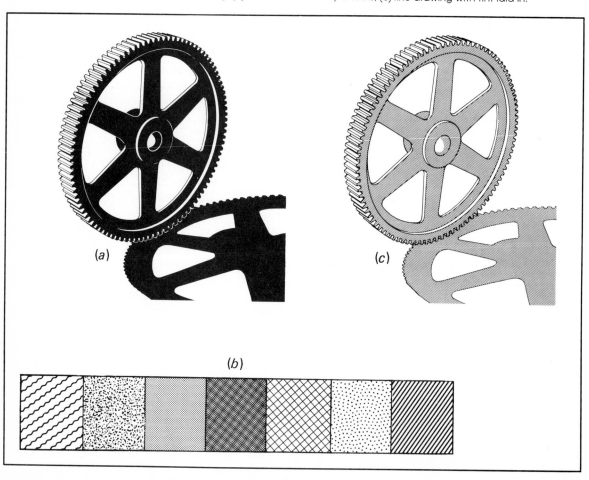

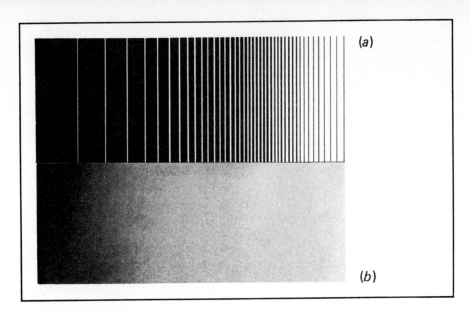

(a)

(b)

Exhibit 16.22
(*a*) Line copy; (*b*) halftone copy.

Halftone plates

Unlike a line drawing, a photograph or painting is a continuous blend of many tones from pure black to pure white. Such illustrations are therefore called *continuous-tone artwork* (Exhibit 16.22). The plates used for them are called *halftone plates*.

How can these various tones of gray be converted into a printable form? The secret lies in a *screen* that breaks up the continuous-tone artwork into dots. These dots are formed on the negative during the camera exposure when a glass or acetate contact screen is inserted between negative and artwork. These screens bear a crosshatch of 50 to 150 or more hairlines per square inch, forming thousands of little windows through which light can pass (Exhibit 16.23).

When you look through a screened window, you are aware for the moment of the screen; but soon the brain adjusts, and you become oblivious to the screen. A camera, however, records exactly what it sees through each of those windows; and what it sees is so tiny that only a dot can come through, varying in size with the blackness of the part of the picture it is seeing. Where the picture is dark, the dots are big and seem close to each other; where it is light, the dots are small. The eye sweeps over the picture and sees a whole photograph.

After photography, the picture, in the form of dots, is printed on a metallic plate, and just like a line plate, it is washed with a preparation that makes the dots acid-resistant. The letterpress plate is splashed with acid that eats away the metal except for the dots, and before long the dots stand out in relief. When a roller of ink is passed over them and paper applied, the ink on top of the dots is transferred to the paper, producing a replica of the original picture. Offset and gravure plates are prepared from the "dotted" copy in the appropriate way for those printing processes (see below).

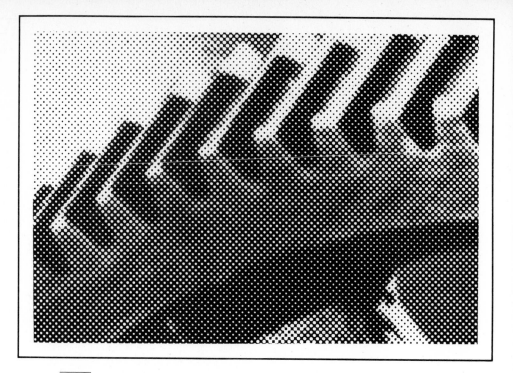

Exhibit 16.23
Magnification of a halftone plate, showing light and dark portions of the photographic copy reproduced as dots of different sizes. Lighter dots are freestanding; but at about the 50-percent value (half black, half white) the dots begin to connect. The centers of the dots are equidistant from each other.

Screens come in a variety of standard sizes so that one chooses the size of dots that will reproduce best on the paper to be used, depending on its smoothness or roughness. The screens most frequently used are 55, 65, 85, 100, 110, 120, and 133 lines each way per inch. The higher the screen number, the more dots per square inch, and the greater the fidelity and detail in the final reproduction (Exhibit 16.24). But the higher the screen, the smoother the paper has to be to have all the dots strike it. That is why newspapers often use a 65-line screen; magazines, a 120-line screen.

The halftone finish. If you want to make a halftone of a photograph of a face, the platemaker can treat the background in a number of ways; that treatment is called its *finish* (Exhibit 16.25). All background can be retained, with the background screen extending to the edge of the rectangular plate. This is called a *square halftone* even if the background is trimmed to some other shape. Or the photoplatemaker can cut away everything in the background, so that the face will appear sharply against the white background of the paper. This is called a *silhouette,* or *outline, halftone,* best for most purposes where the background is not an important feature. In a *vignette* finish the dots fade into the background. This is good but needs very smooth paper.

Combination plates combine continuous-tone and line artwork in the same plate. If, however, you want to print a line subject (such as a black headline) directly across the face of a continuous-tone subject (such as a photo-

PROGRESSIVE STEPS IN FOUR-COLOR PROCESS PRINTING _____

Four plates (yellow, red, blue, and black) combine to produce the desired colors and contrasts.

Yellow

Red

Yellow and Blue

Yellow, Red and Blue

Yellow and Red

Blue

Black

Yellow, Red, Blue and Black

All Colors and Type.

Exhibit 16.24
Halftone screens: (left to right) 65, 110, and 165 lines per inch. The lower the screen ruling, the fewer dots per square inch. The higher the screen ruling, the more dots per square inch. The choice of screen depends on the requirement of a publication, smoothness of the paper, and the amount of detail required.

Exhibit 16.25
(a) Square halftone (background included); (b) silhouette halftone (background omitted).

graph), that is a *surprint*. If the line is to print in white, it is called a *dropout*. If you have a halftone subject on which you want to make frequent changes (such as a change in price) in one place, you actually cut a hole in the plate to make room for that change. That is called a *mortise*.

Two-color halftone plates. A two-color reproduction can be made from monochromatic artwork in one of two ways: a screen tint in a second color can be printed over (or under) a black halftone; the artwork can be photographed twice, changing the screen angle the second time, so that the dots of the second color plate fall between those for the first plate. This plate is called a *duotone*. It can produce a rich effect.

Four-color process printing. The finest reproduction of a color print or painting is by means of a set of four color plates: red, yellow, and blue—which in various combinations produce every color—plus black, which is needed for delineation and contrast. The photoplatemaker photographs (*separates*) the original artwork through filters of different colors, resulting in four negative films. Although these *separation films* are black and white, one of them records all the red; another one, all the yellow; and a third, all the blue portions of the original. A fourth film records shades of black to provide contrast and depth in the shadow portions of the picture.

The four separation films are subsequently screened in order to be reproduced as halftones. From each of the screened films a separate halftone plate is made. When these halftone plates are inked in the corresponding process inks and printed onto paper, a full-color reproduction of the original picture results.

The screen is angled differently for each color so that the dots print side by side, not on top of each other. Thus the colors are not created by *physical* mixing of the printing inks but by an *optical* effect similar to the painting techniques of the nineteenth-century French pointillist painters.

The photoplatemaker will pull a separate proof of each color plate, combinations of two colors and of three colors, and finally a combination of all four colors. These proofs are assembled as a set of *progressive proofs* and sent to the printer together with the set of plates. The "progressives," or "progs," thus serve as a guide in four-color printing (see color insert following p. 398).

OFFSET AND GRAVURE PHOTOPLATEMAKING

Contrary to letterpress publication printing, in which the plate has to be furnished by the advertiser or agency, offset and gravure publications require only films because they can produce their own offset plates or gravure cylinders.

If an agency wishes to retain complete control over the preparatory steps, it usually sends to its own supplier the mechanical and artwork to prepare for the printer. This can be an *offset separation house,* a *gravure service house,* or a *photoengraver* who has branched out into the offset- and gravure-preparatory fields and thus has truly become a photoplatemaker for all major printing processes. Such combination plants are particularly important when media lists contain publications that print by means of different printing processes. Photoengravings as well as separation films for offset and gravure can be made simultaneously in one plant from a single piece of artwork and a single mechanical.

The photographic preparatory steps in the three major printing processes resemble each other closely. In offset and gravure the photoplatemaker produces plates merely for proofing purposes. These plates are not shown to the publications; only the final, corrected films are sent, with proofs and progs pulled from these plates. In letterpress printing actual plates are sent.

Conversions   In order to save time and expense, it is sometimes desirable to convert material from one printing process to another. This can be done by most photoplatemakers.

MAKING DUPLICATE
MATERIAL   It is rather rare for a print ad to run in a single publication. Frequently, advertisers have different publications on their schedules, or they want to issue reprints of their ads or send material to dealers for cooperative advertising. There are various means of producing duplicate material of magazine or newspaper ads.

Duplicate material for magazine
advertisements   If a magazine ad for letterpress has to be duplicated, two methods can be employed: An *electrotype* can be produced, which is a molded, electrolytically formed relief plate bearing an exact duplicate of the original plate; *DuPont Cronapress plates* (called *Cronars*) can be made with DuPont Cronapress film, a pressure-sensitive material onto which an impression of the original plate is made and which is subsequently turned into a negative film from which duplicate halftone plates can be produced, reflecting exactly what was contained in the original.

Duplicate material for offset publications can consist of repro proofs or *3M Scotchprints* (a plasticized repro proofing material) pulled with ink from the original letterpress photoengravings. Or duplicate films can be made from an original mechanical and artwork. For gravure magazines or Sunday supplements duplicate positive films are usually supplied. For black-and-white offset or gravure ads, photographic prints are often substituted for films.

Duplicate material for newspaper
advertisements   There was a time, not so long ago, when almost all daily newspapers were printed by letterpress. Duplicate material prepared for national newspaper campaigns usually consisted of *mats*. The mat was made by pressing a letterpress plate into papier-mâché. When dried, the papier-mâché formed a hard matrix. At the newspaper, molten lead was poured into the

Table 16-1

PRODUCTION SCHEDULE	
WORK	DATE
In order to reach publications by closing date	October 1
Duplicate material must be shipped by	September 28
Duplicate material making must be started by	September 24
Photoplatemaker should deliver final proof by	September 21
Photoplatemaker should have first proof by	September 12
Material should go to photoplatemaker by	August 27
Retouched art and mechanical should be ready by	August 24
Type and mechanical should be ordered on	August 18
Finished artwork (photograph) should be delivered by	August 17
Finished artwork (photograph) should be ordered by	August 9
Creative work (layout and copy) should be approved by	August 6
Creative work should start by	July 26

mat, forming a replica of the original plate and called a *stereotype,* or *stereo.* The use of mats has dwindled because of the decline in letterpress printing of newspapers.

Material for ad insertions in offset or phototype and letterpress newspapers can take on various forms. If an original photoengraving of a newspaper ad is available, inexpensive reproduction proofs can be pulled and sent to the newspapers. If the list contains no metal-composition and letterpress newspapers, the advertiser may choose to prepare the ad photographically. A film master is produced. This serves for the quantity production of photoprints (*screened prints,* or *Veloxes*) or of contact film negatives. Proofs are pulled via an offset plate. Usually photoprints or reproduction proofs are preferred for partial-page ads; film is often requested for full-page insertions and ROP (*run-of-paper*) color ads in newspapers.

The Wall Street Journal uses a unique and new transmission system. A facsimile of each page of this newspaper is relayed by satellite to a reception station, where it is recorded on page-sized photofilm. The film is then used to make lithographic plates, which are placed on presses to reproduce the newspaper in the usual way. The *Journal* has been using this process for several years. It permits the paper to have five different regional editions and utilize the main news items directly from the headquarters plant while allowing for variations in advertising content within each regional edition.

PRODUCTION PLANNING AND SCHEDULING

In order that the creative and the production work may move with the necessary precision, a time schedule is planned at the outset. The *closing date* is the date or time when all material must arrive at the publication. Then the advertiser works backward along the calendar to determine when the work must be begun in order to meet that date.

Let us take a four-color ad to appear in several magazines for which the closing date is October 1. We must plan a production schedule like Table 16.1 (note that *calendar* days are not always *working* days) and Exhibit 16.26.

YOUNG & RUBICAM INTERNATIONAL INC.　　JOB PRODUCTION ORDER/SCHEDULE — **PRINT**　　S3 Rev. 6/74

	DISTRIBUTION	
Client	Name	Function
Product		Account Supervisor
Job #		Account Executive
Subject		Assoc. Creative Dir.
Description		Art Director
		Copywriter
		Art Buyer
		Print Producer

Title (Max. 22 characters)

EVENTS/ITEMS	DUE FROM	DATE	NOTES
Briefing Meeting			
Layout & Copy Due			
Layout & Copy Approved by Client			
Estimate Request Prepared			
Estimate Due			
Art Bids Due			
Type Due			
Art Due			
Final Art & Mechanical Due			
Art & Mechanical Approved by Client			
First Proof Due at Y&R			
Final Proof Approved by Client			
All (Duplicate) Materials Ready to Ship			
Materials Due at First Publication			

PUBLICATION	ISSUE	SPACE	SIZE	4/C B/W	N/B BLD.	PUBLICATION	ISSUE	SPACE	SIZE	4/C B/W	N/B BLD.

Job Quote $	Job Billing Requirements		Antic. Mo. 1st Use (Impact)	Antic. Exp. Date
Prepared by: PRODUCTION COORDINATOR		Date	Authorized by: ACCOUNT MANAGEMENT AUTHORITY	Date

Exhibit 16.26
A schedule. Note the number of steps involved. (Courtesy of Young & Rubicam Inc.)

SUMMARY

It may be helpful to review some of the more important technical terms we have encountered in this chapter. We discussed three major printing processes: *letterpress* (from raised surface), *offset lithography* (from flat surface), and *gravure* (from depressed surface). The form of printing affects the way material is prepared for publication.

Typography deals with the style (or face) of type and the way in which the copy of set. *Typefaces* come in related designs called *families*. The size of type is specified in *points* (72 to the inch). The width of the line in which type is to be set is measured in *picas* (6 to the inch). The depth of newspaper space is measured in (agate) *lines* (14 to the column inch), regardless of the width of the column, which varies from paper to paper.

The chief methods of typesetting are: *metal typesetting* (usually by Linotype, which is cast one line at a time) and *phototypesetting* (type set photographically or electronically onto light-sensitive paper or film). Most phototypesetting is computerized.

If you plan to run ads in letterpress publications, you will have to order *photoengravings*. The two classes are *line plates* (for type and all-line artwork) and *halftones* (for continuous-tone artwork). The *screen* you specify for halftones depends on the smoothness of the printing paper's surface. The smoother the paper, the higher the screen ruling (expressed in lines per inch). You also have to specify the background finish: *square* (includes everything), *outline* or *silhouette* (everything cut away except the subject itself), or *vignette* (dots fading into the background). Vignettes are not good for newspapers.

For a full-color ad you have to order *separations* and a set of plates to be printed in the four *process inks*. For letterpress ads plates are sent to the publications; for gravure and offset lithography films are supplied, with plates made by the photoplatemaker only for proofing purposes. Material for color ads is usually accompanied by *progressive proofs*. Both offset and gravure publications frequently also accept artwork and mechanicals.

Letterpress magazines can be sent *electrotypes* or *Cronar plates*. Duplicate material for offset publications can consist of *repro proofs, 3M Scotchprints, photoprints* (Veloxes or screened prints), or *films*. Gravure publications almost invariably require *film positives*.

In all print-production work a most important element is timing.

In publication printing, which is the kind of printing that concerns most advertisers, the publisher is responsible for supplying the paper and doing the printing. But in direct-mail advertising and other forms of nonpublication advertising, as we have discussed in Chapter 11, the advertiser has to pick the printer, buy the paper, and follow up the entire production job.

QUESTIONS

1. Identify and describe the three major printing processes.
2. What are the chief things to strive for in typography?
3. Why is the choice of a typeface so important?

4. What are four basic styles of typefaces?

5. When do you measure by points? How many to the inch? When do you measure by picas? How many to the inch?

6. How is the depth of newspaper space measured?

7. Explain the factors that influence the readability of typography.

8. Discuss the two chief methods of typesetting.

9. Describe the differences in the use of line plates and halftone plates.

10. What is the principle used in the making of four-color process plates?

11. Explain the importance of production planning and scheduling. Why is timing so critical?

12. What is meant by the following terms?
    a. relief printing
    b. offset printing
    c. rotogravure
    d. screen printing
    e. typeface
    f. serif
    g. point
    h. pica
    i. em
    j. agate line
    k. leading
    l. font
    m. type family
    n. character (as used in measuring type)
    o. galley
    p. composing stick
    q. Linotype
    r. phototypesetting
    s. justified lines
    t. photoproofs
    u. mechanical
    v. photoengraving
    w. tint plates
    x. progressive proofs
    y. photoprints
    z. publication closing date

READINGS

"Blair Graphic Report," (continuing series, published by The Blair Graphics Companies).

GRAHAM, WALTER B.: "Why Precision Lap Register is Critical; Using Register Marks," *Printing Impressions,* March 1981, p. 22.

HANSSENS, DOMINIQUE M., and BARTON A. WEITZ: "The Effectiveness of Industrial Print Advertisements Across Product Categories," *Journal of Marketing Research,* August 1980, pp. 294–306.

NELSON, ROY PAUL: *The Design of Advertising* (Dubuque, Iowa: William C. Brown, 1981).

RUGGLES, PHILIP KENT: "Estimating Time and Cost for a 16-page Booklet," *Printing Impressions,* February 1981, pp. 14–15.

SCHLEMMER, RICHARD M.: *Handbook of Advertising Art Production,* 2nd ed. (Englewood Cliffs, N.J.: Prentice-Hall, Inc., 1976).

TURNBULL, ARTHUR T., and RUSSELL N. BAIRD: *The Graphics of Communication,* 4th ed. (New York: Holt, Rinehart and Winston, 1980).

Typography 2, Annual of the Type Directors Club (Washington, D.C.: Print, 1981).

17

The Television
Commercial

Unlike print ads, a TV commercial enters the homes of prospective buyers and comes alive with sound, motion, people, and the unique ability to demonstrate. A whole new array of techniques is available to you when you write a TV commercial. More people turn at one time to TV than to any other medium (over 65 million people have watched a bowl game). In the average home, the TV set is on 6 hours and 42 minutes a day.* Obviously TV's advertising opportunities are great—but so are its challenges. Your commercial must compete for the viewer's attention not only with the commercials of similar products and services but with all the other commercials attempting to exhort the viewer to some kind of action. In addition, the commercial has to compete with countless short messages of upcoming programs, called *promos,* or *promotions.* Amidst this *clutter,* as promos are also termed, your commercial may well run sandwiched among as many as five other commercials.

The competition for viewers' attention, the short time available to gain this attention (usually 30 seconds), and the tremendous cost of producing and airing TV commercials make creativity a must. The following chapter discusses how to increase the odds of making a commercial that sells.

1979 Broadcast Year Book.

CREATING THE TELEVISION
COMMERCIAL

A TV commercial contains two parts: the audio, made up of spoken words, music, and other sounds, and the video, the part you see on the TV screen. Since there are two parts, you usually begin thinking about creating the commercial with words and pictures simultaneously.

Visual
techniques

Fortunately for the creative person, whether or not a beginning copywriter, a whole gamut of successful visual techniques has been gathered and categorized. These provide a fine reservoir from which to draw in creating your own original commercial.

Spokesperson. An announcer, or "presenter," stands before the camera and delivers your copy directly to the viewer, as a salesperson might do in a store. Displaying and perhaps demonstrating the product, the speaker may appear in *limbo* (plain white background with no set), in a living room, kitchen, or other room of a home, or in a factory, out of doors, or in any surroundings relevant to your product and product story. The problem is to cast your announcer, to choose someone who is likable and believable but not so slick that attention is called to the person instead of to the product.

Testimonial. In a testimonial, selling is attempted by a well-known personality, either an authority on the type of product being advertised or a famous name in another field, such as acting, with a large and loyal following. But the product should be one on which he or she is qualified to speak. In selling a food, the person may be famous for recipes or nutrition. A sports personality's personal experience may enable him to persuade viewers to buy anything from razor blades to beer but not qualify him to give testimony for a medical product. Even people who are unknown can give testimonials, as long as they are credible and viewers can identify with them.

Demonstration. TV is ideal for demonstrating the advantages of a product. A cleanser removing stubborn stains, a refrigerator's new shelf arrangement, and a rent-a-car company's speed in getting the customer into a car—all happen before the viewer's eyes. A word of warning, however: Legally, the demonstration must correspond to actual usage.

Closeups. TV is the medium of closeups. You may want to move in closely to depict a demonstration of your product and to show people reacting favorably to the demonstration. A fast-food outlet may use closeups to show appetizing shots of its frankfurters as they are grilled or served. With this technique the audio is generally delivered off screen; such a *voice-over* costs less than a presentation by someone on the screen.

Slice of life. This approach is based on a dramatic formula: Predicament + solution = happiness. A typical, true-to-life situation is dramatized in the hope of involving the viewer to the point of thinking, "I can see myself in that scene." Since problem solving is a useful format in almost any commercial, slice of life is widely used: *A* meets *B, B* has a problem; *A* has a solution: Buy the product. Next scene: grateful *B* reports success. This is such a popular format that special skill is needed to achieve variety in the setting and presentation of the problem.

Story line. A story-line commercial is similar to a miniature movie episode except that narration is done off screen. A typical video may show a family in the driveway, hoping to leave for vacation but unable to fit all the gear into the automobile. Camera then shifts to the family next door, also leaving on vacation but able to pack everything and everybody into their new station wagon. During these scenes the announcer explains the advantages of the roomy wagon.

Customer interview. Most people who appear in TV commercials are professional actors, but customer interviews also involve nonprofessionals. An interviewer or off-screen voice may ask a housewife, who is usually identified by name, to compare the advertised kitchen cleanser with her own brand by removing two identical spots in her sink. She finds that the advertised product does a better job.

Vignettes and situations. Advertisers of soft drinks, beers, candy, and other lower-priced products find this technique useful in creating excitement and motivation. A fast-paced series of scenes shows people enjoying the product as they enjoy life. Audio over these scenes is often a lively jingle with lyrics based on the situations we see and the satisfaction the product offers.

Direct product comparison. Do you remember "Brand *X*," the product that was never so good as the advertised brand? Well, Brand *X* has gone out of style. Now the trend is to show competitive named products in direct demonstration with your own. Of course your product comes out better. There are two problems with direct product comparisons, however: In case of a lawsuit by a competitor, you must be prepared to prove in court that your product is significantly superior, as stated; second, you must be credible in the way you make your claim, or the commercial may have a reverse effect on your audience.

Still photographs and artwork. Using closeup photography of still photographs and artwork, including cartoon drawings and lettering, you can structure a highly illustrative, well-paced commercial. Supplied at modest cost, the required material may already exist, or it can be shot in candid style or be drawn specifically for your use. Deft use of the camera can give otherwise static visual material a surprising amount of movement. Either zoom lenses, which provide an inward or outward motion, or *panning* the camera across the photographs or artwork gives the commercial motion (panning means changing the viewpoint of the camera without moving the dolly it stands on).

Humor. Combined with practical salesmanship, humor can be effective in a sales message. The challenge is to make the humorous copy relevant to the promise of benefit and not allow it to stray off the copy line. Handled in this manner, humor can convey a serious message. The test is whether people remember the product, not just the humor.

Animation. As opposed to "live action," the use of real people and objects, animation consists of artists' inanimate drawings, which are photographed on motion-picture film one frame at a time and brought to life with apparent movement as the film is projected. Most common is the cartoon. A favorite among children but popular with all ages, the cartoon is capable of creating a warm, friendly atmosphere both for product and message. Animation can also be used to simplify technical product demonstrations. In a razor commercial the actual product may be shown as it shaves a man's face, and an animated sequence may then explain how the blades of the razor remove whisker after whisker. How much animation costs depend upon how elaborate the style. If there is limited movement, few characters, and few or no backgrounds, the price can be low. On the other hand, the Disney style of animation, with many characters and detailed and colorful backgrounds, is much more costly.

Stop motion. When a package or other object is photographed in a series of different positions, movement can be simulated as the single frames are projected in sequence. Stop motion is like artwork photographed in animation. With it the package can "walk," "dance," and move as if it had come to life.

Rotoscope. In the rotoscope technique animated and live action sequences are produced separately and then optically combined. A live boy may be eating breakfast food while a cartoon-animal trademark character jumps up and down on his shoulder and speaks to him.

Combination. Most commercials combine techniques. A speaker may begin and conclude the message, but there will be closeups in between. In fact virtually every commercial should contain at least one or two closeups to show package and logo. Humor is adaptable to most other techniques. Animation and live action make an effective mixture in many commercials, and side-by-side comparisons may be combined with almost any other technique.

Which technique to
select

With such a rich variety of techniques available, you might find it difficult to decide which to use. Answering the following questions may help:

- [ ] Does your promise of benefit and supporting evidence suggest a particular technique? Do you intend to demonstrate your product? Could it win in a side-by-side comparison with other brands? Is any of your copy based on reports of satisfied users? Is your sales story simple and direct enough to warrant the personal touch a speaker may provide?
- [ ] What techniques are your competitors using? Although no law prevents you from following their lead, you may want to choose a different direction in order to give your product its own TV image.
- [ ] From previous advertising has your product or service established a special personality that may suggest continuing a technique?
- [ ] Do consumer attitudes discovered in research interviews suggest any problems to be met or any special advantages to be stressed for your product?
- [ ] Does your campaign already exist in print ads? If so, you will probably want your TV effort to bear a visual resemblance. Often the reverse is true. Many print techniques follow the lead set by TV commercials.
- [ ] How much money is available for production of your commercial? If your budget is modest, you will want to give serious thought to closeups, artwork, simple sets, or locations with a minimum of personnel.
- [ ] What production facilities are available? If you plan to produce your commercial in a large city, facilities will probably be at hand. Otherwise, the nearest TV station or a free-lance film maker may be your best choice.
- [ ] What techniques are used in other commercials? Make it your practice to view TV often and to analyze techniques. This will sharpen your own familiarity with the subject, and you may see techniques that suggest new directions for your product.

Writing the
script

Writing the TV commercial is very different from writing print advertising. First, you must use simple, easy-to-pronounce, easy-to-remember words. And you must be brief. The 30-second commercial has only 28 seconds of audio. In 28 seconds you must solve your prime prospect's problem by demonstrating your product's superiority. If the product is too big to show in use, be certain to show the logo or company name at least twice during the commercial.

Think of words and pictures simultaneously. Usually you divide your paper into two columns. On the left you describe the video action and on the right you write the audio portion, including sound effects and music. Corresponding video and audio elements go right next to each other, panel by panel. In some agencies specially designed sheets of paper, 8½ by 11 inches, are used with boxes down the center for rough sketches of the video portion. These are called "teeny boards" (see Exhibit 17.1).

Write copy in a friendly, conversational style. If you use an off-camera announcer, make certain his dialogue is keyed to the scenes in your video por-

TV Script

Client **DELTA AIR LINES**	City **ATL**		Spot No. **1314**
Date **2/10/82**	Job No. **D-2-9821-9**	Type	Length **:30**
This Spot effective **Feb. 22**	It replaces **1304**	Remarks **"COMING THROUGH"**	

JET FLYING

(MUSIC UNDER)

Delta's coming through

with unbeatable fares

for you.

Unbeatable fares to

STATUE OF LIBERTY

New York...

SUPER: NEW YORK

CHICAGO BUILDING

Unbeatable fares to

SUPER: CHICAGO

Chicago...

Exhibit 17.1
Teeny board now in use in most agencies measures 8½ by 11 inches, fits into folders easily, and copies readily for multiple presentations. (Courtesy of BBDO.)

412

WILD HORSES

To the wide open spaces

SUPER: DALLAS/FT.WORTH
      HOUSTON
      SAN ANTONIO
      AUSTIN

of Texas. And the

SKIERS

Denver Rockies.

SUPER: DENVER

We'll match the domestic
fare on nonstop or single
plane jet service of any
major airline...

JET

SUPER: DISCOUNT SEATS
LIMITED.
CHECK FOR REQUIREMENTS.

on comparable Delta flights...
under the same travel
restrictions.
(MUSIC OUT).

JET

SUPER: UNBEATABLE DELTA
IS READY WHEN YOU ARE.

(JET SFX)
Unbeatable Delta is ready
when you are.

Exhibit 17.1
(continued)

tion. It is not always possible, but matching the audio with the video makes the commercial cohesive and more effective.

Here are some hints for writing the audio portion of your script:

☐ Dedicate your efforts to conveying one basic idea; avoid running in fringe benefits.

☐ Be certain that your words as well as your pictures emphasize your *promise of benefit.* State it, support it, and, if possible, demonstrate it. Repeat your basic promise near the end of the commercial; that is the story you want viewers to carry away with them.

☐ Use short, everyday words.

☐ Read the audio aloud to catch any tongue twisters.

☐ Your audio and corresponding video should relate. Don't talk about one point while demonstrating another.

☐ Don't waste words by describing what is obvious in the picture. Make the words interpret the picture and thereby advance the thought.

To help you visualize your TV commercial at the same time you are writing your copy, these suggestions may be helpful:

☐ Regardless of technique, avoid static scenes. Some type of movement, either within the scene itself or toward or away from the camera, adds interest.

☐ Don't cram the commercial with too many scenes; the viewer may become confused. The only exception is the quick-vignette technique, in which quick changes of active scenes are meant to give a total impression of excitement.

☐ Be sure transitions are smooth from scene to scene. Conceiving your commercial as a flowing progression of scenes makes it easier to help the viewer follow it.

☐ Avoid long shots with the camera distant from the subject. Even the largest TV screens are too small to capture far-off action.

☐ Be sure that backgrounds of your scenes are kept simple and uncluttered. They should point up, rather than detract from, your subject matter.

☐ Try, if possible, to show the brand name. If it is prominent, give a shot of the package; otherwise flash its logotype.

☐ In writing your video description, describe the scene and action as completely as possible. "Open on man and wife in living room" is not enough. Indicate where each is placed, whether they are standing or sitting, and generally how the room is furnished.

The audio—words, sound effects, or music—in a script is as important as the video portion. They both must work together to bring the viewer the message. You need strong copy *and* sound *and* strong visuals. All are vital for an effective commercial.

CREATIVE TEAM AND
WORK
The creative team conceiving the commercial is usually made up of two people—the writer and art director. In some cases the producer is included. After all the elements of the commercial have been agreed upon, the art director actually draws a story board or a teeny board. The visual highlights of the video portion are drawn scene by scene.

Story-board sketches need involve little more than placement of elements such as people and objects within their respective scenes; they need not attempt to show minute detail of backgrounds.

The story board is the key element around which all activity takes place. It serves as a master visualization of the video and audio makeup of the commercial. Account executives and creative management can get a good idea of what is being proposed, and they can approve or make policy corrections. The client sees what the commercial will be. Upon client approval the story board goes into production.

PRODUCING THE TELEVISION
COMMERCIAL
The task of converting the story board or script into a commercial that is ready to appear on the air (see Exhibit 17.2) is the province of TV production. In complete charge of production is the producer, who must combine the talents of a creator, coordinator, diplomat, watchdog, and businessperson. Some producers are on the staffs of large agencies or advertisers. Many work on a free-lance basis, subject to call when needed. The work of the producer is so all-embracing that the best way to describe it is to live through the production of an entire commercial. Let's do that now and pick up the details of the producer's job later in the section headed "Role of the Producer."

Elements of production

At the outset it is helpful to think of production as a two-part process: *shooting* and *editing*. Shooting encompasses the work of filming or videotaping all scenes in the commercial. In fact several "takes" are made of each scene. Sometimes even scenes that may be promising but later deemed unnecessary are shot as well.

Editing, also known as *completion* or *finishing* or *postproduction,* includes selecting scenes that have been shot, arranging them in their proper order, inserting transitional effects, adding titles, combining sound with picture, and delivering the finished commercial. We shall elaborate on all these aspects of editing. Let's begin with the problems of shooting the film, for which a director is appointed by the producer.

The director's function. As the key person in the shooting, the director takes part in casting and directing the talent, directs the cameraman in composing each picture, assumes responsibility for the settings, and puts the whole show together. Before selecting a studio, the agency* finds out which director is available. The director may even be the owner of the studio. Because studios all provide basically the same equipment, the director is more important than the studio.

---

*Usually the agency is the originating point of the creation and production of the commercial. Some large advertisers, however, have their own production operations. Often free-lance producers are then hired for a series of commercials.

1. ANNCR. (MUSIC UNDER): Delta's coming thru with

2. unbeatable fares for you.

3. Unbeatable fares to

4. New York.

5. Unbeatable fares to

6. Chicago.

7. To the

8. Wide open spaces of Texas.

9. And the

10. Denver Rockies. We'll match the domestic fare on nonstop

11. or single plane jet service of any major airline on comparable Delta flights,

12. under the same travel restrictions. Unbeatable Delta is ready when you are.

Exhibit 17.2
Photoscript of the commercial planned in Exhibit 17.1. (Courtesy BBDO.)

Exhibit 17.3a
Concept boards are often used in place of story boards when the commercial has a great deal of action with quick cuts to various cast members in different scenes. The example above is a lacrosse sports-oriented concept board for Pepsi-Cola. The following page shows the completed commercial. (Courtesy Pepsi-Co Co.)

BBDO

Batten, Barton, Durstine & Osborn, Inc.

Client: PEPSI-COLA	Time: 30 SECONDS
Product: PEPSI-COLA	Title: "LACROSSE"	Comml. No.: PEPX 0063

SINGERS: You're the Pepsi Generation.

The spirit of today.

And with every taste of life that's new

Well that Pepsi Spirit

shines right

through.

Catch that Pepsi Spirit.

Drink it in. Drink it in. Drink it in.

Catch that

Pepsi Spirit.

Drink it in.

Drink it in. Drink it in.

Exhibit 17.3b

Shooting on film. Most commercials are shot on film, the oldest form of presenting motion pictures. Although the film of finest quality is 35-millimeter (35mm) film, it is expensive. Less costly is 16mm film, used by most local and some national advertisers. Originally there was a great difference in quality between the 35mm and the 16mm films, but the 16mm film has improved so much that today it's difficult to distinguish between the two.

Unless the action is simple and continuous from beginning to end, the film commercial is generally shot "out of sequence." All indoor scenes (Exhibit 17.4*a*) are shot as a group, regardless of their order within the final commercial, and closeups are also generally filmed together, as are outdoor shots (Exhibit 17.4*b*). They will all be put in place by the editor.

Generally a scene is shot more than once because the first time or two the performances may be unsatisfactory. Even after the director gets an acceptable "take," one more shot may be made for protection. In a normal day's shooting the film camera may expose from 2,000 to 3,000 feet of 35mm film (45 feet will be used in the final 30-second commercial) or 800 to 1,200 feet of 16mm film (18 feet will be used in the 30-second commercial).

Other elements of the commercial

Opticals. Since most commercials contain more than a single scene, optical devices or effects between scenes are necessary to provide smooth visual continuity from scene to scene. These are inserted during the final editing stage. Among the most common are:

☐ *Cut:* One scene simply abuts the next.

☐ *Dissolve:* An overlapping effect; one scene fades out, and the following scene simultaneously fades in.

☐ *Wipe:* The new scene literally "wipes" off the previous scene from top or bottom or side to side or by means of a geometric pattern.

☐ *Matte:* Part of one scene is placed over another so that the same narrator, for example, may be shown in front of different backgrounds; lettering of slogans or product names can be matted, or superimposed, over another scene.

☐ *Zoom:* A smooth, sometimes rapid move from a long shot to a closeup or from a closeup to a long shot.

Sound track. The audio portion of the commercial may be recorded either during the film or videotape shooting or at an earlier or later time in a recording studio. When the sound track is recorded during the shooting, the actual voices of people speaking on camera are used in the commercial. If the sound track is recorded in advance, the film or videotape scenes can be shot to fit the copy points as they occur; or if music is part of the track, visual action can be matched to a specific beat. If shooting and editing take place before the sound track is recorded, the track can be tailored to synchronize with the various scenes.

Music. Music can make or break a TV commercial. It is often used as a background to the announcer's copy or as a jingle (usually sung off screen). Effective music can set the mood and the tone and can even accent the selling words that the copywriter has written. Background music is available as stock music, which is usually prerecorded and sold very reasonably by stock-music companies, or original music, which is especially composed and recorded for your very own commercial. This is usually done by an independent contractor.

The jingle sets to music the slogan or the lyrics written by the agency or by an outside composer. If the melody is original, you must pay a composing fee. If it belongs to a popular or once-popular song, you must get permission from, and usually pay a fee to, the copyright owner. If the music is in the

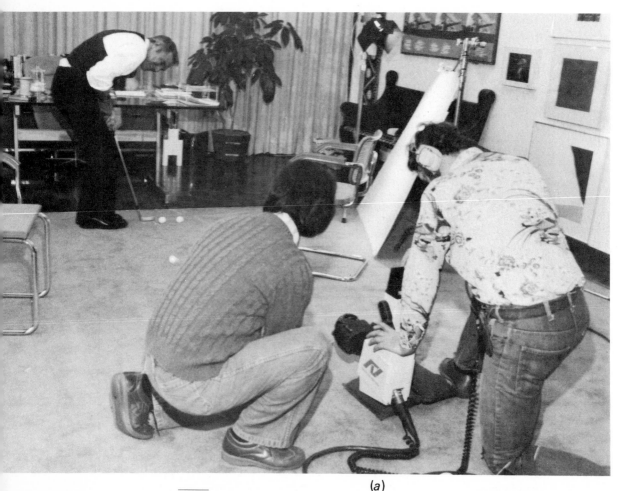

(a)

Exhibit 17.4
(a) Taking an interior scene. (b) Getting ready for an exterior shot of a lacrosse game. (Courtesy of BDA/BBDO.)

public domain, permission is generally not necessary. But in that case other advertisers may be using it as well as you. Regardless of whether the tune is original or standard, the advertiser must usually pay fees for musical arrangements, fees to musicians and singers, studio charges for recording the jingle, and editing charges to complete the sound track.

Once all the scenes have been shot, the film is sent to the laboratory to be processed. Often overnight, all scenes are developed (though not all may be printed), and the film is delivered for viewing. At this point the film becomes known as *rushes* or *dailies*. Once these rushes have been viewed to make certain no reshooting will be necessary, the shooting is officially concluded, and the editing begins.

(b)

Exhibit 17.4
(continued)

Role of the editor

Even when the shooting has been finished, the commercial is by no means ready to be shown. Many shots have been taken out of sequence; some scenes have been reshot several times; extra shots have been taken in case they should be necessary. A separate sound track and possibly a music track have been prepared. Which of the shots shall we use? How should they be assembled with transitional optical effects? How will the sound track be coordinated with the rest of the commercial? The person responsible for answering all these questions is the editor, who must cut out the good shots and splice them by hand. The editor is responsible for coordinating sound and music with the video portion and for assembling and inserting optical effects so that they make sense. In fact, although the producer and the art director may contribute ideas, it is the editor who brings to fruition the efforts of all the creative people who have worked on the commercial.

Table 17.1 and Exhibit 17.5 show how the commercial passes for review up to the delivery to the stations for airing.

Table 17–1

FROM CAMERA TO AIR ON FILM	
PROCESS	WHAT IT'S CALLED
After shooting, the film is processed in a day or two and shown on screen to the producer, director, art director, and film editor.	*Dailies,* or *rushes*
The best take of each scene is selected, cut, and spliced in correct sequence by the editor. The final film is submitted for preliminary client approval.	*Work print,* or *rough cut* (picture changes made most economically at this time)
Once the film has been approved, the film editor prepares opticals and sound tracks on separate reels to be synchronized with the film reel.	(Still time for changes)
Sound and film tracks are combined in one reel.	*Composite print,* or *optical print*
The optical print is approved.	*Answer print*
The answer print is corrected for color, quality, and synchronization.	*Final print*
From the final print, duplicate prints are made and sent to stations.	*Release prints,* or *dupes*
At last the film is on the air!	

```
                    J. WALTER THOMPSON COMPANY


PRODUCTION SCHEDULE FOR SIXTY-SECOND 35MM COLOR TELEVISION COMMERCIAL



        Client approves final script        Friday, August 4
        and storyboard

        Bids                                 Monday - Thursday
                                             August 7 - August 10

        Client approves budget               Friday - August 11

        Pre-production, Casting              Monday - Friday
                                             August 14 - August 25

        Shoot                                Monday - Tuesday
                                             August 28 - August 29

        Edit                                 Wednesday - Thursday
                                             August 30 - August 31

        Client approves rough cut            Friday - September 1

        Record music                         Friday - September 8

        Client approves answer print         Friday - September 15

        Ship air prints to stations          Friday - September 22
```

Exhibit 17.5
A TV-commercial production schedule involves several activities, complete with deadline dates. (Courtesy of J. Walter Thompson Company.)

Videotape   So far, we've been working in the world of film. We now enter the incredible world where everything we've said about shooting and editing is accomplished electronically, by *videotape* recording (also called *VTR*, or *tape*). The videotape process, using a live TV camera, carries the picture impulses through wires, and it records them on either a 1-inch or 0.75-inch magnetic tape. A process newer than film, videotape gives an excellent picture. While most viewers cannot tell whether a commercial was shot on film or on videotape, some professionals argue that videotape offers a more brilliant and realistic look; those favoring film still maintain that it offers a softer, more glamorous quality. Nevertheless, among both local and national advertisers, videotape is increasing in popularity as a method of shooting commercials.

Unique advantages of videotape. Videotape is unique because of the speed with which a commercial is produced. Editing a film commercial usually takes weeks to bring to completion. Tape can be played back immediately after shooting. With videotape you can shoot one day and be on the air the next—a boon to many advertisers, particularly retailers who change commercials every few days to feature sale items.

Videotape has other advantages as well. With videotape you can achieve fascinating trick effects. As one camera focuses on an in-home computer terminal, for example, another camera can focus on the announcer. The two pictures can be combined so that the speaker can actually walk over the keys of the home computer and be about the size of a doll.

Since no time for processing of the videotape is required, shooting ends after the tape has been played back and approved for editing. *If* the commercial has been conceived as one long take from beginning to end that does not require editing, shooting actually ends after the final version has been approved.

Videotape editing. Since the images recorded on videotape are invisible, film methods of editing cannot be employed. The tape editor, therefore, calls upon some very sophisticated equipment in combining the basic elements into the final commercial. Although the equipment is vastly different from that for film, the steps are parallel. First the reel of dailies is screened on a monitor and takes are selected. The various takes are then duplicated and lined up on another monitor in their proper order. This first rough-cut edit, the *work print,* is again the early stage in which the rough commercial can be visualized. Once this version is approved, opticals can be added electronically, and titles can be shot separately and matted over any scene in any position.

Tape's tremendous saving in time minimizes any possible limitations, and many people feel that videotape is the process of the future.

ROLE OF THE PRODUCER

The producer's role begins after the approval of the story board. Conferring with the copywriter and/or the art director, the producer becomes thoroughly familiar with every frame of the story board and encourages the client to make suggestions relating to the actual production (types of performer, for example):

1. The producer prepares the "specs," or specifications, the physical production requirements of the commercial in order to provide the production studios with the precise information they require in order to compute realistic bids. Every agency prepares its own estimate form. The accompanying estimate form (Exhibit 17.6) gives an excellent idea of the chief elements of such estimates. In addition, some advertisers may request a further breakdown of the cost of items such as:

BROADCAST PRODUCTION ESTIMATE

Client _____ Code _____ Job Code _____

Product _____ Code _____ Job Name _____

Media ☐ Radio   ☐ Television

WORK CODE	WORK CATEGORY	ESTIMATED COST	
A5	Pre-Production		
B2	Production		
B3	Animation		
C4	Artwork		
C6	Color Corr Prod		
D4	Record Studio		
D7	Sound Track		
E2	Talent & P + W		
E5	Tlnt Trvl & Exp		
F3	Music		
F4	Musicians (AFM)		
G2	Editorial		
G5	Vtr/Film Trnsfr		
G7	Cassettes		
G9	Prints & Tapes		
H9	Miscellaneous (Com)		
	COMM SUB-TOTAL		
S2	BBDO Trvl & Exp		
S5	Casting at BBDO		
S8	Contingency		
S9	Weather Contingency		
T3	Handling		
T6	Shipping		
T9	Miscellaneous (Non-com)		
V3	Pyrl Tax & Hndlg		
V5	NY Sales Tax		
V6	NJ Sales Tax		
	N/C SUB-TOTAL		
	COMMISSION		
	GROSS TOTAL		

ESTIMATED BY _____

APPROVALS

Producer _____ Date ____

Acct. Exec. _____ Date ____

Client _____ Date ____

DATE INPUT _____

INPUT BY _____

COMPETITIVE BIDS

1. _____ $ _____
2. _____ $ _____
3. _____ $ _____

RECOMMENDED CONTRACTOR

_____

RECOMMENDED EDITOR

_____

COMMERCIAL ID. No.	TITLE	LENGTH	COLOR	35mm	16mm	VTR
1.						
2.						
3.						
4.						
5.						
6.						

Further explanation of charges by work category _____

_____

_____

_____

PROD 857 5/80 REV.

Exhibit 17.6
An estimate sheet for a commercial. (Courtesy BBDO.)

☐ Preproduction and wrapping
☐ Shooting-crew labor
☐ Studio
☐ Location travel and expenses
☐ Equipment
☐ Film
☐ Props, wardrobe
☐ Payroll taxes
☐ Studio markup
☐ Directing
☐ Insurance
☐ Editing

Invariably, changes are made in the specifications, either because the producer thinks they are worth making or at the client's request. Always get a written approval of any changes at the time they are made.

2. The producer contacts the studios that have been invited to submit bids based on their specialties, experience, and reputation, meets with them either separately or in one common "bid session," and explains the story board and the specs in detail.

3. The producer analyzes the studio bids and recommends the studio to the client.

4. He or she arranges for equipment. The studio may own equipment, such as cameras and lights, but more often it rents all equipment for a job. The crew too is freelance, hired by the day. Although the studio's primary job is to shoot the commercial, it can also take responsibility for editorial work. For videotape (see Exhibit 17.7) a few studios own their own cameras and production units; others rent such facilities.

5. He or she arranges the casting. Working through a talent agency, the producer arranges or has the production company arrange auditions. Associates also attend auditions, at which they and the director make their final choices of performers (Exhibit 17.8). The client also may be asked to pass on the final selection.

6. He or she participates in the preproduction meeting. At this meeting the producer, creative associates, account executive, and client, together with studio representatives and director, lay final plans for production: These include what action will take place in each scene, how the sets will be furnished or where the outdoor location will be situated, how the product will be handled, whether the label will be simplified or color corrected for the camera, what hours of shooting will be scheduled—all logistics, in fact, relating to the shooting, which is probably scheduled for only a few days ahead.

7. He or she participates in the shooting and, on behalf of the agency and the client, is the *only* communicator with the director. On the set or location the creative people and the client channel any comments and suggestions through the producer to avoid confusion.

Videotape Contract

Agency Production Number TV	This number MUST appear on all invoices and correspondence. If not, invoice payment may be delayed.	Date

AGREEMENT made by and between BATTEN, BARTON, DURSTINE & OSBORN, INC. (hereinafter called "Advertising Agency") on behalf of _____ (hereinafter called "Advertiser") and _____ (hereinafter called "Contractor"). Advertising Agency on behalf of Advertiser hereby agrees to purchase from Contractor and Contractor hereby agrees to produce and sell to Advertising Agency VTR(s) of television commercial(s) in accordance with storyboards and/or scripts furnished by Advertising Agency, subject to the terms and conditions hereinafter set forth.

1. Specifications:

Commercial Identification No.	Title	Length	Color	B&W

2. Disposition of VTR elements:

(a) Number of mixed master(s) to be delivered_____

(b) Number of release VTR(s) to be delivered_____

(c) Number of release TV film recordings to be delivered_____

(d) All elements to be delivered to:

3. Responsibility for requirements:

(a) The Contractor shall supply the following:

(b) The Agency shall supply the following:

4. Production schedule:

(a) Taping to begin on_____

(b) Rough cut VTR(s) to be screened week of_____

(c) Mixed master VTR(s) to be screened on or before_____

(d) Release VTR(s) to be delivered by_____

(e) Release TV film recordings to be delivered by_____

5. Price and payment schedule:

(a) Total cost: $_____, including mixed master VTR and one release VTR.

(b) Extra release VTR(s) at $_____ each (as an extra charge).

(c) Release TV film recordings at $_____ each (as an extra charge).

(d) Price to be paid in following installments:

1. $_____ on signing this agreement.

2. $_____ on start of taping.

3. $_____ on approval of mixed master VTR(s).

6. Miscellaneous:

(a) The authorized representative of the Advertising Agency in the production of this videotape is _____

(b) The title of Contractor's sample of quality tape is _____

(c) Final edited original master VTR(s) to be stored by _____, with/without insurance.

(d)

This agreement includes additional paragraphs 7 through 31 set forth on the reverse side hereof.

Batten, Barton, Durstine & Osborn, Inc.   by
Agreed and accepted: by

MP 1300 (REV. 2/76)

Exhibit 17.7
A videotape contract, showing the details of what is involved in arranging for videotaping. (Courtesy BBDO.)

427

Commercial Production Report

Client _____ Account Executive _____ Information Received _____
Product _____ BBDO Producer _____ Date Prepared _____
Contractor _____ Shooting Date(s) _____ To Accounting Dept. _____
Recording Studio _____ Film/Tape Recording Date(s) _____ Checks Mailed _____
                    Announcer/Singers   Announcer/Singers

Commercial Identification Number	Title	Length	Film	Tape	SAG	AFTRA
Basic:			☐	☐	☐	☐
Version:						

A MUSIC AFM

Contractor	Date and place of recording	Contract No.	Number of commercials declared
Address			

B SAG/AFTRA Information (Attach Talent Contracts, Time Cards, and Tax Forms)
★(Ethnic Group indicated as follows: Caucasian (C) Negro (N) Puerto Rican (PR) Mexican (M) Oriental (O)

Paid by BBDO	St'd'o	Compensation Scale/Scale +	Name and Ethnic Group ★	★	Camera On	Off	Category	Singers Mult.	Sw't'n'g	Date(s) Worked	Number of Spots	C	Producer's Remarks Upgrade——Downgrade——Outgrade

Commercial Film/Tape Completion Report:

1. MUSIC ☐ Yes ☐ No

If YES, check and fill in one of the following:
☐ Original. You must fill in AFM Information in (A) above.
☐ Picked up from: Film/Tape/Ra No. List Contractor's name and AFM contract number in (A) above.
☐ Licensed from publisher. Copy of license attached.
☐ Stock license. Copy of license attached.

Form No. TV 1399 (August 78)

2. SINGERS ☐ Yes ☐ No

☐ Original (list singers in (B) above.)
☐ Picked up from: Film/Tape/Ra No. _____ (list names in (B) above.)

3. TALENT SAME ☐ Yes ☐ No

If NO, indicate downgrade or outgrade or picked up existing footage from Film/Tape. Indicate commercial Number and name on production report in Section (C) above.

4. EXTRAS ☐ Yes ☐ No

Complete Extras Report and attach to this Completion Report. If Extra upgraded to Principal, list name on Production sheet in Section (B) above. State reason in (C) above.

_____ _____
BBDO Producer (Signature)   Date

Talent Control Department

Exhibit 17.8
Typical commercial production report on talent used for the production of the TV spot.

8. He or she participates in the editing, which begins after viewing of the dailies.

9. He or she conducts the recording session. Either before or after shooting and editing, the producer arranges for the sound track, which may call for an announcer, actors, singers, and musicians. If music is to be recorded, the producer will have had preliminary meetings with the music contractor.

10. He or she schedules screenings. The producer arranges for agency associates and clients to view and approve the commercials at various editing stages and after completion of the answer print.

11. He or she handles the billings and approves studio and other invoices for shooting, editing, and payment to talent.

CONTROLLING THE COST OF COMMERCIAL

PRODUCTION

The cost of producing a TV commercial is of deep concern to both the agency and the advertiser. The chief reason money is wasted in commercials is inadequate preplanning. In production the two major cost items are labor and equipment. Labor—the production crew, director, and performers—is hired by the day, and equipment is rented by the day. If, however, a particular demonstration was improperly rehearsed, if a particular prop was not delivered, or if the location site was not scouted ahead of time, the shooting planned for one day may be forced into expensive overtime or into a second day. These costly mistakes can be avoided by careful planning.

Before we can cite dollar averages for commercials, we have to recognize that there are actually two plateaus of costs. One is paid by the local advertiser, whose 30-second commercial may cost from $5,000 to $25,000; the other is paid by the national advertiser, whose 30-second commercial may cost from $25,000 to $100,000. (There have been cases of a national advertiser paying over $250,000 for one commercial!) This vast difference reflects the varying prices charged by studios and the ability of the local advertiser to work with fewer restrictions.

Union scale   "Restrictions" usually mean *union restrictions.* One of the first facts of life you become aware of in TV production is that it is a highly unionized business. Especially in the large TV centers rate schedules are spelled out for every step.*

Residual fees   Another major expense is the *residual,* or *reuse fee,* paid to performers—announcers, narrators, actors, and singers—in addition to their initial *session fees.* Under the union rules performers are paid every time the commercial is aired on the networks, the amount of the fee depending upon their scale and the number of cities involved. In a commercial aired with great frequency a national advertiser may sometimes pay more in residuals than in the production of the commercial itself. This problem is less severe for the local advertiser because local rates are cheaper than national rates.

The moral is "Cast only the number of performers necessary to the commercial and not one performer more."

---

*The major unions involved are the American Federation of Television and Radio Artists (AFTRA), the Screen Actors' Guild (SAG), the American Federation of Musicians (AFM), the International Alliance of Theatrical and Stage Employees (IATSE), and the National Association of Broadcast Employees and Technicians (NABET).

PHOTOSCRIPTS All advertisers like to be proud of their commercials, and they want to make the best sales promotion use of them. In addition they wish to keep a record of the commercials they've made. For this purpose advertisers often make photoscripts—series of photographic frames taken from key frames of the actual print film, with appropriate copy printed underneath. (See Exhibit 17.3b.)

SUMMARY

More people are exposed to TV than to any other advertising medium; so it is the most important medium to create selling messages for. It is also the most flexible and creative medium, using sight and sound and including color, music, and sound effects. There are many techniques—all effective, but care must be taken to choose the correct one. Writing and visualizing the commercial in simple easy-to-understand terms is essential to success. Producing the finished TV commercial is just as important as conceiving the idea. You must use all types of expert to help you make the idea on paper a reality and yet stay within a client-approved budget.

QUESTIONS

1. In selecting the visual technique for telling your story, you have a wide range of proved techniques from which to choose. Discuss as many as you can, and indicate when you think each would be most appropriate.
2. What guidelines might be used to help in the selection of the visual technique for a given situation?
3. Describe some of the guidelines offered for writing the audio portion of the TV commercial.
4. It is important to visualize the TV commercial as you are writing the copy. What are some helpful suggestions to bear in mind during the process?
5. What is the role of the TV art director?
6. Explain in detail the importance of the story board.
7. What is the role of the creative team in developing a TV commercial?
8. What is meant by TV production?
9. What is the director's function?
10. Production is a two-part process. Explain.
11. Describe the usual way of producing a commercial with a musical background.
12. What is the role of the editor in producing a TV commercial?

13. What are the advantages and limitations of videotape?
14. Explain in detail the responsibilities of a TV producer.
15. What is discussed at a preproduction meeting?
16. What are some of the ways of controlling the costs of TV commercial production?
17. Explain the following:

a. promos
b. clutter
c. limbo
d. voice-over
e. slice of life
f. story line
g. panning
h. rotoscope
i. teeny board
j. TV production
k. shooting
l. editing

m. opticals
n. sound track
o. stock music
p. jingles
q. work print
r. composite print
s. release prints
t. VTR
u. specs
v. residual fees
w. photoscripts

READINGS

FLETCHER, ALAN D., and THOMAS A. BOWERS: *Fundamentals of Advertising Research* (Columbus, Ohio: Grid Publishing, 1979), pp. 191–208.

HEADEN, ROBERT S., JAY E. KLOMPMAKER, and JESSE E. TEEL, JR.: "Predicting Audience Exposure to Spot TV Advertising Schedules," *Journal of Marketing Research,* February, 1977, pp. 1–9.

JENNINGS, JOYCE, FLORENCE L. GEIS, and VIRGINIA BROWN: "Influence of Television Commercials on Women's Self-Confidence and Independent Judgment," *Journal of Personality and Social Psychology,* February, 1980, pp. 203–10.

JEWLER, A. JEROME: *Creative Strategy in Advertising* (Belmont, California: Wadsworth, 1981), pp. 89–102.

McEWEN, WILLIAM J., and CLARK LEAVITT: "A Way to Describe TV Commercials," *Journal of Advertising Research,* December, 1976, pp. 35–39.

McMAHAN, HARRY WAYNE: "So Funny It Ain't Funny: Sort of a Serious Look at Humor," *Advertising Age,* September 13, 1976, pp. 74–75.

"No easy tests for commercial wearout," *Marketing & Media Decisions,* December, 1981, pp. 64–65.

RESNICK, ALAN, and BRUCE L. STERN: "An Analysis of Information Content in Television Advertising," *Journal of Marketing,* January, 1977, pp. 50–53.

The Radio
Commercial

Advertising may be a mass medium, but a radio commercial is from one real person, you, to another important person, the listener. In creating any advertising, you must try to picture a typical person who might buy the product; but in writing radio copy, your challenge is even greater. You also have to visualize what people are doing as you try to talk to them. They may be standing up or moving about, listening to the radio with only one ear as they go about their daily routines. They may be eating, reading, conversing, playing cards, studying, paying bills, or driving a car with an eye on the traffic. Radio reaches an audience more preoccupied than that reached by any other medium.

CREATING THE RADIO
COMMERCIAL

As compensation, however, radio copywriters enjoy almost unlimited freedom in their choices of people and places. With no scenery or transportation costs or limitations, they can summon any characters from any part of the globe. With the aid of sound they can set any stage—a car door slamming, a phone ringing. The writer can picture 100,000 people at a bowl game with a 5-second roar of the crowd. Best of all, the writer can use music, either for background to set the mood or for a jingle to popularize the advertiser's slogan. Such a jingle is called a *musical logo,* or *logotype,* and it helps identify the product and make the message memorable. It is often so memorable that adults and children sing it! (Musical rights for radio are the same as for TV. See Chapter 17.)

Writing the commercial

Like the TV commercial, the basic ingredient of the radio commercial is the promise of a significant and distinctive benefit for the listener, on which the product can make good. Once you have determined your product's promise, the whole world of radio imagery and technique is open to you. With voices, music, and sound effects at your command (Exhibits 18.1 and

Exhibit 18.1
The exciting sound of a racquetball court is directly related to keeping in good physical shape. Fulton Federal's commercial, with its fiscal-fitness theme, is directed to a young, active, affluent audience. (Courtesy of BDA/BBDO.)

BDA/BBDO
Radio Script

Client	Fulton Federal	City	ATL	Spot No.	711

Date	1-8-82	Job No.	F-1-6012-9	Type		Length	:60

This Spot effective	3-2-81	It replaces Spot		Remarks: Racquetball	

SFX: RACQUETBALL COURT

MAN 1: I work hard to keep my body in shape ... racquetball three times
        a week .. a few laps around the track. But I don't have to
        work hard to keep my finances in shape. At lease, not any more.
        I signed up for Fulton Federal's Fiscal Fitness Package.
        Fulton Federal will pay me five and a quarter percent interest
        on my <u>checking</u>. They've always paid me the highest rate on
        my savings. And I could get a VISA card with overdraft protection
        and a discount on the interest rates for a loan on a new car.
        Right now, I'm saving a lot of time and money with bill pay by
        phone. It lets me pay my bills with a single phone call to
        Fulton Federal. I also get 24-hour teller convenience...
        descriptive monthly statements ... 16 great services in all.
        Puls a special planner for my records.

MAN 2: Hey Bob! Ready for another game?

MAN 1: Be right there. But best of all, it gives me more time to play.
        And <u>that</u> I like. Why not get your finances in shape? With the
        Fiscal Fitness Package from Fulton Federal.

BDA/BBDO
Radio Script

Client Fulton Federal	City ATL	Spot No. 712
Date 1-8-82 Job No. F-1-6012-9 Type		Length :60
This Spot effective 3-2-81 It replaces Spot		Remarks: Annual Fiscal

MAN 1: Okay, Mr. Barner. Time for your annual fiscal.

MAN 2: Accountants give physicals?

MAN 1: No. no, <u>fiscal</u>. To check your <u>financial</u> shape. (MAN 2: Huh?)
We use the services in Fulton Federal's Fiscal Fitness Package
as a guide. Okay, take a deep breath...now: do you earn interest
on your checking account?

MAN 2: Interest on my checking??

MAN 1: Sure. Fulton Federal pays five and a quarter percent. (MAN 2:
5¼%?) Now... try to relax, Mr. Barner. (MAN 2: I'll try.)
Do you get the highest interest rate on savings?

MAN 2: Ahh, no!

MAN 1: Can you pay your bills by phone?

MAN 2: Fulton Federal can do that??

MAN 1: Please...just relax.

MAN 2: Sorry

MAN 1: Do you get a discount (MAN 2: Huh?) on a loan for new cars?

MAN 2: No!!

MAN 1: VISA with overdraft protection...

MAN 2: No.

MAN 1: ...24-hour teller convenience...

MAN 2: No.

MAN 1: ...descriptive statements each month to help you balance your budget.

MAN 2: No.

MAN 1: ...over 35 locations to choose from...

MAN 2: I, uh, don't feel so good.

MAN 1: ...a special planner to hold your records...

MAN 2: I'm failing my fiscal, aren't I?

MAN 1: Ahh, maybe you'd better lie down, Mr. Barner...

ANNCR: For all the services in the Fiscal Fitness Package, come to Fulton
Federal, quick!

Exhibit 18.2
(Courtesy of BDA/BBDO.)

18.2), you are free to fashion a mental backdrop of any scene, no matter how spectacular, how modest, or how far away. But you'll have to be imaginative. In radio, words and sounds comprise the copywriter's entire arsenal for communicating the copy story; these make up the entire commercial. You can vitalize the copy with the following devices:

Simplicity. Use known words, short phrases, simple sentence structure. Build around one main point. Avoid confusing the listener with too many copy points.

Clarity. Keep the train of thought on one straight track. Avoid side issues. Use the active voice in simple sentences. Avoid adverbs, clichés, and ambiguous phrases. Delete unnecessary words. (Test: Would the commercial be hurt if the word were deleted? If not, take it out.) Write from draft to draft until your script becomes ummistakably clear and concise.

Coherence. Be certain your sales message flows in logical sequence from first word to last, using smooth transitional words and phrases for easier listening.

Rapport. Remember, as far as your listeners are concerned, you are speaking only to them. Try to use a warm, personal tone, as if you were talking to one or two people. Make frequent use of the word "you." Address the listeners in terms they would use themselves.

Pleasantness. It is not necessary to entertain simply for the sake of entertaining, but there is no point in being dull or obnoxious. Strike a happy medium; talk as one friend to another about the product or service.

Believability. Every product has its good points. Tell the truth about them. Avoid overstatements and obvious exaggeration; they are quickly spotted and defeat the whole purpose of the commercial. Be straightforward; you will convey the feeling of being a trusted friend.

Interest. Nothing makes listeners indifferent faster than a boring commercial. Products and services are not fascinating in themselves; it is the way you look at them that makes them interesting. Try to give your customer some useful information as a reward for listening.

Distinctiveness. Sounding different from other commercials and setting your product apart from others are never easy in a radio commercial. Employ every possible means—a fresh approach, a musical phrase here, a particular voice quality or sound effect there—to give your commercial its own character.

Compulsion. Inject your commercial with a feeling of urgency. The first few seconds are crucial ones; for they are when you capture or lose the listener's attention. Direct every word toward moving the buyer closer to wanting the product. Repeat your promise of benefit; register the name of your product. And don't forget to urge the listener to act without delay. (It's surprising how many commercials don't do this.)

If you were editing the following commercial, how many weaknesses could you spot? Compare your criticisms with the analysis and revision that follow.

> *Announcer:* Go to Hamburg Hut for a really great meal. Hamburg Hut has the best hamburgers and french fries in town. They cook their hamburgers rare, medium, or well done. They also offer thick, creamy shakes and have plenty of clean tables where the meal can be enjoyed. What's more, the Hamburg Hut people are courteous. Remember: Hamburg Huts are almost everywhere, and at Hamburg Hut we serve the best, bar none!

A careful rereading of this commercial shows several weaknesses. First, the copy is incoherent. Second, it contains too many ideas; no major promise of benefit comes through. Third, since the copy talks in terms of the advertiser, with never a mention of "you," there is no rapport with the listener. Fourth, it is riddled with trite phrases such as "best . . . in town," "what's more," and "best, bar none." The copy is hardly distinctive—it fails to stand Hamburg Hut apart from its competitors.

Now note how the commercial improves when we play up its promise of benefit, personalize the message, simplify the copy, and place the thoughts in a more coherent order.

> *Announcer:* How do *you* like *your* hamburgers? Nice and juicy and cooked to your special order? Well, that's the way to get 'em at Hamburg Hut—and *only* at Hamburg Hut. Rare, medium, or well done—cooked to *your order*—topped off with our crispy french fries and thick, creamy shakes. So for hamburgers the way you like 'em, bring your family to Hamburg Hut and tell us: rare, medium, or well done!

Some techniques

Basically a medium of words, radio—more than any other medium—relies heavily on the art of writing strong copy. But just as print ads and TV commercials include pictures and graphics to add impact to the copy, radio creates mental pictures with other techniques. Radio copywriters can choose among many proved techniques to give more meaning to the copy, help gain the attention of the busy target audience, and hold that attention for the duration of the commercial. Some of these techniques, you will note, parallel those in TV.

Straight announcer. In this commonly used and most direct of all techniques, an announcer or personality delivers the entire script, as in the Hamburg Hut example. Success depends both on the copy and on the warmth and believability of the person reciting the commercial.

Two-announcer. In this format two announcers alternate sentences or groups of sentences of copy, enabling the commercial to move at a fast pace and generate excitement. Often used to cover sale items for retail stores, this technique may give a news flavor to the commercial.

Announcer-actor. The listener may identify still more with the situation if the writer intersperses an actor's or actress's voice reacting to or supplementing the message delivered by the announcer.

Slice of life. Writing dialogue that reenacts a true-to-life scene involves the listener in a problem that the advertised product or service can help solve. The announcer may or may not be part of this format.

Jingle-announcer. The jingle (Exhibit 18.3) offers two advantages. As a song, it is a pleasant and easily remembered presentation of at least part of the copy. As a musical sound, it is the advertiser's unique property, which sets the commercial apart from every other ad on radio. Generally, an announcer is used in this flexible technique, which may be structured in countless ways. Most common is the jingle at the beginning of the commercial, followed by announcer copy; the commercial is concluded by a reprise of the entire jingle or its closing bars.

Customer interview. The announcer may talk not with professional talent but with actual consumers, who relate their favorable experience with the product or service or store. As a variation, the satisfied customer may deliver the entire commercial.

Humor. Tastefully handled, humor may be an ingredient in almost any other technique. A slice-of-life scene can have humorous overtones, and even straight announcer copy may be written in a humorous vein. Humor is often appropriate for low-priced package products, products people buy for fun, products whose primary appeal is taste, or products or services in need of a change of pace in advertising because of strong competition (Exhibit 18.4). Never, however, make fun of the product or the customer or treat too lightly a situation that is not normally funny. The test of a humorous commercial is whether the customer remembers the product, not the commercial. Humor is not called for when your product has distinct advantages that can be advertised with a serious approach.

Combination. Radio techniques may be mixed in almost countless ways. To select the right technique for a particular assignment, follow the guidelines we discussed for selecting TV techniques in Chapter 17; they also apply to radio.

LILLER NEAL WELTIN, INC.
1300 Life of Georgia Tower, Atlanta, Ga. 30308

Client: JIM DANDY   Job No: 3364

Subject: '82 Campaign (rev. 2)

Length: :60

Spot No: JDR-60-82-03

Live ☐   Recorded ☒

Date of Broadcast:

RADIO SCRIPT

SINGERS:	He's bright-eyed
	and bushy-tailed
	He's a Jim Dandy Dog!
MAN:	Our dog, Corney, doesn't chase cars...he prefers <u>trains</u>. One goes
	by near us every day...and Corny just loves it. He runs down to his
	favorite big rock, sits on it and watches the train go by...
	wagging his tail the whole time. You know, he was supposed to be
	a bird dog.
SINGERS:	He's a Jim Dandy Dog!
ANNCR.:	To keep Jim Dandy Dogs healthy and alert try Jim Dandy's variety of
	dog food favorites. Like the real meaty flavor of Chunx With Gravy,
	the moist, beefy flavor of Tender Moist Chunx...and of course the
	hearty blend of flavors in traditional Jim Dandy Dog Ration.
	They all supply the balanced nutrition your dog needs to keep
	fit and happy.
SINGERS:	He's bright-eyed
	and bushy-tailed
	He's a Jim Dandy dog.
TAG:	Feed your dog great-tasting Jim Dandy Dog Food. Look for the
	Jim Dandy display at your grocer's.

Exhibit 18.3
A jingle that treats Jim Dandy's theme in a memorable manner makes this factual commercial easy to listen to. (Courtesy of Liller Neal Welton, Inc.)

Exhibit 18.4 (facing page)
A humorous conversation between two Britishers takes Delta Air Lines' fact-filled message about service and makes it more interesting than a straight announcer technique. (Courtesy of BDA/BBDO.)

BDA/BBDO
Radio Script

Client DELTA AIR LINES	City DFW	Spot No. 4841

Date 3/31/82	Job No.	Type	Length :60

This Spot effective 4/20 thru 5/26	It replaces Spot	Remarks: "BILLINGS"

(Upper class English accents)

BILLINGS: Ah, those Americans!!

SIR: What now, Billings?

BILLINGS: Did you know they've been building little cities
all along their West Coast?

SIR: No kidding!

BILLINGS: Los Angeles, San Diego, San Francisco, Seattle/
Tacoma and Portland.

SIR: Clever names.

BILLINGS: Now say you're in Dallas or Ft. Worth...

SIR: Dallas? Ft. Worth?

BILLINGS: You could reach them all on Delta.

SIR: Delta what?

BILLINGS: Delta Air Lines. Seems Delta flies back and
forth at a rate that's positively...positively...

SIR: Come Billings, spit it out.

BILLINGS: Positively convenient, Sir. Delta has 6 nonstops
a day to Los Angeles, one to San Diego, 4 to San
Francisco.

SIR: My stars!!

BILLINGS: And look at Seattle/Tacoma - 2 nonstops daily.
And a pair of thru-jets to Portland.

SIR: Yes, Billings, but how does Delta do in the
final analysis?

BILLINGS: Final analysis, Sir?

SIR: How much bread, Billings?

BILLINGS: Very little. In fact, Delta can save you as much
as 45% off regular Day Tourist on round-trips.

SIR: Really?

BILLINGS: No, ready.

SIR: Ready?

BILLINGS: Ready when you are, sir.

SIR: Who?

BILLINGS: Delta.

SIR: Oh.

Timing of
commercials
Most radio stations accept these maximum word lengths for *live* commercial scripts:

- ☐ 10 seconds, 25 words
- ☐ 20 seconds, 45 words
- ☐ 30 seconds, 65 words
- ☐ 60 seconds, 125 words

When the commercial is prerecorded (see below), you may use any number of words as long as you stay within the time limit.

After you have written the commercial, read it aloud, not only to time it properly but to catch tongue twisters and ensure that it flows smoothly.

Musical
commercials
Often commercials are set to music especially composed for them or adapted from a familiar song. A few bars of distinctive music played often enough may serve as a musical identification of the product. Such a musical logotype usually lasts about 10 seconds. Jingles are also popular ways of making a slogan memorable.

This brings us to the question of musical rights. A melody is in the public domain, available for use by anyone without cost, *after* the copyright has expired. Many old favorites and classics are thus in the public domain and have been used as advertising themes. That is one of their detriments: They may have been used by many others.

Popular tunes that are still protected by copyright are available only by agreement with the copyright owner. You may find a catchy, familiar tune, but it may be costly.

An advertiser can also commission a composer to create an original tune, which becomes the advertiser's property and gives the product its own musical personality.

METHODS OF
DELIVERY
There are two ways of delivering a radio commercial: *live* and *prerecorded.*

The live
commercial
A live commercial is delivered in person by the studio announcer, disc jockey, newscaster, or other station personality or by a sports reporter from another location. Generally read from a script prepared by the advertiser, the commercial is sometimes revised to complement the announcer's style. If time allows, the revised script should be approved in advance by the ad-

vertiser. *Ad-libbing* (extemporizing) from a fact sheet should be discouraged since the announcer may inadvertently omit key selling phrases or, in the case of regulated products, such as drugs, may fail to include certain mandatory phrases.

Some commercials are delivered partly live and partly prerecorded. The prerecorded jingle, for example, can be played over and over with live-announcer copy added. Sometimes the live part (the dealer "tie-up") is left open for the tie-in ad of the local distributor.

The advantage of the live commercial is that the announcer may have a popular following; listeners tend to accept advice from someone they like. Furthermore, particularly when the news announcer also delivers the commercial, some of the believability and timeliness of the news may spill over to the ad.

The prerecorded

commercial

For a regional or national campaign local announcer capabilities are not known, and it is impractical to write a separate script to fit each one's particular style. Commercials for these campaigns are therefore usually prerecorded. Not only are advertisers secure in the knowledge that the commercial is identical each time it is aired, but they can take advantage of myriad techniques impractical for live commercials.

PRODUCING THE RADIO
COMMERCIAL

Although there are certain broad similarities, producing radio commercials is far simpler and less costly than producing TV commercials. First of all, the agency or advertiser appoints a *radio producer,* who converts the script into a recording ready to go on the air. After preparing the cost estimate and getting budget approval, the producer selects a *recording studio,* a *casting director* if necessary, and a *musical director,* orchestra, and singers if the script calls for them.

After the cast has been selected, it rehearses in a recording studio, which can be hired by the hour. For complex productions a rehearsal day may be scheduled ahead of shooting. Since most commercials are shot in short "takes," however, which are later joined in the editing, a formal rehearsal is usually unnecessary. When the producer feels the cast is ready, the commercial is acted out and recorded on tape. Music and sound may be taped separately and then mixed with the vocal tape by the sound-recording studio. In fact, by double- and triple-tracking music and singers' voices, modern recording equipment can build small sounds into big ones. You have to pay for this ability, however. Union rules require that musicians and singers be paid extra fees when their music is mechanically added to their original recording. After the last mix the *master tape* of the commercial is prepared. When final approval has been obtained, duplicates are made on 0.25-inch tape reels or audiocassettes for release to the list of stations.

Steps in radio production

We may summarize the steps in producing a commercial:

1. An agency or advertiser appoints a producer.
2. The producer prepares cost estimates.
3. The producer selects a recording studio.
4. With the aid of the casting director, if one is needed, the producer casts the commercial.
5. If there is to be music, the producer selects a musical director and chooses music.
6. If necessary, a rehearsal is held.
7. The studio tapes music and sound separately.
8. The studio mixes music and sound with voices.
9. The producer sees that the master tape is prepared for distribution on either tape or cassettes and shipped to stations.

You are on the air!

SUMMARY

Radio is the most reasonable, most creative medium you can use.

Costs to produce radio commercials are very low compared to TV. Your imagination is your only limitation. In a few seconds, you use sound effects, character actors, music to set a scene in the listener's mind. As in TV, there are several techniques and types of commercials; but, unlike TV, all radio commercials are simple to produce and economical in cost.

QUESTIONS

1. Describe and explain the characteristics of effective radio copy.
2. Why is compulsion important in radio copy?
3. In attempting to create mental pictures, the radio copywriter has a choice of many proved techniques to give more meaning to the copy and to gain and keep the attention of the target audience. What are these techniques?
4. What is meant by the timing of radio commercials?
5. What are the comparative advantages and limitations of live and prerecorded radio commercials?

6. What is the role of the radio producer?

7. Identify the steps in producing a radio commercial.

8. Since radio is not a visual medium, what are the special challenges of creating effective radio commercials?

9. Describe the following:
   a. two-announcer
   b. jingle-announcer
   c. musical logotype
   d. public domain
   e. ad-libbing
   f. master tape

SUGGESTED EXERCISES

10. Write a 60-second commercial on your favorite toothpaste using a slice-of-life format.

11. Write a 60-second commercial announcing a new model car using background music and two announcers.

12. Write a 60-second commercial using music in the public domain.

13. Write a 60-second commercial using at least three different sound effects.

READINGS

CANTOR, JOANNE, and PAT VENUS: "The Effect of Humor on Recall of a Radio Advertisement," *Journal of Broadcasting,* Winter 1980, pp. 13–22.

HEIGHTON, ELIZABETH J. and DON R. CUNNINGHAM: *Advertising in the Broadcast Media* (Belmont, Cal.: Wadsworth, 1976).

JEWLER, A. JEROME: *Creative Strategy in Advertising* (Belmont, Cal.: Wadsworth, 1981), pp. 75–88.

"The Sounds of Winners: Year's Best Radio Spots," *Advertising Age,* August 24, 1981, pp. 52–54.

TERRELL, NEIL: *Power Technique for Radio-TV Copywriting* (Blue Ridge Summit, Pa.: Tab Books, 1971).

Trademarks and Packaging

Never has a good trademark been so important as in this age of self-service. The trademark directly affects the distinctiveness of the product and therefore the ease with which it is remembered and its sales. The creation of a good trademark is the biggest single contribution a person can add to the marketing success of a product. Although a product often has only one trademark in its lifetime, companies are constantly coming out with new products for which new trademarks will be needed. An advertising person with a knowledge of people, marketing, and copy is in an ideal position to meet the challenge of creating trademarks that give the success of products a big push.

The trademark often becomes the most important asset of a company, growing more valuable each year. A whole body of law has been developed to protect this property against infringers. Getting legal protection is the province of the attorney; however, it begins with the creation of the trademark itself. Hence, in creating or considering an idea for a trademark, you must understand some of the basic legal ground rules.

Packaging is an important part of any marketing and advertising campaign. Simple, modern designs help attract the eye and help customers remember the brand name. Successful products usually have packaging design changes from time to time to bring the products appearance in line with current thinking.

TRADEMARKS

What is a trademark?

A *trademark* is any symbol, sign, word, name, device, or combination of these that tells who makes a product or who sells it, distinguishing that product from those made or sold by others. Its purpose is to protect the public from being deceived and to protect the owner from unfair competition and the unlawful use of his property.

A trademark invariably consists of, or includes, a word or name by which people can speak of the product—"Do you have *Dutch Boy* paint?" That word or name is also called a *brand name*. A trademark may, but does not have to, include some pictorial or design element. If it does, the combination is called a *logotype* (Exhibit 19.1).

Exhibit 19.1
A word alone, even if set in a standard typeface, can be a trademark. When it is formed into a design or combined with one, to add distinctiveness and memorability, it is called a *logotype*.

445

A *trade name,* on the other hand, is the name under which a company does business. *General Mills,* for example, is the trade name of a company making a cake mix whose trademark (not trade name) is *Betty Crocker.* The terms "trademark" and "trade name" are often confused.

A product *can* have several trademarks, as Coca-Cola and Coke. Chief among the basic requirements for making a trademark legally protectable are the following:

☐ *The trademark must be used in connection with an actual product.* The use of a design in an ad does not make it a trademark, nor does having it on a flag over the factory. It must be applied to the product itself or be on a label or container of that product. If that is not feasible, it must be affixed to the container or dispenser of it, as on a pump at a service station.

☐ *The trademark must not be confusingly similar to trademarks on similar goods.* It should not be likely to cause the buyer to be confused, mistaken, or deceived as to whose product he or she is purchasing. The trademark should be dissimilar in appearance, sound, and significance. Cycol was held to be in conflict with Tycol, for oil: Air-O was held in conflict with Arrow for shirts; Canned Light was held in conflict with Barreled Sunlight for paint because of such possible confusion. The two products involved need not be identical. The marks will be held in conflict if the products are sold through the same trade channels or if the public might assume that a product made by a second company is a new product line of the first company. So-Soft tissues, for example, was held in conflict with Snow & Soft paper napkins for this reason. Big Boy! powder for soft drinks was held in confusion with Big Boy stick candy.

☐ *A trademark must not be deceptive.* It must not indicate a quality not in the product or be misdescriptively deceptive. Words that have legally been barred for this reason include Lemon soap that contained no lemon, Half-Spanish for cigars that did not come from Spain, and Nylodon for sleeping bags that contained no nylon.

☐ *A trademark must not be merely descriptive.* "I have often noticed," the head of a baking company might say, "that people ask for fresh bread. We will call our bread *Fresh;* that's our trademark. How nice that will be for us!" But when people ask for "fresh bread," they are describing the kind of bread they want, not specifying the bread made by a particular baker. To prevent such misleading usage, the law does not protect trademarks that are merely descriptive, applicable to many other products. Aircraft for control instruments and Computing for a weighing scale were disallowed as trademarks because they are merely descriptive. The misspelling or hyphenating of a word, such as Keep Kold or Heldryte, does not make a nondescriptive word out of one that, if spelled correctly, would be descriptive of the product. Although a word must not literally be descriptive, it may *suggest* certain qualities, and we shall touch upon this matter shortly.

Forms of trademarks

Dictionary words. Many trademarks consist of familiar dictionary words used in an arbitrary, suggestive, or fanciful manner. They must *not* be used in a merely descriptive sense to describe the nature, use, or virtue of the product. Good examples of dictionary words that meet the foregoing requirements are Dial soap, Glad plastic bags, Sunbeam toasters, Shell oil, and Rise shaving cream. The advantages of using words in the dictionary are that you have so many from which to choose and the public will recognize them. The task is to get them to associate the word with the product. If you have done that, the chances of protection against infringement are good.

Coined words. Most trademarks are words made up of a new combination of consonants and vowels. Kodak is the classic forerunner of this school of thinking. We also have Kleenex, Xerox, Norelco, Exxon—the list is long. The advantage of a coined word is that it is new; it can be made phonetically pleasing, pronounceable, and short. Coined words have a high rank for being legally protectable, but to create one that is distinctive is the big challenge. One drug company tried using a computer to create coined words for its many new products; they were distinctive but just not pronounceable. On the other hand sometimes successful names *are* created by computer or mathematical calculations: The name Exxon was created to replace Esso when the federal government ruled that Esso could no longer be used because of a previous right by another company. Exxon was created by a computer printout of thousands of names and selected after extensive consumer testing showed it to be recognizable as very similar to the service-station signs and logo already in use for Esso.

When a word is coined from a root word associated with a product, there is danger that the basic word may be so obvious that others in the field will use it, with resulting confusion of similar names. In one issue of the *Standard Advertising Register* there were fifteen trademarks beginning with Flavor or Flava. We also have Launderall, Laundromat, Launderette and Dictaphone, Dictograph. But think of a fresh root concept, and you have the makings of a good trademark.

Personal names. These may be the names of real people, such as Sara Lee; fictional characters, like Betty Crocker; historical characters, as in Lincoln cars; mythological characters, as in Ajax cleanser. A surname alone is not valuable as a new trademark; others of that name may use it. Names like Lipton's tea, Heinz foods, or Campbell's soups have been in use so long, however, that they have acquired what the law calls a "secondary meaning"; that is, through usage the public has recognized them as representing the product of one company only. But a new trademark can have no secondary meaning.

Geographical names. A geographical name is really a place name: Nashua blankets, Utica sheets, Pittsburgh paints. These names are old trademarks and have acquired secondary meaning. Often the word *brand* is offered after geographical names. The law does not look with favor on giving one person exclusive right to use a geographical name in connection with a new product, excluding others making similar goods in that area. However, a name chosen because of the fanciful connotation of a geographical setting, rather than to suggest it was made there, may make it eligible for protection, as with Bali bras.

Initials and numbers. Fortunes and years have been spent in establishing trademarks such as RCA TV, AC spark plugs, J & B whisky, A-1 sauce. Hence, they are familiar. In general, however, initials and numbers are the hardest form of trademark to remember and the easiest to confuse and to imitate.

They suggest no visual image by which they can be remembered. One issue of the *Standard Advertising Register* listed the following trademarks: No. 1, No. 2, 2 in 1, 3 in 1, 4 in 1, 5 in 1, No. 7, 12/24, No. 14, 77, and 400.

Pictorial. To reinforce their brand name, many advertisers use some artistic device, as distinctive lettering, a design, insignia or picture, or other visual device. The combination, as we mentioned before, is called a "logotype."

Creating the trademark

The use of a word for a trademark generally gives the owner the right to express the idea in a variety of ways, as with a picture or symbol (such as the trademark Green Giant for frozen and canned vegetables and a picture of a green giant for the same purpose). The total design can then be carried on labels, cartons, packing cases, warehouse signs, and gasoline service stations, both here and abroad. A trademark word or name is more apt to get quick recognition if it is always lettered in a uniform style; this unit is also a logotype. A test of a design is whether it is distinctive enough to be recognized immediately in any size.

Goals of a trademark

A trademark should be characterized as follows:

Distinctive. Its purpose is to *identify* a product. Trade directories are full of trademarks that play it safe and follow the leader, with the result that one directory listed 89 Golds or Goldens, 75 Royals, 95 Nationals, and 134 Stars!

There are styles in trademarks. We have recently been in the This n' That stage: Fresh 'n' Ready, Set 'n' Go, Stir 'n' Serve, Gloss 'n' Toss. These may be legally eligible for protection, but do they rank as distinctive? Or simply bewildering?

The quest for distinction also applies to designs, where circles, ovals, and oblongs are commonplace.

Simple, crisp, short. Good examples: Sanka coffee, Ajax cleanser, Ritz crackers, Crest toothpaste.

Easy to pronounce, and in one way only. The makers of Sitroux tissues changed their name to Sitrue; the makers of Baume Bengué changed it to Ben Gay. To help customers pronounce Suchard, the makers created a charming trade character called Sue Shard and changed the name too. These companies made the best of their old trademarks. But there should be no doubt about the pronunciation of a new trademark.

The great problem with suggestive trademarks is that they may so easily go over that vague boundary that divides them from being descriptive. Even experienced advertisers have this problem. The Sun Oil Company spent upward of $30 million over a 6-year period advertising its brand of gasoline called Custom Blended, only to have the courts finally rule that it was a descriptive term that any gasoline company could use.

A usable design. If a design is used, will it be usable and identifiable in black and white when reduced to small size? It takes a long time for the public to associate a company name with a design; hence many are meant to be used in connection with the product or company name to help reinforce the identification. A design is especially useful on packages, shipping cartons, trucks, and letterheads.

Free of unpleasant connotations, here or abroad. A trademark should be avoided if it can be punned unpleasantly. It should not be offensive abroad. The makers of an American car discovered that its name meant "sudden death" in one Oriental country where they had been trying to do business.

If a trademark conveys some attribute of the product, so much the better. Mere description cannot have legal protection, but a suggestion can: for example, Downy fabric softener, Band-Aid bandages, Accutron watches, Bisquick biscuit mix.

Having reviewed the desirable attributes of the trademark, we come back to the first question: Is it distinctive?

What "registering" a trademark

means   In the United States, the first to use a trademark for a certain category of goods has the exclusive right to it for those goods and for other goods that people might assume to be from the same producer. To let the world know who is using a trademark and to help establish the date on which it was first used, a trademark may be registered with the Patent Office, which has a complete record of all trademarks registered. Registration is not compulsory; but through the Lanham Act it provides 20-year protection, renewable indefinitely. Federal registration applies to goods sold in interstate or foreign commerce. If, within 5 years of registration, old ads or bills of sale prove that someone used a trademark before it was registered by another, the first user has rights over the person who registered it. Nevertheless, most firms apply for federal registration. There is also state registration for those seeking limited protection only.

Once a trademark has been registered, it should carry a notice to that effect wherever it appears, such as ® next to the trademark, or "Registered, U.S. Patent Office," or "Reg. U.S. Pat. Office," or some similar notice. When a trademark is repeatedly used in an ad, some firms require the registration notice on the first use only to reduce the possibility of typographic "bugs."

Putting a lock on

trademarks   We now meet a paradoxical situation, in which the owner of a successful trademark suddenly discovers that anyone can use it—all because certain precautionary steps were not taken. This problem arises when the public begins using a trademark to describe a *type* of product, rather than just a *brand* of that type of product. Originally, Thermos was the trademark owned by the Aladdin Company, which introduced vacuum bottles. In time, people began to ask, "What brand of thermos bottles do you carry?" The courts held that Thermos had become a descriptive word that any manufacturer of vacuum bottles could use as thermos (with a lower-case *t*) and was no longer the exclusive trademark of the originator. Victrola, cellophane, nylon, escalator, aspirin, and linoleum each started off as the trademark of one company but then became generic, a word that is public property because its owners failed to take certain simple steps to put a "lock" on their property.

Nowadays most large corporations follow very strict rules to protect their trademarks with lawyers reviewing every ad and commercial to make certain all legal "notices" are included with the trademark. Because corporations invest millions of dollars to establish their trademarks, they are willing to—and sometimes do—spend hundreds of thousands of dollars to defend their right to use the trademarks and prevent other companies from unlawful infringement or from using very similar trademarks, which impersonate the originals and may confuse the consumer.

The steps to putting a lock on the ownership of a trademark are these: (1) Always make sure the trademark word is capitalized or set off in distinctive type. (2) Always follow the trademark with the generic name of the product: Glad disposable trash bags, Kleenex tissues, Windex glass cleaner. (3) Don't speak of it in the plural, as "three Kleenexes"; rather, say, "three Kleenex tissues." (4) Don't use it in a possessive form (not Kleenex's new features, but the new features of Kleenex tissues) or as a verb (not "Kleenex your eyeglasses," but "Wipe your eyeglasses with Kleenex tissues"). This is a legal matter but the advertising person's responsibility to carry out in the ads. See Exhibit 19.2.

HOUSE MARKS

Up to now we have been speaking of trademarks that identify specific products. We now speak of the *house mark,* the primary mark of a firm that makes a large and changing variety of products. Here the house, or firm, mark is usually used with a secondary mark: Du Pont (primary), Lucite, Dacron, Zerone (secondary); Kellogg's (primary), Special K, Product 19 (secondary). See Exhibit 19.3.

Many companies create a design to go with their house mark. This design alone can appear on everything from a calling card to the sides of a truck and on shipping cases going overseas. It can become an international identification. But it takes time to establish a design; hence companies often use their name along with the house mark.

This brings us to a major marketing-policy decision on how, if at all, the relationship of all the company's products should be presented to the public. We quote from a report on the subject issued by the American Association of Advertising Agencies:

> This is a question of policy. What may be logical for one advertiser may not be at all suitable for another. The food field offers a good example of the two philosophies at work.

Dust was the color of the sky.
Dust was the color of the town.

The young sheriff moved toward the railway platform, pausing only to wipe his moist palms on his holsters.

He watched the Union Pacific engine hurtle around the bend and screech to a clanging, hissing stop. Silently, the Dalton boys swung from the train onto the station platform. Suddenly the sheriff found himself staring down the barrels of three shotguns. The street behind him was empty but for the dust.

There was no turning for help.

As his hands crept slowly toward his gun belt he knew he had to say it now or forever hold his peace. A crooked smile played about the corners of his mouth, as he drawled, "Boys, I want you to hear me and hear me good. Just remember, that Xerox is a registered trademark of Xerox Corporation and, as its brand name, should be used only to identify its products and services."

Exhibit 19.2
Xerox seeks to protect its exclusive right to its trademark.

Exhibit 19.3
House marks and a house mark combined with a trademark of one of the company's products.

Service marks; certification marks

Service mark.

Exhibit 19.4
Service mark.

Exhibit 19.5
Certification mark.

General Foods aims to have each of its many brands stand on its own advertising feet. In their early days they were acquiring companies at the rate of one every three months . . . in virtually every case, each was already established as an advertiser. For many years there was no family identification in the advertising. Then "A Product of General Foods" was included in small type, and more recently there has been an attempt toward family identification through the General Foods Test Kitchen . . .

On the other hand, California Packing has too many products to attempt to establish brand names for each. Consequently all are carried under the house mark, *Del Monte* [now sold to RJR Foods]. They feel that the quality reputation established for the overall mark rubs off on each product. They also point out that this philosophy makes their trademark generically invincible. Who would ask for "a can of Del Monte"?

Some follow a mixed course. National Biscuit has some 200 cookie and cracker packages in its line, a good many of which feature their own brands. Yet all carry the *Nabisco* trademark—usually shown on a corner of the package.

In some cases the association of brand and company is deliberately omitted from advertising, usually because of product competition within the company's line itself. This is a common occurrence with these companies.

This also applies when such associations reflect unpleasantly on the product or corporate image. A food company making fertilizer, for instance. The Quaker Oats "Q" trademark is not with seen in connection with Puss-in-Boots cat food.

Or when the association is meaningless. The *Gillette* mark is not used in advertising Paper-Mate pens.

Thus we see that a consideration of trademarks goes deep into management problems regarding the entire policy of marketing a variety of products made under the control of one company.*

*American Association of Advertising Agencies, *Trademarks—Orientation for Advertising People* (© 1971), pp. 22–23. Published by permission.

SERVICE MARKS: CERTIFICATION

MARKS People who render *services,* as an insurance company, an airline, or even Weight Watchers, can protect their identification mark by registering it in Washington as a *service mark* (Exhibit 19.4). There is also registration for *certification marks,* whereby a firm certifies that a user of his identifying device is doing so properly. Teflon is a material sold by Du Pont to kitchenware makers for use in lining their pots and pans. Teflon is Du Pont's registered trademark for its nonstick finish; Teflon II is Du Pont's certification mark for Teflon-coated cookware that meets Du Pont's standards. Advertisers of such products may use that mark. The Wool Bureau has a distinctive label design that it permits all manufacturers of pure-wool products to use (Exhibit 19.5). These marks are all registered as certification marks. They have the same creative requirements as trademarks—most of all, that they be distinctive.

PACKAGING Whether we talk about a supermarket, hardware store, sporting-goods store, hobby shop, drugstore, toy store, or department store, one thing is certain: A store's environment is an everchanging panorama, with new products, improved products, and new package designs constantly appearing on the scene. This is the arena in which consumer products have to fight for the consumer's patronage.

The package is the most conspicuous identification a product can have (Exhibit 19.6), and it is a major factor in the success of most consumer products. It is very persuasive in the consumer's decision to buy a product and in the retailer's decision to carry the product, but it is important to each for different reasons. With so many demands placed on the package, several people are involved in packaging decisions. The advertising director is one of them especially because advertising and packaging complement each other.

Basic

requirements *From the consumer's viewpoint.* With all the changes in packaging taking place, certain basic requirements never change. The package must protect its contents from spoilage and spillage, leakage, evaporation, and other forms of deterioration from the time it leaves the plant until the product is used up. (How long that might be is an important consideration.) It must fit the shelf of the refrigerator or medicine cabinet in which that type of product is stored. (The Vaseline bottle, which had been round for generations, was redesigned as a rectangular bottle to save room in the crowded medicine chest.) Cereal boxes must fit pantry shelves. If the package is meant to be set on a dressing table, it should not tip easily. The package should be comfortable to hold and not slip out of a wet hand. (Note how shampoo bottles usually provide a good grip.) It should be easy to open, without the user's breaking a fingernail, and to reclose for future use. It should be attractive.

From the store operator's viewpoint. The store manager has additional criteria for judging a package. It must be easy to handle, store, and stack. It

453

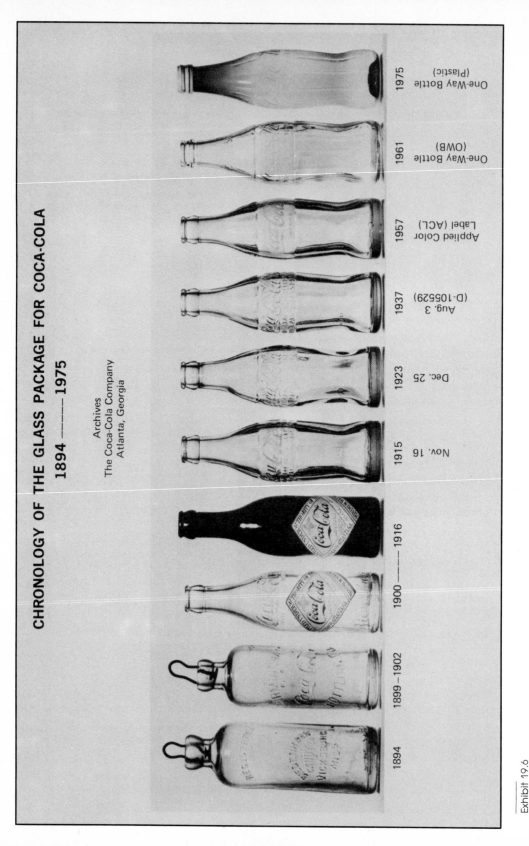

CHRONOLOGY OF THE GLASS PACKAGE FOR COCA-COLA
1894 ———— 1975

Archives
The Coca-Cola Company
Atlanta, Georgia

1894 1899 – 1902 1900 ———— 1916 1915 Nov. 16 1923 Dec. 25 1937 Aug. 3 (D-105529) 1957 Applied Color Label (ACL) 1961 One-Way Bottle (OWB) 1975 One-Way Bottle (Plastic)

Exhibit 19.6
Evolution of the Coca-Cola bottle. The first Coca-Cola bottle (1894) had a rubber stopper, and it popped when the bottle was opened—thus the word *pop* for soft drinks. (Courtesy of the Archives. The Coca-Cola Company.)

should not take up more shelf room than any other product in that section, as might a pyramid-shaped bottle. Odd shapes are suspect; will they break easily? Tall packages are suspect; will they keep falling over? The package should be soil resistant. Does it have ample and convenient space for marking? The product should come in the full range of sizes and packaging common to the field.

For products bought upon inspection, as men's shirts, the package needs transparent facing. (Puritan Shirts even included a plastic hanger for the store's use.) The package can make the difference in whether a store stocks the item.

Small items are expected to be mounted on cards under plastic domes, called *blister cards,* to provide ease of handling and to prevent pilferage. Often these cards are mounted on a large card that can be hung on a wall, making profitable use of that space. And at all times the buyer judges how a display of a product will add to the store.

There are factors other than packaging that may cause a product to be selected, but poor packaging may relegate that product to a poor shelf position. Moving a product from floor level to waist level has increased sales of a product by as much as 80 percent. Good packaging can make that much difference.

Finally, the package should enhance the beauty of its surroundings at the point of use or display.

Designing a new package

Package design embraces the entire physical presentation of the package: its size and shape, the materials of which it is made, the closure, the outside appearance, the labeling.

Fitting the package to marketing goals

Walter P. Margulies, a leading package designer, stresses the fact that package thinking is first of all marketing thinking, and embraces questions such as:

How much emphasis should be placed on the brand name? On the product name?

Toward what segment of the market should the product's basic appeal be aimed?

In what way will the packaging system best communicate product appeal?

Should the graphics try to convey the size, shape, color, in-use applications? If so, how?

In dealing with a food product, is it advisable to include recipes on the package? Which ones? Should they be changed in accordance with the seasons?

Are all package panels being used to their best advantage? Will they effectively sell the product, regardless of the way the package is stacked on the supermarket shelf?

Exhibit 19.7
The old versus the new. The old package is on the left; the new, on the right. (Courtesy Lippincott and Margulies, Inc.)

Can the basic design be extended to encompass other items in the manufacturer's line? Is it flexible enough to permit the addition of new products at some future date?

Is there ample space for the inclusion of extra copy to announce special sales offers?

What about price marking? Has a specific place been set aside where the product can be priced easily by the retailer but not mar the total look of the package?*

These are a mere handful of the multitudinous factors that have to be taken into consideration by those whose job it is to launch a new package.

TIME FOR A CHANGE?

We now jump ahead a number of years and perhaps many millions of dollars in sales for the product we so wisely trademarked and packaged and whose merits have earned it many repeat customers. "What's this?" someone exclaims some morning. "You want to make changes in our good-luck package?" There is no clock of package life that says whether or when you might want to consider a change (Exhibit 19.7). But there are certain telltale market indexes that say it may be time to review the situation. Among them Margulies cites the following:

1. Innovation in physical packaging
2. Exploiting a reformulated product based on a meaningful formula change

*Walter P. Margulies, *Packaging Power* (New York: World Publishing, 1970). Copyright © by Walter P. Margulies; reprinted by permission.

Exhibit 19.8
The old label (left) was redesigned (right) to give the name greater prominence on the store shelf. (Courtesy of International Paper Co.)

3. The force of competitive action
4. Repositioning your product
   General Foods learned that the image of the decaffeinated Sanka brand was that of a castrated bean. The coffee-loving public avoided it. To reposition Sanka, the yellow label, which according to research, suggested weakness, was replaced with a dominantly brown label, "very strong." And the statement "97 percent caffein-free" was given a less significant spot on the label
5. When effective ads force a shift in tactics
   Only when a theme has established itself as distinctive and long-lived
6. When changing consumer attitudes force a shift in marketing tactics
7. Upgraded consumer taste in graphic design
8. Changing retail selling techniques
9. When unrecognized home use determines a new marketing posture

In contrast to these reasons for considering a change Margulies offers the following warnings:

1. Don't change because of a new brand manager's desire to innovate.
2. Don't change to imitate your competition.
3. Don't change for physical packaging innovation only.
4. Don't change for design values alone.
5. Don't change when product identification is strong.
6. Don't change if it may hurt the branding.
7. Don't change if it will weaken the product's authenticity.
8. Don't change if it will critically raise the product's price.

"A decision to stay with the status quo," he adds, "is as important as the one to innovate."* Some companies, however, frequently test new packaging to try to revitalize a product (Exhibit 19.8) or turn an old product into a new one and yet spend less money than if they had started from scratch.

*Ibid., pp. 62–67.

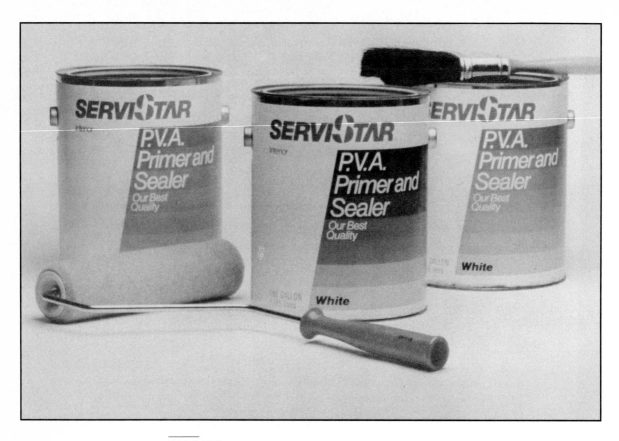

Exhibit 19.9
Two examples of packaging a complete line (page 458 and 459). (Courtesy of Lippincott & Margulies, Inc.)

When a package is to be changed, it is often done on a gradual basis, changing only one element at a time so that old customers will not suddenly feel that this is no longer the product they have known and trusted.

Package design has become so important that a specialized field of package designers has developed, who are often given responsibility for the entire "look" of a firm (Exhibit 19.9).

Testing the package
design   What research techniques can provide information that can be translated into guidelines for a sound package-design program? Among the most common approaches are the following: tachistoscope tests, focus-group interviews, semantic-differential tests, forced-choice association tests, and attitude-study interviews.*

*Walter Stern, "Research and the Designer," *Modern Packaging,* April, 1975, pp. 30–31.

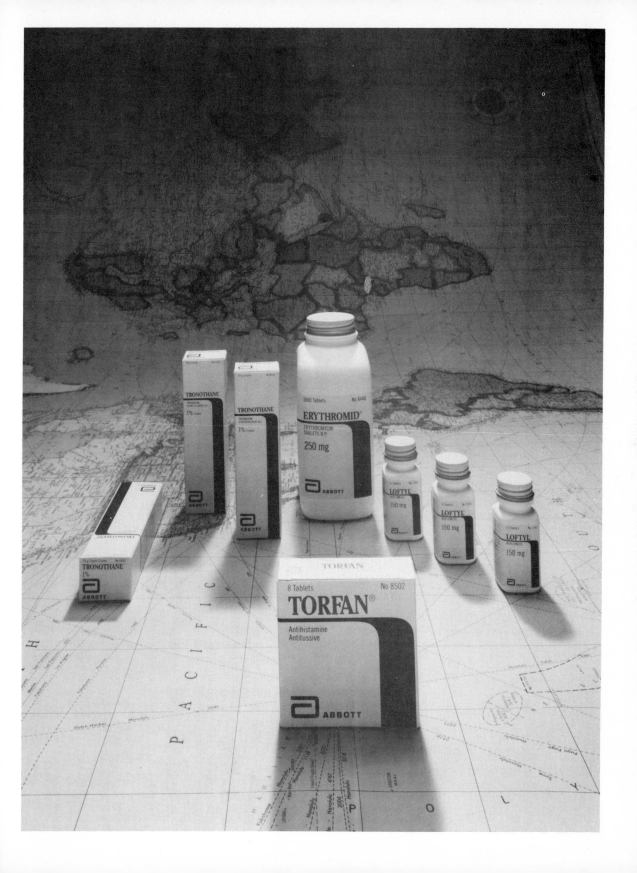

Tachistoscope test. A tachistoscope is a device, similar to a slide projector, that flashes pictures on a screen for very short, controlled periods of time (usually in intervals of a fraction of a second). The respondents are exposed to pictures of a package to determine, for example, how quickly they recognize the brand name, the type of product, package size, illustration, or any other design feature of the package. The results of this test (which is best used in combination with another technique) can be a useful basis for evaluating how the package's message is being received.

Focus-group interview. In an unstructured approach a number (usually from five to ten) of group participants are brought together under the direction of a group discussion leader. They engage in a free-wheeling, open discussion about the subject at hand, which ranges from the general ("How do you feel about breakfast in your home?") to the specific ("What do you look for in a cereal package?"). This approach can provide useful insights into packaging and comparative package designs and is reasonable in cost, no more than $2,000 for the session and report.

Semantic-differential test. This technique uses a series of scales, with each scale consisting of two opposite adjectives, for example, expensive–cheap, natural–artificial, modern–old-fashioned, national–local, sweet–sour, strong–weak, or heavy–light. The semantic-differential method of testing package designs is simple so that several packages can be rapidly rated and compared. It is more reasonable in cost than, but does not provide the depth of, the focus-group session.

Forced-choice association test. Respondents rate package attributes on a scale providing answers that most accurately reflect their opinions on certain questions. (The scale is similar to multiple-choice examinations.) The test permits comparison among various packages or design elements.

Attitude-study interview. Sometimes it is advantageous to conduct interviews to determine consumer attitudes toward packaging. The interviews are normally done at the point of purchase among consumers who have purchased and used the product (or a competitive one), and the respondents are asked a variety of questions pertaining to the product and package. The result is a great deal of data that the packager can use in evaluating a package and in deciding which alternative to choose, if any, for a new package design. An important feature of attitude-study interviews is that the data are usually collected in the actual buying atmosphere of the store.

LEGAL ASPECTS OF PACKAGING

There are both federal and state laws that regulate packaging and labeling. The Fair Packaging and Labeling Act of 1966 says:

Informed consumers are essential to the fair and efficient functioning of a free economy. Packages and their labels should enable consumers to obtain accurate information as to the quality of the contents and should facilitate value comparisons. Therefore it is hereby declared to be the policy of the Congress to assist consumers and manufacturers in reaching these goals in the marketing of goods.

This is the most far-reaching law affecting packaging and labeling. For example, all food packages must display the ingredients prominently (a loaf of bread lists all the ingredients in descending order of their amount); over-the-counter drug products follow the same rule; and drug products must prominently display instructions for use, precautions, and instructions in case of accidental overdose. The Food and Drug Administration is responsible for enforcing the law as it affects foods, drugs, cosmetics, and health devices. The Federal Trade Commission has jurisdiction over "other consumer commodities."

TRENDS IN PACKAGING

Packagers, like most others in industry, have to deal with energy and materials shortages. Whether we talk about plastics, aluminum, glass, paper, or any other packaging material, the problem is the same—supplies are not unlimited, as we once thought. Packagers have been trying to economize by finding substitute materials and by developing simpler and more standardized packages. Alcoa has run extensive advertising to urge people to turn in old aluminum cans for recycling. To save on expensive metal, Band-Aid has switched to a paperboard carton for its bandages. A packaging change born of necessity very often results in a package that consumers like better than the old one, as Taylor Wines found out when it switched from scarce lead foil to PVC (polyvinyl chloride) for the overcap on its bottles—and Taylor got better color identification for the package as a bonus.

The quest continues.

SUMMARY

A good trademark is most important in this age of self-service; it grows more valuable each year. A trademark is any symbol, sign, word, name, or device that tells who makes a product or who sells it and distinguishes that product from products sold by others. Trademarks usually contain a brand name, but not always. A trade name is the name under which a company does business.

There are many forms of trademark: Some use familiar words (like Dial soap or Glad plastic bags), but the words must be used not as a *description* of the product but as the *name associated* with the product; some trademarks are coined words (like Kodak, Xerox, or Exxon)—advantageous because new and legally protectable because original. A trademark usually consists of words and a symbol; the words are usually lettered in a distinctive style, which is known as a logotype.

A trademark should be distinctive, short, easy to pronounce, and free of unpleasant connotations. Trademarks are registered with the United States Patent Office, which has a complete record of all registered trademarks. Registration gives the trademark 20-year protection. Trademarks may be challenged if they are not properly protected when they are used.

Service marks are used by companies that render a service: airlines, insurance companies, and the like.

Packaging is a very important part of selling because the package is the most conspicuous identification a product has. Good packages not only are noticeable but store the product well and are easy to keep and stack on a shelf.

Package design takes in the entire package—size, shape, and materials as well as outside appearance and labeling. Package designs grow old and are sometimes changed to bring the appearance of the product up to date. Such changing is usually done only after a great deal of testing and thought; for an old design may be the consumer's best and most familiar means of identifying the product.

QUESTIONS

1. Define a trademark. What is its purpose?
2. Distinguish among (a) trademark, (b) brand name, and (c) trade name. Give two examples of each.
3. What are the important legal requirements to keep in mind when creating a trademark?
4. Discuss the six forms of trademark cited in the chapter.
5. What are the chief qualities desired of a trademark?
6. Discuss the importance of a trademark from the viewpoint of advertising.
7. What is meant by the registration of trademarks?
8. What are the basic requirements of a package from the consumer's viewpoint? From the retailer's viewpoint?
9. "The package is part of the total product." What is your comment?
10. How do packaging and advertising work together?
11. Explain why packaging thinking is marketing thinking.
12. What are some of the conditions that suggest a need for considering a packaging change? What are some reasons for not changing?
13. Describe the approaches used in package testing.
14. In your opinion, does packaging do a good job? Whatever your answer, justify your position.
15. What do you see as the social responsibilities of packaging? Are they being fulfilled? Why or why not?
16. Cite three examples each of what you believe to be effective packaging and ineffective packaging. Explain the reasons for your choices.

SUGGESTED EXERCISES

17. Think of distinctive names for the following new products:
    a) silk-like fabric,
    b) new high-viscosity motor oil,
    c) new peanut, caramel, chocolate-covered candy bar,
    d) a strong anti-perspirant, deodorant.

18. Design a trademark for a new international conglomerate corporation. List the steps you would take to register the trademark.

19. Choose two packages from products you use every day. Suggest improvements from the following viewpoints:
    a) practicality on the shelf in the store,
    b) attractiveness to the prime prospect for impulse sales,
    c) utility and storage in use at home.

READINGS

The Best in Packaging, Print Casebooks 4 (Washington, D.C.: Print, 1980/81).

DICHTER, ERNEST: *Packaging: The Sixth Sense?* (Boston: Cahners Books, 1975).

"Purina goes after generics," *Advertising Age,* November 23, 1981, p. 1.

"Selling Your Graphic Design and Illustration," *Communicative Arts,* May/June 1981, pp. 74-91.

STATMAN, MEIR, and TYZOON T. TYEBJEE: "Trademarks, Patents, and Innovation in the Ethical Drug Industry," *Journal of Marketing,* Summer 1981, pp. 71-81.

STERN, WALTER: "Research and the Designer," *Modern Packaging,* April 1975, pp. 28-31.

"Technical Advances Push Packaging Forward," *Advertising Age,* April 29, 1974, p. 45.

"Trademarks," *Communication Arts Magazine,* November/December 1981, pp. 153-54.

Managing the Advertising

Advertising is a business conducted largely through advertising agencies. The following chapters deal with the agency role and the role of media-buying services (Chapter 20) and the important part the client's marketing/advertising operation plays in the creation of advertising campaigns (Chapter 21). The last chapter in this part (Chapter 22) deals with the complete campaign. We shall see how the agency and client think through the complex and very disciplined process of bringing a product to market while selecting the target audience, create a strategy to reach the market, and then come up with an ad campaign that not only motivates the consumer but galvanizes everyone in the product company into action to sell the product and make the marketing/advertising campaign a success.

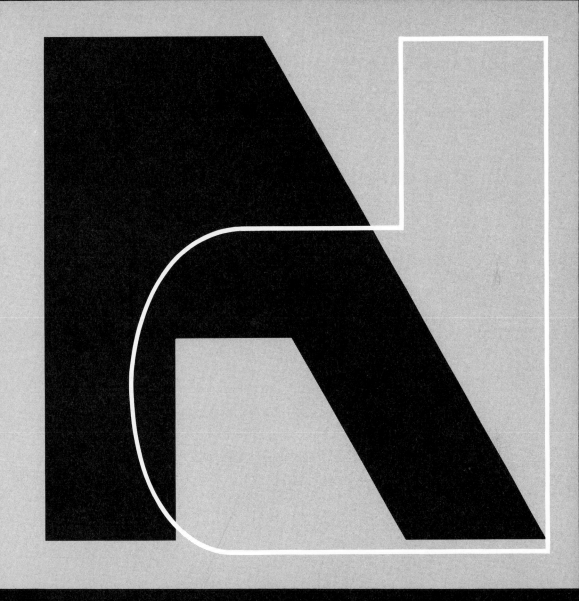

PART FIVE

20

The Advertising Agency, Media Services, and Other Services

THE ADVERTISING
 AGENCY The advertising agency has played an important role not only on the advertising scene but also in American industry and, more recently, in world industry. It has grown with the times; it has changed with the times.

   What is an advertising agency? What does it do? Where does it fit into the marketing picture? What is its role in relation to advertisers and media? How does it get paid? What changes are now taking place in the advertising field? To understand these matters, let's begin at the beginning.

How today's agency
 developed It is not generally known that the first Americans to act as advertising agents were often Colonial postmasters:

> In many localities, advertisements for Colonial papers might be left at the post offices. In some instances the local post office would accept advertising copy for publication in papers in other places; it did so with the permission of the postal authorities. . . . William Bradford, publisher of the first Colonial weekly in New York, made an arrangement with Richard Nichols, postmaster in 1727, whereby the latter accepted advertisements for the *New York Gazette* at regular rates.*

---

  *James Melvin Lee, *History of American Journalism,* rev. ed. (Boston: Houghton Mifflin, 1933), p. 74.

Space salesmen. In 1841 a certain Volney B. Palmer of Philadelphia became the first advertising sales agent to work on a commission basis, soliciting ads for newspapers which at that time had difficulty getting out-of-town advertising. Palmer contacted publishers, offered to get them business for a 50-percent commission, but often settled for less. There was no such thing as a rate card or a fixed price for space or commission: "A first demand for $500 by the papers might be reduced before the bargain was struck to $50." (Today we call that *negotiation.*) Soon there were more agents, offering various deals.

Wholesalers of space. In the 1850s George P. Rowell of Philadelphia became a sort of advertising wholesaler, buying big blocks of space from publishers at very low rates but for cash (most welcome), less agent's commission. He would then sell the space in small "squares"—one column wide—at his own retail rate. Rowell next contracted with 100 newspapers to buy one column of space a month and sold the space in his total list at a fixed rate per line for the whole list: "An inch of space a month in one hundred papers for one hundred dollars." Selling by list then became widespread. Each wholesaler's list, however, was his private stock in trade. (This was the original *media-package deal.*)

The first rate directory. In 1869 Rowell shocked the advertising world by publishing a directory of newspapers with their card rates and with his own estimates of their circulation. Other agents accused him of giving away their trade secrets; publishers howled too because his estimates of circulation were lower than their claims. Nevertheless, he offered to provide advertisers an estimate of space costs based on those published rates for whatever markets they wanted. This was the beginning of the *media estimate.*

The agency becomes a creative center. In the early 1870s Charles Austin Bates, a writer, began writing ads and selling his services to whoever wanted them, whether advertisers or agents. Among his employees were Earnest Elmo Calkins (Exhibit 20.1) and Ralph Holden, who (in the 1890s) founded their own agency, famous for 50 years under the name of Calkins and Holden. They did more than write ads: They brought together planning, copy, and art, showing the way to make all three into effective advertising. Not only was their agency a most successful one for half a century, but the influence of their work helped establish the advertising agency as the creative center for advertising ideas. That many of the names on the list of firms advertising in 1890 (Chapter 1) are still familiar today is a tribute to the effectiveness of that generation of agency people in developing the new power of advertising-agency services. The business had changed from that of salesmen going out just to sell advertising space to that of agencies that created the plan, the ideas, the copy, and the artwork, produced the plates, and then placed the advertising in publications from which they received commission.

Since the early days of Calkins and Holden, there have been many changes in the agency world, and many new services have been—and are

Earnest Elmo Calkins
580 Park Avenue
New York
21

Dear Mr. Kleppner:

You perhaps do not realize what a disorganized muddle
advertising was in the 1880's and 1890's. Most agencies merely
placed copy furnished by clients. The rate cards were farces.
The average agent simply bartered with the medium, magazine or
newspaper, as to cost, beating it down to the lowest possible
amount by haggling.

I consider my greatest contribution as being the first
agency to recognize that advertising was a profession, to be
placed on a much higher plane than a mere business transaction
of placing advertising -- with the copy, the art work, the plan
as the important part. I wrote my first advertising while still
living in my home town, won a prize for an ad, wrote copy for
local business men, worked a year as advertising manager for a
department store, and received an offer from Charles Austin Bates,
who was the first man to make a business of writing advertising
copy. There I met Ralph Holden, and from that association sprang
the name of the old firm of Calkins and Holden. I am now more
than 96 years old.

Cordially,

Earnest Elmo Calkins

Exhibit 20.1
"All of this I have seen, and part of which I have been." Calkins, a pioneer in the advertising-agency business, wrote this letter 3 months before his death in 1964.

being—offered by agencies. But to this day the unique contribution to business for which agencies are most respected is their ability to create effective advertising.

Agency-client relationship established. In 1875 N. W. Ayer & Son of Philadelphia (successors to Rowell and one of our big agencies today) proposed to bill advertisers for what Ayer actually paid the publishers (that is, the rate paid the publisher less the commission), adding a fixed charge in lieu of commission. In exchange, advertisers would place all advertising through agents. This established the relationship of advertisers as clients of agencies rather than as customers who might give business to different salespeople, never knowing whether they were paying the best price.

The Curtis no-rebating rule. In 1891 the Curtis Publishing Company, the giant that published *The Saturday Evening Post* and the *Ladies' Home Journal,* announced that it would pay commissions to agencies only if they agreed to collect the full price from advertisers, a rule later adopted by the Magazine Publishers Association. It was the forerunner of no-rebating agreements, which were an important part of the agency business for over 50 years. (Agency commissions, however, ranged all the way from 10 to 25 percent in both magazines and newspapers.)

Standard commission for recognized agencies established. In 1917 newspaper publishers, through their associations, set 15 percent as the standard agency commission, a percentage that remains for all media to this day (except local advertising, for which the media deal directly with the stores and pay no commission). The commission would be granted, however, only to agencies that the publishers' associations "recognized." One of the important conditions for recognition was that the agencies agree to charge the client the full rate (no rebating). Other criteria for recognition were that the agencies must have business to place, they must have shown competence to handle advertising, and they must be financially sound. Those three conditions are in effect to this day. Anyone may claim to be an agency, but only those who are recognized are allowed a commission.

Agencies still receive commissions from the media for space they buy for clients. Artwork, however, and the cost of production generally are charged by the agency to the advertiser, plus a service charge, usually 17.65 percent of the net—equivalent to 15 percent of the gross. By preagreement a charge is made for other services.

The American Association of Advertising Agencies. The year 1917 also marked the date when the American Association of Advertising Agencies (the 4A's) was formed. This organization has continuously been a great force for improving the standards of agency business and advertising practice. Its members today, large and small, place over 80 percent of all national advertising.

The no-rebate age
(1917 to 1956)
We can summarize the events of the years up to 1956, which have left their mark on the agency world today:

Radio. The main event of 1925 was the notorious Scopes trial, and the main advent was that of radio. Both did a lot for each other. Radio added drama to evolution on trial; it brought the issue of teaching evolution closer to listeners and brought those at home closer to the radio. Tuning in became a major part of American life; especially during the great Depression and during World War II, it established itself as a prime news vehicle. It thus gave advertising a new medium and challenged the agencies to create a new art of advertising, the *radio commercial.* The manufacture of radio sets became a booming new industry that also needed advertising. Radio billings helped many agencies pull through those troubled years. A number of agencies handled the entire production of the program as well as the commercial. By 1942 agencies were billing more for radio ($188 million) than they were for newspapers ($144 million). The radio boom lasted until TV came along.

Television. TV really got going after 1952, when nationwide network broadcasts began. Between 1950 and 1956 TV was the fastest-growing medium. It became the major medium in many agencies. National advertisers spent more on TV than they did on any other medium. TV expenditures grew from $171 million in 1950 to $1,225 million in 1956. In 1981 total TV expenditures were approximately $15 billion. These increases in TV revenues are not adjusted for inflation, which averaged 10 percent per year in the 1970s. However, they are still impressive.

Electronic Data Processing. The computer entered advertising through the accounting department. By 1956 it was already changing the lives of the media department, the marketing department, and the research department—all having grown in competence with the increasing number of syndicated research services. Agencies prided themselves on their research knowledge and were spending hundreds of thousands of dollars for research per year to serve their clients better. One important agency even went so far as to buy its own computer for information storage and media research, and soon other major agencies added the computer to their list of talents.

Business was good, and consumers were attaining a better standard of living than they had ever had before. The period from 1950 to 1956 proved to be the beginning of the biggest boom advertising ever had: Total expenditures jumped from $4,570 million in 1950 to $9,910 in 1956. Over 60 percent of this was for national advertising placed by advertising agencies. And the agency business was good too.

The age of negotiation

(1956 to now) ***Consent decrees.*** In 1956 a great change occurred in the advertiser-agency relationship. The United States Department of Justice held that the no-rebating provision between media associations and agencies limited the ability to negotiate between buyer and seller and that it was in restraint of trade and a violation of the antitrust laws. People involved in such provisions, however, might consent in writing to drop the practices now found unlawful, and any charges would then be dropped. Consent decrees to stop no rebating were entered into by all media associations on behalf of their members.

The Justice Department's ruling in no way affected the 15 percent the agencies received from the media, but it opened the way to review the total compensation an agency should receive for its services, with the 15-percent commission from the media as a basic part of the negotiations. We shall shortly see the many effects this has had on the agency-client relationship.

HOW DOES THE FULL-SERVICE AGENCY

WORK When a new account or a new product is assigned to an agency, work on it will generally proceed along these lines:

What is the marketing

problem? The marketing problem entails research to determine whom we are trying to sell to. Where are they? What are their demographic and psychographic characteristics? How does this product fit into their lifestyle? How do they regard this type of product? This particular product? Competitive products? What one service, above all others, do consumers seek from such a product? In what distinctive way can the product deliver the greatest satisfaction? What media will best reach our market?

The strategy
Based on answers to your questions, your agency formulates a strategy that positions the product in relation to the prime-prospect customer and emphasizes the attribute that will appeal to the prime prospect.

The creative

response Based on the strategy, your agency will decide on the copy appeal, prepare copy, and prepare rough layouts and storyboards.

The media plan
Select media, and prepare schedules with costs.

Total plan
Present roughs of the copy, layout, and production costs, along with media schedules and costs—all leading to total cost.

When approved, proceed with production of ads, issue media orders, and ship plates and prints to media or tapes and films as required.

Notify trade of forthcoming
campaign Inform dealers of the campaign details, giving them time to get ready.

Billing and
payments When ads are run, take care of billing to client and payment of bills to media and to production vendors. As an example of the billing procedure, let us say that through your agency an advertiser has ordered an ad in *Leisure-time* magazine for one page, worth $2,000. When the ad appears, your agency will get a bill from the publisher reading as follows (or something very much like it):

1 page, October *Leisure-time* magazine	$2,000
Agency commission @ 15% [cash discount omitted	
for convenience]	300
Balance due	$1,700

Your agency will then bill the advertiser for $2,000, retain the $300 as its compensation, and pay the publisher $1,700.

The agency commission applies only to the cost of space or time. In addition, as mentioned earlier, your agency will send the advertiser a bill for production costs for such items as finished artwork, typography, and reproduction prints—all at actual cost plus a service charge, usually 17.65 percent of the gross (which is equivalent to 15 percent of the net).

ORGANIZATION OF THE FULL-SERVICE

AGENCY Many of today's agencies were started by two entrepreneurs, one creative, the other an account manager. At first they may have handled all the functions of an agency themselves, but soon they would have to round out their organization to handle the basic areas of full-service-agency responsibility. Although agencies differ in the way they are organized, dividing these areas of responsibility into four main categories will give us a good idea of basic agency structure. For the purposes of this discussion, we put the agency under the command of four major executives: the vice-presidents for (1) the creative department, (2) account services, (3) marketing services, and (4) management and finance. We shall discuss briefly how each department is organized; and also see Exhibit 20.2.

1. Creative

department As the head of the creative department, the creative director is responsible for the effectiveness of advertising produced by the agency. The success of the agency depends on this. The creative director sets the creative philosophy of the agency and its standards of craftsmanship and generates a stimulating environment that inspires writers and artists to do their best work, which in turn inspires the best people to seek work there.

At first writers and artists will work directly with the creative director; but as the business grows, various creative directors will take over the writing

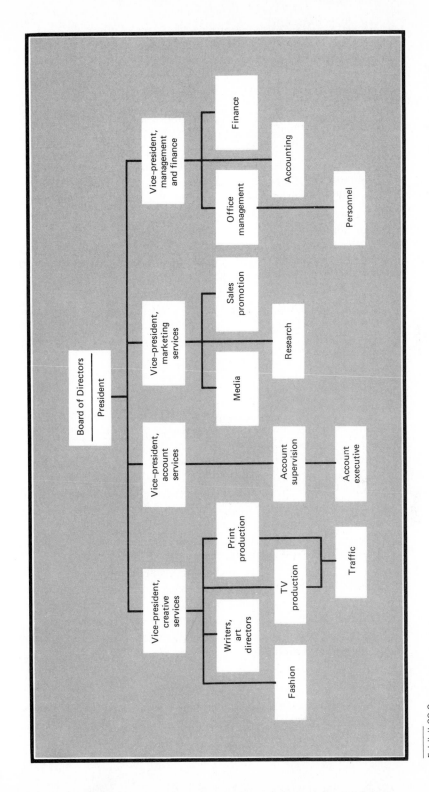

Exhibit 20.2
Organization of a typical full-service agency.

and art activities of different brands. To keep the work flowing on schedule, there will be established a *traffic department.*

2. Account services

The vice-president in charge of account services is responsible for the relationship between agency and client and is indeed a person of two worlds: that of the client's business and that of advertising. The vice-president must, of course, be knowledgeable about the client's business, profit goals, marketing problems, and advertising objectives. He or she is responsible for helping to formulate the basic advertising strategy recommended by the agency, for seeing that the proposed advertising prepared by the agency is on target, and for presenting the total proposal—media schedules, budget, and rough ads or storyboards—to the client for approval. Then comes the task of making sure that the agency produces the work to the client's satisfaction.

As the business grows and the account-services director has several clients, account executives will be appointed to become the continuing contact with the various accounts. Account executives must be skillful in communication and follow-up. Their biggest contribution is to keep the agency ahead of clients' needs. But the account-management director will continue the overall review of account handling, maintaining contacts with a counterpart at the advertiser's office.

3. Marketing services

The vice-president in charge of marketing services will be responsible for media planning and buying, for research, and for sales promotion. The marketing vice-president will appoint a media director, who is responsible for the philosophy and planning of the use of media, for the selection of specific media, and for buying space and time. As the agency grows, there will be a staff of media buyers, grouped according to media (print, TV, or radio), accounts, or territory. The media staff will include an estimating department and an ordering department, as well as one to handle residual payments due performers. The media head may use independent media services, especially in the purchase of TV and radio time, as we shall shortly describe.

The research director will help define marketing and copy goals. Agencies usually use outside research organizations for field work; but in some agencies research and media planning are coordinated under one person. The division of work among the executives may vary with the agency.

The sales-promotion director takes care of premiums, coupons, and other dealer aids and promotions.

4. Management and finance

Like all businesses, an advertising agency needs an administrative head to take charge of financial and accounting control, office management, and personnel (including trainees).

International agency

operations Virtually every large American agency has offices in the lands where its clients conduct their international business. There are such offices in eighty-eight countries. These international offices serve a defensive purpose: If an agency does not have a foreign office to handle an overseas client, that client will turn to the local office of another agency. The door is then open for the competitive agency to take over the American part of the billings, the largest of all.

Chapter 24 deals extensively with international operations. But to fill out the discussion here, we may say that setting up a foreign office is more complex than opening an office within the United States; for each land is a different market, with its own language, buying habits, ways of living, mores, business methods, marketing traditions, and laws. So instead of trying to organize new agencies with American personnel, most American agencies now purchase a majority or minority interest in successful foreign agencies. They usually have a top-management person at the head of an overseas office. Key members of international offices regularly gather at the home office for an intensive seminar on the philosophy and operation of the agency, giving them ideas to carry back and adapt as they see fit.

Competing

accounts The relationship between client and agency is a professional one. A full-service agency will share many of the client's confidences, often including plans for new products; therefore a full-service agency will not, as a rule, accept the advertising of products in direct competition. This practice has led to many conflicts in our age of conglomerates, when a client may buy a company one of whose products competes with one the agency is presently handling. When two agencies consider merging, the first question is "Will any of our accounts conflict?" This subject also presents a problem in dealing with outside creative services and is a conceivably inhibiting factor.

The agency of

record Large advertisers will have a number of agencies to handle the advertising of their various divisions and products. To coordinate the total media buy and the programming of products in a network buy, the advertiser will appoint one agency as *agency of record*. It will make the corporate media contracts under which other agencies will issue their orders, keep a record of all the advertising placed, and transmit management's decisions on the allotment of time and space in a schedule. For this service the agencies involved pay a small part of their commissions (usually 15 percent of their 15 percent) to the agency of record.

Agency

networks In the 1920s Lynn Ellis, an advertising management consultant saw that middle-size agencies that had no branch offices had difficulty in dealing with the regional problems of their clients. He organized such agencies (one agency in each main advertising center) into an *agency network,* to help one another on problems in their respective areas and to exchange ideas, experiences, and facilities. The success of this plan has prompted the formation of other agency networks.

OTHER DEVELOPMENTS IN THE AGENCY

WORLD New services have been springing up outside the agency, contributing to big changes in agency structure:

Independent creative

services Because advertisers were looking around to find top creative talent whose services they could buy on a fee basis, a number of creative shops opened (often called *boutiques*). Usually they were headed by former top-level agency talent and included copywriters and artists. One creative shop won a major advertising award and got so much business that it became a full-service agency, now a very large one.

Media-buying

services Such services are usually referred to as *media services,* and they came to advertising in the late 1960s. They represent independent companies of media specialists, concentrating largely on buying TV and radio time. (We discuss them at greater length later in this chapter.)

Both of these services were born in the 1960s and the 1970s, times of increasing costs and decreasing profits, which caused advertisers to look in all directions to see how they could more effectively handle advertising costs.

Predictably, the boutiques and—most especially—the media-buying services were not allowed to capture business from agencies without a battle. The agencies matched and bettered the media-buying services by buying at better cost efficiencies and offering more services. As a result, there are left today only a few media-buying services that have sizeable national accounts. The same fate befell the creative boutiques.

A la carte

agency Many agencies offer for a fee just that part of their total services that the advertiser wants. The à la carte arrangement is used mostly for creative services and for media planning and placement.

In-house

agency When advertisers found that all the services an agency could offer were purchasable on a piecemeal fee basis, they began setting up their own internal agencies, referred to as *in-house agencies.*

Under the in-house-agency operation an advertiser can employ an agency or a creative service to originate advertising for a fee or markup. A media-buying service will buy the time or space, and an agency will place it for a fraction of their 15-percent commission. Whereas the older *house agency* (see below) was equipped with a complete full-service staff, the in-house agency is an administrative center that gathers and directs varying outside services for its operation and has a minimum staff. The term "in-house" distinguishes the talent-assembling type of agency operation from the self-contained full-service house agency born in the earliest days, when large advertisers owned agencies (even Procter & Gamble had its own Procter and Collier agency); these agencies were geared to perform almost all the advertising functions. But such house agencies generally fell out of favor as the advertisers discovered that they got better advertising when they used independent agencies. Even the few such house agencies operating today may use outside services to supplement their own staffs.

Saving money is not the only or even the chief reason for some firms to use an in-house agency. In the industrial field, dealing with highly technical matters and with constant technical changes and advances, some advertisers have found it more efficient to have their own technical people prepare the ads, to save the endless briefing necessary for outside industrial writers. But they place their ads through an agency of their choice, at a negotiated commission.

The establishment of an in-house-agency operation requires careful planning. Various estimates (running up to $20 million) have been made on how much billing is required for a successful operation. The in-house agency is definitely not for the small advertiser.

FORMS OF AGENCY
COMPENSATION

The two broad sources of agency compensation are the traditional 15-percent media commission, including ways of settling on the final percentage, and strictly a fee basis, whereby the agency commission reverts to the advertiser and the agency receives a fee computed on whatever basis has been agreed upon.

Since 1972 the Association of National Advertisers has conducted biennial surveys among its members to determine their methods of agency compensation. The survey is intended to report variations in the ways of compensating agencies and to provide comparisons that might show trends. Table 20.1 is a summary of the reports of a survey of 257 advertisers. As indicated by the survey results, advertiser-agency compensation arrangements are, as a rule, tailored to the specific service requirements of the advertiser and the willingness and ability of the agency to fulfill those needs at a mutually agreeable cost.*

*Association of National Advertisers, Inc., "Current advertiser practices in compensating their advertising agencies," 1976.

Table 20–1

CLIENT-AGENCY COMPENSATION ARRANGEMENTS		
COMMISSION-RELATED ARRANGEMENTS	NUMBER OF MENTIONS	% OF 275 TOTAL
Traditional 15% media commission plus markup	168	61%
Reduced commission	11	4
Increased commission	3	1
Combination of hourly rates and commissions	4	1
Volume rebate	1	—
Minimum guarantee	12	4
Efficiency incentive compensation plan	7	3
Other	21	8
Total media commission-related	227	82%
Strictly fee arrangements		
Cost plus profit	16	6%
Fixed fee (flat fee, fixed compensation)	18	7
Flat fee plus direct costs	6	2
Supplemental fees (project fees)	3	1
Other	5	2
Total fee	48	18%
Overall total	275	100%

Just as some advertisers move their accounts from independent agencies to form their own in-house agencies, so other advertisers, having tried in-house agencies, have returned to independent agencies. The 4A's made a 2-year study of such shifts among its members, which is summarized in Table 20.2.

MEDIA-BUYING SERVICES
REVISITED

The 1960s were exciting for TV, its first 10 years of nationwide network broadcasting. It was the decade of booming sales of TV sets and TV advertising; in fact sales of TV time doubled during those years. TV media directors of large agencies were spending millions of dollars under great professional pressure to make the most effective use of their budgets by planning the scheduling and by negotiating for the best buys. Meanwhile, in every business office of every TV station there was always concern about unsold time—a cardinal sin because it represented a complete, irreversible loss. The situation was ripe for time buyers, especially in large agencies with large TV schedules, to plan and to place and to negotiate for the best deal for a schedule. Negotiating for time became an art. So much so that some media directors decided to start their own time-buying services, performing whatever part of the total media operation an advertiser or agency might require: planning, scheduling, nego-

478

Table 20-2

	DOLLAR VOLUME		% OF TOTAL 4A VOLUME	
	1980	1979	1980	1979
Movement TO "in-house"	$32,832,000	$26,453,000	0.19%	0.18%
Movement FROM "in-house"	39,435,000	41,810,000	0.23%	0.28%
Net Movement to A.A.A.A. Agencies	$ 6,603,000	$15,357,000	0.04%	0.10%

tiating, verifying. The chief service featured by most of them was at the pocketbook level in negotiating the purchase of time on behalf of the advertiser.

The advent of these services was also in response to some advertisers' need to retain specialists to handle their work, operating on an in-house-agency basis. Some advertisers also saw that competition in media negotiations would result in the best rates for the advertiser—and media services represented competition to the agency's media department. The agencies sharpened their media operations immediately and fought the media-buying services head on: today there are only a few large buying services still in business. The great majority of national advertisers now use the full-service agency, including the media department.

OTHER SERVICES

Barter   Barter is another way for an advertiser or agency to buy media below card rates, especially TV and radio time. It has nothing to do with media services except that they often use it.

When the advertiser is the buyer. Long before radio and TV appeared on the scene, hotels began a practice that they continue to this day: paying for advertising space in exchange for *due bills,* which were good for the payment of rooms and were transferable. They bartered their rooms for advertising space in newspapers and magazines.

Barter in broadcasting began in the early days of radio. Cash was always tight (even as it is today), but studios would have to spend a lot of money for equipment and for gifts to be given away at quiz shows. Some entrepreneurs got the idea that they would get these goods at very low cost, bartering with stations in exchange for blocks of time on the air (again at a very low rate) and then selling that time to advertisers below card rates but at a good profit. The Federal Communications Commission has held that bartering for broadcast time is legal. Firms that handle barter will supply a station anything it needs in barter for time—furniture, equipment, even travel tickets—but the chief subject of barter is program material in the form of films, a constant need of TV stations, which they usually rent from independent film syndicators. Usually included are Hollywood films, films of popular old TV programs, and, more important, films of current popular TV series that the barter houses control. All this involves no cash outflow for the station.

Some barter houses become virtually brokers or wholesalers of time. They build inventories of time accumulated in various barter deals. These inventories, known as *time banks,* are then available to advertisers or agencies seeking to stretch their TV or radio dollars.

Of course, barter has its drawbacks. Often the weaker stations in a market use it most. Some stations won't accept barter business from advertisers already on the air in the market. Much of the time is poor time (even though it is still good value at the low rate paid). The advertiser or agency does not deal directly with the station; it deals with barter houses, who then deal directly with the station. Problems of make-goods can be sticky. Nevertheless, barter is a flourishing practice, used by many well-known advertisers.

The roles are changing, however. Now agencies themselves are using barter on behalf of their clients. This is how it works: The agency goes to a station and offers a syndicated show free. All the station must do is retain 3 or 4 minutes in the half hour for the agency's client. The station is then free to sell 3 or 4 more minutes on its own. The advantage to the advertiser of *trade-out shows,* as they are often called, is not only a possible saving in TV costs but, more important, control over the quality of environment in which the commercial appears. Competitive commercials or commercial overcrowding can be fended off.

The arrangement has proved so successful that a number of agencies have gone into the barter business, creating syndicate shows, bartering time for them on various stations, accumulating their own time banks, and then offering the time to their clients at less than rate-card costs.

Research services

In addition to the syndicate research services previously discussed, which regularly report the latest findings on who may buy our product—who and where they are and how they live and buy or what media they read, watch, or listen to—we also have a vast array of advertising and marketing research services. These services offer custom-made research reports to marketers and their agencies, answering their questions about their own products and their advertising. Studies cover subjects such as advertising effectiveness, TV and print pretesting and posttesting, concept testing, market segmentation, positioning of products, media preferences, purchasing patterns, and similar problems directly affecting advertising decisions.

The variety of techniques used in gathering such information is fascinating. It includes field surveys, consumer mail banks, focus groups, continuous-tracking studies, CATV testing of commercials, image studies, electronic questionnaires, opinion surveys, shopping-center intercepts, and media-mix tests.

Regardless of the technique used in gathering information, when a research report has been submitted, the real value of the effort will be the creative interpretation and use of its findings.

SUMMARY

The advertising agency plays an important role in American industry. It continues to grow and change with the times.

Space wholesalers began what has now become the full-service advertising agency. Later, agencies charged a standard commission, 15 percent, and agreed to a no-rebate rule introduced by the Curtis Publishing Company in 1891. 1917 saw the formation of the American Association of Advertising Agencies (the 4A's), whose members today place 75 percent of all national advertising. The 4A's has striven to improve the standards of agency business and practice.

The no-rebate age (1917 to 1956), when the 15 percent commission system was strictly adhered to, saw the birth of two great new media: radio and TV; but in 1956 the Department of Justice held that the no-rebate provision was in restraint of trade. Consent decrees were entered into by all media associations; and these decrees allowed agency and client to review the total compensation that an agency receives for services.

A full-service agency works on many aspects of the client's marketing problem: prime prospects and their characteristics, competitive products, creative solutions to prime-prospect problems, media plans, and trade campaigns. The agency is usually organized into four divisions: creative department, account services, marketing services, and management and finance. Large accounts require some agencies to have extensive international operations.

There are other types of agency: house agency, in-house agency, à la carte agency, creative boutique, and media-buying service. Agencies usually cannot and will not handle two accounts in the same field that compete in the same market.

Barter is a method of payment for media that uses goods and services in place of cash. Some agencies use barter by producing TV shows and offering them to TV stations in exchange for commercial time.

Research plays a very important part in successful marketing: Studies are done on positioning, concept-testing, advertising effectiveness, TV and print pretesting and posttesting, media preferences, and purchasing problems.

QUESTIONS

1. Define the agency commission system and explain how it works. Has it always been 15 percent? Who pays it? To whom?

2. What are the two main sources of agency compensation? What are some of the variations in the way they are applied?

3. When an agency is said to be "recognized," by whom is it recognized? What is the value in being recognized?

4. Discuss how the work on a new account or a new product usually proceeds in a full-service agency.

5. What are the responsibilities of an account executive?

6. Distinguish among house agency, in-house agency, à la carte agency, and full-service agency.

7. What is the usual policy on an agency's handling competing accounts? Why is it this way?

8. What is meant by the ''agency of record''?

9. What were the reasons behind the development of media services? What are the chief functions of a media service?

10. What are some of the purposes for which advertising research is used?

11. Describe the barter method of buying time. What are its chief advantages? Disadvantages?

12. What are trade-out syndicated programs? What are their advantages for the advertiser? For the station?

SUGGESTED EXERCISE

You head up an ad agency that has just won a new shirt manufacturer's account. List the steps your agency will take to develop a successful advertising program for your new client.

READINGS

BARTLE, JOHN: "Account Planning. What Does It Mean and How Does It Affect the Way an Agency Works," *Admap,* April 1980, pp. 153–57.

BONSIB, RICHARD E.: "Cash-flow: Where Small Agencies Hurt Most," *Advertising Age,* November 9, 1981, pp. 53–54.

COLBERT, JUNE: "How to Get the 'Critical Edge' in Your Agency Presentation," *Advertising Age,* March 22,1976, pp. 41–42.

CROFT, ROY: "Charting the Agency Remuneration Jungle," *Admap,* October 1980, pp. 474–75.

GARDNER, HERBERT S., JR.: *The Advertising Agency Business* (Chicago: Crain Brooks, 1977).

HIXON, CARL: "A Conversation with the 'Scottish Blade' David Ogilvy," *Advertising Age,* September 14, 1981, pp. 61–64.

KINGMAN, MERLE: "A Profile of the Bad Agency," *Advertising Age,* November 23, 1981, pp. 53–54.

"Market/Advertising Research," *Advertising Age,* October 20, 1980, S-1.

MARSHALL, CHRISTY: "Bullish on agency stock," *Advertising Age,* November 2, 1981, p. 3.

RAY, MICHAEL L.: *Advertising & Communication Management.* (Englewood Cliffs, N.J.: Prentice-Hall, Inc., 1982), pp. 275–92.

Standard Directory of Advertising Agencies (Skokie, Ill,: National Register Publishing Company, published annually).

"Trends: Double-Edged Maturing," *Advertising Age,* May 19, 1980, p. 75.

"When agency PR pays off," *Advertising Age,* September 28, 1981, p. 54.

WIND, YORAM and STEPHEN E. SILVER: "Segmenting Media Buyers," *Journal of Advertising Research,* December 1973, pp. 33–38.

21

The Advertiser's Marketing/Advertising Operation

There are two fundamental ways in which the consumer advertising operation is handled by various companies: the traditional advertising-department way and the newer marketing-services approach. Traditionally, all advertising matters are funneled through the advertising department, headed by an advertising manager or director (the terms vary with each company), who operates under the marketing director. The manager's duties, broadly speaking, control the entire advertising strategy and operation: budgeting, monitoring the creation and production of the advertising, planning media schedules, and watching expenditures in line with the budget. As the business grows and new lines are added, assistant advertising managers, usually known as "production advertising managers," under the supervision of the advertising director are appointed to handle the advertising of the different brands of the company (Exhibit 21.1). In this chapter however, we wish to focus not on the advertising department, but on the entire marketing/advertising operation. The first system we shall look at is the marketing services system, undoubtedly the most widely used in the marketing and advertising of consumer goods products.

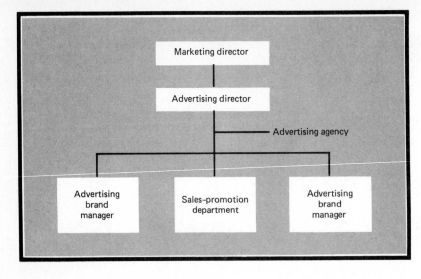

Exhibit 21.1
Simple organization chart of an advertising department.

MARKETING-SERVICES
SYSTEM

The traditional system was the chief one until Procter & Gamble found itself growing with many new brands, each of which had its own marketing problems and all of which together (now about 90) make Procter & Gamble America's largest advertiser. Procter & Gamble developed a new organizational concept, best described as the *marketing-services system.* With variations it has been widely adopted, especially in the package-goods field, for groceries, drugs, and cosmetics.

This system has two parts: One is the marketing activity, which begins with the product managers assigned to different brands; the other, a structure of marketing services, representing all the technical talent involved in implementing a marketing plan, including creative services, promotion services, media services, broadcast programming, advertising controls, and marketing-research services. These are all available to the product manager, as is the help of the agency assigned to that manager's brand. The product manager can bring together the agency professional and his or her counterpart in the marketing-services division, giving the client the benefit of the best thinking of both groups. When different agencies are used, each is assigned to a different group of brands. Each group has a group product manager, who supervises the product managers (Exhibit 21.2).

The product manager's job is to plan strategy and objectives, gather information relevant to the brand, coordinate budget developments and control, and get recommendations from agencies and others up the line for final discussion and approval as quickly as possible. The product manager is a primary liaison between the marketing department and all other departments, as well as the advertising agency. The product manager's plans must be approved by the group product manager, who then submits them for approval to the vice-president for marketing and finally to the executive vice-president.

Under this system the advertising department is a branch of the marketing-services division. The vice-president for advertising, responsible for the review and evaluation of brand media plans, attends all creative presentations to

484

act as an adviser and is an adviser and consultant on all aspects of the advertising. The vice-president for advertising reports to the senior vice-president, director of marketing.

The biggest difference in this operation is that the advertising does not all come through one huge funnel, with one person in charge of all brands. The great advantage, from the corporate viewpoint, is that each brand gets the full marketing attention of its own group, while all brands get the full benefit

Exhibit 21.2
Organization in a large company with a marketing-services division: (a) the marketing department; (b) the marketing-services department, where specialists in creative, media, and research advise product managers and consult with counterparts in agency.

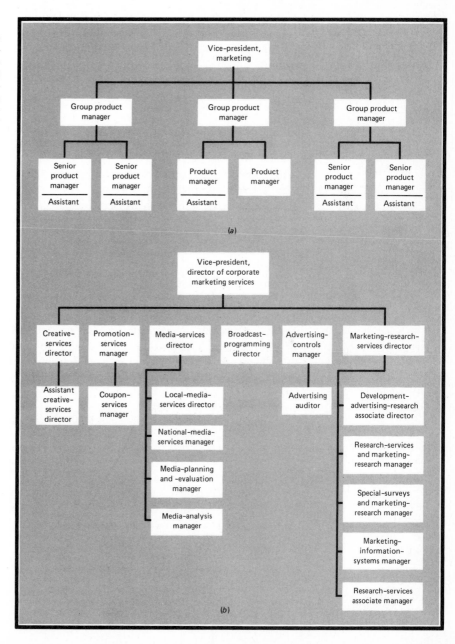

of all the company's special marketing services and of the accumulated corporate wisdom. The more important the decision, the higher up the ladder it goes for final approval.

SETTING THE
BUDGET

The largest variable expense in most companies is for consumer-oriented advertising. Yet with all the technology we can apply to determine how much to spend for advertising, the final decision is a judgmental one. It is different for a company launching a new product, which is the height of risk taking, and for a company with a steadily growing business and many years of background. It differs with the temperament of the top-management group. The approach to making a budget is usually along the following lines:

Percentage of
sales

Companies usually make up their forthcoming budgets in terms of percentage of sales, with the preceding year as a base. If the rate of growth has been consistent with that of earlier years, they may set the budget percentage higher than last year in anticipation of continued increase in business and inflation. If they feel the rate of growth will be slowed, they may lower or maintain the percentage, using the preceding year's sales as a starting figure.

The task
method

By this method, the company sets a specific sales target for a given time, to attain a given goal. Then it decides to spend whatever money is necessary to meet that quota. This might also be called the "Let's spend all we can afford" method, especially in launching a new product. Many big businesses today started that way. Many businesses which are not here today did, too.

The task method is used most widely in a highly competitive environment, as reported in this item taken from the trade press:

> *Johnson & Johnson Takes on Procter & Gamble.* J&J chief Dick Sellers goes after P&G's Pampers (holds estimated 60% share of disposable diaper market) via J&J's Disposable Diaper product. Concentrates advertising efforts in midwest markets. Dick seeks to reach 25% share of each market entered. Earmarks estimated $6 million for advertising campaign to increase awareness of product.*

A Gallagher survey asked 111 large advertisers, "What method was used to arrive at the amount set aside for the budget?" Their responses are shown in Table 21.1. (The first response reveals a lot about how budgets are often arrived at.)

Gallagher Report, September 1975.

Table 21–1

METHODS USED TO ARRIVE AT AMOUNT SET ASIDE FOR AD BUDGET[a]	%
Arbitrarily decided by management on basis of available funds	34.6
Task method combined with percentage of anticipated sales	19.2
Task method: goals set; then cost of reaching goals determined	17.4
Compromise between percentage of anticipated new year sales and last year's sales	11.5
Predetermined percentage of anticipated sales	10.6
Predetermined percentage of this year's sales	4.8
Task method combined with percentage of last year's sales	1.9

[a]*Gallagher Report*, September 1975.

Budgets are under constant scrutiny in relation to sales and usually are formally reviewed quarterly. In addition, budgets are subject to cancellation at any time (except for noncancellable commitments) because sales have not met a minimum quota, money is being shifted to a more promising brand, or management may want to hold back money to make a better showing on its next quarterly statement.

SELECTING AN AGENCY

No matter which side of the fence you are on, the selection of an agency involves criteria worth remembering. If you are being chosen, you will be judged with the following points in someone's mind, or if you are doing the choosing:

1. Determine what types of service you need from an agency, and then list them according to their importance to you. For instance: (1) marketing expertise in strategy, planning, and execution; (2) creative performance in TV, print, radio, or outdoor; (3) media knowledge and clout; (4) sales-promotion and/or trade-relations help; (5) public relations and corporate or image-building ability; (6) market-research strength; (7) fashion or beauty sense; (8) agency size; (9) location in relation to your office. Your special needs will dictate many others.

2. Establish a five-point scale to rate each agency's attributes. A typical five-point scale would be: (1) outstanding, (2) very good, (3) good, (4) satisfactory, (5) unsatisfactory. Of course you should give different values or weights to the more important agency attributes.

3. Check published sources and select a group of agencies that seem to fit your requirements. Use your own knowledge or the knowledge of your industry peers to find agencies responsible for successful campaigns or products that have most impressed you. Published sources include the annual issue of *Advertising Age* that lists agencies and their accounts by agency size and the "Red Book" (*Standard Advertising Register*), which lists agencies and accounts both alphabetically and geographically. In case of further doubt, write to the American Association of Advertising Agencies, 666 Third Avenue, New York, New York 10017, for a roster of members.

4. Check whether there are any apparent conflicts with your accounts at the agency. When agencies consider a new account, that is the first question they ask, along with the amount of the potential billings.

5. Now start preliminary discussions with the agencies that rate best on your preliminary evaluation. This can be done with a letter asking if they are interested or a phone call to set up an appointment for them to visit you or for you to visit the agency. Start at the top. Call the president or the operating head of the agency or office in your area, who will appoint someone to follow up on the opportunity you are offering.

6. Reduce your original list of potential agencies after first contact. A manageable number is usually not more than three.

7. Now again prepare an evaluation list for rating the agencies on the same five-point scale. This list will be a lot more specific. It should cover personnel. Who will supervise your account, and how will the account team be staffed? Who are the creative people who will work on your business? Similarly, who will service your needs in media, production (TV) research, and sales promotion, and how will they do it? What is the agency's track record in getting and keeping business and in keeping personnel teams together? What is the agency's record with media, with payments? Make sure again to assign a weighted value to each service aspect. If TV is most important to you and public-relations aid least important, then be sure to reflect this in your evaluation.

8. Discuss financial arrangements. Will your account be straight 15-percent-commission account, a fee account, or a combination of both? What services will the commission or fee cover, and what additional charges will the agency demand? How will new product work be handled from both a financial and an organizational point of view? What peripheral services does the agency offer, and for how much?

9. Do you feel comfortable with them?

10. If your company is an international one, can the agency handle any of your non-domestic business, and if so, how will they do it?

APPRAISING NATIONAL
ADVERTISING

Continuing questions that all in national advertising and marketing management must address are "How well is our advertising working? How well is our investment paying off?" By what yardsticks can one measure national advertising, whose results cannot be traced as easily as those of direct-response advertising? The following sections point up various factors that you must take into account in evaluating advertising effectiveness.

Advertising goals versus marketing
goals

Many have sought an approach to the problem of appraising national advertising in the light of outside influences. Much of the discussion on the subject centers around a report, by Russell H. Colley, prepared for the Association of National Advertisers. The thesis of this study is that it is virtually impossible to measure the results of advertising unless and until the specific results sought by advertising have been defined. When asked exactly what their advertising is supposed to do, most companies have a ready answer: to increase their dollar sales or to increase their share of the market. But these are not advertising goals, Colley holds; they are total marketing goals. Obviously, national advertising alone is not intended to accomplish this task, but it is rather to be used as part of the total marketing effort. The first step in appraising results of advertising, therefore, is to define specifically what the company expects to accomplish through advertising. The report defines an advertising goal as "a specific communications task, to be accomplished among a defined audience to a given degree in a given period of time."

As an example, the Colley report cites the case of a branded detergent. The marketing goal is to increase the share of industry from 10 to 15 percent, and the advertising goal is set as increasing among the 30 million housewives who own automatic washers the number who identify brand X as a low-sudsing detergent that gets clothes clean. This represents a specific communications task that can be performed by advertising, independent of other marketing forces.

The report speaks of a marketing-communications spectrum ranging from an unawareness of the product to awareness, comprehension, conviction, and action, in successive steps. Exhibit 21.3 is an example of how the *Wall Street Journal* attempts to develop this product awareness. And the way to appraise advertising, according to this view, is by its effectiveness in the communications spectrum, leading to sales.

Differences of opinion. Researchers differ on judging the effectiveness of national advertising on a communications yardstick rather than by sales. A report on the subject by the Marketing Science Institute says:

> In general, total sales are not considered a valid measure of advertising effectiveness, because of the presence of other influencing variables. Sales as a criterion may have some validity if advertising is the most prominent variable, or, in the case of mail-order advertising, when it is the only variable.

On the other hand, there are those who "deplore the general acceptance of measures of advertising short of sales or purchases; they frown on communications measures as the sole criterion." Yet even these critics concede that the effectiveness of communications in general is more readily measurable and, for a given expenditure, more reliable than sales alone. Whatever goal you have selected for your advertising, there are various techniques for finding out how well you have succeeded in achieving it. (See Chapters 5 and 14.)

Testing for change in awareness. Awareness change is particularly important for institutional campaigns as well as for product advertising. For years the Hartford Insurance Company ran a picture of a graceful, but stuffed stag as a trade character in its ads. A new agency acquired the account and replaced the stuffed stag with a live one. More than that, they trained the living beast to be comfortable in scenes with a human family; and whenever a Hartford commercial appeared, the stag appeared too as a participant in the action. The agency had planned in advance for research to determine the effect of the new stag. They made a tracking test and conducted research before the advertising began and after it had been running: In a preadvertising test research showed that more than 70 percent of the people could not identify

1956. Bill Claggett, newly promoted media buyer for the Gardner Advertising Company.

Bill Claggett, when did you start reading The Wall Street Journal?

"In 1956, I was fresh out of Gardner Advertising's training program," recalls William M. Claggett, Vice President and Director of Advertising and Marketing Services of the Ralston Purina Company. "I got a promotion, an office, and a bundle of administrative responsibilities.

"I noticed right off how the management people I worked with—clients as well as agency—always seemed to find the time each day to read The Wall Street Journal. So I started finding time to read The Journal, too.

"When I moved over to the client side at Ralston Purina 15 years ago, my respon-sibilities changed. But my reading habits didn't. I still make time for The Journal—because reading The Journal every day is still the best way I know to keep on top of what's happening in business.

"I don't see how you can be an informed executive without reading it regularly."

Listen to Bill Claggett. If you want all the important, useful business news—and you want it fast and straight—you want The Wall Street Journal. Every business day.

Today. William M. Claggett, Vice President and Director of Advertising and Marketing Services of the Ralston Purina Company.

The Wall Street Journal.
All the business news you need. When you need it.

Exhibit 21.3
The Wall Street Journal keeps its name and image before the public. (Courtesy Wall Street Journal.)

Hartford and its trademark. But after the first few months recall and identification of Hartford Insurance Company increased by 72 percent.

An industrial company, Johnson Controls, provides another example of testing for improvement in awareness. Introducing a total building-automation system that permits all automatic building systems to be monitored, coordinated, and operated by a single computer, they wanted to reach persons who made major decisions regarding building. Johnson ran a campaign in *The Wall Street Journal.* "To check on progress," said the advertising manager, "we set up a research series to objectively measure the results of our total *Journal* campaign. What happened? In just six months, our advertising in *The Journal* increased our top-of-mind awareness by 63%!"

Testing for change of attitude. As in awareness testing, in tests designed to measure changing attitudes a survey must first be made to see what people think about the product or service before the advertising is run. Those opinions are compared with a corresponding survey made after it has been run. Attitude changes are much more readily observed after exposure to a series of ads in an advertising campaign. Some advertisers also wish to know not only whether a change in attitude has occurred but whether it is strongly fashionable enough to cause the consumer to want the product. The following test shows how this may be done:

TESTING CHANGES IN ATTITUDE WITH A TV COMMERCIAL. Various methods have been set up for testing attitude changes within the span of a single TV commercial. In one theater testing plan, women are invited to watch a 30-minute film program, which includes commercials other than the ones being tested. Before the test begins, they are given a list of products and are asked to choose which they would like to take home. After the film showing they are again asked to prepare a list of what they now want to take home. (The amount of the products is large enough to warrant thoughtful consideration of the brands.) By comparing the "pre-" preferences with the "post-" preferences, the tester can weigh the relative effectiveness of the commercial. This test can be repeated with other groups, with alternate commercials.

Appraising the campaign before it is run

There are those who believe that the time to appraise a campaign is before it is run. They would do this by testing idea options in different markets—a familiar practice, of course, with one big drawback: It tips off competition to what you are planning to do, and they will try to beat you to it in other markets, especially if it is a new product or is based on a promotion. To meet this problem, cablecasting has come to the rescue.

Use of cable TV in testing. Cable TV is increasingly used for research because thousands of homes get their TV reception via cable. In some cities cable companies not only relay programs of distant TV stations but can cut in with their own programs, on which they carry spot commercials.

A prominent research firm, AdTel, began by selecting one typical test city, in which 50 percent of the homes had cable TV. It set up a panel of 2,000 subscribers, who were compensated for keeping a diary of their purchases and reporting them each week. The large advertisers for whom AdTel conducts tests either already have a TV schedule in the market or can add it to their list. AdTel is able to cut in on the advertiser's own program, replacing the regular commercial with the test commercials, test ad A being transmitted to half the homes on the panel and test ad B to the other half. The subscribers see the test ads as regular commercials. From their purchase-diary entries over a period of time it is possible to compare actual sales to the subscribers who saw ad A with the sales to the subscribers who saw ad B.

This system, which divides a market into two homogeneous test areas—equally subject to the factors that can foul up the usual tests between two different markets—and which gets a weekly diary report of purchases, has been expanded to other test cities. It is being used to check rate of repurchase and alternative promotional efforts, like sampling and couponing. It also tests different levels of expenditure, to determine the optimum profit. An advantage to advertisers is that it keeps tests of new products away from the eyes of competitors.

Research guidelines

Conditions conducive to research. "As a rule of thumb, in judging whether measurement of results is possible and how comprehensive such measurements can be, the following axioms may be helpful," said the National Industrial Conference Board. To the report, excerpts from which follow, we have added some comments in brackets:

1. The more important advertising is to the sale of a product, the easier it is to appraise results. [Where advertising plays a minor role in the marketing mix, as in the case of raw materials, even a 100-percent improvement in advertising will not add too much weight to the buying decision.]
2. The faster the turnover of a product, the easier it is to appraise the results of advertising. [The shorter the period of time elapsed between the appearance of an ad and the need to make a decision, the better. Fast turnover means early decisions. The price risk of such purchases is usually low.]
3. The fewer selling methods employed in moving a product, the easier it is to appraise the advertising. [If the advertiser is a yarn manufacturer, who sells to the weaver of fabric, who sells to a suit manufacturer, who sells to department stores, the results of advertising to the consumer are much harder to trace than the results of mail-order advertising are.]
4. The less complex the market is (and the less intense the competition), the easier it is to appraise advertising results. [The more competitive a market is, the more business will be done other than by advertising—through deals, promotions, and price changes—obscuring the effects of advertising and the ability to measure it.]

How much testing? The desirability of conducting extensive testing is a function, first, of the importance of advertising to the company. When advertising is very important to the overall marketing program and a lot of money is spent on it, then extensive research on evaluating ads and campaigns is warranted and necessary. Thus most major consumer-goods marketers devote much more energy and research money to testing ads than industrial advertisers do.

A second major factor influencing the extent of advertising testing is how major a change in the advertising program is being contemplated. The greater the change, the greater the need for a wide testing base and for in-depth studies. When a previous campaign is being extended with only minor variations, however, partial evaluation will usually suffice.

SUMMARY

There are two basic ways to handle the advertising operation in a company: an advertising department that supervises the agency and handles all aspects of advertising through the ad manager and a marketing-services system, which uses product managers and specialists in different marketing/advertising services. The selection of an agency involves many factors, the most important of which are how appropriate and experienced the agency is, what kind of work it does for clients, and how well it "fits" with your people.

Budgets are set in various ways, percentage of sales being the most common.

Evaluating national advertising begins by defining what you want the advertising to accomplish. Advertising goals are not the same as marketing goals; advertising is a specific communications task. So changes in awareness are tested periodically by advertisers as an indication of how well advertising is communicating to potential customers. Attitudinal changes are also tested in the same manner, using a benchmark survey to begin with and subsequent surveys to determine the extent of change in attitude. Cable TV is a good way to test because it selects the audience carefully, is easy to control, and can be used without giving away too much information to competition.

Generally, the more important advertising is to the sale of a product, the faster the turnover; and the fewer selling methods used, the easier it is to appraise results.

QUESTIONS

1. We have discussed two fundamental differences in the way that the consumer-advertising operation is handled by various companies. Discuss the distinguishing features of each.

2. Explain the major ways of setting the advertising budget.

3. If you were asked how much advertising money you thought would be needed for launching a new brand of grocery product, how would you go about getting an answer?

4. What is the chapter's suggested ten-step procedure for selecting an advertising agency?

5. "Measuring results from national advertising is not easy." Agree or disagree? Why?

6. Discuss the basic idea behind Colley's approach to evaluating advertising.

7. What is meant by the communications spectrum?

8. Describe how cable TV is being used for research.

9. What conditions are conducive to appraising advertising campaigns?

10. What are the major factors influencing the extent of advertising testing?

SUGGESTED EXERCISE

You head the advertising department of a men's shirt manufacturer. You are asked to find an advertising agency. What criteria will you use?

READINGS

AAKER, DAVID A., and JOHN G. MYERS: *Advertising Management* (Englewood Cliffs, N.J.: Prentice-Hall, Inc., 1982.

ACITO, FRANKLIN, and JEFFREY D. FORD: "How Advertising Affects Employees," *Business Horizons,* February 1980, pp. 53–59.

ANDERSON, ROBERT L. and THOMAS E. BARRY: *Advertising Management* (Columbus, Ohio: Chas. E. Merrill, 1979).

BATHAM, W. G.: "Planning Marketing Research Objectives and Strategies," *Admap,* October 1980, pp. 516–21.

DUBINSKY, ALAN J., THOMAS E. BARRY, and ROGER A. KERIN: "The Sales-Advertising Interface in Promotion Planning," *Journal of Advertising,* Summer 1981, pp. 35–41.

DUFFY, J. O'NEILL: "Five Marketing Challenges: How They Were Met," *Advertising Age,* November 16, 1981, pp. 55–58.

GREYSER, STEPHEN A.: *Cases in Advertising & Communications Management* (Englewood Cliffs, N.J.: Prentice-Hall, Inc., 1981).

KOTLER, PHILIP: *Marketing Management* (4th ed.) (Englewood Cliffs, N.J.: Prentice-Hall, Inc., 1980), pp. 497–525.

McGANN, ANTHONY F. and J. THOMAS RUSSELL: *Advertising Media/A Managerial Approach* (Homewood, Ill.: Richard D. Irwin, 1981), pp. 331–45.

NICKELS, WILLIAM G.: *Marketing Communications and Promotion* (Columbus, Ohio: Grid Publishing, 1976).

"Plan or Perish," *Sales & Marketing Management,* May 18, 1981, pp. 45–46.

SCOTT, LOUIS and JOSEPH A. SMITH: "10 Ways to Wring More Creativity From Your Agency," *Magazine Age,* June 1981, pp. 22–25.

WEBSTER, FREDERICK E., JR.: "Top Management's Concerns about Marketing: Issues for the 1980's," *Journal of Marketing,* Summer 1981, pp. 9–16.

ZELTNER, HERBERT: "When Should You Market Test? Five Guides Help You Decide," *Advertising Age,* January 17, 1977, pp. 46–48.

22

The Complete Campaign

We have developed a new product, tested it in the lab, and tested consumer reaction—gaining all the knowledge we possibly can before putting it in the market place. We are ready to take this new product, place it on the market, and tell the world it is there. This is the moment to take a good, hard look at the chief elements of our advertising campaign.

THE PRODUCT

Is the product good
value?   Does it work? Does it meet all government requirements covering such merchandise? Will it perform properly in the hands of the consumer? Is there any ingredient in the product that may be affected by its standing for a time on the dealer's shelf? Do you foresee any impediment that may affect your ability to maintain quality production and deliveries?

Does it have a good
trademark?   If it uses a package, does that have a good design? Is the product ready for the market?

What's the major

difference?

What is the product's reason for existence as far as the consumer is concerned? Why should one buy it? What value does it offer that other products are not already offering? What is its unique advantage? Will the buyer find that this product in an important way serves the purpose better? The product must have some advantage or distinction from other products in the same category, something that helps solve a prime prospect's problem; see the discussion of Soft 'n Dry in Chapter 14.

Not only should the product have a significant difference, but that feature should be conspicuous or lend itself to demonstration or dramatization. To differentiate their brand of pantyhose from all the others, the makers of L'eggs linked their brand name with a package shaped like an egg.

Is the product in step with the

times?

Changes from many directions, including changes in living styles, affect sales. In the middle 1970s so many people began eating at fast-food restaurants, such as McDonald's and Burger King, that supermarket sales were appreciably affected.

Is the product being replaced by a new type

or a better one?

For example, expensive jeweled-movement watches are being replaced by less costly, more dependable quartz or electronic movements. All in all, is the product part of a growing trend or a waning trend? Is time with it or against it?

It is wise to look at the economic scene for a clue to the way our new product will be received. This reconnaissance will also give us an opportunity to figure out how to present the product so that it *rides with the times*.

THE MARKETING PROGRAM

Positioning the

product

The decision on what you want your product to be known and used for is one of the most important in its success. In one of its own house ads Ogilvy & Mather, a well-known advertising agency, had this to say on the subject:

> The most important decision you will ever make about your advertising is: "How should I position my product?"
>
> Should you position Good Seasons Salad Dressing as a gourmet's delight, for people who appreciate its subtle blend of herbs and spices? Or as a product which competes with bottled salad dressings?

Should you position Shake 'n Bake as a new flavor for chicken? Or as an easier way to get old-fashioned "fried chicken" taste?

The results of your advertising will depend less on how it is *written* than on how it is *positioned.* It follows that the positioning must be decided before the advertising is created.

We positioned Hershey's *oldest* product, Hershey's Milk Chocolate Bar, as the market leader. Familiar, warm, friendly, "the greatest American chocolate bar."

We positioned Hershey's *newest* product, their new Rally Bar, as "the Hershey-covered hunger-stopper."

Selecting the target
market

Who buys the product: men, women, teenagers? What are other significant demographic characteristics of our potential market? Sex? Age? Family size or stage in the life cycle? Income? Occupation? Social class? Is there any part of the country that especially favors this type of product? Do the best prospects have something in common that enables you to reach them as a group?

Who are the heavy users of the product? What distinguishes them from other users? Cereal manufacturers love homes with lots of children; soft-drink manufacturers love homes with teenagers; sporting-goods manufacturers love outdoor enthusiasts; lawn-seed growers love home owners with spacious lawns.

Find the prime prospect's problems. Some advertising agencies look for the needs and desires of prime prospects before positioning the product. By discovering what the prospect wants in a product, you can adjust your product appeal (even the product itself) so that the product has a property or difference that will make it more desirable than other products are in its category.

Picture of the
market

How large are dollar sales in the prospective market? Which products will be most competitive? What are their particular features? What are their sales (estimated)? Is it a market with a few giant companies having the major share and a long list of small firms dividing the remainder? Will the product be priced competitively? What share of the market are we hoping to get, in what time? Is the product sold through franchised dealers or open trade?

Attitude of the trade toward
the product

If our company is well known in the field, salespeople will be welcomed by buyers with a "What's new?" greeting. But if ours is a new company, it will need, even to get attention, striking advertising, a good promotion plan, and a good deal. Possibly this is the time for sampling and cents-off offers in newspaper ads, to get the product on the dealers' shelves. This situation also calls for strong trade-paper support.

THE STORY BEHIND
freixenet

BACKGROUND

Freixenet (freshenet) sparkling wines, bottled in Spain, are distributed in more than fifty countries throughout the world. Although distributed in the U.S. for nearly ten years, marketing support had been minimal until Spring 1981. While sparkling wine and champagne have kept pace with the total market's growth rate in this country, their share level has remained at a relatively small 6 percent. Imported sparkling wines account for only one out of every six gallons distributed.

The Freixenet line consists primarily of Cordon Negro Brut, Carta Nevada (Brut and Semisco), and Brut Nature. Leader of the line is Cordon Negro, a true Brut, austere and very dry with a long-lived effervescence. It is aged four to five years, and priced between the very low-priced domestics and the premium domestics and imports. It is packaged in a distinctive black bottle.

It is important to note that while Americans would consider Cordon Negro "champagne," it cannot be marketed as such. European countries have signed an agreement stating that only those "methode champenoise" wines produced in the Champagne region of France may be called champagne. The U.S. is not a signatory to this agreement; hence New York State and California sparkling wines can be marketed as "champagne" in the U.S. market.

MARKETING OBJECTIVES

1. Achieve 240,000 case sales in 1981.
2. Build brand awareness among the primary consumer and retail target audiences.
3. Stimulate brand trial at point of sale.

STRATEGY

Place primary support on the proprietary brand leader, Cordon Negro, rather than the entire Freixenet line. Begin this support with media advertising in June and July, rather than wait for traditional year-end holiday sales. Concentrate it in compressed time and geography for maximum impact. And maybe most important, while the many French imports are all trumpeting their French heritage, communicate the strong and unique visual identity of the bottle and its price advantage for those special everyday occasions.

EXECUTION

The copy theme developed was "You can't go wrong with Basic Black." It reinforced the Cordon Negro black bottle, implied a stylish sophistication about the product, and communicated a sense of appropriateness about its quality and usage.

RESULTS

Sales projections were comfortably exceeded, and have already earned Cordon Negro the title of "fastest-growing imported sparkling wine in the United States."

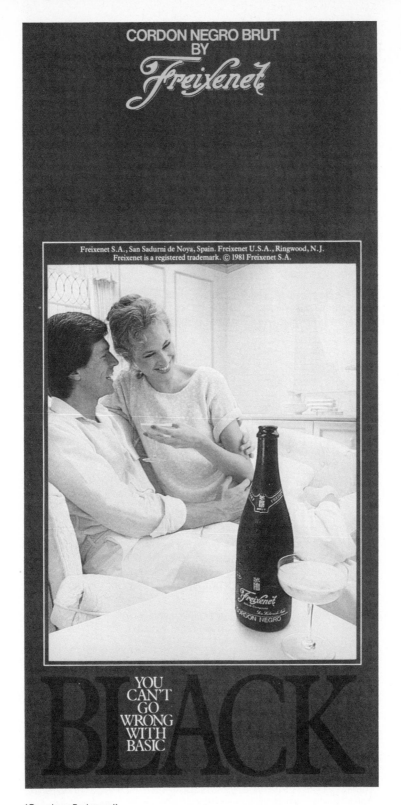

THE STORY BEHIND
haggar company

The objective of the campaign was to reposition Haggar Company from a leading slacks manufacturer to a leader in men's sportswear separates.

BACKGROUND

The Haggar Company had pioneered in marketing a branded product in the men's dress slacks category. Through their advertising agency, Tracy-Locke, Haggar was the first company in the category to use national advertising, starting in the early 1940s. In the 1950s they were the first dress slacks brand to use network television.

While competitive brands had subsequently entered the category, consistent advertising and merchandising had helped Haggar maintain leadership in consumer awareness and acceptance, and dominance in their retail accounts.

In the early 1970s, increasing fashion consciousness among American men led to more diversified wardrobes that included a greater variety of casual and dress wear from jeans to suits. The result was a decline in dress slacks volume.

Competition's early lead in the introduction of leisure tops capitalized on the trend and penetrated Haggar's space and volume at retail.

ACTIONS AND SOLUTIONS

Consumer and trade research was conducted to reassess the strengths of the Haggar brand to help in developing strategies for the future. Results indicated the need and opportunity for Haggar to broaden their base business.

1. The American male's growing acceptance of a wider variety of looks/items in his wardrobe was a long-term trend.
2. Consumer research clearly established the high levels of awareness and acceptance of the Haggar brand. Haggar is perceived as a leader in product quality, comfort, fit, styling, and variety. In fact, Haggar was already perceived as a leading brand of sport coats and tops before they began marketing either.
3. A trade study among retailers reinforced Haggar's image and acceptance in terms of product quality, marketing support, and service to the retailer.

The decision was made and strategies developed for repositioning the Haggar Company from a slacks manufacturer to a diversified men's sportswear company with two objectives.

1. Protect the basic slacks business by giving the consumer new reasons to buy more Haggar brand slacks.
2. Expand the Haggar franchise with a variety of new, fashionable items and looks.

MARKETING STRATEGY

Phase I was the introduction of leisure tops in 1974. With a related color-coordinated separates strategy, Haggar seized category leadership in one year.

LOCKER ROOM:30

COACH: Hey, rookie! C'mon,
the press is waiting!
ROOKIE: Aw, Coach! They're
gonna laugh at me!

COACH: Not at you. At your
clothes. My pros wear
The Haggar Look.

COACH: Like Haggar slacks in
a hard-hitting check.

COACH: Maybe a
crowd-pleasing plaid.

COACH: Or try a new Haggar
sport coat and slacks.

COACH: All of non-glitter
Dacron® polyester. And at prices
that aren't out of the ball park.

COACH: Now get out there.

VO: The Haggar Look.
From America's Best Known
Name in Slacks.

THE HAGGAR LOOK.

Now it'll see him through the week.

Consumers have demanded them. Retailers have demanded them. Now we're delivering. New Haggar sport coats and vests. The latest additions to the Haggar line. And like our leisure tops, they're designed to mix and match with Haggar slacks.

Now you can offer a variety of looks that'll satisfy a customer's fashion needs, Monday through Sunday. Everything from elegant 3-piece suits to sport coat ensembles. From leisure separates to basic slacks. All are exact-sized to minimize alterations.

That's The Haggar Look. Varied. Versatile. Economical. And it's going to see you through your biggest season ever.

Monday

This 3-piece outfit of a 100% Dacron® texturized polyester called Crows-foot™ really helps him get down to business. There's a matching 5-button vest. Plus matching slacks with quarter-top pockets and a gentleman's flare. Dressy or "open collar casual," it's a combination designed to make even "Blue Monday" look good.

Tuesday

Take a walk on the boardwalk, Haggar style. Our Countryarns™ doubleknit of 100% Dacron® polyester makes this sport coat with contrasting plaid slacks right for office hours or after. In all, it's a look that says fashion from the boardwalk to the boardroom.

Wednesday

The sun never set on a better leisure look. The ginger top boasts box-pleated front patch pockets and accent stitching. The slacks are contrasting checks with fashion pockets and a slight flare. Both are Avant Gabs™, 100% Dacron® polyester texturized woven gabardine.

Thursday

Gunpatches, lower inset pockets, and sport coat cuffs give this Single Faille™ ginger top a look that's at home anywhere. The plaid slacks are Haggar Expand-O-Matics® with the exclusive, deep inside elastic waistband. Both of 100% Encron® polyester in a faille-stitch doubleknit.

Friday

Yesterday's leisure top does double duty for tonight's action. It's a Haggar Imperial®, designed with superior construction features like a three-quarter lining and an inside convenience pocket. The matching Single Faille™ slacks are Expand-O-Matics with dual-welted fashion pockets.

Saturday

No matter how his game is going, he'll look great on the links in these Flite-weight® slacks of 80% Dacron® polyester and 20% combed cotton. The feel is light and crisp, so he'll stay comfortable through a full 19 holes.

Sunday

Cool and casually elegant. That's the appeal of this sport coat with slacks and reversible plaid-to-solid vest. The fabric is Mirage™ a comfortable tri-blend of Fortrel® polyester, cotton and acrylic. And the look is versatile enough to dress up with a tie, making Sunday or any day a real breeze.

Phase II began in 1975 with the introduction of Haggar sport coats, vests, and suits.

Strategies for subsequent market segmentation were developed to broaden distribution and market share with different lines of Haggar sportswear designed to appeal to various market segments.

ADVERTISING AND MERCHANDISING

Sales Presentations, trade publication advertising, point of sale materials, co-op advertising for retailer use, and sales training material and seminars for retail sales people communicated the benefits of the related separates strategy and how to sell the new separates concept.

Consumer advertising demonstrated the benefits of the Haggar separates. Television commercials employ a "magical pop change" technique to dramatize wardrobe versatility of Haggar separates.

The campaign, which was consistently effective over eight seasons, positions the product as hero.

The principal character needs help in his appearance. Through the magic of film, he undergoes three quick wardrobe changes. In each he is surprised to find himself transformed in rapid succession by Haggar slacks, a color-coordinated sport coat and slacks, and finally a matching three-piece suit.

As a result of his new look, he is rewarded for his appearance, usually in the form of feminine approval.

RESULTS

In five years Haggar volume increased 40 percent, while industry sales of dress slacks had declined 25 percent. In that five-year period Haggar's share of the dress slacks market increased by 43 percent. Brand awareness more than doubled, and top-of-mind awareness for Haggar was four times that of the nearest competitor. Haggar also achieved leadership in top-of-mind awareness for sport coats.

Since 1975 Haggar has successfully established four separate product lines under the Haggar label:

1. Imperial by Haggar—for upscale discriminating men.
2. Comfort-Plus by Haggar—for "mainstream" market with mature build.
3. Gallery by Haggar—for more youthful men with slightly trimmer build.
4. Body Work by Haggar—high-fashion styling for young men with lean builds.

Courtesy Haggar Company
Advertising Agency: Tracy-Locke/BBDO

THE STORY BEHIND
tostitos brand tortilla chips
by frito-lay, inc.

BACKGROUND

Frito-Lay is the largest operating division of PepsiCo and the number one company in the salted snacks category, with annual retail sales of nearly two billion dollars.

The largest Frito-Lay brand is Doritos brand tortilla chips. It was introduced in 1966 and was the first tortilla chip to be marketed nationally. Between 1974 and 1978, largely due to Doritos' growth, the tortilla chip category more than tripled in size.

As the category expanded, segmentation opportunities were identified in both product characteristics and positioning by Frito-Lay and their advertising agency for Doritos, Tracy-Locke/BBDO.

MARKETING STRATEGY

After extensive product development, the new product was made from stone-ground corn in a new round shape rather than the traditional triangular shape. It was thinner and crispier than the category leader, Doritos. In-home tests were very positive.

To capitalize on the rapid growth and popularity of Mexican foods, Tostitos were positioned as having authentic Mexican taste.

The agency developed the name, packaging, and advertising strategy, and the product was launched in three test markets thirteen weeks after the decision to introduce a new brand to the category.

ADVERTISING

To reflect the authentic Mexican tortilla taste, thin crispy texture, and round shape, the advertising departed from the traditional humorous style of snack foods advertising.

A Mexican restaurant owner in Los Angeles, Fernando Escandon, was chosen as the spokesperson to reinforce the brand's authentic Mexican position. The on-air tests of the commercials produced high communication scores.

The product was introduced in three test markets in December 1977. In April 1978, based on initial test market results, Tostitos was rolled out into six Midwestern states. Projections based on test and expansion markets resulted in national rollout in mid-1979.

Tostitos became the number one corporate priority. Increased capital expenditures and more aggressive marketing spending levels were approved. It became the most comprehensive and aggressive program ever executed at Frito-Lay.

During the rollout, innovative media planning demanded extensive use of regional network and spot TV combinations until national network could be utilized.

Fernando (OC): Tostitos brand tortilla chips.

VO: As a boy I'd run after school to my Uncle Emiliano's bakery.

He made the best tortillas in town. I'd help him stir the stone-ground corn,

and taste the hot, fresh tortilla chips.

Fernando (OC): So today when I tell you Tostitos tortilla chips have an authentic taste, it's from experience.

Light...

(SFX): SNAP.
Crispy... delicious.

Uncle Emiliano, even you'd approve.

Fernando (VO): Tostitos. An authentic tortilla taste.
SFX: CRUNCH.

Introductory programs were employed to gain incremental space at retail. Feature ads, high value coupon drops and direct mail sampling were used to stimulate high consumer trial.

RESULTS

Tostitos was a major success!

In the first full year of national distribution, Tostitos sales exceeded $100 million. According to A. C. Nielsen, it was the largest year-one food brand introduced during the last five years. For perspective, only 20 percent of the new products introduced in 1977 recorded sales of $25 million.

Frito-Lay gained incremental space for snack foods. Attrition on the Doritos brand was only temporary, the total tortilla chip category has expanded, and Doritos has continued its 15-20 percent annual growth trend.

Identifying a market segmentation opportunity, applying the needed resources to capitalize on that opportunity, and making the commitment with the attendant risks led to establishing a major new and growing brand for Frito-Lay.

Courtesy Frito-Lay, Inc.
Advertising Agency: Tracy-Locke/BBDO

THE ADVERTISING PLAN

Establishing

the budget

We have discussed various yardsticks by which budget figures might be reached. For new products particularly, all formula discussion gives way to the final decision on how much a company wishes to venture on what may become one of their most profitable numbers. But to start an advertising plan, a figure must be set, with the understanding that it is subject to change.

At what stage of the advertising spiral is

the product now?

If a product is a new type of article in the pioneering stage, we have to stress the great advantages now available that were never before available in any form. We will have to change a habit and a lifestyle. We must convince people that previous limitations have been overcome, that this product really works. We might stress a demonstration of the product.

If the product is in the competitive stage, we shall bring out its chief distinctive and significant advantages over other products. We seek to present these benefits as dramatically and conspicuously as we can, making sure that, when a person buys the product, it will make good on our claims.

If a product attains a top-of-market share and is in the retentive stage, where it is concerned with a holding action, we know it will have to fight off brand substitutes. But the real problem here is not to stand still in that stage—not to rely on continued loyalty of present customers to your product—but to go after new markets with new uses or else to improve the product greatly or add new products to the line. It is time for a new pioneering effort.

Meeting specific selling

problems

In addition to these broad problems affecting a product, based on the stage in which it finds itself, it is reasonable to expect that every product will have its own special marketing problems, ranging from apathy to active prejudice. We now want to plan the total advertising/marketing strategy that will get the desired action.

Among such specific purposes of campaigns you will recognize those discussed in Chapter 3:

- ☐ Increase the frequency of use of the product
- ☐ Increase the variety of uses of the product
- ☐ Add a new product to a well-known line
- ☐ Reinforce credibility of important claims
- ☐ Launch a special promotional campaign
- ☐ Turn a disadvantage into an advantage
- ☐ Dispel a misconception
- ☐ Enhance the image of a company (institutional advertising)

We can recognize the dual usefulness of these objectives. They suggest an entire marketing strategy and provide the theme or even the ads themselves, which we now turn over to the creative people.

Creating the

advertising

Once the strategy and the theme of the campaign are set, the creative department takes over the task of preparing ads for the print media, the storyboard for TV, and the scripts for radio. While they are working on this, the media department is busy selecting and buying media.

Selecting and buying the

media

Now media planners go to work. They allocate funds to different media in different proportions. Their decisions determine the number of messages that will be delivered per dollar, to whom, and how often; their judgment directly affects the cost/profit ratio of a marketing program.

There is great opportunity for creative and courageous media selection, not always following the crowd in choice of media, use of space or time, and timing. There is also great variability in what media people can get for their dollars through negotiation in the purchase of time and space.

THE SALES-PROMOTION

PLAN   Usually in the first discussions of a campaign for consumer advertising the sales promotion plans are also discussed. These plans may involve dealer displays, premiums, cooperative advertising, and/or couponing offers. When the theme of the campaign has been established for consumer advertising, creative work is begun for sales-promotion material, which is presented along with the consumer-advertising material for final approval. At that time production is carefully planned so that the sales-promotion material will be ready before the consumer advertising breaks.

GETTING THE CAMPAIGN

APPROVED   We now have the campaign complete: the ads, the media schedule, sales-promotion material, and costs for everything spelled out, ready for management's final approval. For that approval it is wise to present a statement of the company's *marketing* goals. The objectives may be to launch a new product, to increase sales by x percent, to increase the firm's share of the market by z percent, or whatever the marketing target may be. Next follows a description of the philosophy and strategy of the advertising, with the reasons for believing that the proposed plan will help attain those objectives. Not until then are the ads or the commercials presented, along with the media proposal and the plans for coordinating the entire effort with that of the sales department. What are the *reasons* for each recommendation in the program? On what basis were these dollar figures arrived at? On what research were any decisions based? What were the results of preliminary tests, if any? What is the competition doing? What *alternatives* were considered? What is the total cost? Finally, how may the entire program contribute to the company's return on its investment? Those who control the corporate purse strings like to have answers to such questions before they approve a total advertising program.

PRESENTING THE CAMPAIGN TO THE

SALES FORCE   The sales force always looks forward to the annual announcement of the company's newest plans. They may gather for the event at a meeting at the home or branch office. There everything may be set up under wraps on a stage, with all the excitement characteristic of the launching of a new venture. Finally, the new advertising campaign is unveiled, along with the product if it is new to the market.

Sometimes a new campaign is launched through closed-circuit TV from the home office to branch-office meetings, to which dealers might be invited. Automobile and household-appliance manufacturers, particularly, bring in sales representatives and the main distributors, to give them a theatrical presentation with music. Or it can all be done on a modest scale; the sales representatives are called in to the sales manager's office, and the advertising manager describes the advertising program.

Usually a kit of the various advertising materials will be given to salespeople, who can show details of the new campaign to the dealers on whom they call.

SUMMARY

The steps in preparing a national campaign for a consumer product may be enumerated as follows (the sequence here is not the same as that of our previous discussion but has been rearranged for convenience in surveying the entire problem):

1. Develop a product that offers good value.
2. Create the trademark.
3. Design the package, if needed.
4. Position the product.
5. Select the target market: Who are the heavy users?
6. Determine the selling price.
7. Determine the form of distribution.
8. Set the appropriation.
9. Establish advertising/marketing strategy and theme.
10. Prepare ads and commercials.
11. Choose the media; prepare schedules; order time and space.
12. Create a sales promotion plan for dealer tie-in.
13. Release the plan to salespeople, dealers, and trade publications.
14. Release ads to the public.
15. Appraise your results.

QUESTIONS

1. What major steps will you take in developing a complete advertising campaign?
2. Ask some of the important questions that you will need answers to in selecting the target market.
3. Select three of the specific advertising objectives mentioned in the chapter. For each discuss a particular current ad or commercial that illustrates an approach to dealing with that objective.
4. Describe the areas you, as advertising director, would cover in a presentation to top management for approval of your advertising program and budget.

5. Explain how you would go about presenting your plan for an advertising campaign to the sales force. How would you achieve dealer cooperation?

6. Why is it important to appraise the results of an advertising campaign? What lessons can be learned? How can the information you get from the appraisal be used?

SUGGESTED EXERCISES

7. A new product is presented to you for your marketing and advertising proposals. What are the chief technical questions you could ask? What would you ask about an existing product for which you will be developing an advertising campaign?

8. Products in the pioneering, competitive, or retentive stage require different kinds of advertising approaches. What direction or approach would you take if you were called upon to advertise different products in each one of the stages?

READINGS

DUNNE, PATRICK, and SUSAN OBENHOUSE (EDS.): *Product Management: A Reader* (Chicago: American Marketing Association, 1981).

FORRNELL, CLAES: "Efficiency in Marketing Communication," Marquette Business Review, Summer 1975, pp. 80–89.

HUGHES, G. DAVID: *Marketing Management: A Planning Approach* (Reading, Mass.: Addison-Wesley, 1981).

MARSIGLIA, TONY: "Getting the (K)nots Out of Your Tie-In Campaign," *ADWEEK,* June 22, 1981, p. 30.

QUERA, LEON: *Advertising Campaigns: Formulation and Tactics* (Columbus, Ohio: Grid Publishing, 1977).

REWOLDT, STEWART H., JAMES D. SCOTT, and MARTIN R. WARSHAW: *Introduction to Marketing Management* (Homewood, Ill.: Richard D. Irwin, 1981).

SCHULTZ, DON E., and DENNIS G. MARTIN: *Strategic Advertising Campaigns* (Chicago: Crain Books, 1979).

SCOTTON, DONALD W., and RONALD L. ZALLOCCO (EDS.): *Readings in Market Segmentation* (Chicago: American Marketing Association, 1981).

UDELL, JON G., and GENE R. LACZNIAK: *Marketing in an Age of Change* (New York: John Wiley, 1981).

WEILBACHER, WILLIAM M.: *Cases In Advertising* (New York: Macmillan, 1981).

WIND, VORAM J.: *Product Policy: Concepts, Methods, and Strategies* (Reading, Mass.: Addison-Wesley, 1981).

Other Worlds of Advertising

Throughout the text we have more or less emphasized national advertising in the United States. This section will deal with two other major areas: retail advertising and international advertising.

In retail advertising the customer meets the product head on. The pace is faster, with deadline pressure on writers and production personnel to make tomorrow's newspaper or broadcast schedule. The success of retail advertising is short term and known immediately: Whereas national advertisers can often only wonder whether any particular ad resulted in more sales or higher profits, the retailer knows—if people line up at the counter the day after an ad runs.

From the personalized world of the retailer we examine the glamour of the international advertiser. As American companies depend on foreign markets for a greater share of sales and overseas companies invade the United States, the world of business is indeed becoming smaller. The multinational advertiser not only must have advertising skills equal to his domestic counterpart but also must be a politician, cultural anthropologist, and international financier. As we shall see in this section, there are virtually no major American advertising agencies that are not dependent on international business for a substantial share of their revenues and profits.

Retail
Advertising

What do you think of when you hear the words "retail advertising"? Many people believe that it's only the kind of newspaper advertising department stores do when they have a big promotion like a winter white sale. Of course, retail advertising still includes such fairly straightforward campaigns; but with the extraordinary growth of different kinds of retail outlet and the many possibilities of local-advertising media, if a campaign is now to become successful, it has to use a more sophisticated and planned style of retail advertising.

Like other styles of advertising, retail advertising must plan to (1) determine overall goals and objectives of the marketing and advertising programs, (2) identify target markets, and (3) develop a copy and media strategy to reach this target. But carrying out the retail-advertising strategy differs markedly from the way the national advertising we have discussed before is carried out.

And it usually includes media other than newspapers. Radio is used frequently with great success because it is reasonable and easy to produce, and can be changed within hours if necessary. TV is also used more frequently now, although not as often as radio. And many successful campaigns use brochures and cata-

DIFFERENCES BETWEEN NATIONAL AND RETAIL
ADVERTISING

National advertising is chiefly done by a marketer, to get people to buy his or her branded goods wherever they are sold. *Retail advertising* is done by local merchants or service organizations to attract customers—in person, by mail, or by telephone—to buy the goods and services they have to offer.

Some firms do both national and retail advertising. The outstanding example is Sears, which produces and advertises goods under its own name and trademark and is one of the largest users of national advertising; but its numerous stores advertise under the Sears name in their communities and thus are local advertisers. Many franchise operations, like the McDonald's fast-food restaurants, use national advertising to spread their reputations around the country and local advertising to get the business of the immediate neighborhood. That both kinds of advertising are used by a single firm should not obscure the basic differences between the two. In national advertising the manufacturer says, "Buy this brand product at any store." The retail advertiser says, "Buy this product here. Better come early!"

In national advertising it is difficult to trace the sales effect of a single insertion of an ad. To trace the effect of a series of ads takes time and is difficult unless the series runs exclusively in one medium. In retail advertising a retailer can usually tell by noon of the day after an ad appeared how well it is doing.

National advertisers speak to a wide and distant audience. Retail advertisers work in the community where they advertise. They know the people, their lifestyles, their tastes; they know who is likely to be in the market for new home furnishings or whether home computers are likely to be desirable.

The national advertiser has chiefly one product or one line of products to sell at a time. The retailer is faced by a relentless river of new styles and offerings to sell within a week, generating a great sense of urgency in the advertising department. It's a fast tempo.

RETAIL
MEDIA MIX

Selecting local media is a "How best to . . . ?" problem: how best to use newspapers, radio, TV, direct mail—the chief media—alone or in combination with each other to sell merchandise and attract store traffic.

Newspapers in retailing

Newspapers continue to dominate retail advertising. Approximately 85 percent of all newspaper revenues (over $12 billion of the almost $15 billion spent in newspapers) come from local advertisers. But as we shall see, other media are aggressively competing for this lucrative retail market. A survey by the National Retail Merchants Association indicated, however, that 97.2 percent of retailers still ranked newspapers as their number-one medium. Newspapers are reacting to the new competitive environment by providing new merchandising services (Exhibit 23.1) and local research data (Exhibit 23.2) to the retailer.

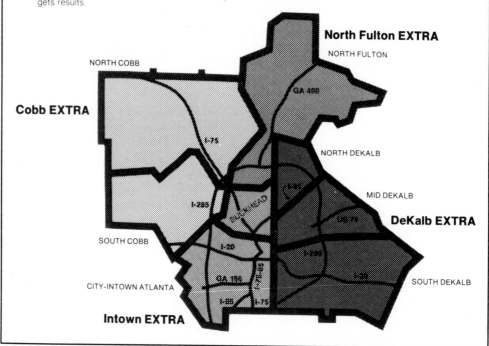

The extra ad-vantage...

Four editorial zones: Cobb County, DeKalb County, Intown (City of Atlanta), and North Fulton County. Each with its own news coverage, local information, and design.

Eight advertising zones: South Cobb, North Cobb, South DeKalb, Mid DeKalb, North DeKalb, City-Intown, Buckhead, and North Fulton. Advertising produced to circulate in the region or regions best serving the advertiser.

Three classified zones: Zone 1 — North, Mid, and South DeKalb. Zone 2 — City-Intown. Zone 3 — Buckhead, North and South Cobb, North Fulton. Regionalized classifieds with circulation coverage that gets results.

Exhibit 23.1
The Atlanta Journal and Constitution provides zoned coverage with its tabloid insert (called Extra) circulated in the metropolitan paper each Thursday. (This, and the next exhibit, are courtesy of the Atlanta Journal and Constitution.)

The use of loose inserts (preprints), which we discussed earlier in Chapter 8, has grown tremendously. Zoned editions (Exhibit 23.1) of metropolitan newspapers make it possible for retailers to advertise in selected areas of a city. Many newspapers have also upgraded their local sales force to provide more professional and faster service to retailers.

Radio and television in retailing

Radio, long a local advertising medium, has been joined by TV as a major force in retail advertising. Radio is effective in reaching people, such as some ethnic audiences and teenagers, who are traditionally not regular newspaper readers. Radio is also an excellent medium to reach specific target mar-

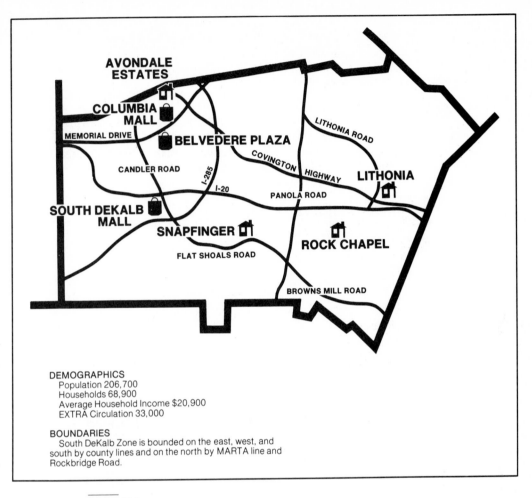

AVONDALE ESTATES

COLUMBIA MALL

MEMORIAL DRIVE

BELVEDERE PLAZA

LITHONIA ROAD

COVINGTON HIGHWAY

LITHONIA

CANDLER ROAD

I-285

I-20

PANOLA ROAD

SOUTH DEKALB MALL

SNAPFINGER

ROCK CHAPEL

FLAT SHOALS ROAD

BROWNS MILL ROAD

DEMOGRAPHICS
  Population 206,700
  Households 68,900
  Average Household Income $20,900
  EXTRA Circulation 33,000

BOUNDARIES
  South DeKalb Zone is bounded on the east, west, and
south by county lines and on the north by MARTA line and
Rockbridge Road.

Exhibit 23.2
A detailed map and demographic breakout of one zone in the Atlanta Journal and
Constitution's zone coverage.

kets. Daytime programs are geared to the housewife and mother; drive time, morning and evening, reaches men.

TV was a comparatively slow starter in the retail field, but the growth of TV-oriented franchise corporations has dramatically increased its use as a retail advertising medium. Many local retailers first experimented with independent TV stations, whose low price structure made TV advertising economically more feasible than large network affiliates did.

TV stations view local advertising as their major growth segment for the future. Especially in large markets they have set up separate retail-advertising sales departments to service local outlets. These sales departments are modeled after similar departments long established in newspapers. They generally have three primary functions:

1. To help with creation of commercials and provide production facilities to retailers
2. To work with retailers to show how TV can complement a total promotion program
3. To deal with both retailers and manufacturers to develop cooperative-advertising funding for TV, the acceptance of coop by national advertisers being a major influence on increases in TV retail advertising

In recent years almost every category of retail TV advertising has increased. The exception to these annual increases has been the automotive and real-estate categories, which saw a decrease because of the high interest rates from 1979 to 1980. The top ten categories of local TV advertising are:*

1. Restaurants and drive-ins
2. Food stores and supermarkets
3. Banks and savings and loans
4. Department stores
5. Furniture stores
6. Movies
7. Auto dealers
8. Discount department stores
9. Radio and cable TV
10. Amusements and entertainment

Direct response in retailing

Retailers have long recognized the advantages of direct-mail advertising to promote special sales or reach a specific segment of their customers. Retail direct mail can consist of various formats, from a postcard to a multipage advertising tabloid.

In addition to traditional direct-mail advertising retailers are beginning to experiment with new technology in their direct-response promotions. One of the newest innovations is the video shopping service, in which cable subscribers pay an annual fee and can then buy discounted merchandise shown on a special shopping-service channel. Comp-U-Card, which is partially owned by Federated Department Stores, Inc., is one of the largest video shopping services currently operating; this service allows a viewer to purchase any item sold through Federated's San Francisco store, I. Magnin, by calling a toll-free number.

Current video shopping services lack the flexibility of allowing viewers to call up categories that they want to purchase. However, Sears, Roebuck & Co., Knight-Ridder Newspapers, Inc., and AT & T have entered into a joint venture, known as Viewtron, to offer a two-way system to customers. Viewtron

---

*Adapted from Television Bureau of Advertising data.

will allow a customer to call up portions of the Sears catalog and order through an adapter attached to the TV set.*

CLASSES OF RETAIL
STORES
Retailing covers a wide variety of store and service operations. There is much shifting and overlapping among them. Drugstores sell radios, food stores carry garden furniture, and discount department stores sell food. Instead of trying to draw sharp distinctions among stores that could fall into several classifications, we shall arbitrarily consider just four contrasting types: discount stores, supermarkets, specialty stores, and traditional department stores.

Discount
stores
Stores that wish to be known for low prices and bargains in everything they sell operate on a smaller markup than department stores do and make every ad look like a page full of bargains. The ad is not an attempt at elegance; rather, it is designed to give the impression that anything the store sells will be at a good price.

Sears, Montgomery Ward, and J. C. Penney. Because these firms control their own production, they can plan far in advance all their merchandise programs, including special sales and special offerings. All the advertising material for each part of the year—newspaper ads, radio scripts, TV spots, store signs, and direct response—is prepared centrally. It is then available directly from the home office or the regional office, upon requisition by the store. In such operations the merchandising manager may decide to feature children's apparel during the 30-day period before Easter, and all the advertising will be prepared for that event. Stores located in warmer climates may decide to run this particular children's ad 4 weeks prior to Easter, while stores in the northern states may prefer to run the ad 10 days prior to Easter. Once this decision is made, the ad has to be positioned in the local papers, signs and in-store displays have to be requisitioned, and salespeople must be advised so that they will be knowledgeable about the advertised goods.

Although these chains may be national, the stores are billed at a low rate, the rule being that, if an ad appears over one name only, it is so eligible.

Supermarkets
Continuous competition make supermarkets vie with each other not only in price but in variety of goods and quality of merchandise. Their chief drawing card is their advertising of weekly price specials, found usually in the Wednesday food sections of newspapers. No supermarket could continue to

---

*John E. Cooney, "With Video Shopping Services, Goods You See on the Screen Can Be Delivered to Your Door," *The Wall Street Journal,* July 14, 1981, p. 52.

exist, however, solely on the patronage of those who come in to buy only the low-priced specials advertised, and they work to acquire a loyal following of steady customers by establishing a distinctive quality or service image for themselves. Stop and Shop, for example, does it by featuring the high quality of its own brand of goods, along with low prices.

Specialty shops

Many stores feature one class of merchandise—women's apparel, household appliances, TV and radio, hardware. There are many regional and national chains of specialty shops that prepare their own advertising, but most specialty shops are independently owned and cater strictly to local trade. For advertising they use newspapers, circulars, radio, and TV. There are TV-production firms that prepare syndicated commercial tapes, which stores can use on TV for series of short flights, as, for example, a series of films for jewelers to advertise jewelry and gifts toward the holiday and wedding seasons. Similarly, there are syndicated services available for use in newspaper advertising. The whole ad, with artwork, is prepared in mat form, allowing space for the local merchant's name. When using mat art provided by a newspaper, you should be guaranteed that the same art will not be used for another ad in the same edition of the newspaper. Local stores often use a local agency or a free-lance advertising person to prepare their advertising on a fee basis.

Traditional department stores

These stores usually sell all types and qualities of merchandise from clothing to furniture. Merchandise is arranged by departments, with salespeople assigned to each. They emphasize customer service, including deliveries, dressing rooms with fitters' services, ease of returning merchandise, restrooms, and restaurants—all with a view to creating a regular clientele. Much of their business is done on credit, and their lists of charge customers are of great value. The introduction of bank charge cards into department stores has reduced the use of "in-store" credit, with a resulting loss of customer identification; but although department stores have bowed to customer demand and accepted bank credit cards, most stores encourage patrons to acquire and use store credit cards. Originally department stores were built in the central city. Today, with the movement of population to the suburbs, department stores have opened branches, typically in shopping malls. In some cases department stores have even closed their large downtown stores, leaving only branch mall stores.

Another major change in department-store operations is their expansion into both discount- and specialty-store subsidiaries. For instance, Woolworth operates both Woolco discount stores as well as specialty shops such as Shirt Closet, Foot Locker, Susie's Casuals, and Richman men's stores. This diversification allows department stores to reach all segments of the public.

Types of department-store advertising. The kind of advertisin/
traditional department store stems directly from the kind of store/
ment wishes to operate, the type of trade it seeks, the range of n
plans to offer, and the image it seeks to project. This affects e/
nected with the operation: store location, decor, degree of emphas.
styles, and types of price range of merchandise. It affects the advertising a..
the organization of the marketing operation (Exhibit 23.3). All advertising of
all stores, however, has these objectives: to sell the specific article advertised,
to bring in store traffic, and to project the store image. The advertising may be
any of three types or a combination of them.

Promotional advertising is devoted to a specific product, such as dresses,
bedspreads, lamps, or china. It reflects the efforts of a buyer to make a particularly advantageous purchase in terms of style, variety, and price. Promotional
advertising can be that of individual items or goods of one particular department. Departmental ads are often built around a theme designed not merely
to sell the particular items advertised but to establish that department as a
headquarters for such goods. Many of the promotional ads run by a department store are on a cooperative basis (discussed below) with a national advertiser.

Next, there is the *advertising of sales,* including storewide special sales
events. Most stores have storewide specials at the end of each season or on
some annual or special promotional basis, such as Washington's Birthday, an
anniversary sale, or a midsummer sale (Exhibit 23.4).

As we mentioned earlier, many department stores are located in shopping malls. Special promotions are often conducted on a joint basis among the
merchants in a mall. The large department stores are usually the reason for
people's coming to the mall and are the traffic builder for smaller shops.

Most traditional department-store advertising is a mixture of the foregoing types, featuring either sales or new merchandise.

Then there is *institutional advertising,* designed to give the whole store a
lift in the esteem of the public, above and beyond its reputation for good merchandising. It may be to help some community project; it may be something
the store is doing to bring pride to the community; it may be some advice to
help a woman in her shopping knowledge of products. It makes no specific
price offerings of merchandise. Institutional advertising as a rule is a one-shot
ad, created only when there is something to say. However, a few large department stores make a regular practice of image-enhancing institutional advertising to maintain long-term customer goodwill and establish the store's position
as a member of the community.

COOPERATIVE ADVERTISING

Although we have already discussed cooperative-advertising allowances chiefly from the manufacturer's point of view, let us review some of
its features from the store's viewpoint. Cooperative advertising is so important

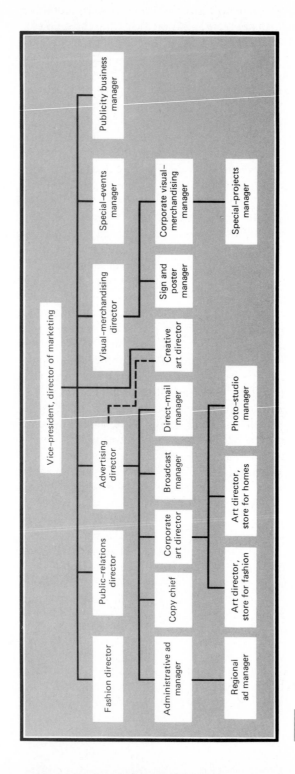

Exhibit 23.3
The marketing operation of a large department store. Note the specialization of the advertising/marketing effort. (Exhibits 23.3 through 23.11 are courtesy of Rich's, a division of Federated Department Stores, Inc.)

Our lowest prices of the season

Starts today!

Shop Downtown 9:30-6:00; Suburban 9:30-9:30

You may win the new Ford EXP sport coupe

Register in Rich's Men's Department for America's new front wheel drive personal sport coupe, designed by Ford for comfort and fuel efficiency. Ballots collected in all 16 Rich's stores and Rich's II. One car awarded from all entries. You must be 18 or older to enter. All contest entries must be in by midnight, May 3, 1981, and are limited to one entry per person. The winner will be selected by random ballot and notified by phone on May 13, 1981. You need not be present to win, no purchase is necessary and no substitutions for prizes will be given. Employees and agents of Rich's, Ford Motor Co., and their families are not eligible.

DOWNTOWN   NORTH DEKALB
BELVEDERE   PERIMETER
COBB   SHANNON
CUMBERLAND   SOUTH DEKALB
GREENBRIAR   SOUTHLAKE
LENOX SQUARE

RICH'S

Exhibit 23.4
A storewide sale opens with a special promotion to gain consumer awareness.

in retailing that in some departments it may run as high as 50 percent of the total advertising expenditure.

Chief advantages

- ☐ Helps the buyer stretch his advertising capability
- ☐ May provide good artwork of the product advertised, with good copy—especially important to the small store
- ☐ Helps the store earn a better volume discount for all its advertising

Cooperative advertising is best when the line is highly regarded and is a style or other leader in the field.

Chief disadvantages

- ☐ Although the store may pay only 50 percent of the cost, that sum may still be out of proportion from the viewpoint of sales and profit.
- ☐ Most manufacturers' ads give more emphasis to the brand name than to the store name.

Manufacturers' ads cannot have the community flavor and the style of the store ads. To localize coop advertising, some retailers will not accept manufacturer-produced ads; instead, the store incorporates product information into an ad that conforms to the retailer's advertising style (Exhibit 23.5).

Retail stores get far more offers for coop advertising than they can possibly use. Everything depends on the importance of the product to the store.

For newspaper advertising the store sends the vendor a tear sheet of its ad, as evidence that the ad ran, together with its bill for the vendor's share of the cost. Since there are no tear sheets for radio and TV advertising, a special form has been adopted to assure the vendor that the commercials ran as scheduled. Designed by the Association of National Advertisers, the Radio Advertising Bureau, and the Television Bureau of Advertising, it combines in one form the commercial script, the bill, and an affidavit to be signed by the station. A copy of this form is sent to the vendor, who then can be sure that the commercial was broadcast as stated on the form containing the station's affidavit. All stores doing cooperative broadcast advertising use such a form. This dependability in billing has undoubtedly led to the greatly increased volume of TV and radio department-store advertising.

There is so much involved in using cooperative advertising that most stores have a business department inside the advertising department to make sure the store collects all the money due it.

Last great weekend **Rich's**
114th Anniversary Sale
Our lowest prices of the season

save 10% to 42%
Save work, save on our everyday low prices

26.99
with rebate*

GE coffeemaker with Brew Starter®

REGULARLY 34.99. Built in clock and timer lets you make coffee while you sleep, then start each day with hot coffee. See through water reservoir with 2 to 10 cup capacity.

*You pay Rich's 31.99. Send rebate coupon to GE, they send you $5 directly. Rebate offer expires 5/31/81.

Small Electrics-all Rich's

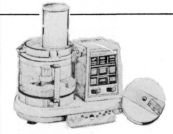

sale 24.99

West Bend electric skillet with Silver Stone® interior

REGULARLY 36.99. Non-stick cooking surface makes clean up fast and easy. Handy 11'' size is perfect for all of your cooking needs. Heavy-gauge aluminum exterior.

17.99
with rebate*

Easy to use Waring Ice Cream Parlor®

REGULARLY 29.99. Makes ½ gallon of homemade ice cream, frozen yogurt or sherbet in about 30 minutes. Uses plain ice cubes and table salt. Shuts off automatically.

*You pay Rich's 22.99. Send rebate coupon to Waring, they send you $5 rebate directly. Rebate offer expires 7/31/81.

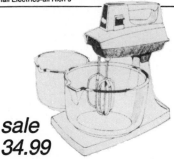

sale 34.99

Sunbeam infinite speed stand mixer

REGULARLY 44.99. Twelve speeds with governor controlled motor to maintain full power on all settings. Removes from stand for portability. 1½ and 4-qt. glass bowls.

32.99 with rebate*

Hamilton Beach two-speed food processor

REGULARLY 46.99. Two speeds for complete processing versatility plus on/off and momentary settings. With steel cutting blade and shredding/slicing disc.

*You pay Rich's 39.99. Send rebate coupon to Hamilton Beach, they send you $7 directly. Rebate offer expires 6/26/81.

29.99 with rebate*

Large Proctor Silex toaster/oven broiler

REGULARLY 44.99. Bake, broil or toast up to four slices of bread with keep-warm to 450° heat range plus broil and automatic toast shut off. Slide out tray.

*You pay Rich's 32.99. Send rebate coupon to Proctor Silex, they send you $3 directly. Rebate offer expires 6/26/81.

For warranty information about specific merchandise, write to:
Penelope Penn, c/o Rich's, 45 Broad Street, S.W., Atlanta, Georgia 30302

Exhibit 23.5
A co-op ad tied in to a storewide sale.

THE STORY BEHIND
a department-store advertising department in action

The entire selling and advertising operation of a department store is reflected in a series of promotional calendars (Exhibit 23.6), beginning with an annual one, prepared before the year starts. As the year advances, seasonal calendars—3-month, 1-month, and finally weekly—are made up. The budget is usually based on the previous year's events but may be increased somewhat because business grows and so does inflation. These plans are designed to make possible a coordinated effort by all involved.

To anyone entering the department-store operating world for the first time the most impressive thing is the long-range planning under which the store operates and the great amount of lead time set for the preparation of advertising. Also impressive is the large number of people involved, each with a different corporate responsibility. Each store has its own operating plan and titles, but the plan that we describe in this section is a typical one, that of Rich's of Atlanta, where a staff of departmental copywriters works within the newspaper department and several are assigned to direct mail; under an organizational scheme such as that shown in Exhibit 23.3 Rich's has also the store buyers and divisional merchandise manager, each of whom is responsible for the operation of a series of related buying areas.

Newspaper advertising. About 3 months before a season begins the preliminary seasonal promotion calendar is prepared. All major events are scheduled and entered on this calendar.

Seven or eight weeks in advance of scheduled publication the monthly plans for advertising are made, to allow time for review and approval by various senior executives. Approved ads can then be in the hands of the advertising department 4 weeks in advance of publication.

Four weeks in advance of a given week the production of that week's advertising begins. The advertising department publishes a master schedule for that week, showing the day the ad is to run, the newspapers involved, merchandise to be featured, vendor money, and size of ad.

Copy preparation. Ads are prepared from information and samples submitted by buyers. If a manufacturer is paying part of the cost of the ad, the invoice must be submitted with copy (Exhibit 23.7).

Once a week the ad copy, vendor invoice, and the merchandise are presented at a meeting of the merchandise manager, buyer, layout and copy people, and the advertising director. The copy is then written, and the layout is designed. The copy and layout are sent to the merchandise manager and buyer for review. Sketches or photographs are made of merchandise. A proof with art and corrected copy is then sent to the merchandise manager and buyer for final corrections. The advertising department has final authority on the layout and the presentation of merchandise. It must be consistent with the standards of the store (Exhibit 23.8).

Results of ads can be obtained immediately by checking the sales the next day. The sales over normal show the success of the ad.

526

SALES PROMOTION PLAN

ALL MARKETS
PERIOD III — 1981 APRIL

SUNDAY	MONDAY	TUESDAY	WEDNESDAY	THURSDAY	FRIDAY	SATURDAY
4/5 * - . . '80 Easter	**6**	**7**	**8**	**9**	**10**	**11**
EASTER PROMOTIONS						
12 Palm Sunday	**13**	**14** Spring Holidays — Cobb & DeKalb County Schools closed (4/13 – 4/17)	**15**	**16**	**17** Good Friday Spring Holidays — Clayton County Schools closed (4/17 – 4/24)	**18**
EASTER PROMOTIONS				D/M Clinique GWP — (In Homes 4/15–17) Atl., Birm.		
19 Easter	**20**	**21**	**22**	**23**	**24**	**25** OPENING DAY ANNIVERSARY SALE
	AFTER EASTER CLEARANCE		COURTESY DAYS — ANNIVERSARY SALE			
			D/M 48 Pg. Book — (In Homes 4/15–18)			
26 8 Pgs. Full color insert — WEDGWOOD ROAD SHOW	**27**	**28**	**29**	**30**	**5/1** Mother's Day Checkbook mailer — in homes (4/30 — 5/1–2)	**2** Last Day — Clinique GWP
			ANNIVERSARY SALE			
			D/M Estee Lauder PWP — Atl. only	(In Home 4/29–30)		

Exhibit 23.6
Section of a typical advertising and promotion calendar. Note that the starting date of the storewide sale is preceded by a 3-day presale promotion ("Courtesy Days").

RICH'S
COOPERATIVE ADVERTISING REQUEST

Tear off and send to Publicity Business Office   Attach Applicable Contracts

Bill to: _____

Attention: _____

Address _____
            Street

_____
City   State   Zip

Dept. _____ / _____
          Buyer's Signature

Name _____ dia and City _____

Date c_ dvertising _____

Radio/TV _____ _____ %/or $ _____

_____ _____ %/or $ _____
Nsp. columns

_____ rt _____ %/or $ _____
other publications (catalogs, inserts, etc.)

Special Instructions: _____

Do not write below this line — for Publicity Business Office use only

Paid Ad Request required for each media regardless of Copy Dept. requirements.   Invoice # _____

             CITY _____ SIZE OF AD _____

DEPT. _____ PHONE _____ SELLING DATE _____ PAPER _____ DAY AD RUNS _____

This information with merchandise, is due in advertising at your scheduled meeting 3 weeks in advance of week ad appears in the paper, for black and white, and 4 weeks in advance for color.
It is your responsibility to see that copy contains no false or exaggerated claims and that copies of fiber or fabric contracts are attached.

FILL OUT COMPLETELY!

Shall we solicit mail and phone orders?
No ☐ Yes: Mo Box ☐ Mail line only ☐
Phone line only ☐ Mail or Phone
line only ☐

Check Stores to be listed:
☐ Downtown   ☐ Southlake
☐ Lenox   ☐ Total Atlanta
☐ Belvedere   ☐ Brookwood
☐ Cobb   ☐ Century Plaza
☐ North DeKalb   ☐ Outlet Hme St
☐ Greenbriar   ☐ Bake Shops
☐ South DeKalb   ☐ PC, CS, & OI
☐ Perimeter   ☐ Augusta
☐ Cumberland   ☐ Columbia

Merchandise in house?_____
If not, when expected?_____

Have we advertised this item
before?_____
Date?_____

Pick up art from previous ad?_____
Date and paper _____

Vendor paid ad?_____
If so, give name of company to
be billed _____

Send Cooperative Advertising Form
to Publicity Business Office.

THE FOLLOWING MUST BE FILLED OUT COMPLETELY

Most important selling point

List 2 other selling features

Be sure to list following information where applicable:
Sale Price:

Reg. or Orig. Price:

% of Savings:

Sizes:

Fabric Fiber Content:

Fabric/Fiber Contract: Yes ☐   No ☐   Attached ☐

Trade Mark Required: Yes ☐   No ☐

Colors:

Any Other Pertinent Information:

         Buyer's Signature
THIS INFORMATION WILL NOT BE ACCEPTED UNLESS FORMS ARE FILLED OUT COMPLETELY.

A   PLEASE FILL OUT AND SEND THIS PORTION OF THE FORM TO THE RECEIVING MANAGER   **A**
D   IF THE MERCHANDISE ON AD IS NOT IN HOUSE   **D**

DEPARTMENT NO. _____ VENDOR NAME _____ AD DATE _____

ORDER NO. _____ DATE EXPECTED _____ BUYER'S SIGNATURE _____
ADV 3 (REV. 2–78)

Exhibit 23.7

A buyer uses this form to request advertising for a cooperative product. Note detailed specifications.

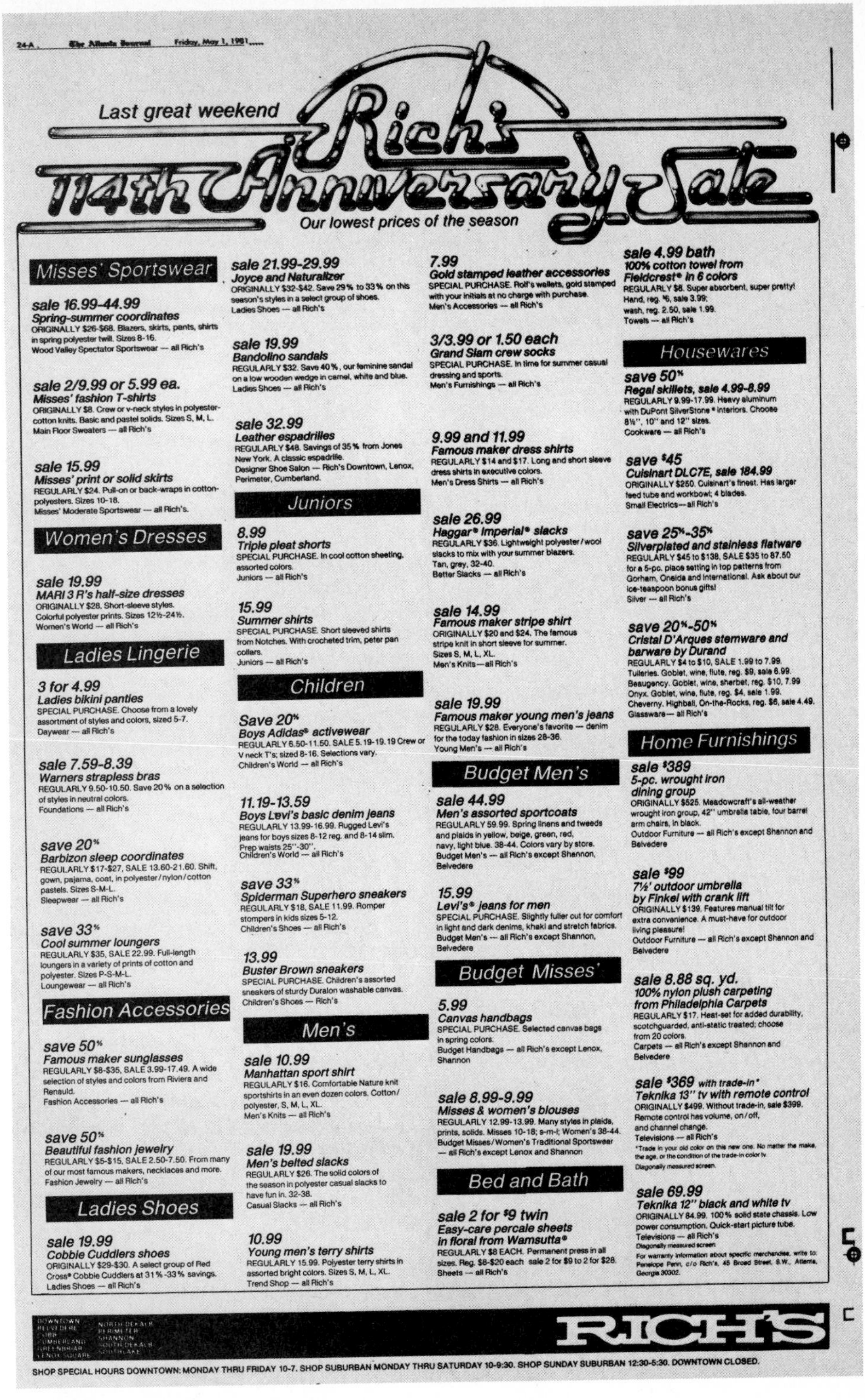

24-A The Atlanta Journal Friday, May 1, 1981

Last great weekend

Rich's 114th Anniversary Sale

Our lowest prices of the season

Misses' Sportswear

sale 16.99-44.99
Spring-summer coordinates
ORIGINALLY $26-$68. Blazers, skirts, pants, shirts in spring polyester twill. Sizes 8-16.
Wood Valley Spectator Sportswear — all Rich's

sale 2/9.99 or 5.99 ea.
Misses' fashion T-shirts
ORIGINALLY $8. Crew or v-neck styles in polyester-cotton knits. Basic and pastel solids. Sizes S, M, L.
Main Floor Sweaters — all Rich's

sale 15.99
Misses' print or solid skirts
REGULARLY $24. Pull-on or back-wraps in cotton-polyesters. Sizes 10-18.
Misses' Moderate Sportswear — all Rich's.

Women's Dresses

sale 19.99
MARI 3 R's half-size dresses
ORIGINALLY $28. Short-sleeve styles. Colorful polyester prints. Sizes 12½-24½.
Women's World — all Rich's

Ladies Lingerie

3 for 4.99
Ladies bikini panties
SPECIAL PURCHASE. Choose from a lovely assortment of styles and colors, sized 5-7.
Daywear — all Rich's

sale 7.59-8.39
Warners strapless bras
REGULARLY 9.50-10.50. Save 20% on a selection of styles in neutral colors.
Foundations — all Rich's

save 20%
Barbizon sleep coordinates
REGULARLY $17-$27, SALE 13.60-21.60. Shift, gown, pajama, coat, in polyester/nylon/cotton pastels. Sizes S-M-L.
Sleepwear — all Rich's

save 33%
Cool summer loungers
REGULARLY $35, SALE 22.99. Full-length loungers in a variety of prints of cotton and polyester. Sizes P-S-M-L.
Loungewear — all Rich's

Fashion Accessories

save 50%
Famous maker sunglasses
REGULARLY $8-$35, SALE 3.99-17.49. A wide selection of styles and colors from Riviera and Renauld.
Fashion Accessories — all Rich's

save 50%
Beautiful fashion jewelry
REGULARLY $5-$15, SALE 2.50-7.50. From many of our most famous makers, necklaces and more.
Fashion Jewelry — all Rich's

Ladies Shoes

sale 19.99
Cobbie Cuddlers shoes
ORIGINALLY $29-$30. A select group of Red Cross® Cobbie Cuddlers at 31%-33% savings.
Ladies Shoes — all Rich's

sale 21.99-29.99
Joyce and Naturalizer
ORIGINALLY $32-$42. Save 29% to 33% on this season's styles in a select group of shoes.
Ladies Shoes — all Rich's

sale 19.99
Bandolino sandals
REGULARLY $32. Save 40%, our feminine sandal on a low wooden wedge in camel, white and blue.
Ladies Shoes — all Rich's

sale 32.99
Leather espadrilles
REGULARLY $48. Savings of 35% from Jones New York. A classic espadrille.
Designer Shoe Salon — Rich's Downtown, Lenox, Perimeter, Cumberland.

Juniors

8.99
Triple pleat shorts
SPECIAL PURCHASE. In cool cotton sheeting, assorted colors.
Juniors — all Rich's

15.99
Summer shirts
SPECIAL PURCHASE. Short sleeved shirts from Notches. With crocheted trim, peter pan collars.
Juniors — all Rich's

Children

Save 20%
Boys Adidas® activewear
REGULARLY 6.50-11.50. SALE 5.19-19.19 Crew or V neck T's; sized 8-16. Selections vary.
Children's World — all Rich's

11.19-13.59
Boys Levi's basic denim jeans
REGULARLY 13.99-16.99. Rugged Levi's jeans for boys sizes 8-12 reg. and 8-14 slim. Prep waists 25"-30".
Children's World — all Rich's

save 33%
Spiderman Superhero sneakers
REGULARLY $18, SALE 11.99. Romper stompers in kids sizes 5-12.
Children's Shoes — all Rich's

13.99
Buster Brown sneakers
SPECIAL PURCHASE. Children's assorted sneakers of sturdy Duralon washable canvas.
Children's Shoes — Rich's

Men's

sale 10.99
Manhattan sport shirt
REGULARLY $16. Comfortable Nature knit sportshirts in an even dozen colors. Cotton/polyester, S, M, L, XL.
Men's Knits — all Rich's

sale 19.99
Men's belted slacks
REGULARLY $26. The solid colors of the season in polyester casual slacks to have fun in. 32-38.
Casual Slacks — all Rich's

10.99
Young men's terry shirts
REGULARLY 15.99. Polyester terry shirts in assorted bright colors. Sizes S, M, L, XL.
Trend Shop — all Rich's

7.99
Gold stamped leather accessories
SPECIAL PURCHASE. Rolf's wallets, gold stamped with your initials at no charge with purchase.
Men's Accessories — all Rich's

3/3.99 or 1.50 each
Grand Slam crew socks
SPECIAL PURCHASE. In time for summer casual dressing and sports.
Men's Furnishings — all Rich's

9.99 and 11.99
Famous maker dress shirts
REGULARLY $14 and $17. Long and short sleeve dress shirts in executive colors.
Men's Dress Shirts — all Rich's

sale 26.99
Haggar® Imperial® slacks
REGULARLY $36. Lightweight polyester/wool slacks to mix with your summer blazers. Tan, grey, 32-40.
Better Slacks — all Rich's

sale 14.99
Famous maker stripe shirt
ORIGINALLY $20 and $24. The famous stripe knit in short sleeve for summer. Sizes S, M, L, XL.
Men's Knits—all Rich's

sale 19.99
Famous maker young men's jeans
REGULARLY $28. Everyone's favorite — denim for the today fashion in sizes 28-36.
Young Men's — all Rich's

Budget Men's

sale 44.99
Men's assorted sportcoats
REGULARLY 59.99. Spring linens and tweeds and plaids in yellow, beige, green, red, navy, light blue. 38-44. Colors vary by store.
Budget Men's — all Rich's except Shannon, Belvedere

15.99
Levi's® jeans for men
SPECIAL PURCHASE. Slightly fuller cut for comfort in light and dark denims, khaki and stretch fabrics.
Budget Men's — all Rich's except Shannon, Belvedere

Budget Misses'

5.99
Canvas handbags
SPECIAL PURCHASE. Selected canvas bags in spring colors.
Budget Handbags — all Rich's except Lenox, Shannon

sale 8.99-9.99
Misses & women's blouses
REGULARLY 12.99-13.99. Many styles in plaids, prints, solids. Misses 10-18; s-m-l; Women's 38-44.
Budget Misses/Women's Traditional Sportswear — all Rich's except Lenox and Shannon

Bed and Bath

sale 2 for $9 twin
Easy-care percale sheets in floral from Wamsutta®
REGULARLY $8 EACH. Permanent press in all sizes. Reg. $8-$20 each sale 2 for $9 to 2 for $28.
Sheets — all Rich's

sale 4.99 bath
100% cotton towel from Fieldcrest® in 6 colors
REGULARLY $8. Super absorbent, super pretty! Hand, reg. $6, sale 3.99; wash, reg. 2.50, sale 1.99.
Towels — all Rich's

Housewares

save 50%
Regal skillets, sale 4.99-8.99
REGULARLY 9.99-17.99. Heavy aluminum with DuPont SilverStone® interiors. Choose 8½", 10" and 12" sizes.
Cookware — all Rich's

save $45
Cuisinart DLC7E, sale 184.99
ORIGINALLY $250. Cuisinart's finest. Has larger feed tube and workbowl; 4 blades.
Small Electrics—all Rich's

save 25%-35%
Silverplated and stainless flatware
REGULARLY $45 to $138, SALE $35 to 87.50 for a 5-pc. place setting in top patterns from Gorham, Oneida and International. Ask about our ice-teaspoon bonus gifts!
Silver — all Rich's

save 20%-50%
Cristal D'Arques stemware and barware by Durand
REGULARLY $4 to $10, SALE 1.99 to 7.99.
Tuileries. Goblet, wine, flute, reg. $9, sale 6.99.
Beaugency. Goblet, wine, sherbet, reg. $10, 7.99
Onyx. Goblet, wine, flute, reg. $4, sale 1.99.
Cheverny. Highball, On-the-Rocks, reg. $6, sale 4.49.
Glassware— all Rich's

Home Furnishings

sale $389
5-pc. wrought iron dining group
ORIGINALLY $525. Meadowcraft's all-weather wrought iron group, 42" umbrella table, four barrel arm chairs, in black.
Outdoor Furniture — all Rich's except Shannon and Belvedere

sale $99
7½' outdoor umbrella by Finkel with crank lift
ORIGINALLY $139. Features manual tilt for extra convenience. A must-have for outdoor living pleasure!
Outdoor Furniture — all Rich's except Shannon and Belvedere

sale 8.88 sq. yd.
100% nylon plush carpeting from Philadelphia Carpets
REGULARLY $17. Heat-set for added durability, scotchguarded, anti-static treated; choose from 20 colors.
Carpets — all Rich's except Shannon and Belvedere

sale $369 with trade-in*
Teknika 13" tv with remote control
ORIGINALLY $499. Without trade-in, sale $399. Remote control has volume, on/off, and channel change.
Televisions — all Rich's
*Trade in your old color on this new one. No matter the make, the age, or the condition of the trade-in color tv.
Diagonally measured screen.

sale 69.99
Teknika 12" black and white tv
ORIGINALLY 84.99. 100% solid state chassis. Low power consumption. Quick-start picture tube.
Televisions — all Rich's
Diagonally measured screen

For warranty information about specific merchandise, write to: Penelope Penn, c/o Rich's, 45 Broad Street, S.W., Atlanta, Georgia 30302.

DOWNTOWN, BELVEDERE, COBB, CUMBERLAND, GREENBRIAR, LENOX SQUARE, NORTH DEKALB, PERIMETER, SHANNON, SOUTH DEKALB, SOUTHLAKE

RICH'S

SHOP SPECIAL HOURS DOWNTOWN: MONDAY THRU FRIDAY 10-7. SHOP SUBURBAN MONDAY THRU SATURDAY 10-9:30. SHOP SUNDAY SUBURBAN 12:30-5:30. DOWNTOWN CLOSED.

Exhibit 23.8
Store-wide sale ends on a hard-sell theme.

Broadcast advertising. There is a regular broadcast budget for storewide events plus merchandise groups based on last year's (yearly) events. The budget request for broadcast is submitted by the buyer, who specifies date of promotion, merchandise description, quantity available, and the sales plan for the period of the promotion, as well as last year's sales, the trend for the periods, and expected plus over normal over the trend. This has to be approved by the divisional merchandise manager, the general-merchandise manager, and the sales-promotion director.

An outside advertising agency is employed to produce radio and TV and to buy media time.

The broadcast department decides whether to use radio, TV, or both, according to type of merchandise. Then, based on information from the merchandise buyer, broadcast decides on the target audience. (Who are the people to go after? Women of a certain age? Kids? Total men? Daytime showing? Sports?) And broadcast decides what markets are to be covered (Atlanta and Augusta, Georgia, Columbia and Greenville, South Carolina, and Birmingham, Alabama). Broadcast also decides when to start the radio or TV schedule and how long the spot will run, radio spots being either 30 or 60 seconds, and TV spots either 10 or 30 seconds. The time spots are determined by the dollars allocated and the availability of time. Summertime presents fewer problems than the fall season, with its new programming and higher rates. Agency media buyers ascertain stations' availabilities and buy the time.

The advertising agency along with the broadcast department handles the concept, script, models, wardrobe, props, type of production (depending on merchandise) and location of studio. Script (Exhibit 23.9) approval is given by the buyer, and the commercial is assembled (see the TV storyboard in Exhibit 23.10). Traffic notifies stations of the schedule and gives them the number of the tape or film to run. Schedules are then made up, showing the day and date of TV or radio spot, station, length of spot, and time of day or night spot will be shown. These are then distributed to all concerned.

Broadcast advertising needs approximately 6 weeks to put together a TV campaign. Radio schedules require less time unless it is a campaign involving custom music and/or specialized production techniques.

Direct mail. Direct mail is becoming more and more important as a method of retail advertising. It wasn't long ago that direct mail consisted of three to four catalogs a year. Now there can be a major catalog every month, plus newspaper preprints, bill inserts, and other sale mailers—all direct mail.

The charge-account customers are the backbone of direct mail. Their roster has been further refined by the development of a "department-of-allegiance" list of customers who have shopped a particular department during a given time. For example, a small Father's Day catalog will be sent to all charge customers who have shopped in the men's area in the last 6 months. Some areas in the store develop their own lists.

The direct-mail manager starts with the budget set up at the preseason planning meeting, at which all the advertising events are scheduled. The manager figures the approximate cost, including an estimate of what vendor money will be available. After everything is budgeted, a final schedule of mailings is prepared by the manager and sent to all who are involved.

Putting through the catalogs. This needs 2 to 3 months' lead time, depending on the size of the catalog. The general-merchandise manager asks the divisional merchandise manager how many pages each buyer wants. The divi-

LILLER NEAL WELTIN, INC. 1300 Life of Georgia Tower, Atlanta, Ga. 30308	Client: RICH'S Subject: Gold Sale Length: :30 Spot No: RR-30-10086 Live☐ Recorded☒ Date of Broadcast: 4/24 - 25	Job No: 3649

RADIO SCRIPT   4-9-81

NAME DROPPER :30 INSTR UNDER ANNCR:

Rich's is celebrating our 114th Anniversary. And to help you get in on the
celebration...we've reduced prices to the lowest of the season. Just listen
to this. Right now, you can save 30% on every piece of beautiful, 14k gold
jewelry in our Fine Jewelry Department. You can save 30% on 14k gold chains,
bracelets, earrings, pendants, charms...and more. Prices start as low as $9.00!
So hurry in today and get in on this savings jubilee...at Rich's...during our
big Anniversary Sale!

Exhibit 23.9
All media carry out the basic theme of the sale.

sional merchandise manager meets with the buyers, and a decision is made on which items will be featured. The buyers meet with the advertising department and present to the art director, copy chief, and copywriters selling features and pricing to be stressed. Coordinators give merchandise to the photo studio. The copy chief and art director set up a page sequence and the emphasis for each page. The copy and merchandise are due in the advertising department approximately 2 to 4 months in advance of mailing. A layout for every page is made and sent to each manager for approval. Seven to eight weeks before going to the printer the writers begin to write their copy. At the same time the photo studio is shooting pictures of the same merchandise for the catalog. It takes approximately 2 to 4 weeks to complete copy and photography. As the copy is written, page by page, it is sent to the buyers for approval. Then the layout and copy are sent to typesetting, which will produce camera-ready repro type. Repro type and photos are now pasted up in the production department to fit the exact page size. These are called "flats." Buyers once again get the opportunity to look at these pages after everything is completely pasted up and color transparencies are attached. After this approval, the flats are circulated throughout the department for a final proofreading. Then they are sent to the typesetting department for final corrections. Everything is then sent to the printer, a sample of the result being shown in Exhibit 23.11.

It takes about only 1 week to print the catalog and collate and staple it. Some copies are delivered to the store to be dispersed to senior merchants, managers, buyers, and advertising people. The rest are sent to a jobber who handles labeling and mailing.

The preceding discussion shows the technique for handling major mailing pieces. For special bill inserts and sale mailers the procedure is similar, except that it is on a smaller scale, with fewer people involved. Many of the small bill inserts are provided by the vendor. These are still handled by the direct-mail department. By the time these inserts are in the mail, work on some new mailing has already been started.*

*Courtesy of Rich's, Inc., Atlanta, a division of Federated Department Stores, Inc.

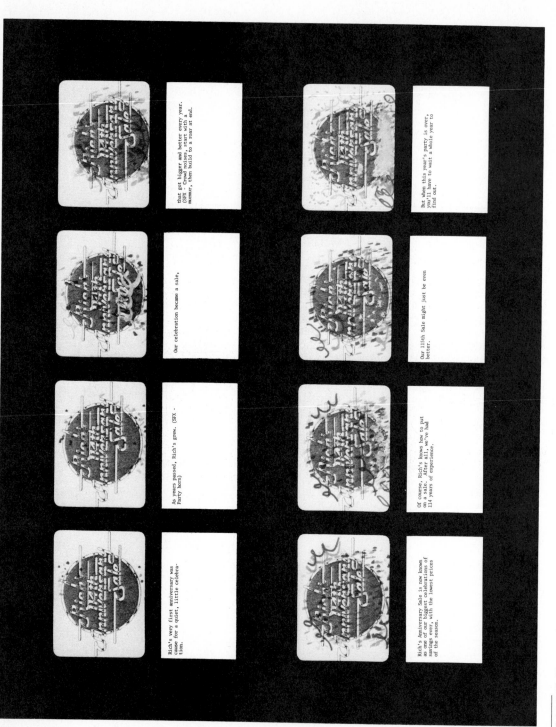

Exhibit 23.10
TV story board for a campaign.

25% off

Handsome coordinates from Pant-her, J.H. Collectibles, Villager

sale 17.99 to 50.99, reg. $23 to $69. Mix 'n match a button-front skirt with two pockets, a patch pocket blazer and a short sleeve striped bow blouse. Super Pant-her styling in easy-care polyester. Pastel colors; in sizes 6 to 14.
Available in Pant-her Sportswear, all Rich's

sale 20.99 to 66.99, reg. $28 to $90. The J.H. Collectibles group includes blouses, knit tops, jackets, pants and skirts with the look of linen, all in easy-wearing polyester/rayons and polyester/cottons. Sizes 6 to 14 in navy, white and kelly green.
Available in Moderate Update Sportswear, all Rich's.

sale 12.99 to 62.99, reg. $18 to $84. Classically styled coordinates from Villager are comfortable polyester/cotton twill and come in a wide variety of sqft colors to set the trend for any spring occasion. 8 to 16.
Available in Wood Valley Sportswear, all Rich's

3

Exhibit 23.11
A page from a catalog for Rich's anniversary sale.

SUMMARY

Retail advertising is the most localized and short term of all types of advertising. Only direct-response advertising, which is itself occasionally used in retail, can measure its success or failure with greater accuracy than retail promotions. The majority of retail advertising is placed in newspapers. However, during recent years retailers have moved into a number of other advertising vehicles to reach their diversified audiences. In recent years we have seen significant shares of retailer budgets moved into radio, TV, and catalogs. Some experiments with in-home shopping through cable links with computer terminals are also part of the retail-advertising inventory.

Retail advertising is becoming more diversified, with specialty shops, discount stores, and suburban shopping malls replacing or offering aggressive competition to the traditional downtown department stores. Retail marketing and advertising are also becoming more sophisticated. Retail promotions, like all successful advertising, are planned and executed according to long-term objectives.

QUESTIONS

1. Discuss the similarities and differences between retail and national advertising.
2. Why do most retailers use their own advertising departments rather than advertising agencies?
3. What role do newspapers, radio, and TV play in retail advertising?
4. From the retailers' viewpoint what are the advantages and disadvantages of cooperative advertising?
5. How have direct-response advertising and the move to suburbs by a substantial number of customers changed traditional retail selling and promotions during the last two decades?
6. What effect has the popularity of specialty and discount stores had on department stores?
7. Retail advertisers have a much easier job evaluating their advertising than national advertisers do. Why?

SUGGESTED EXERCISES

8. How does the TV advertising (if available) differ from the newspaper advertising for a retailer in your area?
9. For local retailers find five newspaper ads that were probably placed on a cooperative basis.

READINGS

BELLENGER, DANNY N. and PRADEEP K. KORGAONKAR: "Profiling the Recreational Shopper," *Journal of Retailing,* Fall 1980, pp. 77–92.

BERMAN, BARRY, and JOEL R. EVANS: *Retail Management: Strategic Approach* (New York: Macmillan, 1981).

BLAIR, A. EDWARD and E. LAIRD LANDON, JR.: "The Effects of Reference Prices in Retail Advertisement," *Journal of Marketing,* Spring 1981, pp. 61–69.

"Food Shoppers Shop Newspaper Ads: FTC," *Advertising Age,* September 15, 1980, p. 4.

INGENE, CHARLES A., and ROBERT E. LUSCH: "Market Selection Decisions for Department Stores," *Journal of Retailing,* Fall 1980, pp. 21–40.

KING, CHARLES W., and LAURENCE J. RING: "Market Positioning Across Retail Fashion Institutions: A Comparative Analysis of Store Types," *Journal of Retailing,* Spring 1980, pp. 37–55.

NEVIN, JOHN R., and MICHAEL J. HOUSTON: "Image as a Component of Attraction to Intra-Urban Shopping Areas," *Journal of Retailing,* Spring 1980, pp. 77–93.

OCKO, JUDY YOUNG, and M.L. ROSENBLUM: *How to be a Retail Advertising Pro* (New York: National Retail Merchants Association, 1977).

"Retail Marketing," *Advertising Age,* November 2, 1981, S-1-20.

ROTHMAN, MARIAN BURK: "A New Look at Services," *STORES,* May 1980, pp. 56–57.

ROTHMAN, MARIAN BURK: "Retail Technology: Making It Work," *STORES,* October 1980, pp. 36–40.

24

International Advertising

If you travel to other countries, you will see American products wherever you go: Cadillacs are bought by oil sheiks, and Coca-Cola is a household word in Fiji. And in the United States you are familiar with Japanese automobiles and Italian typewriters. International marketing activities are definitely on the increase; they stem from the efforts of large corporations: An estimated 80 percent of current American foreign investments is accounted for by some 200 firms, such as General Motors, Ford, and Singer, while about 100 "foreign" multinationals, like Nestlé, Shell, and Lever Brothers, represent the international business of the rest of the world.

As United States corporations' sales in overseas markets have grown and assumed a more important role in overall corporate operations, vast new opportunities for advertising abroad have burgeoned. Indeed, American agencies find it hard to compete for *Fortune* 500 accounts without some international-advertising capability although the development of marketing, communication, and media strategies in foreign environments—many less than totally receptive to advertising—is extremely difficult. Yet a coordinated approach to international management demands a universal, or standardized, advertising concept; and

Table 24-1

	TOP TEN AMERICAN AGENCIES AND THEIR FOREIGN INCOME[a]		
AGENCY AND RANK	TOTAL INCOME, MILLION $	FOREIGN INCOME, MILLION $	FOREIGN INCOME, %
1. Young & Rubicam	340.8	140.8	41.3
2. J. Walter Thompson	322.5	184.7	57.3
3. McCann-Erickson	268.7	204.1	76.0
4. Ogilvy & Mather	245.9	120.4	49.0
5. Ted Bates & Co.	210.6	102.6	48.7
6. BBDO International	175.6	69.8	39.7
7. Leo Burnett Co.	169.7	61.5	36.2
8. SSC & B	166.7	128.6	77.1
9. Foote, Cone & Belding	164.3	55.2	33.6
10. D'Arcy-MacManus & Masius	156.0	88.6	56.8

[a]*Advertising Age*, March 18, 1981, p. 8.

the trend to multinational management combined with local flexibility calls for sophisticated advertising from the agency or agencies entrusted with a multinational account.

American agencies need overseas branches to service domestic accounts, but they can, in fact, increase their profitability by adding strictly foreign accounts to their client list, as shown by Table 24.1, which lists important American-based agencies and the percentage of total income derived from foreign billings. We should note, by the way, that the world's largest agency is in Tokyo: Dentsu, Inc., with an income of $394 million, is the only non-American agency in the top ten worldwide.

ESTABLISHING A FOREIGN AGENCY

BRANCH
The first step in establishing an international operation is to decide what form of operation to use. There are three basic patterns to international-advertising operations:

Starting from scratch
Pioneers in foreign expansion, such as J. Walter Thompson and McCann-Erickson, typically sent an executive team into a country with full responsibility for setting up an overseas office. Often these offices were set up to service one or more domestic accounts; and agencies did not view them as important profit centers and were often not aggressive in soliciting local accounts. Of course there is no reason for continued neglect of local accounts, and today most overseas offices of United States agencies are careful to cultivate such business.

Buying an interest

After 1950 a more common method of establishing an international foothold was by investing in an existing agency. Often these agreements between American and foreign agencies carried an option for the American agency either to gain majority control or to purchase the agency outright within a few years.

Buying into an existing agency has several advantages for the American agency: It gives it immediate visibility and credibility in the host country; it overcomes some of the unfavorable image of a totally foreign (that is, American) company; and finally it may be the only way for an American agency to enter a country where existing regulations prohibit foreign ownership.

Joint ventures

In recent years several types of joint ventures have been developed by American and foreign agencies. Sometimes a joint venture constitutes a formal merger between two existing agencies, with control resting equally in both the agencies. In other cases a joint venture may be a working agreement between two agencies to provide international services when one agency does not desire to set up a full branch office. A dramatic joint venture was the agreement between Dentsu and Young & Rubicam to form Dentsu/Young & Rubicam Tokyo in the fall of 1981. This new venture carries the potential of greatly strengthening the potential of Dentsu's becoming a force in American advertising.

Little comparative research on the merits of various means of overseas expansion by American agencies is available. However, the data that do exist indicate that joint ventures tend to be somewhat more efficient than either totally owned foreign agencies or United States subsidiaries.* (Most studies measure productivity on the basis of agency billings per employee.) This advantage for joint ventures may change in the future as foreign agency personnel continue to upgrade their skills and subsidiaries of American agencies become more acclimated to foreign business practices. At present the joint venture seems to provide a happy marriage of American know-how and foreign personnel's knowledge of local conditions.

HOST-GOVERNMENT PUBLIC-POLICY CONCERNS

Regardless of the mode of entry into a foreign market, advertisers find problems in adapting American techniques to these countries. Although each situation is unique to any agency, client, and country, there are certain concerns that are common to all multinational agencies.

---

*Anthony F. McGann and Nils-Erik Aaby, "United States Influence on Advertising Agency Productivity in Western Europe," *ADMAP*, September, 1975, p. 316.

Table 24–2

CONCERNS OF HOST GOVERNMENTS IN
REVIEWING MULTINATIONAL BUSINESSES[a]

1. Foreign domination of local firms
2. Reduction of opportunity for local firms
3. Foreign interference in internal economic planning
4. Ability to avoid internal economic constraints
5. Creation of technological dependence
6. Extraterritorial interference by the foreign government
7. Negative balance-of-payments effects
8. Unwanted cultural impact

[a]Arnold K. Weinstein, "The U.S. Multinational Advertising Agency and Public Policy," *Journal of Advertising*, Fall, 1977, p. 20.

One of these major concerns is the attitude of host governments toward American businesses in general and toward American advertising specifically. Of course, it is impossible to list *all* the possible problems that can face an American agency in an international setting, but Dr. Arnold Weinstein, a consultant to multinational business, has formulated a list (Table 24.2) of eight common objections that foreign governments have to the establishment of foreign businesses in their countries: How the general concerns are translated into specific regulations depends on the country and the administration in power at any time. However, as American advertising expands into cultures vastly different from our own, such as the Middle East and Asia, it will have to be increasingly attuned to the political and cultural traditions of the host countries.

One of the major problems of the multinational advertiser is interpreting and adapting to the diverse advertising regulations found throughout the world. Added to this burden is the fact that many countries don't have a separate set of advertising regulations. Instead, advertising must conform to a number of regulations that affect the use and ownership of media, product regulations, and other general business regulations that indirectly impinge on advertising. Many of such regulations seem extremely illogical to American companies. Among them are the following:

☐ Argentina has a law that forbids the passing along of advertising costs to customers, with the exception of drugs.
☐ In Colombia all food advertising must have prior government approval.
☐ In Finland children cannot be shown in commercials.
☐ In Lebanon female models may not be used in cigarette advertising.

Other countries have laws and regulations regarding advertising that are very similar to our own:

☐ Belgium has strict laws regarding the advertising of stocks.

☐ Austria can have no TV advertising for cigarettes (a voluntary ban by the Austrian state tobacco monopoly imposed under threat of government regulation).

☐ Germany, Japan, and France, among others, have laws against advertising that promotes unfair competition and against misleading or untruthful advertising.*

ADVERTISING FUNCTION IN INTERNATIONAL ADVERTISING

The basic functions of advertising, research, planning, creative, and media, are the same everywhere. The problem for many American agencies is adapting these techniques to the problems of an unfamiliar marketplace. As in any problem-solving situation, advertising must rely on research to direct planning and execution of the total effort. In international advertising research is crucial since transcultural assumptions can be both misleading and risky.

Research (and planning)

Joseph Plummer, Research Director of Young & Rubicam, has suggested that international advertising must study foreign markets from an audience perspective. That is, the numerical approach used to count total audience and audience segments is not sufficient for fully understanding markets vastly different from our own. He argues that, in addition to demographic research, lifestyle studies may be more important in international-advertising research than they are in this country. He advocates the use of lifestyle studies that encompass the following areas:

☐ *Activities:* how people spend their time at work and leisure

☐ *Interests:* what is important to them in their immediate surroundings

☐ *Opinions:* how they feel about themselves and the larger world

By conducting research in a number of different countries, we can plainly see that opinions and lifestyles vary widely. These differences occur even among countries that we might assume would be very similar. These differences became apparent when Plummer asked people if they agreed with the statements in Table 24.3.

In addition to cross-cultural research it is also necessary to segment foreign audiences just as in American advertising research. While we routinely regard a segmented marketing strategy as necessary in domestic advertising, we often fall into the trap of thinking of consumers in another country as "all alike."

---

*James P. Neelankavil and Albert B. Stridsberg, *Advertising Self-Regulation: A Global Perspective* (New York: Hastings House, 1980), p. 50.

Table 24-3

CROSS-CULTURAL ATTITUDES AND OPINIONS[a]		
"EVERYONE SHOULD USE A DEODORANT," % AGREEMENT	"A HOUSE SHOULD BE DUSTED AND POLISHED THREE TIMES A WEEK," % AGREEMENT	"I ATTEND CHURCH REGULARLY," % AGREEMENT
U.S.A.: 89	Italy: 86	Spain: 77
French Canada: 81	Germany: 70	Italy: 75
English Canada: 77	U.K.: 59	French Canada: 73
U.K.: 71	France: 55	Germany: 70
Italy: 69	Spain: 53	U.S.A.: 65
France: 59	Australia: 33	English Canada: 44
Australia: 53	U.S.A.: 25	U.K.: 36
		France: 23
		Australia: 16

[a]Joseph Plummer, "Consumer Focus in Cross-national Research," *Journal of Advertising*, Spring, 1977, pp. 10, 11.

Creative
considerations

There are two options open to the advertiser who is developing a creative strategy for a multinational product. The first makes the assumption that basic consumer needs and consequently the appeals to these needs are consistent among all buyers. In this case ads, with perhaps minor variations, are used in whatever country the company happens to advertise. A second, more prevalent, view is that some consideration to local preferences should be considered for each country. In this case the particular theme of the advertising and perhaps the brand name of the product will be unique to each country. There are instances of both types of advertising that have been successful (Exhibit 24.1). However, a rule of thumb should be never to assume that an ad can be used in another country without carefully researching it in the local market.

Differences in cultural taste as well as factors such as politics, previous experience with certain types of product (the French traditionally have avoided frozen foods), and consumer affluence will be reflected in what is sold and its advertising. So one of the continuing problems of international agencies is translating product messages from one country to another.

In developing creative copy, advertisers must first determine what product characteristics are of primary importance in a particular country. (For instance, the cleanliness and proper preparation of a product might be very important in an underdeveloped country while taken for granted in the United States.) The advertiser must next be concerned with language, particularly the idioms and nuances so important in persuasive communication. Embarrassing mistranslations of American advertising abroad have become legend:

THE CAN'T-GET-BEARINGS-FAST-ENOUGH BLUES.

AND HOW TO CURE THEM.

Not getting the replacement bearings you need when you need them can be downright depressing.

Downright expensive, too. The money you save on a price break can turn into big losses on idle equipment. Or on the big bearing inventory you have to carry to play it safe.

Your Authorized Timken® Bearing Distributor can chase all your replacement-bearing blues away.

We make over 26,000 tapered roller bearings. Your Authorized Timken Bearing Distributor is likely to have the ones you need to get rolling again in a hurry. So you save on downtime.

He can survey your equipment, then stock the right bearings for you. So you save on inventory.

He can even conduct special clinics to help your people make sure the Timken bearings you buy deliver all the performance they were designed to give. So you save on maintenance. (You could even wind up replacing fewer bearings.)

Talk to your Authorized Timken Bearing Distributor today. And turn those can't-get-bearings-fast-enough blues into always-get-bearings-fast-enough smiles.

The Timken Company, Canton, Ohio 44706, U.S.A.

When you buy a Timken bearing, you buy The Timken Company.

TIMKEN®
REGISTERED TRADEMARK
TAPERED ROLLER BEARINGS

Exhibit 24.1
An example of an ad that is similar in the United States and a foreign country. (Courtesy The Timken Company.)

EL "BLUES" DEL RODAMIENTO QUE LLEGA TARDE.

Y COMO HACERLO UN CANTO ALEGRE.

No obtener los rodamientos de repuesto necesarios cuando usted los necesita puede ser muy deprimente.

Y también demasiado costoso. El dinero que usted ahorra con un precio reducido puede convertirse en grandes pérdidas con un equipo inmovilizado o por el enorme inventario de rodamientos que usted deberá mantener para estar seguro.

El distribuidor autorizado de rodamientos Timken® de su localidad puede quitarle ese "blues" de sus rodamientos de repuesto.

Fabricamos más de 26.000 rodamientos de rodillos cónicos. El distribuidor autorizado de rodamientos Timken de su localidad muy posiblemente tenga los que usted necesita para poder rodar enseguida. De modo que así ahorra usted al no paralizar su funcionamiento.

El puede examinar su equipo y almacenar los rodamientos correctos. Así ahorra usted en inventario.

El puede inclusive dar instrucción especial a su personal para que pueda cerciorarse de que los rodamientos Timken que usted compre dan todo el rendimiento para el que fueron diseñados. Así usted ahorra en mantenimiento. (Hasta podría terminar por reemplazar menos rodamientos.)

Hable hoy con el distribuidor Timken autorizado de su localidad y convierta el "blues" del rodamiento que llega tarde al canto alegre del rodamiento que siempre llega a tiempo.

The Timken Company, Canton, Ohio 44706, U.S.A.

Cuando compra un rodamiento Timken, tiene todo el respaldo de la Compañía Timken.

TIMKEN®
MARCA REGISTRADA
RODAMIENTOS DE RODILLOS CÓNICOS

Exhibit 24.1
(continued)

☐ General Motors' "Body by Fisher" slogan was translated into Flemish as "Corpse by Fisher."

☐ American Airlines' plush "rendezvous lounge" was regarded with suspicion in Brazil, where "rendezvous" in Portuguese means a room hired for love making.

☐ Pepsi encouraged German consumers to "Come Alive with Pepsi" but quickly reworded the ad because the German for "come alive" literally means "come out of the grave."*

Misuse of language is only one of the creative pitfalls that might cause a problem for an international advertiser. As we have pointed out, advertisers must be aware of local regulations and customs that restrict advertising copy in foreign countries.

Media considerations

The international advertiser who tries to carry American media strategy abroad will immediately face a number of barriers even in more developed countries. In Australia the advertiser finds a country about the size of the United States with a population equal to that of the state of Texas. In Canada's Quebec Province bilingual problems plague the advertiser. Canada's language problems are child's play compared with those of India with its 15 languages and 36 percent literacy rate. In countries such as Denmark there is no commercial broadcasting. Cinema advertising is a major medium in some European, Latin American, and Asian countries. Media planning, as we know it in the United States, simply doesn't exist in many parts of the world. Restrictions on commercial media (which the ad in Exhibit 24.2 offers to overcome), a lack of audience information, and often no fixed (or even published) rates (Exhibit 24.3) for commercial space or time combine to make advertising placement an extremely frustrating enterprise.

A continuing problem, especially in the lucrative European markets, is a lack of commercial broadcast time. Major package-goods manufacturers find a scarcity of commercial time a major hindrance to their penetration into foreign markets, especially when competing with established local brands. England is the only European country with anything approaching American advertising availability. In Holland advertising is permitted only 15 minutes per day per channel; in West Germany the figure is 20 minutes per day and none after 8 P.M.; the same type of restriction exists in France, Switzerland, Spain, and Austria. Anthony Garrett, European Vice-President for Procter & Gamble, cited the lack of commercial broadcast time as the " . . . biggest single constraint on our business."†

---

*David A. Ricks, Jeffery S. Arpan, and Marilyn Y. Fu, "Pitfalls in Advertising Overseas," in S. Watson Dunn and E. S. Lorimor, *International Advertising and Marketing* (Columbus, O.: Grid Publishing, 1979), p. 88.

†Eugene Bacot, "P&G Leads Drive for More Europe TV Time," *Advertising Age*, January 19, 1981, p. 1.

HOW CAN YOU MISS IT?

FULL SERVICE OUTDOOR ADVERTISING COMES TO SAUDI ARABIA

Announcing the formation of United Outdoor Advertising—an innovative new company specializing in a wide range of outdoor advertising services. Outdoor is the perfect way to advertise in Saudi Arabia where media is very limited. And no matter what you want to sell, we have an exciting display to suit your needs. From eye-catching (14′ x 48′) illuminated hand-painted bulletins (4.2m x 14.6m) to mylar (7′ x 14′) face back lighted displays (2.1m x 4.2m) to colorful taxi-top canopies. And in May 1981, Spectacolor, the unique animated video display structure, will be available in Jeddah. We will even customize an outdoor structure to your specifications. Make sure your advertising message isn't missed. For a full brochure and rate card, contact: Mr. Ghazi Jameel, General Manager, United Outdoor Advertising, Box 248, Jeddah, Saudi Arabia, Tel.: 660-4488, Telex: 401453

UNITED OUTDOOR ADVERTISING
OF SAUDI ARABIA

Exhibit 24.2
Advertising has become truly worldwide. (Courtesy United Outdoor Advertising.)

Newsweek Asia Ex-Philippines Edition
Average Net Paid Circulation: 146.000

Newsweek Asia Ex-Philippines is printed offset in Tokyo and Hong Kong and distributed to all countries covered by Newsweek Asia with the exception of the Philippines. **Advertising accepted in all 1st cycle issues. Check issue dates on page 3.**

	BLACK & WHITE					
Full Page	$ 8,240	$ 8,075	$ 8,035	$ 7,870	$ 7,705	$ 7,415
	BLACK & ONE COLOR					
Full Page	11,125	10,905	10,845	10,625	10,400	10,015
	FOUR-COLOR					
Full Page	14,010	13,730	13,660	13,380	13,100	12,610

Newsweek Asia Ex-Japan Edition
Average Net Paid Circulation: 120.000

Newsweek Asia Ex-Japan is printed offset in Tokyo and Hong Kong and distributed to all countries covered by Newsweek Asia with the exception of Japan. **Advertising accepted in all 1st cycle issues. Check issue dates on Page 3.**

	1X	13X	17X	26X	39X	52X
	BLACK & WHITE					
Full Page	$ 7,340	$ 7,195	$ 7,155	$ 7,010	$ 6,865	$ 6,605
	BLACK & ONE COLOR					
Full Page	9,910	9,710	9,660	9,465	9,265	8,920
	FOUR-COLOR					
Full Page	12,480	12,230	12,170	11,920	11,670	11,230

Newsweek North Asia Edition
Average Net Paid Circulation: 64,000

Newsweek North Asia is printed offset in Tokyo and distributed throughout Japan, Guam, Korea, certain Pacific islands, People's Republic of China and to military and government personnel. **Advertising accepted in all 1st cycle issues. Check issue dates on page 3.**

	1X	13X	17X	26X	39X	52X
	BLACK & WHITE					
Full Page	$3,915	$3,835	$3,815	$3,740	$3,660	$3,525
	BLACK & ONE COLOR					
Full Page	5,285	5,180	5,155	5,045	4,940	4,755
	FOUR-COLOR					
Full Page	6,655	6,520	6,490	6,355	6,220	5,990

Newsweek South Asia Edition
Average Net Paid Circulation: 102,000

Newsweek South Asia is printed offset in Hong Kong and distributed to all countries covered by Newsweek Southeast Asia, India, Pakistan, Bangladesh and Nepal. **Advertising accepted in all 1st cycle issues. Check issue date on page 3.**

	1X	13X	17X	26X	39X	52X
	BLACK & WHITE					
Full Page	$ 6,240	$ 6,115	$ 6,085	$ 5,960	$ 5,835	$ 5,615
	BLACK & ONE COLOR					
Full Page	8,425	8,255	8,215	8,045	7,875	7,585
	FOUR-COLOR					
Full Page	10,610	10,400	10,345	10,135	9,920	9,550

Newsweek East Asia Edition
Average Net Paid Circulation: 150,000

Newsweek East Asia is printed offset in Tokyo and Hong Kong and distributed to all countries covered by Newsweek Asia with the exception of Bangladesh, India, Pakistan and Nepal. **Advertising accepted in all issues. Check issue dates on Page 3.**

	1X	13X	17X	26X	39X	52X
	BLACK & WHITE					
Full Page	$ 8,570	$ 8,400	$ 8,355	$ 8,185	$ 8,015	$ 7,715
2 Cols	6,430	6,300	6,270	6,140	6,010	5,785
1 Col	3,515	3,445	3,425	3,355	3,285	3,165
	BLACK & ONE COLOR					
Full Page	11,570	11,340	11,280	11,050	10,820	10,415
2 Cols	8,675	8,500	8,460	8,285	8,110	7,810
1 Col	4,745	4,650	4,625	4,530	4,435	4,270
	FOUR-COLOR					
Full Page	14,570	14,280	14,205	13,915	13,625	13,115
2 Cols	11,655	11,420	11,365	11,130	10,895	10,490

Newsweek East Asia Ex-Philippines Edition
Average Net Paid Circulation: 128,000

Newsweek East Asia Ex-Philippines is printed offset in Tokyo and Hong Kong and distributed to all countries covered by Newsweek East Asia with the exception of the Philippines. **Advertising accepted in all 1st cycle issues. Check issue dates on page 3.**

	1X	13X	17X	26X	39X	52X
	BLACK & WHITE					
Full Page	$ 8,165	$ 8,000	$ 7,960	$ 7,800	$ 7,635	$ 7,350
	BLACK & ONE COLOR					
Full Page	11,025	10,805	10,750	10,530	10,310	9,925
	FOUR-COLOR					
Full Page	13,880	13,600	13,535	13,255	12,980	12,490

Newsweek Southeast Asia Edition
Average Net Paid Circulation: 86,000

Newsweek Southeast Asia is printed offset in Hong Kong and distributed in Brunei, Burma, Hong Kong, Indonesia, Laos, Macao, Malaysia, Philippines, Singapore, Sri Lanka, Taiwan and Thailand. **Advertising accepted in all issues. Check issue dates on page 3.**

	1X	13X	17X	26X	39X	52X
	BLACK & WHITE					
Full Page	$5,055	$4,955	$4,930	$4,830	$4,725	$4,550
2 Cols	3,790	3,715	3,695	3,620	3,545	3,410
1 Col	2,075	2,035	2,025	1,980	1,940	1,870
	BLACK & ONE COLOR					
Full Page	6,825	6,690	6,655	6,520	6,380	6,145
2 Cols	5,115	5,015	4,985	4,885	4,785	4,605
1 Col	2,800	2,745	2,730	2,675	2,620	2,520
	FOUR-COLOR					
Full Page	8,595	8,425	8,380	8,210	8,035	7,735

Exhibit 24.3
Example of international rate-card for *Newsweek*. (Courtesy *Newsweek* Magazine.)

In the foreseeable future the scarcity of commercial broadcast time will be a continuing problem for international advertisers. However, there is some evidence of a liberalization of broadcast advertising restrictions, particularly in Western Europe. Belgium recently lifted a 26-year ban on TV and radio advertising. Both Holland and Sweden have increased the number of commercial minutes allowed on TV.

In recent years international advertisers have had the opportunity to use a number of international publications, many of which have been introduced since 1970 (see Exhibit 24.4). A number of leading American consumer and business magazines, such as *Reader's Digest, Time, Newsweek,* and *National Geographic,* have editions throughout the world. In addition a number of foreign-based magazines, such as *Visión* in Latin America and *Eltern* in Europe, offer international editions and aggressively promote them to United States advertisers (see Exhibit 24.5).

Another problem for the international media planner is inflation. Table 24.4 shows the increase in media costs from 1980 to 1981 as compared with the rate of inflation in the economy of particular countries. That is, an index of 100 indicates that media costs have risen at the same rate as the economy as a whole.

FUTURE OF INTERNATIONAL
ADVERTISING
Most of us assume that international marketing and advertising refer to the exportation of American products and advertising messages to other countries. However, as we've learned from the Japanese automotive industry's invasion of this country, international marketing is a two-way street. While American advertising expertise continues to be dominant throughout the world, there is growing evidence that other countries are developing their own advertising industries.

In recent years American advertising agencies have lost accounts to local agencies, and in many countries the leading agencies are no longer American. In Switzerland, a country with long-standing ties to American agencies, only two of the top ten agencies have American connections. In Brazil four of the top five agencies are locally owned.

This is not to suggest a retrenchment by American agencies in the international marketplace. However, American advertising agencies will find the world a more competitive arena in the years to come. It is only a matter of time until major foreign agencies offer substantial competition in this country. Already agencies such as Dentsu have offices in New York and Los Angeles. If an American multinational company feels more comfortable with an American agency, isn't it logical that the same would be true of a Japanese, German, or French company?

A survey conducted by *Advertising Age* indicated that "World markets are continuing to outpace the U.S. market in terms of growth in gross income

When you are thinking about Latin America talk to us at DE ARMAS Publications

Talk to the publishers that can offer you the most —and the most varied magazines in Latin America. Magazines for women, for men and for both. Magazines for the individual, about the home, about special interest, about general interest, about the world.

Our publications:

VANIDADES Continental:- The leading women's magazine in Latin America.

MECANICA POPULAR:- Popular Mechanics . . . in Spanish.

BUENHOGAR:- The Spanish language version of Good Housekeeping.

ALMANAQUE MUNDIAL:- The most complete almanac in Spanish.

COSMOPOLITAN en Español:- For that Cosmo girl . . . in Spanish.

HOMBRE DE MUNDO:- The magazine for the modern Latin American man on the go. . .

FASCINACION:- For the successful working woman.

GEOMUNDO:- A unique guide to the world, its wildlife, its people.

IDEAS PARA SU HOGAR:- The practical guide to help women decorate, garden, sew and learn home crafts . . .

HARPER'S BAZAAR en Español:- Especially for the most sophisticated woman of Latin America.

Plus . . .

INTIMIDADES:- The magazine for the young couple.

COQUETA:- The magazine for the young woman.

THE RING en Español:- The Spanish language version of THE RING.

And . . .

SPECIAL-INTEREST BOOKS:- More than 30 "how to" books on beauty, cooking, decorating, diets, health, car care.

THERE SHOULD BE ONE OF SEVERAL MAGAZINES TO REACH YOUR TARGET AUDIENCE.

For further information, contact:
JOSHUA B. POWERS, LTD. 46 Keyes House, Dolphin Square, London SWIV 3NA, England. Tel.: 01-834-8023

Exhibit 24.4
Foreign language versions of many American magazines are available throughout the world. (Courtesy De Armas Publications.)

Some Facts U.S. Advertisers Should Know About Latin America

FACT: Latin America is no longer a "Sleeping Giant". It is a thriving market for the U.S.

- In 1960, U.S. exports to Latin America totaled 4 billion dollars. By 1980, this figure had risen to over 36 billion.
- Mexico alone is a $15 billion export market for the U.S. It buys more U.S. goods than the U.K., Germany, France or Italy. It is the third ranking U.S. market.
- Between 1979 and 1980 Latin American imports from the U.S. increased by a whopping 37%.
- Latin America imports more from the U.S. than Canada, Africa or Japan. It imports two-thirds as much as the European Economic Community.
- In fact, Latin America imports more from the U.S. than from any other country.
- Argentina, Brazil, Chile, Peru, Venezuela, Colombia and Mexico are *all* billion dollar markets.
- 16.3% of *all* U.S. export revenue comes from Latin America, and the market is getting better every day.

FACT: VISION, La Revista Interamericana, penetrates the booming Latin American market.

- For over 30 years, VISION has reported and interpreted events vital to Latin American development.
- VISION is written *by* Latin Americans, for an upscale Latin American audience. And it is written in the language Latin Americans choose for their serious reading. Their native language. Spanish.
- VISION'S 200,000 readers have the income and influence to buy whatever the U.S. is selling. 93% of VISION readers are male. 94% work in business, government or the professions. Of the businessmen, 91% are top- or middle-managers.
- Advertisers invest more money with VISION and VISAO than with any other multi-country magazines in the market.

For more facts about the Latin American market, attach your card to this ad and mail to: Ron la Villa, VISION Inc, 13 East 75th Street, New York, New York 10021. Please let us know what countries are of particular interest to you.

Exhibit 24.5
A major Latin American magazine attempts to persuade American advertisers to use the publication. (Courtesy Vision Magazine.)

549

Table 24-4

INDEXES OF MEDIA INFLATION (ECONOMY INFLATION INDEX = 100)[a]

NEWSPAPERS

Saudi Arabia	600[b]
Singapore	213
Bahrain	150
Austria	145
Spain	129
Argentina	125
France	119
Australia	118
Lebanon	117
Norway	115
U.K.	114
Brazil	113
Switzerland	111
Hong Kong	107
South Africa	107
Colombia	107
Finland	105
Italy	100
Sweden	88
Germany	83
U.S.A.	74
Netherlands	67
Mexico	67
Canada	64
Greece	62
Belgium	62
Denmark	57
Japan	Nil

MAGAZINES

Saudi Arabia	600
Japan	273
Argentina	200[b]
Finland	195
Singapore	150
Hong Kong	143
South Africa	143
Brazil	136
U.K.	133
Switzerland	133
Norway	108
Colombia	107
Spain	103
Canada	100
Italy	100
France	96
Lebanon	96
U.S.A.	96
Austria	91
Australia	91
Mexico	83
Denmark	81
Netherlands	80
Germany	73
Sweden	71
Belgium	62
Greece	62

TELEVISION

Japan	473
Italy	200
Singapore	188
Belgium	185
Hong Kong	179
Argentina	175
Spain	174
Finland	164
Greece	154
Lebanon	154
Mexico	133
Australia	123
Brazil	119
U.K.	114
Colombia	107
Canada	100
Bahrain	94
Netherlands	93
Switzerland	89
U.S.A.	85
France	81
South Africa	79
Germany	63
Austria	Nil

RADIO

Belgium	246
Bahrain	222
Singapore	188
Spain	181
South Africa	150
Netherlands	147
Mexico	133
Hong Kong	129
Australia	127
Argentina	125
Colombia	125
France	119
Lebanon	109
Canada	100
Brazil	90
Germany	88
U.K.	86
U.S.A.	64
Greece	62
Italy	25
Austria	Nil

CINEMA

Bahrain	222
Argentina	163
Australia	145
Hong Kong	143
Singapore	138
U.K.	124
Sweden	117
France	111
Denmark	105
Finland	85
Norway	85
Mexico	83
Netherlands	80
Brazil	71
Colombia	71
Greece	54
Austria	Nil

OUTDOOR

Saudi Arabia	1800
Argentina	225
Bahrain	222
Spain	161
Hong Kong	143
South Africa	143
Belgium	138
U.S.A.	138
Australia	136
Mexico	133
Singapore	125
U.K.	124
Netherlands	120
Canada	118
Finland	118
Germany	117
Norway	115
Switzerland	111
Sweden	108
Colombia	107
Italy	100
France	96
Brazil	95
Denmark	95
Austria	91
Greece	54

[a]From *Advertising World*, July, 1981, p. 26.
[b]Newspaper rates will increase six times as much as the economy in Saudi Arabia; magazine rates will increase twice as much as the economy in Argentina.

and billings (for agencies), and the gulf may be getting wider."* All indicators show that this growth will accelerate as markets such as China are opened to western multinationals. The same *Advertising Age* study showed that eighteen of the world's fifty largest advertising agencies were controlled by other than American interests. Also the report showed that, of the top twenty-two countries in terms of gross advertising-agency income, the United States ranked sixteenth in rate of growth and twentieth in income growth compared to inflation.

TRENDS IN INTERNATIONAL ADVERTISING

It is obvious that by the year 2000 virtually every major agency throughout the world will be capable, by either direct ownership or some form of joint-venture agreement, of providing international client service. It is also clear that, despite barriers of governmental control of media, advertising will have some role in even the smallest nations.

The quality of advertising and the professionalism of its practitioners will also continue to benefit from the international sharing of ideas and personnel. The United States will continue to dominate the international advertising market, but not without significant competition. This competition not only will exist in the foreign countries where American agencies compete but will very likely come from foreign challenges in this country.

SUMMARY

International marketing and advertising as a major source of revenues is a fairly recent phenomenon for most companies and advertising agencies. Only since the 1950s have American advertising agencies looked upon foreign investment as a major profit center. However, as American companies expanded into international markets after World War II, agencies followed their clients on a worldwide scale. The top ten American advertising agencies have more than 200 foreign branches, with combined income of over $1 billion.

Despite its growth and profitability, foreign advertising investment by American agencies is not easy. Controlling a worldwide network of offices from centralized headquarters is difficult for any business, but particularly a service enterprise such as advertising. The problems of language, foreign exchange,

*Advertising Age, April 20, 1981, p. S-1.

unfamiliar media, and local business practices have caused many agencies to buy into already-established local agencies and maintain a sizable staff of local nationals.

The future prospects for international advertising are excellent. As new markets, such as China and the Middle East open to American business, expansion of American agencies overseas will continue. In addition, as American agencies become more familiar with advertising on a worldwide basis, the problems of the past will lessen, and profitability of these enterprises will increase.

QUESTIONS

1. Why has international advertising become more important in recent years?
2. What effect has American investment abroad had on advertising-agency income?
3. Discuss the various techniques used by American agencies to establish foreign branches.
4. Discuss some of the major political considerations facing multinational American advertising agencies.
5. Relate the research proposals of Joseph Plummer to the marketing concept.
6. Discuss the alternative used by multinational companies in developing creative strategies.
7. Discuss some of the major problems facing the media buyer in a multinational agency.

READINGS

"China," *Advertising Age*, December 14, 1981, S-1-11.

DAVIS, HARRY L., SUSAN P. DOUGLAS, and ALVIN J. SILK: "Measure Unreliability: A Hidden Threat to Cross-National Marketing Research?" *Journal of Marketing*, Spring 1981, pp. 98–109.

DRUCKER, PETER F.: "Japan Gets Ready for Tougher Times," *Fortune*, November 8, 1980, pp. 108–14.

DUNN, S. WATSON, and E. S. LORIMOR: *International Advertising and Marketing*, (Columbus, Ohio: Grid Publishing, 1979).

HENDON, DONALD W.: "The Advertising-Sales Relationship in Australia," *Journal of Advertising Research*, February 1981, pp. 37–51.

HOOPER, WHITE: "A New Wave Has Landed," *Advertising Age*, November 2, 1981, pp. 55–56.

HORNIK, JACOB, and STEVEN C. RUBINOW: "Expert-Respondents' Synthesis for International Advertising Research," *Journal of Advertising Research,* June 1981, pp. 9–18.

KOTLER, PHILIP: *Marketing Management,* 4th ed. (Englewood Cliffs, N.J.: Prentice-Hall, Inc., 1980), pp. 663–79.

NAKANISHI, MASAO: "Marketing Developments in Japan," *Journal of Marketing,* Summer 1981, pp. 206–8.

"Nissan Change May Work, but Price High," *Advertising Age,* July 27, 1981, p. 2.

RENFORTH, WILLIAM, and DOUGLASS G. NORVELL: "Marketing to Become Sophisticated, Efficient in 1980s in Latin America," *Marketing News,* October 17, 1980, p. 1.

VANDERVORT, BRUCE: "Advertisers Flee Boring Swiss Television," *Advertising Age,* October 26, 1981, p. 70–72.

VERNON, RAYMOND: "Gone are the Cash Cows of Yesterday," *Harvard Business Review,* November/December 1980, pp. 150–55.

Advertising as an Institution

As we reach the concluding section of this book, we take a final overview of advertising as a major institution of society. Advertising is much more than an adjunct to business and marketing: It can provide a role model for society's expectations and acts as an agenda-setting device as to what is "in" or "out," important or trivial, worthwhile or valueless. Such functions are a responsibility not taken lightly by advertisers or those who scrutinize them. In this section we shall look at the diverse attitudes toward advertising as an economic tool, its inherent value to consumers as an information source, and its role in determining or modifying social values. But before the final chapter, dealing with advertising's social aspects, and closely associated with these views of advertising, the legal and regulatory framework that has been put in place as a safeguard against misleading or untruthful advertising will be examined. Every level of government—local, state, and federal—has a number of laws dealing specifically with the way advertising should be conducted, and no group is more aware of the importance of high standards of performance than the advertisers themselves. Few industries have a more formalized or effective system of self-regulation than advertising does. Honest advertisers realize that great damage can be done by a small minority of dishonest practitioners and have taken steps to prevent the use of misleading advertising.

PART SEVEN

25

Legal and Other Restraints on Advertising

The legal and regulatory environment in which advertising operates has become increasingly complex during the last two decades. Advertisers and their agencies have large legal staffs to check all product claims and advertising presentations. In spite of this care, companies still run afoul (often innocently) of the legal restraints concerning advertising.

The intent of this chapter is not to give definitive coverage of all aspects of advertising law. We shall examine the major regulatory bodies, statutory restraints, and major court decisions that affect advertising. The prudent advertiser may not know all aspects of the law but will recognize *potential* problems and seek legal counsel before they become real.

The fact is that advertising is a technique; techniques have no morality of their own but reflect the mores of the times and the standards of their users. In the last several decades we have witnessed a reexamination of the libertarian notion of *caveat emptor,* "let the buyer beware," which was based on the classical economic perception of a free marketplace of goods and ideas and perfect knowledge on the part of the participants in that marketplace. That is, both buyers and sellers had equal information, and both groups, being rational, would make correct economic choices without government interference into business transactions.

By the twentieth century the complexities of the marketplace had led to the rejection of the principle of caveat emptor. In its place came the idea that consumers cannot hope to have perfect knowledge of the marketplace and must be protected by legal guarantees as to the authenticity of advertising claims. To protect the public from false and misleading advertising, numerous laws have been passed. Chief among these is the Federal Trade Commission Act, which we discuss first. We shall then touch upon some other federal and state laws affecting advertising, as well as mentioning other steps to protect the consumer from misrepresentation in advertising.

FTC

When the Federal Trade Commission Act was passed in 1914, Congress held that "unfair methods of competition are hereby declared unlawful." The law was thus designed to protect one business from another. Commercial behaviors injurious to consumers but not to competitors were not regarded as unfair and were not thought to be within the scope of the FTC's jurisdiction. It was not until 1922, in the case *FTC v. Winsted Hosiery Company,* that the Supreme Court held that false advertising was an unfair *trade* practice. In 1938 passage of the Wheeler-Lea amendments broadened this interpretation to include the principle that the FTC could protect consumers from deceptive advertising. This law also gave the FTC specific authority over false advertising in the fields of food, drugs, therapeutic devices, and cosmetics. Today the FTC has a wide sweep of power over advertising of products sold or advertised across state lines.

Some basic FTC rules and legal

findings   Over the years there have emerged ground rules for applying the FTC law to advertising. Based largely on the regulations of the FTC and on court decisions, these rules include the following important points:

FTC guidelines. The FTC, after consulting with members of over 175 industries, compiled and published official trade practices, which also called attention to illegal practices in each industry. The rules were offered as guidelines for legal operation. (However, the FTC Improvements Act of 1980 placed a 3-year moratorium on the FTC's ability to develop industry-wide rules regarding unfair advertising.)

Total impression. The courts have held that the overall impression an ad gives is the key to whether it is false or misleading. Thus in one case, although the term "relief" was used in an ad, the net impression from the entire context was that the product promised a "cure" for the ailment. Similarly, words like "stops," "ends," and "defeats" may improperly imply permanent rather than temporary relief. If an ad has even a "tendency to deceive," the FTC may find it illegal.

Clarity. The statement must be so clear that even a person of low intelligence would not be confused by it. The tendency of the law is to protect the credulous and the gullible. If an ad can have two meanings, it is illegal if one of them is false or misleading.

Fact versus puffery. The courts have held that an advertiser's opinion of a product is tolerated as the legitimate expression of a biased opinion and not a material statement of fact. However, a statement that might be understood by a sophisticated person as trade puffery can be misleading to a person of lower intelligence. Much controversy over misleading advertising hovers around the questions "When is a statement trade puffery, and when is it a false claim?" All factual claims must be supportable: If you say, "This is an outstanding leather briefcase," and the case is made of vinyl, that is misrepresentation. If you say, "This is an outstanding briefcase," that is a subjective matter of opinion and is considered puffery, which is not a legal matter.

The question of taste. In general the precedents of advertising law indicate that bad taste (except in advertising that is lewd) is not in itself deceptive or unfair. Hence bad taste is not an issue that would involve the FTC (although, of course, it might adversely affect sales).

Demonstrations. Demonstrations of product or product performance on TV must not mislead viewers. In some cases product substitutions may be made in a commercial if the intent is not to give a product qualities that it does not otherwise possess. For instance, the hot lights used in filming TV commercials would not allow realistic portrayals of some food products. Additives or substitutes may be made if the intent is only to show the product in a normal way or setting and not to upgrade the consumer's perception of the product.

Warranties. The major legislation dealing with warranties is the Magnuson-Moss Warranty Act, which became effective in July, 1975. The act does not require that products carry a warranty but sets up a framework for disclosure of consumer warranties. The act requires that the following information must be provided to consumers at the time of purchase: (1) the nature and extent of the guarantee (most guarantees are *limited* rather than *full* warranties, and the limitations must be specifically stated); (2) the manner in which the guarantor will perform (what items will be replaced or when refunds will be made and under what conditions); (3) the identity of the guarantor (if the product is defective, should the consumer look to the retailer, distributor, or manufacturer for resolution of his claim?).

"Free." Along with related words, "free" is a popular word in advertising: "Buy one—get one free," "2-for-1 sale," "Gift," "Bonus," and "Without charge." If there are any terms or conditions for getting something free, they must be stated clearly and conspicuously with the word free. If a purchaser must buy something to get something else free, the purchased product must be at its lowest price (same quality, same size) in 30 days. A free offer for a single size may not be advertised for more than 6 months in a market in any 12-month period.

Lotteries. Lotteries are schemes for the distribution of prizes won by chance. If a person has to pay to enter a lottery conducted by an advertiser (except government lotteries), the United States Postal Service calls it illegal and bans the use of the mail for it. If a lottery is advertised in interstate commerce, the FTC also holds it illegal and will proceed to stop it. Prizes in many sweepstakes (which are a form of lottery) are allowable if money need not be paid to enter the sweepstakes. Sponsors of sweepstakes must actually give away all prizes or cash advertised and must disclose the approximate odds of winning. The next time you see a sweepstakes announcement, check whether these conditions are explicitly conformed to.

Methods of FTC enforcement

Cease-and-desist orders. Historically the most used weapon of the FTC has been the issuance of a cease-and-desist order. Normally the advertiser will sign a *consent decree,* in which he promises to stop the practice(s) cited but admits no wrongdoing. Any further violation is subject to a fine of $10,000 per offense.

Corrective advertising. Although a cease-and-desist order stops a particular advertising practice, it does not repair any past damage that may have been done by false or misleading advertising. Now a new philosophy has been put into operation: To counteract the residual effects of the deceptive advertising, the FTC may require the advertiser to run advertising at his or her own expense "to dissipate the effects of that deception." The commission appears to require corrective advertising chiefly when major advertising themes are the bases for consumers' choices. In the first case of corrective advertising Listerine was ordered to insert messages in $10 million worth of advertising that Listerine did not cure colds or lessen their severity, a long-running theme of Listerine advertising.

Affirmative disclosure. The FTC recognizes that deception can occur through a lack of information as well as by the communication of misleading information. The principle of affirmative disclosure is based on the fact that consumers make reasonable assumptions about advertised products. For instance, we assume that a product carries no health risks, but if it does, the FTC requires that this must be disclosed to the buyer.

Standards of disclosure and substantiation. The FTC has also enforced truthful advertising practices by requiring that claims be substantiated and methods of comparison standardized. Disclosure and substantiation requirements come from both FTC rules ("Guides for Household Furniture Industry," say) and laws passed by Congress but enforced by the FTC (Truth-in-Lending Act): The Civil Aeronautics Board keeps records on customer complaints about airline service and these can be the basis for comparative ads. (Exhibit 25.1.)

The Robinson-Patman Act. The FTC, through its antitrust division, enforces another law affecting marketing and advertising, the Robinson-Patman Act. In brief this law requires a seller to treat all competitive customers on proportionately equal terms in regard to discounts and advertising allowances. This is not a law for or against advertising and promotional allowances; it simply says that, if they are granted to one customer, they must be offered to competing customers on the same proportionate terms in relation to sales. The FTC, which is in charge of the enforcement of this act, offers the following examples of how the law is interpreted:

EXAMPLE 1: A seller may properly offer to pay a specified part (say, 50 percent) of the cost of local advertising up to an amount equal to a set percentage (such as 5 percent) of the dollar volume of purchases during a specified time.

EXAMPLE 2: A seller should *not* select one or a few customers to receive special allowances (for example, 5 percent of purchases) to promote a product, while making allowances available on only some lesser basis (for example, 2 percent of purchases) to customers who compete with them.

EXAMPLE 3: A seller's plan should *not* provide an allowance on a basis that has rates graduated with the amount of goods purchased, as, for instance, 1 percent of the first $1,000 purchased per month, 2 percent of the second $1,000 per month, and 3 percent of all over that.

EXAMPLE 4: A seller should *not* identify or feature one or a few customers in his own advertising without making the same service available on proportionately equal terms to customers competing with the identified customer or customers.

For advertisers whose dollar allowance is not big enough to run meaningful newspaper space, the manufacturer may offer the dollar equivalent in direct mail bearing the store imprint or some other promotional offer. Enforcement of the Robinson-Patman Act has been difficult.

Changing role of the FTC

Since the FTC is funded by Congress and its members appointed by the President, it cannot be divorced from the political process. During the Carter administration the FTC took an activist stance: It undertook or proposed studies of trade practices in the legal, medical, mortuary, and cereal industries; the FTC also suggested the banning of sugary foods from TV commercials directed to children between ages 8 and 11.

THIS COUNTRY PREFERS DELTA.

Delta flies the most passengers in the United States.*

Delta also has the fewest passenger complaints.* This year. Last year. The year before that. And the year before that. And the year before that. And the year

*According to C.A.B. records.

Exhibit 25.1
Delta turns government regulation to its advantage.

Under Reagan appointee James Miller the FTC has been less likely to advocate government interference in the marketplace. The current FTC, without liberals such as long-time Commissioner Paul Rand Dixon, has reflected the Reagan administration's concerns about excess regulation. Miller has proposed that Congress set limits on what he sees as virtually unlimited authority by the FTC. He has said that he is in favor of looser standards for advertising substantiation; is a liberal on the issue of cigarette hazard disclosures; and thinks that consumers are less gullible than regulators believe they are.*

---

*Stanley E. Cohen, "Miller Opens to Mixed Reviews," *Advertising Age* (November 30, 1981), p. 26.

THE FEDERAL FOOD, DRUG, AND
COSMETIC ACT
Closely tied to the Federal Trade Commission Act is the Federal Food, Drug, and Cosmetic Act, passed in 1938, giving the Food and Drug Administration broad power over the labeling and branding—as contrasted with the advertising—of foods, drugs, therapeutic devices, and cosmetics. It is under this law that food and drug manufacturers must put their ingredients on the labels.

The term labeling has been held to include any advertising of the product appearing in the same store in which the product is sold; it does not have to be physically attached to the package. In the case of one drug preparation, the package itself was properly labeled, but stores also sold a soft-cover book on health, written by the maker of the drug, mentioning it, and making unprovable claims for it. The drug manufacturer was in trouble with the Food and Drug Administration for false labeling and for false advertising.

OTHER FEDERAL CONTROLS OF ADVERTISING

Alcohol tax unit of the United States
treasury department
The liquor industry has a unique pattern of labeling and advertising under both federal and state laws. For an interesting historical reason the federal laws are under the jurisdiction of the Treasury Department: The first American excise tax was the one levied under Alexander Hamilton, Secretary of the Treasury, on alcoholic beverages. That department, through its Alcohol Tax Unit, is interested to this day in their labeling, standards of size of bottles for tax purposes, and advertising.

Each state also has its own liquor-advertising laws. In some states you cannot show a drinking scene; in others you can show a man holding a glass, but not to his lips; in another you can picture only a bottle. In few industries does an advertising person need a lawyer more often than in liquor advertising.

Securities and Exchange
Commission
The SEC is the government agency that controls all advertising of public offerings of stocks or bonds. It insists on full disclosure of facts relevant to the company and the stock to be sold so that the prospective investor can form an opinion. Its insistence on the facts that must be published—including a statement of negative elements affecting the investment—is very firm and thorough. The SEC never recommends or refuses to recommend a security; its concern is with the disclosure of full information.

United States postal

service   The postal service has the authority to stop the delivery of mail to all firms guilty of using the mails to defraud—which is enough to put any firm out of business. It deals mainly with mail-order frauds.

FEDERAL LAWS AND

ADVERTISING   In addition to federal regulatory agencies the Supreme Court has played a major role in defining acceptability of certain types of advertising. The court, while broadening the scope of advertising practice, has confined its decisions to narrow issues in the specific cases on which it has ruled. It would be incorrect, based on current precedents, to say that advertising has the full protection that noncommercial speech has. Two areas of law are discussed below to give us an idea of the broadened, but still limited, protection enjoyed by advertising during the last 25 years.

Advertising and the First

Amendment   Until very recently the courts have held that commercial speech did not have any of the First Amendment protections afforded other communication. In several cases during the 1960s and 1970s the courts extended some level of free-speech protection to advertising messages. However, prior to 1976 the ads at issue involved messages other than those dealing with the promotion of a service or product. For instance, as late as 1975 the Supreme Court overturned a Virginia law making publicizing a New York abortion clinic in a Virginia newspaper a criminal offense. However, the court was careful to note that the ad involved an issue of public interest and did not constitute a purely commercial message. This and other similar opinions left open the question of Constitutional protection for strictly commercial advertising.

Then in 1976 the court addressed the question of purely commercial speech in the case of *Virginia State Board of Pharmacy v. Virginia Citizens Consumer Council.* The court ruled that a state law banning the advertising of prescription-drug prices was unconstitutional. The court, in effect, ruled that society benefits from a free flow of commercial information just as it benefits from a free exchange of political ideas.

However, it would be incorrect to claim full Constitutional guarantees for commercial speech. In 1979, in the case of *Friedman v. Rogers,* the court upheld the right of the state of Texas to prevent an optometrist from using an "assumed name, corporate name, trade name, or any other than the name under which he is licensed to practice optometry in Texas." In its decision the court ruled that First Amendment protection for commercial speech is not absolute and that regulation of commercial speech can be allowed even when some restrictions would be unconstitutional " . . . in the realm of noncommercial expression." In effect the court is saying that each case of commercial-speech restraint will be decided on its own merits.

Advertising of professional services

Two restrictions against legal advertising had long prevailed, one imposed by state laws and one by bar associations, which had the power to drop the membership of an attorney who advertised. In the case of *Bates v. State Bar of Arizona* the Supreme Court ruled that state laws forbidding advertising by attorneys were unconstitutional on First Amendment grounds. Bar associations and other professional associations still have regulatory powers over the accuracy and scope of their members' advertising, but the associations cannot entirely prohibit their members from advertising.

The FTC has addressed the issue of trade- and professional-association restrictions on members from the standpoint of restraint of trade. Prohibiting advertising could work a discriminatory hardship on new members of a profession, who are attempting to become established, as against those already in practice. In July, 1981, both the American Bar Association and the American Medical Association testified before the Senate asking for congressional action against any attempts by the FTC to regulate association rules pertaining to members of a profession.* The problem is still fluid.

STATE AND LOCAL LAWS RELATING TO ADVERTISING

While the pattern of the federal statutory scheme is generally one of broad language that is not essentially confined to specific industries, most states and some cities have narrower laws directed at one or more designated practices or industries. The result has been a hodgepodge of state mandates on liquor, bedding, stockbrokers, banks, loan and credit companies, employment agents, business-opportunity brokers, real-estate brokers, and a variety of others. Many localities have strict sign ordinances aimed at outdoor advertising.† New York City has regulations concerning the advertising of rates in the travel and hotel industries.

The first and basic state statute in the regulation of advertising, which still represents a landmark in advertising history, is the *Printers' Ink* Model Statute, drawn up in 1911, attempting to punish "untrue, deceptive, or misleading" advertising. *Printers' Ink* magazine, the pioneer trade paper of advertising, has died; but its model statute, in its original or modified form, exists in forty-four states.

---

*"MDs, Lawyers Rap FTC," *Advertising Age,* July 20, 1981, p. 23.

†In 1981 the Supreme Court struck down a San Diego ordinance banning all offsite outdoor boards. However, the opinion was based at least partially on the fact that noncommercial (political and public-service) advertising was prohibited. Justices White, Marshall, Powell, and Stewart noted that the banning of outdoor advertising was not per se a Constitutional question. (*Advertising Age,* July 13, 1981, p. 14).

COMPARISON
ADVERTISING

Comparison advertising compares a product with a named competitive product (see Chapter 14 for uses of comparison advertising). Comparison advertising is not new: In 1930 J. Sterling Getchell, head of the agency bearing his name, introduced the Chrysler car, never on the market before, by inviting comparison with General Motors and Ford cars and using the headline "Try all three." For many years car advertisers would stress a feature or the track record of their cars against other named brands. But the received wisdom of the advertising trade generally was that, if you mentioned a competitor's name, you were giving him free advertising.

The big push for comparative advertising came in 1972, when the FTC urged ABC and NBC to allow commercials that named competitors. Until then only CBS had permitted such messages, whereas ABC and NBC would allow nothing but "Brand X" comparisons. Since then comparative advertising has become a popular, although extremely controversial, technique. As of October, 1980, 38 percent of complaints handled by the NARB (an industry regulator discussed later in this chapter) involved comparative advertising.*

Many advertising agencies urge that their clients consider comparative advertising with great caution. When you compare your product with that of a competitor and mention it by name, you must be able to substantiate in court any adverse statement you make about that product. An advertiser who thinks his product has been misrepresented in a comparative advertisement may sue the competitor for triple damages under provisions of the Lanham Act. It is also important that an advertiser does not claim overall superiority over his competition when products are compared only on selected features: Better mileage alone does not make a better car. Despite the risks of comparative advertising, it is being used by more and more advertisers.

Types of comparative advertising

There are three basic approaches to comparative advertising:

Head-to-head comparisons. The most common comparative ads are those where a single competitor is challenged. Avis versus Hertz, Heinz Ketchup versus Hunt's, and Tums versus Rolaids are well-known examples of one-to-one comparisons. Here the advertiser must substantiate claims against only a single brand. On the other hand this type of advertising is not effective unless there is a clear leader in the field against which you can make a comparison (Exhibit 25.2).

Your brand against the world. In recent years some advertisers have become bolder and made blanket claims against a number of other brands. This

---

*Graham H. Phillips, "To Compare or Not To Compare: That Is the Question," *Ad-Media,* March, 1981, p. 10.

DeanWitter is
4 times better
than the average.

For nearly three years, Dean Witter Reynolds' "Recommended List" has outperformed the Dow Jones Industrial Average by more than 4 to 1. That's not only a consistently high level of performance, but a standard that would please even a hard-to-please investor.

The Actual Proof Of Performance

An independent accounting firm compared the performance of all the securities on our "Recommended List" against the Dow during the period from January, 1978 through September, 1980. The results? Our list appreciated in value by 66.2%, over four times more than the Dow's 14.4% gain.* It also outperformed Standard & Poor's "400" Industrials and "500" Composite by a considerable margin.

Of course, we know that the impressive past performance of our "Recommended List" doesn't guarantee the same success with those recommendations or with any other recommendations in the future. But with our uncompromising research standards and timely recommendations, we think we're bound to put a smile on your face—even if you're the most demanding investor.

Our Research Standards Aren't Standard

The outstanding performance record of our "Recommended List" is due in part to our uncompromising research standards. At Dean Witter, we don't just investigate the companies we consider for the "Recommended List," we turn them inside out. We check every possible angle to be sure those recommendations are sound. We also weigh each stock's upside potential against its downside risk. Should a stock meet all our criteria, then, and only then, does it become a candidate for the "Recommended List"—and that should help you feel more secure about your investments.

A Recommendation Is Only As Good As Its Timing

Because market values fluctuate so quickly, we go out of our way to make sure our research data is current and our recommendations are on time as well as on target. That's part of the reason the track record of our "Recommended List" is so solid. Demanding investors expect that level of performance. That's why Dean Witter Reynolds is winning over more and more of them. No wonder Dean Witter Reynolds is one investment firm you'll be glad to hear from.

*Both indices are exclusive of dividends and commissions. "Recommended List" results were achieved only if all recommendations were followed. A report on the performance of individual stocks, including advances and declines, is available at branch offices.

> Dean Witter Reynolds Inc.   000
> Client Information Services
> P.O. Box 5013, Clifton, NJ 07012
>
> Please send me complete information on Dean Witter Reynolds' "Recommended List," including Dean Witter Reynolds' "Monthly Investment Outlook," containing an index of the latest "Recommended List" and a copy of the comparative performance report.
> Name_____
> Address_____
> City_____State_____Zip_____
> Home Phone_____Business Phone_____
> If you are currently a Dean Witter Reynolds client, please indicate your Account Executive's name and office _____

Mail this coupon or call toll-free

800-526-7443, ext.140

In New Jersey: 800-522-4503, ext. 140

 ## DEAN WITTER REYNOLDS
One investment firm
you'll be glad to hear from.

Member SIPC.

Exhibit 25.2
Head-to-head comparisons can be effective when the product category has few brands. (Courtesy Dean Witter Reynolds.)

FACE FACTS:

Pine-Sol® Cleans Grease Better.

It's a fact. Concentrated Pine-Sol cleans grease better than <u>any</u> other leading liquid cleaner! Katie the Cleaning Lady proves it on TV. Now prove it yourself in your own home.

Another fact: Pine-Sol is more than just a cleaner—it's a cleaner-disinfectant. So Pine-Sol cleans, kills household germs and odors, and leaves a fresh scent!

Pine-Sol cleans grease better, kills germs and leaves a fresh scent.

Exhibit 25.3
A comparison that doesn't name the competition. Can you guess what the ''other'' cleaner is? (Courtesy American Cyanamide Company.)

type of comparison is more dangerous since it opens you to counterclaims and demands for substantiation from a number of brands. Often these ads are based on industrywide standards, as in the Delta ad in Exhibit 25.1.

Brand X comparisons. In this type of comparison no direct mention is made of competition. However, in many cases the unnamed competitor is very obvious (Exhibit 25.3), and not naming the competitor directly will not necessarily free an advertiser from liability.

As we have previously pointed out, aside from any legal considerations comparative advertising risks doing the competitor a favor. In some ways it is a compliment to be the object of comparison, and so you must be careful not to provide free advertising for the competition. This is especially true if differences between the products compared are not substantial and meaningful to consumers.

REGULATION BY
MEDIA
The media are among the oldest continuous controllers of advertising content. National magazines keep a close eye on all ads, especially on those of new advertisers with new products, to make sure their readers will not be misled. The greatest number of problems is found in newer magazines that, anxious to sell space, are not vigilant about some of the mail-order advertisers.

Newspapers also have their codes of acceptable advertising. Most of them exercise control over even the comparative price claims made in retail advertising. A store may be asked to change a headline such as "These are the lowest-price sheets ever offered," to "The lowest-price sheets we have ever offered." "The greatest shoe sale ever" will be changed to "Our greatest shoe sale ever."

One of the most generally accepted industry advertising codes was that of the National Association of Broadcasters (NAB). Most of the major television and radio stations adhered to the code's advertising provisions. However in March 1982, a federal district court held that certain aspects of the NAB code were in violation of antitrust legislation, a view also held by the Justice Department in an earlier decision.

The court decision dealt only with two specific areas of the code. These were NAB limits on commercial time and the number of products that could be promoted in commercials of less than 60 seconds (known as piggybacking). In response to these attacks on the code, and the general uncertainty of its legal standing, the NAB suspended all television and radio ad standards. The NAB is presently reviewing the status of its broadcast code to determine if a modified code could be legally adopted or if the suspension should be permanent.

The suspension of the NAB code does not mean, of course, that no broadcast advertising standards exist. Each of the networks, and most major broadcast stations, have a broadcast standards department, which is often stricter than the former NAB code. If there is any question about a commercial, advertisers and their agencies will normally take storyboards or scripts of proposed commercials to the networks or stations for approval prior to production.

Generally, from one network to another standards are consistent about commercials networks will approve for airing. However, this is not always true: For instance, in the spring of 1981 NBC and ABC accepted commercials for Vanish toilet-bowl cleaners while CBS refused. The commercials claimed that competitive products might corrode plumbing fixtures. After threatened court action by a competitor, the two networks withdrew approval of the commercials pending review.*

---

*"Vanish Spots Pulled; NBC Out of Suit," *Advertising Age,* July 13, 1981, p. 2.

SELF-REGULATION BY INDIVIDUAL ADVERTISERS
AND INDUSTRIES
The most meaningful of all forms of advertising self-regulation is that of the individual advertiser. It is wholly voluntary, not the result of group pressure. It reflects the policy of top management, its sense of public responsibility, and its enthusiasm to survive and grow in a competitive arena where consumer confidence is vital. Almost every sizable advertiser maintains a careful system of legal review and appraisal, backed by factual data to substantiate claims. At Lever Brothers Company all copy developed by the advertising department and agencies is submitted first to a research-and-development division, where it is analyzed in the light of records and reports of experimental data. It must then be passed by the legal department, and only after this second approval is it released for publication.

Many industries have established their own codes of standards of advertising practice. Most of them relate to local advertising of products by their distributors or dealers or franchise owners, especially products such as air conditioners, water softeners, or other products with new or servicing features. Voluntary trade codes usually prove ineffective; for the associations lack the power of enforcement because of antitrust laws, which preclude any action that might be regarded as interfering with open competition.

The leading organizations of the advertising industry have created a self-regulating mechanism that avoids conflict with antitrust laws. It uses peer pressure on advertisers whose advertising is questionable, and it has an original and effective system for helping to prevent misleading advertising or, failing that, helping the law to curb it if it is run. It is an offspring of the Better Business Bureau, created by the advertising industry to curb misleading advertising, especially at the local level.

Better Business
Bureaus*
In 1905, various local advertising clubs formed a national association that today is known as the American Advertising Federation. In 1911 this association launched a campaign for truth in advertising, for which purpose various vigilance committees were established. These were the forerunners of the Better Business Bureaus, which adopted that name in 1916 and became autonomous in 1926. Today the movement has 151 separate bureaus operating in major cities and supported by more than 126,000 firms, who contribute over $19 million per year. The bureau system handled about 6.5 million inquiries and complaints from business and the public in 1980. In the same year the Council of Better Business Bureaus (the national organization) conducted a study of fifty-five work-at-home promotions and defined acceptance guidelines for the media, released findings on a study of comparative pricing practices in catalog showroom merchandisers, issued a bulletin, "Add-on-Rates in Credit Advertising," for the guidance of the media, continued the development of ad-

---

*Information Concerning the Better Business Bureaus and the National Advertising Review Council is supplied courtesy of the Council of Better Business Bureaus, Inc.

vertising and selling standards for specific industries, and completed plans for a major collaborative program with the American Advertising Federation for broadening local advertising self-regulation. Its published service, *Do's and Don'ts in Advertising Copy,* is a standard reference work on the subject.

Until recently the Better Business Bureaus had worked chiefly at the local level. They have no legal power to enforce their findings, but the influence in communities is a force to protect the public. In 1971, however, the bureaus assumed a new responsibility and role as part of the National Advertising Review Council.

The National Advertising Review Council

In response to the many voices of different consumer groups against deceptive advertising, the chief advertising organizations formed the most comprehensive self-regulating apparatus ever established in advertising. Called the National Advertising Review Council, its chief purpose is "to develop a structure which would effectively apply the persuasive capacities of peers to seek the voluntary elimination of national advertising which professionals would consider deceptive." Its objective is to sustain high standards of truth and accuracy in national advertising. It consists of the Council of Better Business Bureaus and the three leading advertising groups: the American Advertising Federation, the American Association of Advertising Agencies (the 4A's), and the Association of National Advertisers. The council has two operating arms: the National Advertising Division (NAD) of the Council of Better Business Bureaus and the National Advertising Review Board (NARB).

The NAD full-time professional staff has had a lot of experience working with advertisers on complaints. If a complaint appears valid, personal contact is used to get the advertiser to correct the deceptive item. Decisions are reprinted in a release published monthly.

In the event of an impasse the case is passed to the NARB, composed of fifty people, five of whom are assigned to a case—like a court of appeals. If they feel the action was justified and the advertiser still does not wish to correct the deceptive element, the rules provide for the whole matter to be referred to the appropriate government agency. The entire process is diagrammed in Exhibit 25.4. In over 10 years of operation no advertiser who participated in the complete process has declined to abide by the NARB decision. Indeed, only 2 percent of NAD's decisions have required NARB review.

In discussing the National Advertising Review Council, we should understand that it cannot:

☐ Order an advertiser to stop running an ad
☐ Impose a fine
☐ Bar anyone from advertising
☐ Boycott an advertiser or a product

What it can do is to bring to bear the judgment of the advertiser's peers that what is being done is harmful to advertising, to the public, and to the of-

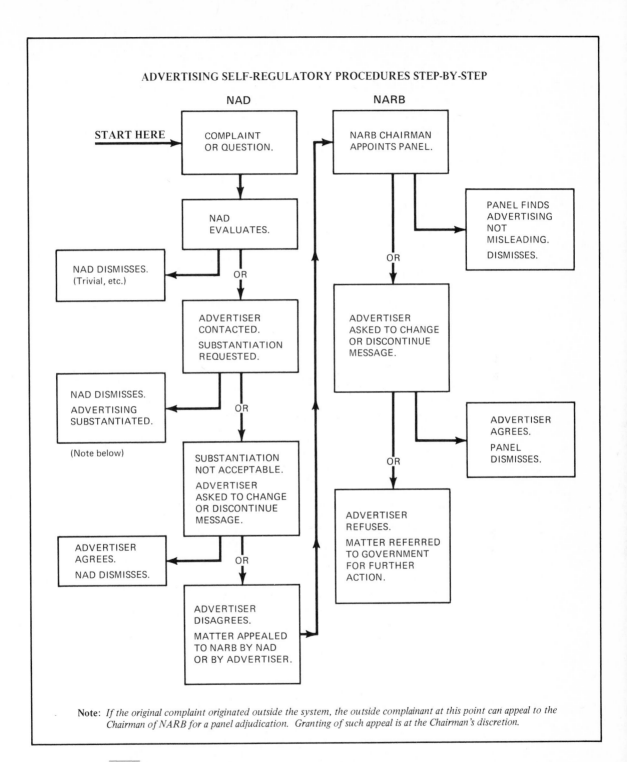

ADVERTISING SELF-REGULATORY PROCEDURES STEP-BY-STEP

NAD

NARB

START HERE → COMPLAINT OR QUESTION.

NARB CHAIRMAN APPOINTS PANEL.

NAD EVALUATES.

PANEL FINDS ADVERTISING NOT MISLEADING. DISMISSES.

NAD DISMISSES. (Trivial, etc.)

OR

ADVERTISER CONTACTED. SUBSTANTIATION REQUESTED.

OR

ADVERTISER ASKED TO CHANGE OR DISCONTINUE MESSAGE.

NAD DISMISSES. ADVERTISING SUBSTANTIATED.

OR

ADVERTISER AGREES. PANEL DISMISSES.

(Note below)

SUBSTANTIATION NOT ACCEPTABLE. ADVERTISER ASKED TO CHANGE OR DISCONTINUE MESSAGE.

OR

ADVERTISER AGREES. NAD DISMISSES.

OR

ADVERTISER REFUSES. MATTER REFERRED TO GOVERNMENT FOR FURTHER ACTION.

ADVERTISER DISAGREES. MATTER APPEALED TO NARB BY NAD OR BY ADVERTISER.

Note: *If the original complaint originated outside the system, the outside complainant at this point can appeal to the Chairman of NARB for a panel adjudication. Granting of such appeal is at the Chairman's discretion.*

Exhibit 25.4
Self-regulation advertising involves many aspects. (Courtesy of NARB.)

fender. This has great moral weight. The situation is also reinforced by the knowledge that, if the results of an appeal to the NARB are not accepted, the whole matter will be referred to the appropriate government agency and that that fact will be released to the public, together with any statement the advertiser wishes to make. This step, unique in business self-regulation machinery, avoids any problem of violating antitrust laws, presents the entire matter to public view, and still leaves the advertiser subject to an FTC ruling on the advertising. The following case report is typical:

BACKGROUND REVIEW

The National Advertising Division (NAD) of the Council of Better Business Bureaus received a complaint in January, 1980 from the Schering-Plough Corporation alleging that "creaseproof" advertising claims made for Formula 2 Eyecolor by Revlon were misleading to consumers. Print advertising claimed: "The first creaseproof eyeshadow and liner pencil in one. Only Formula 2 Eyecolor has a unique color-setting formula. Color that shadows without creasing."

Since it is the NAD's policy to question all pertinent claims in an advertising campaign, NAD also questioned these claims made in the same advertisement: "Color that lines without creasing. Waterproof. Irritant-free." Also in television advertising: " . . . you need color that lasts without creasing. It lines without creasing."

The complainant maintained its research showed that the product is not creaseproof. The Plough test, involving 22 participants, alleged that after four hours, 73% of the participants considered that the product had creased. To the more experienced eye of a cosmetologist, creasing occurred in 50% of cases. After eight hours, the figures were 91% for the subjects, and 55% for the cosmetologist.

The advertiser rejected this research, charging that it was biased, technically flawed, and invalid.

In support of the "creaseproof" claim, Revlon presented the results of three consumer wear tests it conducted. These tests were comprised of seven to nine panelists each, and were administered under controlled conditions. The test results report distinctions by cosmetologists. A tabulation of these results, made by NAD, showed that by combining "slight" and "moderate" creasing, 23.5% of panelists had some degree of creasing after four hours, and 44.5% showed creasing after six hours. The advertiser maintained that "slight" creasing, observed by a professional cosmetologist, is not perceptible to the layman and should be categorized as "no creasing."

The complainant contended that "creaseproof" is an absolute statement, and a product either creases or it does not. Revlon maintained that to be "creaseproof" a product is not required to be totally impervious to creasing, but rather to be impervious to creasing to a significant degree.

NAD FINDINGS

Based on substantiating information provided by the advertiser, NAD had no problem with the following claims which NAD had questioned in addition to the creaseproof claim: " . . . unique color-setting formula," "waterproof," "irritant-free" and "color that lines without creasing" and they are not submitted for review by the Panel.

Based on Revlon's tests alone, NAD concluded that the creaseproof claim for Formula 2 Eyecolor had not been adequately substantiated. Of concern were varying results from test to test as to the degree of creasing, or time involved before creasing occurs, and equating "slight" creasing to no creasing. Also, NAD felt the testing was done under somewhat artificial conditions which did not take into account the many variables that women with different types of skin and habits would encounter in a "normal" day. Absent any standard for "creaseproof," the NAD felt a reasonable expectation of performance would be 85% of women using the product should find it to be literally creaseproof for a minimum of eight hours, representing a normal days' wear without touching up.

Revlon did not agree with NAD's definition and meaning of creaseproof, and thus joined NAD in requesting a review of the matter by the NARB.

NARB FINDINGS

In the course of the hearing the Panel reviewed written submissions from the NAD, the complainant and Revlon, and heard oral testimony from representatives of the three entities.

No evidence was submitted nor was there indication from any of the parties that there existed information as to the public perception of the term "creaseproof." In the absence of such data, the Panel concludes that many potential purchasers may assume an absolute standard of performance. We note that consumers have had experience in dealing with other "proof" claims such as fireproof, rustproof, etc.

Since the test protocol used to measure creaseproof performance varies from company to company, and there appears to be no commonly accepted standard of measurement, the Panel believes that the term "creaseproof" without further qualification has the tendency and capacity to mislead.

We believe the advertiser can satisfactorily establish a limited degree of creaseproof performance and should it wish to claim this characteristic for this product, it should be done in manner which discloses the percentage of subjects and the length of time that they experienced the creaseproof benefit. Without such qualifications, consumers have no criteria for judging the meaning of the term "creaseproof," and many are quite likely to be misled into assuming a higher standard than in fact exists.

DECISION

Accordingly, the Panel concludes that the unqualified term "creaseproof" is perceived as an absolute and, therefore, is inherently misleading.

The Panel suggests that it would be in the public interest for the cosmetics industry to address itself to the need for consumer research to measure public perceptions and to develop appropriate standards, and protocols for measuring such standards.

By the end of 10 years 655 of the approximately 1,800 national-advertising cases reviewed by the NAD had resulted in either substantially modified advertising or discontinuance of the advertising claim by the advertiser (see Table 25.1). The Children's Advertising Unit of the NAD had similar action in 108 additional cases involving advertising to children.

Table 25–1

NAD STATISTICAL CASE RECORD[a]	CUMULATIVE[b]
Total complaints	1,864
Disposition:	
Dismissed:	
Adequate substantiation	715
Dismissed:	
Advertiser modified or discontinued	763
Administratively closed	322
Referred to NARB by NAD	15[c]
Pending	48
Sources of complaints:	
Consumers	239
Consumer organizations	179
Competitors	374
Local Better Business Bureaus	318
NAD monitoring	697
Other	57

[a]As of July 1, 1981.
[b]June, 1971, to July, 1981.
[c]Twenty-two cases appealed to NARB by outside complainants or advertisers.

COPYRIGHTING ADVERTISING

Copyrighting has nothing to do with the problems of the legal controls over advertising, which we have been discussing here. But since copyrighting is a legal procedure related to advertising, it seems appropriate to have this discussion join its legal relatives at this point.

Nature of copyrights

A copyright is a federal procedure that grants the owner of it the exclusive rights to print, publish, or reproduce an original work of literature, music, or art (which includes advertising) for a specific period of time. January 1, 1978, marked a memorable day in copyright history; for on that day a new law made the period of time of copyright protection the life of the author plus 50 years (since 1909 it had been for only a maximum of 56 years).

A copyright protects an "intellectual work" as a whole from being copied by another; however, it does not prevent others from using the essence of, say, an advertising idea and from expressing it in their own way. Copyrighting does not protect a concept or idea or theme but only the expression of it. To be copyrightable, an ad must contain a substantial amount of original text or picture. Slogans and other short phrases and expressions cannot be copyrighted even if they are distinctively arranged or lettered. Familiar symbols and designs are not copyrightable (also see Chapter 19).

Copyrighting

policy

Some companies make it a policy to copyright all their publication advertising. Most national advertisers, however, deem copyrighting unnecessary in their publication advertising unless it contains a piece of art or copy that they think others will use. Retail newspaper advertising moves too fast for the advertiser to be concerned about having it bodily lifted. Direct-response advertisers often copyright their publication and direct-mail advertising because, if an ad is effective, it may be used over a long period of time and could readily be used, with minor changes, by another.

How to register a

copyright

Registering a copyright is one of the simple steps that can be handled directly by the advertiser, but it must be followed precisely.

1. Write to the Register of Copyrights, The Library of Congress, Washington, D.C. 20559, for the proper application form for what you plan to protect.
2. Beginning with the first appearance of the ad, the word Copyright or the abbreviation Copr. or the symbol© should appear with the name of the advertiser. Add the year if foreign protection is planned. For a booklet or other form of printed advertising, other than publication ads, the copyright notice "shall be affixed to the copies in such manner and location as give reasonable notice of a claim of copyright."
3. As soon as the ad is published, two copies, with the filled-out application form and fee, should be sent to the Register of Copyrights.

SUMMARY

Advertising more than most businesses operates within a complicated environment of local, state, and federal statutes and regulations. In addition the advertising industry itself cooperates with various trade associations, media, and consumer groups, such as Better Business Bureaus, to promote better advertising through self-regulation.

There is no disagreement among responsible parties that truthful and informative advertising is the ideal for which advertisers should strive. For the advertiser the problem is one of meeting the requirements of numerous, sometimes conflicting and constantly changing advertising regulations. Since the last century, advertising has developed a sense of professionalism and high standards of performance. As in any business, there are unfortunate exceptions to the rules of professionalism. However, the advertiser who uses untruthful or misleading methods will soon find himself confronted with a number of constraints from both within and without the advertising industry.

QUESTIONS

1. Discuss some major reasons for the current increase in legal and regulatory restrictions over advertising compared with those of 50 years ago.
2. What is the FTC?
3. What are its criteria for considering an ad false and misleading?
4. Discuss the use of corrective advertising. Do you believe the technique is an effective deterent to misleading advertising?
5. What are some other government agencies involved in advertising regulation, and what is the primary role of each?
6. Define or discuss the following:

   a. *caveat emptor*
   b. total-impression criteria
   c. limited warranty
   d. cease-and-desist order
   e. affirmative disclosure
   f. substantiation of claims
   g. Lanham Act
   h. use of the word "free"

7. What is the current status of advertising and First Amendment protection?
8. What is the position of the American Medical Association and the American Bar Association on FTC efforts to liberalize advertising among doctors and lawyers?
9. In general, how do local advertising ordinances differ from federal laws and regulations?
10. What has been the role of the FTC in comparative advertising over the last decade?
11. Discuss the merits and limitations of the three most used approaches to comparison advertising.
12. What role do the media play in monitoring truthful advertising? Give some examples.
13. Discuss the role of the National Advertising Review Council in promoting truthful advertising, including its limitations.

SUGGESTED EXERCISES

14. Find three examples of advertising using product puffery. Do you find them acceptable, or could they mislead an unsophisticated consumer?
15. Find an example of a good comparison ad and one that is not. Briefly give your reasons in each case.

READINGS

"Battle lines drawn over copyrights," *Advertising Age,* November 16, 1981, p. 78.

Council of Better Business Bureaus, *NAD/ NARB Decisions* (Washington: Council of Better Business Bureaus, published monthly).

DYER, ROBERT F., and TERENCE A. SHIMP: "Reactions to Legal Advertising," *Journal of Advertising Research,* April 1980, pp. 43–51.

EDWARDS, LARRY and TODD FANDELL: "FTC's Miller: Ad Proof Still Concerns Me," *Advertising Age,* November 16, 1981, p. 1.

HANCOCK, WILLIAM A.: *Executive's Guide to Business Law* (New York: McGraw-Hill, 1979), p. 12-1.

LaBARBERA, PRISCILLA A.: "Advertising Self-Regulation: An Evaluation," *Business Topics,* Summer 1980, pp. 55–63.

LAMB, CHARLES W., JR., and MARY ANN STUTTS: "The Impact of Corrective Advertising upon Consumers' Attitudes, Beliefs, and Behavior," *Journal of the Academy of Marketing Science,* Fall 1979, pp. 307–15.

McDONALD, STEPHEN W., and C. P. RAO: "A Post Evaluation of the Magnuson-Moss Warranty Act," *Akron Business & Economic Review,* Summer 1980, pp. 38–41.

MURDOCK, GENE W., and JAMES PETERSON: "Strict Product Liability for Advertising Agencies: A Pro/Con Discussion," *Journal of Advertising,* Fall 1981, pp. 5–10.

ROTFELD, HERBERT J., and IVAN L. PRESTON: "The Potential Impact of Research on Advertising Law," *Journal of Advertising Research,* April 1981, pp. 9–18.

SHIMP, TERENCE A., and IVAN L. PRESTON: "Deceptive and Nondeceptive Consequences of Evaluative Advertising," *Journal of Marketing,* Winter 1981, pp. 22–32.

SIGELMAN, LEE, and ROLAND E. SMITH: "Consumer Legislation in the American States: An Attempt at Explanation," *Social Science Quarterly,* June 1980, pp. 58–70.

Economic and
Social Aspects
of Advertising

26

Mass communication and advertising are business institutions that have a wide impact, and like other institutions that permeate many aspects of our daily lives, advertising is controversial, subject to questions about its productivity and waste, and (as we have seen in Chapter 25) vulnerable to control and regulation. Moreover, we ought to keep in mind that, since advertising is not a single and sharply defined enterprise, a case can be made "proving" almost any positive or negative characteristic of it; the various categories of advertising (national, classified, institutional, retail, and so on) have features unique to them as well as general characteristics in common. Within these categories there are numerous examples of how advertising is used and misused.

This chapter will view some of the general aspects of the advertising process, previous chapters having shown advertising as a problem-solving tool for specific brands and industries. The following discussion should be viewed as a broad-brush and free-wheeling approach rather than as an attempt to provide application to any particular advertising situation. We shall touch on the economic value of advertising in a competitive market, the value of advertising as an educational tool, the role of advertising as a persuader for a certain point of view, and the impact the consumerism movement has had on advertising.

ADVERTISING AND THE ECONOMIC
AND SOCIAL PROCESS

Economic
perspective   Much of the contemporary scrutiny of advertising involves its role as
an economic force. Certainly advertising as an institution must be judged on
its contributions to productivity and growth as well as to the enlightenment of
consumers. This section will address some of the major topics of advertising as
they relate to a competitive economy and capitalism in general.

Value Goal of a Product and Advertising Cost. Even if we grant all the
advantages that advertising brings us, the question still often arises, "Doesn't
the consumer have to pay for all that advertising?" The answer is yes. The consumer who buys a product has to pay a share of all the costs that go into making and selling the product. But to say that consumers pay their share of advertising is not the same as saying that they are paying *more* money because of
that advertising. The answer to the question depends largely on the *value goal,*
which is the value a business plans to offer in a product and the form that
value is to take. It is the reason for the product's existence.

The value goal may be to produce a dependable product at the lowest
possible price, as in the case of Timex watches. Here the whole business was
dedicated to that low-price goal: mechanism of the works, design, choice of
materials, planning of production—everything was aimed at producing the
lowest-cost dependable watch. But it took advertising to create the sales to
amortize the cost of the special machinery needed and to get the volume of
business necessary to keep that production line busy at its cost-saving level.
Here it is legitimate to say that advertising helped reduce the cost of the product to the consumer.

Or the value goal of the business may be to offer the most luxurious
product in its field, like the Piaget watch, which has been advertised as "the
most expensive watch in the world." Here everything was planned with one
goal in mind: to make the finest watch possible, regardless of cost. Advertising
tells people why the watch is worth the money. Certainly, in this case advertising is not an instrument for reducing cost. The same applies to the luxury or
premium end of most product lines, for example, Chivas Regal Scotch whiskey, a most expensive brand.

Because of the differences in the value goals of various enterprises, it is
not possible to make a single sweeping statement about the effect of advertising on the cost of a product to the consumer. The fact remains that for most
products designed for widespread consumer use the value goal of management
is to produce a better product at a lower cost to the buyer.

Cost competition. Some economists have criticized advertising as part of
a conspiracy by business to sell products on the basis of imaginary virtues
rather than in terms of competitive pricing. In effect they argue that advertis-

Exhibit 26.1
(opposite page) The creative impact of the competitive system, in which advertising plays an important part. Advertising makes known the advances in our technology; and in doing so, it creates markets, spurs competition, and stimulates creativity. (From Fran Maierhauser, **The Evolution of Electric Appliances.** Courtesy of *Rural Kentuckian Magazine.*)

ing contributes to a less-than-free economy by helping to create "brand monopolies." It is charged that advertising is used as a substitute for either price competition or beneficial product improvements. Instead of being of overall economic value to society, advertising, critics claim, is used as a primary means of creating noncompetitive price structures and persuading customers to switch brands among a few large firms within each product category. The implications of this view of advertising are twofold: Advertising results in brand switching with no overall economic gain for consumers, and advertising causes higher prices to the buying public.

On the first point the number of new products introduced each year and the growth in the gross national product (GNP) during this century show the so-called monopoly of existing products to be largely unfounded. Once a new product shows promise of success, other producers can be expected to come out with their versions, designed to improve upon the original. Soon many others will enter the new market, each offering special features. This pattern is our competitive way of life. Every marketer will advertise improvements that may not seem large, but the total effect is a better product and a wider choice for consumers (Exhibit 26.1). It may be hard to judge the growth of house plants, standing in a row, if comparison is made one with another. But if you compare the growth of the whole row from one time to another, the difference is clear. Similarly, products may seem alike; but if you compare yesterday's product with today's product, the improvement in the entire class will be impressive.

Rance Crain, President of *Advertising Age,* sees the advertising and marketing successes of the future to be to those who are willing to innovate: "There'll be greater reward for companies that take the risks to innovate—and greater loss for companies saddled with the outmoded risk-aversion strategy of the '70's."*

As to the second point, that advertising only causes higher prices, numerous examples refute this charge:

DATRIL AND TYLENOL. For years Tylenol was an over-the-counter drug for people who could not tolerate aspirin but who wanted the relief that aspirin affords. An effective substitute for aspirin, Tylenol was not advertised, and it sold for $2.85 per 100 tablets. Then Datril came along with the identical formula, giving the same results, and was offered at $1.85 for 100 tablets. It was extensively advertised. Tylenol dropped its price, and prices dropped for some time thereafter until inflationary pressures raised them again.

---

*Rance Crain, "Product Innovation, Ad Daring Essential for Booming '80s," *Advertising Age,* November 13, 1980, p. 6.

From This

General Electric, 1905

Westinghouse, 1908

General Electric, 1913

Hotpoint, 1923

Frigidaire, 1947

Frigidaire, 1963

this 5-lb. roast cooked in just 35 minutes!

ROPER
COMBINATION MICROWAVE RANGE

Beautifully browned roasts . . . cooked just the way your family likes them at super speeds . . . is *only one* of the remarkable things your new Roper does. Combination cooking for all foods with regular heat *plus* super-fast microwave energy at the same time cooks up to 75% *faster* . . . saves costly energy, too! The Roper Combination Microwave Range does everything your way . . . in one big oven . . . with no special dishes, no extra elements, no extra finishing. No special recipes needed . . . no complicated time or temperature conversions for combination cooking. The *newest* from the *oldest* name in cooking is so different, so advanced and so easy that you'll just have to try it to believe it.

An American Tradition of Quality for over a Century

three cooking choices!

1 Combination Cooking with regular heat and Microwave at the same time . . . you can even cook a complete meal at one time . . . and up to 75% faster!

2 Super-fast, energy-saving Microwave Only in a big oven . . . plus separate Defrost Cycle.

3 Regular roasting, baking or broiling with regular heat.

PLUS: Self-Cleaning Oven with automatic cycle to clean itself completely. Roll-out Storage Drawer for utensils.

  **SALES**

KANKAKEE, ILLINOIS 60901

Exhibit 26.1
(*cont.*)

EYEGLASSES. Until recent changes in the law, about three-fourths of the states prohibited opticians and optometrists from advertising. In those states eyeglasses were at least 25 percent higher than in such states as Texas, Iowa, Utah, Colorado, Minnesota, and others that permitted advertising of eyeglasses.

PRESCRIPTION DRUGS.

> In 1976, in what was regarded as a landmark victory for the consumer movement, the Supreme Court ruled 7 to 1 that states may not forbid pharmacists from advertising prices of prescription drugs. The Federal Trade Commission staff said that lifting restrictions on drug-price advertising could save consumers over $300 million a year.*

It is not always easy to tell the effects of advertising alone in reducing prices, but the foregoing are clear examples of where it has reduced prices.

Creation of unneeded purchases. There is no doubt that advertising contributes to people's making new purchases before old products are completely worn out. When a housewife redecorates, she may discard furniture or draperies that still have life in them and, strictly speaking, creates economic waste. However, it is often pointed out that our economic system and standard of living are based on the premise of continually expanding demand. The positive side of the expansionist character of advertising was summed up some 40 years ago by Professor Neil H. Borden of Harvard University:

> Advertising's outstanding contribution to consumer welfare comes from its part in promoting a dynamic, expanding economy. Advertising's chief task from the social standpoint is that of encouraging the development of new products. It offers a means whereby the enterpriser may hope to build a profitable demand for his new and differentiated merchandise which will justify investment.†

Whether one views advertising as a critic or proponent, the claim that it is the primary cause of sales grossly overstates advertising's influence. The new-product failure rate, depending on data sources and product categories, is somewhere between 50 and 80 percent. The package-goods category has one of the lowest rates of successful product introduction in spite of the fact that packaged goods are among the most heavily advertised products. There is simply no evidence that advertising can coerce consumers into unwanted purchases. To suggest otherwise insults the intelligence of consumers and is contrary to the facts.

It is interesting that many economists now say that we must begin to reeducate the American people concerning the level of consumption that can

---

The New York Times, May 25, 1978.

†Neil H. Borden, *The Economic Effects of Advertising* (Homewood, Ill.: Irwin, 1942), p. 881.

HOW TO SAVE FUEL DURING YOUR SUMMER VACATION

ENGINE TUNING, TIRE PRESSURE, AND HOW YOU DRIVE MAKE A BIG DIFFERENCE.

You're sure to be on the move this summer. With gas more expensive, you may find a few simple reminders on the best ways to get maximum mileage helpful. They won't take a lot of time, and may save you a fair amount at the gas pump.

A car that is properly tuned and maintained will be the most fuel-efficient. Newer GM cars require less routine maintenance than older ones, but all cars require some periodic checkups. Fouled spark plugs, improper spark timing or clogged oil and air filters all can reduce mileage significantly. So be sure to follow the maintenance program in your GM Owner's Manual and Maintenance Schedule.

Underinflated tires waste lots of gas. Tires that are too soft have a higher rolling resistance, which forces the engine to work harder and to use more fuel. So have the tire pressures checked periodically or use a tire gauge yourself to be sure your tires are inflated to the pressure recommended in the GM Owner's Manual.

Air conditioning also takes fuel, so try not to use it except when it's absolutely necessary. Whenever possible, use the vent position on the air conditioner to circulate air; it'll be quieter and cleaner than opening the windows all the way. If you can park in the shade, it'll be much cooler when you get into the car, and you'll be less likely to want to switch on the air conditioner.

Keeping the proper amount of coolant in the radiator will help prevent your car from overheating. It won't save fuel, but it may save expensive towing costs. A lot of people think it's okay just to add extra water, but that can actually cause the mixture in your radiator to boil. Coolant—a 50/50 mixture of ethylene glycol antifreeze and water—raises the boiling temperature and will therefore help prevent overheating.

Your driving habits are probably the most important factor of all in saving fuel. The best advice we can give is to drive at moderate speeds and accelerate evenly. For example, jackrabbit starts take much more gasoline than gradual acceleration. Frequent stops will also cost you fuel, because every "pump" of the accelerator means extra gas going through the carburetor. Also, "riding the brake" creates a lot of unnecessary friction and wastes gas.

Extra weight in your trunk, such as tire chains, golf clubs you don't plan to use, even unnecessary luggage, takes more gas to haul. And finally, driving at high speeds substantially reduces fuel economy. So observing the 55 mile per hour speed limit makes economic sense and may save lives, too. Tests confirm that you can get approximately 20% better mileage by driving at 50 miles per hour than at 70 miles per hour.

Attention to routine maintenance and moderation in how you drive are the keys to getting the best mileage from your car during this summer. That'll save you money and help make sure that there's enough gas for others to enjoy a summer vacation, too.

This advertisement is part of our continuing effort to give customers useful information about their cars and trucks and the company that builds them.

General Motors
People building transportation
to serve people

Exhibit 26.2
Ad advocating more responsible consumption. (Courtesy General Motors.)

reasonably be maintained in the future. Many of these demarketing messages are being carried through advertising (Exhibit 26.2).

Product information. One of the major areas of advertising criticism concerns the amount and type of information it provides. Critics charge that information provided by advertising is either incomplete or misleading or untruthful.

Untruthful or purposely misleading advertising cannot be defended. Businesses that use such tactics constitute only a minority of advertisers and are concentrated among a few small firms, usually at the local level. One of the most difficult problems faced by advertising is determining what is totally truthful. What constitutes acceptable product puffery in the eyes of one consumer is branded misleading advertising by another. However, as buyers have become more sophisticated and business has matured, the examples of outright misrepresentation and fraud that were so common at the turn of the century have been largely eliminated.

Honest advertising, quite apart from any ethical considerations, is simply good business. Firms depend on return sales for their economic survival. Products bought because of exaggerated or misleading advertising will rarely result in return purchases. Consumers expect advertising to present a reasonable portrayal of product quality, and advertisers by and large do just that.

Whereas untruthful advertising is universally condemned among both advertisers and consumers, adequate advertising information is a more complex issue. Many people who criticize advertising for a lack of complete information fail to understand its many forms and functions in the sales process.

For instance, direct-response advertising seeks to crowd into a given amount of space or time all the information about the product that a person might desire before making a decision to buy. But when we speak of national advertising, we are speaking of only one step in the buying process, that of acquainting a person with the availability of the product, its chief usefulness, and its advantages (in TV that often has to be done in 30 seconds) and encouraging him or her to buy the product or to make further inquiries if necessary. Automobile buyers, for example, are invited to go to a dealer with whatever questions they may have and even try the car. The buyer of foods or drugs will find further information on the package, much of it required by law.

For household appliances, such as stoves, refrigerators, or laundry equipment, advertising usually supplies enough information to enable the prospective purchaser to decide whether or not to seek further information. Advertising for a service, such as an airline, refers interested persons to a travel agent or possibly invites them to send a coupon for further information. Retail advertising offers products that the customer can examine at the store and about which the customer can look to the package, label, or salesperson for further facts. Not every ad is responsible for supplying all the information buyers might need; it may merely lead them to sources of more information. As a rule, the costlier or more technical a product is, the more information about it is given in the advertising.

perspective   In recent years a good deal of advertising criticism had been directed against its contribution to the American quality of life. Although criticism of the social effects of advertising is not a new phenomenon (for example, Thomas S. Hardings's *The Popular Practice of Fraud* in 1935 or Carl F. Taeush's *Policy and Ethics in Business* in 1931), the advent of TV as a selling medium has brought about additional concerns to critics of advertising.

It is difficult to find distinct categories for the wide-ranging social concerns relative to the advertising process. The present section summarizes some of the most discussed issues in the relationship between advertising and other facets of American society.

Social values.   One of the oldest and most prevalent criticisms of advertising concerns its effect on our social values and general lifestyle. Critics claim that advertising promotes greed and envy by constantly pointing out what we do not have and encouraging us to seek additional material wealth. They charge that advertising is particularly disruptive among low-income segments of the population, who have little or no chance of achieving the affluence portrayed in advertising. In addition to the overemphasis on material values in advertising, it is frequently pointed out advertising presents a totally fictitious view of life: A seemingly endless number of dramatized vignettes indicates that our most pressing problems are clogged sinks, bad breath, and body odor. Often these "problems" have been presented in a middle-class, largely white, male-dominated context.

Both of these charges have some validity. It is obvious that advertising promotes the acquisition of material goods; it is also apparent that many of those who are not able to avail themselves of these economic opportunities will be dissatisfied with their situation. However, in this regard advertising promotes those values which society, or at least the business sector, wants promoted. Advertising is simply a mirror of the enlightened economic self-interest on which our capitalistic system functions. We might contrast our economic system and the role played by advertising in it with those controlled economies where advertising is seldom used or is controlled by government. The extent to which advertising is used in an economy is a good indicator of the affluence of a society and the freedom with which new businesses can start. Advertising serves only a limited function where allocation of goods and selection of the producers of products is determined by government.

Likewise, advertising presentations are sometimes accused of being unrealistic or even offensive to certain groups. In recent years advertisers have attempted to correct this by meeting with representatives of various special-interest groups. Through feedback from organizations such as the Urban League and the National Organization for Women advertising now reflects American society in a more common-sense fashion.

Freedom of the press.   To its defenders advertising represents the most efficient means of maintaining the kind of broadly distributed, free press envisioned by our forefathers. There are a limited number of means of supporting the press: government support through a nationalized press system; support by users with extremely high subscription costs and a tax of some sort for the broadcast media; or advertising. Many feel that advertising is the most democratic medium since it provides a broad base of support for the media with a minimum of governmental interference.

In addition to supporting the media, advertising also provides a forum for diverse points of view. By buying time or space, individuals or organizations can become minieditors to answer contrary opinions appearing in the media or to present new and perhaps unpopular ideas (Exhibit 26.3).

A contrary view of advertising support of the media is that it exercises too much influence over the media in exchange for its support. It is true that most of the mass media tend to support middle-of-the-road causes. The greater the audience for a medium, the more it can charge advertisers. However, the notion that advertisers dictate the content of the media is simply incorrect. The number of news specials and documentaries that appear throughout a year attest that the media often present unprofitable or selective content. As a practical matter, the medium that attempts to mold its news and entertainment content to the wishes of any one enterprise will soon find that it loses credibility with *all* its advertisers as well as the public.

ADVERTISING AND THE CONSUMER
MOVEMENT

Since advertising is the major contact consumers have with a company's products, it is important that advertising as an institution be judged as a positive force by the consuming public. The public's concern with product quality and promotional honesty, under the general term *consumerism,* had its genesis in two events during the 1960s: The first was President John F. Kennedy's consumer bill of rights, to safety, to be informed, to choose, and to be heard;* second was the publication of Ralph Nader's book *Unsafe at any Speed,* published in 1966. Consumerism can be defined as an action-oriented movement designed to fulfill the rights articulated by President Kennedy over a decade ago. In addition consumerism denotes the right to obtain mechanisms for the redress of legitimate consumer complaints. In the past few years many critics have extended the term consumerism to include an expectation that business will not harm the general quality of life.

Impact of consumerism on advertising

The demand for more complete and reliable information is one of the main objectives of the consumer movement, which, to quote Stephen Greyser, is "the movement to augment the power of buyers versus that of sellers in the marketing systems." He continues:

---

*See Consumer Advisory Council, "First Report, Executive Office of the President" (Washington: United States Government Printing Office, October, 1963).

The ominous impasse in the Middle East

In June, 1973, in a message similar to this one, Mobil warned about the tensions then widening in the Middle East and cautioned that "nobody can afford another war in the Middle East." We asked the American people to consider the importance of Middle East oil to the U.S. economy and living standards—not just at that time, in 1973, but also for the years to come. And we urgently requested national and international action to achieve a settlement, and the base for a durable peace, in the Middle East.

We were criticized for writing that 1973 message, and some said we were doing the bidding of the Arabs. What those who criticized us failed to recognize, even though we stated it, was that a war would hurt us all—not just the Arabs and Israel, but the entire world. Unfortunately, our call went unheeded, and the war we had seen looming soon erupted. The baneful effects of that renewed cycle of violence in the Middle East have been manifest to all the world.

Yet all of this may seem a temperate flurry in comparison to the tempest now brewing in the Middle East because of the tragic situation in Iran and the Soviet invasion of Afghanistan. Each crisis in the Middle East has acted as a catalyst to bring on yet another. The Arab-Israeli confrontations of 1973 led to the transformation of oil from a commodity to a powerful instrument of international politics and diplomacy. And this new significance of oil has played no small part in tempting the Soviet Union to undertake activities threatening a confrontation with global consequences.

This is an old danger given fresh urgency: every U.S. president for over 30 years has been aware that the unresolved conflicts in the Middle East might one day lead to a direct confrontation between the Soviet Union and the Free World. We have admired President Carter's steadfast dedication to achieving what he described, at a press conference on February 15, as "... a comprehensive peace in the Middle East, the alleviation of tension, the involvement of others in the negotiating processes, the realization of Palestinian rights, and the perpetuation of the security of Israel and the peaceful nature of Israel's relationship with her neighbors." In a broader forum, the United Nations earlier passed a resolution (No. 242) dealing with many of the same principles.

And yet the Arab world, even more apprehensive than the U.S. about the encroachment of Soviet military power—in South Yemen, Ethiopia, and now Afghanistan—remains uncertain about U.S. reliability and intentions because of the prolonged stalemate in resolving the remaining political questions that impede a Middle East settlement.

With Russian troops already engaged in subduing Afghanistan, and a vulnerable Iran just across the border from Soviet tanks, we are rapidly using up the time left to us to conclude negotiations aimed at a just and equitable peace among the parties to the Arab-Israeli dispute in the Middle East.

The potential for war in this region now looms so large that it virtually demands a united front among the United States, those industrialized nations who historically and currently have major economic interests in the area, Israel, and the Arabs. Every option, every promising new avenue, every possible effort should therefore be explored in order to achieve that "comprehensive peace" sought by the President—a peace which will assure both the security of Israel and the rights of the Palestinian people.

A settlement of the Arab-Israeli dispute and its removal as an internal source of instability in the region would be a major step forward in the realization of unity among the nations of the West and most, if not all, of the Middle East. The strength of this unity would be a powerful deterrent to confrontation with expansionist Soviet activity.

In 1973 we said conditions were heading for a war and a possible oil embargo. Unfortunately, our predictions materialized.

In 1980 we are saying that conditions once again are raising the specter of war and a possible oil embargo. But today's conditions are even more threatening than those of 1973. We now have the Russians occupying Afghanistan with an appetite for further expansion in the Middle East.

Every effort must be made now by Israel, its Arab neighbors, and the United States to settle the Palestinian problem so that we and all our friends in the Middle East can be united against the Russian threat.

Exhibit 26.3
Ad designed to inform the public of a corporate point of view. (© 1980 Mobil Corporation.)

Consumerism . . . has found advertising to be a prime object of attention because advertising visibly touches Americans virtually all day long. Among the areas in which advertising has been affected in recent years by pressures from consumer activists and the regulatory community are:

Advertising substantiation, whereby advertising now must have advance substantiation for the factual claims in their advertising;

Corrective advertising, whereby those advertisers guilty of false and misleading advertising must admit their guilt in a given amount of future advertising;

Broadening of interpretations of "deception" in advertising, including attacks on brand claims that are truthful but not unique to the advertised brand.*

Advertising and good

taste In recent years the mass media, especially TV, have routinely discussed subjects that would not have been even considered only a few years earlier. Advertising has also recently liberalized product categories and types of presentation, particularly those on TV.

Although advertisers enjoy greater freedom, they also have a greater responsibility to treat topics in an inoffensive and tasteful manner. A survey conducted by Warwick, Welsh & Miller, a New York advertising agency, found that a large segment of the public finds a number of commercials objectionable. Among the brands cited in the study as having objectional advertising were Calvin Klein and Jordache jeans, Underalls pantyhose, and Rolaids antacid. The study also listed a number of product categories and the attitudes of respondents toward these categories, as shown in Table 26.1.

Table 26–1

PRODUCT CATEGORY	ATTITUDES TO COMMERCIALS[a]		
	IN GOOD TASTE, %	IN POOR TASTE, %	NET IMPRESSION
Feminine hygiene	12	70	−58
Laxatives	18	51	−33
Bras and girdles	18	50	−32
Jeans	24	48	−24
Pantyhose	26	39	−13
Antacids	34	27	+ 7
Island resorts	38	19	+ 19
Cosmetics	43	18	+ 25
Perfumes	43	18	+ 25

[a]Courtesy of Warwick, Welsh, & Miller, New York.

_____
*Stephen A. Greyser, "Consumerism's Growing Impacts on Advertising," *AdEast,* March, 1977.

Whether to buy and what to buy: the consumer

has the choice
We bask in our freedom to make choices in the things we can buy, but all of us have made choices that we later regretted. Most such purchases are errors of judgment made on unadvertised products as well as on advertised products. Under our system of government we have the responsibility of deciding for ourselves how to spend what remains of our money after taxes, what things are necessary or important to us, and what we want to work for. Would it be reasonable to refrain from telling about a product because some readers or viewers of the ad could not afford it?

A service is performed by the person who shows people how they can live better or get better satisfaction in their way of living. This is not the exclusive province of advertising: Store windows do it; a visit to a friend may do it; a magazine, a book, or a lecture may do it. But advertising doesn't limit itself to telling about these satisfactions; it is forever informing us how they may be attained more easily, more quickly, and at less cost—the favorite words of advertising headlines.

The price of having choices. One of the prices we have to pay for living in a society that offers choices to meet different tastes is the responsibility of setting our own scale of values. Which of the goodies you learn about are for you? Which are not? What is your list of priorities? This effort is a small price for having the privilege of choice.

Historian Daniel Boorstin has defined advertising as "the reminder of choices." He observed:

> It is a mission then of the advertising industry to try to keep these choices alive. You keep them alive by describing them realistically. If you—the advertising industry—can do this, then in another way you will be adding a tonic to American life.*

Advertising not only is essential but is growing more so. John Crichton, the late president of the 4A's, said:

> The truth of the matter is that the advertising business in this country keeps growing. There are more advertisers each year, and they spend more money. Given the realities of our market—our retail mechanism—there is no hope for any other kind of selling, other than advertising. One will not see the revival of massive sales forces. One will not see the informed retail sales clerk. What one will see more and more is self-service and automation. The choice will be made by the consumer before he enters the store. His basic information will stem from advertising. All national marketers know this. Increasingly the vast retail chains are putting it into operation. It is not really debatable. The facts are there for anyone to see.†

---

*Daniel J. Boorstin, "The Good News of Advertising," *Advertising Age,* November 13, 1980, p. 20.

†John Crichton, *Report of the President,* Papers of the Annual Meeting of the American Association of Advertising Agencies, 1976.

And with this observation we conclude our discussion of advertising. This book has sought to capture the essence of advertising thinking today, a brief moment in the long history of advertising. From Chapter 1 on we have seen how advertising has its roots in the history of the human desire to tell the world about what people have to sell. In our industrialized society there are many who have products and services to offer, and there are many interested in knowing about such things and able to buy them. In the free world there are media through which people can reach each other. Techniques will change, styles of advertising will change, the forms of advertising will change. But the need for advertising will continue to grow.

SUMMARY

First and foremost, advertising should be viewed as an economic force. There is no doubt that advertising is an essential component in an economy that depends on high levels of production and sales for its survival. Because advertising has such a high profile, it is often placed under closer evaluation than other business enterprises.

Even under this sometimes critical examination advertising's role in the economic and social order is impressive. For instance, no other institution could carry out simultaneously the diverse roles of

☐ selling goods and services
☐ providing consumer information and product comparisons
☐ supporting the mass media of the country and keeping them free of government or special-interest control
☐ providing a platform for divergent ideas of a political and social nature

No one would argue that advertising is without flaws. However, it is important to note that there are really no more effective or practical means of accomplishing the many tasks carried out by advertising. In the future, as society becomes more impersonal and fragmented, the role of advertising may take on even greater importance as a source of information and ideas.

QUESTIONS

1. Advertising causes consumers to purchase unwanted products. Discuss.
2. Advertising does not provide complete product information. Discuss.
3. If advertising were not used to bring products before the public, what alternatives would there be?
4. What is meant by the "value goal of a product"? Select three products with which you are familiar, and describe what you judge were the value goals in producing them.

5. What is the relationship between mass production and advertising, in terms of cost to the consumer?

6. "The consumer is king." Agree or disagree? Why?

7. How does advertising affect the public's freedom of choice?

8. What, in your opinion, are the things advertising does best? The things it does not do so well and could improve?

9. "This product costs less because we don't advertise." Discuss.

10. What do you think are the social responsibilities of advertising? How well does it fulfill them?

11. Is advertising essential? Why or why not?

12. Discuss advertising's role in a free press.

SUGGESTED EXERCISES

13. Analyze an ad that utilizes each of the following: working women, a minority, the elderly, and housewives. Is the portrayal of these groups realistic? Why or why not?

14. Cite three examples of ads that contributed to your buying a product.

READINGS

BARKSDALE, HIRAM C., and WILLIAM D. PERREAULT: "Can Consumers Be Satisfied?" *Business Topics,* Spring 1980, pp. 19–30.

BROADBENT, SIMON: "Price and Advertising: Volume and Profit," *ADMAP,* November 1980, pp. 532–40.

"Can Advertising Regulate Itself," *Marketing & Media Decisions,* July 1981, pp. 37–39.

NEIMAN, JANET: "Boycott? 2 Leaders disagree," *Advertising Age,* April 27, 1981, p. 1.

ROTZOLL, KIM B., JAMES E. HAEFNER, and CHARLES H. SANDAGE: *Advertising in Contemporary Society* (Columbus, Ohio: Grid Publishing, 1976).

"Smith Outlines Eight Trends to Watch," *Advertising Age,* August 24, 1981, p. 22.

"Study Supports Recession Ads," *Advertising Age,* April 28, 1980, p. 4.

WHIPPLE, THOMAS W., and ALICE E. COURTNEY: "How to Portray Women in TV Commercials," *Journal of Advertising Research,* April 1980, pp. 53–60.

P.S.

Getting and Succeeding In Your Advertising Job

When you're ready for your first job in advertising or marketing, where do you begin? What do you need to know?

Another book than this one could be written on the subject, and many have. Here are a few tips: Consider a career in advertising as a career in marketing and advertising; there is much overlapping of both those fields. A man or woman who begins as a salesperson in a firm and rises to be a marketing executive may leave the company to become the chief executive of an advertising agency. An assistant account executive may someday become advertising director of a large company with a multimillion dollar ad budget.

The advertising agency is the most publicized institution in advertising, but it employs only about one-fourth of all people in the field. Other advertising employers include national, retail, industrial, and direct-response advertisers, TV and radio producers, sales-promotion services, and research companies. A full description of career opportunities in advertising is given in *Advertising, a Guide to Careers in Advertising,* a booklet prepared by the American Association of Advertising Agencies.* It discusses the many different kinds of work done by agencies and by adver-

---

*For a copy write to American Association of Advertising Agencies, Materials Department K, 666 3rd Avenue, New York, New York 10017.

tisers, the great diversity of talent employed in advertising, and the qualifications needed for various jobs.

Join advertising clubs. Colleges offering advertising courses usually have ad clubs and many cities have ad clubs for young people (21–30) sponsored by the AAF (American Advertising Federation) Exhibit PS 1 shows how one such club attempts to help beginners break into advertising.

The most important things to have for a career in advertising are an inquisitive mind and a persistent attitude: All successful advertising professionals have inquisitive minds, constantly asking questions and looking for new ways to approach problems, new solutions to creative problems; and persistence is essential for success in advertising, whether you are an account executive, a creative person, a media planner, an ad director, or a media sales person. Look constantly for work and for new problems to solve and for new solutions to seemingly routine problems. The key to success in advertising is *innovation.*

Although, as we've pointed out, the ad agency is the most visible and glamorous part of the advertising business, it is the most difficult to break into. Very few agencies have training courses today; nevertheless, they often accept beginners to work in various departments. The beginning pay may seem low, but after 6 months to a year—when beginners have had a chance to reveal their aptitudes—the novices' rise in the agency can pick up momentum. In about 2 years beginners suddenly realize how many opportunities are open for those with "about 2 years' experience." By the time they are in their early 30s, they may well be making far more money than some of their classmates who started in other fields with higher starting salaries but slower potentials for moving up. The advertising-agency world is one in which a person who reveals talent and competence is not denied the opportunity of earning good money because he or she is "too young" or because of others' seniority, as is the case in some other fields.

To the young person embarking on a career in advertising agency David Ogilvy offers the following advice:

> After a year of tedious training, you will probably be made an assistant account executive. The moment that happens, set yourself to become the best informed person in the agency on the account to which you are assigned. If, for example, it is a gasoline account, read textbooks on the chemistry, geology, and distribution of petroleum products. Read all the trade journals in the field. Read all the research reports and marketing plans that your agency has ever written on the product. Spend Saturday mornings in service stations pumping gasoline and talking to motorists. Visit your client's refineries and research laboratories. At the end of your second year, you will know more about gasoline than your boss; you will then be ready to succeed him or her.*

---

*From David Ogilvy, *Confessions of an Advertising Man* (New York: Atheneum, 1963), pp. 151–152. Copyright 1963 by David Ogilvy Trustee. Reprinted by permission of Atheneum Publishers, New York, and Longmans, Green & Co. Limited, London.

Take A Look At Our Book.

Our Portfolio Can Help You Land A Job.

Atlanta Ad Club II has a "portfolio" of invaluable job information for you. Everything from a Guide to Resume Writing. To a comprehensive contact list of Atlanta agencies, T.V. stations, art shops, and In-house ad departments. To coupons and give-aways. To membership information on the best, most active club in town, Ad Club II. Plus, we'll tell you about our job referral service, called E/E (Employer/Employee) Match.

So fill out the coupon below. And send it with $2 (to cover mailing costs) to: The Portfolio, Atlanta Ad Club II, P.O. Box 18907, Atlanta, Georgia 30326.

The Ad II Portfolio. It'll help you land that first job in advertising.

Name_____

Address_____

City_____ State_____ Zip_____

Exhibit P.S. 1
Ad Club II recruiting ad for job seekers. (Courtesy of Ad Club II, Atlanta, GA.)

Sidney and Mary Edlund, in their book, *Pick Your Job and Land It!* give good advice on turning your interview into an offer:

☐ Have a clear picture of what the job calls for.
☐ Gather all the facts you can about the firm and its products.
☐ Draw up in advance an outline of the main points to be covered.
☐ Appeal to the employer's self-interest. Offer a service or dramatize your interest.
☐ Back up all statements of ability and achievement with proof.
☐ Prepare some questions of your own in advance. Keep etched in mind the two-way character of the interview: mutual exploration.
☐ Prepare for the questions normally asked.
☐ Anticipate and work out your answers to major objections.
☐ Close on a positive note.
☐ Send a "thank you" note to each interviewer.
☐ And follow up your best prospects.*

Once you get a job in the field, be sure you do everything you can to advance yourself. The best way to do that is to do everything you can to advance the company you work for. You are hired to contribute to the company's success, and the more successful the company becomes because of your efforts and creativity, the more successful your career will be in that company and your chosen field.

---

*See also Melvin W. Donaho and John L. Meyer, *How to Get the Job You Want: A Guide to Résumés, Interviews, and Job-Hunting Strategy* (Englewood Cliffs, N.J.: Prentice-Hall, Inc., 1976). A Spectrum Book.

Sources of Information

PERIODICALS

GENERAL ADVERTISING PUBLICATIONS

Adweek
820 2nd Avenue
New York, New York 10017

Advertising Age
740 North Rush Street
Chicago, Illinois 60611

Journal of Advertising
University of Wyoming
Laramie, Wyoming 82070

Journal of Marketing
250 South Wacker Drive
Chicago, Illinois 60606

MARKETING

Marketing & Media Decisions
342 Madison Avenue
New York, New York 10017

DIRECT MARKETING

Direct Marketing
224 7th Street
Garden City, New York 11530

Zip
545 Madison Avenue
New York, New York 10022

MAGAZINES

Magazine Age
6931 Van Nuys Boulevard
Van Nuys, California 91405

PACKAGING

Modern Packaging
205 East 42nd Street
New York, New York 10017

RESEARCH

Journal of Advertising Research
Advertising Research
Foundation, Inc.
3 East 54th Street
New York, New York 10022

Journal of Marketing Research
222 South Riverside Plaza
Chicago, Illinois 60606

SALES PROMOTION

Incentive Marketing
633 3rd Avenue
New York, New York 10017

TELEVISION AND RADIO

Broadcasting
1735 DeSales Street, N.W.
Washington, D.C. 20036

Television/Radio Age
1345 Avenue of the Americas
New York, New York 10019

INTERNATIONAL ADVERTISING

Advertising World
380 Lexington Avenue
New York, New York 10168

REFERENCE BOOKS AND INFORMATION SERVICES

**Editor and Publisher
Market Guide**
850 3rd Avenue
New York, New York 10022

The Media Book
75 East 55th Street
New York, New York 10022

Media Market Guide
Conceptual Dynamics
P.O. Box 332
Wakefield, New Hampshire
03598

Sources of Information

Newspaper Circulation
Analysis (NCA)
Standard Rate & Data
Service, Inc.
866 3rd Avenue
New York, New York 10022

N. W. Ayer & Sons Directory
of Newspapers and Periodicals
N. W. Ayer & Sons, Inc.
West Washington Square
Philadelphia, Pennsylvania
19106

Standard Directory of
Advertisers (The Red Book)
Standard Directory
of Advertising Agencies
National Register Publishing
Co., Inc.
5201 Old Orchard Road
Skokie, Illinois 60076

ASSOCIATIONS OF ADVERTISERS AND AGENCIES

The Advertising Council
825 3rd Avenue
New York, New York 10017

American Advertising
Federation (AAF)
1225 Connecticut Avenue, N.W.
Washington, D.C. 20036

American Association of
Advertising Agencies (AAAA, 4A's)
666 3rd Avenue
New York, New York 10017

American Marketing
Association (AMA)
250 South Wacker Drive
Chicago, Illinois 60606

Association of National
Advertisers (ANA)
155 East 44th Street
New York, New York 10017

Business & Professional
Advertising Association (BPAA)
41 East 42nd Street
New York, New York 10017

International Advertising
Association (IAA)
475 5th Avenue
New York, New York 10017

National Advertising
Review Board (NARB)
850 3rd Avenue
New York, New York 10022

National Council of Affiliated
Advertising Agencies
6 East 45th Street
New York, New York 10017

SYNDICATED MEDIA-RESEARCH SERVICES

Syndicated media-research services conduct regular surveys to reveal the publications people read, stations they listen to, ads they read, programs they listen to or watch, their reaction to programs and commercials, types of products they use and which brands, and demographic information. Each service focuses on some special phase of the total picture. Since they are continually working to make their output more helpful, no effort is made here to describe the specific services each offers. For latest information communicate directly with them.

The Arbitron Company, Inc.
1350 Avenue of the Americas
New York, New York 10019

Broadcast Advertisers
Report, Inc. (BAR)
500 5th Avenue
New York, New York 10036

FC&A
The Buyer Guide to
Outdoor Advertising
P.O. Box 79
Searsport, Massachusetts 04974

Leading National
Advertisers, Inc. (LNA)
347 Madison Avenue
New York, New York 10017

Mediamark Research, Inc.
341 Madison Avenue
New York, New York 10017

A. C. Nielsen Company
Nielsen Plaza
Northbrook, Illinois 60062

Simmon Marketing
Research Bureau
219 East 42nd Street
New York, New York 10017

Standard Rate & Data
Service, Inc.
5201 Old Orchard Road
Skokie, Illinois 60076

Starch, Inra, Hooper, Inc.
East Boston Post Road
Mamaroneck, New York 10544

Glossary

A

AAA. *See* American Academy of Advertising.

AAAA (4A's). *See* American Association of Advertising Agencies.

AAF. *See* American Advertising Federation.

ABC. *See* Audit Bureau of Circulations or American Broadcasting Company.

ABP. *See* American Business Press, Inc.

ACB. *See* Advertising Checking Bureau.

Account executive. Member of the agency staff who is the liaison between advertiser and agency, presenting the advertiser's problems to the agency and the agency's recommendations and proposed ads to the advertiser. Responsible for keeping in close touch with the advertiser's needs and plans and for seeing that approved plans are carried out by the agency.

Across the board. A TV or radio program scheduled for broadcast in the same time period on different days during the week (usually Monday through Friday).

ADI. *See* Area of dominant influence.

Adjacency. A program or time period that immediately precedes or follows a scheduled program on a single radio or TV station.

Ad-lib. To extemporize lines not written into the script or the musical score. Lines or music so delivered.

Advertising. A method of delivering a message impersonally to many people over the sponsor's name.

Advertising agency. An organization rendering advertising services to clients.

Advertising Checking Bureau (ACB). A private organization through which most newspaper publishers send their tear sheets to national advertisers for checking purposes.

Advertising Council. The joint body of the AAAA and the ANA and media, through which public-service advertising is produced and presented.

Advertising network. A group of independently owned, noncompeting advertising agencies that agree to exchange ideas and services in the interests of their clients.

Advertising Research Foundation (ARF). An association of research people devoted to furthering the use and effectiveness of marketing and advertising research.

Advertising specialty. An inexpensive gift bearing the advertiser's name and trademark, given without cost to a selected list.

Advertising spiral. The graphic representation of the stages through which a product might pass in its acceptance by the public. The stages are *pioneering, competitive,* and *retentive.*

Advertorial. An ad that advocates some philosophical or political position rather than selling a product or service.

Affidavit. A sworn statement. A TV or radio station must make an affidavit that a commercial appeared as stated on invoice.

Affiliate. An independently owned TV or radio station that agrees to carry programs provided by a network.

AFTRA. *See* American Federation of Television and Radio Artists.

Agate line. A unit measurement of publication advertising space, one column wide (no matter what the column width) and one-fourteenth of an inch deep.

Agency. *See* Advertising agency.

Agency charges (TV). All items, including talent session fees, artwork, commission, taxes, and so on, appearing on the TV production budget, exclusive of the production-studio bid.

Agency commission. Compensation paid by a medium to recognized agencies for services rendered in connection with placing advertising with it. Usually 15 percent. Some media also allow 2 percent of the net (85 percent) as a cash discount for prompt payment. This is passed on to the client for prompt payment.

Agency network. A voluntary affiliation of one agency in a major city to act as local office or provide local service for other members of that network. There are a number of different networks.

Agency of record. The advertising agency designated by the advertiser to coordinate the total media buy and the programming of products in a network buy. It keeps a record of all advertising placed. Used in situations where large advertisers have several agencies handling the advertising of their various divisions and products.

Aided recall. A research technique that uses prompting questions or materials to aid a respondent's memory of the original exposure situation, as

"Have you seen this ad before?" In contrast to *unaided recall:* "Which ad impressed you most in this magazine?"

Air check. A recording of an actual broadcast which serves as a file copy of a broadcast and which a sponsor may use to evaluate talent, program appeal, or production.

A la carte agency. One that offers parts of its services as needed on a negotiated-fee basis; also called *modular service.*

AM. *See* Amplitude modulation.

American Academy of Advertising (AAA). The national association of advertising teachers in colleges and universities and of others interested in the teaching of advertising.

American Advertising Federation (AAF). An association of local advertising clubs and representatives of other advertising associations. The largest association of advertising people. Very much interested in advertising legislation.

American Association of Advertising Agencies (AAAA, 4A's). The national organization of advertising agencies.

American Broadcasting Company (ABC). One of three major TV networks. Also has four radio networks (Contemporary, Entertainment, FM, and Information).

American Business Press, Inc. (ABP). An organization of trade, industrial, and professional papers.

American Federation of Television and Radio Artists (AFTRA). A union involved in the setting of wage scales of all performers.

American Newspaper Publishers' Association (ANPA). The major trade association of daily- and Sunday-newspaper publishers.

Amplitude modulation (AM). The method of transmitting electromagnetic signals by varying the *amplitude* (size) of the electromagnetic wave, in contrast to varying its *frequency* (FM). Quality not as good as FM but can be heard farther, especially at night. *See* Frequency modulation (FM).

ANA. *See* Association of National Advertisers.

Animation (TV). Making inanimate objects apparently alive and moving by setting them before an animation camera and filming one frame at a time.

Announcement. Any TV or radio commercial, regardless of time length and within or between programs, that presents an advertiser's message or a public-service message.

Announcer. Member of a TV or radio station who delivers live commercials or introduces a taped commercial.

ANPA. *See* American Newspaper Publishers' Association.

Answer print (TV). The composite print of the TV commercial with all elements in place.

Antique-finish paper. Book or cover paper that has a fairly rough, uneven surface, good for offset printing.

Appeal. The motive to which an ad is directed and which is designed to stir a person toward a goal the advertiser has set.

Approach (copy). The point of view with which a piece of copy is started—factual or emotional.

Approach (outdoor). The distance measured along the line of travel from the point where the poster first becomes fully visible to a point where the copy ceases to be readable. (There are *long* approach, *medium* approach, *short* approach, and *flash* approach.)

Arbitrary mark. A dictionary word used as a trademark that *connotes nothing* about the product it is to identify, for example, *Rise* shaving cream, *Dial* soap, *Jubilee* wax.

Area of dominant influence (ADI). An exclusive geographic area consisting of all counties in which the home-market station receives a preponderance of total viewing hours. Developed by American Research Bureau. Widely used for TV, radio, newspaper, magazine, and outdoor advertising in media scheduling. *See also* Designated Market Area (DMA).

Area sampling. *See* Sample; sampling.

ARF. *See* Advertising Research Foundation.

ASCAP (American Society of Composers, Authors, and Publishers). An organization that protects the copyrights of its members and collects royalties in their behalf.

Ascending letters. Those with a stroke or line going higher than the body of the letter—*b, d, f, h, k, l,* and *t*—and all capitals. The descending letters are *g, j, p, q,* and *y.*

Association of National Advertisers (ANA). The trade association of the leading national advertisers. Founded 1910.

Association test. A research method of measuring the degree to which people correctly identify brand names, slogans, and themes.

Audience, primary. In TV and radio the audience in the territory where the signal is the strongest. In print, the readers in households that buy or subscribe to a publication.

Audience, secondary. In TV and radio the audience in the territory adjacent to the primary territory, which receives the signal but not so strongly as the latter. In print the number of people who read a publication but who did not subscribe to or buy it. Also called *pass-along circulation.*

Audience, share of. The number or proportion of all TV households that are tuned to a particular station or program.

Audience composition. The number and kinds of people, classified by their age, sex, income, and the like, in a medium's audience.

Audience flow. The TV household audience inherited by a broadcast program from the preceding program.

Audience fragmentation. The segmenting of mass-media audiences into smaller groups because of diversity of media outlets.

Audimeter. The device for recording when the TV set in a household is on, a part of the research operation of the A. C. Nielsen Company.

Audio (TV). Sound portion of a program or commercial. *See* Video.

Audit Bureau of Circulations (ABC). The organization sponsored by publishers, agencies, and advertisers for securing accurate circulation statements.

Audition. A tryout of artists, musicians, or programs under broadcasting conditions.

Audition record. A transcription of a broadcast program used by a prospective sponsor to evaluate it, generally before the broadcast.

Availability. In broadcasting a time period available for purchase by an advertiser.

B

Background. A broadcasting sound effect, musical or otherwise, used behind the dialogue or other program elements for realistic or emotional effect.

Back-to-back. Describes the situation in which two commercials or programs directly follow each other.

Bait advertising. An alluring but insincere retail offer to sell a product that the advertiser in truth does not intend or want to sell. Its purpose is to switch a buyer from buying the advertised merchandise to buying something costlier.

Balloons. A visualizing device surrounding words coming from the mouth of the person pictured. Borrowed from comic strips.

Balopticon (balops). A type of TV animation made possible through the use of a Balopticon machine.

Barter. Acquisition of broadcast time by an advertiser or an agency in exchange for operating capital or merchandise. No cash is involved.

Basic bus. A bus, all of whose interior advertising is sold to one advertiser. When the outside is also sold, it is called a *basic basic bus.*

Basic network. The minimum grouping of stations for which an advertiser must contract in order to use the facilities of a radio or TV network.

Basic rate. *See* Open rate.

Basic stations. TV networks are offered in a list of stations that must be included. These are the basic stations. There is also a supplementary list of optional additions.

Basic weight. The weight of a ream of paper if cut to the standard, or basic, size for that class of paper. The basic sizes are: writing papers, 17 by 22 inches; book papers, 25 by 38 inches; cover stocks, 20 by 26 inches.

BBB. *See* Better Business Bureaus.

Bearers. (1) Excess metal left on an engraving to protect and strengthen it during the process of electrotyping. (2) Strips of metal placed at the sides of a type form for protection during electrotyping.

Better Business Bureaus. An organization, launched by advertisers and now with wide business support, to protect the public against deceptive advertising and fraudulent business methods. Works widely at local levels. Also identified with the National Advertising Review Board.

Billable services. *See* Collateral services.

Billboard. (1) Popular name for an outdoor sign. Term not now generally used in the industry. (2) The TV presentation of the name of a program sponsor plus a slogan, used at the start or close of a program and usually lasting 8 seconds.

Billing. (1) Amount of gross business done by an advertising agency. (2) Name credits of talent in order of importance.

Black and white. An ad printed in one color only, usually black, on white paper. Most newspapers are printed in black and white.

Blanking area. The white margin around a poster erected on a standard-size board. It is widest for a 24-sheet poster, for example; narrower, for a 30-sheet poster; and disappears on a bleed poster.

Bleed. Printed matter that runs over the edges of an outdoor board or of a page, leaving no margin.

Blister pack. A packaging term. A preformed bubble of plastic holding merchandise to a card. Used for small items. Also called *bubble card.*

Block. (1) A set of consecutive time periods on the air or a strip of the same time on several days. (2) Wood or metal base on which the printing plate is mounted. (3) British term for photoengraving or electrotype.

Blowup. Photo enlargement of written, printed, or pictorial materials, for example, enlargement of a publication ad to be used as a poster or transmitted through TV.

BMI. Broadcast Music, Inc. Chief function: to provide music to radio and TV shows with minimum royalty fees, if any.

Boards (outdoor). Poster panels and painted bulletins. Term originated in the period when theatrical and circus posters were displayed on board fences.

Body copy. Main text of ad, in contrast to headlines and name plate.

Body type. Commonly used for reading matter, as distinguished from display type used in the headlines of advertisements. Usually type 14 points in size or smaller.

Boldface type. A heavy line type; for example, the headings in these definitions.

Bond paper. The writing paper most frequently used in commercial correspondence, originally a durable quality used for printing bonds and other securities. The weight in most extensive use for letterheads is 20 pounds.

Book paper. Used in printing books, lightweight leaflets, and folders, distinguished from writing papers and cover stocks. Basic size: 25 by 38 inches.

Bounce back. An enclosure in the package of a product that has been ordered by mail. It offers other products of the same company and is effective in getting more business.

Boutique. A service specializing in creating ads. Often calls in independent artists and writers. This term is usually applied to small groups. Larger groups refer to themselves as *creative services,* and they may develop into full-service agencies.

Box-top offers. An invitation to the consumer to get a gift or premium by sending in the label or box top from a package of the product (with or without an additional payment).

BPA. *See* Business Papers Audit of Circulation, Inc.

Brand name. The spoken part of a trademark, in contrast to the pictorial mark; a Trademark word.

Bridge. Music or sound-effect cue linking two scenes in a TV or radio show.

Broadcast spectrum. That part of the range of frequencies of electro-magnetic waves assigned to broad-casting stations. Separate bands of frequencies are assigned to VHF and UHF TV and AM and FM radio.

Brochure. A fancy booklet or mono-graph.

Bubble card. *See* Blister pack.

Bulk mailing. A quantity of third-class mail that must be delivered to the postoffice in bundles, assorted by state and city.

Bulldog edition. A morning paper's early edition, printed the preceding evening and sent to out-of-town readers on night trains or planes. If an advertiser does not get copy in early, it will miss this edition.

Buried offer. An offer for a booklet, sample, or information made by means of a statement within the text of an ad without use of a coupon or typographical emphasis. (Also called *hidden offer*.)

Business Papers Audit of Circulation, Inc. (BPA). An organization that audits business publications. In-cludes controlled, or "qualified," free circulation.

Buying services (media). A profes-sional organization that plans and executes media schedules for agencies and advertisers. Also known as *media services,* operating chiefly in the broadcast field.

Buying space. Buying the right to in-sert an ad in a given medium, such as a periodical, a program, or an outdoor sign; buying time is the corresponding term for purchase of TV or radio broadcast privilege.

C

Cable networks. Networks available only to cable subscribers. They are transmitted via satellite to local cable operators for redistribution ei-ther as part of basic service or at an extra cost charge to subscribers.

Cable television. TV signals that are carried to households by cable. Pro-grams originate with cable oper-ators through high antennas, satel-lite disks, or operator-initiated programming.

Calendered paper. Paper with a smooth, burnished surface, attained by passing the paper between heavy rolls called *calenders.*

Call letters. The combination of letters assigned by the Federal Communi-cations Commission to a broad-casting station. They serve as its of-ficial designation and establish its identity.

Camera light. Pilot light on TV cam-eras indicating which camera is on the air.

Camera lucida ("lucy"). A device used in making layouts, enabling the art-ist to copy an illustration larger, smaller, or in the same size.

Campaign. A specific advertising effort on behalf of a particular product or service. It extends for a specified period of time.

Caption. The heading of an ad; the descriptive matter accompanying an illustration.

Casting off. Estimating the amount of space a piece of copy will occupy when set in type of a given size.

Cathode-ray tube (CRT). Electronic tube used by high-speed photocom-position machines to transmit the letter image onto film, photopaper, microfilm, or an offset plate.

CATV. *See* Cable television.

Center spread. In print the space occu-pied by an ad or the ad itself on the two facing pages of a publication bound through the center. Other-wise called *double-page spread.* In outdoor two adjacent panels using coordinated copy.

Certification mark. A name or design used upon, or in connection with, the products or services of persons other than the owner of the mark, to certify origin, material, mode of manufacture, quality, accuracy, or other characteristics of such goods or services, for example, *Seal of the Underwriters' Laboratories, Sanfor-ized, Teflon II.*

Chain. (1) A group of retail outlets with the same ownership, manage-ment, and business policy. (2) A regularly established system of TV or radio stations interconnected for simultaneous broadcasting through associated stations. (3) A group of media outlets under common own-ership.

Chain break. Times during or between network programs when a broad-casting station identifies itself (2 sec-onds) and gives a commercial an-nouncement (8 seconds). The announcements are referred to as chain breaks or *ID's* (for identi-fication).

Channel. A band of radio frequencies assigned to a given radio or TV sta-tion or to other broadcasting pur-poses.

Checking copy. A copy of a pub-lication sent to an advertiser or agency to show that the ad ap-peared as specified.

Circular. An ad printed on a sheet or folder.

Circulation. Refers to the number of people a medium reaches. (1) In publication advertising *prime* circu-lation is that paid for by the reader, in contrast to *pass-along* circulation. (2) In outdoor and transportation advertising people who have a rea-sonable opportunity to observe dis-play. (3) In TV usually referred to as *audience.*

Circulation waste. Circulation for which an advertiser pays but which does not reach prospects.

Classified advertising. In columns so labeled published in sections of a newspaper or magazine set aside for certain classes of goods or services, for example, Help Wanted, Posi-tions Wanted, Houses for Sale, Cars for Sale. The ads are limited in size and illustrations.

Class magazines. Term loosely used to describe publications that reach select high-income readers, in con-trast to magazines of larger circula-tions, generally referred to as *mass magazines.*

Clear. (1) To obtain legal permission from responsible sources to use a photograph or quotation in an ad or to use a certain musical selection in a broadcast. (2) To clear time is to arrange with a TV station to provide time for a commercial program.

Clear-channel station. A radio station that is allowed the maximum power and given a channel on the frequency bank all to itself. Possibly one or two sectional or local stations may be removed from it far enough not to interfere. (*See also* Local-channel station, Regional-channel station).

Clear time. *See* Clear.

Clip. A short piece of film inserted in a program or commercial.

Closed circuit (TV). Live, videotape, or film material transmitted by cable for private viewing on a TV monitor.

Closing date, closing hour. (1) The day or hour when all copy and plates or prints must be in the medium's hands if an ad is to appear in a given issue. The closing time is specified by the medium. (2) The last hour or day that a radio program or announcement may be submitted for approval to a station or network management to be included in the station's schedule.

Cluster sample. A random or probability sample that uses groups of people rather than individuals as a sampling unit.

Clutter. Refers to proliferation of commercials (in a medium) that reduces the impact of any single message.

CMX (TV). Computer editing, in which the videotape of the TV commercial is edited at a console with two side-by-side monitors.

Coarse screen. A comparatively low, or coarse, *screen*, usually 60, 65, or 85 lines to the inch, making a *halftone* suitable for printing on coarse paper.

Coated paper. Coating gives paper a smooth, hard finish, suitable for the reproduction of fine *halftones*.

Coaxial cable. In TV the visual part is sent on AM frequency; the audio part, on FM. Both frequencies are sent through the same cable, the *coaxial* cable.

Coined word. An original and arbitrary combination of syllables forming a word. Extensively used for trademarks, as Acrilan, Gro-Pup, Zerone. (Opposite of a dictionary word.)

Collateral services. An agency term to describe the noncommissionable forms of service that different agencies perform, such as sales promotion, research, merchandising, and new-product studies. Done on a negotiated-fee basis, both for clients and nonclients.

Collective mark. An identification used by the members of a cooperative, an association, collective group, or organization, including marks used to indicate membership in a union, an association, or other organization (for example, Sunkist).

Color proof. Combined impressions from separate color plates.

Column-inch. A unit of measure in a periodical one inch deep and one column wide, whatever the width of the column.

Combination plate. A *halftone* and *line plate* in one engraving.

Combination rate. (1) A special space rate for two papers, such as a morning paper and an evening paper, owned by the same publisher. Applies also to any other special rate granted in connection with two or more periodicals. (2) The rate paid for a combination plate.

Comic strip. A series of cartoon or caricature drawings.

Commercial. The advertiser's message on TV or radio.

Commercial program. A sponsored program from which broadcasting stations derive revenue on the basis of the time consumed in broadcasting it.

Community-antenna television (CATV). Cable television.

Comparative advertising. *See* Comparison advertising.

Comparison advertising. Used interchangeably with the term *comparative advertising*, it directly contrasts an advertiser's product with other named or identified products.

Competitive stage. The advertising stage a product reaches when its general usefulness is recognized but its superiority over similar brands has to be established in order to gain preference. (*Compare* Pioneering stage; Retentive stage.) *See also* Spiral.

Composite print (TV). A 35-mm or 16-mm film print of a TV commercial, complete with both sound and picture.

Composition. Assembling and arranging type for printing. (Also called *typography* or *typesetting*.)

Composition (cold). Strike-on, or direct-impression, typesetting by a typewriter.

Composition (hand). Metal type already molded and picked out of its case by hand to compose the copy.

Composition (hot). Type molded for the needs of the copy being set, as by a line-casting machine (for example, the Linotype).

Composition (photo). Type set photographically or electronically onto photosensitized paper or film.

Comprehensive. A layout accurate in size, color scheme, and other necessary details to show how a final ad will look. For presentation only, never for reproduction.

Computerized composition. The use of a stand-alone or built-in computer in phototypesetting (or, rarely, line-casting) equipment for the purpose of justifying and hyphenating, storing (as for telephone directories, price and parts lists, and so on), and typographically manipulating copy after it has been keyboarded but before it is set into type.

Concept. The combining of all elements (copy, headline, and illustrations) of an ad into a single idea.

Consumer advertising. Directed to people who will personally use the product, in contrast to trade advertising, industrial advertising, or professional advertising.

Consumer goods. Products that directly satisfy human wants or desires, such as food and clothing; also products sold to an individual or family for use without further processing; as distinct from industrial goods.

Contest. A promotion in which consumers compete for prizes and the winners are selected strictly on the basis of skill. *See* Sweepstakes.

Continuity. A TV or radio script. Also refers to the length of time a given media schedule runs.

Continuity department (TV). Determines whether or not a commercial is up to the broadcast standards of the station.

Continuity premium. A premium that is part of an ongoing program. The longer a consumer participates, the more valuable the gift becomes. Trading stamps are the most used continuity premiums.

Continuous tone. Shading in a picture that is not formed by screen dots.

Contract year. The period of time, in space contracts, running for 1 year, beginning with the first ad under that contract. It is usually specified that the first ad shall appear within 30 days of the signing of the contract.

Controlled-circulation business and professional publications. Sent without cost to people responsible for making buying decisions. To get on, and stay on, such lists, people must state their positions in companies and request annually that they be kept on the list. Also known as *qualified-circulation publications.*

Convenience goods. Consumer goods bought frequently at nearby (convenient) outlets, as distinct from shopping goods, for which a person compares styles, quality, and prices.

Conversion table. Table showing what the equivalent weight of paper stock of a given size would be if the sheet were cut to another size.

Cooperative advertising. (1) Joint promotion of a national advertiser (manufacturer) and local retail outlet on behalf of the manufacturer's product on sale in the retail store. (2) Joint promotion through a trade association for firms in a single industry. (3) Advertising venture jointly conducted by two or more advertisers.

Cooperative mailing. Sent to a select list comprising all the inserts of a group of noncompetitive firms trying to reach the same audience. A way of reducing mailing costs.

Copy. (1) The text of an ad. (2) Matter for a compositor to set. (3) Illustrations for an engraver to reproduce. (4) Any material to be used in the production of a publication. (5) The original photograph, drawing, painting, design, object, or anything

that is in process of reproduction for printing purposes.

Copy approach. The method of opening the text of an ad. Chief forms: factual approach, emotional approach.

Copy platform. The statement of the basic ideas for an advertising campaign, the designation of the importance of the various selling points to be included in it, and instructions regarding policy in handling any elements of the ad.

Copyright. Legal protection afforded an original intellectual effort. Application blanks for registry are procurable from the Copyright Office, Library of Congress, Washington, D.C. 20559. Copyright notice must appear on ads for this protection.

Copy testing. Measuring the effectiveness of ads.

Copywriter. A person who creates the text of ads and often the idea to be visualized as well.

Corrective advertising. To counteract the past residual effect of previous deceptive advertising, the FTC may require the advertiser to devote future space and time to disclosure of previous deception. Began around the late 1960s.

Cover. The front of a publication is known as the first cover; the inside of the front cover is the second cover; the inside of the back cover is the third cover; the outside of the back cover is the fourth cover. Extra rates are charged for cover positions.

Coverage. *See* Reach.

Coverage (TV). All households in an area able to receive a station's signal, even though some may not be tuned in. *Grade A* coverage: those households in the city and outlying counties that receive signals with hardly any disturbance. *Grade B:* those on the fringes of the market area, receiving signals with some interference.

Cover stock. A paper made of heavy, strong fiber; used for folders and booklet covers. Some cover stocks run into the low weights of paper known as book paper, but most

cover stocks are heavier. Basic size, 20 by 26 inches.

CPM (cost per thousand). Used in comparing media cost. Can mean cost per thousand readers or viewers or prospects. Must be specified.

Crash finish. A surface design on paper, simulating the appearance of rough cloth.

Crew (TV). All personnel hired by the production company for shooting a TV commercial.

Cronar film and Cronar plates. A conversion method by which either type of letterpress engraving is transferred directly to film by mechanical means (balls or fingers). This film can then be used to make offset plates, gravure cylinders, or very faithful duplicate letterpress plates.

Cropping. Trimming part of an illustration. Cropping is done either to eliminate nonessential background in an illustration or to change the proportions of the illustration to the desired length and width.

CRT. *See* Cathode-ray tube.

CU. Close-up (in TV). *ECU is extra close-up.*

Cue. (1) The closing words of an actor's speech and a signal for another actor to enter. (2) A sound, musical or otherwise, or a manual signal calling for action or proceeding.

Cumes. Cumulative audience. The number of unduplicated people or homes reached by a given schedule over a given time period.

Customer profile. A composite estimate of the demographic characteristics of the people who are to buy a brand and the purchase patterns they will produce.

Cut. (1) The deletion of program material to fit a prescribed period of time or for other reasons. (2) A photoengraving, electrotype, or stereotype; derived from the term *woodcut.* In England called a *block.*

Dailies (TV). All film shot, developed, and printed, from which scenes are selected for editing into the completed TV commercial. The term may also apply to videotape shooting. Also known as *rushes*.

Dayparts. Time segments into which a radio or TV day is divided, from first thing in the morning to the last thing at night. The parts are given different names. The cost of time depends upon the size of the audience at the time of each different daypart.

DB. *See* Delayed broadcast.

Dealer imprint. Name and address of the dealer, printed or pasted on an ad of a national advertiser. In the planning of direct mail, space is frequently left for the dealer imprint.

Dealer tie-in. A national advertiser's promotional program in which the dealer participates (as in contests, sampling plans, cooperative-advertising plans).

Deals. A *consumer* deal is a plan whereby the consumer can save money in the purchase of a product. A *trade* deal is a special discount to the retailer for a limited period of time.

Decalcomania. A transparent, gelatinous film bearing an ad, which may be gummed onto the dealer's window. Also known as a *transparency*.

Deckle edge. Untrimmed, ragged edge of a sheet of paper. Used for costlier forms of direct mail.

Deck panels (outdoor). Panels built one above the other.

Definition. Clean-cut TV and radio transmission and reception.

Delayed broadcast. A TV or radio program repeated at a later hour to reach people in a different time belt.

Delete. "Omit." Used in proofreading.

Demarketing. A technique of discouraging sales of scarce goods or limiting sales to unproductive market segments.

Demographic characteristics. A broad term covering the various social and economic characteristics of a group of households or a group of individuals. Refers to characteristics such as the number of members of a household, age of head of household, occupation of head of household, education of household members, type of employment, ownership of home, and annual household income.

Depth interview. A research interview conducted without a structured questionnaire. Respondents are encouraged to speak fully and freely about a particular subject.

Depths of columns. The dimension of a column space measured from top of the page to the bottom, in either agate lines or inches.

Designated market area (DMA). A rigidly defined geographical area in which stations located, generally, in the core of the area attract most of the viewing. A concept developed by the A. C. Nielsen Company. *See also* Area of dominant influence (ADI).

Diary. A written record kept by a sample of persons who record their listening, viewing, reading, or purchases of brands within a specific period of time. Used by syndicated research firms who arrange with a selected sample of people to keep such diaries and to report weekly, for a fee.

Die cut. An odd-shaped paper or cardboard for a direct-mail piece or for display purposes, cut with a special knife-edge die.

Diorama. (1) In point-of-purchase advertising these are elaborate displays of a scenic nature, almost always three-dimensional and illuminated. (2) In TV a miniature set, usually in perspective, used to simulate an impression of a larger location.

Direct-mail advertising. That form of direct-response advertising sent through the mails.

Direct Mail/Marketing Association (DMMA). Organization to promote direct-mail and direct-response advertising.

Direct marketing. Selling goods and services without the aid of wholesaler or retailer. Includes direct-response advertising and advertising for leads for salespeople. Also direct door-to-door selling. Uses many media; direct mail, publications, TV, radio.

Director. The person who writes or rewrites and then casts and rehearses a TV or radio program and directs the actual air performance.

Direct process. In two-, three-, and four-color process work, color separation and screen negative made simultaneously on the same photographic film.

Direct-response advertising. Any form of advertising done in direct marketing. Uses all types of media: direct mail, TV, magazines, newspapers, radio. Term replaces *mail-order advertising*. *See* Direct marketing.

Disk. Circular carrier of negative fonts used in phototypesetting equipment such as Photon or Fototronic.

Disk jockey. The master of ceremonies of a radio program of transcribed music (records).

Display. (1) Attention-attracting quality. (2) Display type is in sizes 18 points or larger. Italics, boldface, and sometimes capitals are used for display; so are hand-drawn letters and script. (3) Display space in newspapers usually is not sold in units of less than fourteen column lines; there is no such minimum requirement for undisplay classified ads. (4) Window display, interior display, and counter display are different methods of point-of-purchase advertising. (5) Open display puts the goods where they can be actually handled and examined by the customer; closed display has the goods in cases and under glass.

Display advertising. (1) In a newspaper, ads other than those in classified columns. (2) Advertising on backgrounds designed to stand by themselves (as window displays) or mounted (as a tack-on sign).

Dissolve (TV). Simultaneous fading out of one scene and fading in of the next in the TV commercial.

DMA. See Designated market area.

Dolly. The movable platform on which a camera is placed for TV productions when different angles or views will be needed.

Double billing. Unethical practice of retailer's asking for manufacturer reimbursement at a higher rate than what was paid for advertising time or space.

Double-leaded. See Leading.

Double-page spread. Facing pages used for a single, unbroken ad. Also called *double spread* and *double truck* or *center spread* if at the center of a publication.

"Down-and-under." A direction given to a musician or sound-effects person playing solo in a broadcast. It means, "Quiet down from your present playing level to a volume less than that of the lines of dialogue that follow."

Drive time (radio). A term used to designate the time of day when people are going to, or coming from, work. Usually 6 A.M. to 10 A.M. and 3 P.M. to 7 P.M., but this varies from one community to another. The most costly time on the rate card.

Drop-in. In broadcasting, a local commercial inserted in a nationally sponsored network program.

Drop-out halftone. *See* Halftone.

Dry-brush drawing. A sketch made with a brush and extra-thick, dry ink or paint.

Dry run. Rehearsal without cameras.

Dubbing. The combining of several sound tracks for recording on film.

Dubbing in. Addition of one TV film to another, for example, adding the part containing the advertiser's commercial to the part that carries the straight entertainment.

Dubs (TV). Duplicate tapes, made from a master print, sent to different stations for broadcast.

Due bill. (1) In a media barter deal the amount of time acquired from a station by a film distributor, owner, or producer. (2) An agreement between an advertiser (usually a hotel, restaurant, or resort) and a medium, involving equal exchange of the advertiser's service for time or space.

Dummy. (1) Blank sheets of paper cut and folded to the size of a proposed leaflet, folder, booklet, or book, to indicate weight, shape, size, and general appearance. On the pages of the dummy the layouts can be drawn. Useful in designing direct-mail ads. A dummy may also be made from the proof furnished by the printer. (2) An empty package or carton used for display purposes.

Duograph. A two-color plate made from black-and-white artwork. The second color is a flat color and carries no detail. Less expensive than a *duotone.*

Duotone. Two halftone plates, each printing in a different color and giving two-color reproductions from an original one-color plate.

Duplicate plates. Photoengravings made from the same negative as an original plate or via DuPont Crona-press conversion.

E

Early fringe. The time period preceding prime time, usually 4:30 to 7:30 P.M., except in Central Time Zone, where it extends from 3:30 to 6:30 P.M.

Ears (newspaper). Boxes or announcements at the top of the front page, alongside the name of the paper, in the upper right- and left-hand corners. Sold for advertising space by some papers.

Earth station. A TV receiving station designed to capture signals from satellites for relay to broadcasting stations or in time, possibly directly to receiving sets.

ECU (TV). Extra-close-up in shooting a picture.

Editing (TV). Also known as "completion," "finishing," and "post production." The second major stage of TV-commercial production, following shooting, in which selected scenes are joined together with opticals and titles and sound track into the finished commercial.

Electric spectaculars. Outdoor ads in which electric lights are used to form the words and design. Not to be confused with illuminated *posters* or illuminated *painted bulletins.*

Enameled paper (enamel-coated stock). A book or cover paper that can take the highest-screen halftone. It is covered with a coating of china clay and a binder and then ironed under high-speed rollers. This gives it a hard, smooth finish, too brittle to fold well. Made also in dull and semidull finish.

End-product advertising. Advertising by a firm that makes a constituent part of a finished product bought by the consumer. For example, advertising by DuPont that stresses the importance of Teflon in cooking ware.

English finish (EF). A hard, even, unpolished finish applied to book papers.

Engraving. (1) A photoengraving. (2) A plate in which a design is etched for printing purposes.

Equivalent weight of paper. The weight of a paper stock in terms of its basic weight. *See* Basic weight.

Ethical advertising. (1) Standards of equitable, fair, and honest content in advertising. (2) Addressed to physicians only, in contrast to ads of a similar product addressed to the general public.

Extended covers. A cover that is slightly wider and longer than the pages of a paper-bound booklet or catalog; one that extends or hangs over the inside pages. Also called *overhang* and *overlap. See also* Trimmed flush.

Extra (TV). A commercial performer who does not take a major role or receive reuse payments, or *residuals.*

F

Face. (1) The printing surface of type or a plate. (2) The style of type.

Facing text matter. An ad in a periodical opposite reading matter.

Fact sheet. A page of highlights of the selling features of a product, for use by a radio announcer in ad-libbing a live commercial.

Fade. (1) Variation in intensity of a radio or TV signal received over a great distance. (2) *Fading in* is the gradual appearance of the TV screen image, brightening to full visibility. (3) To diminish or increase the volume of sound on a radio broadcast.

Family life cycle. Concept that demonstrates changing purchasing behavior as a person or family matures.

Family of type. *Typefaces* related in design, as Caslon Bold, Caslon Old

Style, Caslon Bold italic, Caslon Old Style italic.

Fanfare. A few bars of music (usually trumpets) to herald an entrance or announcement in broadcasting.

FCC. *See* Federal Communications Commission.

FDA. *See* Food and Drug Administration.

Federal Communications Commission (FCC). The federal authority empowered to license radio and TV stations and to assign wavelengths to stations "in the public interest."

Federal Trade Commission (FTC). The agency of the federal government empowered to prevent unfair competition and to prevent fraudulent, misleading, or deceptive advertising in interstate commerce.

Field-intensity map. A TV or radio broadcast-coverage map showing the quality of reception possible on the basis of its signal strength. Sometimes called a *contour map*.

Field-intensity measurement. The measurement at a point of reception of a signal delivered by a radio transmitter. Expressed in units of voltage per meter of effective antenna height, usually in terms of microvolts or millivolts per meter.

Fill-in. (1) The salutation and any other data to be inserted in individual form letters after they have been printed. (2) The blurring of an illustration due to the closeness of the lines or dots in the plate or to heavy inking.

Firm order. A definite order for time or space that is not cancellable after a given date known as a *firm-order date*.

Fixed position. A TV or radio spot delivered at a specific time, for example, 8 A.M.

Flag (outdoor). A tear in a poster, causing a piece of poster paper to hang loose. Plant owner is supposed to replace promptly.

Flat color. Second or additional printing colors, using line or tints but not *process*.

Flat rate. A uniform charge for space in a medium, without regard to the amount of space used or the frequency of insertion. When flat rates do not prevail, *time discounts* or *quantity discounts* are offered.

Flight. The length of time a broadcaster's campaign runs. Can be days, weeks, or months but does not refer to a year. A flighting schedule alternates periods of activity with periods of inactivity.

FM. *See* Frequency modulation.

Following, next to reading matter. The specification of a position for an ad to appear in a publication. Also known as *full position*. This preferred position usually costs more than *run-of-paper* position.

Follow style. Instruction to compositor to set copy in accordance with a previous ad or proof.

Font. An assortment of type characters of one style and size, containing the essential twenty-six letters (both capitals and small letters) plus numerals, punctuation marks, and the like. *See* Wrong font.

Food and Drug Administration (FDA). The federal bureau with authority over the safety and purity of foods, drugs, and cosmetics and over the labeling of such products.

Forced combination. A policy of allowing advertising space to be purchased only for a combination of the morning and evening newspapers in the community.

Form. Groups of pages printed on a large single sheet. This book was printed in 32s. (thirty-two pages to one sheet, or *form*).

Format. The size, shape, style, and appearance of a book or publication.

Forms close. The date on which all copy and plates for a periodical ad must be in.

4A's. American Association of Advertising Agencies.

Four-color process. The process for reproducing color illustrations by a set of plates, one of which prints all the yellows, another the blues, a third the reds, the fourth the blacks (sequence variable). The plates are referred to as *process plates*.

Free lance. An independent artist, writer, TV or radio producer, or advertising person who takes individual assignments from different accounts but is not in their employ.

Frequency. (1) the number of waves per second that a transmitter radiates, measured in kilohertz (kHz) and megahertz (MHz). The FCC assigns to each TV and radio station the frequency on which it may operate, to prevent interference with other stations. (2) Of media exposure the number of times an individual or household is exposed to a medium within a given period of time. (3) In statistics the number of times each element appears in each step of a distribution scale.

Frequency modulation (FM). A radiotransmission wave that transmits by the variation in frequency of its wave, rather than by its size (as in AM modulation). An FM wave is twenty times the width of an AM wave, which is the first source of its fine tone. To transmit such a wave, it has to be placed high on the electromagnetic spectrum, far from AM waves with their interference and static. Hence its outstanding tone.

Fringe time. In TV the hours directly before and after prime time. May be further specified as *early fringe* or *late fringe*.

FTC. *See* Federal Trade Commission.

Full position. A special preferred position of an ad in a newspaper. The ad either (1) follows a column or columns of the news reading matter and is completely flanked by reading matter or (2) is at the top of the page and alongside reading matter.

Full-service agency. One that handles planning, creation, production, and placing of advertising for advertising clients. May also handle sales promotion and other related services as needed by client.

Full showing. (1) In an outdoor-poster schedule, a 100-intensity showing. (2) In car cards one card in each car of a line or city in which space is bought. The actual number of posters or car cards in a 100-intensity showing varies from market to market.

G

Galley proofs. Sheets, usually 15 to 20 inches long, on which the set type is reproduced for reading before it is made up into pages.

Gaze motion. Arranging elements in such a way that they "point" to the center of attention in an ad.

General rate (newspapers). Offered to a nonlocal advertiser. It is also called a *national rate*.

Geostationary (TV). The position of a synchronous satellite, which rotates around the earth at the equator at the same rate as the earth turns. Used for satellite transmission.

Ghost. An unwanted image appearing in a TV picture, for example, as a result of signal reflection.

Ghosted view. An illustration giving an X-ray view of a subject.

Grain. In machine-made paper the direction of the fibers, making the paper stronger across the grain and easier to fold with the grain. In direct mail it is important that the paper fold with the grain rather than against it.

Gravure printing. A process in which the printing image is etched below the nonprinting area. Instead of plates or forms, gravure printing usually employs a cylinder that is fully inked. The surface is then wiped clean, retaining ink only in the cups (sunken area). Tone variations are mainly achieved by etching cups to different depths. *See* Rotogravure.

Grid (TV). A system of presenting rates. It assigns various values to each time period. Higher values are assigned to nonpreemptible announcements and to announcements that are telecast during peak periods. Time can be offered and sold in terms of grids.

Gross national product (GNP). The total annual output of the country's final goods and services.

Gross rating points (GRP). Each rating point represents 1 percent of the universe being measured for the market. In TV it is 1 percent of the households having TV sets in that area. In radio it is 1 percent of the total population being measured, as adults, male/female, teenagers. In magazines it is 1 percent of the total population being measured, as 1 percent of all women or all men of different ages or teenagers, based on census records. In outdoor it is the number of people passing a sign in one day. The percentage is figured on the population of that market. This includes people who pass the sign more than once a day. Gross rating points represent the total of the schedule in that medium in that market per week or per month.

Ground waves. Broadcasting waves (AM) that tend to travel along the surface of the earth and are relatively unaffected by the earth's curvature. *See* Sky waves.

Group discount. A special discount in radio station rates for the simultaneous use of a group of stations.

GRP. *See* Gross Rating Points.

Gutter. The inside margins of printed pages.

H

Halftone. A photoengraving plate whose subject is photographed through a screen (in the camera) that serves to break up the reproduction of the subject into dots and thus makes possible the printing of halftone values, as of photographs. Screens vary from 45 to 300 lines to the inch. The most common are 120- and 133-line screens for use in magazines and 65-to 85-line screens for use in newspapers. *Square halftone:* The corners are square, and it has an all-over screen. *Silhouette,* or *outline, halftone:* The background is removed. *Vignette halftone:* Background fades away at the edges. *Surprint:* A line-plate negative is surprinted over a halftone negative, or vice versa. *Combination plate:* Line-plate negative is adjacent to (but not upon) halftone negative. *Highlight,* or *dropout, halftone:* Dots are removed from various areas to get greater contrast.

Hand composition. Type set up by hand, as distinguished from type set up by machine. (*Compare* Linotype composition.)

Hand lettering. Lettering that appears drawn by hand, as distinguished from type that is regularly set.

Hand tooling. Handwork on an engraving or plate to improve its reproducing qualities, charged for by the hour. Unless the plate is a highlight halftone, hand tooling is needed to secure pure white in a halftone.

Head. Display caption to summarize contents and get attention. *Center heads* are centered on type matter; *side heads,* at the beginning of a paragraph; *box heads,* enclosed by rules; *cut-in heads,* in an indention of the text.

Head-on position. An outdoor-advertising stand that directly faces direction of traffic on a highway.

Heaviside layer. A blanket of ions that encloses the earth. Bounces AM waves back at night, enabling AM stations to be heard at far distances. Named after an English physicist, Oliver Heaviside.

Heavy-half users. People who buy 50 percent or more of the total volume sold. They are usually less than 50 percent of the total number of users of the product.

Hertz. Frequency per second. *See* Kilohertz.

Hiatus. *See* Flight.

Hidden offer. Without calling attention to the offer, something useful or interesting offered free at the end of an ad that is wholly or largely copy. Response to the offer reveals how much attention the ad is drawing.

Holdover audience. The audience inherited from the show immediately preceding.

Horizontal publications. Business publications addressed to people in the same strata of interest or responsibility, regardless of the nature of the company, for example, *Purchasing, Maintenance Engineer, Business Week. See also* Vertical publications.

House agency. Owned and operated by an advertiser. May handle accounts of other advertisers, too.

Households using television (HUT). Number of households in a market or nationally watching any TV program.

House mark. A primary mark of a business concern, usually used with the trademark of its products. *General Mills* is a house mark; *Betty Crocker* is a trademark. Du Pont is a house mark; Teflon II is a trade-mark.

House organ. A publication issued periodically by a firm to further its own interests. It invites attention on the strength of its editorial content. Also known as *company magazine* and *company newspaper*. Used mostly in the industrial or professional world.

I

Iconoscope (TV). The special TV camera that picks up the image to be sent.

ID. A TV station break between programs or within a program, used for station identification. Usually 10 seconds, with 8 seconds for commercial.

Industrial advertising. Addressed to manufacturers who buy machinery, equipment, raw materials, and components needed to produce goods they sell.

Industrial goods. Commodities (raw materials, machines, and so on) destined for use in producing other goods, also called *producer goods* and distinct from *consumer goods.*

Inherited audience. The portion of a TV or radio program's audience that listened to the preceding program on the same station.

In-house agency. An arrangement whereby the advertiser handles the total agency function by buying individually, on a fee basis, the needed services (for example, creation, media services, and placement) under the direction of an assigned advertising director.

Insert (freestanding). The loose inserts placed between the pages or sections of a newspaper.

Insertion order. Instructions from an advertiser authorizing a publisher to print an ad of specified size on a given date at an agreed rate; accompanied or followed by the copy for the ad.

Inserts (magazine). A card or other printed piece inserted in a magazine opposite the advertiser's full-page ad. Insert is prepared by advertiser

at extra cost. Inserts appear in many forms and shapes. Not sold separately.

Institute of Outdoor Advertising (IOA). Organization to promote outdoor advertising and provide information to advertisers concerning the outdoor industry.

Institutional advertising. That done by an organization speaking of its work, views, and problems as a whole, to gain public goodwill and support rather than to sell a specific product. Sometimes called *public-relations advertising.*

Intaglio printing. Printing from a depressed surface, such as from the copper plate or steel plate that produces engraved calling cards and announcements; *rotogravure* is a form of intaglio printing. (*Compare* Letterpress and Lithography.)

IOA. *See* Institute of Outdoor Advertising.

Ionosphere. A canopy or layer that forms in the upper atmosphere, against which AM radio signals are reflected back to earth. FM signals are not.

IP (TV). Immediately preemptible rate. *See* Preemption.

ISKI (TV). A standardized coded method of identifying the tapes of commercials so that stations can make sure of using the right commercials in the right sequence.

Island display. A store display placed at the head of an aisle in a store, a choice location.

Island position. (1) In a publication page an ad surrounded entirely by editorial matter. (2) In TV a commercial isolated from other advertising by program content.

Iteration. A trial-and-error method of getting a mathematical solution to a problem that cannot be reduced to a formula in advance. Used in determining which of a given list of media will provide the widest reach at the lowest cost.

J

Jingle. A commercial set to music, usually carrying the slogan or theme

line of a campaign. May make a brand name and slogan better remembered.

Job ticket. A sheet or an envelope that accompanies a printing job through the various departments, bearing all the instructions and all records showing the progress of the work.

Judgment sampling. *See* Sample.

Junior unit. In print a page size that permits an advertiser to use the same engraving plates for small and large-page publications. The ad is prepared as a full-page unit in the smaller publication (such as *Reader's Digest*) and appears in the larger publication (such as *House & Gardens*) as a junior unit, with editorial matter on two or more sides.

Justification of type. Arranging type so that it appears in even-length lines, with its letters properly spaced, as on this page.

K

Keying an advertisement. Giving an ad a code number or letter so that, when people respond, the source of the inquiry can be traced. The key may be a variation in the address or a letter or number printed in the corner of a return coupon.

Key plate. Plate in color process with which all other plates must *register*.

Key station. The point at which a TV or radio network's principal programs originate. There may be several.

Kilohertz. Formerly called kilocycle. A way of measuring the frequency per second at which radio waves pass a given point. The words *per second* had long been dropped, and *frequency* alone was not a complete definition. Therefore an international body of scientists decided that a new word was needed for *frequency per second,* and they chose *hertz,* after Heinrich Rudolph Hertz, who produced the first radio waves in a laboratory. 1 kilohertz = 1,000 waves per second; 1 megahertz = 1,000,000 waves per second. Stations are identified by these frequencies.

Kinescope (TV). Recording on film of a live or videotape TV commercial, electronically reproduced from the kinescope tube.

King-size poster. An ouside transit display placed on the sides of vehicles. Size: 30 by 144 inches. *See Queen-size poster.*

Known-probability sampling. *See* Sample.

Kraft. A strong paper used for making tension envelopes, wrappers for mailing magazines, and the like.

L

Laid paper. Paper showing a regular watermarked pattern, usually of parallel lines.

Lanham Act. The Federal Trademark Act of 1946, supplanting the previous federal trademark acts.

Layout. A working drawing showing how an ad is to look. A printer's layout is a set of instructions accompanying a piece of copy showing how it is to be set up. There are also rough layouts, finished layouts, and mechanical layouts, representing various degrees of finish. The term *layout* is used, too, for the total design of an ad.

lc. Lower-case letters.

Leaders. A line of dots or dashes to guide the eye across the page, thus:
....

Lead-in. (1) In relation to *audience flow* the program preceding an advertiser's program on the same station. (2) The first few words of a copy block.

Leading (pronounced "ledding"). The insertion of metal strips (known as *leads*) between lines of type, causing greater space to appear between these lines. Leaded type requires more space than type that is set solid. The term is also used for additional line spacing in phototype-setting, although no lead is used.

Lead-out. In relation to *audience flow* the program following an advertiser's program on the same station.

Ledger. A high-grade writing paper of tough body and smooth, plated surface. Used for accounting work and for documents.

Legend. The title or description under an illustration. Sometimes called *cut line* or *caption*.

Letterpress. Printing from a relief, or raised, surface. The raised surface is inked and comes in direct contact with the paper, like that of a rubber stamp. *See* Offset, Rotogravure.

Lettershop. A firm that not only addresses the mailing envelope but also is mechanically equipped to insert material, seal and stamp envelopes, and deliver them to the post office according to mailing requirements.

Limited-time station. A radio station that is assigned a channel for broadcasting for a specified time only, sharing its channel with other stations at different times.

Linage. The total number of lines of space occupied by one ad or a series of ads.

Line. A unit for measuring space: fourteen lines to a column inch.

Line copy. Any copy suitable for reproduction by a *line plate*. Copy composed of lines or dots, distinguished from one composed of tones.

Line drawing. Made with brush, pen, pencil, or crayon, with shading produced by variations in size and spacing of lines, not by tone.

Line plate. A photoengraving made without the use of a screen, from a drawing composed of lines or masses, which can print on any quality stock.

Linotype composition. Mechanical typesetting, molding a line of type at a time. The Linotype machine is operated by a keyboard. (*Compare* Hand composition.) Widely replaced by photocomposition.

Lip synchronization (lip sync). In TV recording voice as a performer speaks. Requires more rehearsal and equipment and costs more than narration.

List broker. In direct-mail advertising an agent who rents the prospect lists of one advertiser to another advertiser. The broker receives a commission from the seller for this service.

List compiler. Person who sells lists of names to direct-mail advertisers.

Listening area. The geographic area in which a station's transmitting signal can be heard clearly. The area in which transmission is static free and consistent is called the *primary listening area.*

Lithography. A printing process by which originally an image was formed on special stone by a greasy material, the design then being transferred to the printing paper. Today the more frequently used process is *offset* lithography, in which a thin and flexible metal sheet replaces the stone. In this process the design is "offset" from the metal sheet to a rubber blanket, which then transfers the image to the printing paper.

Live. In TV and radio a program that originates at the moment it is produced, in contrast to a program previously taped, filmed, or recorded.

Local advertising. Placed and paid for by the local merchant or dealer, in contrast to national, or general, advertising of products sold by many dealers.

Local-channel station. A radio station that is allowed just enough power to be heard near its point of transmission and is assigned a channel on the air wave set aside for local-channel stations. (*Compare* Regional-channel station, Clear-channel station.)

Local program. A nonnetwork, station-originated program.

Local rate. A reduced rate offered by media to local advertisers. It is usually lower than that offered to national advertisers.

Log. A continuous record by a station, reporting how every minute of its time is used, as required by the FCC for its review when considering renewal of licenses.

Logotype, or logo. A trademark or trade name embodied in the form of a distinctive lettering or design. Famous example: Coca Cola.

Lower case (lc). The small letters in the alphabet, such as those in which this is printed, as distinguished from UPPER-CASE, or CAPITAL, LETTERS. Named from the lower case of the printer's type cabinet, in which this type was formerly kept.

Lucy. *See* Camera lucida.

M

Machine-finish (MF) paper. The cheapest of book papers that take halftones well. A paper that has had its pores filled ("sized") but is not ironed. Thus it possesses a moderately smooth surface. Smoother than *antique,* but not so smooth as *English-finish* or sized and *super-calendered* paper.

Mail-order advertising. See Direct-response advertising (the current term of preference).

Mail-order selling. *See* Direct marketing (the current term of preference).

Makegood. (1) In *print* an ad run without charge, in lieu of a prior one that the publisher agrees was poorly run. A print ad run in lieu of a scheduled one that did not appear. (2) In *TV* or *radio* a commercial run by agreement with advertiser, in place of one that did not run or was improperly scheduled. All subject to negotiation between advertiser (or agency) and medium.

Makeready. In letterpress, adjusting the plates for the press to ensure uniform impression. The skill and care in this work serve to make a good printing job.

Makeup of a page. The general appearance of a page; the arrangement in which the editorial matter and advertising material are to appear.

Makeup restrictions. To prevent the use of freak-sized ads which would impair the value of the page for other advertisers, publishers require that ads have a minimum depth in ratio to their width.

Mandatory copy. Copy that is required, by law, to appear on the advertising of certain products, such as liquor, beer, and cigarettes. Also refers to information that, by law, must be on labels of certain products, as foods and drugs.

Market. A group of people who can (1) be identified by some common characteristic, interest, or problem; (2) use a certain product to advantage; (3) afford to buy it; and (4) be reached through some medium.

Marketing concept. A management orientation that views the needs of consumers as primary to the success of a firm.

Market profile. A demographic and psychographic description of the people or the households of a product's market. It may also include economic and retailing information about a territory.

Market research. Gathering facts needed to make marketing decisions.

Market segmentation. Dividing a total market of consumers into groups whose similarity makes them a market for products serving their special needs.

Master print (TV). The final approved print of a commercial, from which duplicates are made for distribution to stations.

Masthead. Part of a page devoted to the official heading of the publication and frequently followed by personnel or policy information. In newspapers it is usually on the editorial page.

Matrix ("mat"). (1) A mold of papier mâché or similar substance, made by pressing a sheet of it into the type setup or engraving plate. Molten lead is poured into it, forming a replica of the original plate, known as a *stereotype.* Mainly employed by newspapers. (2) The brass molds used in the Linotype. Used in letterpress printing. Both going out of use.

Matter. Composed type, often referred to as: (1) *dead matter,* of no further use; (2) *leaded matter,* having extra spacing between lines; (3) *live matter,* to be used again; (4) *solid matter,* lines set close to each other; (5) *standing matter,* held for future use.

Maximil line rate. The milline rate of a newspaper computed at its maximum rate. *See* Milline rate.

Mechanical. A form of layout. An exact black-and-white copy of the ad as it will appear in printed form. Each element is pasted to an art board in precise position, ready for the camera.

Media Imperatives. Based on research by Simon Media Studies, showed the importance of using both TV and magazines for full market coverage.

Media strategy. Planning of ad media buys, including: identification of audience, selection of media vehicles, and determination of timing of a media schedule.

Medium. (1) The vehicle that carries the ad as TV radio, newspaper, magazine, outdoor sign, car card, direct mail, and so on. (2) The tool and method used by an artist in illustrations, as pen and ink, pencil, wash, or photography.

Merchandising. (1) "The planning involved in marketing the right merchandise or service at the right place, at the right time, in the right quantities, and at the right price," (America Marketing Association). (2) Promoting advertising to an advertiser's sales force, wholesalers, and dealers. (3) Promoting an advertised product to the trade and the consuming public, whether by media, point-of-purchase display, in-store retail promotions, guarantee seals, tags, or other means.

Merge/purge (merge & purge). A system used to eliminate duplication by direct-response advertisers who use different mailing lists for the same mailing. Mailing lists are sent to a central merge/purge office that electronically picks out duplicate names. Saves mailing costs, especially important to firms that send out a million pieces in one mailing. Also avoids damage to the goodwill of the public.

MF. Machine-finish paper.

Milline rate. A unit for measuring the rate of advertising space in relation to circulation; the cost of having one agate line appear before 1 million readers. Calculated thus:

$$\frac{1{,}000{,}000 \times \text{line rate}}{\text{quantity circulation}} = \text{milline}$$

Used in newspaper advertising.

Modern Roman. *See* Old-style Roman.

Modular agency. Also called *à la carte agency.*

Month preceding. "First month preceding publication" means that the closing date is in the month that immediately precedes the publication date on the cover of a periodical.

Motivational research. *See* Research.

Multiple-cable-system operator (MSO). Single firm that owns more than one cable system.

N

NAB. *See* Newspaper Advertising Bureau or National Association of Broadcasters.

NAD. *See* National Advertising Division.

NARB. *See* National Advertising Review Board.

National advertising. Advertising by the marketer of a trademarked product or service sold through different outlets, in contrast to *local advertising.*

National Advertising Division (NAD). The policy-making arm of the National Advertising Review Board.

National Advertising Review Board (NARB). The advertising industry's major organization for policing misleading ads.

National Association of Broadcasters (NAB). Trade association to promote both radio and TV.

National brand. A manufacturer's or producer's brand distributed through many outlets, distinct from a *private brand.*

National plan. Advertising-campaign tactics aimed at getting business nationwide, simultaneously. When properly used, it is the outgrowth of numerous local plans.

Negative-option direct response. Technique used by record and book clubs whereby a customer receives merchandise unless the seller is notified not to send it.

Nemo. Any broadcast not originated in the local studio.

Net audience. Total audience for a schedule in a medium, less duplication.

Network. Interconnecting stations for the simultaneous transmission of TV or radio broadcasts.

Newspaper Advertising Bureau (NAB). Association to promote newspaper advertising, especially coop and greater use of newspapers by national advertisers.

Next to reading matter (n.r.). The position of an ad immediately adjacent to editorial or news matter in a publication.

Nielsen Station Index (NSI). These reports, issued by the A. C. Nielsen Company, provide audience measurement for individual TV markets.

Nielsen Television Index (NTI). National audience measurements for all network programs.

Nonilluminated (regular). A poster panel without artificial lighting.

Nonoptimizing approaches to media planning. Computer solutions that offer several acceptable media schedules but no single right answer.

Nonstructured interview. An interview conducted without a prepared questionnaire. The respondent is encouraged to talk freely without direction from the interviewer.

Nonwired networks. Groups of radio stations whose advertising is sold simultaneously by station representatives.

NSI. *See* Nielsen Station Index.

NTI. *See* Nielsen Television Index.

O

OAAA. *See* Outdoor Advertising Association of America.

O & O stations. TV or radio stations owned and operated by networks.

Off camera. A TV term for an actor whose voice is heard but who does not appear in a commercial. Less costly than on camera.

Off-screen announcer. An unseen speaker on a TV commercial.

Offset. (1) *See* Lithography. (2) The blotting of a wet or freshly printed sheet against an accompanying sheet. Can be prevented by slip-sheeting. Antique paper absorbs the ink and prevents offsetting.

Old English. A style of black-letter or text type, now little used except in logotypes of trade names or names of newspapers.

Old-style Roman (o.s.). Roman type with slight difference in weight between its different strokes, as con-

trasted with Modern type, which has sharp contrast and accents in its strokes. Its serifs for the most part are oblique; Roman serifs are usually horizontal or vertical.

On camera. A TV term for an actor whose face appears in a commercial. Opposite of *off camera.* Affects the scale of compensation.

One-time rate. The rate paid by an advertiser who uses less space than is necessary to earn a time or rate discount, when such discounts are offered. Same as Transient rate, Basic rate, and Open rate.

Open end. A broadcast in which the commercial spots are added locally.

Open rate. In print the highest advertising rate on which all discounts are placed. It is also called Basic rate, Transient rate, or One-time rate.

Opticals. Visual effects that are put on a TV film in a laboratory, in contrast to those that are included as part of the original photograph.

Optimizing approaches to media planning. Computer solutions that offer a single best media schedule.

Out-of-home media. Outdoor advertising; transportation advertising.

Out-of-Home Media Services (OHMS). Firm that provides agencies with a national buying service for both outdoor and transit advertising.

Outdoor Advertising Association of America (OAAA). The trade association of the outdoor-advertising industry. Oldest advertising association.

Overtime (TV). TV production hours beyond the normal shooting day, when crew costs double, sometimes triple.

P

Package. (1) A container. (2) *In radio* or TV, a combination assortment of time units, sold as a single offering at a set price. (3) A special radio or TV program or series of programs, bought by an advertiser (for a lump sum). Includes all components, ready to broadcast, with the addition of the advertiser's commercial.

(4) In *direct-response* advertising a complete assembly of everything to be included in the mailing, including the envelope, letter, brochure, and return card.

Package insert. A card, folder or booklet included in a package, often used for recipes, discount coupons, and ads for other members of the product family. When attached to outside of package, called *package outsert.*

Package plan (TV). Some combination of spots devised by a station and offered to advertisers at a special price. Package plans are usually weekly or monthly buys.

Painted bulletins. Outdoor signs that are painted rather than papered. More permanent and expensive than posters, they are used only in high-traffic locations.

Participation. In TV and radio an announcement within a program, as compared with one scheduled between programs.

Pattern plate. (1) An electrotype of extra heavy shell used for molding in large quantities to save wear on the original plate or type. (2) An original to be used for the same purpose.

Pay cable. An additional service offered to cable subscribers at an extra charge. Home Box Office is an example of a pay-cable service.

Photocomposition (phototypesetting). A method of setting type by a photographic process only. Uses no metal.

Photoengraving. (1) An etched, relief printing plate made by a photomechanical process—as a halftone or line cut. (2) The process of producing the plate.

Photoplatemaking. Making plates (and the films preceding the plates) for any printing process by camera, in color or black and white.

Photoprint. The negative or positive copy of a photograph subject.

Photoscript (TV). A series of photographs made at the time of shooting a TV commercial picture based on the original script or storyboard. Used for keeping record of commercial, also for sales-promotion purposes.

Photostat. One of the most useful aids in making layouts or proposed ads.

A rough photographic reproduction of a subject; inexpensive and quickly made (within half an hour if desired).

Phototypesetting. The composition of phototext and display letters onto film or paper for reproduction. Letters are projected from film negative grids and are also stored in a binary form in computer core to be generated through a CRT system. *See also* Photocomposition.

Phototypography. The entire field of composing, makeup, and processing phototypographically assembled letters (photodisplay and phototext, or type converted to film) for the production of image carriers by plate makers or printers.

Photounit. The print-out or photoexposure unit of a phototypesetting system. When activated by keyboarded paper or magnetic tape, the unit exposes alphanumerical characters onto film or paper from negative fonts, disks, or grids.

PI (per-inquiry) advertising. A method used in direct-response radio and TV advertising, whereby orders as a result of a commercial are sent directly to the station. The advertiser pays the station on a per-inquiry (or per-order) received basis.

Pica, pica em. The unit for measuring width in printing. There are 6 picas to the inch. Derived from *pica,* the old name of 12-point type (1/6 inch high). A page of type 24 picas wide is 4 inches wide (24 ÷ 6 = 4).

Picture resolution. The clarity with which the TV image appears on the TV screen.

Piggyback (TV). The joining of two commercials, usually 15 seconds each, back to back for on-air use. A practice going out of use.

Pilot film (TV). A sample film to show what a series will be like. Generally, specially filmed episodes of TV shows.

Pioneering stage. The advertising stage of a product in which the need for such product is not recognized and must be established or in which the need has been established but the success of a commodity in filling those requirements has to be established. *See* Competitive stage, Retentive stage, Spiral.

Plant operator. In outdoor advertising the local person who arranges to lease, erect, and maintain the outdoor sign and to sell the advertising space on it.

Plate. The metal or plastic from which impressions are made by a printing operation.

Plated stock. Paper with a high gloss and a hard, smooth surface, secured by being pressed between polished metal sheets.

Playback. (1) The playing of a recording for audition purposes. (2) A viewer's or reader's report on what message he or she derived from a commercial or ad.

Point (pt.). (1) The unit of measurement of type, about 1/72 inch in depth. Type is specified by its point size, as 8-pt., 12-pt., 24-pt., 48-pt. (2) The unit for measuring thickness of paper, 0.001 inch.

Point-of-purchase advertising. Displays prepared by the manufacturer for use where the product is sold.

Point-of-purchase Advertising Institute (POPAI). Organization to promote point-of-purchase advertising.

Poll. An enumeration of a sample. Usually refers to sample opinions, attitudes, and beliefs.

POPAI. *See* Point of Purchase Advertising Institute.

Position (magazine). The place in a magazine where an ad or insert appears. Best position is up front (or as close to it as possible), right-hand side.

Position (newspaper). Where in paper, on what page, and on what part of page the ad appears.

Position (TV and radio). Where in the program your commercial is placed.

Positioning. Segmenting a market by creating a product to meet the needs of a selective group or by using a distinctive advertising appeal to meet the needs of a specialized group, without making changes in the physical product.

Poster panel. A standard surface on which outdoor posters are placed. The posting surface is of sheet metal. An ornamental molding of standard green forms the frame. The standard poster panel is 12 feet high and 25 feet long (outside dimensions).

Poster plant. The organization that provides the actual outdoor advertising service.

Poster showing. An assortment of outdoor poster panels in different locations sold as a unit. The number of panels in a showing varies from city to city and is described in terms of a 100 showing, a 50 showing, a 25 showing. This identification has no reference to the actual number of posters in a showing, nor does it mean percentages.

Posting date (outdoor). The date on which posting for an advertiser begins. Usually posting dates are every fifth day, starting with the first of the month. However, plant operators will, if possible, arrange other posting dates when specifically requested.

Posting leeway (outdoor). The five working days required by plant operators to assure the complete posting of a showing. This margin is needed to allow for inclement weather, holidays, and other contingencies as well as the time for actual posting.

PPA (Periodical Publishers Association). A group of magazine publishers that passes an agency credit. For newspaper credit, *see* ANPA.

Predate. In larger cities a newspaper issue that comes out the night before the date it carries, or a section of the Sunday issue published and mailed out during the week preceding the Sunday date.

Preemption, preemptible time. (1) Recapture of a time period by a network or station for important news or special program. (2) By prior agreement the resale of a time unit of one advertiser to another (for a higher rate). Time may be sold as nonpreemptive (NP) at the highest rate, 2 weeks preemptible (lower rate), or immediately preemptible (IP), the lowest rate.

Preferred position. A special, desired position in a magazine or newspaper, for which the advertiser must pay a premium. Otherwise the ad appears in a *run-of-paper (ROP) position,* that is, wherever the publisher chooses to place it.

Premium. An item, other than the product itself, given to purchasers of a product as an inducement to buy. Can be free with a purchase (for example, on the package, in the package, or the container itself) or available upon proof of purchase and a payment (*self-liquidating premium*).

Primary circulation. *See* Circulation.

Primary service area. The area to which a radio station delivers a high level of signals of unfailing steadiness and of sufficient volume to override the existing noise level both day and night and all seasons of the year, determined by field-intensity measurements.

Prime rate. The TV and radio rate for the times when they reach the largest audience.

Prime time. A continuous period of not less than 3 hours per broadcast day, designated by the station as reaching peak audiences. In TV usually 8:00 P.M. to 11:00 P.M. E.S.T. (7:00 P.M. to 10:00 P.M. C.S.T.).

Principal register. The main register for recording trademarks, service marks, collective marks, and certification marks under the Lanham Federal Trademark Act.

Printers Ink Model Statute (1911). The act directed at fraudulent advertising, prepared and sponsored by *Printers' Ink,* which was the pioneer advertising magazine.

Private brand. The trademark of a distributor of products sold only by that distributor, in contrast to manufacturers' brands, sold through many outlets. Also known as *private labels* or *house brands.*

Process plates. Photoengraving plates for printing in color. Can print the full range of the spectrum by using three plates, each bearing a primary color—red, yellow, blue—plus a black plate. Referred to as *four-color plates. See also* Process printing.

Process printing. Letterpress color printing in which color is printed by means of process plates.

Producer. One who originates and/or presents a TV or radio program.

Product Differentiation. Unique product attributes which set off one brand from another.

Production. (1) The conversion of an advertising idea into an ad mainly by a printing process. (2) The building, organization, and presentation of a TV or radio program.

Production department. The department responsible for mechanical production of an ad and dealing with printers and engravers or for the preparation of a TV or radio program.

Production director. (1) Person in charge of a TV or radio program. (2) Head of department handling print production.

Professional advertising. Directed at those in professions such as medicine, law, or architecture who are in a position to recommend use of a particular product or service to their clients.

Profile. (1) A detailed study of a medium's audience classified by size, age, sex, viewing habits, income, education, and so on. (2) A study of the characteristics of the users of a product or of a market.

Progressive proofs. A set of photoengraving proofs in color, in which: the yellow plate is printed on one sheet and the red on another; the yellow and red are then combined; next the blue is printed and a yellow-red-blue combination made. Then the black alone is printed, and finally all colors are combined. The sequence varies. In this way the printer matches up inks when printing color plates. (Often called "progs.")

Proof. (1) An inked impression of composed type or of a plate for inspection or for filing. (2) In photocomposition a proof is made on photographically or chemically sensitized paper. (3) In engraving and etching an impression taken to show the condition of the illustration at any stage of the work. Taking a proof is "pulling a proof."

Psychographics. A description of a market based on factors such as attitudes, opinions, interests, perceptions, and lifestyles of consumers comprising that market. *See* Demographic characteristics.

Public-service advertising. Advertising with a message in the public interest. When run by a corporation, often referred to as *institutional advertising.*

Public-service announcements. Radio

and TV announcements made by stations at no charge, in the public interest.

Publisher's statement. Statement of circulation issued by a publisher, usually audited or given as a sworn statement. All publication rates are based on a circulation statement.

Qualified circulation. The term now being applied to those controlled-(free) circulation trade magazines sent only to people who have representative positions in the field and who apply in writing annually for continuation on the free list.

Queen-size poster. An outside transit advertising display placed on the sides of vehicles (usually the curb side). Size: 30 by 88 inches. *See* King-size poster.

Radio Advertising Bureau (RAB). Association to promote the use of radio as an advertising medium.

Randomization. In consumer research a method of securing random (unbiased) selection of respondents. *See) Sample; sampling.

Rate card. A card giving the space rates of a publication, circulation data, and data on mechanical requirements and closing dates.

Rate holder. The minimum-sized ad that must appear during a given period if an advertiser is to secure a certain *time* or *quantity discount*. It holds a lower rate for an advertiser. Used mostly in local advertising.

Rate protection. The length of time an advertiser is guaranteed a specific rate by a medium. May vary from 3 months to 1 year from the date of signing a contract.

Rating points (outdoor). Used in estimating the number of people to whom an outdoor sign is exposed. Each board is rated in terms of 1 percent of the daily passersby in relation to population. In making up a showing of different sizes in a market, the total number of rating points of those signs is added and

referred to as the *gross rating point* of that showing for that market. The count includes duplication of people who may pass a sign more than once a day.

Rating point (TV). (1) The percentage of TV households in a market a TV station reaches with a program. The percentage varies with the time of day. A station may have a 10 rating between 6:00 and 6:30 P.M., and a 20 rating between 9:00 and 9:30 P.M. (a real hit!). (2) In radio the percentage of people who listen to a station at a certain time. *See* Gross rating points.

Reach. The total audience a medium actually covers.

Reading notices. Ads in newspapers set up in a type similar to that of the editorial matter. Must be followed by "Adv." Charged for at rates higher than those for regular ads. Many publications will not accept them.

Ream. In publishing and advertising, 500 sheets of paper. Thousand-sheet counts now being used as basis of ordering paper.

Rebate. The amount owed to an advertiser by a medium when circulation falls below some guaranteed level or the advertiser qualifies for a higher *space* or *time discount*.

Recognized agency. An advertising agency recognized by the various publishers or broadcast stations and granted a commission for the space it sells to advertisers.

Reduction prints (TV). 16-mm film prints made from 35-mm films.

Regional-channel station. A radio station that is allowed more power than a local station but less than a clear-channel station. It is assigned a place on the frequency band set aside for regional-channel stations. *See also* Local-channel station and Clear-channel station.

Register. Perfect correspondence in printing; of facing pages when top lines are even; of color printing when there is correct superimposition of each plate so that the colors mix properly.

Registering trademark. In the United States the act of recording a trademark with the Commission of Patents, to substantiate claim of first use. The law differs from many in

South America and some in Europe. Whoever is the first to *register* a mark is its owner. One result is that trademark pirates in South America and Europe watch for new American trademarks, register them, and thus become owners. Then they wait for American firms to enter their markets. At that time they may permit use of the trademark for a price.

Register marks (engraving). Cross lines placed on a copy to appear in the margin of all negatives as a guide to perfect register.

Release. A legally correct statement by a person photographed, authorizing the advertiser to use that photograph. For minors the guardian's release is necessary.

Relief printing. Printing in which the design reproduced is raised slightly above the surrounding, nonprinting areas. Letterpress is a form of relief printing contrasted with intaglio printing and lithography.

Reminder advertising. *See* Retentive stage.

Remote pickup. A broadcast originating outside the studio, as from a football field.

Representative (rep). An individual or organization representing a medium selling time or space outside the city of origin.

Repro proofs (reproduction proofs). Exceptionally clean and sharp proofs from type for use as copy for reproduction.

Research. (1) Structured research: A list of questions is prepared, and subjects are given choices of responses. (2) Unstructured research: Subjects are asked open-ended questions to probe underlying reasons for specific behavior. Also called *motivational,* or *in-depth, research.*

Residual. A sum paid to certain talent on a TV or radio commercial every time the commercial is run after 13 weeks, for life of commercial.

Respondent. One who answers a questionnaire or is interviewed in a research study.

Retail advertising. Advertising by a local merchant who sells directly to the consumer.

Retentive stage. The third advertising

stage of a product, reached when its general usefulness is everywhere known, its individual qualities are thoroughly appreciated, and it is satisfied to retain its patronage merely on the strength of its past reputation. *See* Pioneering stage, Competitive stage, Spiral.

Retouching. The process of correcting or improving artwork, especially photographs.

Reversed plate. (1) A line-plate engraving in which white comes out black, and vice versa. (2) An engraving in which right and left, as they appear in the illustration, are transposed.

Riding the showing. A physical inspection of the panels that comprise an outdoor showing. Also, riding through a market, selecting locations for signs.

Robinson-Patman Act. A federal law, enforced by the FTC. Requires a manufacturer to give proportionate discounts and advertising allowances to all competing dealers in a market. Purpose: to protect smaller merchants from unfair competition of larger buyers.

Roman type. (1) Originally, type of the Italian and Roman school of design, as distinguished from the blackface Old English style. Old style and modern are the two branches of the Roman family. (2) Typefaces that are not italic are called *roman*.

ROP. *See* Run-of-paper position.

ROS. *See* Run of schedule.

Rotary plan (outdoor). Movable bulletins are moved from one fixed location to another one in the market, at regular intervals. The locations are viewed and approved in advance by the advertiser.

Rotary press. A printing press having no flat bed, but printing entirely with the movement of cylinders.

Rotation (broadcasting). A technique of moving commercials into different dayparts to expose all categories of viewers and listeners.

Rotogravure. The method of intaglio printing in which the impression is produced by chemically etched cylinders and run on a rotary press; useful in large runs of pictorial effects.

Rotoscope. A technique that combines live and animated characters.

Rough. A crude sketch to show basic idea or arrangement. In making layouts, this is usually the first step.

Rough cut (TV). The first assembly of scenes in proper sequence, minus opticals and titles, in the TV commercial. Also called *work print.*

Routing out. Tooling out dead metal on an engraving plate.

Run-of-paper (ROP) position. Any location that the publisher selects in a publication, in contrast to *preferred position.*

Run of schedule (ROS). Commercial announcements that can be scheduled at the station's discretion anytime during the period specified by the seller (for example, ROS, 10 A.M. to 4:30 P.M., Monday through Friday).

Rushes (TV). The first, uncorrected prints of a commercial. Also called *dailies.*

S

SAAI. *See* Specialty Advertising Association International.

Saddle stitching. Binding a booklet by stitching it through the center and passing stitches through the fold in the center pages. Enables the booklet to lie flat. When a booklet is too thick for this method, *side stitching* is used.

SAG. Screen Actors' Guild.

Sales promotion. (1) Sales activities that supplement both personal selling and marketing, coordinate the two, and help to make them effective, for example, displays. (2) More loosely, the combination of personal selling, advertising, and all supplementary selling activities.

Sample; sampling. (1) The method of introducing and promoting merchandise by distributing a miniature or full-size trial package of the product free or at a reduced price. (2) Studying the characteristics of a representative part of an entire market, or universe, in order to apply to the entire market the data secured from the miniature part. A *probability sample* is one in which every member of the universe has a known probability of inclusion. A *random sample* is a probability sample in which, with a fixed

mathematical regularity, names are picked from a list. A *stratified quota sample* (also known as a *quota sample*) is one drawn with certain predetermined restrictions on the characteristics of the people to be included. An *area sample* (or *stratified area sample*) is one in which one geographical unit is selected as typical of others in its environment. In a *judgment sample* an expert's experience and knowledge of the field are employed to choose representative cases suitable for study. A *convenience,* or *batch, sample* is one selected from whatever portion of the universe happens to be handy.

Satellite earth station. A receiving station for domestic satellite transmission, usually to cable-casting systems. (Over 100 such stations in operation in 1978. Number estimated to double in 3 years.)

Satellite station. (A term born before we had sky satellites.) A small local TV station that has a feeder line running to a distant larger station (a parent station) so that programs can be relayed from the larger station. Not to be confused with *satellite earth station.*

Saturation. A media pattern of wide coverage and high frequency during a concentrated period of time, designed to achieve maximum impact, coverage, or both.

SC. Single column.

sc. Small caps.

Scaling down. Reducing illustrations to the size desired.

Scatter plan (TV). The use of announcements over a variety of network programs and stations, to reach as many people as possible in a market.

Score. To crease cards or thick sheets of paper so that they can be folded.

Scotchprint. A reproduction proof pulled on plastic material from a letterpress plate or form. Normally used in conversion of color plates from letterpress to offset.

Screen (photoengraving). (1) The finely cross-ruled sheet used in photomechanical plate-making processes to reproduce the shades of gray present in a continuous-tone photograph. Screens come in various rulings, resulting in more (or fewer) "dots" to the square inch on the plate, to conform with the requirements of different grades and kinds of printing paper. (2) In TV the surface on which a picture is shown.

Screen printing (silk screen). A printing process in which a stenciled design is applied to a textile or wire-mesh screen and a squeegee forces paint or ink through the mesh of the screen. *See* Silk screen.

Script (TV). A description of the video, along with the accompanying audio, used in preparing a storyboard or in lieu of it.

Secondary meaning. When a word from the language has long been used as a trademark for a specific product and has come to be accepted as such, it is said to have acquired a "secondary meaning" and may be eligible for trademark registration.

Secondary service area (radio). The area—beyond the *primary service area*—where a broadcasting station delivers a steady signal; that signal must be of sufficient intensity to be a regular program service of loudspeaker volume, day and night, all seasons. *See* Primary service area.

SEG. Screen Extras Guild.

Segmentation. *See* Market segmentation.

Segue (pronounced "segway"). From Italian, "it follows," the transition from one musical theme to another without a break or announcement.

Self-liquidating premium. A premium offered to consumers for a fee that covers its cost plus handling.

Serif. The short marks at top and bottom of Roman lettering. Originally chisel marks to indicate top and bottom of stone lettering.

Service mark. A word or name used in the sale of services, to identify the services of a firm and distinguish them from those of others, for example, Hertz Drive Yourself Service, Weight Watchers Diet Course. Comparable to trademarks for products.

Sets in use. The number of TV sets and radios turned on at any given time.

Sheet. The old unit of poster size, 26 by 39 inches. The standard-size posters are 24 sheets (seldom used)

and 30 sheets. There are also 3-sheet and 8-sheet posters.

Shooting (TV). The first stage of TV production, which covers the filming or videotaping of all scenes up through delivery of the *dailies.*

Short rate. The balance advertisers have to pay if they estimated that they would run more ads in a year than they did and entered a contract to pay at a favorable rate. The short rate is figured at the end of the year or sooner if advertisers fall behind schedule. It is calculated at a higher rate for the fewer insertions.

Showing. Outdoor posters are bought by groups, referred to as *showings.* The size of a showing is referred to as a 100-GRP showing or a 75- or 50-GRP showing, depending on the gross rating points of the individual boards selected.

Showing transit (exterior). A unit for buying outdoor space on buses. The cards vary according to size, position, and cost per bus.

Showing transit (interior). A unit for buying card space inside buses and subways. A showing usually calls for one card per bus or per car per market.

SIC. *See* Standard Industrial Classification.

Side stitching. The method of stitching from one side of a booklet to the other. Stitching can be seen on front cover and on back. Used in thick-booklet work. Pages do not lie flat. *See* Saddle stitching.

Signal area. The territory in which a radio or TV broadcast is heard. Can be primary, where most clearly heard, or secondary, where there may be more interference.

Signal. The communication received electronically from the TV or radio broadcast station. One speaks of a "strong signal" or a "weak signal."

Signature. (1) The name of an advertiser. (2) The musical number or sound effect that regularly identifies a TV or radio program. (3) A sheet folded and ready for binding in a book, usually in multiples of 32; but 16's and 8's are also possible. A mark, letter, or number is placed at the bottom of the first page of every group of 16 or 32 pages to serve as a guide in folding.

Silhouette halftone. *See* Halftone.

Silk screen. A printing process in which a stenciled design is applied to a screen of silk, organdy, nylon, Dacron, or wire cloth. A squeegee forces paint or ink through the mesh of the screen to the paper directly beneath.

Simulation (computer). The process of introducing synthetic information into a computer for testing, an application for solving problems too complicated for analytical solution.

Simulcast. The simultaneous playing of a program over AM/FM radio.

Siquis. Handwritten posters that in sixteenth- and seventeenth century England were forerunners of modern advertising.

SIU. Sets in use (TV).

Sized and supercalendered paper (s. and s.c.). Machine-finish book paper that has been given extra ironings to ensure a smooth surface. Takes halftones very well.

Sized paper. Paper that has received a chemical bath to make it less porous. Paper sized and ironed (calendered) is known as *machine finish.* If it is again ironed, it becomes *sized and supercalendered (s. and s.c.).*

Skin pack. A packaging method whereby a plastic film is pulled tightly around a product on a card. Used for "card merchandising."

Sky waves. The electromagnetic waves that shoot toward the sky from a station. During the day they all go through the Heaviside electronic layer, which blankets the earth. At night the AM waves bound back at an angle; hence AM broadcasts can be received at night over vast distances. *See* Ground waves.

Slip-sheeting. Placing a sheet of paper (tissue or cheap porous stock) between the sheets of a printing job to prevent them from *offsetting,* or smudging, as they come from the press.

Small caps (sc or sm. caps). Letters shaped like upper case (capitals) but about two-thirds their size—nearly the size of lower-case letters. THIS SENTENCE IS SET WITH A REGULAR CAPITAL LETTER AT THE BEGINNING, THE REST IN SMALL CAPS.

SMSA. *See* Standard Metropolitan Statistical Area.

Snipe. A copy strip added over a

poster ad, for example, a dealer's name, special sale price, or another message. Also referred to as an *overlay.*

Sound effects. Various devices or recordings used in TV or radio to produce lifelike imitations of sound, such as footsteps, rain, or ocean waves.

Space buyer. The official of an advertising agency who is responsible for the selection of printed media for the agency's clients.

Space discount. Given by a publisher for the linage an advertiser uses. (*Compare* Time discount.)

Space schedule. Shows the media in which an ad is to appear, the dates on which it is to appear, its exact size, and the cost.

Specialties. *See* Advertising specialty.

Specialty Advertising Association International (SAAI). Organization to promote specialty advertising.

Spectacular. An outdoor sign built to order, designed to be conspicuous for its location, size, lights, motion, or action. The costliest form of outdoor advertising.

Spiral (advertising). The graphic representation of the stages through which a product might pass in its acceptance by the public. The stages are *pioneering, competitive,* and *retentive.*

Split run. A facility available in some newspapers and magazines, wherein the advertiser can run different ads in alternate copies of the same issue at the same time. A pretesting method used to compare coupon returns from two different ads published under identical conditions.

Sponsor. The firm or individual paying for talent and broadcasting time for a radio or TV feature; the advertiser on the air.

Spot (TV and radio). (1) *Media use:* purchase of time from an independent station, in contrast to purchase from a network. When purchased by a national advertiser, it is, strictly speaking, *national spot* but is referred to as just *spot.* When purchased by a local advertiser, it is, strictly speaking, *local spot* but is referred to as *local TV* or *local radio.* (2) Creative use: the text of a short announcement.

Spread. (1) Two facing pages, a *double-page* ad. (2) Type matter set full measure across a page, not in columns. (3) Stretching any part of a broadcast to fill the full allotted time of the program.

Spread posting dates. Division of outdoor posting dates: One-half the panels of a showing may be posted on one date, the other half later, say, 10 to 15 days.

Staggered schedule. Insertions alternated in two or more periodicals.

Standard Industrial Classification (SIC). The division of all industry, by the Bureau of the Budget, into detailed standard classifications identified by code numbers. Useful in making marketing plans.

Standard Metropolitan Statistical Area (SMSA). An allocation of territories in a metropolitan area as defined by the Bureau of the Budget, brought to county-line basis. Used in sales planning and scheduling.

Stand by. *Cue* that a program is about to go on the air.

Stand-by space. Some magazines will accept an order to run an ad whenever and wherever the magazine wishes, at an extra discount. Advertiser forwards plate with order. Helps magazine fill odd pages or spaces.

Station breaks. Periods of time between TV or radio programs or within a program as designated by the program originator.

Station clearance. *See* Clear.

Station satellite. A station, often found in regions of low population density, that is wholly dependent upon another, carrying both its programs and commercials. Purpose is to expand coverage of the independent station and offer service to remote areas. Nothing to do with TV from satellites.

Steel-die embossing. Printing from steel dies engraved by the intaglio process, the sharp, raised outlines being produced by stamping over a counterdie. Used for monograms, crests, stationery, and similar social and business purposes.

Stet. A proofreader's term: "Let it stand as it is; disregard change specified." A dotted line is placed underneath the letter or words to

which the instructions apply.

Stock footage (TV). Existing film that may be purchased for inclusion in a TV commercial.

Stock music. Existing recorded music that may be purchased for use in a TV or radio commercial.

Storecasting. The broadcasting of radio programs and commercials in stores, usually supermarkets.

Storyboard. Series of drawings used to present a proposed commercial. Consists of illustrations of key action (video), accompanied by the audio part. Used for getting advertiser approval as a guide in production.

Strip. (1) In *TV or radio* a commercial scheduled at the same time on successive days of the week, as Monday through Friday. (2) In *newspapers* a shallow ad at the bottom of a newspaper, across all columns.

Subcaption (subcap). A subheadline.

Subscription television (STV). A pay-television service that broadcasts a scrambled signal. Homes with a decoder can receive a clear signal for a monthly charge.

Substance No. Usually followed by a figure, as substance No. 16. In specifying paper stock, the equivalent weight of a given paper in the standard size.

Superstations. Local independent TV that is transmitted by satellite to cable systems around the country.

Supplements (newspaper). Loose inserts carried in a newspaper. Printed by advertiser. Must carry "supplement" and newspaper logotype to meet newspaper postal requirements.

Surprint. (1) A photoengraving in which a line-plate effect appears over the face of a halftone, or vice versa. (2) Printing over the face of an ad already printed.

Sustaining program. Entertainment or educational feature performed at the expense of a broadcasting station or network; in contrast to a commercial program, for which an advertiser pays.

Sweepstakes. A promotion in which prize winners are determined on the basis of chance alone. Not legal if purchaser must lay out money to get it. *See* Contest.

Sworn statement. When a publisher does not offer a certified audited report of circulation (as many small and new publishers do not), it may offer advertisers a sworn statement of circulation.

Syndicate mailings (direct-response advertising). The mailing pieces a firm prepares for its products but then turns over to another firm to mail out to the latter's lists. Terms are negotiated individually.

Syndicated research services. Research organizations regularly report on what TV and radio programs are being received, what magazines are read, what products are being used by households, where, and other information. Sold on subscription basis.

Syndicated TV program. A program that is sold or distributed to more than one local station by an independent organization outside the national network structure. Includes reruns of former network entries and movies that are marketed to stations by specialized firms that had a hand in their production.

Syndication, trade-out. *See* Trade-out syndication.

T

TAB. *See* Traffic Audit Bureau.

Tag (TV). A local retailer's message at the end of a manufacturer's commercial. Usually 10 seconds of a 60-second commercial.

Take-one. A mailing card or coupon attached to an inside transit ad. The rider is invited to tear off and mail for further information on the service or offering by the advertiser.

Tear sheets. Copies of ads from newspapers. Sent to the agency or advertiser as proof of publication.

Telephone coincidental. A broadcast-audience research technique that contacts respondents by telephone during the broadcast being measured.

Television Advertising Bureau (TvB). Association to promote the use of TV as an advertising medium.

TF. (1) Till-forbid. (2) To fill. (3) Copy is to follow.

Thumbnail sketches. Small layouts used to view various alternatives before finished layouts are drawn.

Till-forbid; run TF. Instructions to publisher meaning: "Continue running this ad until instructions are issued to the contrary." Used in local ads.

Time classifications (TV). Stations assign alphabetical values to specific time periods for easier reference in reading rate cards. The values generally extend from *A* through *D*. In an average market the classification might work as follows: *AA* and *A* for *prime time; B* for early evening and late news; *C* for daytime (afternoon) and late night; *D* for the periods from 1 A.M. until sign-off and from sign-on until noon.

Time clearance. Making sure that a given time for a specific program or commercial is available.

Time discount. Given for the frequency or regularity with which an advertiser inserts ads. Distinguished from *quantity discount,* for amount of space used.

Tint. A reproduction of a solid color.

To fill (TF). Instructions to printer meaning: "Set this copy in the size necessary to fill the specified space indicated in the layout."

Total audience plan. In TV and radio a spot package consisting of a combination that will hit all a station's listeners in a specified time span.

Tr. Transpose type as indicated, a proofreader's abbreviation.

Trade advertising. Advertising directed to the wholesale or retail merchants or sales agencies through whom the product is sold.

Trade character. A representation of a person or animal, realistic or fanciful, used in conjunction with a trademark to help identification. May appear on packages as well as in advertising (for example Green Giant).

Trademark. Any device or word that identifies the origin of a product, telling who made it or who sold it. Not to be confused with *trade name.*

Trade name. A name that applies to a business as a whole, not to an individual product.

Trade-out syndication. A TV program series produced by an advertiser and containing that advertiser's commercials is offered to stations. There are no charges on either side. Stations save the expense of the programs, and advertisers keep other ads away from their own. Stations are free to sell a selected amount of the time at specific points in the program.

Trade paper. A business publication directed to those who buy products for resale (wholesalers, jobbers, retailers).

Traffic Audit Bureau (TAB). An organization designed to investigate how many people pass and may see a given outdoor sign, to establish a method of evaluating traffic measuring a market.

Traffic count. In outdoor advertising the number of pedestrians and vehicles passing a panel during a specific time period.

Traffic department. In an advertising agency the department responsible for prompt execution of work in all departments and getting complete material to the forwarding department for shipment on schedule.

Traffic-flow map (outdoor). An outline map of a market's streets scaled to indicate the relative densities of traffic.

Transcription program library. A collection of transcription records from which the radio station may draw. Stations subscribe to various transcription libraries.

Transient rate. Same as One-time rate in buying space.

Transition time. *See* Fringe time.

Transparency. Same as *decalcomania.*

Traveling display. An exhibit prepared by a manufacturer of a product and lent to each of several dealers in rotation. Usually based on the product and prepared in such a way as to be of educational or dramatizing value.

Trimmed flush. A booklet or book trimmed after the cover is on, the cover thus being cut flush with the leaves. *Compare* Extended covers.

Triple spotting. Three commercials back to back.

TvB. *See* Television Advertising Bureau.

TV week. Sunday to Saturday.

25 × 38-80. (Read "twenty-five, thirty-eight, eighty.") The method of expressing paper weight, meaning that a ream of paper 25 by 38 inches in size weighs 80 pounds. Similarly, 25 × 38-60, 25 × 38-70, 25 × 38-120, 17 × 22-16, 17 × 22-24, 20 × 26-80, 38 × 50-140. Used as a standard for paper sold in any size.

Typeface. The design and style of a type letter.

Type family. A group of type designs that are variations of one basic alphabet style. Usually comprising roman, italic, or boldface, they can also vary in width (condensed or extended) and in weight (light to extrabold). Some families have dozens of versions.

Type page. The area of a page that type can occupy; the total area of a page less the margins.

U

Ultrahigh frequency (UHF). TV channels 14 to 83, operating on frequencies from 470 to 890 MHz.

Unaided recall. A research method for learning whether a person is familiar with a brand, slogan, ad, or commercial without giving a cue as to what it is. "What program did you watch last night?" *See* Aided recall.

V

VAC. Verified audit circulation by an auditing organization, which believes every publication selling advertising should have an audit available, whatever the circulation method (paid or free).

Value goal. The amount and form of value a company sets out to offer in a product.

Vertical publications. Business publications dealing with the problems of a specific industry, for example, *Chain Store Age, National Petroleum News, Textile World. See also* Horizontal publications.

Very-high frequency (VHF). The frequency on the electromagnetic spectrum assigned to TV channels 2 to 13, inclusive. *See* Ultrahigh frequency.

Video (TV). The visual portion of a broadcast. *See* Audio.

Videotape recording. A system that permits instantaneous playback of a simultaneous recording of sound and picture on a continuous strip of tape.

Videotape (TV). An electronic method of recording images and sound on tape. Most TV shows that appear live are done on videotape.

Vignette. A *halftone* in which the edges (or parts of them) are shaded off gradually to very light gray.

Voice-over. The voice of a TV commercial announcer or actor or singer recorded *off camera.* Costs less than if delivered *on camera.*

VTR (TV). Videotape recording of a commercial.

W

Wait order. An ad set in type, ready to run in a newspaper, pending a decision on the exact date (frequent in local advertising).

Warm up. The 3- or 5-minute period immediately preceding a line broadcast, in which the announcer or star puts the studio audience in a receptive mood by amiably introducing the cast of the program or discussing its problems.

Wash drawing. A brushwork illustration, usually made with diluted India ink or watercolor. In addition to black and white, it has varying shades of gray, like a photograph. *Halftones,* not *line plates,* are made from wash drawings.

Wave posting (outdoor). Concentration of poster showings in a succession of areas within the market. Usually coincides with special promotions in each of these areas.

Weather contingency (TV). An estimated emergency fund to cover daily pay for union crew and equipment rental if unfavorable weather interferes with scheduled shooting of a commercial.

Web printing. Also called *roll-fed printing.* In contrast to *sheet-fed printing,* paper is fed into the press from rolls. This method is used in rotogravure, newspapers, magazine presses, packaging presses, and increasingly in offset. Do not confuse with *wet printing* though both may take place simultaneously.

Wet printing. Color printing on specially designed high-speed presses with one color following another in immediate succession before the ink from any plate or cylinder has had time to dry.

wf. Wrong front.

Widow. In typography applied to the last line of a paragraph when it has only one or two words.

Wild spot (TV). A commercial broadcast by noninterconnected stations.

Window envelope. A mailing envelope with a transparent panel, permitting the address on the enclosure to serve as a mailing address as well.

Work-and-turn. Printing all the pages in a signature from one form and then turning the paper and printing on the second side, making two copies or signatures when cut.

Work print (TV). *See* Rough cut.

Wove paper. Paper having a very faint, clothlike appearance when held to the light.

Wrong font (wf). Letter or letters from one series mixed with those from another series or font. *This sentence is the wrong front.*

Z

Zinc etching. A photoengraving in zinc. Term is usually applied to line plates.

Zone plan. Concentration on a certain limited geographical area in an advertising campaign. Also known as *local plan.*

Zoom (TV). A camera-lens action or optical effect that permits a rapid move in toward, or pull back away from, the subject being photographed in a commercial.

Index

R

S